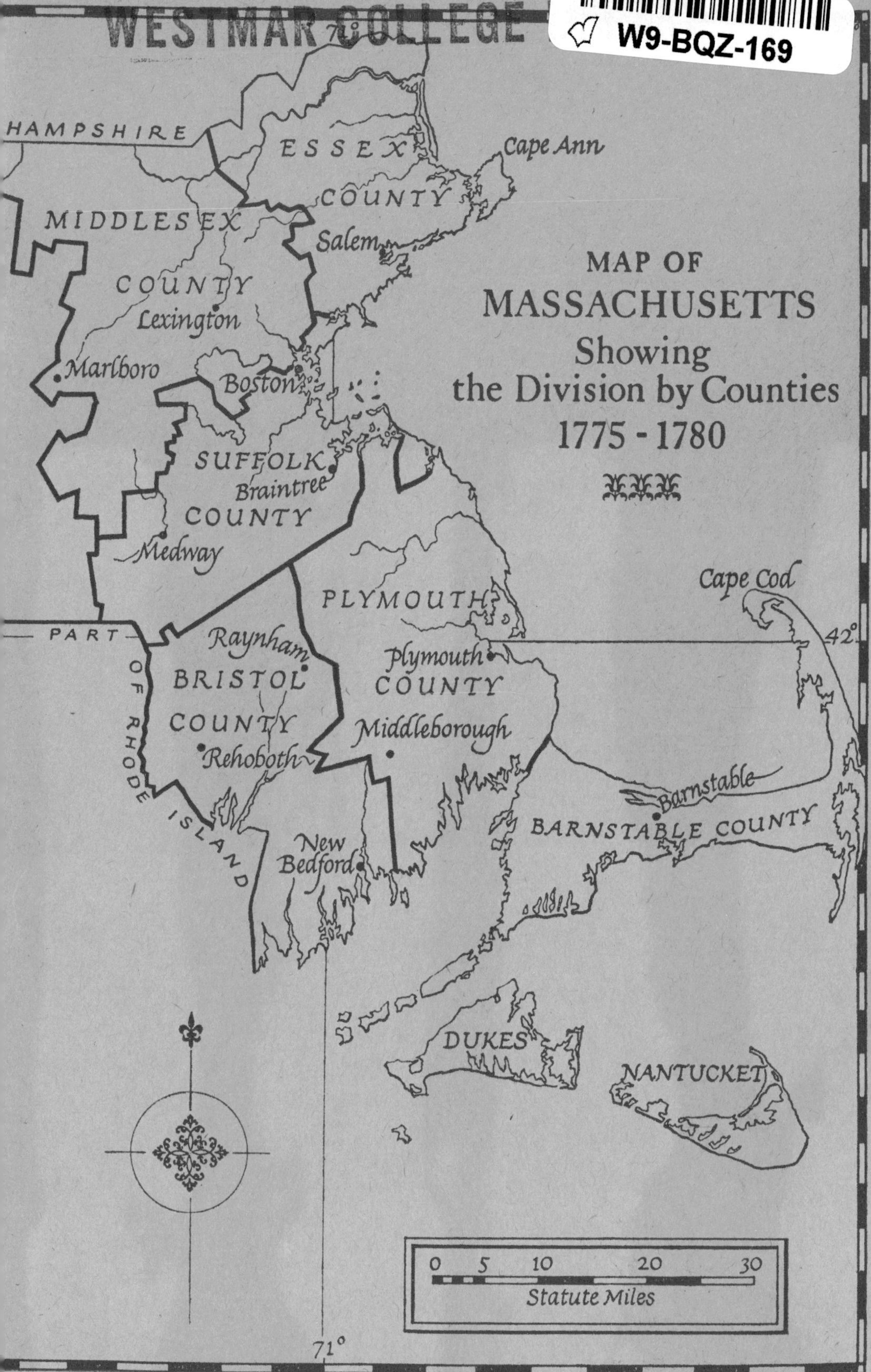
MAP OF
MASSACHUSETTS
Showing
the Division by Counties
1775 - 1780
HAMPSHIRE
ESSEX
COUNTY
Cape Ann
MIDDLESEX
COUNTY
Salem
Lexington
Marlboro
Boston
SUFFOLK
Braintree
COUNTY
Medway
PLYMOUTH
Cape Cod
PART
OF RHODE ISLAND
Raynham
BRISTOL
COUNTY
Rehoboth
Plymouth
COUNTY
Middleborough
42°
Barnstable
BARNSTABLE COUNTY
New Bedford
DUKES
NANTUCKET
71°
0 5 10 20 30
Statute Miles

This book is an attempt to understand the American Revolution in terms of the ideas of the mass of the people who participated in it. Rarely is it possible to hear the voice of the people in a revolution except as it filters through the writings of articulate individuals who may not be representative. But when the province of Massachusetts broke away from England, it cut itself off from the recognized source of political authority. The revolutionary political leaders were deeply concerned that order be maintained and unequivocal approval be secured from the people — the *new* source of authority — for their actions in setting up a government.

Therefore on several occasions during the effort to draft a constitution for Massachusetts after 1776, the citizens of the new Commonwealth were asked to convene in their three hundred town meetings to debate and convey to the legislators in Boston their political theories, needs, and aspirations, and to ratify, or reject, various specific proposals. The resulting extensive debates, which constitute a unique body of material documenting the political thought of the ordinary citizen, were transcribed and forwarded to the legislature.

This important collection of sources, most of it previously unpublished, is presented here along with related explanatory material. In an extended introduction, the editors interpret the American Revolution and its sustaining political framework in light of these documents, analyzing the forces that were singular and those that were universal in the shaping of American democracy. Comparisons are made with popular uprisings in other parts of the world and at other times, and the whole is integrated into a general discussion of the nature of revolution and its relationship to constitutional authority.

Oscar Handlin, author of many books and a Pulitzer Prize winning historian, is [illegible] Warren Professor of History, Harvard University. His wife, Mary F. Handlin, is Research Editor, Center for the Study of the History of Liberty in America, at Harvard University.

Center for the Study of the History of Liberty in America

The Popular Sources of Political Authority

A PUBLICATION OF THE CENTER FOR THE STUDY
OF THE HISTORY OF LIBERTY IN AMERICA
HARVARD UNIVERSITY

THE POPULAR SOURCES OF POLITICAL AUTHORITY

DOCUMENTS ON THE MASSACHUSETTS CONSTITUTION *of* 1780

EDITED WITH AN INTRODUCTION
by
OSCAR AND MARY HANDLIN

THE BELKNAP PRESS OF
HARVARD UNIVERSITY PRESS
Cambridge, Massachusetts
1966

DISTRIBUTED IN GREAT BRITAIN BY OXFORD UNIVERSITY PRESS, LONDON

THE CENTER FOR THE STUDY OF THE HISTORY OF LIBERTY IN AMERICA
IS AIDED BY A GRANT FROM THE CARNEGIE CORPORATION OF NEW YORK

LIBRARY OF CONGRESS CATALOG CARD NUMBER 66-18247

PRINTED IN THE UNITED STATES OF AMERICA

To

SAMUEL ELIOT MORISON

TEACHER AND COLLEAGUE

Acknowledgments

In the course of preparing this work we have acquired many obligations toward the individuals and the institutions whose cooperation made it possible.

The bulk of the documents here reproduced, and on which our understanding of the constitutional process in Massachusetts depended, are stored in the Massachusetts Archives in Boston. In compiling this volume, as in our research for an earlier book, we were immensely aided by the patience and helpfulness of Leo Flaherty and Helen Flaherty, devoted civil servants who have displayed an admirable familiarity with and solicitude for, the materials under their charge. We are also grateful to the State Archivist, Dr. Richard Hale, Jr., and to Secretaries of State Edward J. Cronin, Joseph Ward, and Kevin White for facilitating our work.

We have in addition profited from the assistance of the custodians of the Harvard College Library, the New York Public Library, the Boston Public Library, the Massachusetts Historical Society, the Berkshire Atheneum (Pittsfield), and the American Antiquarian Society. The officials of the towns and cities, upon whose records we have drawn, have been helpful in supplying us with material.

In preparing this difficult manuscript we were fortunate to be able to count upon the efficient services of Katherine E. Top, Barbara Evans, and Nancy Jackson.

The research on this work was conducted under the auspices of the Center for the Study of the History of Liberty in America. We are indebted for the ability to carry this work forward, as for the operations of the whole Center, to the Carnegie Corporation of New York. We have profited constantly from the advice and criticism of our colleagues associated with the Center—the late V.O. Key, Jr., David Riesman, George Albert Smith, Jr., Paul A. Freund, and Carl Kaysen. We are particularly grateful to Crane Brinton and Paul H. Buck, who gave the manuscript a critical and perceptive reading. We have also been fortunate to be able to discuss many of the issues involved with Bernard Bailyn, who shares our interest in the problems with which this book deals. We and all those who have worked in this field, are indebted to the efforts of Samuel Eliot Morison who, fifty years ago, first systematically exploited the collections which are touched on here. For the interpretations advanced in this work, however, we are solely responsible.

O. H.
M. H.

Cambridge, Massachusetts
May 1966

Contents

II

The Constitution of 1778, January 1777—November 1778

III

Formation of the Constitution of 1780, February 1779—March 1780

IV

Ratification, May 1780—June 1780

Appendix

The Popular Sources of Political Authority

You and I, my dear friend, have been sent into life at a time when the greatest lawgivers of antiquity would have wished to live. How few of the human race have ever enjoyed an opportunity of making an election of government, more than of air, soil, or climate, for themselves or their children! When, before the present epocha, had three millions of people full power and a fair opportunity to form and establish the wisest and happiest government that human wisdom can contrive? I hope you will avail yourself and your country of that extensive learning and indefatigable industry which you possess, to assist her in the formation of the happiest governments and the best character of a great people.*

* To George Wythe in John Adams, *Thoughts on Government* (Philadelphia, 1776), in *Works of John Adams,* ed. C. F. Adams, IV (Boston, 1851), 200.

Introduction

Revolution is so prominent among the forces that shape the world of the twentieth century that it is tempting to seek analogies with the past. In a tumultuous age marked by swift political change, historians understandably search the experience of earlier eras in the hope of making out the universal rules governing these convulsions.

They have been encouraged to do so by a persistent assumption, more than a century old, that all revolutions are inherently the same. Any overturn of an existing political and social system, it was believed, had an essential anatomical structure and a predictable course independent of variations in the context in which it occurred. Always it involved a breach in existing authority that permitted a "large lower class" to challenge the position of "a small upper class" in the struggle for power. The laws that governed such contests were equally applicable to the Gracchi brothers and to Fidel Castro.[1]

Such uniformities seemed particularly plausible when located in the events that transformed Europe and America in the last quarter of the eighteenth century. The Enlightenment was international and there were substantial similarities among the social systems of all the areas involved. "Western Civilization as a whole, at a critical moment in its history," seemed to have been swept "by a single revolutionary movement, which manifested itself in different ways and with varying success in different countries, yet in all of them showed similar objectives and principles." The American, French, Dutch, Swiss, and other revolutions were "related products of a common impulse, or different ways of achieving, under different circumstances and against different degrees of opposition, certain recognizably common goals." The determination of "constituted bodies" of government—"parliaments, councils, assemblies, and magistracies of various kinds"—to defend themselves by appeals to legitimacy

[1] A typical exposition of this point of view may be found in Alfred Meusel, "Revolution and Counter-Revolution," *Encyclopaedia of the Social Sciences* (New York, 1934), XIII, 367ff. While these assumptions received their modern formulation in the nineteenth century, their origins reach as far back as Aristotle, *Politics,* Book V, ed. Ernest Barker (Oxford, 1946), 203ff. See also P. A. Sorokin, *Sociology of Revolution* (Philadelphia, 1925); L. P. Edwards, *The Natural History of Revolution* (Chicago, 1927); Crane Brinton, *The Anatomy of Revolution* (New York, [1952]).

and to the law of nature "against either superior authorities on the one hand or popular pressures on the other" precipitated a "democratic revolutionary movement," when persons systematically excluded attempted to "change the basis of authority and representation, reconstitute the constituted bodies, or obtain a wholly new constitution of the state itself." In time, however, "an aristocratic resurgence" stopped the moves for democratization, to varying degrees but with unmistakable common effect.[2]

This approach has been fruitful insofar as it has stressed the pervasiveness of a common vocabulary that expressed the aspirations of aggrieved men everywhere in the Western world. But it has obscured a more critical problem, the extent to which concepts, similar in the abstract, received specific meaning from the concrete situation in which they were embedded. The Enlightenment and the political ideas derived from it certainly passed across national boundaries. Men spoke of natural rights, of a social compact, of a constitution, and of consent of the governed in France and England and the Netherlands as they did in Pennsylvania and Virginia. But the connotations attached to those phrases varied with the practical circumstances and the historical antecedents against which they were interpreted.[3]

So, too, the events in the Paris of 1789 bore surface similarities to those in the Philadelphia of 1776; and participants on both sides of the Atlantic, for a time, even considered the one sequence a continuation of the other. But the characters, the courses, and the outcomes of the two revolutions have meaning only in terms of the different political and social systems in which they emerged and at which they were directed. Revolution was not a phenomenon with a generic quality of its own; it was an incident in the life of a particular society.[4]

The American Revolution was a phase in the political development of the eighteenth-century colonies which, well before the first shots were fired, had already diverged significantly from their European antecedents. This revolution can only be understood in the context of the distinctive features of the environment in which it took form and developed. To that end it will be useful to examine, in one state, the interaction among

[2] R. R. Palmer, *The Age of the Democratic Revolution,* I (Princeton, 1959), 4, 9, 23.

[3] Oscar and Mary Handlin, "James Burgh and the American Revolutionary Theory," Massachusetts Historical Society, *Proceedings,* LXXIII (1963), 38ff.; Bernard Bailyn, "Political Experience and Enlightenment Ideas in Eighteenth-Century America," *American Historical Review,* LXVII (1962), 339ff.

[4] See Ernest Barker, *Oliver Cromwell and the English People* (Cambridge, Eng., 1937), 86ff.

the ideas of the Enlightenment, the existing institutions of government, and the unspoken assumptions of the people about their relationship to power.

As Massachusetts ceased to be a chartered province under the British King and became an independent commonwealth governed by a constitution of its own making, it passed through a revolution. The men who effected the change were as informed as those of any Western nation about the abstract ideas of natural rights, constitutions, and liberty. But their experiences had sensitized their capacity for receiving, digesting, and acting upon those ideas in a way markedly different from their counterparts across the Atlantic.

The critical difference arose from the distinctive social setting. In eighteenth-century America the gap between the constituted bodies of government and the people had narrowed so that the rulers operated not only with the consent but with the active participation of those over whom they held authority. A revolution under these conditions was therefore not the result of an effort by excluded elements to reach for a share of power. It was rather an attempt to adjust political forms to existing practices and to give them reasonable order in the light of underlying ideas about man and society.

In Massachusetts the revolutionary leadership bore a peculiar relationship to its following. The groups which held or sought power by virtue of wealth, organizational ability, or talent did not impose a settlement upon the mass. Their power was tentative and conditioned upon the ability to secure the consent of the governed. And the order devised in six years of experiment required constant consultation of the wishes of the people. The obligation to refer disputed issues back to the constituents of the state also compelled those swayed by divergent interests and ideas to compose their differences and to search for tolerable compromises that would elicit widespread acquiescence. The subtle process by which leaders informed and were informed by their followers is the subject of this volume.

The occasion for reconsidering the nature of its polity arose from the conflict between Massachusetts and the Crown. More than two years before the Declaration of Independence, the dispute with Great Britain catapulted the colony into a quest for a new mode of governing itself that did not end until the adoption of the state Constitution in 1780. The

Parliamentary Act of 1774, which directed that the Council be appointed by royal writs of mandamus, instead of elected annually by the House of Representatives, seemed at first only to raise the remote issue of the inviolability of the provincial charter under which the colony had been ruled for eighty years. But each step in questioning the power to alter that framework led to a rejection of imperial control. Yet as imperial control was rejected, the charter to which the aggrieved appealed could no longer function, for it was itself a royal document, under the terms of which the Crown reserved a vital role in government.

When Governor Thomas Gage dissolved the General Court on June 17, 1774, he scarcely understood that another such body would never sit. He expected the sullen representatives to return to their homes and then come back later in the year after the new arrangements had been effected. He did not, therefore, hesitate to issue writs on September 1 for the election of a Court to meet at Salem on October 5.

But the events of the intervening months altered his expectations and his plans. The dispersal of the General Court, instead of leaving him the sole custodian of power in the province, cut him off from its local sources. Town government in the three hundred communities of the colony continued to operate as before; the selectmen summoned meetings of the freemen who debated issues and decided upon the course to follow. Furthermore, everywhere committees of correspondence provided these localities with the means of communicating with one another and of agreeing upon joint action.[5]

The Governor also lost control of the county, the intermediary territorial unit. He appointed its chief officers, the judges, sheriffs, and coroners; but when they ceased to command local support, they lost their effectiveness and other agencies pre-empted their authority. "A people may let a king fall, yet still remain a people," sagely observed Abigail Adams. "But, if a king let his people slip from him, he is no longer a king."[6]

Throughout their history necessity had familiarized the Massachusetts men with the means of cooperative action. Since the seventeenth century, the towns had sent commissioners to county meetings to assess taxes, elect the county treasurer, and transact other business of local concern

[5] Harry A. Cushing, "Political Activity of Massachusetts Towns during the Revolution," American Historical Association, *Annual Report for the Year 1895* (Washington, 1896), 105ff.

[6] To John, Braintree, May 7, 1776, in Charles Francis Adams, ed., *Familiar Letters of John Adams and His Wife Abigail Adams, during the Revolution* (Boston, 1875), 169.

with which the provincial government in Boston could not deal.[7] These practices were adapted to the new emergency as a matter of course. County conventions, composed of delegates from the towns, took over much of the actual business of administration.

The designation given these gatherings was significant. The term, convention, was familiar from the practice of the Congregational churches. Since the ministers had lost their formal role in the polity, they had met annually in "General Convention" on the day the Assembly elected councilors to propose "Matters of public Importance, referring to the Interest of Religion in the Churches." The conventions assumed no power of decision, yet their advice for *"the preserving and promoting of true PIETY* in the Land" was influential; and they frequently made "Motions . . . unto the *General Assembly* for such *Acts* and *Laws"* as were desirable.[8]

The ministers who first assembled in this manner no doubt knew of the earlier use of the word to apply to a regular, quasi-governmental gathering of representatives of the Scottish burghs to concert action in dealing with the Crown and Parliament. In England, too, occasional exceptional Parliaments, such as that which restored Charles II in 1660 and that which vacated the throne of James II in 1688, were known as conventions. In all these contexts the term referred to a body which met, directly or indirectly to exercise or influence power outside the established structure of government. In the Bay Colony too, "private Fellow Subjects, conven'd from divers Towns" in convention, as in 1768, when more normal procedures were inadequate to express their grievances. The adoption of the same device in Massachusetts in 1774 recognized the urgency of the situation and was a sign of the ability to deal with it.[9]

[7] See st. 1692–93, chs. 4, 41, 49; st. 1695–96, ch. 6; st. 1702–03, ch. 4 (*Acts and Resolves, Public and Private, of the Province of the Massachussetts Bay* [Boston, 1869–86], I, 29ff., 91ff., 106ff., 213ff., 515ff.); also John Fiske, *Civil Government in the United States Considered with Some Reference to Its Origins* (Boston, 1892), 53; C. H. J. Douglas, *Financial History of Massachusetts* (New York, 1892), 27, 62; Irving Brant, *James Madison*, I (New York, 1941), 149.

[8] Cotton Mather, *Ratio Disciplinae Fratrum Nov-Anglorum. "A Faithful Account of the Discipline Professed and Practised in the Churches of New-England"* (Boston, 1726), 176ff.; *An Historical Sketch of the Convention of the Congregational Ministers in Massachusetts* (Cambridge, Mass., 1821); John W. Harding, *Historical Sermon* (Boston, 1888), 4, 5.

[9] Massachusetts Convention, *Result of the Conference . . . at Boston the Twenty-Second Day of September, 1768*, Broadside (Boston, 1768). Shortly after the Revolution, Samuel Adams gave concise expression to the concept of the convention to John Adams and Noah Webster, April 16, 30, 1784, in *Writings*, ed. H. A. Cushing (New York, 1904–08), IV, 296, 305ff. See also Theodora Pagan, *The Convention of the Royal Burghs of Scotland* (Glasgow, 1926); L. F. Brown, "Religious Factors in the Convention Parliament,"

A succession of county conventions that year expressed grave doubts about Great Britain's power to interfere with the administration of the colony. The convention of all the towns and districts in Suffolk County on September 6, 1774, declared Parliament's "fatal edict, which proclaims a power to frame laws for us in all cases whatsoever" an "unparalleled usurpation of unconstitutional power." It appealed to "that inalienable and inestimable inheritance which we derived from nature, the constitution of Britain, which was covenanted to us in the charter of the province," called for repeal of the law, and rejected as unconstitutional courts under justices holding office "by any other tenure than that which the charter and the laws of the province direct." It urged the mandamus councilors to resign lest they "be considered by this county as obstinate and uncorrigible enemies to this colony," and it requested the several towns to choose members for a Provincial Congress to meet in Concord.[10]

Other conventions elsewhere professed loyalty to the King, but stressed the urgent necessity for maintaining the colony's "natural and charter rights." Privileges confirmed by a charter could not be forfeited by one of the "contracting parties" simply because the other party found it inexpedient to continue them. The appointment of councilors who would be "absolute tools and creatures" struck at the essential "equilibrium in the legislative body." To maintain "constitutional" government, only those civil officers whose commissions were issued before July 1, 1774 would be obeyed.[11]

The inviolability of the charter in these statements was linked to two other concepts, also specifically spelled out: that the colonies enjoyed an inalienable British inheritance and that they were "entitled to all the natural rights of mankind . . . subject to the control of no power on earth, but by their own consent."[12] The word constitution, to which the protesters appealed, conveyed all three connotations—the specific charter, the legacy of British law, and natural rights. Yet none was as clear as repetition made it seem. What compact, natural rights, constitution, equilibrium in the legislative body, and consent meant was yet to be explored in a practical sense, as Massachusetts sought to establish a new mode of governing itself.

English Historical Review, XXII (1907), 51ff.; D. L. Keir, *Constitutional History of Modern Britain* (London, 1960), 269, 270.

[10] William Lincoln, ed., *Journals of Each Provincial Congress of Massachusetts in 1774 and 1775* (Boston, 1838), 601–604.

[11] Middlesex Convention, August 30, 31, 1774, *ibid.,* 611–613.

[12] Plymouth Convention, September 26, 27, 1774, *ibid.,* 622.

These declarations persuaded Governor Gage on September 28 to proclaim that it was "inexpedient" to convene a General Court. The "extraordinary resolves which have been passed in many of the counties," and "the present disordered and unhappy state of the province" justified postponement to "some more distant day." Despite this proclamation, some ninety representatives met at Salem on October 5, 1774, went through the formalities of waiting for the Governor to administer the oaths, and, on Gage's failure to appear, organized themselves into a convention on October 6, under the chairmanship of John Hancock. A report of a committee chosen to canvass the next steps found the Governor's cancellation of the meeting of the General Court "unconstitutional, unjust, and disrespectful to the province," and the convention then voted to form themselves into a Provincial Congress "to be joined by such other persons as have been or shall be chosen for that purpose."[13]

Many towns had instructed their representatives "to adhere firmly to the charter of the Province, and not consent to any act that can possibly be construed into an acknowledgement of the validity of the act of the British Parliament, for altering the government of the Massachusetts Bay; more especially to acknowledge the Hon. Board of Counsellors, elected last May, by the General Court, as the only rightful and constitutional Council of the Province."[14] But a mere retraction of the offensive measures of 1774 would no longer satisfy everyone. Some people in the western counties explained "that no security can be given them that they shall enjoy their estates without molestation, even if the late charter should be again restored in all its parts, since the possession of their lands may be rendered precarious by any alterations in the charter which the parliament shall think fit to make." It was necessary in addition to forestall future usurpations; now was the time for a more basic settlement. The compact had been broken. Let the people frame a new one proposing "a certain limited subjection to the king, as they shall judge convenient, which he may accept or reject, as he pleases."[15]

For the moment "caution and prudence" were necessary. Indirect negotiations with the royal authorities were still in progress and moderate men were yet dragging their heels. Above all Massachusetts had no desire to strike out on its own without the approval of the rest of the

[13] *Ibid.*, 3–6; Mercy Warren, *History of the Rise, Progress and Termination of the American Revolution* (Boston, 1805), I, 160ff.

[14] William Barry, *History of Framingham* (Boston, 1847), 91.

[15] Joseph Warren to Samuel Adams, September 12, 1774, in Richard Frothingham, *Life and Times of Joseph Warren* (Boston, 1865), 376.

Continent. The void in that province was more precipitous and more extreme than in "the other colonies" whose "charters have not yet been torn to pieces by the harpies of power" and which still retained "their usual forms of trials by juries, in courts duly constituted." Even though many in the Bay Colony were certain that they had "a right to determine for themselves under what government they will live hereafter," they had to tread warily until others fell in line in the face of parliamentary intransigence.[16]

Meanwhile there were immediate problems of maintaining order. The successive Provincial Congresses, of which there were three between October 1774 and July 1775, continued to meet "to collect the wisdom of the province . . . to concert some adequate remedy for preventing impending ruin, and providing for the public safety." They acted, not officially as General Courts, but rather as conventions or revolutionary committees to link the Massachusetts towns with the Continental Congress in Philadelphia on the one hand, and with General Gage on the other. But they also had to see to it that the taxes went to the use of the colony and not of the royal representatives, and to provide for the "defence and safety" of the province by mustering the militia—in other words to exercise the powers of civil government.[17] The members still shied away from an overt acknowledgment of the consequences and put off what problems they could until "a general assembly shall be convened in this colony."[18] But the fact remained that the provisional device of a Provincial Congress created a substitute for the General Court, and the only governing agency for the province.

Through the winter of 1774 the delegates continued to urge both the need for defying the Governor and the urgency of preserving proper procedures. The meanest peasant deserved "the same security in his life and property, as his sovereign has in his crown." But the House of Commons, consisting of "persons who are by no means accountable to you," had "claimed and exercised the power of granting your money without your consent." When such tyrants trampled on freedom, "resistance is so far from being criminal, that it becomes the christian and social duty of each individual."[19]

Yet there was to be no irresponsible action. As late as April 1, 1775, the Congress resolved that if writs should be issued for a general assem-

[16] Warren to Samuel Adams, September 4, 1774, *ibid.*, 357.
[17] Lincoln, *Journals of Each Provincial Congress*, 17, 19, 27ff., 32, 38ff.
[18] *Ibid.*, 67.
[19] *Ibid.*, 91ff.

bly, the several towns "ought to obey such precepts, and choose their members as usual; and instruct them to transact no business with the council, appointed by mandamus; and if they should be dissolved, to meet in a Provincial Congress, for the purpose of considering and transacting the affairs of this colony."[20]

Shortly thereafter, however, the events at Concord and Lexington thrust the delegates closer to an open rupture with the Crown. The prospect for reconciliation faded. Early in May, the Congress revoked its suggestion that the people participate in the election of an assembly, because "consequences of a dangerous nature would result from the operation of that resolution"; and the Committee of Safety, which was acting as a provisional directory, declared that "the public good of this colony requires, that government in full form ought to be taken up immediately."[21]

The ultimate step of creating a new political system waited upon approval from the Continental Congress in Philadelphia. On May 16, 1775, Massachusetts requested "explicit advice" about "the taking up and exercising the powers of civil government." The province had raised a military force and made all the preparations for defense that its confused state would admit. "But, as the sword should, in all free states, be subservient to the civil powers," it trembled at "having an army, although consisting of our own countrymen, established here, without a civil power to provide for and control it." Yet since the problem equally affected its sister colonies, it had "declined . . . to assume the reins of civil government" without their advice and consent.[22]

A second plea pointed to the "embarrassments, delays, disappointments and obstructions, in executing every undertaking necessary for the preservation of our lives, and much more of our property," to the "alarming symptoms of the abatement of the sense, in the minds of some people, of the sacredness of private property," and to "the extreme difficulty of maintaining the public peace" under existing circumstances.[23]

The anomalous situation troubled such men as Joseph Warren. They had taken up arms and had presumed to exercise certain fiscal powers. By whose warrant? And could they be sure that others in the colony would not also take it into their heads to follow their own inclinations? Without some civil authority to guide them, the soldiery might "lose the

[20] *Ibid.*, 116.
[21] *Ibid.*, 192; Frothingham, *Warren*, 477.
[22] Lincoln, *Journals of Each Provincial Congress*, 229ff.
[23] *Ibid.*, 319ff.

ideas of right and wrong" and "plunder, instead of protecting, the inhabitants." There would then follow unimaginable difficulties.[24]

Divided counsels in Philadelphia, however, delayed action. The Continental Congress was still probing the possibilities for mediation and seeking a consensus among all the colonies. Sensitive to opinion in Great Britain and in Europe, it preferred the final break to follow some overwhelming, irremediable, and glaring iniquity of the Crown.

At last, on June 9, 1775, the Continental Congress acted. It advised the Provincial Congress to "write letters to the inhabitants of the several places, which are entitled to representation in assembly, requesting them to choose such representatives; and that the assembly, when chosen, should elect counsellors; which assembly and council should exercise the powers of government, until a governor of his majesty's appointment will consent to govern the colony according to its charter." Precepts for the election of a General Court to meet at Watertown on July 19 were accordingly issued.[25]

The outcome, which amounted to a pretense that the old charter was still valid, disappointed many Massachusetts leaders. Joseph Warren, for one, thought it inconceivable that the colony would be advised, "to take up that form established by the late charter, as it contains in it the seeds of despotism, and would, in a few years, bring us again into the same unhappy situation in which we now are." He had hoped that a new government "might be so happily moulded, that the only road to promotion" would be "through the affection of the people. This being the case, the interest of the governor and the governed will be the same; and we shall no longer be plagued by a group of unprincipled villains." The revolutionaries had missed an opportunity to adopt "a constitution worthy of freemen." But, although they did not altogether "admire the form of government presented," they were "all submission" in the face of the exigencies of the moment.[26]

The Provincial Congress followed the advice from the Continental Congress because it was "impressed with the indispensable necessity of rescuing this people from the danger they are in, of falling into a state of anarchy" and so that its "public resolutions may be taken and executed

[24] Warren to Samuel Adams, May 17, 26, 1775, in Frothingham, *Warren,* 485, 495.

[25] Lincoln, *Journals of Each Provincial Congress,* 359; John Adams, *Works,* ed. C. F. Adams (Boston, 1850–56), IV, 213, 214; Mercy Warren, *History of the American Revolution,* I, 225ff.

[26] Warren to Samuel and John Adams, May 14, June 21, 1775, in Frothingham, *Warren,* 483ff., 512.

with greater despatch." On June 20, 1775, it ordered the towns "to cause the freeholders and other inhabitants . . . that have an estate of freehold in land, within this province or territory, of forty shillings per annum, at the least, or other estate to the value of forty pounds sterling," to assemble "to elect and depute one or more freeholders, resident in the same town, according to the numbers set" by an earlier act to convene at Watertown on July 19. On that day the newly constituted House of Representatives met and elected a council.[27]

Far from settling the question of authority, the recommendations of the Continental Congress brought the whole issue out into the open by recognizing the right of Massachusetts to organize itself without royal permission. Until then, the Provincial Congress had gone about its business without Governor Gage's leadership, under the pretense that this unpleasant but inevitable expedient had been forced on it by Parliament's unconstitutional acts. It had governed, but had disclaimed the authority to govern. Now the advice from Philadelphia was to assume that authority. As in the past, the voters were to qualify; the towns were to elect deputies; the House of Representatives was to organize, although still without the Governor. Resumption of the old charter therefore meant resumption only of so much of it as seemed viable in 1775. With the Governor removed, the Council of twenty-eight appointed by the House as it had been before the crisis became the sole executive, exercising some judicial and legislative powers as well.[28]

The concern with the niceties of procedure persisted. "When we deviate from the established rules," wrote the Berkshire County Committee of Correspondence, "we are lost in the boundless field of uncertainty and disorder." A determination to maintain orderly forms therefore tempered the desire to make a new start. Soon after the reconstituted General Court met it passed "An Act to Confirm and Establish the Resolves of the Several Provincial Congresses of this Colony." It noted that the colony had "for many months past been deprived of the free exercise of its usual powers of government," and that congresses had had to act on "many matters of the greatest importance for the recovery and preservation of that liberty, which God, nature and compact have given to this people." Fearing that the legality of these transactions might in the future be questioned, "unless confirmed and established in some

[27] Lincoln, *Journals of Each Provincial Congress,* 359, 365.

[28] On the Council, see A. B. Hart, ed., *Commonwealth History of Massachusetts,* III (New York, 1929), 70ff.

known constitutional manner," the General Court established the deeds of the Provincial Congresses "as lawful and valid to all intents." [29]

The new arrangements were "not considered as permanent." Samuel Adams, for instance, thought the time near "when the most timid will see the absolute Necessity of every one of the Colonies setting up a Government within it self." A new framework would soon take form. But meanwhile there was business to do, a war to be fought, and order to be restored.[30]

The General Court set about raising and financing an army, fitting out armed vessels, and defining economic objectives. It had to provide for a currency, squeeze taxes from those who could pay, and support communities which had suffered from the hostilities. It learned that even when there was unanimity in enacting these measures, there remained the problem of eliciting obedience, and it discovered that plans reasonable in the abstract often had unanticipated and incalculable consequences. Down to 1780, it struggled to sustain the revolutionary enterprise in practice while its own legality remained a subject of constant concern.

The question of the source of authority continued to intrude. In November 1775, the Continental Congress's recommendation that South Carolina and New Hampshire constitute governments without reference to their earlier charters reaffirmed for some people the desirability of a totally fresh reconsideration of how Massachusetts would rule itself. The departure of the loyalists in March 1776 removed one of the drags that had prevented the rebels from acting in accord with the realities of the situation. In May, the Continental Congress advised all the provinces to establish new forms of government. In July, the independence of the colonies was recognized by declaration as it had already been achieved in actuality. And each succeeding month made reconciliation with the Crown less likely and raised again and again the troubling question: why did a free state continue to govern itself by the terms of a royal charter?

The same question emerged repeatedly in the course of practical efforts to make the old arrangements work under new conditions. The General Court needed the consent of those it governed and therefore had to deal

[29] Below, No. 1; Peter Force, *American Archives,* Fourth Series (Washington, 1837–46), V, 807; *The Charters and General Laws of the Colony and Province of Massachusetts Bay* (Boston, 1814), 687–688.

[30] Samuel Adams to James Warren, November 4, 1775, December 26, 1775, in Samuel Adams, *Writings,* III, 233, 244; Hart, *Commonwealth History,* III, 71.

with representation. In August 1775 it restored to incorporated districts the privilege of sending deputies, of which they had been deprived "against common right, and in derogation of the rights granted to the inhabitants . . . by the charter."[31] But the issue was more complex than this calm pronouncement recognized. Before 1774, each town with thirty or more freeholders had enjoyed the privilege of sending one deputy to the Assembly; Boston, the largest, could elect four and was aggrieved because the system fell so far short of giving it the weight it felt its size justified. It and the other populous eastern places could readily be outvoted by a combination of small towns with only a fraction of their population. In May 1776 An Act Providing for a More Equal Representation in the General Court removed the upper limit and gave each place the right to a delegate for every additional hundred voters. That, however, made the size of the House unwieldy and raised fears that the whole province might be dominated by the metropolis.[32]

What was being represented, the incorporated communities or the individual inhabitants? That question could not be answered without reconsidering the whole basis of government. A memorial of Essex County towns unhappily had inquired, "If a new System of Government, or any material Alteration in the old is to be in the Contemplation of the next general Assembly; Is it not fitting that the whole Community should be equally concerned in adjusting this System?"[33]

In its concern with proper procedures, Massachusetts also edged up to the problem of the control of power. The militia was the effective coercive force, but there was no clear guide to the forms for its administration. Before 1774, the governor had appointed its chief officers, while the captain of each company designated the sergeants and corporals. In Gage's absence the people had presumed to select the captains and the Provincial Congress had acquiesced in a process by which those so designated had proceeded to choose the line officers, cautioning them only "to pay strict obedience to the orders and directions of the . . . committee of safety."[34]

[31] Below, No. 2; st. 1775–76, ch. 3 (*Acts and Resolves,* V, 419, 511).

[32] Below, No. 7; st. 1692–93, ch. 38 (*Acts and Resolves,* I, 88); st. 1775–76, ch. 26 (*ibid.,* V, 502, 542); also Essex County Convention, April 25, 26, 1776, below, No. 6; James Savage, *Address Delivered before the Massachusetts Lyceum, January 26, 1832* (n.p., n.d. [Boston, 1832]), 6–10; Hart, *Commonwealth History,* III, 79.

[33] Essex County Convention, Ipswich, April 25, 26, 1776, MA 156/192–195. See also John Adams to James Warren, June 5, 1777, in *Warren-Adams Letters,* ed. W. C. Ford (Massachusetts Historical Society, *Collections,* LXXII–LXXIII [1917–18]), I, 327.

[34] Lincoln, *Journals of Each Provincial Congress,* 32ff., 241.

This situation, however, did not make the army subordinate to effective civil power and control and troubled the Continental and Provincial Congresses, particularly after the outbreak of fighting in April 1775. But any effort to change the mode of selecting officers raised the ticklish question of who had inherited the royal governor's prerogative. The Continental Congress, in general instructions issued on July 18, 1775, had left it to the discretion of each colony whether to continue their former practices or to give the appointive power to the respective provincial assemblies.[35] The Council considered itself heir of the governor's power and therefore claimed the exclusive right to handle the matter. The House of Representatives, however, also claimed a role and in addition some towns would recognize only such officials as the people themselves elected. The Council itself was apologetic; in November, it expressed its "firm Attachment to the natural Rights of Men" and explained that "if there is an Incompatibility between those Rights and the Charter-Constitution of this Colony," it could only lament its obligation to observe the constitution. To prevent the colony from falling into disorder, the Council finally decided "to gratify the House of Representatives in this claim but not by any means any further to deviate from the Charter." Again the question of the charter-constitution![36]

These uncertainties became more dangerous as the revolutionary situation unfolded. The acts of the Provincial Congress directed at winning the war commanded general assent from all those with a stake in victory. But the same measures also influenced the personal welfare of various groups in the society. Money and supplies were necessary to carry on the fight; but fiscal policy and price-control laws affected differently the merchants, farmers, artisans and seamen, the creditors and debtors, the

[35] The Continental Congress, John Adams explained, was unable to make a complete break with the past because the gentlemen in other colonies were "habituated to higher notions of themselves, and the distinction between them and the common people, than we are." It therefore sought to widen the distance between officers and men and to control appointments in the Councils. See John Adams to Joseph Hawley, November 25, 1775, in E. C. Burnett, ed., *Letters of Members of the Continental Congress* (Washington, 1921–38), I, 259ff.; also Samuel Adams to James Otis, November 23, 1775, *ibid.*, I, 256ff.; John Adams to James Otis, November 23, 1775, *ibid.*, I, 258; John Hancock and Thomas Cushing to the Massachusetts Council, November 24, 1775, *ibid.*, I, 258ff.

[36] *Acts and Resolves,* V, 523, 525. On the general development of the militia, see editor's notes, *ibid.*, V, 520ff.; Province Charter (*ibid.*, I, 18); st. 1693–94, ch. 3 (*ibid.*, I, 128–130); Lincoln, *Journals of Each Provincial Congress,* 32ff., 89ff., 121, 135, 230, 241, 243ff., 245; *Massachusetts Soldiers and Sailors of the Revolutionary War* (Boston, 1896), I, xvii; MA 195/393; also Frothingham, *Warren,* 495; Samuel Adams to James Warren, January 7, 1776, in Samuel Adams, *Writings,* III, 250–251. For early demands for popular elections, see, e.g., W. S. Heywood, *History of Westminster* (Lowell, 1893), 154.

residents of the eastern commercial towns and the backwoodsmen. Each interest, as it became defined in the shifting fortunes of war, struggled to shape government according to its own lights. Since the pattern of colonial politics was disrupted, each actual use of power involved a reshuffling of relationships, to be viewed with suspicion. The Berkshire farmers looked upon the proceedings of the remote legislature with distrust while the Salem traders learned with dismay of the closing of the courts in the West. The Baptist minority worried about the intentions of the Congregationalist majority; Stockbridge complained about its neighbor, Lee; and the inhabitants of "a Goar of Land Adjoying to the north Line of Chesterfield" felt discriminated against by the town meeting—"when men or money is wanting we were never neglected, but when Privelidges are to be Destributed then we are neglected."[37]

Everything was in flux. New people acquired wealth and aspired to power; Mrs. Cabot's freed Negro Titus filled his coffers as agent for some privateersmen, took to wearing "cloth shoes, ruffled shirts, silk breeches and stockings," and danced minuets at Commencement. Those among the former leaders who did not emigrate had to make room for the newcomers; "these little lofty animals" could do "a world of mischief" unless guided by the superior qualities of those familiar with responsibility. Well might the General Court command "the good People" to "lead Sober, Religious, and peaceable Lives," avoiding "all Debauchery, Profaneness, Corruption, Venality, all riotous and tumultuous Proceedings, and all Immoralities whatsoever." In the midst of a noble revolution, "Avarice, venality, Animosity, contention, pride, weakness and dissipation" prevailed in the cottage as in the mansion. The first step in stabilizing the entire society was to settle the question of legitimacy in the political system.[38]

None doubted that a new constitution more consonant with the natural rights of man was necessary. But though the term constitution had often been used, experience offered few guides to the means of devising one. Massachusetts men occasionally hoped that the Continental Congress would instruct them and they also observed the experiments in other

[37] *Acts and Resolves,* V, 828, 831.

[38] F. E. Oliver, ed., *Diary of William Pynchon of Salem* (Boston, 1890), 48, 103; Abigail to John Adams, June 15, 1777, in L. H. Butterfield, ed., *Adams Family Correspondence* (Cambridge, Mass., 1963), II, 265; Proclamation of the General Court, January 23, 1776, below, No. 4; "OPQ," in *Massachusetts Spy,* below, No. 8; Oscar and Mary F. Handlin, "Revolutionary Economic Policy in Massachusetts," *William and Mary Quarterly,* Third Series, IV (1947), 3ff.

states with interest, for the effort of free men, of their own accord, reasonably to frame a government was an unprecedented, exciting, and frightening enterprise in which the penalties of failure were as great as the rewards of success.

The leaders, among them John and Samuel Adams and James Sullivan, were encumbered by the logic of their earlier debate with Britain. The oft-repeated argument that "resistance to innovation and the unlimited claims of Parliament, and not any particular new form of government, was the object of the Revolution" had left the implication that the "free constitution" to which they appealed was the ancient political order of Britain, "the grand charter of British liberties." When the break with the Crown became irremediable, it seemed only necessary, from this point of view, to adopt "a plan as nearly resembling the government under which we were born, and have lived, as the circumstances of the country will admit. Kings we never had among us. Nobles we never had. Nothing hereditary ever existed in the country. . . . But governors and councils we have always had, as well as representatives. A legislature in three branches ought to be preserved, and independent judges."[39]

These men, therefore, at first sought a "piece by piece" adaptation, fearing that a total revision "would be attended with the greatest anarchy, as it would leave the people for a time without any rulers." The General Court was, in any case, "daily altering our old, unmeaning form of government" and should continue to do so. "May not Laws be made and Regulations establishd under this Government, the salutary Effects of which the People shall be so convincd of from their own Experience, as never hereafter to suffer them to be repeald or alterd." Meanwhile it was desirable to strive for " a Change of Manners" for only if the populace was itself virtuous would it be able to safeguard its liberty under whatever scheme of government.[40]

In many parts of the province, however, a polity which rested upon the royal charter was tainted at its source and dangerous to future freedom.

[39] See below, p. 18; Force, *American Archives*. Fourth Series, IV, 833; Samuel Langdon, *Sermon Preached before the Honorable Congress of the Colony of the Massachusetts-Bay* (Watertown, 1775), in J. W. Thornton, *Pulpit of the American Revolution* (Boston, 1860), 249ff.; John Adams to Mercy Warren, July 20, 1807, in Massachusetts Historical Society, *Collections*, Fifth Series, IV (1878), 351; John Adams, *Works*, III, 17ff., 20.

[40] James Sullivan to John Adams, May 9, 1776, in Thomas C. Amory, *Life of James Sullivan* (Boston, 1859), I, 76ff.; also New-England Historic, Genealogical Society, *Proceedings Commemorative of the Organization of Government in 1780* (Boston, 1880), 21; Samuel Adams to James Warren, December 26, 1775, in Samuel Adams, *Writings*, III, 244ff.; John to Abigail Adams, May 27, 1776, in C. F. Adams, *Familiar Letters of John and Abigail Adams*, 177.

The inhabitants of Pittsfield, on December 26, 1775, explained that "since the Suspension of Government," they had "lived in peace, Love, safety, Liberty and Happiness." It had been a mistake, "hasty and precipitate," to fall back upon a mode of government so generally reprobated "and if once adopted by the people we shall perhaps never be able to rid ourselves of it again." A new beginning was necessary; the Continental Congress could not have intended to force the old detested charter upon them.

To such people, a constitution had come to mean a written document establishing the frame of government to which they themselves assented; and until they could have one, they preferred to remain, as they had "for some Time past in a State of Nature." They demanded the privileges of "confessing Judgment in Cases of Debt." They also requested that the Court "issue out . . . orders to the good people of this province that their Votes may be collected in the Election of a Governor and Lieutenant Governor to act in Concert with the Honourable Board and house of Representatives," and "that every Town may retain the previlege of nominating their Justice of the peace and every County their Judges as well as the Soldiers of every Company of the Militia their officers." If the people did not have those rights the Pittsfield men were "indifferent who assumes it whether any particular persons on this or on the other side of the water." Although hopeful that their "Rulers would not admit of collecting private Debts for the present," they would be submissive to a constitution of their own which would rest upon "such a broad Basis of Civil and religious Liberty as no length of Time will corrupt and which will endure as long as the Sun and Moon shall endure." Meanwhile, on the basis of these "premises" and "on account of obnoxious persons being appointed to rule us," they ordered the Quarter Sessions Court of the county "to desist from any future Sessions."[41]

That final pronouncement revealed the inescapable imperative of the Massachusetts situation. The people of Pittsfield—and elsewhere—could, if they wished, prevent the courts from sitting; they did not have to

[41] Below, p. 27 and No. 3; J. E. A. Smith, *The History of Pittsfield, (Berkshire County,) Massachusetts, from the Year 1734 to the Year 1800* (Boston, 1869), 343–345; *Acts and Resolves,* V, 1028–1033, 1275–1276. See also Proceedings of the Hampshire Convention, March 11, 1776, in James R. Trumbull, *History of Northampton* (Northampton, 1902), II, 389ff.; John to Abigail Adams, August 14, 1776, in C. F. Adams, *Familiar Letters of John and Abigail Adams,* 212ff.; John Winthrop to John Adams and Adams to Winthrop, June 1, 23, 1776, in Massachusetts Historical Society, *Collections,* Fifth Series, IV (1878), 306–310; Force, *American Archives,* Fourth Series, V, 807, 1275ff.; Lee N. Newcomer, *Embattled Farmers* (New York, 1953), 134ff.

accept any government but that to which they consented; and none could rule without their acquiescence. This was hardly that state of nature founded upon "the eternal fitness of things" theory had made familiar. It seemed rather to mark that "fallen and degenerate" time when it became necessary to constitute a body politic to guard men against "the tyranny of hundreds of imperious masters . . . the vilest slavery, and worse than death." [42] Yet the leaders in Boston and Philadelphia could not hold to the concept of an evolving "antient Constitution" as their English counterparts did. Nor indeed could they impose any theories upon the emerging polity without taking account of the prejudices and interests of their fellow citizens. John Adams, who had his own ideas of the proper form of government, in 1775 wisely acknowledged that "any form that our people would consent to institute, would be better than none, even if they placed all power in a house of representatives." The people might err; but "their will be done; if they suit themselves they will please me." [43]

For four years between 1776 and 1780, Massachusetts grappled with the problem of converting the consent of the governed from a political theory into a political process. To John Adams and others it had from the start been clear that this was their "most difficult and dangerous business," that there was more peril in the experiment in self-government "than from all the fleets and armies of Great Britain." [44] Yet the task could not be evaded.

To some it had seemed "most natural," back in 1775, to have the Continental Congress "appoint a committee to prepare a plan of government, to be reported to Congress and there discussed, paragraph by paragraph, and that which should be adopted should be recommended to all the States." But few Americans had been able to conceive of a practical way to consolidate "this vast continent under one national government." Only the utterly visionary ventured to imagine that a single scheme

[42] Samuel West, *Sermon Preached before the Honorable Council . . . May 29th, 1776* (Boston, 1776), in Thornton, *Pulpit of the American Revolution,* 271, 274; see also Langdon, *Sermon,* 249ff.; Mercy Warren, *History of the American Revolution,* I, 226.

[43] John Adams to James Warren, May 3, June 11, 1777, in *Warren-Adams Letters,* I, 322, 329; and to Francis Dana, August 16, 1776, in John Adams, *Works,* IX, 430; and also *ibid.,* III, 17; Pittsfield Petitions, May 29, 1776, below, No. 9. For the English background and usage, see J. L. de Lolme, *The Constitution of England* (London, 1775); J. G. A. Pocock, "Burke and the Ancient Constitution," *Historical Journal,* III (1960), 128ff.

[44] John Adams, *Works,* III, 13. See also Elisha P. Douglass, *Rebels and Democrats* (Chapel Hill, [1955]), 162ff.

adopted in Philadelphia would everywhere prove acceptable. Instead the work was to begin from the bottom. The people were to "erect the whole building with their own hands, upon the broadest foundation," and that "could be done only by conventions of representatives chosen by the people in the several colonies" which would then confederate.[45]

Conventions of representatives, "freely, fairly, and proportionably chosen" could elicit the consent of the people. If there were any doubt about popular approval, "the convention may send out their project of a constitution, to the people in their several towns, counties, or districts, and the people make the acceptance of it their own act." Those who supposed "the people" knew "nothing about constitutions" were mistaken, for "in every considerable portion of the people, there will be found some men, who will understand the subject as well as their representatives, and these will assist in enlightening the rest."[46]

The process of devising a new constitution for Massachusetts therefore partook of the nature of a dialogue between the representatives in Boston who framed the proposals and the citizens in their towns who gave or withheld their consent. The interchange provided the means for expressing shared assumptions about the polity of a free society.

There was widespread resistance to any suggestion that the popular role be passive only. From June 1776 onward, various committees of the General Court labored to contrive the form of government "Best calculated to promote the greatest good of the People and of the United Colonies." In September 1776, the House of Representatives "recommended to the Male Inhabitants of Each Town in this State, being Free and Twenty-One Years of Age or upwards" that they assemble in meetings to "consider and determine whether they will give their Consent that the present House of Representatives . . . together with the Council . . . should . . . enact such a Constitution . . . for this State, as . . . will most conduce to the Safety, Peace and Happiness of this State, in all after Successions and Generations; and if they would direct that the same be made Public for the Inspection and Perusal of the Inhabitants, before the Ratification thereof by the Assembly."[47]

The response was less than enthusiastic. Some towns did not answer

[45] John Adams, *Works,* III, 16, 22. See also R. H. Lee to John Adams, May 18, 1776, *ibid.,* IX, 374; John Adams to Horatio Gates, March 23, 1776, and to Patrick Henry, June 3, 1776, in Burnett, *Letters of Members of the Continental Congress,* I, 406, 471.

[46] John Adams, *Works,* III, 20; also West, *Sermon,* 278.

[47] Below, No. 12. See also John Adams to James Warren, April 22, 1776, in *Warren-Adams Letters,* I, 233ff.; Fred E. Haynes, "Struggle for the Constitution of Massachusetts" (Harvard University Archives, 1891), 82.

at all. Others vigorously denied the power of the House and Council to create a new frame of government, insisting that only a convention specifically convened for the purpose could undertake the task; a constitution formed by the legislature could also be modified by it and therefore would be no check upon arbitrary power. Even the towns willing to have the General Court propose a plan wished to retain a veto. A multitude of provisos and qualifications made a mathematical determination of yeses, noes, and doubtfuls impossible. The Revolution had by this time exposed a variety of assumptions, attitudes, and beliefs about government theretofore hidden beneath the common Enlightenment phraseology. Every town had its own theorists who applied abstract concepts, as they understood them, to the questions at issue; and only the shared experience of reducing these ideas to practice would reveal the extent of agreement among them.[48] The responses to the Resolve of 1776 indicated that loyalty and obedience would remain tenuous until the adoption of a new constitution that conformed to the expectations of the people; and among those expectations were formulation by a convention and a degree of popular involvement that would make the concept of consent meaningful. Only a procedure that gave an active role to the citizens assembled in their towns would meet the needs of the situation.

Although the Council for a time was reluctant to do so, the General Court, on May 5, 1777, instructed the towns at the next election to empower their representatives to join with the Council in reconstituting themselves as a convention for the sole purpose of forming a constitution, which, if accepted by two-thirds of the freemen, would become the new frame of government.[49] The legislature then elected, having thus transformed itself into a convention, in June 1777, appointed a committee to prepare a draft. After six months of effort, the committee submitted a tentative report and asked "leave to sit again." But the conven-

[48] The returns are given below, No. 13. See also Worcester and Sutton statements, Nos. 14, 15; MA 137/138ff.; 210/242; Harry A. Cushing, *History of the Transition from Provincial to Commonwealth Government in Massachusetts* (New York, 1896), 184ff. Not all the town responses reached Boston or survived, but some not in the archives are locally preserved. See, e.g., William A. Benedict and Hiram A. Tracy, compilers, *History of the Town of Sutton, Massachusetts, from 1704 to 1876* (Worcester, 1878), 99–100. For early statements on the constitutional convention, see the Middleborough and Concord resolves, in No. 13, MA 156/147, 182.

[49] Below, Nos. 16 and 17; also MA 158/81–83; 213/472–473; 214/3–9. An earlier version had left the task to the House alone. On the attitude of the Council which feared a diminution of its authority, see James Warren to John Adams, July 10, 1777, in *Warren-Adams Letters,* I, 341. See also Cushing, *Transition from Province to Commonwealth,* 204–226; Fred E. Haynes, "Struggle for the Constitution of Massachusetts" (Harvard University Archives, 1891), 86–96.

tion was aware of the political necessity for action and hoped that debate in the full body would resolve the questions at issue. It therefore ordered the committees' report printed and by February 28, 1778 had approved a constitution for submittal to the towns.[50]

In the subsequent canvass, the document was overwhelmingly defeated. William Gordon, chaplain of the House, and historian of the Revolution, originated a charge—since then frequently repeated—that the Constitution of 1778 had been purposely left defective and "laid before the publick ere it was ripened" with the hope that it would be rejected. The members of the convention, "tho' called the sons of liberty" had craftily worked out this means of retaining power in their own grip.[51]

But a reading of the minutes, the working copies, and amendments throws a different light on the matter. The frame of government was submitted as it was because the members of the convention feared that further delays would hamper the war effort; and it was imperfect because the novel experience of constitution-making raised more problems than could be resolved in haste. The deletions and insertions reflected three orders of difficulty: ineptitude, inability to agree upon wording where there was no substantive difference of opinion, and actual disagreement about certain provisions.[52]

The appropriate phrases did not come readily to mind. Was it necessary, in describing the powers of the General Court to make laws, to specify that it could also "repeal the same"? Was it useful in asserting that the Senate and House of Representatives should be "two separate and distinct bodies" to add "of men"? Troublesome disagreements took time even when there was no dispute about the provision involved. The article on the laws to remain applicable in the new state (Number XIX in the original draft, and Number XXXII in the draft submitted to the towns) suffered many changes simply in the effort to eliminate any source of future doubt.[53] And then there were unexpected questions, on the answers to which the delegates did not agree, when new mechanisms of

[50] MA 156/268–274; below, No. 20.

[51] To George Washington, July 17, 1777 April 15, 1778, and to Horatio Gates, April 28, 1778, in Massachusetts Historical Society, *Proceedings*, LXIII (1930), 346, 397, 401; S. E. Morison, *History of the Constitution of Massachusetts* (Boston, 1917), 16; see also Theophilus Parsons to John Waite, March 12, 1776, in Theophilus Parsons, *Memoir of Theophilus Parsons* (Boston, 1861), 40; James Savage to Theophilus Parsons, May 4, 1857, *ibid.*, 81ff.

[52] The documents are in MA 156/passim; below, No. 19.

[53] MA 156/206, 249.

government were to be contrived. A second house of the legislature was to be elected by units larger than the towns. How? A chief executive was desirable. How was he to be selected and what powers should be given him? Debate on such matters was unavoidable.[54]

In truth, it was easy enough to generalize about emerging from a state of nature—the old charter was to be discarded and the people would build afresh on the basis of reason. Yet when the delegates envisaged the new structure, experience tied them to the old; they thought at once of a governor, a council, a House of Representatives elected in the towns, and a judiciary dispensing justice according to an accretion of familiar law. These institutions, formerly corrupted by the insidious influence of royal authority, now would be purified. But to dovetail the amorphous ideals with reality was difficult; "Better heads than mine should be employed in this business," wrote James Warren. Alas, there were no better heads. The magnitude of the task, rather than a conspiracy, explained the deficiencies of the Constitution of 1778.[55]

The people in the towns rejected that document because of its imperfections and because many disagreed also with its provisions for control of the militia and for representation. There were complaints, as well, about the lack of a Bill of Rights, about exclusion of Negroes from the suffrage, and about the inadequacy of the safeguards to property. In the light of those defects, the Newburyport lawyer, Theophilus Parsons, who helped compose the incisive criticism of the Essex Result, agreed with the farmers of Pittsfield that a state of nature was surely preferable.[56]

No one, however, actually imagined that the citizens of Massachusetts would long continue to live in a state of nature; the improvised political system continued to function de facto, but some courts were still prevented from sitting and protests from county conventions in the West made it apparent that it was "necessary, for carrying into more effectual exertion the means of common safety, that some mode of government should be adopted." [57] The failure of the Constitution of 1778 shortly led to a renewed trial which would profit by the experience of the first effort.

[54] MA 156/204, 208, 226, 227, 232, 233, 257. Even John Adams was uncertain on these points; see Adams to James Warren, May 12, 1776, in *Warren-Adams Letters,* I, 242.

[55] Warren to John Adams, August 10, 1777, in *Warren-Adams Letters,* I, 350; also "Z.A.," *Boston Gazette,* May 11, 1778.

[56] Below, No. 22; see also the Spencer and Westminster returns, MA 160/7, 17ff.; *Boston Gazette,* May 11, 1778; Parsons, *Parsons,* 47, 54, 359ff., 362, 367.

[57] Opinions of Meetings of the Committees of Berkshire and Hampshire Towns, below, Nos. 23, 24, and 25; Smith, *Pittsfield,* 343–345; MA 180/150, 336; Hart *Commonwealth History,* III, 77ff.

On February 19, 1779, the House, declaring that it was "doubtful from the Representations made to this Court, what are the sentiments of the major part of the good People of this State, as to the expediency of now proceeding to form a new Constitution of Government," resolved that all qualified to vote for representatives should respond before the last Wednesday of May, 1779 to two questions: *"First.*—Whether they choose, at this time, to have a new Constitution or Form of Government made. *Secondly.*—Whether they will empower their Representatives for the next year to vote for the calling a State Convention, for the sole purpose of forming a new Constitution; provided it shall appear to them, on examination, that a major part of the People present and voting at the meetings, called in the manner and for the purpose aforesaid, shall have answered the first question in the affirmative?" The Council having concurred on the next day, the questions were sent to the towns for action.[58]

Both queries, having been answered in the affirmative, with returns from over two-thirds of the towns, the House on June 15, 1779 recommended that a convention, "for the sole purpose of framing a new Constitution," be elected, "consisting of such number of Delegates, from each Town . . . as every different Town is entitled to send Representatives to the General Court." A printed copy of the Constitution agreed upon in convention was to be transmitted to the towns, to be laid before a regular meeting "in order to its being duly considered and approved or disapproved by said Towns and Plantations." The Constitution was to be established if it was "approved of by at least two thirds of those, who are free and twenty one years of age, belonging to this State, and present in the several meetings." Neither in choosing delegates nor in voting to ratify were property qualifications to apply.[59]

"A large number of Delegates" convened on September 1, 1779 in the convention so elected; but the attendance was by no means constant in the seven months of its labors. There were times when only a handful of members voted on crucial issues and the business often dragged on with painful slowness.

Yet the constitution-making process did not fall into the hands of a

[58] *Journal of the Convention for Framing a Constitution of Government for the State of Massachusetts Bay, from . . . September 1, 1779, to . . . June 16, 1780 . . .* (Boston, 1832), 189ff.; below, No. 26.

[59] For the returns, see below, No. 29; also below, Nos. 27 and 28. The call for the convention is given below, No. 30. See also *Journal of the Convention,* 5, 6. The action of the towns is summarized below, No. 31. See also S. E. Morison, "Vote of Massachusetts on Summoning a Constitutional Convention," Massachusetts Historical Society, *Proceedings,* L (1917), 245.

small group of interested activists. Among the participants were John and Samuel Adams, John Hancock, James Bowdoin, Benjamin Lincoln, Theophilus Parsons, James Sullivan, and Caleb Strong, indeed almost every prominent actor in the revolutionary drama in Massachusetts. Some of these men, and John Adams in particular, had already given much thought to the proper framework of government; but the document which resulted from their efforts did not simply express the views of a group of exceptional individuals. However respected were the leaders they were well aware that their work would be successful only if it won the approval of the people in the towns. And experience, since 1774, had shown that approval could as readily be withheld as granted.

Victories on the floor of the convention were therefore futile unless they were such as would be ratified later in the meetings. The function of the delegates was not only to debate and to vote but also to be able to "explain, to the satisfaction of their constituents" the "grounds and reasons of every decision." Some members indeed requested and received instructions from the towns.[60] Divisions of opinion appeared frequently in the debates and in the balloting; but whether as many as 250 votes were cast or as few as 30, every majority knew that its success was qualified by the ultimate threat of a reversal at the hands of the people. "There never was an example," John Adams pointed out, "of such precautions as are taken by this wise and jealous people in the formation of their government. None was ever made so perfectly upon the principle of the people's rights and equality. It is Locke, Sidney, and Rousseau and De Mably reduced to practice."[61]

The very organization of the convention showed a sensitivity toward the need for a consensus. Many remote towns, confident that they would ultimately have the opportunity to review the work of the convention, preferred to spare themselves the expense and did not trouble to send delegates. As a result Nantucket and Dukes counties, still exposed to British raids, were unrepresented and Cumberland and Lincoln were far below the strength to which they were entitled. On the other hand, the eastern delegates were there in full force. But those present did not try to take advantage of the fortuitous turns of attendance. Instead the task of preparing a draft was assigned to a committee on which all the counties received places (Suffolk, Essex, Middlesex, Worcester, Hampshire, 3

[60] *Journal of the Convention*, 7, 49. For instructions, see below, No. 31; also Dudley, MA 160/283; Gorham, MA 160/288.

[61] John Adams, *Works*, IV, 216.

each; Plymouth, Bristol, York, and Berkshire, 2 each; and Barnstable, Cumberland, Lincoln, and Nantucket and Dukes, 1 each).

An adjournment permitted most of the members to return to their homes while the committee did its work. The convention reassembled between October 28, 1779 and November 11, 1779, then adjourned once more until January 5, 1780. But at the turn of the year, an unusually harsh winter brought travel to a standstill and fear of the smallpox in Boston kept some delegates away so that at the appointed day few members appeared. Three weeks later, when the actual work resumed, only sixty persons were present. Newspaper advertisements coaxing the absentees to attend were largely ineffective; but a determined group toiled on until the Constitution was completed on March 2 and submitted to the people for ratification. The towns were asked to discuss the draft and report to the convention when it reconvened on June 7, 1780.[62]

The returns revealed the extent of the discussion in the town meetings. Circumstances varied markedly from place to place. Some communities took perfunctory action; others held repeated sessions, examined each provision carefully and produced reasoned disquisitions on the theory and practice of government. Some voted on the document as a whole; others on each clause; and still others joined to their decision qualifications of greater or lesser significance. When the convention examined the results in June it declared the Constitution ratified; but, though it tried to do so, it was not able to cast up a coherent statistical account that would show just how many were in favor and how many opposed.

Nor is it possible to do so almost two centuries later.[63] The process of ratification was not a referendum that produced a clear-cut outcome. It was rather the occasion for discussion of fundamental issues such as men rarely have the opportunity to confront. The citizens of Massachusetts ultimately acquiesced in the decision to adopt the Constitution set before them, not because a precise calculation informed them that more than two-thirds had voted yes, but because having canvassed the issues presented to them, they were aware that they agreed among themselves in

[62] Below, Nos. 32, 33, 34; *Journal of the Convention,* 53, 161; Samuel to John Adams, January 13, 1780, in Samuel Adams, *Writings,* IV, 177. The *Journal* shows that this convention was much more punctilious in procedures than that of 1778. (The manuscript, in Volume 276 of the Massachusetts Archives, was not transcribed here because it is reprinted in an acceptable edition in *Journal of the Convention.*) For the exact mode of ratification, see S. E. Morison, "Struggle over the Adoption of the Constitution of Massachusetts, 1780," Massachusetts Historical Society, *Proceedings,* L (1917), 358ff.

[63] See, e.g., *Manual for the Constitutional Convention 1917* (Boston, 1917), 21, 22; Morison, "Struggle over the Adoption of the Constitution," 367, 396ff., 410, 411; Douglass, *Rebels and Democrats,* 208ff.

more respects than they disagreed. "I stile it glorious," wrote Joseph Hawley, who had opposed ratification, "altho, I humbly conceive it has several great blemishes, on account whereof it will until corrected be liable, in my poor opinion, to very weighty Exception; but still it remains glorious in respect of the great Quantity of excellent matter contained in it." The dissidents in Middleborough, a town where the Baptists were strong, therefore evoked no response in their call for repudiation of the Constitution.[64]

In devising their Constitution, the people of Massachusetts drew upon their previous experience to reduce to particulars a general body of theory about the nature of society and of the state. But since, on some matters, they were divided in interests and attitudes, they also interpreted specific issues in the light of the anticipated effects upon the control of the government. The discussion in the convention, the text of the Constitution, and the returns of the towns thus reflected the influences of commonly held assumptions about the polity, of colonial precedent, and of immediate problems in the use of power.

The "body-politic" was formed "by a voluntary association of individuals." The revolutionary debate, the course of settlement for a century and a half, the structure of the Congregational churches, and the corporate origins of the colonial charters took this statement out of the realm of abstract propositions and made it a literal description of society. In Massachusetts, the people had indeed entered into "a social compact" in which they had covenanted among themselves to "be governed by certain laws for the common good."[65]

Actuality and theory had alike demonstrated that the state created by that act of consent was "one moral whole"; beyond the interests of each person and each group was a common interest in which all had a stake. The delegate to the convention who proposed to change the name of the state to Oceana had in mind James Harrington's influential definition of that interest. However, the popular understanding of the concept developed

[64] Joseph Hawley, Statement, October 28, 1780, Hawley Papers, New York Public Library; Mary C. Clune, "Joseph Hawley's Criticism of the Constitution of Massachusetts," *Smith College Studies in History,* III (1917), 52ff.; also Arthur Lord, "Some Objections Made to the State Constitution, 1780," Massachusetts Historical Society, *Proceedings,* L (1916), 54ff.; Samuel to John Adams, July 10, 1780, in Samuel Adams, *Writings,* IV, 199.

[65] The quotations are from the preamble to the Constitution of 1789, below, No. 34. See also Thad W. Tate, "The Social Contract in America, 1774–1787: Revolutionary Theory as a Conservative Instrument," *William and Mary Quarterly,* Third Series, XXII (1965), 375–391.

not from any single book but out of years of experience; and it was sharpened by the urgency of fighting a war and creating a nation. Therefore there was no dispute over the propriety of ordaining the Declaration of Rights and Frame of Government as the Constitution of the *Commonwealth* of Massachusetts. The end and design of government was "to promote the welfare and happiness of the community." [66]

A precise description of rights and duties in the Commonwealth was essential because men, while naturally good and responsive to pure reason, were subject to corruption when intoxicating power fell into their hands. There were no illusions about the benevolence of human nature. That the most virtuous might yield to temptation was a possibility ever to be anticipated; and each provision of the Constitution was to be scrutinized from that point of view. The legislature represented the people; yet "in every Assembly, Members will obtain an Influence by Noise not Sense, by Meanness not Greatness, by Ignorance not Learning, by contracted Hearts not large Souls." A governor was essential. Yet it was not enough to require that public funds be paid out only by a warrant signed by him with the advice and consent of the Council: What if the chief executive refused to sign "till he first be fully Supplied with money for his own use"? In any case, Cambridge pointed out, the tax collector was a menace "to the Liberty of the Subjects" and would "swallow up a considerable part" of the revenue since he would always find "favourable Opportunities to carry on iniquitous practices without being detected." Popular surveillance alone was inadequate to check abuses, for the royal government, "being calculated rather to make *servile Men* than *free Citizens*," had inured the minds of many "to a cringing Obsequiousness, too deeply wrought into Habit to be easily eradicated." Indeed, breast-beating sermons and the laments of moralists repeatedly pointed out that the people, yielding to "soft and luxurious" manners, had "already degenerated from the pure morals and disinterested patriotism of" their ancestors.[67]

[66] *Journal of the Convention*, 43; John Adams to Francis Dana, August 16, 1776, in John Adams, *Works*, IX, 430; West, *Sermon*, 296; "Essex Result," Parsons, *Parsons*, 365–366; Oscar and Mary F. Handlin, *Commonwealth: A Study of the Role of Government in the American Economy* (New York, 1947), 30–32; Charles Blitzer, *An Immortal Commonwealth* (New Haven, 1960), 144ff.

[67] John Adams to James Warren, April 22, 1776, in *Warren-Adams Letters*, I, 234; John Adams to Joseph Hawley, August 25, 1776, in John Adams, *Works*, IX, 434; Samuel Adams to James Warren and to Elbridge Gerry, October 24, November 27, 1780, in Samuel Adams, *Writings*, IV, 212, 228; "Essex Result," Parsons, *Parsons*, 378; Phillips Payson, *A Sermon Preached before the Honorable Council, and the Honorable House of Represent-*

Only a balanced and orderly allocation of responsibilities would develop respect for persons in authority and permit the use of power for the common good. "A power without *any* Restraint is Tyranny." Any possibility of deviations, even the suspension of laws in an emergency, was regarded with trepidation, for "it must most Surely Introduce Anarky or a Government of Men and why should we open a door in our Constitution for Either." [68]

One of the first actions of the convention had been to recognize the need for a Declaration of Rights that would secure the "natural, essential and unalienable rights" of men who were all born equally free and independent. The fatal deficiencies of the Constitution of 1778, in this respect, were fresh in the minds of all. Yet while it was clear that some such statement was essential, there was considerable vagueness about its precise character. The delegates had therefore not found it necessary to wait for the preparation of the Declaration before proceeding to frame the government; they simply assumed that the general principles on which there was widespread agreement could be put off until later.[69]

The Declaration of Rights, as finally adopted, consisted of thirty articles which ranged from general hortatory statements to specific pronouncements on various matters in which the acts of government might affect the inhabitants. Some subjects such as the right to habeas corpus, which presumably should have fallen within this section, were actually treated in the body of the Constitution. Some clauses that were included were redundant or merely set forth maxims or platitudes incapable of practical application.

This was not a reasoned articulation of general principles, the "clear truths, of the most important and unalienable rights of human nature" such as Joseph Hawley wanted, but rather a listing of anticipated contingencies in which it might be desirable to safeguard the individual against oppressive measures.[70] The imagination of the drafters ran largely to past instances of the arbitrary use of power; and the remedies proposed were influenced by earlier formulations in Bills of Rights in England and in Virginia.

atives. . . May 27, 1778 (Boston, 1778), reprinted in Thornton, *Pulpit of the American Revolution,* 332ff., 338; Cambridge, MA 277/5; Middleborough, MA 277/40.

[68] Address of the Convention, below, No. 33; Petersham, MA 277/104; also Eastham, MA 277/49; Worcester, MA 277/120; Payson, *Sermon,* 331.

[69] *Journal of the Convention,* 22, 23, Constitution of 1780, Preamble; Part I, Article I.

[70] Joseph Hawley, Criticisms of the Constitution (fragment), Hawley Papers, Box 2, p. 8, New York Public Library; Clune, "Joseph Hawley's Criticism," 31ff.

The provision to safeguard the freedom of the press attracted some attention; a few towns wished it strengthened to protect the critics of "weak, or wicked Rulers" while others feared that it might be misused "to the Dishoner of god by printing herasy and so forth and like wise injurious to private Charactors." [71] The provision with regard to habeas corpus (which was not in the Declaration of Rights, but in Chapter VI, Article VII) seemed to some respondents to require strengthening. So too, some returns asked for more careful description of the power of juries and of lawyers; and others requested firmer reassurance against the danger of the use of mercenaries and explicit guarantees of the right of the people to bear arms.[72] There were some objections to the privileges given to the University at Cambridge, since the legislature might in time "find it Necesary to Curtail that Rich and Growing Corporation Least it should Endanger the Liberties of the Commonwealth." [73] Some communities, indeed, thought that education in general was not a fit subject for state action. "The inhabitants of Each Town have the Sole Right and are the Properest Judges of what Schooles are the most Suteall." [74] There were a few indignant demands that slavery be explicitly condemned. "When we have long struggled, at the expence of much treasure and blood, to obtain liberty for ourselves and posterity, it ill becomes us to enslave others who have an equal right to liberty with ourselves." [75] On most of these matters, however, there was little debate in the convention, only verbal amendment in the text and but slight discussion in the towns.

The most prominent exceptions were the clauses linking church and state which had touched off "very extensive" debate in the convention and considerable revision in the text and which attracted the attention of numerous town meetings.[76]

After assuring every man the liberty of "worshipping GOD in the manner and season most agreeable to the dictates of his own conscience,"

[71] Milton, MA 277/73; Dunstable, MA 277/10. See also Samuel Adams to John Adams, May, 1780, in Samuel Adams, *Writings*, IV, 187; Payson, *Sermon*, 341.

[72] Groton, MA 277/14; Barnstable, MA 277/47, 48; Roxbury, MA 277/75; Milton, MA 277/73; Boston, MA 277/61; Royalston, MA 277/106; Bellingham, MA 277/60; Belchertown, MA 276/40; Northampton, MA 276/58.

[73] Petersham, MA 277/104; also Mendon, MA 277/97; Bellingham, MA 277/60; New Salem, MA 276/17; Middleborough, MA 277/40; Rochester, MA 277/44.

[74] Bellingham, MA 277/60; also Colrain, MA 276/45; Sutton, MA 277/112. For popular attitudes toward education, see also Samuel Adams, *Writings*, III, 235ff.; Payson, *Sermon*, 334–336.

[75] Braintree, MA 277/63; Petersham, MA 277/104; Rochester, MA 277/44.

[76] *Journal of the Convention*, 39, 45; Morison, "Struggle over the Adoption of the Constitution," 368ff.

the Declaration of Rights empowered the legislature to "authorize and require" the towns "to make suitable provision, at their own expense, for . . . the public worship of GOD, and for the support and maintenance of public protestant teachers of piety, religion and morality." The taxes contributed by each individual were to be applied to support the minister "of his own religious sect or denomination, provided there be any on whose instruction he attends." Otherwise, it was to go to the minister of the parish in which the money was raised. The legislature also received "authority to enjoin upon all the subjects an attendance upon the instruction of the public teachers . . . at stated times and seasons, if there be any on whose instructions they can conscientiously and conveniently attend." But "every denomination of christians, demeaning themselves peaceably" was to be "equally under the protection of the law: And no subordination of any one sect or denomination to another shall ever be established by law."[77]

The contradictions implicit in an effort to support religious worship while preventing the subordination of one sect to another were glaringly apparent. Middleborough protested that Article III might compel individuals under some circumstances to pay money contrary to the dictates of their consciences.[78] That that town should object was not surprising for it was the residence of the Baptist minister, Isaac Backus, who had already denounced such taxation. In 1777 he had pointed out that the old charter of 1691 which had granted liberty of conscience to all Christians except Papists had been construed to mean that "the General Court might, by laws, encourage and protect that religion which is the general profession of the inhabitants." The minister, chosen by the majority in a town, was paid by a tax levied on all and was, in consequence, "in reality the king's minister; and the salary for him is raised in the king's name, and is the king's allowance unto him." Power thus used was "as real a breach of public faith in our charter, as ever it was for the British Court to take from us the right of choosing our own Governors, and then to burn our towns and cut our throats for not paying them as much money as they demanded." Now the Constitution repeated the error.[79]

The ultimate solution, many responses pointed out, was to remove the

[77] Articles II, III; Article XXXIV of the Constitution of 1778 had guaranteed freedom of worship only "to every denomination of Protestants."

[78] MA 277/40.

[79] Isaac Backus, *History of New England,* 2d ed., I (Newton, 1871), 532ff. The general Baptist position and an incisive criticism of the provisions of the Constitution of 1780 are given in Isaac Backus, *Truth Is Great, and Will Prevail* (Boston, [1781]). See also Joseph Hawley, Criticisms, 9–10.

organization and administration of the churches from the province of government. Granville denied "after the most mature Consideration" that "the People have a Right to invest their Legislature with a Power to interfere in Matters that properly belong to the Christian Church." Such interference was "an Incroachment on the Kingly Office of Jesus Christ, who Stands in no need of the help of any civil Legislature whatever," and was "consequently . . . an Affront to him." West Springfield explained that if the legislature could "oblige all the Citizens to attend on the public Worship of God at stated Times and Seasons," it could "prohibit the worship of God at any other time . . . and also define what that worship shall be and so the right of private Judment will be at an End." [80]

Yet even those who argued for complete separation of church and state set limits upon the application of the principle. The convention had considered, but rejected, proposals to define the Christian religion as Protestant; it had been content simply to call for an oath of office abjuring civil or spiritual allegiance to any "foreign Prince, Person, Prelate, State or Potentate." That precaution did not satisfy everyone. Wilmington which wanted assurance that the majority of any town "Shall not have it in Their Power to Settle a Public Teacher over the Consciences of the Minority," nevertheless confined the right of "free Liberty of Conscience" to "Calvinists and Armenians." The same liberty was certainly not to extend to Catholics. Sandisfield considered the Constitution lax in requiring that the governor be a Christian without specifying of what denomination. "Since it is a Community of Protestants that are Covenanting and emerging from a State of nature and for their posterity it is necessary to say that not only the Governor but all executive Legislative Judicial and Military officers shall be of the Protestant Christian religion." "We Mean Not," Paxton declared, "to have any other but protestants to Rule us but as occasion May Requier in the army." Northbridge wished "to ward against Roman Catholicks Pagons or Mahomitents from Having any Seat in Government, from whom the People of God Have So much Suffred in past ages." Lexington wanted a similar "guard against introducing Persons into Offices of Trust and Places of Power . . . whose *Religion itself* leads them to hold Principles, and avow Practices inimical to Liberty, subversive of Government and dangerous to the State." Wareham requested that Article II be amended so "that Roman Catholicks may not Enjoy equal priviledges with Protestant Christians yet Never-

[80] MA 276/49, 71. See also Leicester, MA 277/95; Needham, MA 277/74.

theless to enjoy a Toleration in Particular places as the Legislature shall Direct." To Wells it seemed "that a Papist is at least as unsuitable to be Chosen and admitted to the Office of Governor in this Commonwealth, as one that makes no profession of the Christian Religion."[81]

These comments reflect a pervasive uncertainty about the application of generally accepted propositions about freedom of conscience to the practical relationships of church and state in the Commonwealth. Implicit in Barnstable's preference to restrict civil and military office to Protestants was the assumption that there would be an established religion in Massachusetts: "We are in no Doubt," the town wrote, "but that in most of the kingdoms of Europe Every person must be of the Establisht Religion of the State as a necessary Quallification for office." General professions of a belief in religious liberty therefore were not incompatible with demands for guarantees of a Protestant Christian state in the requirements for officeholding or for more exacting wording of oaths or for provisions "to Prohibit Labour and unnescesary travaling and Recreations on the first Day of the Week."[82]

Furthermore, there was a lingering conviction even among those who urged the separation of church and state that some provision for instruction in morality was essential. Backus' Middleborough argued that "all men have an Equal Right in all Cases with Respect to the Choice of their publick Teachers." But the town insisted also that it was "the Right as well as the Duty of all men in Society to invest their Legislature with power and authority to Require (for Equal Benefit to Each and Every Denomination of Christian people) that all men Shall give an account or by Some means Let it be publickly known what Denomination of Christian people they join with or mean to join with in attending the publick worship of god (So far as is necessary) So that no ill conveniance take place in Consequence of ignorance therein." Some such arrangement was necessary in order "to instruct the People in the Knowledge of the divine Being, his Perfections and Government of future Rewards and Punishments of the Sacredness of Oaths and importance of good Morals."[83]

The citizens who framed these responses were dealing with an abstraction and with an actuality. They believed in freedom of the conscience. "The religion of America is the religion of all mankind. Any person may worship in the manner he thinks most agreeable to the Deity; and if he

[81] MA 277/34, 276/20, 277/103, 277/101, 277/16, 277/46, 277/56.

[82] MA 277/47; Bellingham, MA 277/60. See also Natick, MA 277/21; Sutton, MA 277/112; Constitution of 1778, Article XXIX.

[83] MA 277/40; Roxbury, MA 277/75; also Abington, MA 277/35; Bellingham, MA 277/60; Medway, MA 277/72.

behaves as a good citizen, no one concerns himself as to his faith or adorations, neither have we the least solicitude to exalt one sect or profession above another." So much was the inalienable right of every individual.[84]

Yet a moral basis was also necessary to social order. People learned their obligations to each other from public instruction in religion; hence the concern of the government. "Let the restraints of religion once be broken down, as they infallibly would be by leaving the subject of public worship to the humors of the multitude," and it would be hopeless to "preserve order and government in the state." [85] It was therefore not within the province of the polity to support the church, but religion could provide sanctions to maintain social order.

But long before 1780, dissent had divided the communities of the Commonwealth and the law had begun to adjust to a situation in which church and state were no longer identical as they had been in the seventeenth century. The Constitution had to formulate a position on the issue while the adjustment was still in process. Article III therefore was not so much the articulation of a theory as the description of such compromises, shaped by experience, as would be "likely to hit the taste of the public." The Declaration of Rights did not establish the Orthodox Congregational churches; yet it left them undisturbed where they were dominant. The loose terms in which it referred to teachers of morality and to the equality of sects aimed to appease the Baptists and Quakers and to attract the widest support possible. The disregard of the rights of Catholics or Jews or Muslims—while theoretically inconsistent—reflected the simple fact that there were no significant numbers of these people in the state. In the quarter century after 1780, when their numbers did grow, the constitutional provision proved hardly an inconvenience; nor did it restrain the spread of Unitarianism, Universalism, and Deism in the same period.[86]

The delegates in convention also had to square theory with actuality in hammering together a frame of government. The Constitution set up

[84] "An American," *Massachusetts Spy* (Boston), July 16, 1778, in Samuel Adams, *Writings*, IV, 34; "Mentor," *Boston Gazette*, January 26, 1778; see also "Essex Result," Parsons, *Parsons*, 360, 386, 389.

[85] Payson, *Sermon*, 339, 340; West, *Sermon*, 297–299; Theophilus Parsons, *Defence of the Third Article of the Massachusetts Declaration of Rights; as Delivered . . . in the Case of Barnes vs. Falmouth* (Worcester, 1820), 4–7; Simeon Howard, *Sermon Preached before the Honorable Council and the Honorable House of Representatives . . . May 31, 1780* (Boston, 1780), in Thornton, *Pulpit of the American Revolution*, 373, 374.

[86] See John Adams' statement of 1812 in W. D. Williamson, *History of the State of Maine* (Hallowell, 1839), II, 483*n;* also Hart, *Commonwealth History*, III, 196ff.; Jacob C. Meyer, *Church and State in Massachusetts* (Cleveland, 1930), 90ff.; Oscar Handlin, *Boston's Immigrants: A Study in Acculturation* (Cambridge, Mass., 1959), 180ff.

machinery to permit the people to govern themselves by fixed laws of their own making; that was the essense of a free republic. A bicameral legislature, a governor advised by a council, and an independent judiciary, the devices that were to assure the use of power for common ends, were agreed upon after six years of experiment. The canvass of opinion in the two conventions and in the towns revealed some difference of viewpoint with regard to these structural matters. But the sharpest intellectual issues were defined with reference to another range of questions—who should participate in the polity; how could a legislature express the will of the citizens; and who should wield the instruments of power?

It was no easy task to reconcile theory and practice in framing the answers. Until the Constitution was ratified, the people presumably existed in a state of nature and could have contrived any political order their ingenuity might have suggested. But in actuality they lived in a functioning polity, the features of which significantly influenced the scheme that was ultimately adopted.

People were reluctant to overturn the customary adaptations of years of practice. On the issue fundamental to the participation in the polity, for instance, the Constitution made property not only a requisite for the ballot but, in increasing amounts, for the tenure of office. In this respect, it reversed the position of the Constitution of 1778, seemed to set higher requirements than prevailed before 1774, and appeared to deny the proposition that all men were equally entitled to consent to be ruled and to take a part in government. Yet if few towns came out unequivocally for universal manhood suffrage as "a natural right, which ought to be considered as a principle corner-stone in the foundation for the frame of government to stand on," that was not because the property qualification was unimportant.[87] The returns frequently dealt with the subject and at least thirty-four of them opposed the proposed limitations. But the discussion was not mounted in abstract terms; only once was it mentioned in connection with Article IX of the Declaration of Rights. The men at the meetings debated the problem as it affected them in concrete cases and as it arose in specific clauses of the frame of government. The result was not a clear decision for or against the property qualification

[87] Stoughton, MA 277/76; *Journal of the Convention,* 75, 121, 136; *Manual for the Constitutional Convention 1917,* 25, 26. On this point, Robert E. Brown, *Middle-Class Democracy and the Revolution in Massachusetts, 1691–1780* (Ithaca, 1955), 396, is misleading. The ratification of the Constitution was not an indication of the lack of internal discontent over qualifications for voting. The returns cited show that there was such discontent, but the Constitution-making process was more complex. See also James Sullivan to James Warren, March 24, 1777, in Amory, *Sullivan,* I, 96.

but a canvass of opinion about the ways in which it might affect the polity.

The Address of the Convention had explained why the Constitution of 1780 restricted the suffrage to male inhabitants, twenty-one years old and having an annual income of £3 from a freehold or £60 in any estate. "Persons who are Twenty one Years of age, and have no Property, are either those who live upon a part of a Paternal estate, expecting the Fee thereof, who are but just entering into business, or those whose Idleness of Life and profligacy of manners will forever bar them from acquiring and possessing Property." The deserving young, it was argued, would "think it safer for them to have their right of Voting for a Representative suspended for [a] small space of Time, than forever hereafter to have their Privileges liable to the control of Men, who will pay less regard to the Rights of Property because they have nothing to lose."[88]

Some towns directly challenged this explanation. The restrictive provisions would "exclude many good members of Society," Richmond asserted, "and the bad Members of Society" could better be excluded by other tests. Only "misbehaviour" or "Vicious Conduct" should forfeit the "free Liberty to Vote" which was guaranteed in the first and ninth articles of the Constitution.[89] That liberty rested not on a "civil right" but on a "natural right," which ought to be considered as a "principle corner-stone in the foundation for the frame of government to stand on: consequently it is unsystematical and contrary to the rules of architecture to place, or make it dependent on the frame."[90]

The future implications were ominous. The number disenfranchised by property requirements was, Dorchester claimed, "daily increasing and possibly may increase in such proportion, that one half the People of this Commonwealth will have no choice in any Branch of the General Court." "Shall we be content and satisfied," asked Northampton, "to see these our deserving brethren on election days, standing aloof, and sneaking into corners, and ashamed to show their heads, in the meetings of freemen, because, by the constitution of the land, they are deemed intruders, if they should appear at such meetings?" The justice of the complaint moved Monson and Granby which approved the concept of property

[88] Address of the Convention, below, No. 33.

[89] Richmond, MA 276/19; Tyringham, MA 276/22; Ashfield, MA 276/39; New Marlborough, MA 276/15; Northampton, MA 276/58; Richmond, MA 276/19; Mansfield, MA 276/33; Norton, MA 276/34; Belchertown, MA 276/40; Colrain, MA 276/45; Ludlow, MA 276/54.

[90] Stoughton, MA 277/76.

qualifications nevertheless to recommend a reduction in the required amount.[91]

But even the most extreme affirmation of the right to vote as "natural" recognized that there were proper limitations upon it. No one questioned the restriction of the suffrage to those twenty-one years old and male. One suggestion, made in the course of the convention, that women vote, went unechoed in the responses. Northampton alone considered it necessary to explain why "infants" and "women" were excluded with a summary reference to Locke's treatment of "paternal power" and to the Essex Result; the exclusion seemed beyond dispute.[92]

Likewise, everyone took for granted that only qualified inhabitants could participate. Indeed some towns which unequivocally criticized the property qualifications proposed other stringent conditions of their own. Thus Northampton suggested residence in the Commonwealth "for the space of three years next preceeding" an election. And Belchertown would have excluded foreigners who "ought not to have and Exercise that Right until they obtain the Freedom of some Town where they inhabit by the unanimous Approbation of the select Men of the same." Thence it was but a short step to accept taxability as a prerequisite not only for office-holding but for voting. "No Person that dont pay Publick Taxes ought to be Chosen into the House of Representatives—or Senate." And those who did pay deserved the suffrage. The "many sensable, honest, and naturly Industreouss men [who] by Numberless Misfortins Never Acquire and possess Propperty of the value of sixty pounds" had a right to the ballot provided that they "paid taxes in the same Town (unless bly law excused)."[93]

There was a theoretical as well as a practical justification for substituting taxability for property as the qualification for voting. Those who contributed to the "support and defence of the Community" had earned a place in the body politic, had become "citizens of the Commonwealth." An "association . . . which without consent totally excludes many such adult male persons, from any participation in the appointment of the legislature" was in fact "no constitution and does not make a body politick." The Revolution had rested on that premise. Parliament's claim to the right to tax the unrepresented colonists had been "a principle cause of the present War." Every person obligated "to pay taxes ought to have

[91] MA 276/48, 55, 58; MA 277/67. See also Westhampton, MA 276/70.

[92] MA 276/58.

[93] MA 276/40, 58; Charlestown, MA 277/6; Braintree, MA 277/63; Southborough, MA 277/109; Mansfield, MA 276/33.

a share in the Choice of those that tax them." Those who "have hitherto been called upon to Vote themselves Independent of Great Britain and to stand forth in the defence of their darling Right and priviledges . . . will not now give up so dear a priviledge as that of Representation."[94]

These statements did not necessarily imply a denial of the importance of property. Thus Rochester ingeniously proposed that all twenty-one-year-old males paying a poll tax be entitled to vote, while those with estates be given additional votes in proportion to the amount of taxes paid. Dorchester buttressed its argument for the elimination of property qualifications for voting by noting "the Property and Estates of the People will be sufficiently guarded by the Senate who represent the same." Pembroke, having demanded the "erasment of the Qualification of Property in the Electors" of Senators nevertheless accepted the qualifications for serving as Senator. And Northampton, which recorded the most forceful criticism against the qualification for voting for Representatives, quibbled about the amount but not about the principle of the same qualifications for Senatorial electors.[95]

Actually, a few towns categorically objected to the property qualifications of the elected as well as of the electors and "voted intirely to expunge it from the Constitution." They defended not only the untrammeled right to vote but also the right to choose legislators whose "best and only necessary Qualification" was "Social virtue and Knowledge." Others wanted the towns to "be the Judge of the Qualifications of those they Chuse to Represent them." If all men were born free and equal, and had certain natural, essential, and unalienable rights, and if all elections were to be free, then the inhabitants had "a right to Such men, to represent them, whether rich or poor, as will feel the distress of the poor . . . otherwise, all men cannot be said to be born free and equal."[96]

But most of the towns which complained about the voting provisions did not find anything unseemly in the same requirements for serving as Representative, Senator, or governor. Some accepted the principle that officeholders, unlike voters, should be propertied, but demanded a reduction or some other alteration in the specified amount.[97] Others requested

[94] Tyringham, MA 276/22; Northampton, MA 276/58; Braintree, MA 277/63; Norton, MA 276/34.

[95] MA 277/41, 44, 67; Northampton, MA 276/58.

[96] Wilbraham, MA 276/72; Athol, MA 277/83; see also Colrain, MA 276/45; Tyringham, MA 276/22; Richmond, MA 276/19; Eastham, MA 277/49; Braintree, MA 277/63; Dudley, MA 277/90; Douglas, MA 277/89.

[97] E.g., Westhampton, MA 276/70; Richmond, MA 276/19; Ludlow, MA 276/54; Scituate, MA 277/45; West Springfield, MA 276/29; Petersham, MA 277/104.

increases for "no man ought to be advanced to places of Important Trust That has not a Considerable Interest to Share the fate of others in Time of War and other Such General Calamities—as a person having nothing of value to loose in a State may be Tempted for the Sake of Gain to change sides with Enemies and thereby Endanger its Safety or otherwise Betray the Liberties for his own Emolument."[98] Still others debated the fairness of the requirement (Chapter I, Section III, Article III) that a representative "shall cease to represent [his town] immediately on his ceasing to be qualified." Adverse Providence, Southborough noted, could force retirement from the House, a circumstance the town judged "to be a Disparagement to a Gentleman"; and Douglas asked that the office be forfeited only if the incumbent "lose his estate by his own imprudence."[99]

Significantly, there were towns silent on the property qualifications of governor, Senator, or Representative, which went out of their way to insist upon such requirements for delegates to the Continental Congress. Chelsea thought "no person shall be a member of Congress . . . unless he possesses a Right in freehold double to the Sum that by this Constitution Quallifies any person to be a Senator." Norton proposed that delegates have the same prerequisites as the governor, "Except property which we think should be fixed at least at five hunderd pounds Each." In doing so these joined towns like Reading which believed that Congressmen "should have the Qualifications of Estate and Residence in the State equal to the highest officer in the state—for the following Reasons——— they have the Right of apportioning each State's Quotas of the Continental Charges—of making Peace or War—And of entring into alliances with foreign Powers as They shall judge proper." Responsible position implied responsibility which could best be gauged by the ability to acquire worldly goods.[100]

On the other hand, the power granted the legislature to increase the property qualifications for office raised questions. That many towns which opposed those qualifications should attack the provision was not surprising. "Why we Dont Except this Article," Shelburne explained, "is because we think that the Qualifications mentioned in said Article are too High already." Before the legislature increased qualifications, Ludlow argued, it should have "the Consent of the People . . . Because wee

[98] Wareham, MA 277/46.
[99] MA 277/89, 109.
[100] MA 276/34; MA 277/65; Reading, MA 277/23.

conceive that should the Legislature have the Power to incrase etc. it would totaly subvert the natural rights of the People."[101] But the same criticism also emanated from towns which had accepted all other provisions involving property. "If at any Time the majority of the general Court should Consist of men of the first fortunes they may pass such Laws as will Exclude men of Common condition from a seat which will manifestly tend to destroy the Liberties of the People."[102]

The range of opinion on the role of property as a requisite for participation in the government revealed the interpenetration of theory and experience. Law and custom had defined the freeholder, the head of a household with a stake in society, as the basic integer in the polity. The conditions of eighteenth-century life in Massachusetts excluded relatively few by that definition; the fact that occasional Negroes and other poor folk were sometimes "not alowed in voating in the town meating. . . nur to chuse anoficer" did not yet seem incompatible with the concept of consent of the governed. "Our people," wrote John Adams in 1776, "have never been very rigid in scrutinizing into the qualifications of voters," and he presumed that they would "not now begin to be so." That understanding quieted the qualms, raised by revolutionary appeal to equality, about the propriety of exclusions on the basis of wealth. Property thus loosely interpreted could be a measure of men's ability to take active positions of command so long as the rules were properly established by the people. The Constitution—with its sliding scales—was a mechanism that almost all could accept within the context of local conditions of control.[103]

[101] MA 276/54, 62; also Richmond, MA 276/19; Dartmouth, MA 276/29; Rochester, MA 277/44; Bellingham, MA 277/60; Dedham, MA 277/66; Norton, MA 276/34; Mansfield, MA 276/33; New Marlborough, MA 276/15; Sandisfield, MA 276/20; Stoughton, MA 277/76; Taunton, MA 276/38; Worcester, MA 277/120.

[102] Groton, MA 277/14; also Ware, MA 276/68; Attleborough, MA 276/27; Lexington, MA 277/16.

[103] MA 186/134. See, on the whole issue, the long letter, John Adams to James Sullivan, May 26, 1776, in John Adams, *Works*, IX, 375ff.; Benjamin W. Labaree, *Patriots and Partisans: The Merchants of Newburyport, 1764–1815* (Cambridge, Mass., 1962), 12ff. The injection of the term, and concept, of "democracy" into recent historical discussions of the suffrage has produced a prolonged and fruitless controversy. That the right to vote was widely exercised in most places is clear; whether that amounts to "democracy" is another and less important matter. See: Brown, *Middle-Class Democracy*, 99; John Cary, "Statistical Method and the Brown Thesis on Colonial Democracy," With a Rebuttal by Robert E. Brown, *William and Mary Quarterly*, Third Series, XX (1963), 251–276; J. R. Pole, "Suffrage and Representation in Massachusetts," *William and Mary Quarterly*, Third Series, XIV (1957), 565ff.; J. R. Pole, "Historians and the Problem of Early American Democracy," *American Historical Review*, LXVII (1962), 626ff.

An analogous accommodation of theory to practice ran through the debate about the way in which the governor and the bicameral legislature would express the will of the people. The argument in favor of a "balanced" government in which "checks" would prevent any concentration of power from "becoming formidable and injurious to the Commonwealth" was plausible.[104] But the detailed arrangements to make the balance effective were necessarily complex.

Experience and the exigencies of war had revealed, for instance, that proper power had to be entrusted to a chief executive.[105] But memories also went back to the decade before the Revolution when the royal governor's control of an extensive patronage and his prominent role in the judicial and legislative processes had been a threat to popular liberties. Even though many officials were now to be elected, the danger still seemed great. The Constitution of 1778 therefore had made the governor presiding officer of the Senate which shared his power and had also provided explicitly that he was to have "no negative" in "any matter . . . but shall have an equal voice with any Senator, on any question before them."[106] It was thus in accord with the arrangements in Virginia and Pennsylvania which also provided for a weak executive.

The more liberal grant of power in the Constitution of 1780 aroused some trepidation. Petersham wanted no governor at all lest the people be "Droved into parties By the influence of Rich and Powerful Men who will act in Competition with each other" and spread the "Corruption that Naturally Flows from Bribery and undue Influence."[107] Many more towns questioned the propriety of the governor's veto or suggested curtailment of his other powers.[108] On the other hand, there were people who regarded the chief executive as "the most fit person" to limit "an incontroulable Power of Legislation in the Hands of those who are only the Representatives of particular and smaller Districts of the Common-

[104] Address of the Convention, below, No. 33; "Essex Result," Parsons, *Parsons,* 373, 379.

[105] See, e.g., William Gordon to George Washington, July 17, 1777, in Massachusetts Historical Society, *Proceedings,* LXIII (1930), 346.

[106] Constitution of 1778, Article XXII; see also MA 156/204.

[107] MA 277/104. See also Hardwick, MA 277/92; Warwick, MA 276/69.

[108] Sandisfield, MA 276/20; Wilbraham, MA 276/72; Edgecomb, MA 276/77; Shutesbury, MA 276/63; Southampton, MA 276/64; Lincoln, MA 277/17; Grafton, MA 277/91; Norton, MA 276/34; Stoughton, MA 277/76; Colrain, MA 276/45; Sunderland, MA 276/67; Middleborough, MA 277/40. On the pardoning power, see Westminster, MA 277/118; Sunderland, MA 276/67. On reports from officials, see Greenwich, MA 276/51; Colrain, MA 276/45; Sandisfield, MA 276/20; Belchertown, MA 276/40; Hardwick, MA 277/92; New Braintree, MA 277/99. On salary, see Norton, MA 276/34; Sutton, MA 277/112; Brookline, MA 277/64; Holliston, MA 277/15; Middleborough, MA 277/40; Oakham, MA 277/102.

wealth," since he was "the Center of Union to all the several parts and members of the political Body; who is chosen and constituted by the whole Community to be in a peculiar manner the Guardian of the Constitution and of the Rights and Interests of the whole State." [109]

The suggestions, in the convention, that the governor be the third branch of the legislative department reflected the prevailing confusion about the arrangement of the lawmaking power. Although a few towns objected to the whole principle of bicameralism, there was general agreement about the desirability of two houses that could check each other's activities. In the precedents with which Americans were familiar each body represented a different estate, as Lords and Commons did in England. The absence of any such division in Massachusetts society made an alternative necessary. The House was to speak for all the people of the Commonwealth, the Senate for its virtue and wisdom, as measured by property. Even critics who objected to the plan set forth in the Constitution generally favored some scheme by which two houses would balance each other. Mansfield, for instance, believed that the Senate should "Represent persons as well as propperty" and the House "propperty as well as persons for sure both branches make but one General Court, and each Branch aught Equally to consult the safty, Prosperity, and the happiness of the Whole." [110]

There remained considerable vagueness and uncertainty about the innovation. Some towns wished the Senate to be chosen by the House; others proposed changes in its size or preferred that it take the place of the Council.[111] Still others worried about the adequacy of the requirement for a quorum, or demanded a printed legislative journal, or suggested that the towns reserve the right to review legislation.[112]

The most difficult problem, however, was a familiar one—how to allocate the places in the House of Representatives, which inherited the functions of the colonial assembly and was ascribed the attributes and prestige of the House of Commons. More attention was devoted to this

[109] Wells, MA 277/56; Groton, MA 277/14; "Essex Result," Parsons, *Parsons,* 395ff.

[110] See *Journal of the Convention,* 44; for towns opposed to a bicameral legislature, see Athol, MA 277/83; Grafton, MA 277/91; Rehoboth, MA 276/35; Bellingham, MA 277/60. For the analogy with Parliament see Northampton, MA 276/58. For objections to the constitutional plan, see Petersham, MA 277/104; Mansfield, MA 276/33.

[111] E.g., Middleborough, MA 277/40; Mansfield, MA 276/33; Wrentham, MA 277/79; Norton, MA 276/34; Oakham, MA 277/102; Medway, MA 277/72; Medfield, MA 277/70.

[112] Worcester, MA 277/120; Royalston, MA 277/106; Dudley, MA 277/90; Petersham, MA 277/104; Braintree, MA 277/63; Newton, MA 277/22; Athol, MA 277/83.

issue than to the character of the Senate, structured by the Constitution to reflect the distribution of property in the state, in accord with the recommendation of the Essex Result.[113]

If Massachusetts was indeed in a state of nature, then all men subscribing to the social contract deserved equal representation wherever they lived. On that abstract basis, the Essex Result had insisted that the legislature should be "an exact miniature" of its constituents, "the whole body politic . . . reduced to a smaller scale."[114] But in fact the towns conducted much of the business of government and regarded the members of the General Court as their deputies whom they instructed and by whom they expected to be obeyed.[115] Even the tiniest therefore insisted on some representation. Yet to satisfy them would either slight the more populous or make the House unmanageably large. The dilemma had long been bothersome, only now it could not be blamed on "a secret poison" spread by the Crown "for the corrupt Designs of an abandoned Administration."[116]

Complaints about the inequity of representation in 1775 and 1776 had left a vivid impression on the framers of the Constitution of 1778; an involved debate had produced an intricate scheme which gave every town one seat but also allotted additional places to the larger ones according to a graduated scale. The proposal had not been happily received and was in part responsible for the rejection of the Constitution.[117]

The members of the convention of 1780 were acutely sensitive to the issue. An Address to the citizens, submitting the draft Constitution, acknowledged that "Representation ought to be founded on the Principle of equality." But this, it pointed out, did not mean "that each Town in the Commonwealth shall have Weight and importance in a just proportion to its Numbers and property." Even in a "System of Government arising from the State of Nature," it would be "unpracticable" to establish "an exact Representation." And Massachusetts was providing for its legislature not out of a state of nature but with "nearly three hundred

113 Parsons, *Parsons,* 370ff., 376, 391; Morison, "Struggle over the Adoption of the Constitution," 386ff.

114 Parsons, *Parsons,* 360, 376, 384ff., 389, 390.

115 Kenneth Colegrove, "New England Town Mandates," Colonial Society of Massachusetts, *Publications,* XXI (1919), 411ff.

116 Pittsfield Memorial, December 26, 1775, No. 3.

117 See above, p. 13; Article VI of Constitution of 1778; materials on the drafting of the provision are in MA 156/207, 284, 235ff. See also Samuel Adams to John Adams, September 16, 1776, in John Adams, *Works,* IX, 442; John Adams to James Warren, June 22, 1777, in *Warren-Adams Letters,* I, 334–335.

Coroporations" already in existence. Considering their claims, the convention fixed upon a plan that gave towns of 150 ratable polls one member, towns with 375 two, and still larger towns one member for every 225 polls above 375. Those places already incorporated but lacking the newly established minimum would not be penalized but could continue to send a representative.[118]

Much of the comment in the responses dealt with details of the scheme and obscured a basic confusion in the thinking on the subject.[119] Did representation aim to secure equality among the towns or among the people?

The smaller places inclined toward the view that the community was the entity for which each member of the House would speak. Therefore, Wilbraham argued, the number of inhabitants was "much too unsteady and wavering to place Representation upon." Incorporation was "the best Rule whereon to found a just Representation." "Each Town," Washington claimed, "has an undeniable Rite to Equel Representation." And Ward "heartily" wished "that representation might be weighed by Towns rather than by the Number of polls, which would be Similar to the proceedings of the Honorable Congress and Some Neighbouring, well regulated States that have been attended with very wholsome Effects." [120]

Yet it was hard to deny the justice of giving the more populous towns additional seats. In fact some of the larger places questioned the propriety of giving the smallest ones any recognition at all. "The admission of small Corporations to send a Representative," Roxbury voted, was "inconsistent with the fundamental principle" of representation *"founded on the principle of equality."* Such a plan in the future might give "the *Minority of People, the Majority of Power and Influence."* [121]

Two concepts had become intertwined—apportionment according to corporateness and according to population. Through the eighteenth century, despite the resistance of royal authority, there had been a rapid proliferation of towns and their offshoots, for it was only on that local

[118] Address of the Convention, below, No. 33; *Journal of the Convention,* 118ff., 123ff., 135ff.

[119] E.g., Sandisfield, MA 276/20; West Stockbridge, MA 276/24; Mansfield, MA 276/33; Norton, MA 276/34; Leverett, MA 276/53; Monson, MA 276/55; Pelham, MA 276/61; Southwick, MA 276/65; Springfield, MA 276/66; Sunderland, MA 276/67; West Springfield, MA 276/71; Framingham, MA 277/12; Bellingham, MA 277/60; Shelburne, MA 276/62; Concord, MA 277/8; Medfield, MA 277/70; Southborough, MA 277/109; Stoughton, MA 277/76.

[120] MA 276/23, 72; MA 277/116.

[121] MA 277/75; see also Leverett, MA 276/53.

basis that power could effectively be organized. The General Court had frequently granted incorporation and had also let communities organize as quasi-corporations "with all the Privileges of Towns in General . . . except that of sending a Representative to the General Assembly." In some cases, in fact, it had allowed these districts to "continue a part of the town" from which they were separating, for the purpose of choosing representatives. And the Revolution had made it difficult to deny a voice in the General Court to anyone who paid taxes. "Are not our Dificulty Simaler to those of the Colloneys that we are all Engaged aganst?" asked the inhabitant of one unrepresented place.[122]

The history of settlement had diffused these corporations and had also blurred their character. If a town was entitled to representation, why not every political entity which in practice operated like a town? If special adjustments permitted inhabitants to vote outside their own community, was it not the person rather than the town that deserved representation? The issue had been canvassed repeatedly in the convention and various responses returned to it.[123] There appeared to be no solution, but to represent all towns, and the more populous more than the others.

The drawback was that the Constitution's proposal would result in an unwieldy chamber. *"Great bodies move slowly,"* Worcester warned. "A very few of the most populous Towns will have it in their power to constitute a Quorum . . . and being near the State house . . . their members can easily and constantly attend; while those at a distance from their local situation and many other Causes, be unavoidably absent . . . *whereby in* a thin house Laws might be passed which would not be calculated for the General Good."[124] The citizens of the western counties also foresaw that they would be at a disadvantage. The more distant towns would "generally omit the full Exercise of their Rights," thus relinquishing to the more fortunately located corporations "more than an equal Proportion of Influence in the Conduct of Public Affairs in general." To equalize the disparity Springfield demanded "that each and every Town, even the largest, should be expressly limitted to a certain moderate Number of Representatives, which they should not exceed, that

[122] Joseph Bennet to Joseph Hawley, December 4, 1775, Hawley Papers, Box 2, New York Public Library; "Petition of the Inhabitants of the Easterly Part of the Township of Sunderland To Be Set Off—March, 1773," J. M. Smith, *History of the Town of Sunderland* (Greenfield, Mass., 1899), 47; J. H. Temple, *History of the Town of Palmer* (Springfield, Mass., 1889), 175ff.

[123] E.g., Stoughton, MA 277/76; Roxbury, MA 277/75.

[124] MA 277/120.

this should be so done, that the Number should be reduced, its Increase duly restrained, and the Mischiefs or Dangers aforesaid prevented." [125]

These arguments all rested on the assumption "That each Town has rights, Liberties, and Priviledges peculiar to the same, and as dear to them as those to any other, and which they have as just a right as any others to have guarded and protected." "This State," Lincoln pointed out, "is Constituted of a great number of Distinct and very unequal Corporations which Corporations are the Immediate Constituant part of the State and the Individuals are only the Remote parts in many respects—in all acts of the Legislature which Respect particular Corporations each Corporations hath both a Distinct and seperate Interest Clashing with the Interest of all the rest." Many representatives for a single town would, therefore, strengthen its cause in the General Court, to the point where "they Could Compleately Tyraniz over all the Rest." [126]

Paradoxically, however, the small communities that wished payment out of state funds for attendance at, as well as for travel to, the General Court argued from a diametrically opposed position. "Each member of said house," explained Worcester, "is the Representative of the whole State and not meerly of the Corporation by which he is elected," and therefore should be paid by the state. Belchertown declared that all members of the General Court should be "supported and paid out of the publick Chest . . . Because they are Representatives not meerly of this or that particular Town (which would suppose them to have the interest of that Town only to provide for) But of the whole Body of the People—and though they are to guard the Rights of the Town where they are chosen as they are presumed to know the state of it, yet they are equally to guard the Rights of the whole." [127]

A few responses perceived the implications of this concept; the towns need not be the unit of representation. New Salem and Mendon suggested that for the purpose of representation the state be divided "into Equal Districkts of a proper Bigness" with the members "paid wholly out of the State Treasury." Bridgewater spelled out what was implicit in these proposals: "A Representation Cannot be had in any manner So Eaqual as that of Choosing Representatives by Districts: and ascertaining the number Each District shall be intitled to send, according to the

[125] MA 276/66.
[126] MA 277/17; also Sunderland, MA 276/67.
[127] Worcester, MA 277/120; Belchertown, MA 276/40; also Petersham, MA 277/104.

number of Electors in each District." Only thus could the objective of a House representing persons be attained.[128] But that proposal, however plausible in the abstract, was not feasible in the Massachusetts of 1780.

The discussion took the tortuous course it did because the men who spoke or wrote on the issue earnestly desired to square theory and actuality. They were not in a state of nature, but wished to behave as if they were—to act by the light of pure reason and yet to preserve familiar institutions.

Woven into the debate about who should participate in the polity and about the structure of the government was a realistic appraisal of still another question. Who should actually wield the power the Constitution formalized? That is, who would designate the military and civil officers, and for what terms?

The conditions of an ongoing war lent exceptional importance to the militia, a subject already the cause of considerable controversy. An act of January 22, 1776 had formalized the earlier compromise by which the House and the Council had agreed to share the appointing power; and the Constitutions of 1778 and 1780 had each dealt with the matter. In the subsequent canvasses of opinion, the citizens scrutinized these provisions with care.[129]

The act of 1776 had allowed the militiamen to elect the captains and subalterns of their companies while the Council and the House—each with a negative over the other—selected the field officers, brigadiers, and major generals. The convention of 1778 had sought to create a more coherent chain of command. A proposal that "Military officers shall be appointed by the General Court by Ballot, each branch to have a right to originate or negative the choice" failed to pass. Instead, a preliminary draft gave the governor and the Senate power to appoint "all General, Field, and Staff Officers, both of the Militia and of the troops" raised by the state. The captains and subalterns of the militia were to "be chosen by the People agreeable to the present Militia Act, unless altered by some future Act of the General Assembly." On the other hand, captains and subalterns of other troops raised by the state were also to be appointed by the governor and Senate. In the course of its consideration by the convention, the sentence dealing with the militia was deleted, probably

[128] MA 276/17; MA 277/35; MA 277/97; also Wells, MA 277/56.

[129] See above, p. 13ff.; st. 1775–76, ch. 10 (*Acts and Resolves,* V, 445ff.); Constitution of 1778, Article XIX; Constitution of 1780, Chapter II, Section I, Article X; also Amory, *Sullivan,* II, 370, 371.

with the intention of subsuming the captains and subalterns of the militia under the phrases "troops raised by and in the pay of this State," so that the governor and Senate would appoint all military officers.[130]

The convention of 1780 was more judicious and more ingenious. The militiamen twenty-one years of age and upwards were to elect the company captains and subalterns who would choose the regimental field officers, who in turn would select the brigadiers. The Senate and the House, each with a negative upon the other, would appoint the major generals, while the governor designated the commanders of other troops and commissioned all the officers.[131]

The concession to local and popular control still did not go far enough to please everyone. There were complaints that the governor's power to appoint officers outside the militia might sometimes put "large quantities of warlike Stores" at the disposal of persons "who May not ame at the Good of the Commonwealth." [132] Other objections went to the opposite extreme: "the method of appointing Officers by Election" caused "dissatisfaction and discontent . . . in Consequence of which military Authority has been weakened and relaxed so that it has often been scarce possible for the Officers to execute the Order of their Superiors," since they were "liable to be under control by being dependent on the Soldiers for their Commissions and therefore cannot act free and independent." Such officers would therefore be "liable to be degraded or superseeded in Case of a Vacancy by the Soldiers, if they do not act in Conformity to their Wills and capricious Humors, without Reason, or against Reason." It was better to have the governor select all military officers in his role "as Captain General." [133]

However the officers were to be chosen, there were recurrent demands that their terms be set at one year or, at least, at some fixed period "to the End that those who are unfit for their Posts may be easily dropped, and such as are Worthy as they come on the stage Elected." It was understandable that "when persons grow old they are fond of their offices though everybody (except themselves) are sensible they are unfit to Continue in office." [134]

[130] MA 156/205, 217, 231.
[131] Chapter II, Section I, Article X; *Journal of the Convention,* 113, 114, 124–127, 132ff.
[132] Westhampton, MA 276/70; also Sutton, MA 277/112; Greenwich, MA 276/51; Shrewsbury, MA 277/108; Shelburne, MA 276/62; Pelham, MA 276/61.
[133] Wells, MA 277/56; Biddeford, MA 277/53; Stockbridge, MA 276/21; York, MA 277/57.
[134] Belchertown, MA 276/40; Hatfield, MA 276/52; also South Brimfield, MA 276/43; Shutesbury, MA 276/63; Westfield, MA 276/68.

There were also doubts about the propriety of the age requirement for voting in the election of officers. "Every soldier that is Liable to be Draughted for Sarvic ought to have his vote for his officers." Almost a third of the militia consisted of youths between the ages of sixteen and twenty-one whose experience gave them not only the right to choose but also "Sufficien Knowledge of the Qualifications of an officer." [135]

The appointment of civil officials proved as thorny a problem. The Constitution of 1778 had distinguished between those with terms of one year who were to be chosen by the General Court (Secretary, Treasurer-General, and Commissary-General) and those who held their places during good behavior (judges, sheriffs, registers of probate courts, coroners, notaries, naval officers, and the attorney-general) who were to be designated by the governor and Senate. The Constitution of 1780 adopted the same essential distinction with only minor modifications. In both, provisions against plural officeholding were inserted to guard against corruption and against excessive concentration of power.[136]

The responses which challenged this arrangement occasionally suggested a shift to the legislature of the whole power to appoint and dismiss; the governor, after all, did not "know in so extensive a State who are proper for Officers" and would be tempted "to sell offices to the highest bidder." [137] But the dissidents more often demanded that all positions be filled by popular election. "Surely," Middleborough pointed out, "if all officers are at all times accountable to the people for their conduct in office: the people ought to Chuse them: and if the Right and privilege of Chusing any one officer be given out of the hands of the people: by the Same Rule the people may by Degrees Loose the privilege of Chusing Every officer. and then groan under the government of a Venal

[135] Shelburne, MA 276/62; Pelham, MA 276/61; also Douglas, MA 277/89; Granville, MA 276/49; Rochester, MA 277/44; Plympton, MA 277/43; West Springfield, MA 276/71; Westfield, MA 276/68; Sunderland, MA 276/67; Southwick, MA 276/65; Montague, MA 276/56; Monson, MA 276/55; Ludlow, MA 276/54; Granby, MA 276/48; Chesterfield, MA 276/44; West Stockbridge, MA 276/24; Tyringham, MA 276/22; Lanesborough, MA 276/13; Hancock, MA 276/12; Becket, MA 276/11; Adams, MA 276/10; Milford, MA 277/98; Wilbraham, MA 276/72; Sutton, MA 277/112; Conway, MA 276/46–47; Westhampton, MA 276/70.

[136] Constitution of 1778, Articles IV, XIX, XXIV–XXVI; Constitution of 1780, Chapters II, III, VI. For the importance of the independent judiciary see John Adams to James Warren, May 12, 1776, in *Warren-Adams Letters,* I, 242. For plural officeholding, see Samuel Adams to James Warren, November 4, 1775, in Samuel Adams, *Writings,* III, 237; Ellen E. Brennan, *Plural Office-Holding in Massachusetts, 1760–1780* (Chapel Hill, 1945).

[137] Sutton, MA 277/112; also Palmer, MA 276/60; Ware, MA 276/68; Oakham, MA 277/102; Shrewsbury, MA 277/108; Shelburne, MA 276/62; Acton, MA 277/1; Granby, MA 276/48; Upton, MA 277/114; Westminster, MA 277/118; Southborough, MA 277/109; Sandisfield, MA 276/20; Rehoboth, MA 276/35.

and most Wreched Set of Villains." That any one man or number of men should choose officers for other men was inconsistent "with the Right of Nature."[138] Let the people of each county who "generally know thire worthyest men" elect local officials. There would then be less reason to fear that "ambitious and artfull men" would perpetuate "the Same pernitious influence" by working for the governor's election.[139] It was not safe "to put any more athority into one Mans hand than what is of absolute necessity. —— and if the Govenor should give himself so much Time as would be nesesary for that purpose he neglect other business of more importance."[140]

Rural towns, which felt the inconvenience of remote registries of deeds and courts of probate, were particularly sensitive to the issue of local control. Unless such business could be transacted in each town, travel costs and fraud increased "the burden the Fatherless and Widow have long laboured under" and resulted in many small estates being "almost totally Dissipated before a final settlement could be obtained."[141]

That some officers could be re-elected, that judges served during good behavior, and that salaries could not be reduced or withheld were also worrisome details. It was desirable that public servants be "Animated to Officiate faithfully" by dependence upon the people. To permit any "Standing Salleries or pentions" would diminish that dependence. "Persons in Office for a long or unlimited Term" will be "too independent of their Constituents" and "will Naturally Become the most insolent haughty and imperious monsters that can be Ranked among the human Species." Annual elections, for a limited number of terms with salaries controlled by the legislature, were preferable.[142] Furthermore, there was a persistent demand for strengthening the provisions against plural office-holding.[143]

The Address of the Convention had anticipated these objections. Officials chosen by popular election would forever be "under the Control

[138] MA 277/40; also Greenwich, MA 276/51; Howard, *Sermon*, 364ff.

[139] Barnstable, MA 277/47, 48; Granby, MA 276/48; Sandisfield, MA 276/20; Southwick, MA 276/65; Belchertown, MA 276/40; Sunderland, MA 276/67; Bellingham, MA 277/60.

[140] Winsor, MA 276/26.

[141] Foxborough, MA 277/68; also Petersham, MA 277/104; Northfield, MA 276/57; Belchertown, MA 276/40; Wrentham, MA 277/79; Milford, MA 277/98.

[142] Colrain, MA 276/45; Athol, MA 277/83; Richmond, MA 276/19; Middleborough, MA 277/40; also Shutesbury, MA 276/63; Dunstable, MA 277/10; Warwick, MA 276/69; Tyringham, MA 276/22; Bellingham, MA 277/60; Milton, MA 277/73; Boston, MA 277/61; Wilbraham, MA 276/72.

[143] Acton, MA 277/1; Shrewsbury, MA 277/108; Northborough, MA 277/100; West Springfield, MA 276/71. See also above, n. 136.

of ambitious, artful and interested men, who can obtain most Votes for them." Nor was it prudent to entrust the selection of judges to a legislature which was "too numerous to be accountable for putting weak or wicked Men into Office" and which, being charged with instituting and trying impeachments, should not be involved in appointments over which it might have to sit in judgment. Tenure during good behavior and "fixed and ample Salaries" would make the "judges . . . at all Times feel themselves independent and free" in decisions that affected every citizen's life and property.[144]

No more than with regard to property qualifications or apportionment in the House, was it possible to reach a complete consensus with regard to the control of power in the new commonwealth. The Constitution achieved an approximate accommodation of theory and practice that left some citizens dissatisfied, but none so aggrieved as to be unwilling to give it a trial.

The new frame of government demanded no firmer commitment than that. It embraced enough common assumptions so that the groups, still genuinely divided against one another, could continue to struggle within it for acceptance of their own views of representation, the suffrage, or religious freedom and could expect also to seek their own advantage within the forms thus established. Nor was the Constitution itself regarded as unalterable. This was not the perfect, immortal product of a genius "Legislator" that Harrington had described. The convention assumed from the start that its handiwork would be amendable and it provided for a total review of its product by a new convention in fifteen years if the people then wished it. Some responses complained that revision should have been mandatory and that the period of trial was too long; and some asked that the process be continuous. Whenever a majority of the towns agreed on the need, a convention "ought to be impowered Not only to propose Amendments" but also to "Remove Every Encroachment Made By the Legislature" on "the Reasonabl Liberties of the people."[145] Insofar as the voters in the town meetings were ratifying

[144] Address of the Convention, below, No. 33; also "Essex Result," Parsons, *Parsons,* 360, 382ff.

[145] *Journal of the Convention,* 156–159, 161–165. See also Petersham's proposal of a standing "Coart of Convention," MA 277/104. For other comments on the amending process, see Ward, MA 277/116. About eighty towns requested revision in a period shorter than fifteen years. See, e.g., Northampton, MA 276/58; Wilmington, MA 277/34; Woburn, MA 277/33; Weston, MA 277/32; Tewksbury, MA 277/28; Stow, MA 277/27; Sudbury, MA 277/26; Sherborn, MA 277/24; Newton, MA 277/22; Natick, MA 277/21; Malden, MA 277/19; Lincoln, MA 277/17; Holliston, MA 277/15; Framingham, MA

a social compact, their actions were tentative only; power still resided in the sovereign people.

More precisely stated, however, they were not actually emerging from a state of nature and beginning afresh, but living under institutions that they were modifying and could continue to modify. For the very first paragraph of the Constitution's preamble had reassured them that whenever a government failed to further the enjoyment of "their natural rights," the sovereign people had "a right to alter the government, and to take measures necessary for their safety, prosperity and happiness."[146]

The documents which follow reveal the popular involvement in the constitution-making process. The bulk of them consist of the responses sent by the towns in commentary upon the proposals submitted to them in 1778 and 1780. The answers differ strikingly. Some are perfunctory; others are the outcome of extensive debate which produced elaborate essays upon the theory and practice of government. Such diversity was to be expected in view of the diversity of communities in the state. But running through the replies, whether from the coastal cities or the rural towns of the interior, was a continuing concern and intimate involvement with the momentous political issues of the Revolution. Even places which sent no responses were deeply concerned. The failure to reply was sometimes the result of the inability to agree and sometimes, as in the case of Salem, the result of a decision to allow the delegates orally to communicate the ideas of the meeting to the convention.

Each place had its leaders—the lawyers, ministers, teachers, gentry, or farmers who served as selectmen and commanded the respect of their neighbors. But the documents themselves, in their diction and orthography as well as in their sentiments, reveal the closeness of the ties between such people and those for whom they spoke. In the responses, the polished phrases of the formal political essay dropped away and thoughts

277/12; East Sudbury, MA 277/11; Dunstable, MA 277/10; West Springfield, MA 276/71; Westfield, MA 276/68; Sunderland, MA 276/67; Southampton, MA 276/64; Shelburne, MA 276/62; Pelham, MA 276/61; Leverett, MA 276/53; Greenwich, MA 276/51; Granby, MA 276/48; Belchertown, MA 276/40; Taunton, MA 276/38; Norton, MA 276/34; Easton, MA 276/31; New Salem, MA 226/17; New Marlborough, MA 276/15; Acton, MA 277/1; Westborough, MA 277/117. See also Samuel Adams to John Adams, March 15, 1780, in Samuel Adams, *Writings,* IV, 183; William Gordon to John Adams and Francis Dana, March 8–11, to John Adams, July 22, October 19, 1780, in Massachusetts Historical Society, *Proceedings,* LXIII (1930), 430ff., 437, 442. On Harrington, see Blitzer, *Immortal Commonwealth,* 163, 175ff.

146 See also Samuel Adams to John Adams, November 25, 1790, in Samuel Adams, *Writings,* IV, 344; West, *Sermon,* 285, 302ff.

were expressed in the Biblical language that men of all estates heard in the meetinghouse.[147]

The close connection between leaders and followers was unique to this revolution. No such communication with the populace informed the men who seized power in England more than a century before or in France more than a decade later. The Cahiers of 1789, for instance—even those which demanded constitutional uniformity—were framed within the procedures and terms set by established and scarcely questionable institutions. Not until the right of petition was accorded would the rulers begin to hear the voice of the French populace; and there was no mechanism for feeding information about popular desires to the men who tried to establish new forms of government to replace the old régime.[148]

The constitution-making process did not follow the same course in the other American states. All recognized that their authority derived from the sovereign people, but in none was the participation of the citizens as conscious and explicit as in the Bay State. Therein lies the utility of its development in illuminating the meaning of the American Revolution.

The distinctive qualities of its revolution were the products of both the social and the institutional structures of Massachusetts. Local power, in the neighborhood and countryside, was the key to the mastery of the colony and state as it had been for centuries in England. The crucial difference lay in who exercised that power and how. Long before 1774, the mass of the population—farmers, artisans, and traders—had learned to use that power and to qualify the dominance of the great landowning, officeholding, and mercantile families.[149] The Massachusetts townsmen were sensitive to the dangers of an aristocracy; and they possessed effective instruments for making their wishes known. Recurrent controversies

[147] Alice M. Baldwin, *New England Clergy and the American Revolution* (Durham, 1928), 135.

[148] See the procedures traced in Ch. -L. Chassin, *Les Élections et les cahiers de Paris en 1789* (Paris, 1888–89); also Edme Champion, *La France d'après les cahiers de 1789* (Paris, 1897), 29ff.; P. Bois, *Cahiers de doléances du tiers état de la Senéchaussé de Chateau-du-Loir* (Gap, 1960), lviii; Jean Belin, *La Pensée des petitionnaires. La Réforme des institutions et l'enchainement des vocables politiques* (Paris, 1939); Beatrice F. Hyslop, *French Nationalism in 1789 according to the General Cahiers* (New York, 1934) 97ff.; Georges Lefebvre, *La Révolution française* (Paris, 1963), 123ff.

[149] See Helen M. Cam, *Liberties & Communities in Medieval England* (Cambridge, Eng., 1944), xi. David Syrett, "Town-Meeting Politics in Massachusetts, 1776–1786," *William and Mary Quarterly,* Third Series, XXI (1964), 352–366, not only depends on "admittedly fragmentary evidence" for its conclusion "that Massachusetts elections and town meetings during the 1770's and 1780's were similar to most other Anglo-American political institutions of the late eighteenth century," but also disregards entirely the character of popular controls.

familiarized the people of the state with a body of political theory which did not remain abstract, but was reduced to meaningful categories that described their own experience. When the crisis of Revolution came and the Tory gentry withdrew, that theory supplied not only an explanation for what had happened but also a guide for reconstructing the polity. The concepts of consent of the governed, of a social compact arising out of a state of nature, of natural rights and the balance of power were familiar to every sector of the population for these general ideas were closely related to political and social actuality. With the collapse of royal government, power devolved back to the members of the town meetings; and men, continually concerned with legitimacy, struggled to frame a polity in which authority could safely be lodged with the concurrence of the whole Commonwealth. The process by which they did so gave their revolution a peculiar national quality.

At the completion of the task, a preacher exclaimed: "Is not a country a constitution—an established frame of laws; of which a man may say, 'we are here united in society for our common security and happiness. These fields and these fruits are my own: the regulations under which I live are my own; I am not only a proprietor in the soil, but I am part of the sovereignty of my country."[150] Hence the awesome significance of the task to those engaged in it. "If America preserves her freedom," one of them said, "she will be an asylum for the oppressed and persecuted of every country; her example and success will encourage the friends and rouse a spirit of liberty through other nations, and will probably be the means of freedom and happiness to Ireland, and perhaps in time to Great Britain, and many other countries."[151]

The documents reproduced are, for the most part, deposited in the Massachusetts Archives, the State House, Boston, and are published with the kind permission of the Secretary of State.[152] These and other sources have been drawn together to present a step-by-step account of the development of the Constitution of 1780. The documents are presented in a

[150] Samuel Cooper, *Sermon Preached before His Excellency John Hancock . . . October 25, 1780* (Boston, [1780]), 27.

[151] Howard, *Sermon,* 390ff. Perry Miller has called attention to the continuity of these phrases with those of Puritan theology ("From the Covenant to the Revival," James W. Smith and A. L. Jamison, eds., *Shaping of American Religion* [Princeton, 1961], I, 322ff.). But the rhetoric in the 1770's no longer corresponds to the traditional contents; instead it is used to express purely secular and rationalistic concepts.

[152] References to material in the archives are given as: MA, followed by the volume/folio numbers.

form intended to be clear and comprehensible and yet to reproduce on the printed page the original quality of the written manuscript. The language, spelling, punctuation, and style have been left intact. In the interest of comprehensibility abbreviations have been expanded and superior letters brought down—where the meaning was clear—in accordance with the directions of the *Harvard Guide to American History* (Cambridge, Mass., 1954), 98. Words crossed out on the manuscript are given in angle brackets. The signatures of the ordinary men who helped compose these documents were often difficult to decipher. Where possible they have been checked against local sources; but on occasion it was necessary to make the closest approximation feasible.

I

The Problem Explored

August 1775—November 1776

I

An Act to Confirm the Resolves of the Provincial Congresses, August 23, 1775

Each of the Provincial Congresses had been the actual governing agency for the colony of Massachusetts from October 1774, to the time when, upon the advice of the Continental Congress in Philadelphia, precepts for the election of a new General Court were issued in July 1775. A determination to maintain orderly forms prompted the General Court to confirm the legality of the measures passed by these Provincial Congresses. The following act, reprinted from *The Charters and General Laws of the Colony and Province of Massachusetts Bay* (Boston, 1814), 687–688, established the deeds of the Provincial Congresses "as lawful and valid to all intents."

An Act to Confirm and Establish the Resolves of the Several Provincial Congresses of this Colony.

WHEREAS this oppressed colony has for many months past been deprived of the free exercise of its usual powers of government, which has necessarily occasioned the publick business thereof to be conducted by congresses, and as many matters of the greatest importance for the recovery and preservation of that liberty, which God, nature and compact have given to this people, have been resolved, done and transacted by provincial congresses, some of which have not yet had their full effect, and whereas the legality of such resolves, doings and transactions may hereafter be called in question, and may occasion much litigation, unless confirmed and established in some known constitutional manner.

SECT. 1. Be it therefore enacted by the council and house of representatives of this colony in general court assembled, and by the authority of the same, that all and every the resolves, doings and transactions of the several provincial congresses of this colony, from and after the fourth day of October one thousand seven hundred and seventy-four, to the twentieth day of July one thousand seven hundred and seventy-five, be, and they hereby are confirmed and established as lawful and valid to all intents, constructions and purposes whatsoever, as fully and effectually as if the same resolves, doings and transactions had been done by any general court or assembly of this colony.

SECT. 2. And be it further enacted by the authority aforesaid, that whenever any person or persons shall be sued or prosecuted before any superiour court of judicature, court of assize and general goal delivery, or before any inferiour court of common pleas, or any court of general sessions of the peace, or before any single magistrate, for any thing done in obedience to or in compliance with any of the resolves, doings, recommendations or other proceedings of said congresses, such person or persons shall and may give this act, and the record of the resolves, doings and transactions of the several provincial congresses aforesaid in evidence under the general issue; and the same thus given in evidence shall avail to all intents and purposes as if the same were specially pleaded, any law, usage or custom to the contrary notwithstanding.

SECT. 3. And be it further enacted by the authority aforesaid, that the records of the resolves, doings and transactions of the several provincial congresses aforesaid, be immediately lodged and for ever hereafter kept in the secretary's office of this colony, and that the secretary shall copy and authenticate all such records of said resolves, doings and transactions as shall be demanded of him to be used in any of the courts aforesaid, which copies so authenticated shall be received as full evidence in said courts of all such resolves, doings and transactions. [Passed August 23, 1775]

2

An Act on Representation, August 23, 1775

The newly constituted General Court needed the consent of those it governed and therefore had to deal with representation. In August 1775 it restored to incorporated districts the privilege earlier denied them of sending deputies to a general court or assembly. The act of August 23, 1775, is reprinted from *Charters and General Laws of the Colony and Province of Massachusetts Bay,* 796–798.

An Act Declaratory Of The Right Of Certain Towns And Districts In The Colony of The Massachusetts Bay In New England To Elect And Depute A Representative Or Representatives To Serve For And Represent Them In Any Great And General Court Or Assembly, At Any Time To Be Held And Kept For The Service Of The Said Colony.

WHEREAS there are divers acts or laws heretofore made and passed by former general courts or assemblies of this colony for the incorporation of towns and districts, which against common right, and in derogation of the rights granted to the inhabitants of this colony by the charter, contain an exception of the right and privilege of choosing and sending a representative to the great and general court or assembly,

SECT. 1. Be it therefore enacted and declared by the council and house of representatives in general court assembled, and by the authority of the same, that henceforth every such exception contained in any act or law heretofore made and passed by any general court or assembly of this colony, for the erecting or incorporating any town or district, shall be held and taken to be altogether null and void; and that every town and district in this colony, consisting of the number of thirty or more freeholders and other inhabitants qualified by charter to vote in the election of a representative, shall henceforth be held and taken to have full right, power and privilege to elect and depute one or more persons, being freeholders and resident in such town or district, to serve for and represent them in any great and general court or assembly hereafter to be held and kept for this colony, according to the limitations in an act or law of the general assembly, entitled an act for ascertaining the number and regulating the house of representatives, any exception of that right and privilege contained or expressed in the respective acts or laws for the incorporation of such town or district notwithstanding.

And whereas in and by an act or law of this colony, entitled an act for erecting part of the town of Newbury into a new town by the name of Newburyport, it is enacted and provided that the said town of Newburyport should have the right of choosing and sending from time to time but one person to represent them in the great and general court of this colony, and that the inhabitants of the town of Newbury, from and after the time of the making and passing the said act, should have a right to choose and send no more than one person to represent them in the great and general court of this colony,

SECT. 2. Be it enacted and declared by the authority aforesaid, that henceforth each of the said towns of Newbury and Newbury port shall have the full power and right of choosing and sending as many persons to represent them respectively in the great and general court or assembly of this colony as each of the said towns would have had a right to have chosen and sent to the said general court by virtue of the abovementioned act or law, entitled an act for ascertaining the number and regulating the house of representatives, in case there had not been any restrictions upon the said towns touching their rights and privilege of choosing and sending persons to represent them respectively in the great and general court or assembly, contained or expressed in the said act for the constituting and making that part of the former town of Newbury now called Newburyport a distinct town.

SECT. 3. And be it further enacted and declared by the authority aforesaid, that every corporate body in this colony which in the act for the incorporation thereof is said and declared to be made a district, and has by such act granted to it, or is declared to be vested with the rights, powers, privileges or immunities of a town with the exception abovementioned, of choosing and sending a representative to the great and general court or assembly, shall henceforth be and shall be holden, taken and intended to be a town to all intents and purposes whatsoever. [August 23, 1775]

3

Pittsfield Memorial, December 26, 1775

The inhabitants of Pittsfield expressed the conviction that the royal charter was not a proper foundation for a new government. They wanted a new, written constitution confirming privileges which they outlined in their petition, found in MA 180/150. This memorial, in the handwriting of Thomas Allen, was assigned the date December 26, 1775, by J. E. A. Smith, *The History of Pittsfield, (Berkshire County,) Massachusetts, from the Year 1734 to the Year 1800* (Boston, 1869), 343–345.

The Petition Remonstrance and Address of the Town of Pittsfield to the Honourable Board of Councellors and House of Representatives of the Province of the Massachusetts Bay in General Assembly now setting in Watertown—

May it please your Honors,

The Inhabitants of the Town of Pittsfield unalterably attached to the Liberties of their Country, and in the fullest Approbation of Congressional Measures, with all humility Defference and Candor beg leave to manifest the painful anxieties and Distresses of our minds in this definitive Crisis not only in behalf of ourselves but this great and powerful Province, and declare our abhorrence of that Constitution now adopting in this province. Nothing but an invincible Love of Civil and religious Liberty for ourselves and future posterity has induced us to add to your accumulated Burdens at this Great Period.——

Our forefathers left the delightful Abodes of their Native Country, passed a raging Sea that in these then solitary Climes they might enjoy Civil and religious Liberty, and never more feal the hand of Tyranny and Persecution; but that despotic persecuting power from which they fled reached them on these far distant shores, the weight of which has been felt from their first Emigration to the present Day. After the Loss of the Charter of this province in the reign of Charles the second a popish Tyrant, a new one was obtained after the Revolution of King William of glorious Memory which was lame and essentially defective and yet was of great value for the support of tolerable order, 'till we had grown up to our present strength to seek that by force of Arms which was then unjustly denied us.

The nomination and appointment of our Governors by the King has been the Sourse of all the Evils and Calamities that have befallen this province and the united Colonies. By this means a secret poison has been spread thro' out all our Towns and great Multitudes have been secured for the corrupt Designs of an abandoned Administration. Many of these Men who had drank of this baneful poison could not be confided in to aid and assist their Country in the present Contest, which was one Reason of the Necessity of a Suspension of Government. At this Door all Manner of Disorders have been introduced into our Constitution till it has become an Engine of Oppression and deep Corruption and would finally had it been continued, have brought upon us an eternal Destruction. The want of that one previlege of confessing Judgment in Cases of Debt has overwhelmed great Multitudes in Destruction and affoarded Encouragement to mercenary Lawyers to riot upon the spoils of the people.—

We have been ruled in this Country for many years past with a rod of Iron. The Tyranny, Despotism and oppression of our fellow Subjects in this County have been beyond belief. Since the Suspension of Government we have lived in peace, Love, safety, Liberty and Happiness except the Disorders and Dissentions occasioned by the Tories. We find ourselves in Danger of [*torn*] to our former state and of undergoing a yoke of Op[pression?] which we are no longer able to bear.

We have calmly viewed the nature of our antient mode of Government—its various sluices of Corruption and oppression—the dangerous Effects of nominating to office by those in power, and must pronounce it the most defective discordant and ruinous System of Government of any that has come under our Observation. We can discern no present necessity of adopting that mode of Government so generally reprobated by the good people of this province; or which will inevitably be so as soon as the great, rational Majority of the people have had Time for proper Reflection. The adopting this Mode of Government to the length we have gone has in our view been hasty and precipitate. It was surprising to this Town and directly contrary to the Instructions given to their Representatives. By this Means a considerable Number of incurable Enemies to a better Constitution has been made and if once adopted by the people we shall perhaps never be able to rid ourselves of it again.

We have seen nothing done by the Continental Congress which leads us to conclude that they would limit us to this mode of Government. We do not know of their having given us any Advice that must necessarily be construed in opposition to what they gave [*torn*]ernments of New Hampshire and South Carolina [*torn*] Who if they think it necessary are to chuse such form of government as they in their Judgment shall "think will best promote the happiness of the people and preserve peace and good order during the present dispute with Great Britain." Certainly the Continental Congress could have no Intention of forcing upon us a Constitution so detested by the people and so abhorrent to common Sence, and thus to reward us for our unparalleled Sufferings. We have been led to wish for new previleges which we still hope to obtain, or remain so far as we have done for some Time past in a State of Nature.—

We have with Decency and Moderation attended to the various arguments of those gentlemen lately created our Rulers, particularly, we have heared it urged as the Advice of the venerable Continental Congress, we have sufficiently attended to that and various other Arguments in favor of reassuming our antient Constitution, and are of opinion there is no such advice, the qualifying Expressions leaving ample room to new model our Constitution, but if there is, we are of opinion that unlimited passive obedience and Non Resistance to any human power whatever is what we are now contending with Great Britain and to transfer that power to any other Body of Men is equally dangerous to our Security and happiness.—

We chuse to be known to future posterity as being of the Number of those who have timely protested against the Reassumption of this discordant Constitution and shall be restless in our endeavours that we may obtain the previlege of electing our Civil and military officers. We assure your Honors that some of those who have been appointed to rule us are greatly obnoxious to people in General, especially those who have protested against the Just proceedings of a Congress lately held at Stockbridge. We beg leave further to assure your Honors that a Court has been held in this Town in a Clandestine Manner and great Dishonour hereby done to the Dignity of magistracy.—

We therefore pray your Honors to issue out your orders to the good people of this province that their Votes may be collected in the Election of a Governor and Lieutenant Governor to act in Concert with the Honourable Board and house of Representatives. After which we pray that every Town may retain the previlege of nominating their Justice of the peace and every County their Judges as well as the Soldiers of every Company of the Militia their officers. If the right of nominating to office is not invested in the people we are indifferent who assumes it whether any particular persons on this or on the other side of the [wa?]ter. When such a Constitution is assumed you'll [f?]ind us the most meek and inoffensive Subjects of any in this province, though we would hope in such a case that the wisdom of our Rulers would not admit of collecting private Debts for the present as we imagine that Measure would be of great Detriment to our common cause as it would put much Money into the hands of our Enemies and create Divisions among ourselves. But if this just and reasonable request is denied us, we pray, that as we have lived in great love peace and good order in this County for more than 16 Months past in the most vigorous unintermitted Exertions in our Countrys cause, that you would dispense with a longer Suspension of this antient Mode of Government among us which we so much detest and abhor. The Government of our respective Committees is lenient and efficacious.. But if it is necessary for the carrying into more effectual Execution the Means of our Common safety that some Mode of government should be adopted we pray it may be one De novo agreeable to that forementioned Advice of the Continental Congress and no more of our antient form be retained than what is Just and reasonable. We hope in the Establishment of such a new Constitution regard will be had for such a broad Basis of Civil and religious Liberty as no length of Time will corrupt and which will endure as long as the Sun and Moon shall endure. And as in Duty bound will ever pray.

per order of the Town. ISRAEL DICKINSON Town Clerk

N. B. Upon the foregoing premises and on account of obnoxious persons being appointed to rule us The Court of this County of Quarter Sessions etc. is ordered to desist from any future Sessions.—

Our resolves may be seen at Mr. Thomas's which were entered into at the same Time this petition was accepted by this Town.

4

Proclamation of the General Court, January 23, 1776

To encourage "Piety and Virtue" and suppress "vice and Immorality" the General Court issued a proclamation urging the people to lead sober lives and requesting persons of influence to contribute by example to a reformation in manners and respect for law. The proclamation is in MA 138/281–282 and Peter Force, *American Archives,* Fourth Series (Washington, 1837–46), IV, 833–835. Bracketed words are supplied from Force's version, since they are indecipherable or completely deteriorated in the archives document.

By the Great and General Court of the Colony of Massachusetts-Bay

A Proclamation.

The frailty of human Nature, the Wants of Individuals, and the numerous Dangers which surround them, through the course of Life, have, in all Ages and in every Country, impelled them to form Societies, and establish Governments.

As the Happiness of the People, ⟨alone⟩ is the sole End of Government, so the Consent of the People is the only Foundation of it, in Reason, Morality, and the natural Fitness of Things; and therefore every Act of Government, every Exercise of Sovereignty, against, or without, the Consent of the People, is Injustice, Usurpation, and Tyranny.

It is a Maxim, that, in every Government, there must exist, Somewhere, a Supreme, Sovereign, absolute, and uncontroulable Power; But this Power resides, always in the body of the People, and it never was, or can be delegated, to one Man, or a few; the great Creator, having never given to Men a right to vest others with Authority over them, unlimited, either in Duration or Degree.

When Kings, Ministers, Governors, or Legislators, therefore, instead of exercising the Powers intrusted with them, according to the Principles, Forms, and Proportions Stated by the Constitution, and established by the original Compact, prostitute those Powers to the Purposes of oppression;—to subvert, instead of supporting a free Constitution;—to destroy, instead of preserving the Lives, Liberties, and Properties of the People:—

they are no longer to be deemed magistrates vested with a Sacred Character, but become publick Enemies, and ought to be resisted.

The Administration of Great Britain, despising equally the Justice, Humanity, and Magnanimity, of their Ancestors, and the Rights, Liberties, and Courage of Americans, have, for a Course of years, laboured to establish a Sovereignty in America, not founded in the consent of the People, but in the mere Will of Persons a thousand Leagues from us, whom we know not, and have endeavoured to establish this Sovereignty over us, against our Consent, in all Cases whatsoever.

The Colonies, during this Period, have recurred to every peac[eable recourse] in a free Constitution, by Petitions and Remonstrances, to o[btain justice,] which has been not only denied to them, but they have been tr[eated with unex]ampled Indignity and Contempt; and, at length, open Wa[r, of the most] atrocious, cruel, and sanguinary kind, has been commenced [against them]. To this, an open, manly and successfull Resistance has, hith[erto been made.]

Thirteen Colonies are now firmly united in the Conduct of this most just and necessary War, under the wise Councils of their Congress.

It is the Will of Providence, for wise, righteous, and gracious Ends, that this Colony should have been singled out, by the enemies of America, as the first object both of their Envy and their Revenge; and after having been made the Subject of Several merciless and vindictive Statutes, one of which was intended to subvert our Constitution by Charter, is made the Seat of War.

No effectual Resistance to the System of Tyranny prepared for us could be made, without either instant Recourse to Arms, or a temporary Suspension of the ordinary Powers of Government and tribunals of Justice. To the last of which Evils, in hopes of a Speedy Reconciliation with Great Britain, upon equitable Terms, the Congress advised us to Submit: and Mankind has seen a Phenomenon without Example in the political World, a large and populous Colony, Subsisting, in great Decency and order, for more than a year, under such a Suspension of Government.

But, as our enemies have proceeded to such barbarous Extremities, commencing Hostilities upon the good People of this Colony, and, with unprecedented malice, exerting their Power to Spread the Calamities of Fire, Sword, and Famine through the Land, and no reasonable Prospect remains of a Speedy Reconciliation with Great Britain, the Congress have resolved "That no obedience being due to the Act of Parliament for altering the Charter of the Colony of Massachusetts-Bay, nor to a Governor or Lieutenant-Governor, who will not observe the Directions of, but endeavour to subvert that Charter, the Governor and Lieutenant-Governor of that Colony are to be considered as absent, and their offices vacant; and, as there is no Council there, and Inconveniences arising from the Suspension of the Powers of Government are intollerable, especially at a Time when General Gage hath actually levied War and is carrying on Hostilities against His Majesty's peaceable and loyal Subjects of that Colony; that, in order to conform as near as may be, to the Spirit and Substance of the Charter, it be recommended [to] the Provincial Convention to write Letters to the Inhabitants of the [s]everal Places which are intituled to Representation in Assembly, [r]equesting them to chuse such Representatives, and that the Assembly, when chosen, do elect Counsellors; and that Such Assembly and Council exercise the Powers of Government, untill a Governor of his Majestys Appointment will consent to govern the Colony according to its Charter.["]

In Pursuance of which Advice, the good People of this Colony have chosen a full and free Representation of themselves, who, being convened in assembly, have elected a Council, who, as the executive Branch of Government, have constituted necessary officers through the Colony. The present generation, therefore, may be congratulated on the Acquisition of a Form of Government, more immediately in all its Branches, under the Influence and Controul of the People, and therefore more free and happy than was enjoyed by their Ancestors: But, as a Government so popular can be Supported only by universal Knowledge and Virtue, in the Body of the People, it is the Duty of all Ranks to promote the Means of Education, for the rising Generation, as well as true Religion, Purity of Manners, and Integrity of Life, among all orders and degrees.

As an Army has become necessary for our Defence, and, in all free States the civil must provide for and controul the military Power, the Major Part of the Council have appointed Magistrates and Courts of Justice in every County, whose Happiness is so connected with that of the People, that it is difficult to suppose they can abuse their Trust. The Business of it is, to see those Laws inforced, which are necessary for the Preservation of Peace, Virtue, [and good order.] and the great and general Court expects, and requires, that all necessary Support and Assistance be given, and all proper obedience yielded to them, and will deem every Person, who shall fail of his Duty in this Respect towards them, a disturber of the peace of this Colony and deserving of examplary Punishment.

That Piety and Virtue, which, alone can Secure the Freedom of any People, may be encouraged, and Vice and Immorality suppressed, the great and general Court have thought fit to issue this Proclamation, commanding and enjoining it upon the good People of this Colony, that they lead Sober, Religious and peaceable Lives, avoiding all Blasphemies, contempt of the holy Scriptures, and of the Lord's day and all other Crimes and Misdemeanors, all Debauchery, Prophaneness, Corruption, Venality, all riotous and tumultuous Proceedings, and all Immoralities whatsoever; and that they decently and reverently attend the public Worship of God, at all Times acknowledging with [gratitude, his merciful interposition in their behalf, devoutly confiding in him, as the God of armies, by whose favour and protection, alone, they may hope for success in their present conflict.

And all Judges, Justices, Sheriffs, Grand-Jurors, Tything-Men, and all other] civil officers, within this Colony, are hereby Strictly enjoined and commanded that they contribute all in their Power, by their Advice, Exertions, and Examples, towards a general Reformation of Manners, and, that they bring to condign Punishment, every Person who shall commit any of the Crimes or Misdemeanors aforesaid, or that shall be guilty of any Immoralities whatsoever; and that they use their Utmost Endeavours to have the Resolves of the Congress, and the good and wholesome Laws of this Colony, duly carried into execution.

And as the Ministers of the Gospel, within this Colony, have, during the late Relaxation of the Powers of civil Government, exerted themselves for our Safety, it is hereby recommended to them, still to continue their virtuous Labours, for the good of the people, inculcating, by their public Ministry and private example, the Necessity of Religion, morality, and good order.

Council, January 19, 1776.

Ordered, That the foregoing Proclamation be Read at the opening of Every Superiour Court of Judicature, etc., and Inferiour Common Pleas, and Court of General Sessions for the Peace within this Colony, by their Respective Clerks and at the annual Town meetings in March, in Each Town, and it is hereby Recommended to the several Ministers of the

Gospel throughout this Colony, to Read the same in their Respective assemblies on the Lords Day next after Receiving it, immediately after Divine service.

Sent down for concurrence.

Perez Morton, Deputy Secretary. [1776]

Consented to

William Sever,	Charles Chauncey,
Walter Spooner,	Joseph Palmer,
Caleb Cushing,	John Whetcomb,
John Winthrop,	Jedediah Foster,
Thomas Cushing,	Eldad Taylor,
Moses Gill,	John Taylor,
Michael Farley,	Benjamin White,
Samuel Holten,	James Prescott

In the House of Representatives, January 23, 1776.

Read and concurred.

William Cooper, Speaker, Pro Tem.

Consented to. . . . By order of the General Court:

Perez Morton, Deputy Secretary

God Save the King.

5

Report of a Lecture by Thomas Allen on February 18, 1776

In a lecture at the house of Doctor Thomas Tarbell in Richmond, the Reverend Thomas Allen of Pittsfield used as his text Matthew 10:17, Beware of men. Allen spoke of the "designing men" who had deceived the Continental Congress into thinking that the people were content with the mere re-establishment of the General Court. He forcefully echoed the grievances of the Pittsfield Memorial (No. 3) of a few months previous, and asserted he preferred no government at all to one without a constitution. The report bv hostile listeners is found in MA 137/77–78.

County of Berkshire ss. March 2d Ad 1776

Elijah Brown and David Rosseter Esquires Messers Elisha Blin. Benjamin Peirson Joseph Raymond William Lusk, each of Lawfull age deposeth and saith, That they attended a lecture at the Dwelling house of Doctor Thomas Tarbell in Richmont on the Evening next after the Eighteenth Day of Febuary Current, preached by the Rev. Thomas Allen, of Pittsfield, from those words in the 10th Chapter of Matthew 17th verse, beware of men; After a Short Explanitory Introduction, in which he attempted to Demonstrate what was the Reason of this Caution of our Saviour to his Disciples which was to the following Purpose viz: That men when compared with beasts of prey, were most to be feared and guarded against, he observed that our Saviour did not Caution his Disciples against those, but against men, That men would Use all manner of Deceit and Craft to Circumvent and entangle them,—That men would haul them before Councils, and Magistrates and to Prison, and that they should Suffer many ways and on many accounts, by the hands of wicked and Deceitfull men, When he proceeded to the Improvement of his Sermon, which was altogether Political,—he gave it as his Opinion that the words of the Text might with Propriety be applied to the present Circumstances of this Province, He attempted to Shew the badness of the Constitution of this Colony—He Said it was rotten to the Core gave it as his Opinion that it was by no means best to Suffer it to take place But that it was the Duty of the People to oppose it, and that he had rather be without any Form of Goverment than to Submit to this Constitution He Said it was very Oppressive—That he had often Seen the Tears of those who were oppressed by it, and that they had no Comforter, that on the side of the Oppressors was Power but they had no Comforter —he Said the People of this Province had lived in peace and good order for more than a year, without Goverment, as the General Assembly themselves had Confessed—That altho. the Continental Congress had advised to the assumption of this form of Goverment, yet they were to be considered as failable Creatures: that they had failed in one Instance already as they themselves had confessed.—that no Power ought to be given to any man or Body of men so far as to Deprive any man of Judging for himself and that if the People upon Strict Examination Judged that they (the Congress) had abused their power they were to be opposed in the Same manner, as the King and Parliment ought to be opposed—In Speaking of the Congress and General Court, the Said Mr. Allen frequently repeated the words, beware of men—and Said it concerned the People to See to it that whilst we are fighting against oppression from the King and Parliment, That we Did not Suffer it to rise up in our own Bowels, That he was not so much concerned about Carrying our Point against Great Brittain, as he was of haveing Usurpers rising up amongst ourselves, he further Endeavoured to Insinuate into the minds of the People that our Provincial Congress and General Court had been, and were Composed of designing men—he Said the Provincial Congress had deceived the Continental Congress, that they had petitioned to them for our former mode of Goverment, and induced them to believe the people were attached to it. that if we Suffered it to take place we Should find it very Difficult to rid ourselves of it—that the General Court had taken up the old Constitution contrary to the minds of the People. He further Said that by the old Constitution the King appointed the Governer that the Governer put in the Officers and in Consequence they were all Dependant on the King. It therefore Mattered not whether they were appointed by North, our Council Hutchinson, Gage, our General Court, or any other man or Body of men. for they (the officers) were not put in by the great Majority of the People. that all those who have taken Commisions ought to Deliver them into the hands of the People: Mr. Allen often during his Sermon refered to Something he Should read by and by, for Evidence that the members of the General Court were Designing men, and inconsistant with themselves.—In the Close of his Sermon he Said here is a Proclimation which I Shall read to you, which is Directly

Contrary to what I have now Delivered. I will read it to you and you must hear for yourselves and Judge for yourselves. He then read the late Proclimation of the General Court and Said he had received it but the Day before, Nevertheless he had made a few remarks which he would read to us, among other things he Said the Proclimation was Inconsistant, for that theirin it was Set forth that the Suspension of Goverment was intolerable and at the Same Time Said that the People had behaved in great Decency and order for more than Twelve Months, and further the Said Mr. Allen in Shewing the Necessity of Opposing the present Goverment of this Colony Urged that the General Court is Composed of men who are Seeking places for themselves and Sons

Sworn the 2nd Day
of March
Above written—
Before
Tim. Edwards Jus. Pac.

Elijah Brown
David Rosseter
Elisha Blin
Benjamin Peirson
Joseph Raymond
William Lusk

6

Essex County Convention, Ipswich,

April 25, 26, 1776

The Essex County memorial to the Council and the House of Representatives of Massachusetts complained that the representation of the populous, wealthy towns was inadequate and demanded an adjustment that would reduce the influence of poor and sparsely settled communities. The memorial is found in MA 156/192–196.

To the Honourarable the Council and the Honourable the House of Representatives for the Colony of the Massachusetts-Bay in general Court Assembled April 1776.——

The Subscribers delegated, by the several Towns in the County of Essex to our Names affixed, to represent them in County Convention, to be held at Ipswich in said County on the twenty fifth of this Instant April, for the Purposes appearing in this Memorial, beg Leave to Represent——

That, in the present Important Crisis, when every member of the Community must be anxiously solicitous for the public Weal, and when a new, and we trust a glorious Empire is forming on the Basis of Liberty, the present State of Representation in this Colony has gained the Attention of the Towns from whence we are delegated, and we are chosen to meet in a County Convention for the Purpose of endeavouring to procure one more equal, than is at present enjoyed——

When the natural Rights which Men possess are given up to Society, they ever expect to receive an equivalent, from the Benefits derived from a social State; Freeman submitting themselves to the Controul of others, and giving up the entire Right of Legislation and Taxation without reserving any Share to themselves, can receive no possible equivalent for the Concession; for they become absolute Slaves; But if they delegate a Number from themselves to conduct these important Articles of State, over whom they retain a suitable Controul, they enjoy a qualified Liberty, in many Respects preferable to what they relinquish.——

If this Representation is equal, it is perfect, as far as it deviates from this Equality, so far it is imperfect; and approaches to that State of Slavery; and the want of a just Weight in Representation is an Evil nearly akin to being totally destitute of it——An Inequality of Representation has been justly esteemed the Cause which has in a great Degree sapped the foundation of the once admired, but now tottering Fabric of the British Empire; and we fear that if a different Mode of Representation from the present, is not adopted in this Colony, our Constitution will not continue, to that late Period of Time, which the glowing Heart of every true American now anticipates.——

In the early Period of our Settlement, when thirty or forty Families were first permitted to send each a Representative to the general Assembly, there can be no Doubt, but the proportionate Equality was duly adjusted; nor is there much more Doubt, but that, as just an equality took Place in the Representation of the several Corporations of the british Empire, when the Rule was first established there—That striking, that unjust Disproportion, which fills us with Disgust and Detestation, has arisen in Britain, chiefly from the great Increase of Numbers and Wealth in some places of that Empire and a Decrease in others, and continued from a blind Attachment to the Forms of Antiquity in some, and a wicked Disposition in others, who found an effectual Way to turn this Inequality to their own Advantage, though to the Destruction of the State——

We cannot realize that, your Honours, our wise political Fathers, have adverted to the present Inequality of Representation in this Colony, to the Growth of the Evil or to the fatal Consequences which will probably ensue from the Continuance of it——Each Town and District in the Colony is by some late Regulations permitted to send one Representative to the general Court, if such Town or District consists of thirty Freeholders, and other Inhabitants qualified to elect if of one hundred and twenty to send two——No Town is permitted to send more than two except the Town of Boston, which may send four——There are some Towns and Districts in the Colony in which there are between thirty and forty Freeholders and other Inhabitants qualified to elect, only; there are others besides Boston, in which there are more than five hundred,——The first of these may send one Representative;—The latter can send only two, if the Towns as to Property are to each other in the same respective Proportion, is it not clear to a Mathematical Demonstration, that the same Number of Inhabitants of equal Property in the one Town, have but an Eighth Part of the Weight in Representation with the other, and with what colourable Pretext we would decently enquire——

If we regard Property as the Rule of Representation, it will be found that there are certain thirty Towns and Districts in the Colony, which altogether pay to the publick Expence, a sum not equal to what is paid by one other single Town in this County; yet the former may have a Weight in the Legislative Body, fifteen Times as large as the latter; nay it will be found by Examination, that a Majority of Voices in the Assembly may be obtained from the Members of Towns, which pay not more than one fourth Part of the publick Tax——The County of Essex, which we represent in Convention, pays more than one sixth part of the publick Tax; and they have not a Right to send one Tenth Part of the Number of Representatives which may be by Law returned to the general Assembly; This county contains one or two thousand Polls more than any other County in the Colony—The Town of Ipswich is in Property (and we suppose in Numbers) nearly equal to the several Towns and Districts of Hadley, South Hadley, Amherst, Granby, Deerfield, Greenfield, Shelburne and Conway (and more than equal to the like Number of other Places in the Colony) who are or may be represented in the general Court; Ipswich can send only two Members; the other Towns and Districts above mentioned may send ten Members at the least; can the Division of two Towns into eight, Towns and Districts furnish an Argument for the disproportionate Representation which of Consequence has taken Place; if the Property and Numbers remain the same, the Reason is to us Paradoxical——

If a new System of Government, or any material Alteration in the old is to be in the Contemplation of the next general Assembly; Is it not fitting that the whole Community should be equally concerned in adjusting this System?——

The many evil Consequences that will naturally and must inevitably arise from this Inequality of Representation, we trust, we need not attempt to mark out to a wise and free House of Americans; the Delineation would be disagreeable as well as indecent——Nor would we arrogantly suggest, to your Honours, the Mode of Redress, we confide in your Wisdom and Justice, and if an Equality of Representation takes Place in the Colony, we shall be satisfied, whether it has Respect to Numbers, to Property or to a Combination of both.

In County Convention
Ipswich April 25th. 1776.

John Pickering jun
Jona. Gardner jun } Salem

Stephen Choate, Daniel Noyes	Ipswich
Richard Adams Jr.	Newbury
John Lowell, Jona. Jackson	Newburyport
Jonathan Glover	Marblehead
Samuel Burrel [?]	Lynn
Samuel Phillips, Daniel Spafford	Andover
Jereh. Mighill	Rowley
Samuel Nye	Salisbury
Thomas West	Haverhill
John Low, Winthrop Sargent	Glocester
David Merrill	Almsbury
Peter Russell	Bradford
Tyler Porter	Wenham
John Lee	Manchester
Jonathan Swan	Methuen
Asa Perley	Boxford

Essex County In County Convention Ipswich April 26th. 1776.

Voted That John Lowell Esquire Mr. Stephen Choate and Colonel Daniel Spafford or any two of them be a Committee of this Convention to present their Memorial to the General Court and that They be directed to desire with the Leave of the Honorable House to be heard on their Floor, in support of said Memorial, if they should think necessary——

Attest Daniel Noyes Clerk

Beverly, 1776 (156/196)

At a Legal Meeting of the Inhabitents of the Town of Beverly April 30th 1776——

Captain Benjamin Lovett Jr was Chosen to Sign in their behalf the memoraial of the Late County Convention held at Ipswich on the 25th of April Instant

True Copy attest Joseph Wood T. Cler

Danvers, 1776 (156/196)

At a Meeting of the Inhabitants of Said Danvers the first day of May 1776, For the purpose of hearing and Concuring with the Convention held at Ipswich within and for the County of Essex, on the 25th April last, Respecting a Memorial to the Great and General Court, Agreed upon by Delegates representing the Major part of the Towns in Said County of Essex,

This Town after a full hearing and due Examination of said Memorial, Past the Following Vote

Voted, that this Town do Unanimously Concur with the Sentiments of Said Delegates, as Agreed upon in Said Memorial——

True Extract from the Minuts
Attest Stephen Needham T. Clerk

7

An Act for More Equal Representation, May 4, 1776

In response to petitions such as the one from Essex County (see above, No. 6), an act was passed increasing the number of representatives the larger towns could send to the General Court. The act provided that each town of 225 freeholders have the privilege of sending three members, each town of 320, four members, and larger towns, a proportionate number. The act is st. 1776, ch. 328, in *Charters and General Laws of the Colony and Province of Massachusetts Bay,* 694.

An Act Providing for a More Equal Representation in the General Court

WHEREAS the present representation of this colony is not so equal as it ought to be, and this court being desirous to have the same as proportionate as it can in the present state of the colony be made,

SECT. 1. Be it therefore enacted by the council and house of representatives in general court assembled, and by the authority of the same, that each town in this colony which contains two hundred and twenty freeholders and other inhabitants qualified to vote for representatives, as by the charter is provided, shall at all times have the privilege of sending three members to represent them in the great and general court of this colony, and that those towns which have three hundred and twenty freeholders and other inhabitants qualified as aforesaid may send four, and in that proportion for any greater number of freeholders and other inhabitants qualified as aforesaid, any law to the contrary notwithstanding.

SECT. 2. And be it further enacted and declared, that this act shall be construed and taken to empower every town in this colony to elect and depute representatives to serve for and represent them in the next general assembly as well as if it had been made and passed before the issuing of the writs for the choice of representatives for the next general assembly.

Provided, that nothing in this act shall extend or be construed to extend to alter or deprive any town of the privilege of sending as many representatives as they have heretofore been empowered to send. [May 4, 1776]

8

O.P.Q., "To the Electors," May 18, 1776

The author of "To the Electors," disturbed by the state of society in a time of upheaval, called for patriotic concentration on the war effort and warned against hasty measures that might endanger the interests of commerce. The letter was printed in the *Massachusetts Spy* (Boston), May 18, 1776.

Number, I.

To the ELECTORS OF REPRESENTATIVES *for the Colony of* MASSACHUSETTS BAY, *and to the* ELECTORS OF COUNSELLORS *for the same*

MY FRIENDS AND FELLOW COUNTRYMEN,

The subject upon which I am now to address you, is so important in itself and in its remotest consequences, as to require that unreserved freedom and simplicity which, while it may seem to need, will apologize for an apology—for when every thing which is valuable in life is at stake, to sacrifice to the graces would be criminal.

The government to be formed, and the administration of that government, are of vast importance; the men, therefore, who are to constitute and to have the appointment of those who are to execute it, ought to be chosen with the utmost care and caution.—They should be men of the best understanding, the strictest integrity and the purest patriotism.

We have by melancholy experience found the misfortune of placing our confidence in men of weak and contracted minds, in men of sordid and selfish spirits, in cursing and designing men and in pretended patriots,—let us, now we have the opportunity, resume our misplaced confidence, and delegate the powers of government to those, and to those only, who will act upon the genuine, the unadulterated principles of the constitution, and conscientiously endeavour, in the execution of the trust reposed in them, to promote the greatest happiness of the greatest numbers—who will not devote their time, their abilities and the powers with which they are vested, in advancing their personal profits and honors, and those of their respective families and friends.—Who will not do every thing in their power to destroy the commercial part of the community, without considering that the value of our lands is enhanced in proportion to the demand, which an extensive commerce, the opulence of the merchant, and the number of mechanics necessarily occasion, and that excessive burdens always operate as prohibitions, and that therefore, the end in view will be frustrated by the very means taken to accomplish it.

We have had in some former houses, men who under the banners of the constitution, have, either through ignorance or design, been undermining its foundations; and in some late ones, those who have been so exceedingly prudent of the public monies, or *so much more advantageously employed,* as to leave the capital of the province, *committed to their care and guardianship,* to be fortified and secured by the impoverished and distressed inhabitants, at their own expence and that of a few patriotic neighbours,—but for whose spirited exertions, we might have had a melancholy experimental comment, in the military operations of the ensuing season, upon that trite, but very emphatical characteristick of the wisdom of the late legislature, expressed in the proverb by *saving at the spiket and letting out at the bung.*

From such statesmen, such politicians, good Lord deliver us!

Our situation, my friends, is exceedingly critical—it is no time to contend for the preservation and use of a charter, which in its most perfect and peaceful operation gave us scarcely the shadow of right—it is no time to debate about the prerogatives, which that charter might have given to the upper or the lower house—it is no time to scramble for posts and places—it is no time to contrive expedients for depressing one part of the community, to exalt another; which is at all times contrary to the spirit of patriotism and to the equitable maxims of our holy religion: It is, in fine, no time to deliberate upon the internal police of the colony, but to exert all the powers of our minds and bodies, to devote all our estates and influence, to secure the colony from invasion, and to prepare for the instant defence of our lives, our liberties, and properties, against the tyranny of the British government, and the force of the British arms.

Wherefore, my friends, let no man have your suffrages, whose conduct in any former house, on whose known or even suspected principles, not only in politics, but in private life, may lead you to think he could in any instance postpone the public to his private interests—who possesses any place in the executive department, other or higher than that of a justice of the peace—who has ever manifested a disposition to oppress or distress the trading part of the colony—or whose inattention or avarice had like to have exposed the capital to destruction, by leaving it in the most unguarded state, and by it have sacrificed the colony.

Such men are always dangerous in the legislature, but incomparably more so at this time—and though they may pay their addresses to you, by an apparent design to advance your interest, believe me, they would eventually destroy it.

The uniting the legislative and executive powers in the same person, the unjust and oppressive taxation of the trading and monied interests, the proposed method of representation and pay of representatives, the state of the militia and the fortifications, shall be the subject of a future speculation; in which, by a minute deduction of facts, and reasons drawn from first principles, I shall endeavour to convince you of the necessity of placing your confidence in such men, and such only, as I have recommended, and at the same time justify my intruding my advice upon you.

If there is wisdom in the measures at which I have hinted and which shall be more particularly considered, I confess it is beyond my penetration, and I should thank any person who would instruct me in it—and if the men who have originated or prosecuted them are patriots, I confess myself a stranger to patriotism.

I revere a government in which regal power has no part, and which I hope will be universally established in these colonies—but would most sacredly guard the fountains of that government, least any thing should gain admittance, which might contaminate its purity, obstruct its due course, or destroy its salutary influences.

There is something in genuine patriotism, I had almost said, adorably amiable; it is the fairest transcript, *but one,* within the compass of the human mind, of that *good will to men,* which brought the son of God from Heaven, and Angels to celebrate his incarnation. I doubt not that the sovereign of the universe approves of every struggle for the rights of humanity; however he may see fit to punish, in that very struggle, the vices of the community by which it is supported. Happy, beyond expression happy, must I therefore esteem these colonies, in a cause, which they can with conscious integrity commit to him that judgeth and avengeth in the earth. May the God of armies and the wonderful counsellor be our guide and guardian; that by the wisdom and unanimity of our councils, and by the vigor and success of our arms, America may become, and ever continue, the dread of tyrants and the asylum of the oppressed; while her virtue, freedom and happiness shall be her unrivaled glory, the admiration and joy of successive generations. O.P.Q.

Number II

To the ELECTORS *of* REPRESENTATIVES *for the Colony of* MASSACHUSETTS-BAY, *and to the* ELECTORS *of* COUNSELLORS *for the same.*

MY FRIENDS AND FELLOW COUNTRYMEN,

OBSTA PRINCIPIIS, is a maxim of such importance both in relegion and politics that it cannot be too frequently or too earnestly inculcated.

At the first establishment of a civil constitution, so important as ours is like to be to ourselves, and by its connections to the whole continent, we should strenuously oppose, in its first appearance, every thing which is contracted, and which has a tendency to bring the colony into disrepute. These colonies to form an invincible union should be severally modeled upon the most generous principles of the constitution, and every Assembly composed of such men, and such only, as are incapable of postponing the public to their private interests.

In my last, I contented myself with general advice founded on general though forcible reasons.

I shall now in confirmation of the same, and the more seriously to engage the public attention and a correspondent conduct, proceed to the minute consideration of the several particulars, which I then proposed to resume.

Sensible that I shall need the candor of my readers, I must beg leave to presume on that indulgence, which any one may reasonably expect whose desires are simply to the honour and service of his native province, although his views of the measures taken to promote them may not be exactly co-incident with theirs.

In the first place, I shall attempt to convince you, that *the placing the legislative and executive powers in the same hands,* is unconstitutional, impolitic, oppressive and absurd.

Among the first fruits of the fair seeds of opposition to the tyranny of the British administration, from whence we may justly expect a glorious harvest of freedom and happiness, is a clear understanding of the constitution of civil government amongst all orders and ranks of people:— It will be therefore, too much like proving a self-evident proposition, to labour the unconstitutionality of an investiture of such inconsistent powers in the same person.

I shall only point out the wisdom of the early provision made to guard against it; which will shew that the reasons of that provision existed in the nature and necessity of government, before any express constitution took place, and consequently are fundamental to that constitution: This will at the same time evince its absurdity, impolicy and mischievous tendency.

The first reason might arise from experience and observation, that the highest improvements in every art and science, as well as in every kind of business in life, is made by attending to but one thing at a time; and from the evident confusion which the interference of a multiplicity of concerns militant with each other necessarily occasions.

Another motive for making the executive and legislative separate departments was, doubtless, the undue weight and influence which those who were in both might have in the legislature;—an influence to which the British Parliament has ever been subject (and these colonies have but too sensibly felt its ill effects) though they have apparently censured and disclaimed it, by the disqualifying bill; by which a precept must issue for a new choice upon an executive appointment, giving the people an opportunity, if they see cause, to restore to the crown-officer his legislative capacity.—An influence by which we of this colony have formerly suffered, but which by the seasonable exertions of some patriotic members in both houses, we have, till of late, been happily freed from, and if we were as consistent as we ought to be in all our public conduct to the spirit of the constitution, should ever remain so.

The last reason which I shall mention, to shew the absurdity of making laws for the same person to execute, is that appeals from executive courts lay to the legislative, at least, to the upper house: And for a judge to determine upon appeals from his own judgment, is so repugnant to the common law, yea to the first principle of justice and equity, that it need only be mentioned as incident to the investiture of the legislative and executive powers in the same person, to shew its absurdity, its impolicy, its unconstitutionality and oppressive tendency.

To shew that the inhabitants of this colony are now suffering, and if by a change of men in the next choice of representatives and counsellors, they do not prevent it, will continue to suffer, all the inconvenience which arise from blending the executive and legislative powers, I shall just observe,

That since, by the approbation of the honourable the Continental Congress, the General Assembly was formed in May last, the members of that assembly have divided among themselves, and their particular friends, all the civil and military offices in the colony. That the public business has been exceedingly impeded, by the attention necessary to executive offices perpetually changing the acting members, and but seldom leaving enough to make a majority or a governor; at a time when the constant attendance of the best members (and such are those *principally* among whom the executive offices are distributed) was of the highest importance to the colony, and to individuals.

And, That as soon as the executive courts return to their accustomed business, every inconvenience, before mentioned, will be encreased and confirmed,—unless the elections of this month shall happily relieve us.

I shall close this subject with observing the surprizing difference between the assembly which left all the executive officers out of the council and that which has devoted all their ingenuity and great part of their time in distributing their respective offices among them—when the principles which actuated the former at the early periods of the opposition, might reasonably be expected much more forcibly to actuate the latter in the present stages of it; and while the conduct of the former was perfectly consonant to the spirit of the opposition, the proceedings of the latter bear too near a resemblance to those of the administration we so justly oppose.—But,

"Tempora mutantur et nos mutamur in illis."

[I had prepared, agreably to my engagement, some serious strictures upon the military conduct of our late legislature, but the fortifications of the town and harbour of Boston being undertaken and almost compleated by and at the expence of the inhabitants, through their neglect, being both in a moral and political view censure sufficient, and fully evidential of the confidence proper to be placed in such men, at such a time as this, I shall wave all I had to say of the prudence and care of the province in this important respect; and after apologizing for one more omission arising from the unexpected alteration which has taken place in the proposed representation bill; and by which an enormous landed influence, a vast clog upon the wheels of government, the introduction of a large majority of people into public business, unacquainted with it and incapable of it, an immense and disproportionate burden on the trading part of the community;—and what would have compleated our misery the immortality of such a mischievous body, are happily removed, shall proceed to]

The last thing upon which I engaged to remark at this time, which is *the oppressive taxation of the trading and monied interests,* which obtained in the last assembly: Than which I know of nothing which could have been devised more unjust, or of a more baneful tendency.

This measure will drive all trade out of the colony, to such places as have the wisdom and foresight to give it every possible encouragement—and this colony will be proportionally impoverished; having no vent for their surplus produce, either for exportation or consumption—For no person who has a trading stock, or who has money to let out on interest will tarry in the colony where he is obliged to pay not only three times the tax for that profit or interest, which he ever paid before (which, were it his proportion and arose wholly from the encreasing charges of government by reason of the war, he would chearfully pay, were it much more) but three times his proportion—as the court have ordered, for the relief of the landed interest on a prospect of great war charges, directing the assessors, in what is usually called the state bill, to assess stock in trade and money at interest at the rate of 180l. on the 1000l. whereas it usually was assessed in the proportion of only 60l.

Shall I repeat it, that while real estate stands just as it has done for many years, only with an exception in favor of necessary repairs, "All monies at interest either within or without the colony," are by the last tax bill ordered to be set at three times the yearly lawful interest thereof, and "incomes by trade at three times the sum of such incomes." Money and incomes used to be set, "the former at six per cent, the real interest, the latter at what the assessors in their consciences thought the real income"; now both are trebled; and the consciences of the Assessors thro' the colony are to be stretched by this act in due proportion;—this is the most extraordinary exertion of power over the consciences of men I ever heard of.

The evident intent of this iniquitous bill is to lay the burden of the encreasing charges of government, on account of the war, on the trading and monied interests. The consequences of which will be, that the monied men, whose expences, and whose accommodating the farmer with money on loan, are exceedingly beneficial, and who instead of reaping an advantage, as the farmer does by the war in the enhanced price of his produce, of his labour and transportation, and by the rise of his lands, really suffers in his necessary charges in proportion to the other's gain, will quit the colony and repair to that which lays no tax on money at interest. And the trader whose commerce is so very beneficial to the community, and would be so much more beneficial in proportion to its extent as that they would gain much by not taxing him at all, will also seek a settlement where he will not be obliged to pay out of his profits the taxes of all his neighbours in addition to his own.

Will the end in view be answered?—Will not the enormous and now encreasing influence of the landed interest at court, ruin the colony—will not the very persons who are intended to be relieved have ail his charge to pay, when by straining to over burden the merchants and monied men, they generally withdraw, and leave them to the just effects of their iniquitous policy.

Formerly it was sufficient reason against high taxes of monies at interest, that it would be unjust to the lender or injurious to the borrower—for the former was limited, to prevent extortion, to six per cent—and the latter would be disappointed of his purpose if an excessive tax obliged the former to transfer his money into the public funds in England (which could then be done) or to remove himself out of the province.

Another reason, which ought to have some weight, is, that money lent is, in effect, twice taxed if not oftner. The lender parts with it to the husbandman, he purchases lands or stock, which are again taxed; or if he lets it to a trader, he purchases goods which are taxed in their place.

The last reason I shall mention is that most governments do not tax monies at interest at all.

A gentleman of great abilities in Massachusetts Assembly once said "no wise government ever did tax money at interest."

Were the men who could press such a bill capable of moral sense, I could make them blush at the view of those arguments which arise from natural conscience, and from the divine principles and equitable precepts of the religion they possess; but as the presumption is, that the conviction resulting from them is to operate to their utter exclusion from any future share in the administration of government, I shall address them, as the preceeding, to the electors of the ensuing assembly.

Wherefore, my friends, let me beg your patience a little longer, while I ask you a few plain, but serious questions.

In the first place, had the fortune of war placed the inhabitants of the frontier towns in the same situation as those of the sea ports, what would have been their sentiments respecting this matter?

Had the destructive policy of our unnatural enemies succeeded to their wish, and the Canadians and Indians driven them from their peaceful recesses into the heart of the country, or to the sea ports, obliging them to leave all their interests to the mercy of those lawless ravagers, and to support their families among strangers, and at an enhanced price, with the small pittance which they were able to save, at the risque of their lives and liberties, out of the flames, would they have thought it reasonable or just, instead of being relieved of their accustomed proportion of the public charge, to have had it trebled upon them?—Even though some late houses of assembly, from a conviction that they had always paid a disproportionate part of the taxes, had reduced them near one half? Would the prospect of an increase of public charge justify it? Would it not rather plead in their favour?

Should is [it] be said, that they were not injured, because they were taxed by their own representatives in a constitutional way,—they would readily and very justly reply, that the force of that representation was in a great measure abated, if not wholly destroyed, should the sea ports have taken the advantage of their situation and encreased the number and influence of their members; hereby rendering their boasted representation of much the same value with that proposed to the colonies by some minions of power, in the British Parliament, in order to secure unlimited taxation, and but little more than virtual.

Secondly, Whether there is any essential difference in the moral qualities of oppression, or any other iniquity, arising merely from the different situation of its subject? Or whether my being an inhabitant of one part of the colony, makes it more equitable to oppress me than if my residence was in another? If not,

Thirdly, Whether the late tax bill, is reconcileable to that grand maxim of commutative justice, "Whatsoever ye would that men should do unto you, do ye even so unto them." And if not,

Lastly, Whether you can consistently and conscientiously give your votes for returning the same members to court, as have past so unrighteous and oppressive acts: And whether you would not shew yourselves more truly and justly tenacious of the reputation, the virtue, and the interests of the colony by electing, in their place, men of honest minds, enlarged views and inflexible patriotism; who, setting aside all selfish and party considerations, will devote their time, abilities and influence, to the promoting those things, and those only, by which the public security, interest and happiness may be advanced.

Happy is it for us, my friends, that our constitution of civil government (though not so pure and perfect as it might be, and I hope soon will be) is free from the curse of triennial and septennial parliaments; that the revolution of a single year puts it in our power to correct some errors, and to prevent worse. And that it must be our own fault, if in a government so often reverting to first principles, and revolving upon the electors, any capital deviation from those principles, and consequent acts of oppression or iniquity are suffered to continue.

O. P. Q.

9

Pittsfield Petitions, May 29, 1776

In order to defend itself against accusations of lawlessness, Pittsfield attempted to define the principles under which it had suspended the courts. In rebuttal of the charge of a minority that they simply wished to evade the payment of their debts, the petitioners supported the call for the formation of a fundamental constitution by references to social compact theory. The petitions are found in MA 181/42–47.

To the Honourable Council, and the Honourable House of Representatives of the Colony of Massachusetts Bay in General Assembly met at Watertown May 29th. 1776—

The Petition and Memorial of the Inhabitants of the Town of Pittsfield in said Colony,

Humbly Sheweth,

That they have the highest sense of the Importance of Civil and religious Liberty.—The destructive nature of Tyranny and lawless power, and the absolute necessity of legal Government to prevent Anarchy and Confusion.

That they, with their Brethren in other Towns in this County, were early and vigorous in opposing the destructive Measures of British Administration against these Colonies.—That they early signed the Non-Importation League and Covenant, raised Minute Men, agreed to pay them, ordered their public Monies to be paid to Henry Gardiner Esqr receiver General, cast in their mite for the Relief of Boston, and conformed in all things to the Doings of the Honourable Continental and Provincial Congresses.

That they met with the most violent opposition from an unfriendly party in this Town in every step in every Measure they pursued agreeable to the Common Councils of this Continent, which nothing but the most obstinate persevereance has enabled them to overcome and surmount; Which, together with other Inconveniences we have laboured under, affoard the true Reason why we have been so behind in the payment of our public Taxes.—

That they with the other Towns in this County, have come behind none in their Duty and attachment to their Countrys Cause and have exerted themselves much beyound their strength on all occasions. A fresh Instance of their Zeal was conspicuous on our late Defeat at Quebec, when a considerable Number of Men were raised and sent off in the Dead of Winter and lay dying with Sickness before the walls of Quebec before any one Man from this Colony had so much as left his own habitation for the Relief of our Distressed Friends in Canada.—

That from the purest and most disinterested Principles, and ardent Love for their Country, without selfish Considerations and in conformity to the Advice of the wisest Men in the Colony, they aided and assisted in suspending the executive Courts in this County in August 1774.

That on no Occasion have they spared either cost or Trouble, without hope of pecuniary reward, vigorously and unweariedly exerting ourselves for the support and in the Defence of our Countrys cause notwithstanding the most violent Discouragements we have met with by open or secret Enemies in this Town and County and in a Neighbouring province.

That 'till last fall your Memorialists had little or no Expectation of obtaining any new previleges beyound what our defective Charter secured to us.—

That when they came more maturely to reflect upon the nature of the present Contest, and the Spirit and obstinacy of Administration—What an amazing Expence the united Colonies had incured? How many Towns had been burnt or otherwise damaged? what Multitudes had turned out to beg and how many of our valiant Heroes had been slain in the Defence of their Country and the Impossibility of our being ever again dependant on Great Britain or in any Measure subject to her Authority—When they further considered that the Revolution in England affoarded the Nation but a very imperfect Redress of Grievances the Nation being transported with extravagant Joy in getting rid of one Tyrant forgot to provide against another—and how every Man by Nature has the seeds of Tyranny deeply implanted within him so that nothing short of Omnipotence can eradicate them—That when they attended to the Advice given this Colony by the Continental Congress respecting the Assumption of our antient Constitution, how early that Advice was given, the Reasons of it and the principles upon which it was given which no longer exist, what a great Change of Circumstances there has been in the Views and Designs of this whole Continent since the giving said Advice—That when they considered, now is the only Time we have reason ever to expect for securing our Liberty and the Liberties of future posterity upon a permanent Foundation that no length of Time can undermine—Tho' they were filled with pain and Anxiety at so much as seeming to oppose public Councils yet with all these Considerations in our View, Love of virtue freedom and posterity prevailed upon us to suspend a second Time the Courts of Justice in this County after the Judges of the Quarter Sessions had in a precipitate and clandestine Manner held one Court and granted out a Number of Licences to Innholders at the rate of six shillings or more each and divided the Money amongst themselves with this boast that now it was a going to be like former Times and had discovered a Spirit of Independance of the People and a Disposition triumphantly to ride over their heads and worse than renew all our former Oppressions.

We further beg leave to represent that we were deeply affected at the Misrepresentations that have been made of us and the County in general, as Men deeply in Debt, dishonest, ungovernable, heady untractable, without principle and good Conduct and ever ready to oppose lawful Authority, as Mobbes disturbers of peace order and Union, unwilling to submit to any Government, or ever to pay our Debts, so that we have been told a former House of Representatives had it in actual Contemplation to send an armed force to effect that by violence which reason only ought to effect at the present Day.

We beg leave to lay before your Honors our Principles real Views and Designs in what we have hitherto done and what Object we are reaching after, with this Assurance if we have erred it is thro' Ignorance and not bad Intention.—

We beg leave therefore to represent that we have always been persuaded that the people are the fountain of power.

That since the Dissolution of the power of Great Britain over these Colonies they have fallen into a state of Nature.

That the first step to be taken by a people in such a state for the Enjoyment or Restoration of Civil Government amongst them, is the formation of a fundamental Constitution as the Basis and ground work of Legislation.

That the Approbation of the Majority of the people of this fundamental Constitution is absolutely necessary to give Life and being to it. That then and not 'till then is the foundation laid for Legislation. We often hear of the fundamental Constitution of Great Britain, which all political Writers (except ministerial ones) set above the King, Lords, and

Commons, which they cannot change, nothing short of the great rational Majority of the people being sufficient for this.

That a Representative Body may form, but cannot impose said fundamental Constitution upon a people. They being but servants of the people cannot be greater than their Masters, and must be responsible to them. If this fundamental Constitution is above the whole Legislature, the Legislature cannot certainly make it, it must be the Approbation of the Majority which gives Life and being to it.—

That said fundamental Constitution has not been formed for this Province the Corner stone is not yet laid and whatever Building is reared without a foundation must fall into Ruins.

That this can be instantly effected with the Approbation of the Continental Congress and Law subordination and good government flow in better than their antient Channels in a few Months Time.—That till this is done we are but beating the Air and doing what will and must be undone afterwards, and all our labour is lost and on divers Accounts much worse than lost.

That a Doctrine lately broached in this County by several of the Justices newly created without the Voice of the People, that the Representatives of the People may form Just what fundamental Constitution they please and impose it upon the people and however obnoxious to them they can obtain no relief from it but by a New Election, and if our Representatives should never see fit to give the people one that pleases them there is no help for it appears to us to be the rankest kind of Toryism, the self same Monster we are now fighting against.

These are some of the Truths we firmly believe and are countenanced in believing them by the most respectable political Writers of the last and present Century, especially by Mr. Burgh in his political Disquisitions for the publication of which one half of the Continental Congress were subscribers.

We beg leave further to represent that we by no means object to the most speedy Institution of Legal Government thro' this province and that we are as earnestly desirous as any others of this great Blessing.

That knowing the strong Byass of human Nature to Tyranny and Despotism we have Nothing else in View but to provide for Posterity against the wanton Exercise of power which cannot otherwise be done than by the formation of a fundamental Constitution. What is the fundamental Constitution of this province, what are the unalienable Rights of the people the power of the Rulers, how often to be elected by the people etc. have any of these Things been as yet ascertained. Let it not be said by future posterity that in this great this noble this glorious Contest we made no provision against Tyranny amongst ourselves.

We beg leave to assure your Honors that the purest and most disinterested Love of posterity and a fervent desire of transmitting to them a fundamental Constitution securing their sacred Rights and Immunities against all Tyrants that may spring up after us has moved us in what we have done. We have not been influenced by hope of Gain or Expectation of Preferment and Honor. We are no discontented faction we have no fellowship with Tories, we are the staunch friends of the Union of these Colonies and will support and maintain your Honors in opposing Great Britain with our Lives and Treasure.

But if Commissions should be recalled and the Kings Name struck out of them, if the Fee Table be reduced never so low, and multitudes of other things be done to still the people all is to us as Nothing whilst the foundation is unfixed the Corner stone of Government unlaid. We have heared much of Governments being founded in Compact. What Compact has been formed as the foundation of Government in this province?— We beg leave further to represent that we have undergone many grievous oppressions in this County and that now we wish a Barrier might be set up against such oppressions, against which we can have no security long till the foundation of Government be well established.—

We beg leave further to represent these as the Sentiments of by far the Majority of the people in this County as far as we can Judge and being so agreeable to Reason Scripture and Common Sence, as soon as the Attention of people in this province is awakened we doubt not but the Majority will be with us.

We beg leave further to observe that if this Honourable Body shall find that we have embraced Errors dangerous to the safety of these Colonies it is our Petition that our Errors may be detected and you shall be put to no further Trouble from us but without an Alteration in our Judgment the Terrors of this World will not daunt us we are determined to resist Great Britain to the last Extremity and all others who may claim a similar Power over us. Yet we hold not to an Imperium in Imperio we will be determined by the Majority.—

Your Petitioners beg leave therefore to Request that this Honourable Body would form a fundamental Constitution for this province after leave is asked and obtained from the Honourable Continental Congress and that said Constitution be sent abroad for the Approbation of the Majority of the people in this Colony that in this way we may emerge from a state of Nature and enjoy again the Blessing of Civil Government in this way the Rights and Liberties of future Generations will be secured and the Glory of the present Revolution remain untarnished and future Posterity rise up and call this Honourable Council and house of Representatives blessed

and as in Duty bound will ever pray
Attes. Israel Dickinson Town Clerk

To the Honorable House of Representatives in General Court Convened at Watertown on the 29th Day of May 1776

We The Subscribers Freeholders and Inhabitants in the Town of Pittsfield in the County of Berkshire Beg leave to Inform the Honorable House That we Conceive it has been the Constant Sence and Opinion of your Honours that no Minister of the Gospel ought, to be admitted to a Seat in the House of Representatives in the General Court of this Colony; on the General Principle that no Persons, not Contributing to the Support of Publick Burthens, and payment of Publick Taxes, ought to have a Voice in giveing or granting, the Property of others, not so Exempted, or in Meking, and Passing any acts, or Laws, not Equally Binding on themselves, and their Constituants unless for mere Political Purposes Excused—

We further would inform your Honours that notwithstanding the Same has also been the Sence of this Town, as appears by the Instructions they gave their Representatives the year Past, injoining them to Do their utmost to prevent any Minister of the Gospel from haveing a Seat in the House of Representative The Inhabitants of said Town have by some Extraordinary Means Chosen one Mr. Valentine Rathbone to Represent them in this Honorable Court—Which Said Rathbone we aver to your Honours, is and has been ever Since he lived in this Town the Minister or Elder of a Baptist Church and Congregation in this Town, and that he had never paid any Taxes either Public or private in the Town, or been assessed to the payment thereof but has from year to year for four or five years past given Certificates to the members of his Church and Congregation In the Capacity of an Elder thereof, in order to obtain their Exemption from the payment of Ministerial Charges etc—We Therefore pray your Honours would Take the premises into your wise Consideration, and that the Said Mr. Rathbone may be Dismissed from giveing his attendance as a Member of this Honorable Court, and this we are the more imboldened to ask as the Town have also made Choice of another Person to Represent them whom We Conceive to be not thus incapacitated and who upon Notice will Doubtless attend—And as in Duty Bound Shall pray

James Jn Colt
Charles Goodrich
Daniel Cadwell
Erastus Sackett
Jacob Ensign
Ebenezer Soane
Jacob Ward

[read May 31 and dismissed]

10

Boston's Instructions to Its Representatives, May 30, 1776

The process of devising a new constitution for Massachusetts was characterized by an exchange between the representatives in the General Court and the citizens who sent them. Boston instructed its representatives to use their own wisdom and discretion in matters of public concern, but included some rather specific indications of its thoughts on proper governmental forms. The instructions are in *A Report of the Record Commissioners of the City of Boston, Containing the Boston Town Records, 1770 through 1777* (Boston, 1887), 236, 237–238.

Monday May 30th 10 O'Clock Town met according to Adjournment——

. . .

Touching the internal Police of this Colony, it is essentially necessary, in Order to preserve Harmony among ourselves, that the constituent Body be satisfied, that they are fully and fairly represented——The Right to legislate is originally in every Member of the Community; which Right is always exercised of a State: But when the Inhabitants are become numerous, 'tis not only inconvenient, but impracticable *for all* to meet in One Assembly; and hence arose the Necessity and Practice of legislating by a few, freely chosen by the many.——When this Choice is free, and the Representation, equal, 'tis the People's Fault if they are not happy: We therefore entreat you to devise some Means to obtain an *equal Representation* of the People of this Colony in the Legislature. But care should be taken, that the Assembly be not unweildy; for this would be an Approach to the Evil meant to be cured by Representation. The largest Bodies of Men do not always dispatch Business with the greatest Expedition, nor conduct it in the wisest manner—

It is essential to Liberty that the legislative, judicial and executive Powers of Government be, as nearly as possible, independent of and separate from each other; for where they are united in the same Persons, there will be wanting that natural Check, which is the principal Security against the enacting of arbitrary Laws, and a wanton Exercise of Power in the Execution of them.——It is also of the highest Importance that every Person in a Judiciary Department, employ the greatest Part of his

Time and Attention in the Duties of his Office.——We therefore farther instruct you, to procure the making such Law or Laws, as shall make it incompatible for the same Person to hold a Seat in the legislative and executive Departments of Government, at one and the same time:—That shall render Judges in every Judicatory through the Colony, dependent, not on the uncertain Tenure of Caprice or Pleasure, but on an unimpeachable Deportment in the important Duties of their Station, for their Continuance in Office: And to prevent the Mutiplicity of Offices in the same Person, that such Salaries be settled upon them, as Will place them above the Necessity of stooping to any indirect or collateral Means for subsistence.——

We wish to avoid a Profusion of the public Monies on the one hand, and the *Danger of sacrificing our Liberties to a Spirit of Parsimony on the other:*——Not doubting of your Zeal and Abilities in the common Cause of our Country, we leave your Discretion to prompt such Exertions, in promoting any military Operations, as the Exigency of our public Affairs may require: And in the same Confidence in your Fervor and Attachment to the public Weal, we readily submit all other Matters of public Moment, that may require your Consideration to your own Wisdom and Discretion.——

The foregoing Draught of Instructions to our Representatives, having been read and considered, the Question was put——"Whether the same shall be accepted, and given to our Representatives, as their Instructions" ——Passed in the Affirmative unanimously.——

11

Topsfield's Instructions to Its Representatives, June 14, 1776

On April 22 and 24 Topsfield chose a committee to meet with committees from other towns at Ipswich to act "respecting a more just and equal choice and representation in the General Court." Topsfield's instructions to its representatives are found in George Francis Dow, ed., *The Historical Collections of the Topsfield Historical Society,* XXVIII (Topsfield, Mass., 1925), 78–79.

To Mr John Gould Representative of Topsfield, [in General Court]
Sir,

A resolution of the Honorable House of Representatives, Calling upon the Several Towns in this Collony to express their minds with respect to American Independence of the Kingdom of greate Britten, is the ocasion of our giving you Instructions, this being the greatest question that ever Came before this town.

A few years ago, Sir, such a question would have put us in a greate surprise, and we apprehend would have been Treated with the uttmost contempt. We then thought ourselve happy in being the Subjects of the King of greate Britten, it being our pairent State; and we have always Looked upon it as our Duty as well as Interest, to defend and support the honor and Dignity of the Crown of greate Britten; and we have alway freely done it, both with our Lives and fortunes, counting ourselves happy when in the strictest union and connection with our pairent State.

But the Sene is now Changed; our minds and sentiments are now altered. She that we call our mother Country and pairent State is now without any Just Cause or Injury done by these Colonies, become their greatest enemies. The unprovoked Injuries these Colonies have received; the unjustifiable and unconstitutional Claims that have been made on these Colonies by the Court of greate Britten, to Tax us and take away our Substance from us, and that at any time and for any use that they please without our consent, and the cruel prosecuting these their Claims, have been cruel and unjust to the Highest degree; the whole of their governours appointed and sent into these colonies, are so well known, and have been by much abler hands set fourth in such a clear, true and plaine Light, we think it needless to Innumerate any further particulars.

For these reasons, Sir, as well as many others that might be mentioned, we are Confirmed in the opinion that the unighted Colonies will be greatly wanting in their duty, both to the greate governer of the univers, to themselves, and posterity, if Independence of the kingdom of greate Britten is not declared as soon as may be,—these being our Sentiments. But we would not be understood that we mean to dictate, Leaving that momentous afaire to the well known wisdom, prudence, Justice, and Integrity of that honorable body, the Continental Congress, under whose direction it more Immediately belongs.

And, in respect to a forme of government for the future, we take it, that belongs to an after question; and we could wish that no Court or congress on this continent, might spend their time in debateing about forms and serimonies, equall or unequal representation in Court, at present. As enovasions are always dangerous, we hartily wish that the antiant rules in the Charter, which this province has been so much contending for, might be strictly adheared to till such time as the whole of the people of this Colony have Liberty to express their Sentiments in respect to that afaie, as fully as they have in the cause of Independence. For we are full in the opinion, that the sentiments of the people in general, are never fully collected by the vote or opinion of a few persons meat together, (tho appointed), when they desend into matters of greate Importance that are wholly new, and especially when the whole of the people are Immediately concearned theirin.

Haveing thus freely spoken our Sentiments in respect to Independence etc.—We now Instruct you, Sir, to Honorable, the Continental Congress, the strongest assuerances that if, for the Safety of the united Colonies, they shall declare America to be Independant of the Kingdom of greate Britten, your Constituants will support and defend the measure with their Lives and fortunes to the uttmost of their power.

12

Resolution of the House of Representatives, September 17, 1776

From June 1776 onward, various committees of the General Court had worked to devise a form of government best suited to the interests of the people of Massachusetts. In September the House of Representatives recommended that the towns meet and vote on whether the existing legislative body should enact a constitution. The handbill is found in MA 156/197.

Handbill Copy of the Resolution of the House of Representatives, 17 September, 1776.

In the House of Representatives, September 17th, 1776. Resolved, That it be recommended to the Male Inhabitants of each Town in this State, being Free and Twenty-one Years of Age or upwards, that they assemble as soon as they can in Town-Meeting, upon reasonable previous Warning to be therefor given, according to Law; and that in such Meeting, they consider and determine whether they will give their Consent that the present House of Representatives of this State of the *Massachusetts-Bay* in *New-England,* together with the Council, if they consent in one Body with the House, and by equal Voice, should consult, agree on, and enact such a Constitution and Form of Government for this State, as the said House of Representatives and Council as aforesaid, on the fullest and most mature Deliberation shall judge will most conduce to the Safety, Peace and Happiness of this State, in all after Successions and Generations; and if they would direct that the same be made Public for the Inspection and Perusal of the Inhabitants, before the Ratification thereof by the Assembly. And that each Town as soon as may be after they shall have passed on the Question aforesaid, cause their Votes or Resolutions thereon to be certified into the Office of the Secretary of this State. And all Towns having a Right according to Law to a Representation in the General Assembly, and not having chose a Representative in Pursuance of the Precepts issued in *April* last, are at the Meeting aforementioned, impowered if they see Cause upon this Occasion, to return a Member or Members in the same Manner as they were by the Laws of this State impowered to do in Consequence of the Precepts aforesaid.

Also, Ordered, That *David Cheever,* Esq; procure the foregoing Resolve to be Published in Hand-Bills, and sent to the Selectmen of each Town.

J. Warren, Speaker.

13

Returns of the Towns on the House of Representatives Resolution of September 17, 1776

The response of the towns in September and October 1776 to the proposal that the existing House of Representatives and Council enact a constitution for the state was less than enthusiastic. Some towns did not answer at all; others, while agreeing that the legislature should form a constitution, reserved the right of the people to approve it; and still others insisted that only a convention chosen for the purpose could establish legal government. The responses revealed that loyalty and obedience would remain tenuous until the citizens assembled in their towns were actively involved in the constitution-making process. Unless otherwise indicated, the returns are found in MA 156/121–198. In three cases the returns are supplied from other sources.

Gloucester [New Gloucester, Maine] (156/121)

Town of Glocester, Instructions to the Assembly respecting a form of Government September 18—1776 [*Inscription annotated* Doubtful]

According to a Resolve of the Honorable House of Representatives September 17th. 1776

At a meeting of the Inhabitants of the town of Glocester September 30, 1776 having been duly warned

Voted unanimously that, they give their Consent that the present House of Representatives of this state of the Massachusetts-Bay in New England, together with the Council, if they Consent in one Body with the House, and by equal Voice, should consent, agree on, and enact such a Constitution and Form of Government for this State as the said House of Representatives and Council as aforesaid, on the fullest and most mature Deliberation shall judge will most conduce to the safety, peace and happiness of this State, in all after Successions and Generations; and they direct that the same be made Public for the Inspection and perusal of the Inhabitants, before the Ratification thereof by the Assembly.

Ordered that the above be Certified into the office of the Secretary of this State

James Porter Town Clerk

Truro (156/121)

Persuent to Directions from the Honourable House of Representatives of the State of the Massachewsetts Bay isued the 17th of September 1776 to the Selectmen of Truro: the male inhabitants thereof from 21 years old and upward accordingly assembled in legal meeting and gave their harty assent the Honourable Council and Honourable house of the State afore said should propose such a form or forms of Goverment as they shall judge most beneficial for after successions and Publish the same to the inspection and perusal of the inhabitants of this Town befor the Ratification of the same: voted allso that the Town Clerk procure a true coppy of this Result to be convid to the Secretarys office of this State——

a true coppy attested per Daniel Paine
town clerk

[*Annotation at bottom of document* Doubtful]

Sandisfield (156/121)

In pursuance of a Resolve in the house of Representatives passed September 17th 1776 a Meeting was Called and the Town being Legally Assembled passed the following Vote = viz = Voted unanimously that the present house of Representatives of this State with the Council in one body and with equal Voice Consult and Agree on such a Constitution and form of Government for this State as they shall judge will most Conduce to the safty and happeness of this State in all after succesions and generations and that the same be made publick for our inspection and Perusal before the Ratification thereof

Test Samuel Smith Moderator
Sandisfield September 30th 1776

Colrain (156/122)

At a legal Town meeting of the Inhabitants of the Town of Colrain held on the 25th Day of September 1776 Voted unanimously, That the present Honorable House of Representatives of this State together with the Council jointly acting in one Body. and with Equal voice should consult and agree on such a Constitution and form of Government for this State, as the said House of Representatives and Council aforesaid on the fullest and most mature Deliberation shall judge will most conduce to the safety peace and happiness of this State in all after successions and generations, and that the same be made public for the inspection perusal and approbation of the people before the ratification thereof——

Attest per James Stewart
Town Clerk

Sheffield (156/122)

Sheffield September the 26 1776

Att a Legal Town meating held the twenty Sixth of September Currant Captain William Day was Chosen moderator of the Same and the Said meating was ajournd to the twenty Eighth currant and the Town then proceeded to act and passed the following Vote; Voted thatt we will Concent that the Present House of Representatives and the Council Consult agree upon and enact Such a Form of Goverment and Constitution as they on the most mature Deliberation shall judg will most Conduce to the Safty Peace and Hapiness of this State——on this Condition that the Same be made Publick and agreed to by the Peopel att Large before it be Finally ratified by the Said Generall Court or any futer Assembly

Test William Day
Moderator

Conway (156/123)

Conway the 26th of September 1776

at a Legal meeting of the Inhabitants of Conway from 21 years oald and Upwards assembled at the meetinghous in said Town agreable To a precept or handbill Resolved in the hous of Representatives of the 17th. Instant

Voted that This Town is willing that a form of Government should be adopted by the present houses agreable to the above said handbill——

Voted that Copies of the Form adopted by the General Court be Sent to Each Town for perusal for their Consent or Rejection and Their Resolves be Trasmited to the Secretary of State——

A Trew Coppe fron the Minutes attest
Oliver Wetmore Town Clerk

Greenfield (156/123)

At a Legal Town meeting of the inhabitants of the Town of Greenfield held on the 26 Day of September 1776

Voted unanimously, That the present Honorable House of Representatives of this state together with the Councel jointly acting in one Body and with Equal voice should consult and agree on such Constitution and form of Government for this State as the said House of Representatives and Council aforesaid on the fullest and most mature Deliberation shall judge will most Conduce to the Safety peace and happeness of this State in all after succession and generations, and that the same be made Publick for the inspection perusal and approbation of the people before the Ratification thereof——

Attest. Samuel Wells
Town Clerk

Wilmington (156/123)

At a Legal Meeting of the Freeholders of the Town of Wilmington on Monday the 30th Day of September AD 1776——

Voted that the present House of Representatives Together with the Council, if they Consent in one body, and by Equal Voice Should Consult, agree on, and Enact Such a Constitution, and form of government for this State, as will most conduce, to the Safety peace and Happiness of this State, in all after Successions and generations;——

Voted that the said form of government for this State, be made public by printed copys, to be laid before the inhabitants of said Town, for their Inspection and perusal, before the ratification thereof by the Assembly;——

A True extract from the Records Attest
Cadwr. Ford Jnr T CK

To the Honorable John Avery
Dep Secretary Boston

Scarborough (156/124)

At a Town Meeting held at Scarborough the first Day of October 1776 voted that this Town Consent that the present House of Representatives with the Honorable Counsel of the State of the Massachusetts form a Constitution of Government for Said State and that each Town in said State have the Prusual before Ratified agreabl to the Resolve of Said court

a true coppy attest
Samuel Small
Town Cler

Littleton (156/124)

The folloing is a Rosolve of the Town of Littleton in the County of Middlesex in the State of the Massachusetts Bay

We the Inhabitents of the Town of Littleton being Assembled in Town Meeting to take under Considerration A Resolve of the House of Representatives of September 17 1776 With Regard to Setling a Constitution and form of Goverment for this State. We do Consent that the Honorable Council and House of Representatives of this State that they in one Body and equal Voice Shuld Plan a Constitution and form of Goverment for this State and that form or plan to be Published and Sent to the Several Townes for there Inspection and perusal and that no Constatution of Goverment be Ratified or Confermed without the Consent of the People or the Mager Part of them——

Orderd that this Resolve be Certified into the Office off the Secretary of this State——

A true Copey Attest
per William Henry Prentice Town Clerk

Methuen (156/125)

Att Meeting Inhabants of the Town of Methuen on october the 2d: 1776 the Town Voted and Choose Captain John Bordwell modertor for said Meeting, put to Vote Whether it be the minds the Town that the present House of Representivs with the Counsel should agree on such consteution for this State a they think for the Good of the State and publish the same for the approbation of the people befour it Retified.

At past in the affomative

a true Coppy Atts Richard Whitter
Town Clerk

Stoughton (156/125)

At a Town meeting Legally assembled at Stoughton October the 2 : 1776 The Town Voted the following resolutions viz——

1 — Resolved that good Goverment is the Basis of Liberty and absolutely necessary to the safety and well fair of a people

2 Resolved that as the end of Goverment is the happiness of the People so the sole power and right of forming and Establishing a plan thereof is essentially in the People——

3 Resolved that as this State is at present Destitute of a fixed and established form of goverment it is absolutely necessary that one be immediately formed and established agreeable to the recommendations of the Grand Congress——

4 Resolved that as the present house of Representatives have passed a resolve to see if the Several Towns in this state would empower them the said house to gether with the Council to enact a form of goverment for this state it appears to unadviseabl and irrational, and a measure that ought by any means to be complied with for these Reasons. (viz) that are totally unacquainted with the Capacities Patriotism and Characters of the members that Compose the said house and Council—(excepting our own members)—also because they were never elected by the people for that purpose and also because the present embarrassed state of our publick affairs calls for the steady attention of every member of said Court——

5. Resolved that it is the Duty and Interest of this Town immediately to choose one or more members, to join with the member of the other Towns in this State to form and publish a plan of Goverment for Said State——

6. Resolved that in order to carry the aforegoing Resolutions into execution as soon as the importance of the matter will admit it appears to us best that the members of the several Towns in each county in this

State (chosen for the express purpose aforesaid) should meet together in County Conventions and when so met should Draft a form of goverment for the whole state, then that the members of the several counties of this state should meet to gether by them selves or by their Committes in a State Convention or Congress, and Compare the several forms of goverment together whereby the wisdom of the whole state may be collected and a form of goverment may be Extracted——

7. Resolved that it appears to us absolutely necessary for the Liberty and safety of this state that the plan of goverment when formed and published, should not be Established till the people of this state have had time and opportunity of thoroughly Examineing the same, and shall consent that it be established by the said State Convention or Congress——

Stoughton October the 2. 1776

A True Copy Attest
Theophilus Lyon
Town Clerk Pro. Tem.

Northampton (156/126)

At a meeting of the Inhabitants of the Town of Northampton from twenty years of age and upwards being free and Legally Assembled at the Town house in said Town on thursday the third day of October Anno Domini 1776

In the first place Joseph Hawley Esquire was chosen Moderator

And then the Question was put Whether the Town will give their consent that the present House of Representatives of this State of the Massachusetts Bay in New England together with the Council (if they consent) in one Body with the House and by equal voice should consult agree on and enact such a Constitution and Form of Government for this State as the Said House of Representatives and Council as aforesaid on the fullest and most Mature Deliberation Shall Judge will most conduce to the Safety Peace and Happiness of this State in all after Successions and Generations And it Passed in the Affirmative

The Question was then Put Whether they would Direct that the Same should be made Publick for the Inspection and Perusal of the Inhabitants before the Ratification thereof by the Assembly. And it Passed in the Affirmative

A true Copy of the Record Attest Elijah Hunt
Town Clerk of the Town of Northampton

Northampton Octob. 7th 1776

West Springfield (156/127)

At a Meeting of the Inhabitants of the Town of West Springfield legally assembled on Thursday 3rd Day of October 1776—in Pursuance of a Resolve of the general Court of this State passd—17th Day September last etc———

Deacon Jonathan White chosen Moderator

Voted.—That it is the Opinion of this Town that the present House of Representatives of this State, together with the Council, if they consent in one Body with the House, and by equal Voice, should consult, and agree on such a Constitution, and Form of Government, as they, in their Wisdom shall think most salutary for this State; and that they would cause the same to be made public in each Town within this State, for the Perusal, and Inspection of the Inhabitants; which shall be either confirmed, or disannulled—by the Legislature according to the Votes of the several Towns of this State approving or disapproving the Same.———

Voted—That the Town Clerk be directed to send a Coppy of the above Proceedings into the Secretary's office of this State.

A true Coppy from the Minutes

Attr Chauncy Brewer Town Clerk

West Springfield October 15th 1776

To be lodged in the Secretary's office

Dunstable (156/128)

Middlesex County At a meting of the Inhabitance of the Town of Dunstable Legally Assembled in publick Town meting on the third Day of October 1776 adjornd Till the 10th Day, then Held According to adjornment to Take under Consideration a motion of the Honourable House of Representatives of the State of the Massachusetts Bay in New

England viz (Whether the Town will Give there Consent that the present House of Representatives To Gether with the Councell if they Consent in one body with the House and by Equel Voice Should Consent Agree on and Enact Such a Constitution and form of Government for the State as the said House and Councell aforesaid Shall Judg will most Conduce to the Safty Peace and hapiness of this State—The Question being put Accordingly the Inhabitance Unanomusly gave there Consent that the said House and Councel Consult agree on and Enact such Constitution and form of Government for this State as they Shall Judg most advantagious———But at the Same Time Direct that the Same be made publick In Such maner as that the Inhabitance may have an opertunity for perusing the same Before the Ratifycation there off———

Attest

Josiah Blodget Jur Town Clerk

Reading (156/122) *

In Conformity to a Recommendation of the Honorable House of Representatives of September 17th—1776—respecting a Constitution and Form of Government for the State of Massachusetts Bay: In consequence of a previous Warning therefor, according to Law [the?] Inhabitants of Reading assembled in Town Meeting on the third of October Instant, and Voted as their Mind in the Case that———

"The General Court of this State of Massachusetts-Bay should publish a Form of Government for the Inspection of the several Towns before it be enacted"

Attest. Jacob Emerson Town Clerk pro Tempore

Reading October–15th–1776

Kittery (156/129)

York County. At a Meeting of the Male Inhabitants Twenty one Years of age and upwards of the Town of Kittery Duly warned in Publick Town Meeting Assembled third Day of October: 1776. Then and theair to Consider and Act upon a Resolve of the Honorable House of Representatives of this State Relative to Enecting Such a Constitution and

* Numbered 122, but bound in on 128.

Form of Government for the Same as will most Conduce to the Safety Peace and Happiness Thereof etc.——as in Said Resolve is Expressed——

Voted that the Honorable Charles Chancey be Moderator of this Meiting

After having Said Resolve Read and taking the minds of the Inhabitants thereon——Voted the Honorable James Gowen and Charles Chancey Esquire Captain John H. Bartlet Major John Shapleigh. Captain Samuel Weeks. . Misters Nathaniel Remick: and William Stacey, be a Committee to Draw A Proper Vote agreable to the minds of the Inhabitants as now Exprest——Then Voted, that this Meeting be Adjourned to the Seventeenth. Instant at two of the Clock after-noon——

At the Adjournment October the 17th the Said Committee Reported A Draught of a Vote as Follows. Viz. That the Inhabitants of this Town give their Consent that the Honorable House of Representatives together with the Honorable Council of this State Form a Constitution of Government for the Same with this Reserve, That Such form of Government as They may Agree upon be made Publick for the Inspection and Perrusal of the Inhabitants of Each Town and that A Meeting for that Purpose be Called to se Wheather the Inhabitants will give there Consent or not to Such Form of Government before the Ratification thereof——

The foregoing Report being Destinkly Read Several times Then the Question was Put Wheather the Same be Excepted and it Pased in the Affirmative——

A True Coppey From the Minuts of the Meeting
Attest Dens. Fernald Town Clerk

Kittery Octoober the 18th 1776

New Providence (156/130)

To the Honorable the Council and House of Representatives of the State of Massachusetts Bay, to Meet by adjournment on Thursday the ninth of this instant October——

May it Please Your Honours. We the Inhabitants of a New Plantation Called New Providence in the County of Berkshire and State aforesaid having Received Your Honors Hand Bill Giving us Liberty to Show our Minds, Whither We were Willing that the Council together With the House of Representatives of this State, Should make a Constitution and form of Goverment for this State or Not Where upon we Proceeded and Warned the Inhabitants of this Place to meet on the thirtieth of September Past——

who then and there came to the Following Resolutions——

1ly Voted Unanimously, that the Said Council and House of Representatives Should make a Constitution and Form of Government for this State——

2ly Voted Unanimously, that as Soon as the Said Form of Goverment be Compleated The Same be made Publuk throughout this State, before the Ratification thereof——

Signed in Behalf and by order of the
People of aforesaid New Providence
Samuel Low Clerk

Dated New Providence Oct. 4, 1776

Ashfield (156/131)

To the Honorabel House of Representatives of the State of the Massachusets Bay in New England Assembled for the good of this State Having Reseved your Resolve of September the 17 1776 Directing the Several Towns to Call A Meting for the Spesal Pirpos of Causing thair Vots or Resolves to be Returned to the Secertarys Office of this State, the Town After having Ben Previously Warned, Met on thusda 26th of September instant and After Debating the Matur Ajurned to October the 4 : 1776 Then Met and in the Fullest and most Mature Dilibrate Maner Came into the folowing Resolves

Viz 1 Voted that it is our mind that we would have the forme of Sivil Goverment Set up for the Good of this Stat

2 Voted that the Presant Reprasentatives of the Peopel Shall forme the Constitution Exclusive of the Counsel for the Good of this State and Returne it to the Sevarals' Towns for their Exceptanc Before the Ratifycation thairof

3 Voted that we will take the Law of God for the foundation of the forme of our Goverment for as the Old Laws that we have Ben Ruled by under the British Constitution have Proved Enefectual to Secuer us from the more then savige Crualty of tiranical Opressars and Sense the God of Nature hath Enabeled us to Brake that yake of Bondage we think our Selves Bound in Duty to God and our Country to Opose the Least Apearanc of them Old Tiranical Laws taking Place again

4 Voted that it is our Opinniun that we Do not want any Goviner but the Goviner of the Univarse, and under him a States Ginaral to Consult with the wrest of the united Stats for the Good of the whole

5 Voted that it is our Opinian that Each Town is invested with a Natve Athority to Chuse a Comitte or Number of Juges Consisting of A Number of wise understanding and Prudant Men that Sall Jug and Detarmin all Cases betwixt Man and Man, Setel Intesttute Estates and Colect all Debts that have Ben Contracted, or may be Contracted within their Limite and all contravarsies what Socuer Exept in the Case of Murdor and then it will be Nesesary to Call in Eleven men from Eleven Nabouring Towns that Shull be Cose for that Porpos Anuly to Joge and Condem Such Moderrers

6 Voted that it is our opinion that the Town Clark shal Regester all Deads within the Leminits of Said Town

7 Voted that it our opinan that the Asembelly of this Stat consist of one Colecttive body the members of which body shall Anually be Alected

8 Voted that we Do Not want any Laws made to Govern in Eclasastics Afairs fairmly Believing the Divine Law to be Safficiant and that by which we and all Our Religion affairs aught to Governed by

9 Voted that it is our opinion tha the Representitive of this State Be Payed out of the Publick Treshurar of this State which monies shall be Colected of the whole State

10 Voted that it is ower opinion that all acts Pased by the Ginaral Cort of this State Respecting the Seviral Towns Be Sent to the Sevarals Towns for thair acceptants Before thay shall be in force

Ashfield October 4th: 1776

A tru copy Test Aaron Lyon Clark P T

Warwick (156/132)

Att a meeting of the freeholders and other Inhabitants of the town of Warwick October the 4—1776 by warrant Directed from the Selectmen Requisting the Constables to Notify and warn Evry Individial that was Set fourth in the hand Bills Directed to the Several towns in this State for the purposes mentioned in Said hand Bills, and as it Seemed, to appear there was Some Deficienty in the Constables warning it was objected against by one man when upon Some Desputes arose, upon which the Question was accordingly put whether the town would act upon the Notice they had——which passed in the affarmitive

1ly Voted and Chose Lieutenant Thomas Rich Moderator

2ly A motion made and Seconted whether the town will give their consent that the present house of Representitives with the Council Enact and agree on a Constitution or form of Goverment—and passed in the Negative

3ly A motion made and Seconted that the present house of Representitives of this State make a form of Goverment and Send it out to the Inhabitants of Each town in this State for their Inspection and perusal ——and passed in the affarmitive

4ly A motion made to Chuse a Committee of three men, to forme Some Instructions for the Representitive of Said town and Voted and Chose Amos Marsh, Josiah Rawson and Peter Fisk

5ly Voted that the following Instructions of the above committee be sent into the Secretaries office

To Lieutenant Thomas Rich——

Sir Having by a Late vote impowerd and Directed you to Joyn the other members of the General Assembly in forming a plan of goverment for this State, and being fully Sensible that it is a matter of the greatest importance Both to the present and future Generations that Such a plan be adopted as shall be most free from the Seeds of tyrany, have the greatest tendency to preserve the rights and Liberties of the people, and the most Likely to preserve peace and good order in this State, we therefore begg Leave to Lay before you the following Short hints Respecting a form of Goverment which we apprehend if adopted will have a tendency to answer the purposes above mentioned——

1ly that there be but one Branch in the Legislative authority of this State viz the Representitives from the Several towns with a president or Speaker at the head

2ly that an equal Representation may be made and the Ballance of power properly preserved, Let each Incorporate town Send one member, and the Largest towns not more than four or five and other towns in same purportion

3ly that in making choice of Representitives evry male Inhabitant that is twenty one years of age (being free) to have the previledge of Voteing——

4ly that in Case sufficent Evidence appears to a town that their member or members are guilty of acting contrary to the Rights and Liberties of the people, then to have the priveledge at any time in the year to Recall him or them and Chuse a New——

5ly that not Liss then Eighty members make a house

Dated at Warwick
October the 4—1776

Amos Marsh
Josiah Rawson Committee
Peter Fisk

A true coppy of the proceedings of Said Meeting
Atest Amos Marsh town clerk

Great Barrington (156/133)

October 4th 1776

at a Legal Town Meeting of the Inhabetints of Great Barrington

1t voted: Doctor William Whiting Moderator

2d voted . . that the Hous of Representatives of this State of the Massachusentts Bay togather with the Council Consenting as one Body be Impowed to Consult and agree on such a Constitution and form of Goverment for this State as the House of Representatives and Council afore said shall on the fullest and most deleberated consideration and in their Great Wisdom Judge most conducive to the Safety and good order of this State for the Present and Succeeding Gennerattons

3d voted: that the Constitution and form of Goverment when agreed on by the Authority aforesaid: be made Public for the Inspection and Perusal of the free Peopel of this State: and their Assent before Ratification

Daniel Nash
Town Clerk

Charlemont (156/133)

Charlemont Octo 7th 1776

At a meeting Legally Assembled the Inhabitants of this Town In Compliance with a Resolve passed in the House of Representatives September 17. 1776. Unanimously Voted

1t that the present Assembly proced to form a Constitution for this State

2d That the Same be made Public for Inspection before the Ratification of it by the Assembly:

Jona. Hastings
Josuiha Hings Select Men
James White

Groton (156/134)

Groton October 7th 1776

At a Legal Town meeting Unanimously Voted——their Consent that the present house of Assembly, with the Council, agree upon a form of Government for this State, agreeable to their Resolve of 17th September last etc. and that the forme be made publick for the Inspection and perusal of the Inhabitants, before the Ratification of the same by said Assembly——

Extracts from the minutes
Oliver Prescott Town Clerk

Medway (156/134)

At a Legal Meeting of the Inhabitants of the Town of Medway On the 7th of October A D 1776

Put to vote to see if the Town Will give their Consent that the Present house of Representatives of the State of the Massachusetts Bay Together with the Council if they Consent in One Body with the house and by Equal Voice Should Consult and Agree On Such a Constitution and form of Government for this State, As the said house of Representatives and Council As Aforesaid, On the most mature Deliberation Shall Judge will most Conduce to the Safty Peace and Happiness of this State
Resolved in the Affirmative——

Put to vote to See if the Town Would Direct that the Constitution and form of Government for the State of Massachusetts Bay, Be made Publick for the inspection and Perusal of the Inhabitants before the Same be Ratifyed and Confirmd by the General Assembly——
Resolved in the Affirmative——

Attest Elijah Clark Town Clr

Westford (156/135)

Westford October the 7th 1776

at a Town Meeting Regurlerly assembled at the Meeting House in said Westford the following votes was passed, viz, firstly voted and chose Deacon John Abbott moderator for said Meeting

2ly Voted That they freely consent the present Great and General Court of This State Shall form a plan of Goverment for this State——— Provided that This Town Before the Ratification Thereof———be Served with a Coppy of The Same for Their Perusal and approbation or Disapprobation etc.———

Jno. Abbott Moderator

The foregoing is a True Coppy

att. Jos. Read Town Cler P. T

Deerfield (156/135)

Att a Legal Town Meeting held in Deerfield on the seventh Day of October 1776———The Question was put whether this Town will consent that The present House of Representatives of this State of the Massachusetts Bay in New England, together with the Council, if they consent in one Body with the House and by equal Voice, should consult, agree on, and enact such a Constitution or Form of Government for this State, as the said House, and Council as aforesaid, shall upon the most mature Deliberation, judge will most conduce to the Safety, Peace, and Happiness of this State, provided the same be made publick for the perusal and Inspection of the Inhabitants of this State, before the Ratification thereof by the Assembly, and passed in the Affirmative———

A true Extract from the Records
Deerfield October
8th 1776 Per David Dickinson, T. Clerk

Hutchinson (156/136)

Hutchinson Oct: 7 1776

These may Certifye that the Town meett on the Day above Specified and

Unanimusly Voted that the present House of Representive and Counsel in Conjunction Shoul form a Contiution and Lay the Same Before the Contstiututienss for Their Accetptance

Peter Fessenden	Secletmen
John Mason	and
Ezra Jones	Moderator

Rehoboth (156/136)

Att a meeting of the Freehoders and other Inhabitants of the Town of Rehoboth from Twenty one year and upwards on the Seventh of october 1776———

Voted that this town do not consent that the Present house of Representatives togather with the Council of this State of the massachusetts Bay Enact Such a constitution and form of Government for this State for all after Sucsesions and generations

For the following Reason (viz)

Because we have not had a Plan for Peruesal and as we look upon it to be the Right of the peopel at Large to give their consent to either a part or the whole or to propose such amendments as they think proper———

also Voted that the Town Clerk Deliver a copy of the above to our Pesent Representative

a True Copy Attest Jesse Parin Town Clerk

Beverly (156/137)

At a Legall meeting of the Inhabitnts of the Town of Beverly on October 7th 1776 agreeable to a resolve of the Honorable House of Representetives of the State of the Massachusetts Bay on the 17th of September Last———

it was put to Vote to se if the Town will give their Consent that the Present House of Representetives of this State of the Massachusetts Bay in New England to gather with the Council if they Consent in one Body with the House and by Equil Voice Should Consult agree on and Enact Such a Constatution and form of government for this State as the Said Hous of representetives and Council as aforesaid on the Fullest and most mature Deliberation Shall Judge will most Conduce to the Safty

Peace and Happyness of this State in all after Successions and generations and if they whould Direct that the Same be made Publick for the Inspection and Perusal of the Inhabitents be fore the Rattafication hereof by the Assembly and it Passed on the Negative

True Copy Attest
Joseph Wood T. Cler

Boxford (156/138)

At a Meeting of the Free-Holders and other Inhabiteints of the Town of Boxford Legally assembled on Monday the 7th day of October 1776——

Captain John Chusing Moderator——

it was put to Vote to See if the Town would Consent that the Present House of Representatives of this State together with the Council Should Consult agree upon and enact such a Constitution and form of Government for this State as they Shall on the Most full and Mature Deliberation Judge to be Most conducive to the peace and Hapiness of this and all Succeeding Generations And it past in the Negative——
a true Copy from the Records attest per me

Aaron Wood Town Clerk

Berkley (156/138)

At a Legal Town Meeting Held at Berkley on Monday the Seventh Day of October 1776——
Voted that the Present House of Representetive To gether with the Council form a plan of Goverment and Send it out to the Several Towns in This State for their Inspection be fore it is Ratified and Confermed——

Atest Samuel Tobey Jur Town Clerk

Marshfield (156/138)

At a Legal meeting of the Inhabitants of the Town of Marshfield on the Seventh Day of October AD 1776.——unanimously voted that the

Present Honorable House of Representatives, Together with the Honorable Council jointly acting with Equal voice, Consult, and agree upon a Constitution and form of Government for this State, and Send the Same to the Several Towns for the Inspection and Perusal of the Inhabitants, before the Ratification of the Same———

Attest Neh. Thomas Town Clerk

Marblehead (156/139)

At a meeting of the Male Inhabitants of this Town being free and Twenty One years and upwards, Legally Convoked the Twenty third Day of September 1776

Voted Azor Orne Esquire Moderator

Voted That the Present Honorable House of Representatives of this State of the Massachusetts Bay in New England together with The Honorable Council, if they consent in one Body with the House And by Equal Voyce Should Consult agree on, and Enact Such a Constitution and form of Government for this State, as the said House of Representatives and Council as aforesaid on the Fullest and most Mature Deliberation shall Judge will most conduce to the Safety peace and Happiness of this State in all after Successions and Generations; and if they would direct that the same be made public for the Inspection and perusal of the Inhabitants, before the Ratification thereof by the Assembly. And that this Town as soon as may be, after they shall have passed on the question aforesaid, cause their votes or Resolutions thereon to be Certified into the office of the Secretary of this State.

Voted. that an attested Copy of the Resolutions of this Town respecting forming a Constitution, be transmitted to the Secretarys office of this State.

Copy Attest Benja. Boden Town Clerk

Marblehead October 7. 1776

Wells (156/140)

At a Meeting of the Male Inhabitants of the Town of Wells being free and Twenty one years of Age or upwards Legally Warned and held at the Meeting House in the First Parish in Wells on Monday the 7th day of October 1776

John Wheelwright Esquire was Chosen Moderator
Then the Resolve passed by the House of Representatives of this State the 17th day of September 1776 Respecting the Settlement of a Constitution and Form of Government for the same was Read And after the said Resolve was fully Considered It was by said Inhabitants Voted that they Consent that the present House of Representatives of said State with the Council if they think proper Consult upon and draw up such a Constitution and Form of Government as shall on the fullest and most mature Deliberation by them be Judged will most Conduce to the Safety Peace and Happiness of said State and that the said Form of Government be made publick for the Inspection and Perusal of the Inhabitants thereof And if the said Constitution and Form of Government shall be approved of by the Inhabitants of this State then that the same be enacted and Ratified to Continue in all after Successions and Generations———
Voted that a True Copy of the Proceedings of the Town at this Meeting be Transmitted to the office of the Secretary of this State as soon as may be

The aforegoing is a true Copy of the Proceedings of the Town of Wells at their meeting Held in Compliance with the above Resolve of the State
Atts Nathaniel Wells Town Clerk
To the Honorable Sam Adams Esqr Secretary of this State at his Office at Watertown

Wrentham (156/141)
Wrentham October 7th, 1776

At a general town meeting. (Pursuant to a resolve of the General Court passed September 17th 1776) of the inhabitants of this town, being Duly warned Quallified and Assembled as the above said resolve directs, at the Publick meeting house in the first Precinct in this town———

After Considerable debate, it was proposed to the town, Whether they will give their Consent that the present house of Representatives of this State of Massachusets Bay, together with the Council, if they Consent in one Body with the house, and by Equal Voice Should Consult, agree on, and Enact, Such a Constitution and form of Government, for this State, as the said house of Representatives and Council as aforesaid, on the fullest and most mature Deliberation, Shall Judge will most Conduce to the Safty peace, and Happiness, of this State, in all after Successions and Generations; and that the same be made Publick for the Inspection and Perusal of the Inhabitants of this State, before the Ratification thereof by the Assembly——

Voted in the Affirmitive——

further Voted, that the town Clerk, Make out a true Copy of this vote, and send the same to the Secretarys Office of this State——

True Coppies
Attest. John Messinger Town Clerk

South Hadley (156/141)

To the Honorable Assembly of the State of the Massachusetts Bay in obediance to your Resolve have had a Town Meeting Octoer 7 and Put it to Vote Whather the Present Assembly with the Councel Should form a Sistam of Government for this State, Past in the Nagetive for these Resons viz our People being gon so many of them from us and the prsent distressing Situation of Affares think best to Neglect it for the prsent

South Hadley 28th 1776 by order of the Town
David Nash Town Clerk

Duxbury (156/142)

Att a Town meeting Legally convened at the meeting house in the town of Duxbury on monday the 7th of October 1776 The Question was proposed to the Town whether they would give their Consent that the present House of Representatives together with the Council of this State should consult and determine upon a form of Government for this State and publish the same before it be ratifyed and confirmed agreeable to a Resolve of the Great and General Court of the 17th of September 1776 and it passed in the Negative unanimously——

This was the vote at the Meeting Attest per John Wadsworth
Town Clerk

Bridgewater (156/143)

At a Town meeting Held in Bridgwater Pursuant to a Resolve of the General Court on monday the seventh Day of October 1776 and having Settled their meeting by the Choice of Danel. Johnson Esquire moderator and after Reading to the Inhabitants the Resolve of said Court the Town voted to Chuse a Committee of Five men to make a Draught of a vote to be laid before the Town for their acceptance and the Town made Choice of Benjamin Wellis Esquire John Fobes Captain David Kingman Doctor Phillip Bryant and Josiah Richards and the Draught of the Vote being Read to the assembly which was to see if the Town would agree that the present members of the Honourable Counsel of this State to gether with the House of Representatives of this State Should Joyntly by Equal voice and in one house Consult agree upon and adopt Such a Constitution and Form of Government for this State as shall be most Conducive to the Safty peace and Happiness of this State in all future Generations, and that the Same be offered to the Several Towns belonging to this State for their Consent and aprobation and that no Form of Government be Ratified and Confirmed till it has been consented to by the major part of the Inhabitants of the Several Towns in this State. and it was voted in the affirmative

The above is a True Coppie of the Vote of the Town of Bridgwater att the above meeting

Atts Nathaniel Brett Town Clerk

Cambridge (156/144)

At a legal meeting of the Male Inhabitants of the Town of Cambridge from Twenty one years Old and upwards, on the Seventh Day of October 1776 Voted That we the Inhabitants of the town of Cambridge do consent that the Honorable Council and House of Representatives of this State according to their wisdom jointly consult and agree upon such a Constitution of Government as they shall Judge most conducive to the Happiness of this State; and that the same be published and dispersed among the Towns, and opportunity given for the several towns to vote thereupon before the said Form and Constitution be enacted and established, And that no establishment be enacted without the Consent of the

Majority of the People, and that both branches of the General Assembly be united in one Body, when they shall enact such constitution as aforesaid.

A true Copy Attest Andrew Bordman Town Clerk

Hubbardston (156/145)

At a Town meeting in Hubbardston Leagally Assembled at the meeting house on Monday the Thirtyeth Day of September AD 1776 the Second Article was to See if the Inhabitants of this Town that are free and Twenty one years of age will give their Consent that the presant house of Representatives of this State of the Massachusetts bay in New England to gether with the Council; if they Consent in one body with the house and by Equal Voice Should Consult agree on and Enact Such a Constitution and form of Goverment for this State afore said on the fullest and most mature Deliberation Shall Judge will most Conduce to the Safty peace and happiness of this State in all after Successions and Generations and for the Inspections and perusal of the Inhabitants before the Ratification there of by the Assembly———

The Question being put to the Inhabitants of Hubbardston agreeable to the article above said, it Past.s in the Negetive———

Extracts from the minutes John Woods Town Clerk

Hubbardston October the 7th 1776

Bernardston (156/145)

At a Meeting of the Male Inhabitants of Bernardston from Twenty one years of Age and upwards holden on the 30th day of September Anno. Domini 1776———

After Chusing a Moderator the Question was put. "Whether they will give their consent that the Present house of Representitives of this State of the Massachusetts-Bay in New England together with the Councel, if they consent in one body with the house, and by equal voice, Should consult Agree on, and Enact Such a Constitution and form of Government for this State, as the said house of Representitives and Councel as aforesaid, on the fullest and most mature Deliberation Shall judge will most conduce to the Safety, peace, and happiness of this State, in all after

Successions and Generations, and if they will direct that the same be made Publick for the Inspection and Perusal of the Inhabitants, before the Ratification thereof by the Assembly" And it passed in the Affirmative by a great Majority———

A True Copy

Bernardston
October 7th 1776

Attest John Burke
Town Clerk

Norton (156/146)

At a Legal meeting of the freeholders and other Inhabitants of the Town of Norton Legally Warned and Assembled on monday the Seventh Day of October 1776 and continued by adjournments to Tusday the Twenty Second Day of this Instant October Taking under Consideration a Late Resolve of the present Honorable House of Representatives of this State Respecting their Consent that said House with the Honorable Council Should agree on and Enact a form of Government for Said State passed the following Resolves viz———

1tly That the Establishing a good form of Goverment is absolutly necessary in order to lay a foundation for the future Safety happiness and Wellfare of a people———

2dly That as the End of goverment is the good of the people So the power and right of forming and Establishing a plan there of is Essentially in them———

3dly That as this State is at present with out a form of Goverment it is highly necessary that one Should Soon be formed———

4thly That we cannot give our consent to the proposals of the said Honorable House in their Resolve of the Seventeenth of September Last the present Honorable House with the Honorable Council Should Enact a form of goverment for this State for these Reasons viz—1st that the present House and Council was not Seperately Elected by the people for that Special purpose which we think it highly Resonable they Should be in a matter of Such Importance———2dly The Requision of the Honorable House being So pregnant with power we cannot think it will be conducive to the future good of this people to comply with their proposal———

5thly That we Humbly conceive that if the present General Assembly in a Convenient time Should be Disolved and a State Convention Called and Convened for this Important purpose it might Conduce much to the peace and quiet of the people of this State and we hope would be a Salutary measure to obtain the End proposed———

6thly That we think it would be verry Conducive to said End with Regard to a form of Goverment if Each County Should meet by their Delegates and Consult with Regard to What form of goverment they may think it would be best for this State to come into and when they have so Done to lay the Result of their Several meetings before the proposed General Convention that they may the better Collect the minds of the people and Select from the Whole Such a form of Goverment as Shall by them be thought most likely to terminate in the Safety peace and happiness of the people———

7thly That it appears to us absolutely necessary for the Liberty and Safety of this State that the plan of Goverment when formed should be published for the perusal of the people and not Established without their approbation———

8thly That a Coppey of these Resolves be Sent to the Secretarys office of Said State attested by the Clerk of said Town———

A True Coppey
Witnes.................................... John King Town Clerk

Middleborough (156/147–148)

Middleborough, October 7th 1776

At a leagal Meeting of this Town to Declare our Minds on a Resolve Passed in the house of Representives September 17 last and give Instructions to our Reprsentve if we See Cause Relitiv to State affairs we Say as follows

1st Consedering that the mode of Goverment already adopted may answer the Exigences of this State for the time being Considering also the Publick troubles and Distresses we are under (which must be a great Impediment to Such a calm Deliberat and Extensive Attention as is Neefull in order to place a new form of Lasting Goverment) we humbly move whether it is not best to post Pone this weighty affair to sume after Date of Time.

2dly We highly approve the Conduct of the Honorable House in Making Application to the Pople of this State for their opinions on this weighty Matter and Should have been Glad to hear that the Honorable Council had been invited and joined in the Motion:

3dly as to the leading Question in the Resolve we Say: if The Major

Part of the People of this State are for Planing a form of Goverment forthwith. we readely fall in: and furthermore we have no objection to the Presant Honorable Council and Honorable House Consulting and agreeing a mong themselves upon Such a Constituion and form of Goverment as they judge most conducive to the Safty Peace and Happiness of this State this however we Should not Consent to were it not for the Liberty we have to Peruse the plan before it is Enacted or Established as a Code of Law for the State Because till we See it we Shall not know but the Plan may be Very offincive So offincive as to be capable of admitting the Same Person To a Place in the Legislative judiciary and Executive Department Which we Shall oppose to the utermost of our Capacity as well as Som other Usages that have been Practiced for a greate many years But tho we readley Submit to the major Voice of the people yet we Think it would be rather Preferable to Select a Body of men Som from Each Countey Whose Sole Business it Should be to Strike out or Plan a New Constution subject to the Correction the approbation or Disapprobation both of the Court and People.

We are Deeply Sensable we cannot Do Well Without Good Goverment and inf the presant Council and house Proceed forthwith in the Business (as it is a most weighty affair and will requier Great Wisdom attention and application) we hope and pray thay will be Assisted by the alwise Ruler of the World and directed to Such an equal Good and Rightas Plan of Goverment as Shall be most for the Safty and happiness of the State Now and through all Succeeding Generations.

The following Instructons we give to our Representive Deacon Benjamin Thomas.

Sir. We Direct you to let it be known in Court as our oppinion That the legisative body of this State ought to consist of three Branches: a *President* a *Council* and house of Representives the President to Stand not Exceding one year and to be clothed with Such authority as best tends to the Dispatch of Public Business and the Good of the State in Generial.

The *Councial* to consist 30: or 33 Members and Stand one year Two of the Members Shall be Chosen out of Each County and by the Inhabitents of Said County (Except two of the Counteys that are Small[est?] and few in its Numbers and Estate thay Shall Chuse Each of them one.) the Remaning Number Shall be Chose by the Representives When met.

The House of *Represtentves* Shall be Chose yearley by the Joint Voice of the pople and let purticualer Care be taken for an equal Representation thro the State that Such towns or Districts as are Small may have the Liberty of Joining with a Neighbouring Soicitey in the above Said Choice

Furthermore we Derict you Strenuasly to insist that no one Person (a common justice of Peace Exceped) Shall be Capable of holding the Place or office of Leagislator and Judge at the Same Time and as is altogeather Unreasonable for any Select Body of Men in a Community to have the Exclusive Power of Voting their own Salary or Voting money from the Comunity into their own Pockets we think Proper that a Committee Composed of one Member from Each Countey Said Members to be Chose by its respective Countey fix the Rewards of all Sallires and Donations We Direct you Sir to make and Endever to Support this as well as the other articals also that you make a motion to have the Courts of Justices Restrained for a Short time from acting on any Case Exepting Crimonal ones as it will tend to quiet and Lengthn out the Peace and harmony of the Pople which at the Presant Day is of the Gratest Consequence

for the Rest we only advise you to join with the honorable House in all those Measuers which tend to the Safty and welfar of the Publick———

Abner Borrows Town Clerk

Copey attest
Middleborough October 7th 1776

Pembroke (156/149)

At a Town Meeting held at Pembroke on the Eighth Day of October A D 1776

At Said Meeting the Question was Put to Know the Towns mind whether they would Consent that the Present House of Representatives Joyned With the Councel if they Consent in one Body With the House and By Equal voice Should Consult agree on and Enact Such a Constitution and form of Govermen for this State as the House of Representatives and Councel as aforesaid on the fullest Deliberation Shall Judge will most Conduce to the Safty Peace and Happiness of this State in after Successions and Generations) and it is Desired That Twenty one of the

Same May be Sent to the Committe of Corrispondance for the Perusal of the Town of Pembroke Before the Same be Ratifyed On the Conditions afore Said it Passed in the Afformative unanomusly——

A True Copey Attest Jno. Turner Town Clerk

Lynn (156/150)

At a Town meeting Legualy assembled This Eight Day of October 1776——

Voted that the Present House of Representative of this State of the Massachusetts Bay, to Gether with the Council, if they Consent in one Body with the Hous, and By Equal Voice, may Consult agree on, and Enact, Such a Constitution and form of Goverment for this State, as they Shall Judge will most Conduce to the Safety, Peas, and Happiness, thereof, in all after Generations, in Case that the Same Shall be Published and Laid befoure the Several Towns of this State for their approbation befour the Ratification by the assembly——

Lynn October 30 1776

a Trew Coppy attest
Benja. Newhall Town Clerk

To the Secretary of the State
of the Massachusetts Bay

Newburyport (156/150)

Newbury Port, October 8th, 1776

In Town Meeting voted that the Delegates of this Town be directed to use their utmost Influences that the Honorable Council and House of Representatives, in their respective Capacities, (and not in one Body, and by equal Voice,) should "consult, agree on, and enact such a Constitition and Form of Government for this State, as They shall, on the fullest and most mature Deliberation, judge, will most conduce to the Safety, Peace and Happiness of the Same, in all after Successions and Generations, and that it be made public, before the Enacting, for the Perusal" and Approbation of the People——

A true Copy attest Nicolas Pike Town Clerk

Sunderland (156/151)

Sunderland 8th October A.D. 1776

At a Meeting of the Male Inhabitents of said Town of Sunderland, being free and of the Age of twenty one years, pursuent to the recomendation of the House of Representatives, September 17th, 1776 for the purposes contained in said recomendation.

The Question being put (viz) whether the Members of this Meeting will give their consent that the house of Representatives of the State of Massachusetts Bay in New England, together with the the Councel, if they consent in one body and by Eaqual Voice Enact Such a form of Government for this State, as the said house of Representatives, together with the Council afore said, shall judge will most conduce to the Safety, Peace and Happiness of this State, in all after Successions and Generations, with this restriction (viz) that before the ratification theirof they, the Inhabitents of this Town Shall have the perusal theirof, reserving to themselves this liberty to Disscent theifrom if the plan proposed should be thought not Safe; Resolved in the Affirmative.

further resolved in said meeting that the above resolution be Certified into the office of the Secretary of this State.

Attest Simon Cooley Town Clerk

Medford (156/152)

At a Town Meeting Legally Conveened in Medford, on the Eight October 1776

Benjamin Hall Esquire Chosen Moderator

Voted That this Town upon a due Consideration of the Resolve in the House of Representatives of the 17th of September, 1776, Relative to the Settlement of a Form of Government; Consent That this present House of Representatives together with the Councill, should Consult, Agree, upon a Constitution and Form of Government for the Future; But not Enact the Same, until it is Throughly Revised and Examined by the Said Town, and a Report made accordingly———

A Copy Attest—
Richard Hall Town Clerk

Belchertown (156/153)

To the Honorable Assembly of the State of Massachusetts In obedience to a Resolve of the House of Representatives of said State of the 7th of September 1776 At meeting of the Inhabitants of Belcherstown on Tuesday the 8th of October Instant it was Considered whether we thought it Expedient to Give our Consent that the Present Assembly of this State should now form a Constitution for the State those who wear assembled in said Meeting wear unanamously of oppinion that it was not best to which opinion we wear Led by Sundry Considerations Espeacially because it is an affair of Great Importance and wants perhaps more time for Deliberation than the present Exigences of the State will allow.

Further more Great Numbers of the Inhabitants of this Town being absent in the War we thought it not adviseable to Consent to the Seting up of a Constitution at present as we Could not have their minds Concerning the Matter and we Judge it to be So in most other Towns So that their Can not be a proper Consent of the people of this State by the voice of those who Can now assemble in Town meeting.

We mean not to object to the haveing a Constitution, but wish and hope for a wise one in Due time, but we think it Concerns the youngerly men Especially who are in the war to have a voice in the affair which Can not now be had Voted unanemously

A True Coppy of the Vote Attes Nathaniel Dwight
Cler of Belcherstown

And it was then put to vote whether the Town would Chews a Member To Represent the said Town in the General Assembly aforsaid and it passed in the affirmative.

And a vote was Called and they Did then Elect and Depute Mr. Daniel Smith a Free holder of Belcherstown to Serve for and Represent them in the Sessions of the Great and General Court———

Dated at Belcherstown October 8th 1776

Nathaniel Dwight Select men
Caleb Clark of
Benjamin Morgan Belcherstown

The Person Chosen as AboveSaid
Notified thereof and Summoned
to attend accordingly
by me James Smith Conl

Gageborough (156/154)

Gageborough Oct. the 9th 1776
Sir
These are to Certify that at a Meeting of the Inhabitants of the Town of Gageborough the Seventh Instant pursuent to a Resolution of the House of Representatives of the Massachusetts Bay September the 17th 1776 Recommending to the male Inhabitants of each Town in this State in public Town meeting to consider and determine whether they will give their consent that the present House of Representatives of this State of the Massachusetts Bay in New-England together with the Council if they Consent in one Body with the House and by equal Voice should consult agree on and enact Such a Constitution and form of Government for this State as the Said House of Representatives and Council as aforesaid shall Judge will most conduce to the Safty peace and Hapiness of this State etc. Mr. Elisha Brown Moderator. Upon motion made the Question was put and past in the affirmative provided that the Same be made public for the Inspection and perusal of the Inhabitants of the State before the Ratification thereof by the Assembly Voted that the above vote be Certified into the Secrataries office by the Town Clerk.

Elisha Brown Moderator
A True Copy Atts. Joseph Hascall Town Clerk

Hingham (156/155)

At a Meeting of the Town of Hingham in pursuance of and agreeable to a Recommendation of the House of Representatives of this State of the 17 of September last Holden at Hingham aforesaid this 9 Day of October, 1776———Rosolved That the Town of Hingham give their con- that the present House of Representatives of this State of Massachusetts-Bay in New England, together with the Council, if they consent in one Body with the House, and by equal voice, should consult, and agree on, such a Constitution and Form of Government for this State, on the Said House of Representatives and Council aforesaid, on the fullest and most mature Deliberation shall judge should most conduce to the Safety, piece and Happyness of this State, in all after Successions and Generations———

And That whereas we consider it as a matter of the last importance to this People, and that their Piece, Happyness, and safety, depends on the Constitution's being *Duely Guarded on every Side;* and that the wisdom of the whole may be necessary thereto therefore Resolved 2dly That they as a part of the Body politick Direct that the Form of Government be made public for the inspecion, perusal and *animadversion* of the Inhabitants before the Ratification thereof by the General Assembly

The above passed Nem: Con:

Then Resolved that the Clerk Certify and forward the above votes to the Office of the Secratary of this State.

Extract from the Minutes
S. Norton Clerk p T.

Barnstable (156/156)

At a Town meeting legally warned and held at Barnstable on the 9th day of October AD 1776

The Honorable Daniel Davis Esquire was Chosen Moderator. Voted that this Town do consent that the present House of Representatives of this State of the Massachusetts Bay in New England together with the Council if they consent in one body with the House and by equal voice should consult agree on and enact Such a Constitution and form of goverment for this State as the said House of Representatives and Council as aforesaid on the fullest and most mature deliberation shall Judge will most Conduce to the Safety peace and hapyness of this State in all after Successions and generations and that they do direct that the same be made publick for the inspection and perusal of the inhabitants before the ratification thereof by the Assembly in order that this town may approve or disapprove of the same. Voted that the foregoing vote and resolution be Certified into the office of the Secretary of this State and that the Town Clerk be directed to authenticate a fair attested Copy thereof and forward the same to the Secretary as soon as may be.

A true Copy attest Josiah Crocker, Town Clerk

Williamstown (156/157)

Persuant to the within Handbil the Inhabitants of Williamstown Legally met in Town-meeting the 9th Day of October 1776 and after

Choosing a Moderrator for said Meeting pased the following Resolve and unanimously voted (Viz) that we give our consent that the Presant House of Representatives together with the Councel in one Body and by equal voice form a Constitution for this State and that the Same be made Public for the Inspection and perusal of the Inhabitents of this Town before the Ratification thereof by the Assembly.

Nehemiah Woodcock Moderator
Daniel Horsford Clerk Per. Tem

In the fore mentioned Meting warse thought advisable that we have a member in the House in forming Said Constitution as [its?] being the Foundation of our future Peace and Happeness and as the one Chose for the Presant year is now Ingaged in the Army of the United States Mr. Nehemiah Woodcock is Chose to Represent Said Town in General Court in his absence. And as the first Representative for Said Town is one of the Selectmen and Mr. Woodcock another Consequently there is but one Selectman to Certify

Robart Hawkins Select man
Daniel Horsford Clerk Per. Tem

Monson (156/158)

Agreable to a resole of the Late House the Inhabitans of Monson Being Leagely wornd mat on Wednesday the 9th Day of October instent and Voted that the Preasent house togeather with Honorable Councel Draw up such a form of Gourvenment as thay shall think proper and sand out for the perusel of the peopel

Monson October the 10 1776 Attest Abijah Newell By Order of the Select men

Granby (156/158)

In Pursuence to a late order of Court.———Att a Regular meeting of the Inhabitants of the Town of Granby on Wednesday the Ninth Day of October 1776. After Chuseing a Moderator, Voted that this Town do Give their Consent, that the Present House of Representitives of this

State, Together with the Counsel, make or Enact a Constitution and form of Goverment, for this State——

2d: Voted that this Town do Direct that Said Constitution or Proposed form of Goverment, be made Public, for their Inspection and Perusal, before the Ratification thereof.——

A True Copey Attest.——
Nathan Smith Town Clerk——

Dated att Granby October 12th 1776.

Bedford (156/159)

At a General Town meeting Legally Assembled at Bedford on the tenth Day of October AD 1776——

Then, Considered and Acted Uppon a Resolve of the Representatives Passed on September the 17th 1776 of this State of the Massachusetts Bay in New England, Viz, Whether they will Give their Consent That the present Representatives together with the Council, if They Consent in one body with the house and by Equal Voice Should Consent, agree on, and Enact Such a Constitution and Form of Goverment For this State, as the said house of Representatives and Council as aforesaid, on the Fullest and most matuer Deliberation Shall Judge will most Conduse to the Safety, peace and happiness of this State, in all after Successions and Generations——

Voted in the afirmative that they should procead agreable to The Resolve, with Giving this Town a Coppay of their——Procedings For the inspection and perusal, of, the inhabitants Before the Ratification there of by the assembly——

A true Coppay of the Vote
Attest John Webber Town Clerk

Southampton (156/159)

Mr. Secretary, Sir——att a meeting of the Inhabitants of Southampton on thirsday the tenth Day of October——1776——Voted to Give thire Consent that the present house of Representatives of this State of the Massachusetts Bay in New-England together with the Counsel, Should form a Constitution for this State agreable to there resolves——A true Coppy Drawn per——Ebenezer Kingsley Town Clerk of Southampton

Arundel (156/160)

At a Lawfull Town Meeting Held at Arundel the 11th of October 1776 the inhabitants of Said Town voted that the Presant House of Representatives of this State Together with the Council Shall Exhibate Such a Constitution and form of goverment for this State as the Said House of Representetives and Council Shall Judge will most Conduce to the Safety, Peace and Happiness of this State and that the Same Shall be Published for the Inspection and General Consent of the People Previous to its Ratification

the above is a True Coppy from Arundel Town Book as it wase voted at Said meeting attest

Per. Benja. Downing Town Clerk

Boston (156/160–161)

At a Meeting of the Inhabitants of the Town of Boston at the Old Brick Meeting House October 11, 1776 9.O'Clock A:M: and continued by Adjournment to the 16th. of said Month, in consequence of, and agreable to, a Resolve of the Honorable House of Representatives of this State, passed the 17th. of September last———

Benjamin Kent Esquire Moderator———

The Resolve of the Honorable House of Representatives of this State passed the 17th of September last, was read, and considered, and the Question being put—Viz—"Whether this Meeting, will give their consent, that the present House of Representatives of this State of Massachusetts Bay in New England, together with the Council if they consent in one Body with the House, and by equal Voice Should consult agree on, and enact Such a Constitution and form of Government for this State, as the said House of Representatives and Council as aforesaid, on the fullest and most mature deliberation shall Judge will be most conducive to the Safety Peace and Happiness of this State, in all after Successions and Generations; and if they would direct that the same be made public for the Inspection and perusal of the Inhabitants, before the Ratification thereof by the Assembly"———Passed in the Negative unanimously——— Voted, that the follow Reasons be given, why this Meeting have declined empowering the House and Council in one Body, to form and enact a Constitution of Government to be laid before the People for their perusal and inspection——Viz——1st To form Government and establish a Constitution for the present and Succeeding Generations, is a task or consideration the most important—it extends as well to our Religeous as Civil Interests, and includes our all—it effects every Individual, every Individual therefore ought to be consulting, aiding and assisting———

2d. A Subject of such general and indeed infinite concernment, ought to be proceeded in with the greatest caution, and maturest deliberation—the means or channels of information should all lay open to the People, and not restricted or confined to any particular Assembly however respectable——

3d Precipitancy is to be guarded against, time and opportunity should be taken by the People, whose Right it is to form Government; to collect the wisest Sentiments on this Subject, not of the present House only, but also of the Council and every other Society or Member of the State, that would favor the Public with their Sentiments, in order that they may possess themselves of such Principles, and wise Maxims, founded on the best Precidents, and thereby be enabled to form a Judicious and happy Constitution of Government.

Att. William Cooper Town Clerk

[Boston Town Records, October 11, 1776, in *Report of the Record Commissioners of the City of Boston, Containing the Boston Town Records, 1770 through 1777* (Boston, 1887), 247–248.]

3 o'Clock P.M. met according to Adjournment.——

The Committee appointed to draw up and state the Reasons, which operated to the Town's Voting in the Negative——when the Question was put, relative to impowering the House and Council in One Body to form a Constitution of Government to be laid before the People for their Perusal and Inspection——Reported as follows, Vizt.

1t. We apprehend the People have some higher Privileges, than A bare Inspection and Perusal of the Constitution under which they are to live.

2d. The present General Court were not chosen for the Purpose of forming a Government, which, of Right, originates with the People.

The above Report having been read——after long Debate, it was Voted, that the farther Consideration thereof be referred to the Adjournment.

Voted, that this Meeting be adjourned to Wednesday the 16th. instant, 10 o'Clock A. M.——

Dedham (156/162)

At a Meeting of the Freeholders and other Inhabitants of the Town of Dedham regularly Assembled at the Meeting House in the First Precinct in Said Town——on Monday the 14th Day of October A.D. 1776.

Voted——That the House of Representatives of the State of the Massachusetts Bay—with the Council, agreeable to a Resolution passed in said House September 17th 1776.——Consult and agree upon a Constitution and form of Goverment for Said State, (as Soon as Conveaniently may be) and Send the same to the Several Towns in said State—for the Inspection and Perusal of the Inhabitants, before the same be Enacted.

A true Copy.

Attest.

Isaac Whiting Town Clerk

Billerica (156/162)

Billerica, October 14, 1776. The Town of Billerica being assembled this day, on adjournment of a legall meeting, warned, in Complyance with a Recommendation from the house of Representatives, in order for the freemen of Said town to express their minds, Relative to the erecting Some form of Government in this State, after Deliberately Discusing the matter, came into the following votes,——

First That the Tyranny of Great Britain, (which has Compelled the United provinces of America to Dissolve their, Connection with her) having Broken up the Constitution of this Province, it has now become necessary, for the prevention of anarchy, for the preservation of internal peace and good order, and for the Mutual Security of the Inhabitants in the enjoyment of their property and just rights, that some form of Government be Speedily erected: and therefore

2ly That it be Submitted to the present house of Representatives in Conjunction with the Council, to Draw up Such a plan of Government, as they, in their wisdom, Shall Judge best adopted to promote the lasting welfare and happiness of this State, Depending on it, that before Such plan of Government be Ratified and established, by an Act of the Court, it be made publick for the inspection of the people, that they also may have an opportunity to Judge of it, and to propose such alterations as they may think best to be made, if it shall appear in any respects Disagreable to them.

Billerica October 21:1776 William Stickney Esqr Moderator
Copy Examined Joshua Abbot Town Clerk

Berwick (156/163)

At a General Meeting of the Burghers, Free-men and Inhabitants of the Town of Berwick, in the County of York, within the State of the Massachusetts-Bay, on the 14th day of October 1776. Due Warning being given for the same.———

Agreeable to a Resolve of The Honorable, The House of Representatives, for the said State, of the 17th day of September last, to know the minds of the Good People in each Town within this State, Whether the present House of Representatives, Together with the Council of this state (if they Consent to Join) shall prepare a Constitution and Form of Government for this state.———

After due deliberation thereupon, We the Inhabitants aforesaid, do Consent and agree, Nemine Contradicente, That a Constitution and Form of Government be so far prepared, as that the same may be made Publick, for the Revisal and approbation of this and all other Towns within this state, before the same be Enacted and passed into a Constitutional Law.———

We Cannot, nor indeed are we able, at this Critical Juncture, to dictate or prescribe any Plan of Government for a free and Independant State; Solely Relying on you the Grand Council of this once happy Colony, now duly Assembled as Representatives of the Good people; But would most Respectfully desire, that whatever Form of Government, may by you be Framed; may be the most Easy and plain to be understood by People of all denominations, whereby a Line may be drawn, that the Rulers and the Ruled may know their duty; and that Tyranny on the one hand, and Anarchy on the other, may be avoided as much as possible.———

A True Copy from the Minutes
Attst Nahum Marshall Town Clerk

Chelmsford (156/164)

Chelmsford Octob 14 1776

This Town having been legally warned, mett together in the meeting house, Agreeable to the recommendation of the present House of Representatives of the State of Massachusett Bay, in New England——and Having chosen Oliver Barron Esquire Moderator—Proceeded to the consideration of the subject matter of said recommendation, and came into the following Votes

First. That we give our consent, that the present house of Representatives, together with the Council of said State, in one body with the House, and by equal voice, should consult, agree on, and enact such a Constitution and form of Government for this State, as the said House of Representatives, and Council Aforesaid, on the fullest, and most mature deliberation, shall Judge will most conduce to the Safety, peace and happiness, of this State, in all After successions and generations——

Secondly, Voted, That the constitution of Government for this State, agreed upon by said House and said Council be made publick, for the inspection, and perusal of the inhabitants of said State, before it be ratified, by said House and Council

Thirdly Voted. That When we have had opportunity, to have considered, and to have expressed our sentiments, by vote on said Constitution of Government so agreed on, we will cause our votes on Resolutions, respecting the same, to be certified into the Office of the Secretary of this State.——

A True Copy of Record Attest David Spaulding Town Clerk

Halifax (156/165)

At a Town meeting in Hallifax October 14th 1776

1st Voted that the present house of Representitives of this State of the Masachusets-Bay in New-England togather with the Council, if they Conscent in one Body with the house and by Equal voice, Should Conscent agree on and Enact Such a Constitution and form of Government for this State, as the Said house of Representitives and Council as afor Said on the fullest and most mature Deliberation Shall Judge will be most Conducive, to the Safety peace and happiness of this State in all after Successions and Generations, and that they make the Same Publick for the Inspection and Perusal of the Inhabitance befor the Ratification by the Assembly

2nd Voted to Send no Representitive to the General Assembly

A True Coppy from the Record
per Moses Inglee Town Clerk

Brimfield (156/166)

At a Meeting of the Male Inhabitants of the Town of Brimfield, being Free, and Twenty One Years of Age or upwards, held at the Meeting House in Said Brimfield on Monday the Fourteenth Day of October 1776——

Voted, That the said Inhabitants of Brimfield, Consent that the present House of Representatives of this State of Massachusetts Bay, together with the Council, should if they think proper, consult and agree on such a Constitution and Form of Government for this State as they Shall judge will most conduce to the Safety, Peace and Happiness of the State, and make the same Publick for the Consideration and Approbation of the Inhabitants of the State before the Enacting and Ratifying thereof by the Assembly——

Copy from the Record——
Att. Ja Bridgham Town Clerk

Wareham (156/167)

At a Town Meeting in Wareham October 14th 1776 To Consider of the within Request of the Honorable General Assembly——Resolved as follows——

1 That we Judge it best; that the Plan of Government by late Charter (viz) by the House of Representatives and Council be Still Continued and Strictly adheared to and that no Alteration be made therein Respecting a form of Government at least During the present war——

2dly that Should the Major Part of the Towns in this State Vote for A New form of goverment to be Erected we desire that no form of goverment be Erected on any account untill the Plan of goverment Be Made Publick and that the Inhabitants May have the Perusall Thereof and to

give their approbation before any ratifycation of the same be Made———
A True Copy Attest Andrew Mackie Town Clerk

Dracut (156/168)

At a Meeting of the Inhabitants of the Town of Dracutt on Monday the 14 Day of October 1776 Agreable to a Resolve of the Great and General Court of the State of the Massachusetts Bay Recommending A meeting of the Inhabitants of Said Town to See if they will Consider and Determin Whether they will Give their Consent that the Present House of Representatives of this State Together with the Council if they Consent in One Body with the House and by Equal Voice Should Consult Agree: on and enact Such a Constitution and Form of Government for this State as the Said House of Representatives and Council aforesaid on the Fullest and Most Mature Deliberation Shall Judge will most Conduce to the Safty Peace and Happiness of this State in all after Successions and Generations—and if they would Direct that the Same be made Publick for the Inspection and Perusal of the Inhabitants Before the Ratification thereof by the Assembly———

1st Made Choice of John Varnum Esquire Moderator of Said Meeting

2 Voted that the Presant House of Representatives together with the Honourable Council of this State Draw up Such a Constitution or Form of Government as they in their Wisdom Shall think will be for the peace and Happiness of this State and that the Same be Made Publick Before the Ratification thereof by the Assembly for the Inspection and Perusal of the People only always Reserving that Such Form of Government may be Subject to Such Alteration as this State hereafter may find to be of Necessaty and Conveniency for Said State

John Varnum Moderator of Said Meeting

A True Copy as of Record———

William Hildreth Town Clerk

Taunton (156/169)

At a meeting of the Inhabitants of the Town of Taunton that ware free men and twenty one years of age and upward held at Said Taunton on the 30th Day of September AD. 1776, warned according to Law by Reasonable previous notice thefor given. and then made Choise of Benjamin Williams moderator to Govern Said meeting

N.B Town Clerk absent Attest Richard Godfrey Selectmen
Simeon Williams of
Ichabod Leonard Taunton

and then the said Town at the above said meeting voted to adjourn the same to the Seventh Day of October next at four of the Clock after noon at a meeting of the Inhabitants of Said Town held at Said Taunton on the Seventh Day of October Ad. 1776 by an adjournment from the 30th. Day of September Last and then mett and Voted to adjourn said meeting to Monday the 14th Day of October Currant at four of the Cloik after noon———at a meeting of the abovesaid Inhabitants of Said Town held at Said Taunton by several adjournments from the thirtyeth Day of September Last to Monday the fourteenth Day of October AD. 1776 and then mett and voted as followeth To wit voted on the second article in the warrant for Calling said meeting namly voted that the present House of Representatives of this State Together with the Councel if they Consent in one Body with the House and by Equal Voice make a Draught of What Form of Constitution and Plan of Government is most beneficial for the peace and hapiness of this People; and then Send the Same to Each Town in this State to be Considered on and not To be Confirmed by said Court untill it has been approved of by the major part of the Towns in Said State by meetings Called for that purpose

A Copy Transcribed from the minutes of said Vote attest

Benjamin Williams moderator of said meeting

N.B Town Clerk absent

Holliston (156/170)

To the Secretary of the State of the Massachusetts Bay In Observance of a Resolve of the House of Representatives of this State September 17th 1776 the Town of Holliston Legally Assembled the 7th Day of this Instant and passed the following Votes on the Question in said Resolve viz:

1st That the said House together with the Council in one body Consult agree on and Enact a form of Goverment for this State

2ly That the said form be made Public for the Inspection and Perusal of the Inhabitants before the Ratifiction thereof by the Assembly

Holliston October the 14th 1776

A True Coppy from the minutes
Attest Aaron Phipps Town Clerk

Norwich (156/170)

To the Great and General Court Now Siting at Wortertown Greetings We the inhabitants of Norwich in the County of Hampshier upon a Town Meeting Leagely Worned to Consider of a Resolve of Court of the Seventeenth of September, Resolved that the present house of Representativs With the Counsil Afix a form of Goverment for this State of the Massachusets Bay and Send it out for the inspection of the People——
Also Maid Choice of Lew David Scott to Represent us in the Greate and General Court Now Seting at Wortertown——

Norwich Otob 14 1776.

Jona Ware
Wm Carter
Select Men of Norwich

Attleborough (156/171)

At a Town meeting legally assembled at Attleborough, October the 14th 1776. In consequence of a Resolve of September 17th 1776 passed by the Honorable House of Representatives for the State of Massachusetts-Bay, The following Resolves were passed——

1st Resolved that good Government is the Basis of Liberty, and absolutely necessary for the Safty and Welfare of a People——

2dly Resolved that as the End of Government is the Happiness of the People; so the Sole Power and right of forming a Plan thereof is essentially in the People——

3dly Resolved, that as this State is at present destitute of a fixed and established form of Government, it is epedient and necessary that one be formed and established as soon as conveniently may be; agreeable to the Recommendation of the Continental Congress——

4thly Resolved, that wheres the present honorable House of Representatives have passed a Resolve of September 17th 1776, referring to the Consideration and Determination of the male Inhabitants etc. of this State; whether they will impower the said Honorable House with the Council etc.; to agree on, and enact a Constitution and Form of Government for this State, we can by no means consent to give them such a Power, for two Reasons especially (viz) because we apprehend the present honorable House is not a fair Representation of the Inhabitants of this State,—many Towns (not having this important matter in view) having chosen and sent fewer than their just Proportion of Members to that Honorable Boddy.——and also because the right of the Inhabitants of the Said State by their Votes in Town-meeting to negative the Said form, or any Article in it when drawn is not expressly acknowledged in the Said Resolve. For——5thly it is resolved that it appears absolutely necessary for the Safty and Liberty of this State, that the Plan of Government when formed and published should be thoroughly examined and actually approved and consented unto by the good People of this State and convenient time for that Purpose be allowed before the establishment thereof—the establishment itself to be by a State Convention by them appointed for that purpose

6thly Resolved that the honorable House be requested, to call upon the Several Towns in this State to chose one, or more Members for the purpose of draughting and publishing a Form of Government for this State, to be approved by the Several Towns,—in order to which Draught we would humbly purpose the following method (viz) that the Members so chosen for the several Towns in each County, meet together in County Conventions and therein draught Said Forms—, which done, that they by themselves, or their Committee meet in a State Convention or Congress and compare their Several Forms together, whereby the Wisdon of the whole State may be collected and a Form extracted, to be published for the Inspection and approbation of the Several Towns, also that the time for the meeting of the Said County and State Conventions for carrying into execution the Said Process, be appointed by the Court; and finally, that after the Said Form shall have been published, examined and consented to by the Several Towns in this State, or the major part of them,—the Said State Convention to be impowered by their Constituents to establish the Same.

Dated at Attleborough
October the 28.1776—

test Jonathan Stanley Town Clerk

Stoughtonham (156/172)

At a Town Meeting Legaly Held, in the Town of Stoughtonham by adjournment from October the 14th 1776 To this 30th Day of October 1776 Mr. Daniel Richards Moderator———
Voted, that it appears Absolutely Necessary and Rational, for the Liberties and Safety of this State, that Constitutional Government Be Formed and Established And this Town, do Consent that the General Court for the Time being, do form Such plans of Government, as Shall be for the Good of the Community, Provided, Such Plans of Government So formed be Published and Laid Before the People for their Deliberate Consideration and Consent, as the Establishing Such Plan, is Essentially in the People Agreable to the Resolutions of the Grand Continential Congress———

A True Copy

Attest Benja. Hewins Town Clerk

Sudbury (156/172)

At a Town meeting in Sudbury Legally warned October 14th 1776 The Town being Met to Consider and determin Whether the Town would Desier the present General Court of this State to Consult and Agree on a form of Government for this State According to the Resolve of the House of Representatives on the 17th of September 1776, the Vote being put up it passed in the Negative

A true Copy from the Minutes

Attest James Thompson Town Clerk

Walpole (156/173)

Walpole October the 14:1776 Then Assembled the Inhabitants of this Town and Voted that the present House of Representitives of this State together with the Council if they consent in one Body with the House and by equal Voice should Consult and agree on such a Constitution and form of Government for this State as the said House of Representitives and Council as aforesaid, on the fullest and most mature deliberation shall Judge will most conduce to the Safty Peace and Happiness of this State Provided they will direct that the same be made Publick for the Inspection and Perusal of said Town before the Ratification thereof by said Assembly.———

A True copy from the Minutes
Attest Benj. Kingsbury junior Town Clerk

Plympton (156/173)

At a Town Meeting held at Plimton on Octob 14 1776 Lieutenant Zabede Chandler was Chose Moderator
Said Town Taking under Consideration What was Recomended to the Saveral Towns in this Provence Respacting the General Assemblys Laying a plan or form of Goverment for This State upon which the folowing Vot Passt
Voted that it is the opinion of This Town that the mathod Recomended by the General assembly of This State With Regard to Thear Enacting Such a Consetution or form of Goverment as is There in Sot forth Will Promot the Intrest and hapyness of This State

A True Copy per me Josiah Perkins Town Clerk
Plimton, October 15 1776

Haverhill (156/174)

Att a Town Meeting legally warned—and held in Haverhill on Monday 14 instant October 1776———Whereof Jonathan Webster Esquire was Moderator———
Voted and passed in the Affirmative That the present Honorable House of Representatives of the State of the Massachusets Bay New England, Together with the Honorable Counsel (if They consent in One Body with the House, and by equal Voice) Should Consult, agree on, and enact Such a Constitution and Form of Government for this State, as the Said House of Representatives and Counsel as aforsaid, on the fullest, and most mature Deliberation Shall Judge will most Conduce to the Safety, Peace and Happiness of this State, in all after Successions and Generations.———

Also Voted that the Town will direct that the same be made Publick for the Inspection, and Perusal of the Inhabitants before the Ratification thereof by the Assembly——

A true Copy of Record——

Exd. Att. John Whittier Town Clerk

Haverhill October 15th 1776

Barnstable (156/175)

At a Town meeting hild in Falmouth Barnstable County October the 15 1776 Nathanael Shiverick Esquire Moderator etc.——Voted that we give our Consent that the presant House of Representitives of this State of the Massucttes Bay in New England together with the Council if they consent with one bodey with the House and by Equil voyce Should Consult agree on and enact Sutch a Constitution and Forme of government for this State as the Said House of Representatives and Counceil as aforesaid on the fullest and most mature Deliberation shall Judg will most Conduce to the Safty peace and Happiness of this State in all after Successions and generations for the inspection and perusal of the inhabitants before the Ratification theirof by the assembley.

A Trew Coppey from the minutes per me——

Joseph Bourn Town Clerk

Freetown (156/175)

At a Town meeting Leagulay warned and met by ajornment on Saterday the 12th of October 1776 at the meeting house in Freetown Resolved that the General Court be Directed to form a polecy of goverment agreable to their Resolve of the 17th of September Last and Lay the Same before the Towns for their inspection and approbation before the Same passes to be inacted for a Law——

A Trew Copy from the minets for and by order of the selectmen——

Attest Sam Barnaby Town Clerk

Dated at Freetown October the 15th 1776

Danvers (156/176)

At a Leagal Meeting of the Inhabitants of the Town of Danvers October the 17th 1776
The Town took into Consideration the Resolve of the Honorable House of Representatives of the 17 of September last pased the follwing Vots (viz)
Voted that we approve of the present Council and House of Representatives to Draw a Form of Goverment for this State to be presented to the Several Towns theirin for their approbation or Disapprobation
Voted that the Town Clerk be directed to Transmit an Attested Copy of this vote to the Generael Court

Attest

Stephen Needham Town Clerk

Dartmouth (156/177)

Pursuant to a Resolve of the House of Representatives September 17th 1776. the Town of Dartmouth Meet on the Nineteenth day of October. A D: 1776 in a legal Town meeting and passed the following Resolves to Wit——
1ly Resolved, that the pesent House of Representives of the State of the Massachusetts Bay togeather with the Council in one Body with the House and by equal voice do propose and frame a Constitution and form of Government for the Said State; and Said form to be printed and Sent into every Town in Said State for the inspection approbation or the Rejection of the Inhabitants of the Said State:——
2ly Resolved, that the State be not hasty in Establishing Said form of Government, but that proper Means be used in order to Collect the wisdom of the Whole State.
Therefore 3ly Resolved, that During the time that Said form of Government is under Consideration any person or persons may have Liberty to print any Corrections or emendations of Said Form of Government, and that Said Alteration and Emendations be Laid before the Several Towns ——togeather with Said form of Government that so they may be Enabled to Adopt the best Constitution.——
4ly Resolved, that we Judge it best the Towns do not proseed to Stablish a Constitution till the State in general judge themselves ripe for Detereminieng upon so Weighty an affair——

5ly Resolved, that the foreging Resolves be taken into a fair Draft by the Town Cark, and Sent to the Secretary of this State and also, to be inserted in the Newspaper at Watertown three Weak Sucsesely a We also Recommend the same practice in Every other Town in this State———

A True Coppy Compd. Benjamin Akin Town Clar

Lexington (156/178–179)

At a Meeting of the Freemen in Lexington, duly Notified, and legally Assembled, on October 9th. and by adjournment October 21, 1776, in Pursuance of a Resolve of the Honorable House of Representatives of this State. "To Consider and determine Whether they will give their Consent, that the present House of Representatives of this State of the Massachusetts Bay in New England, together with the Council, if they Consent in one Body with the House, and by equal Voice, Should consult, agree on, and enact Such a Constitution and Form of Government for this State as this Said House of Representatives and Council aforesaid, on the fullest, and most mature Deliberation Shall judge will most conduce to the Safety, Peace and Happiness of this State, in all after Successions and Generations, and if they would direct that the Same be made public for the Inspection and Perusal of the Inhabitants before the Ratification thereof by the Assembly":—after hearing, considering and maturely deliberating upon the important Question before them, came into the following Votes.———

That always desirous of being impressed with the Justest Sentiments of the Wisdom, Integrity and Fidelity of so respectable a Body as the Honorable House of Representatives of this State, in that high Department assigned them by their Constituents, it is with an oft peculiar anxiety we find ourselves oblidged in Faithfulness to ourselves and Posterity, to withold a chearful Compliance with any Resolve or Proposal of them, as we are constrained to do upon the Question before Us, by the following Considerations, which to us (at least) appear interesting and Important.———

1. It appears to us that as all Government Originates from the People, and the Great End of Government is their Peace, Safety and Happiness; so it is with the People at large, or where that is impracticable, by their Representatives freely and equally elected and impowered for that Pur-

pose, to form and agree upon a Constitution of Government, which being considered and approved by the Body of the People, may be enacted, ratified and established.———

2 That the present House of Representatives were not elected for the Purpose of agreeing upon and enacting a Constitution of Government, for this State, neither had their Constituents the least Information of any thing of this Kind, in the Precept upon which they were elected: and therefore the proposing themselves to the People, and asking their Consent as Candidates for this Service, appears to Us to be a Clog to that Freedom of Election which ought always to be exercised, by a free People, in Matters of Importance, more especially in an affair of such lasting Concernment as this.———

3 —That no Provision is made in the Resolve for those Towns, which have not chosen so many Representatives, as they have a Right to send, to chuse others to compleat their Number upon this important Occasion. By which it may happen, not through the Neglect of the People but for want of Opportunity, the Representation may be Unequal.———

4 —That in Case we do not See our Way clear to Consent, as proposed in the Question before us, it does not appear, that any Provision is made in the Resolve, for Our having any Voice at all in the Matter, as Our Representative will not be considered as Impowered, by his Constituents, for this Purpose.———

5 —That it is greatly to be feared, if the proposal in this Resolve is complied with the People of this State, upon this most Interesting Occasion, it will be pled as an established Precedent, in all future Time, for the Decency and Propriety of Persons offering themselves Candidates for the Election of the People, to Offices of Trust and Importance;—A Practice which hath always been held, by the judicious and virtuous, dangerous to the Liberties of the People, and a Practice by which corrupt and designing Men, in every age, have too often availed themselves of Places of Power and Authority, to the great Disadvantage of those that elected them, if not to the Gross Violaton of their most Sacred Rights———

6 Lastly that the Resolve gives us to expect a Publication of the proposed Form of Government, for the Perusal of the Inhabitants, before the Ratification of the Same, yet it does not appear from thence, that there is any just Provision made for the Inhabitants, as Towns, or Societies, to express their approbation, or the Contrary, in Order to Such Ratification by the Assembly.———

For these obvious Reasons, therefore we cannot see our way clear to comply with the Proposal of the Honorable House of Representatives, in the Question before Us.———

Voted and resolved, That as our former Constitution (the Charter) is at an End, and a New Constitution of Government, as soon as may be is absolutely Necessary, if not to the Being, Yet to the well being of this State; and as the Present General Court are considered as the Eyes of the People, and the Guardians as well as Watchmen of the State, it be most earnesly recommended to our Worthy Representative, and that He be hereby instructed, to use his utmost Endeavour and Influence, that either by Precepts for a New Assembly, impowered for this Purpose, or by Special Notification, for the Choice of Persons for the express Purpose of forming a New Constitution, or in any other Way which their Wisdom may direct, consistent with the Liberties of the People, Measures may be taken to give the People an Opportunity to carry this Matter to Effect, and as soon as may be consistent with the Exigence of the Public Affairs, freely to give their Votes for such Persons as they judge will best serve the Public, themselves and Posterity in a Concernment of so great Importance, to the present and all Succeeding Generations.———

A true Copy from the Minutes
Attest Joseph Mason Town Clerk

Raynham (156/180)

[Printed copy of resolve 9/17/1776]

In pursuance of the above Resolve the Inhabitants of the Town Raynham, being Qualified as Recomended in Said Resolve and being Duely Notified meet at the Publick Meeting House in Said Raynham on Monday 21:st day of October A D 1776 and Voted that the present House of Representatives with Counsel in Manners as Mentioned in their Resolve shall proceed to form a Plan of Goverment for this State for the prensent and all after Successions and Generations, and that the Same be Made Publick for the inspection of the Inhabitants of this State Before Ratification thereof

Zeph Leonard Town Clerk

Marlborough (156/181)

At a Meeting of the Freeholders and other Inhabitants of the Town of Marlborough, Being Free and Twenty-one Years of Age and upwards, on the 21st. of October 1776 To take into Consideration a Resolve of the

House of Representatives of the 17th. of September 1776, Respecting their giveing their Consent that the Present House, together with the Council Should Enact a Constitution and Form of Government for this State———

They haveing taken the Same into Consideration, and the Question being put, whether they Consent as aforesaid Passed, in the Negative. Nem. Con.———

And would offer their Reasons as follows. viz———

That some Towns in this State who have not had one Member in the House, are Impowered to Return their whole Number of Members, that they were Impowered to do in Consequence of the Precepts Issued in April Last; while other Towns, who have Sent one Member and had a Right to Send two or more, are not Impowered to Return their whole Number at this time, when there ought to be the most Equally Just Representation.———

That a great Part of the People, who are now Impowered to Vote, are not Represented, by the present House; haveing had no Voice in the Election———

That altho we do not Consent as abovesaid, yet we are Desirous, that there may be Enacted a Constitution and Form of Government as soon as may be under an Equall and Just Representation.———

Voted that the Town Clerk Transmit a Copy of the above into the Office of the Secretary of this State.

Edward Barns Moderator

A True Copy Attest Wins. Brigham T Clerk

Concord (156/182)

At a meeting of the Inhabitents of the Town of Concord being free and twenty one years of age and upward, met by adjournment on the twenty first Day of October 1776 to take into Consideration a Resolve of the Honorable House of Representatives of this State on the 17th of September Last, the Town Resolved as followes———

Resolve 1st. That this State being at Present destitute of a Properly established form of Goverment, it is absolutly necesary that one should be emmediatly formed and established———

Resolved 2 That the Supreme Legislative, either in their Proper Capacity, or in Joint Committee, are by no means a Body proper to form and Establish a Constitution, or form of Goverment; for Reasons following.

first Because we Conceive that a Constitution in its Proper Idea intends a System of Principles Established to Secure the Subject in the Possession and enjoyment of their Rights and Priviliges, against any Encroachments of the Governing Part———
2d Because the Same Body that forms a Constitution have of Consequence a power to alter it. 3d—Because a Constitution alterable by the Supreme Legislative is no Security at all to the Subject against any Encroachment of the Governing part on any, or on all of their Rights and priviliges. Resolve 3d. That it appears to this Town highly necesary and Expedient that a Convention, or Congress be immediately Chosen, to form and establish a Constitution, by the Inhabitents of the Respective Towns in this State, being free and of twenty one years of age, and upwards, in Proportion as the Representatives of this State formerly ware Chosen; the Convention or Congress not to Consist of a greater number then the House of assembly of this State heretofore might Consist of, Except that each Town and District shall have Liberty to Send one Representative or otherwise as Shall appear meet to the Inhabitents of this State in General
Resolve 4th. that when the Convention, or Congress have formed a Constitution they adjourn for a Short time, and Publish their Proposed Constitution for the Inspection and Remarks of the Inhabitents of this State. Resolved 5ly. That the Honorable House of assembly of this State be Desired to Recommend it to the Inhabitants of the State to Proceed to Chuse a Convention or Congress for the Purpas abovesaid as soon as Possable.

A True Copy of the Proceedings of the Town of Concord at the General Town meeting above mentioned———atts. Ephraim Wood Junr. Town Clerk
Concord October the 22. 1776

Topsfield (156/183)

Att a Legal Town meeting in Topsfield held by adjournment 22 nd. of October A D 1776———
The Committee that was Chosen to Consider and Report to the Town what they Should Judge proper for the town to do respecting giveing their Consent that the present House of Representatives with the Council, Should Anact a forme of Constitution and forme of Government for

the future, made report, as followeth———It Being a time (as we apprehend) that the perplexing affairs of this State are Sufficient to take up the whole attention of the general Court, properly to Conduct the Same and although the members of the present House of Representatives are numerus, many of them are new, and we are not aquainted with them. And we Cannot but hope that before the next Choice of Representatives, the Late Act of Tolleration for townes to Send to Court, Such numbers of persons, which Act we fear was Obtained only to Serve the Interest of perticuler parties under a pretence of Equal representation, will be repealed and the Court will return to, or near to, the antient rule, of representation in the general Court, and we hope members will be then Chosen that will Look upon it their duty not only to represent perticuler parties, nor their owne town only, but the whole State in general, and then, and not till then, we Shall have and Equal representation in the general Court———Therefore this Town are not willing that the present House of Representatives and Council Should an act and pass a Constitution and forme of government for this State of Massachusetts Bay for the future, But we are willing that the present house of Representatives, and the Council Should Draw Such a Draft of Constitution and forme of Government as they Shall Judge will most Conduce to the Safety peace and happiness of this State, and also Cause a Printed Copy thereof to be Sent to Every Town and destrict in this State, for the Inspection and perusal of the Inhabitants, till after the next may Sessions of the general Court, That the Several towns, if they see Cause may then Instruct their Representatives to Cause the whole or Such part thereof, or with Such Allterations as they may think proper to make, to be anacted, and pass into a Law for this State

Which was accepted after being Sundry times read over and also voted that the Town Clerke draw the Same into a faire draft and attest the Same, and forward it to the Secretary of this State by the first opertunity

Test Samuel Smith Town Cler———

Milton (156/184)

At a Legal Town Meeting in Milton on the 23d Day of October 1776 the following Vote was passed, Viz.

The Town having met in Legal Town-Meeting to consider and determine whether they will consent, that the present House of Representatives of this State, together with the Council, shall Enact a Constitution and Form of Government for this State, are of Opinion; that it would be highly injurious to this State, and to the great American Cause to have the minds of their Representatives Employed in an Affair of this Nature, while the men Proportioned to this State for the ensuing Campaign remain unraised——they view the raising of, and well-providing for, a new army at this Important Crisis, of Infinitely Greater Consequence than the now forming a new System of Government, and therefore they are oblieged to give their Vote, and Do accordingly give it in the Negative.

A True Copy
attest Amariah Blake Town Clerk

Ashby (156/185)

Ashby October the 24th 1776 At a Legal Town Meeting of the Town of Ashby on the Hand-Bill Sent out by the House of Representitives to se if the Town will consent that the Present House of Representitives and Council (being agreed) Should Form and Ratify a Constitution for this State.

After having Chosen a Committee (Imediately) to Consider and Report on said Resolve: Said Committee having met and attended Said Servise Do Report as Followes (viz) 1st. it appears to us, that if the Present General Court are Properly Constituted to act in any Matter Senc the Declaration of Independency (which is Disputed) Yet there is a very Unequal Repprensentation of the Several Towns in this State at Present; in that some Towns are Allowed to Send Such a Large Number of Members Bairly in consideration of Number, With out any Regard had to Lande and Real Estates, Which appears to be in Consequence of an act Passed in a former General Cort. And Where as Mature Consideration Appeare to be Necessary to be Used in such a case of such importance; Because we Look Upon it Erational and Unjust for us to act Any thing that Shall Opperate in any measure for Such an Extensive and Everlasting affect; while So Many of our Brethren are Gone into the army as Would be Plainly Voting away their Writes in there absence——

A true Extract from the Minutes.

Attest, John Lawrence Jur. Town Clerk——

Dorchester (156/186)

Att a Meeting of the Male Inhabitants of the Town of Dorchester, of Twenty one years of age upwards, being free, October 28th. 1776, by Adjournment from the 14th of this Instant October.———

As the Great and General Court has at present much Business before them, and is likely to have this year, Voted That we judge it best that the Consulting and agreeing upon a Constitution and Form of Goverment, Should be Postponed for the present.———

A true Copy, Attest Noah Clap Town Clerk.———

Bradford (156/186)

At a Legal Meeting of the Male Inhabitents of the Town of Bradford on Adjournment, held October 31st 1776, to Receive a Report of the Committee chosen by the Town, to take into Consideration a Resolve of the Honorable House of Representatives Passed September 17th 1776. Relating to the House and Council, in one Body, forming a Plan of Government for this State, Reported as follows,

That we are not willing, nor do we Consent, that the house of Representatives and Council, acting in one Body, as proposed in a Resolve of the House of Representatives, of September 17th, 1776, Should Agree on and enact a Constitution and form of Goverment for this State———

But we are willing and desire, that the Honorable Council and Honorable House of Representatives (Each acting in their Respective Capacities) Proceed to form a Plan of Goverment for this State, and exhibit attested Copies thereof to its Several Towns, for Inspection and Approbation, before it is Ratified and Confirmed.———

The Question being put whether the Town would accept the Above Report, and it Passed in the Affirmative.

A true Copy Attest

Benj: Muzzy Cler

Brookfield (156/187)

November 4th 1776

At a Legal Meeting of the Inhabitants of Brookfield Voted that this Town Consent that the Present house of Representitives of this State with the

Council jointly may Plan a Constitution or form of Government and Publish the Same for the Inspection of the Publick but that the Same be not Rattifyed and Confairmed untill after the new Election of members for the assembly———

A true Coppy of the Record Attest

Jabez Crosby Town Clark

York (156/187)

At a Meeting of the Male Inhabitants of the Town of York being free and twenty one Years of Age or upwards held at York on Monday the 4th Day of November 1776, by Adjournment from the 14th. of October preceeding.

the Honorable John Bradbury Esquire Moderator.

After reading over the Resolve of the Honorable House of Representatives passed the 17th. of September last, respecting the Form of a Constitution for this State, and mature consideration thereon,

Voted as the Opinion of this Town, that the General Assembly of the State of the Massachusetts Bay in General Court Assembled, are from long Usuage under the former Administration, the Supream Legistive Power or Authority in this State, and to whose Acts all the Individuals in the State ought to be held and pay due obedience——That in case the General Court in their Wisdom shall see meet to alter and Amend the Present, or form a new Constitution (which this Town would advise to be as near the former as conventiently maybe) and make the same Public before they shall Enact the same to be binding on the Inhabitants of this State; this Town when such Amendments or New form of Constitution shall be laid before them, will Signify their Approbation or Disapprobation thereof.

A true Copy Daniel Moulton Town Cler

Acton (156/188)

Acton, Nov. the 4th 1776

At a Meeting of the Male Inhabitants of the Town of Acton, Being free and Twenty one years of Age and upward Legally Assembled To Se if this Town will Agree that the Present House of Representitives Together with the Council Enact a form of Goverment for this State the Town Resovled as follows

1st Resolved that, as this State is at Present Destitute of an Established form of Goverment it is Necessary one Should be Immediately formed and Established

2ly Resolved that the Supreme Legislative in their Capacity are by no means a Body Proper to form and Establish a Constitution for the following Reason (viz) Because that a Constitution Properly formed has a System of Principles Established to Secure the Subjects in Possession of their Rights and Previleges against any Incroachments of the Governing Part and it is our Oppenion that the Same Body that forms a Constitution have of Consequence a Power to alter it, and we Conceive that a Constitution Alterable by the Supreme Legislative Power is no Security to the Subjects against Incroachments of that Power on our Rights and Priveliges

3ly Resolved that this Town think it Expediant that a Convention be Chosen by the Inhabitants of the Several Towns and Districts in this State to form and Establish a Constitution for this State

4ly Resolved that the Honorable Assembly of this State be Disired to Recommend to the Inhabitants of this State to Chuse a Convention for the Above Purpose as Soon as Possable

5ly Resolved that the Convention Publish their Proposed Constitution Before they Establish it for the inspection and Remarks of the Inhabitants of this State.

A true Coppy of the above Proceedings of the Town
Attest Francis Faulkner Town Clerk

Needham (156/189)

Pursuant to a Late Resolve of the General Court of the State of the Massachusetts Bay———

Hereby is Certified, That at a Meeting of the Inhabitants of the Town of Needham, Being free and Twenty One Years of Age or Upwards, Legally Assembled, October the 29th: 1776.

It was Put to the Vote of the Town; To See if it be the mind of the Town, That the Council and house of Representitives, To Act as One Joynt Body in forming a New Constitution of Goverment, and that they Publish the Same in Every Town in this State; And if it be Agreeable to the Inhabitants at Large, Then to be Ratifyed and Confirmed; And it Past in the Affirmative——

A True Copy Taken Out of Needham Town Book of Records Examined: Needham November the 6th, 1776.

Attest: Robert Fuller Town Clerk

North Yarmouth (156/190)

At a meeting of the Freeholders and other Male Inhabitants of the Town of North Yarmouth, of the Age of twenty one Years and Upwards, at the Meeting-house in said Town Monday November 11th 1776.
Voted That the present House of Representatives of this State of the Massachusetts Bay in New England, together with the Council, in one Body with the House, and by Equal Voice, consult and agree upon such a Constitution and Form of Government for this State, as the Said House of Representatives and Council as aforesaid, on the fullest and most mature Deliberation shall judge will most conduce to the Safety Peace and Happiness thereof——
Voted That when Said Constitution and Form of Government Shall be so agreed upon the same be made publick for the Inspection and Perusal of the Inhabitants of this State and sufficient time given for Animadversion thereon before the Ratification thereof by the Assembly.——

A True Copy from the Records of Said Town
Examined Per David Mitchell Town Clerk

Sherborn (156/190)

At a Meeting of the Inhabitants of Sherburn on Monday the 11th Day of November 1776 it was Voted Unanimously that the Presant General Court of this State Form Such a Constitution and Form of Government as they shall Judge will most Conduce to the Happiness Peace and Safety of the Inhabitants theirof, and that the Same be made Publick for the Inspection and approbation of the Inhabitants of this State Before the Ratification theirof by the Said General Court

Attest Daniel Whitney Town Clerk

Sherburn November the 11th 1776

Greenwich (156/191)

At a Legal Town meeting held at the publick meeting house in Greenwich on Friday the 15th Day of November 1776 at 2 of the Clock afternoon, first voted and Chose Deacon Simon Stone Moderator
2ly voted that the Town gives their voice and Consent that the present house of Representatives of this State of Massachusits bay in New england togeather with the Council if they Consent in one Body with the house and by Equal voice should Consult agree on and Enact Such a Constitution and form of Government for this State as the Said house of Representatives and Council as aforesaid on the fullest and most mature Deliberation Should Judge will most Conduce to the Safety Peace and Happiness of this State in all after Successions and Generations and if they would Direct that the Same be made publick for the Inspection and perusal and approbation of the Inhabitants before the Ratification thereof by the assembly

Simon Stone Modr

A True Coppy-Attest Isaac Powers Town Clerk

Weymouth (156/191)

At A Meeting Legally warned and Convened at the Meeting-House in the Second Precinct of the Town of Weymouth on monday the 18d of November A.D. 1776——To Consider and Determine whether they will Give their Consent that the present House of Representatives of this State of the Massachusetts Bay together with the Council if they Consent in one Body with the House and by equil Vote Sould Consult etc. as is Exprest in the Resolve of the House of Representatives on 17 of September last——and after Same Debate thereon the Question being put by the Moderator it passed in the Negative———

A True abstract from the Minutes

Josiah Waterman, Town Clerk

Bellingham (156/198)

The Answer of the Inhabitants of the Town of Bellingham to the Resolve of the Honorable House of Representatives heretoe Annexed

Dated September 17. 1776. as Voted in Town Meeting Called in Conformity to Said Resolve, on Due Notice for that End held at Bellingham on the 28th of October and by Adjournment on the 2d of December after.

We are of opinion that the Setling a form of Government for this State is a matter of the Gratest Importance of a Civil Nature that we were Ever Concerned in and ought to be Proceeded in with the Gratest Caution and Deliberation.

It appears to us that the late General Assembly of this State in their Proclamation Dated January 23. 1775. have well Expressed.

That Power Alwaise resides in the Body of the People.

We understand That all of the Males above 21 Years of age meeting in Each Separate Town and acting the Same thing and all their acts United together make an act of the Body of the People. We Apprehend it would be proper that the form of Government for this State to origenate in Each Town and by that means we may have the Ingenuity of all the State and it may Qualifie men for Publick Stations.

Which might be Effected if the Present Honorable House of Representatives would Devide this State into Districts of about 30 miles Diameter or less if it may appear most Convenient, So that None be more than 15 miles from the Center of the District that there may be an Easey Comunication beteween Each Town and the Center of its District, and that no town be divided And That Every town chuse one man out of 30 of their Inhabitants, to be a Committee to meet as Neer the Center of the District as may be, to meet at about 6 weeks after the House of Representatives have Issued their order for the Towns to meet to Draw a form of Government, and the Same Committee to carry with them the form of Government their Town has Drawed, to the District meeting and compare them together, and Propose to their Towns what alterations their Towns in their opinion ought to make, and Said Committee in Each District adjourn and Carry to their Several Towns and lay before them (in Town Meeting for that End,) the form of Government, Said District has agreed toe, and the towns agree toe or alter as they Se meet, after which the District Committee meet according to Adjournment and revise the form of Government, after which Each District Committee chuse a man a Committee to meet all as one Committee at Watertown at 12 Weeks after the Date of the order of the House of Representatives, for the Towns first meeting to Draw a form of Government, which Committee of the Whole State may be Impowered to Send Precepts to the Several towns in this State to chuse one man out of 60. to meet in Convention at Watertown or such other Town as Said Committee Shall Judge best, Six weeks from the time of Said Districts, last Sitting, the Said one man out of 60, to meet in Convention to Draw from the forms of Government Drawn by Each Districts Committee One Form of Government for the Whole State; after which Said Convention Send to Each Town the form of Government they have Drawed for the Towns Confirmation or Alteration and then Adjourn Notifying Each Town to make Return to them of their Doings at Said Convention Adjournment.

And at Said Adjournment Said Convention Draw a General Plan or form of Government for this State, So that they Ad nothing to nor Deminish nothing from the General Sence of Each Town. And That Each Town be at the Charge of all the men they Imploy in this affair.

test———

Aaron Holbrook town Clerk

Sutton, 1776 *

The town was also called upon to take action on the following article in the warrant for the meeting of October 7th [1776]:

"To see whether the above mentioned Inhabitants will give their Consent that the present House of Representatives, of this State of the Massachusetts Bay, in New England, together with the Council, if they Consent in one Body with the House, and by equal voice should consult, agree on, and enact such a Constitution and Form of Government for this State, as the said House of Representatives and Council, as afore said, on the fullest and most mature Deliberation, shall judge will most conduce to the Safety, Peace, and Happiness of this State, in all after Successions and Generations: and if they would direct that the same be made publick, for the Inspection and Perusal of the Inhabitants before the Ratification there of, by the Assembly.

Deacon Willis Hall, Mr. Samuel Dagget, Deacon Ebenezer Pierce, Mr. Nathan Putnam, and Colonel Timothy Sibley were appointed a Committee to draw up a Form of vote upon the above article."

The committee brought in the following report, which was accepted and adopted:

* William A. Benedict and Hiram A. Tracy, comps., *History of the Town of Sutton, Massachusetts, from 1704 to 1876* (Worcester, Mass., 1878), 99–100.

"At a legal meeting of the Town of Sutton, upon the Hand-Bill, sent out by the House of Representatives, to see if Towns will consent, that the present House of Representatives and Council should form and ratify a Constitution for this State.

Resolved that this Town can, by no means, consent to what is there proposed, for the following reasons (viz.)

1. Because we think it irrational for us to consent to the setting up any Constitution unknown to us, or to vote for any thing, before we see what it is we vote for.

2. Because we look upon the present House of Representatives, not only, to be a very unequal Representation of the State; But also an illegal one, many of them being chosen by virtue of a pretended Law, made after the Precepts went out for the Election of the House.

3. Because we look upon it irrational and unjust for us, to act anything that shall operate, in any measure, for such an everlasting effect, while so many of our Brethren and Neighbors are gone into the army, and would be plainly a voting away their Right, in their absense."

Lancaster [10/7/1776] *

Voted that the Town Impower the present house of Representatives to Draw up a Form of Government and Transmit Back for the Town's Ratification.

* H. S. Nourse, *Military Annals of Lancaster, Massachusetts. 1740–1865* (Lancaster, Mass., 1889), 153.

14

Resolution of Worcester County Towns, November 26, 1776

The following statement from the towns in Worcester County, published in the *Massachusetts Spy,* December 4, 1776, indicates the desire that the new constitution be formed by a special convention rather than by the existing legislature.

At a meeting of the Committees of [*S*]*afety* etc. *From a majority of the Towns in the County of Worcester, held by adjournment, at the Court House in said Worcester. November* 26, 1776. Voted,

THAT the Members inform the Convention what were the general sentiments of the inhabitants of their respective Towns, concerning a Resolve of the House of Representatives, on the 17th of September last, respecting the formation of a system of Government.

Lancaster, Rutland, Harvard, Princeton. Paxton, Southborough, Hardwick, Uxbridge, New-Brantree, Oakham, Shrewsbury, Winchendon, Consented, subject to the approbation or rejection of the people.

Oxford, Dissented by reason of unequal representation and brethren absent.

Sutton, Bolton Sturbridtge, Holden, Northbridge, Dissented for unequal representation.

Worcester, Postponed acting on said resolve, till the third Monday in December next, to have the voice of their brethren in the Army.

Leicester, Dissented, presuming the people were excluded the right of approbation or rejection.

Dudley, Charlton, Objected to the present House.

Petersham, The same and against any Council.

Brookfield, Consented with right of approbation or rejection, and Government to be established by a future House.

Mendon, Not to comply with said resolve.

[*S*]*pencer,* The same, the Court not being in a proper situation.

Templeton, Fitchburg, Douglas, Objected to the present Court.

Northborough, Upton, Westborough, Ashburnham, Had no resolve, nor acted thereon.

Grafton, Did not act thereon.

Westminster, Had no resolve or acted thereon. Voted,

That a system of Government is necessary to be established in this State, so soon as it may be done with safety.

Whereas the Honorable the Continental Congress have thought fit, with the consent, and for the safety, peace and happiness of the American States to declare them free and independent on the Crown of Great-Britain etc. And have recommended to said States the forming such systems of Government as may be most agreeable to their respective situations and circumstances;

And whereas the present House of Representatives, to bring forward this important business have asked the consent of the people to impower that body with the Council, to form such a system of Government for this State;—The Committees of Safty etc. from a great majority of the Towns in the County of Worcester, convened at the Court House in said Worcester, on Tuesday the 26 of November 1776, for the purpose of reconciling the various sentiments of the inhabitants respecting said request, and preserving unanimity in the County; and also considering the loose and disjointed State, the people of the Massachusetts-Bay, have been in for divers years past, in which time, many errors have crept in and been supported with the remains of the late constitutions; that the evils are daily increasing and in all probability will continue till a fixed and permanent form of Government be established. Therefore to prevent, (as much as in themselves) anarchy and confusion, and the undue influence or power of individuals in monopolizing incompatible offices in the hands of particular persons, on the one hand and on the other to strengthen the hands of Government, against an unatural enemy, and lay a permanent foundation for safety, peace and happiness for this and succeeding generations; said Convention have come into the following votes, etc. with intention to lay the same before their respective Towns for their consideration.

Whereas an act passed in the late General Court. making the representation of the State very unequal and unsafe, this Convention is of opinion that the present General Court is not the most suitable body to form a system of Government for this State, moreover the business being of the greatest importance, will require more time and closeer attention than can be spared, by a house of representatives, from the ordinary and daily concerns of the State. Therefore voted, That a State Congress chosen for the sole purpose of forming a Constitution of Government is (in the opinion of this Convention) more eligible than an House of Representatives. Voted, That it be recommended to our respective Towns, that they instruct their Representatives, to exert their influence, that writs be issued from the General Court impowering and directing the Towns to chuse members, to form a State Congress, by a mode of representation agreeable to the last charter and as practised in the year 1775, for the purpose of forming a plan of Government, which, when formed, to be laid before the people for their inpection, approbation, rejection, or amendment, (if any they have to propose) and when approved by the people, that said Congress solemnly establish the same, issue out writs for convening a legislative body agreeable to said Constitution and dissolve.

Voted, That the proceedings of this Convention be submitted to the consideration of the other counties in this State, and request the favour of their sentiments on the subject.

Voted, To publish the foregoing in the Boston, Worcester and Hartford News-Papers, also in Hand Bills.

By order of the Convention

JOSEPH HENSHAW, Chairman

II

The Constitution of 1778

January 1777—November 1778

15

Sutton Requests a County Convention, January 1777

Sutton, aggrieved by the Act for more equal representation of May 4, 1776 (No. 7), which increased the influence of larger towns, called for the organization of a Worcester County Congress to meet and seek redress of this and any other grievances the delegates wished to consider. The proceedings are recorded in Benedict and Tracy, comps., *History of the Town of Sutton,* 101–103.

[January 20, 1777, call for a meeting]

To see if the Town will choose one or more Delegates, to meet in County Congress, with any such other Towns as will join with us in this method for a redress of the Grievance by the Law made last Spring for the new modelling the Representation of this State; or any other Grievance that shall be thought proper by any of the Towns joining in such Congress. And also, to see if the Town will invite the other Towns in the County, to join with them in such Congress, by a Note of our proceedings in the Worcester News Paper.

[The town "Voted to choose delegates," and also "to give invitation to the other Towns in the County to join with us in such Congress, by a Note in the Worcester News Papers." The delegates were instructed as follows:]

The Inhabitants of the Town of Sutton in legal Town Meeting assembled January 27th.

To Captain Henry King and Captain Samuel Trask, whom we have now chosen Delegates, to join in County Congress with such other Towns in this County as shall adopt the like method for the obtaining redress of the grievance by the Law made last Spring, for the new modelling the Representation of this state; or any other grievances that any of the Towns joining in such Congress shall think proper. We hereby direct you to repair to the House of the Widow Stearns, Inn holder, in Worcester, on Wednesday the 26th day of Febr. next, at ten o'clock in the forenoon; then and there, to join with such other Towns as may meet you by their Delegates, and form into a County Congress, to consult, deliberate upon, and unite, in some method, for the redress of the grievance aforesaid or any other grievance there moved, either by petition to the

General Court, or by recommending a form of Instructions to the Several Towns, to give their Representatives, or both, as shall be thought most effectual. And that you invite the other Counties in this State, to adopt the like method, and to correspond with you by Committees, that this County and others, may harmonize in their measures. And we farther direct and order you to continue yourselves by adjournment, (if the other Towns will join in it) so that you remain a County Congress, until next May meeting, for choosing Representatives, at which time, if it be agreeable to the County in general, we propose to continue such Congress by the choice of new Delegates, for a future time, as shall be thought proper. You are also to make return to us, at next March Meeting, what you find and agree upon at your first Congress; and so on, from time to time, as we shall require. And we think, that your first adjournment ought not to be deferred longer than the beginning of May next; in order that, if the above grievous act should not by that time be repealed, some other Constitutional measures might be agreed upon for redress; or if it should be repealed, any other matters, then thought of, for the good of the public, might be agreed upon to instruct the Representatives, at the next Election, or any other business proper for a County Congress that may occur at that time.

And you are, from time to time, to attend to and pursue, as far as you can, all such Instructions as you shall receive from us, your constituents.

And we hereby, also invite all the other Towns in this County, to join with us, in such Congress.

And, for that purpose, order that the above be inserted in the Worcester News Paper as soon as possible.

And also, that the above Delegates take care that the above be immediately put into Hand-Bills and distributed to the Selectmen of the Several Towns in this County at the expense of this Town.

16

Resolution Authorizing the General Assembly to Frame a Constitution, April 4, 1777

The House of Representatives, responsive to the demands for a new constitution, resolved that the towns at their next election choose representatives who, in addition to their ordinary duties, would be vested with the power of forming a constitution, subject to the approval of two thirds of the people present and voting at the several town meetings. The resolution is found in MA 156/200–202. Words crossed out on the manuscript are given in angle brackets. Other corrections in the manuscript are given in footnotes.

State of Massachusetts Bay
In the House of Representatives April 4th 1777

That the happiness of Mankind depends very much on the Form and Constitution of Goverment they live under. that the only object and design of Goverment should be the good of the people. are truths well Understood at this day and truths taught by reason and Experience very clearly at all times. and yet by far ⟨the bulk⟩ the greater part of Mankind are governed only for the advantage of their ⟨Governors⟩ Masters, and are the miserable slaves of a single or a few despots whose Ideas or humanity never Extend beyond the limits of their own Gr[andeur?] or Interest. and indeed among the Multitude of Mankind who have lived ⟨in the world⟩ and the variety of people who have succeeded each other in the several ages of the world. very few have ever had an oppertunity of choosing and forming a Constitution of Goverment for themselves.——this is a great privilege and such an opportunity the good People of this state by the distinguished favours of a kind Providence now Enjoy and which the Interst and happiness of ⟨mankind⟩ themselves and posterity loudly call upon them to Improve with wisdom and prudence——⟨God in his Providence has permitted⟩ the Infatuated Policy of Britain, instead of destroying has in all probability (by the Goodness of God) promoted and accelerated the happiness of the people of the United States of America. the Cruelty and Injustice of Britain has driven ⟨America⟩ us to a declaration of Independence and a dissolution of ⟨its⟩ our former Connections with them and made it necessary for each of the ⟨state⟩ United States to form and constitute a Mode of Goverment for themselves . . . [sic] and Whereas by the suffrages of the good People of this State it has become more especially our duty to Consult and promote the happiness of our Constituents and haveing duly Considered the ⟨necessity and advantages⟩ advantages and necessity of immediately forming a fixed and permanent Constitution of Goverment ⟨in which the several powers of the Legislative and Executive parts shall be clearly defined and determined⟩ and Conceiving it to be the Expectation of our Constituents that we should originate and recommend to them the most suitable method for Effecting this valuable and Important purpose. do Resolve——That it be and hereby is recommended to the several Towns and places in this state——Impowered by the Laws thereof to send Members to the General Assembly. that at their next Election of a Member or Members to represent them they make Choice of Men in whose Intigrity and Abilities they can place the greatest Confidence. and in addition to the Common and ordinary powers of Representation vest them with full powers to form such a Constitution of Goverment as they shall Judge best Calculated to promote the happiness of this state and when Compleated to Cause the same to be printed in all the Boston News papers and also in hand Bills one of which to be transmitted to the selectmen of each town or the Committee of each plantation. to be by them laid before their respective Towns ⟨for their⟩ or plantations at a regular meeting for that purpose to be called. to be by each Town and Plantation Considered. and a return of their approbation or Disapprobation to the Clerk of the House of Representatives [1] at a reasonable time to be fixed on by said House Specifieing the Numbers present in Such meeting voteing for and those voteing against the same ⟨of Representatives⟩ [2] and if upon a fair Examination of said returns [3] it shall appear that said form of Goverment be approved of by ⟨a majority of⟩ at least two thirds of those ⟨people⟩ within this State who are Free and twenty one years of age and present in the several meetings.[4] then the Same ⟨to⟩ shall be deemed ⟨to be⟩ and Established as the ⟨Form and⟩ Constitution and form of Goverment of the State of Massachusetts Bay according to [5] which the Inhabitants thereof shall be Governed in all

[1] The words "to the Clerk of the House of Representatives" are interlineated.

[2] The text of these lines was several times altered. An earlier form read: "to be fixed on by the said House of Representatives for which purpose the Numbers present in Meeting voteing for the form so sent out. and those voteing against it shall be returned to the Clerk of the House of Representatives."

[3] The words "of said returns" are interlineated.

[4] The words "who are Free and twenty one years of Age and present in the several meetings" are interlineated.

[5] The words "according to" are interlineated.

succeeding Generations unless altered by <the authority of the Peop> their own Express Direction or that of a fair Majority of them. and it is further recommended to the selectmen of the several Towns in the return of their Precepts for the Choice of Representatives to signify their haveing Considered this resolve and their doings thereon and it is also Resolved that Mr Story. Mr Freeman. and Captain Page——be a Committee to get these Resolves printed in hand Bills and sent to the several Towns and Plantations in this State as soon as may be and also to cause the same to be published in all the Boston News papers three weeks successively——

Sent up for Concurrence

17

Resolve of May 5, 1777

After considerable discussion in the Council and House, reflected in the changes in the House resolution of April 4, 1777 (No. 16), the General Court adopted the plan there outlined. The resolution is ch. 1169 in *Acts and Resolves, Public and Private of the Province of the Massachusetts Bay,* XIX (Boston, 1918), 932–933; MA 142/64.

That, the Happiness of Mankind depends very much on the Form and Constitution of Government they live under, and that the only Object and Design of Government should be the Good of the People, are Truths well understood at this day, and taught by Reason and Experience, very clearly, at all Times. And Yet, by far the greater Part of Mankind are governed only for the Advantage of their Masters, and are the miserable Slaves of a single or a few Despots, whose Ideas or Humanity never extend beyond the Limits of their own Grandeur or Interest; and indeed among the Multitudes of Mankind who have lived, and the Variety of People who have succeeded each other in the several Ages of the World, very few have even had an Opportunity of choosing and forming a Constitution of Government for themselves. This is a great Privilege, and such an Opportunity the good People of this State, by the distinguishing Favor of a kind Providence, now enjoy, and which the Interest and Happiness of themselves and Posterity loudly call upon them to improve with Wisdom and Prudence. The infatuated Policy of Britain, instead of destroying, has rather, by the Goodness of God, promoted and accelerated the Happiness of the People of the United States of America. The Injustice and Cruelty of Britain has driven us to a Declaration of Independence, and a Dissolution of our former Connections with them and put it in the Power of each of the United States to form and constitute a Mode of Government for themselves. And Whereas it is our peculiar Duty to consult and promote the Happiness of the good People of this State, having duly considered the Advantages of forming, as soon as may be, a new Constitution of Government, and conceiving it to be the Expectation of many, that we should recommend the most suitable Method for effecting this valuable and important Purpose: We do

Resolve, That it be and hereby is recommended to the Several Towns and Places in this State, impowered by the Laws thereof to send Members to the General Assembly, that at their next Election of a Member or Members to represent them, they make choice of Men in whose Integrity and Abilities they can place the greatest Confidence; and in addition to the common and ordinary Powers of Representation, instruct them in one Body with the Council, to form such a Constitution of Government, as they shall judge best calculated to promote the Happiness of this State; when compleated, to cause the same to be printed in all the Boston News-Papers, and also in Hand-Bills, one of each to be transmitted to the Selectmen of each Town, or the Committee of each Plantation, to be by them laid before their respective Towns or plantations, at a regular Meeting of the Inhabitants thereof, to be called for that Purpose; in order to its being by each Town and Plantation duly considered. And a Return of their Approbation or Disapprobation to be made into the Secretary's Office of this State, at a reasonable Time to be fixed on by the General Court, specifying the Numbers present in such Meeting, voting for, and those voting against the same. And if upon a fair Examination of the said returns by the General Court, or such Committee as they shall appoint for that purpose, it shall appear, that the said Form of Government is approved of by at least two Thirds of those who are free and twenty-one Years of Age, belonging to this State and present in the several Meetings, then the General Court shall be impowered to establish the same as the Constitution and form of Government of the State of Massachusetts Bay, according to which the Inhabitants thereof shall be governed in all succeeding Generations, unless the same shall be altered by their own express Direction, or that of at least two Thirds of them.

And it is further recommended to the Selectmen of the several Towns, in the Return of their Precepts for the Choice of Representatives, to signify their having considered this resolve, and their Doings thereon.

18

Boston Objects, May 26, 1777

Despite the Resolve of May 5, 1777 (No. 17), the Boston town meeting unanimously instructed its representatives to oppose the General Court's intention of forming a constitution and to press for a convention specially chosen for that purpose. The instructions are found in *Report of the Record Commissioners of the City of Boston, 1770 through 1777*, p. 284.

Monday 26th. of May, 3 O'Clock P.M. met according to Adjournment.——

The Committee appointed to prepare Instructions for the Gentlemen chose to represent this Town in the next General Assembly, Reported the following Draught, Vizt.

To the Honorable John Hancock Esquire, David Jeffries, Caleb Davis, Oliver Wendell, John Brown, John Pitts and Ellis Gray, Esquires.

Gentlemen,

You have been chosen by the Voice of the Town of Boston to represent them in the Great and General Court, and as it must be agreable to you to know the Minds of your Constituents in all important Matters, we think fit to give you the following Instructions.——

With respect to the General Courts forming a new Constitution, you are directed by a unanimous Vote of a full Meeting, on no Terms to consent to it, but to use your Influence, and oppose it. Heartily, if such an Attempt should be made, for we apprehend this Matter (*at a suitable time*) will properly come before the people at large, to delegate a *Select Number for that Purpose, and that alone,* when some things which we esteem *absolutely necessary* to a good Form, may be viewed by a General Court, in the Light of *self denying Ordinances,* which it is natural to consider, are always disagreable to human Nature: Among other things we have *peculiarly in View making the Council intirely independent of the House, and to prevent the lately too prevalent Custom of accumulating Offices in One Persone:* We could wish to establish it, as a certain Rule, that no One person whatever, be entrusted with more than One Office at a time (and for the Discharge of it, let there be honorable Allowance) and to keep the *Members of the General Court from accepting any:* This we apprehend will have a happy Effect at large, and is agreable to the Custom of all States until Corruption and Bribery destroy the Principles of Vertue.——

19

Journal of the Convention, June 17, 1777—March 6, 1778

In June 1777 the Council and the House of Representatives transformed themselves into a convention for the purpose of forming a constitution, and appointed a committee to prepare a draft. The committee submitted its report on December 11, 1777, and the convention proceeded to a consideration of it on January 15, 1778. On February 28, 1778, the report, as amended, was passed. The journal is found in MA 156/266–293. Folios 266–268, which record the meeting of March 4, 1778, are placed in the archives at the beginning of the journal. They have here been transcribed in their proper chronological position.

State of Massachusetts Bay

At a Convention of the Members of the Hon. Council,—and the Members of the Hon. House of Representatives—begun and held at Boston in the County of Suffolk on Tuesday the 17th Day of June A.D. 1777 for the purpose of forming a new Constitution of Government for this State pursuent to a Resolve of the General Court of the 5th May A D 1777——

The Hon. Jeremiah Powell Esq was chosen Chairman and

Samuel Freeman Esq Clerk

The Resolve aforesaid was then read—and after some Debates on the matter at large it was On Motion Voted—That a Committee be appointed to draw up such a Constitution or Form of Government as they shall judge best calculated to promote the happiness of this State—and report the Same to this Convention——

Voted That this Committee consist of one Member from each County —to be appointed by the Members from the Several Counties and an additional Number of five to be chosen by this Convention [at] large by written Vote——

The Members from the Several Counties then withdrew—and having accordingly [appointed?] the Committee—reported their Names as follows—viz

For the County of Suffolk	Hon Thomas Cushing Esq.
For the County of Essex	John Pickering Esq.
For the County of Middlesex	Hon. James Prescott Esq.

For the County of Hampshire	Hon. John Bliss Esq
For the County of Plymouth	George Partridge Esq
For the County of Barnstable	Hon Daniel Davis Esq.
For the County of Bristol	Hon. Robert T. Paine Esq.
For the County of York	Joseph Simpson Esq.
For the County of Dukes County	
For the County of Nantucket	
For the County of Worcester	Seth Wasburn Esq.
For the County of Cumberland	Hon. Jeremiah Powell Esq.
For the County of Lincoln—	Hon. John Taylor Esq.
For the County of Berkshire—	Mr. John Bacon

Who were appointed

The Convention then assigned 10 o'clock to morrow morning for the choice of the additional five——

Then the Convention adjourned to to-morrow 10 o'clock A M

Wednesday June 18. 1777

Met according to Adjournment

The Hon Jeremiah Powell Esq—being absent—

The Convention appointed the Hon Thomas Cushing Esq Chairman PT.

Then the Convention proceeded agreeable to the Order of the Day to the appointment of five Gentlemen on the Committee for draughting a Form of Government and [Doctor?] Holten and [Doctor?] Taylor and General Warren were appointed a Committee to receive count and sort the Votes——

Who having attended that Service reported that the following Gent were chosen—viz

Hon James Warren Esq.
Azor Orne Esq.
Noah Goodman Esq.
Captain Isaac Stone
Eleazer Brooks Esq.

Then the Convention adjourned to Friday next at 12 oClock——

Friday June 20

The Convention met according to adjournment——

Voted that the Convention be adjourned to Thursday next at 12 o'clock ——and that the Chairman be impowered to call the same together, at any earlier time if it shall be necessary——

Thursday June 26.

The Convention met according to adjournment.

Voted That the Eldest Counsellor who would [*illegible*] preside at the Hon. Board be Chairman of this Convention——

Then the Convention adjourned to Monday next a 3 oClock PM

Monday June 30. 1777

The Convention met according to adjournment and having Voted that the Chairman be impowered to call the Convention together whenever he shall judge it necessary, before the Time to which it shall be adjourned during the Sitting of the General Court——adjourned to the Second Thursday of the next sitting of the General Court at 10 oClock in the forenoon

---

Thursday August 14. 1777

The Convention met according to Adjournment no business

Adjourned to the second Thursday of the next siting of the General Court at 11 o'clock in the forenoon——

Thursday Sept. 18th 1777

The Convention met according to adjournment——and having enjoined their Committee to sit at every opportunity. adjourned to Thursday the second day of October next at 10 o'Clock in the forenoon——

Thursday October 2d 1777

The Convention met according to adjournment and their Committee not being ready to report adjourned to Thursday the 16th Current at 11 o'clock am.

Thursday October 16th. 1777

The Convention met according to Adjournment.——and their Committee not being ready to report adjourned to the second Wednesday of the next session of the General Court at 11 o'clock in the forenoon——

Wednesday. December 3. 1777

The Convention met according to adjournment——the Chairman of their Committee informed the Convention that a quorum of the Committee was not in Town—and that they were not ready to report—and moved that further time be allowed them to prepare their Report whereupon the Convention to Thursday the eleventh current at 11 o'clock am.

Thursday. December 11th 1777

The Committee appointed to draw up a Form of Government, brought in a Report——and asked leave to sit again.

The Report was twice Read and then a motion was made that the same be printed for the inspection and perusal of the Members——Before the question was determined the Convention (after debate on the Motion) adjourned to three o'clock in the afternoon.[1]

Afternoon

The Convention resumed the Consideration of the Motion made in the forenoon for printing their Committees Report and after further debate thereon——

Ordered that the Report be printed under the direction of the Committee, and that each Member of the Convention have one Copy for his inspection and perusal——

Ordered. That the number to be printed, be 300——That the Printer be directed to suffer no Copy to be taken from his Office, but to deliver the whole when printed together with the Original, to the Clerk, for the Use of the Members——and that the Printer be under Oath to print no more than the Number aforesaid, and that he break up and destribute the Types in presence of one of the Committee And that no Member be permitted to deliver a Copy to or Suffer a Copy to be taken by any Person who does not belong to this Convention——And the Clerk is likewise enjoined not to deliver any Copy or Copies to any Person—except to the Members of this Convention——[2]

Ordered That these Restrictions be printed at the End of the Report——

Then the Convention adjourned to Saturday next at 12 oClock——

Saturday December 13th 1777

The Convention met according to Adjournment——

Voted That this Convention when adjourned, be adjourned to the 2d Thursday of the next Session of the General Court——

Ordered That the Clerk cause a notification of the Adjournment to be inserted in one of the Boston Papers—with a N.B. desiring the other Printers in the State to publish the same——and to cause a similar notification to be printed at the end of the Report, informing the Members that the Report is to be taken into consideration at that Time——

Voted That the President be impowered to call this Convention together at any time sooner than that to which it shall be adjourned, if it shall be judged necessary——

[1] The report of the committee with the clerk's minutes is in MA 156/203–209.

[2] An extract from these minutes is in MA 156/210, 264–265. A draft of the Constitution reported by the committee with revisions is in MA 156/211–235.

Then the Convention adjourned to the 2d Thursday of the next Session of the General Court at 11 oClock in the forenoon

---

Thursday January 15th 1778

The Convention met according to adjournment——

Voted that the Secretary of the State may attend this Convention at any time whenever he shall incline——and that a Chair be provided for him.

Voted to proceed to the X

The Report of a X

The Form of Government reported by the Committee appointed to prepare one was then read and

On Motion——the Convention voted to proceed to the Consideration of the Same by Paragraph——[3]

And accordingly considered the first Article and passed upon the Same——

Afternoon

The Convention proceeded to the Consideration of the Report of the Committee——and having passed upon the 2. 3. 4. and 5 article and entered on the consideration of the 6th——adjourned to 3 oClock to morrow afternoon

Friday January 16. 1778

The Convention proceeded to the consideration of their Committees Report——and having passed upon the 7. 8. and 9th Articles and ordered the 6 to be recommitted—adjourned to Tuesday next at 10 oClock in the forenoon

Tuesday January 20. 1778

The Convention met and adjourned to Thursday next at 10 oClock in the forenoon

Thursday January 22d 1778

The Convention met according to adjournment and having considered the 10th and 11th Article [ordered?] the 10th to be recommitted, [dep. upon the 1st part of the 11th] and then adjourned to 4 o'clock in the afternoon——

Afternoon

The Convention proceeded to the further Consideration of the 11th Article——

[3] The revised version of the Constitution is in MA 156/236–263.

And on a Motion made by Coll Brooks which was seconded—that the Words "All other Civil Officers [and to the End] be deled the question after debate was put and it passed in the Negative——

It was then moved that the question be put whether the Officers mentioned in this Paragraph should be appointed by the Governor and Senate ——and it being put—passed in the negative This Question was then put—whether the Said Officers should be appointed by the General Court——and it passed in the affirmative

Then the Convention adjourned to 3 o'Clock to morrow afternoon——

Friday 23d. 1778

Afternoon

The Convention met according to adjournment——It was moved by Brig Danielson that previous to any further debates on the Report the Galleries should be cleared——Seconded by Mr Jackson——Some Debates being had thereon the question was put and in [it] [lost?] in the negative——

On Motion. The question was put whether the Vote which passed yesterday determining that the Officers mentioned in the latter part of the eleventh Article viz from the Words "All the Civil Officers etc—— should be appointed by the General Court should be reconsidered—— and it passed in the Negative——

Ordered That the 11th Article be recommitted for the purpose making the regular amendments therein agreeably to the Sense of the House

The Convention considered and passed upon the 12th Article——It was then moved than an addition be made to it respecting Persons who through Age may be rendred incapable of Serving in the Offices therein mentioned and the question being put it passed in the affirmative

The following addition was then proposed, viz

"Provided that neither of the before mentioned Officers shall be considered as capable of holding the Office to which he may be appointed after he shall arrived to the Age of 65 Years (unless he shall be continued in his Office by annual appointments"——and after Debate the question was put whether the Said addition be made——and it passed in the negative

Then the Convention adjourned to Monday next at 3 oClock in the afternoon——

Monday January 26th 1778

The Convention met according to adjournment and passed upon the 13th. 14th. and 15th. Articles of the Report and the 16th Article being read. It was moved that the same be recommitted and that the Committee be directed to vary the Report in such a manner as that the Legislative and Executive Powers shall be distinct.——After debate the question was put and it passed in the Negative——

It was moved that the Vote for making an addition to the 12th Article be reconsidered and the question being put, it passed in the negative

It was then moved by Mr. Bacon that the following addition be made. viz

"Provided that no one shall be capable of holding the Office either of a Justice of the Superior Court, a Chief Justice of the Inferior Courts of Common Pleas, or a Judge of Probate of Wills, after he shall have arrived at the age of Seventy Years"

After debate thereon the question was put and it passed in the negative——

The Convention then on motion, reconsidered their vote for making an addition to the 12th. Article——

The Convention then passed upon the 16 and 17 and 18 Articles—and after entring upon the Consid of the 19, adjourned to 3 oClock to morrow afternoon

Tuesday January 27 1778
Afternoon

The Convention met according to adjournment—and passed upon the 20, 21, 22 and 23d Articles—and the two last paragraphs of the 19th, the former part of which was referred for further consideration——and then the Convention adjourned to 3 o'clock to morrow afternoon——[4]

Wednesday, January 28th 1778——
Afternoon

The Convention met according to adjournment——and took into consideration the 24th Article——and after debates thereon adjourned to 3 oClock to morrow afternoon

Thursday January 29th 1778

The Convention met according to adjournment—and proceeded to the consideration of the 24th Article—and after full debate[5] thereon passed upon the first Paragraph, and then adjourned to 3 oClock to morrow afternoon

---

Friday January 31. 1778

The Convention met according to adjournment——and again took

[4] Marginal note: "to be Deled."
[5] Marginal note: "to be deled."

into consideration the 24th Article of the Report—and having debated largely thereon

Ordered on Motion—That

Mr President—Mr Greenough Brigadier Danielson, Captain Stone of Oakham Major Goodman—Mr Pickering Mr Philips Coll Grout and Mr Spooner——be a Committee to take the same into consideration and report——

Then the Convention adjourned to Tuesday next at three oClock in the afternoon

---

Tuesday February 3d. 1778

The Convention met according to adjournment——

The Committee appointed to take into consideration the 24th Article of the Report

Reported and as follows–viz

That a Town of 100 Voters may send 1 Member

300—2	3000—11
520—3	3400—12
760—4	3800—13
1020—5	4260—14
1300—6	4720—15
1600—7	5200—16
1920—8	5700—17
2260—9	6220—18
2620—10	6760—19
	7320—20

On Motion. The Convention reconsidered the Vote which passed the 29th ultimo for accepting the first Paragraph of the 24th Article——

It was moved that every incorporated Town within the State have a right to send a Representative——and after debate the question was put —and it passed in the negative——

The question was then put upon the Report above mentioned—and it passed in the affirmative—(81–134)——

Then the Convention adjourned to 3 oClock to morrow afternoon——

Wednesday February 4th 1778

The Convention met according to adjournment——It was moved that the following Addition be made to the 24th Article viz

"Provided always That the Great and General Court shall once in every seven years direct app[rove?] and declare what number each County Town and Place shall elect and depute to serve for and represent them respectively in the said Great and General Court——and after debate thereon the question was put and it passed in the Negative——

The Convention passed upon the 25th Article and then adjourned to 3 oClock to morrow afternoon——

Thursday February 5 1778

The Convention met according to adjournment——and passed upon the 26th and 27 Articles——

Ordered that a clause be added to the 27th Article for increasing the number of Senators as the Number of Voters in the several Districts shall increase

The Convention then considered the 28th Article and having ordered the same to be recommitted——adjourned to 3 oClock to morrow afternoon——

Friday February 6 1778

The Convention met according to adjournment and passed upon the four last Articles of the Report——

On Motion Ordered that a Clause be brot in making Provision for *Liberty of Conscience*

The Report was recommitted and

Then the Convention adjourned to Tuesday next at three oClock in the afternoon

Tuesday February 10 1778

The Convention met according to adjournment——

The Committee reported sundry amendments according to order which were considered by the Convention [same?] passed on, also clause for Liberty of Conscience——The Report was then recommitted and then the Convention adjourned to 3 oClock to morrow afternoon——

Wednesday February 11. 1778

The Convention met according to adjournment

The Committee again reported—and the Convention considered the clause for allowing a Liberty of Conscience viz A and There the Convention adjourned to 3 oClock to morrow afternoon——

Thursday February 12 1778

The Convention met according to adjournment—and resumed the consideration of the clause brot in by the Committee making provision for liberty of conscience——and after debate thereon the question was put whether the same be accepted and it passed in the negative——

It was then motion [D. Holten?] Voted—That the following be an Article in the Constitution—viz

"The free exercise and enjoyment of Religious Profession and Worship shall for ever be allowed to every Denomination of Protestants within this State"

It was moved *again* that the Words "Indians Negroes and Molattoes" be expunged from the 23d and the question being put it passed in the negative——18 only out of 101 for the Question

On Motion the Convention after debate reconsidered their Vote for appointing Civil and Military Officers by the General Court——

The Convention then accepted the 11th Article of the Committees Report——and having passed on the other amendments reported by the Committee—adjourned to Tuesday next at 3 oClock in the afternoon

Tuesday February 17. 1778

Afternoon

The Convention met according to adjournment——The Committee reported a Preamble to the Constitution of Government——Read and ordered to be recommitted——

The Committee likewise reported an Article for establishing the Form of an Oath to be taken by the Civil Officers of Government—Read and passed——

It was moved that the 28th Article be so altered that the Senators should be chosen by the House of Representatives——After Debate the Motion was withdrawn——

Then the Convention adjourned to 3 oClock to morrow afternoon——

Wednesday February 18th 1778

The Convention met according to adjournment. The Committee reported again a Preamble to the Constitution of Government——Read and passed

The Sixth Article was again taken into consideration—and after large debates thereon—ordered that the same be recommitted at large——Then the Convention adjourned to Tuesday next at 3 oclock in the afternoon——

Tuesday February 24th 1778

The Convention met according to adjournment——The Committee reported an amendment to the Sixth Article of the Report——which was read amended and accepted as follows, viz "Provided always that the Governor shall exercise the Power given him by this Constitution over the Militia and Navy of the State according to the Laws thereof or the Resolves of the General Court"——

It was moved That the 11th. Article of the Report be reconsidered——and the previous question whether the same shall be again taken into consideration—being put, it passed in the negative.

It was moved that a clause be added to the 24th Article determining that each Town shall pay the Expence of its own Representatives—as heretofore——and on motion the previous question was put whether the said Motion should be considered, and it passed in the negative——

Honorable Mr Cushing and Mr Pickering by order of the Convention brought in the following Article——

Read and passed—viz

——The Governor shall have no negative etc.——

The Report was read throughout——Then the Convention adjourned to Thursday next at 4 oClock in the afternoon——

Thursday February 26th 1778

The Convention met according to adjournment It was moved by Captain Stone Oak That the words "and no Person shall be obliged to pay towards the support of any Teacher or Teachers except of his own Profession or where they shall usually attend Public Worship" be added to the Article that provides for Liberty of Conscience.

And on Motion the question was put whether the question shall be put on the said Motion—and it passed in the negative.

It was moved that the 24th Article in the Report respecting Representation be reconsidered, and the following substituted in its Stead viz

"Each Incorporated Town within this State shall be intituled to send one Representative to the General Court——Any Town have five hundred Voters may send two having ten hundred may send three——and so on each five hundred more giving another Member——On Motion the previous question was put, whether there shall be any alteration in said Article—and it passed in the negative——(38–92)

The Convention adjourned five oClock to morrow afternoon to determine and pass upon the Report in whole—and enjoined the Members to attend punctually at that Time.——

Then the Convention adjourned to 5 oClock to morrow afternoon——

Friday February 27th 1778

The Convention met according to adjournment

It was moved That a clause be brought into the Report determining that a Governor shall not continue in Office more than three years out of six——and the question after a short debate, being put, it passed in the Negative——18.

It was moved That every incorporated Town have a Right to send a Representative—and that each Town pay its own Representative or Representatives and after some debate thereon the question was put and it passed in the Affirmative——66–93

A Clause for that purpose was inserted accordingly——

Then the Convention adjourned to 10 oClock to morrow morning——

Saturday February 28th 1778

The Convention met according to adjournment and after some debate adjourned to half an hour after 4 oClock in the afternoon——

Afternoon——

Met according to adjournment.

The Convention ordered That the following Article be inserted in the Report——being laid upon the Table by Mr Pickering and agree to by the Committee—viz

——Delegates at Congress

The Question was then put upon the Report in whole as amended and it passed in the Affirmative——39 out of 53

Ordered that Mr. President Mr. Pickering and the Clerk of the Convention be a Committee to arrange the several Articles of the Report properly, and then cause 600 Copies of the same to be correctly printed and distributed——agreeably to the Resolve of the General Court [noted?] in the Preamble of the said Report,——

Then the Convention adjourned to Thursday next at three oClock in the afternoon

State of Massachusetts Bay——

In the House of Representatives March 4th: 1778

WHEREAS in consequence of a Resolve of the General Court of this State passed May 5th 1777——the present House of Representatives were at their respective elections instructed in one Body with the Council "to form such a Constitution of Government as they shuld judge best calculated to promote the happiness of this State" And the Council and House of Representatives having accordingly in Convention assembled agreed to a Form of Government to be laid before the Inhabitants of this State agreably to said Resolve——It is Therefore,

RESOLVED that a printed Copy of said Form of Government be forthwith transmitted to the Selectmen of each Town and the Committee of each

Plantation, and the said Selectmen and Committee are hereby directed to lay the same before their respective Towns or Plantations at a regular meeting of the male Inhabitants thereof being free and twenty one Years of Age, to be called for that purpose, in order to its being duly considered and approved or disapproved by said Towns and Plantations: and the said Selectmen and Committees are hereby further directed to make a return of the doings of their respective Towns and Plantations into the Secretary's Office of this State, by the Fifteenth Day of June next, Specifying in such return the number present in such Meeting voting for, and the number voting against said Form of Government and where the Inhabitants of any Town or Plantation voting in such Meeting are unanimous the Selectmen or Committee are directed in their return to Specify the Number so voting and whether for or against said Form of Government, as it is necessary that the whole Number voting for, and the whole Number voting against said Form of Government, throughout the State be known.——

And it is hereby recommended to the Several Towns and Plantations within this State to instruct their respective Representatives upon this Subject that so the General Court may be properly impowered to establish this Form of Government; if upon a fair Examination of the Returns aforesaid by the General Court or such a Committee as they shall appoint for that Purpose it shall appear, that it is approved of, by at least two thirds of those who are Free, and twenty one Years of Age belonging to this State and Present in the several Meetings.——

Sent up for Concurrence J Warren Speaker

In Council Read and Concurred John Avery Dy. Sy.

Consented to by the Major Part of the Council——

A true Copy Attest Jno. Avery Dy. Secy.

Thursday March 5 1778
Afternoon

The Convention met and adjourned to 5 oClock to morrow afternoon

---

Friday March 6 1778

The Convention met according to adjournment

Ordered That the Committee who were appointed to cause the Form of Government to be printed in Pamphlets—see that it is printed in all the Boston News Papers——

Then the Convention was dissolved——

20

The Rejected Constitution of 1778

The Constitution adopted by the Council and House of Representatives, sitting in convention, was submitted to the towns for approval. The Constitution is reprinted from *Journal of the Convention for Framing a Constitution of Government for the State of Massachusetts Bay . . . 1779* (Boston, 1832), 255–264.

A CONSTITUTION AND FORM OF GOVERNMENT for the State of Massachusetts Bay, *agreed upon by the Convention of said State, February 28, 1778—to be laid before the several towns and plantations in said State, for their approbation or disapprobation.*

State of Massachusetts Bay.

IN CONVENTION, February 28, 1778

Whereas, upon the Declaration of Independence, made by the Representatives of the United States, in Congress, assembled, by which all connexions between the said States and Great Britain were dissolved, the General Assembly of this State thought it expedient, that a new Constitution of Government for this State should be formed; and, apprehending that they were not invested with sufficient authority to deliberate and determine upon so interesting a subject, did, on the fifth day of May, 1777, for effecting this valuable purpose, pass the following resolve:

"RESOLVED, That it be, and hereby is recommended to the several towns and places in this State, empowered by the laws thereof to send members to the General Assembly, that, at their next election of a member or members to represent them, they make choice of men, in whose integrity and ability they can place the greatest confidence; and, in addition to the common and ordinary powers of representation, instruct them with full powers, in one body with the Council, to form such a Constitution of Governement as they shall judge best calculated to promote the happiness of this State; and, when completed, to cause the same to be printed in all the Boston newspapers, and also in handbills, one of which to be transmitted to the Selectmen of each town, or the committee of each plantation, to be by them laid before their respective towns or plantations, at a regular meeting of the inhabitants thereof, to be called for that purpose, in order to its being, by each town and plantation, duly considered, and a return of their approbation or disapprobation to be made into the Secretary's office of this State, at a reasonable time, to fixed upon by the General Court; specifying the numbers present at such meeting voting for, and those voting against the same; and, if upon a fair examination of said returns by the General Court, or such a committee as they shall appoint for the purpose, it shall appear, that the said Form of Government is approved of by at least two thirds of those who are free, and twenty-one years of age, belonging to this State, and present in the several meetings, then the General Court shall be empowered to establish the same as the Constitution and Form of Government of the State of Massachusetts Bay; according to which the inhabitants thereof shall be governed in all succeeding generations, unless the same shall be altered by their express direction, or at least of two thirds of them. And it is further recommended to the Selectmen of the several towns, in the return of their precepts for the choice of Representatives, to signify their having considered this resolve, and their doings thereon."

And whereas the good People of this State in pursuance of the said resolution, and reposing special trust and confidence in the Council and in their Representatives, have appointed, authorized and instructed their Representatives, in one body with the Council, to form such a Constitution of Government as they shall judge best calculated to promote the happiness of this State, and when completed, to cause the same to be published for their inspection and consideration.

WE, therefore, the Council and Representatives of the People of the State of Massachusetts Bay, in Convention assembled, by virtue of the power delegated to us, and acknowledging our dependence upon the all wise Governor of the Universe for direction, do agree upon the following Form of a Constitution of Government for this State, to be sent out to the People, that they may act thereon, agreeably to the aforesaid resolve.

I.—THERE shall be convened, held and kept, a General Court, upon the last Wednesday in the month of May of every year, and as many other said times as the said General Court shall order and appoint: which General Court shall consist of a Senate and House of Representatives, to be elected as this Constitution hereafter directs.

II.—THERE shall be elected annually a Governor and Lieutenant Governor who shall each have, by virtue of such election, a seat and voice in the Senate; and the style and title of the Governor shall be His Excellency; and the style and title of the Lieutenant Governor shall be his Honor.

III.—No person shall be considered as qualified to serve as Governor, Lieutenant Governor, Senator or Representative, unless qualified respectively at the time of their several elections, as follows, viz: The Governor and Lieutenant Governor shall have been inhabitants of this State five years immediately preceding the time of their respective election; the Governor shall be possessed, in his own right, of an estate of the value of one thousand pounds, whereof five hundred pounds value, at the least, shall be in real estate within this State; the Lieutenant Governor shall be possessed, in his own right, of an estate of the value of five hundred pounds, two hundred and fifty pounds thereof, at the least, to be in real estate, within this State; a Senator shall be possessed, in his own right, of an estate to the value of four hundred pounds, two hundred pounds thereof, at the least, to be in real estate, lying in the district for which he shall be elected. A Representative shall be possessed, in his own right, of an estate of the value of two hundred pounds, one hundred pounds thereof, at the least, to be in real estate lying in the town, for which he shall be elected. Senators and Representatives shall have been inhabitants of districts and towns, for which they shall be respectively elected, one full year immediately preceding such election; provided, that when two or more towns join in the choice of a Representative, they may choose an inhabitant of either of said towns, being otherwise qualified as this article directs.

IV.—THE Judges of the Superior Court, Secretary, Treasurer General, Commissary General, and settled Ministers of the Gospel, while in office; also all Military Officers, while in the pay of this or of the United States, shall be considered as disqualified for holding a seat in the General Court; and the Judges and Registers of Probate, for holding a seat in the Senate.

V.—EVERY male inhabitant of any town in this State, being free and twenty one years of age, excepting negroes, Indians and mulattoes, shall be entitled to vote for a Representative or Representatives, as the case may be, in the town, where he is resident; provided he has paid taxes in said town (unless by law excused from taxes) and been resident therein one full year, immediately preceding such voting, or that such town has been his known and usual place of abode for that time, or that he is considered as an inhabitant thereof; and every such inhabitant qualified as above, and worth sixty pounds, clear of all charges thereon, shall be entitled to put in his vote for Governor, Lieutenant Governor and Senators or Representatives, shall be by ballot, and not otherwise.

VI.—EVERY incorporated town within this state shall be entitled to send one Representative to the General Court; any town having three hundred voters may send two; having five hundred and twenty voters may send three; having seven hundred and sixty may send four; and so on, making the increasing number necessary for another number, twenty more than the last immediately preceding increasing number, till the whole number of voters in any town are reckoned. And each town shall pay the expense of its own Representative or Representatives; and the inhabitants of any two or more towns, who do not incline to send a Representative for each town, may join in the choice of one, if they shall so agree.

VII.—THE Selectmen of each town shall some time in the month of April, annually, issue their warrant or warrants, under their hands and seals, directed to some constable or constables, within their towns respectively, requiring him or them to notify the inhabitants qualified to vote for a Representative, to assemble in some convenient place in such town, for the choice of some person or persons, as the case may be, to represent them in the General Court the ensuing year: the time and place of meeting to be mentioned in warrant or warrants for calling such meeting.

AND the Selectmen of each town respectively, or the major part of them, shall make return of the name or names of the person or persons elected by the major part of the voters present, and voting in such meeting, to represent said town in the General Court the ensuing year, into the Secretary's office, on or before the last Wednesday of May then next ensuing; and when two or more towns shall agree to join for such a choice, the major part of the Selectmen of those towns shall, in the manner above directed, warn a meeting to be held in either of the said towns, as they shall judge most convenient for that purpose, and shall make return as aforesaid, of the person chosen at such meeting.

VIII.—THE number of Senators shall be *twenty eight;* (exclusive of the Governor and Lieutenant Governor) their election shall be annual, and from certain districts, into which the State shall be divided as follows, viz: The middle district to contain the counties of Suffolk, Essex and Middlesex, within which ten Senators shall be elected: the southern district to contain the counties of Plymouth, Barnstable, Bristol, Dukes' County and Nantucket, within which six Senators shall be elected: the western district to contain the counties of Hampshire, Worcester and Berkshire, within which eight Senators shall be elected: the northern district to contain the counties of York and Cumberland, within which three shall be elected: the eastern district to contain the county of Lincoln, within which one shall be elected. And as the numbers of inhabitants in the several districts may vary, from time to time, the General Court shall, in the way they shall judge best, some time in the year one thousand seven hundred and ninety, and once in twenty years ever after, order the number of the inhabitants of the several districts to be taken, that the Senators may be apportioned anew to the several districts, according to the numbers of the inhabitants therein. And the General Court may, at such new apportionment, increase the number of Senators to be chosen as they may see fit; provided that the whole number shall never exceed thirty six, exclusive of the Governor and Lieutenant Governor.

IX.—THE inhabitants of the several towns in this State, qualified as this Constitution directs, shall, on the first Wednesday in the month of November, annually, give in their votes in their respective towns, at a meeting, which the Selectmen shall call for that purpose, for Senators for the year ensuing the last Wednesday in May then next. The votes shall be given in for the members of each district separately, according to the foregoing apportionment, or such as shall be hereafter ordered; and the Selectmen and town Clerk of each town shall sort and count the votes, and, by the third Wednesday in December then next, transmit to the Secretary's office a list, certified by the town clerk, of all the persons, who had votes as Senators for each district at such meeting, and the number each person had affixed to his name. The lists, so sent in, shall be examined by the General Court at their then next sitting, and a list for each district of those voted for, to the amount of double the number assigned such district (if so many shall have votes) taking those who had the highest numbers, shall be made out and sent by the first of March, then next after, to the several towns of this State, as a nomination list, from which said towns shall, at their meetings for the choice of Governor in the month of May, vote for the Senators assigned the respective districts; which votes shall be counted and sorted and lists certified as before directed, made out and sent in to the Secretary's office, by ten o'clock in the forenoon of the last Wednesday in said May, and not afterwards; which lists shall be examined by the House of Representatives for the first time of the election of Senators, and ever afterwards by the Senate and House of Representatives on said last Wednesday of May, or as soon after as may be; and those persons in each district, equal to the number assigned such district, who have the greatest number of votes, shall be Senators for the ensuing year, unless it shall appear to the Senate that any member or members thereof were unduly elected or not legally qualified; of which the Senate shall be the judges. And the Senate, when so constituted, shall continue in being till another Senate is chosen, and the members thereof gone through all the steps necessary to qualify them to enter on the business assigned them by this Constitution.

X.—THERE shall forever hereafter, on the first Wednesday in the month of May annually, be held, in each town in this State, a meeting of the inhabitants of such towns respectively, to give or put in their votes for Governor, Lieutenant Governor and Senators, which meeting the Selectmen shall cause to be notified in the manner before directed for the meeting for the choice of Representatives: and the town clerk shall return into the Secretary's office by ten o'clock in the morning of the last Wednesday of said May, and not afterwards, an attested copy of all the persons, who had votes for Governor and Lieutenant Governor respectively, certifying the number of votes each person so voted for had; which lists shall be, on said last Wednesday of May, or as soon after as may be, examined by the Senate and House of Representatives; and the persons, who, on such examination, shall appear to have the greatest number of votes for those offices respectively, provided it be a majority of the whole number, shall be by the two Houses declared Governor and Lieutenant Governor, the Senate and House of Representatives shall, as soon as may be, after examining said lists, proceed by joint ballot to elect a Governor or Lieutenant Governor, or both, as the case may require, confining themselves to one of those three, who had the greatest number of votes collected in the several towns for the office to be filled.

XI.—IF any person chosen Governor, Lieutenant Governor, Senator or Representative, whose qualification shall be questioned by any one member of the Senate or House of Representatives, within twenty four days after his appearing to enter upon the execution of his office, shall not make oath before a Senator, the Speaker of the House of Representatives, or some Justice of the Peace, that he is qualified as required by this constitution, and lodge a certificate thereof in the Secretary's office, within ten days after notice given him of such questioning by the Secretary, whose duty it shall be to give such notice, his election shall be void; and any person claiming privilege of voting for Governor, Lieutenant Governor, Senators or Representatives, and whose qualifications shall be questioned in town meeting, shall by the Selectmen be prevented from voting, unless he shall make oath that he is qualified as this Constitution requires; said oath to be administered by a Justice of the Peace, or the town clerk, who is hereby empowered to administer the same, when no Justice is present.

XII.—WHENEVER any person, who may be chosen a member of the Senate, shall decline the office, to which he is elected, or shall resign his place, or die, or remove out of the State, or be any way disqualified, the House of Representatives may, if they see fit, by ballot, fill up any vacancy occasioned thereby, confining themselves in the choice to the nomination list for the district, to which such member belonged, whose place is to be supplied, if a sufficient number is thereon for the purpose; otherwise the choice may be made at large in said district.

XIII.—THE General Court shall be the supreme legislative authority of this State, and shall accordingly have full power and authority to erect and constitute judicatories and courts of record, or other courts; and, from time to time, to make and establish all manner of wholesome and reasonable orders, laws and statutes; and also, for the necessary support and defence of this government, they shall have full power and authority to levy proportionable and reasonable assessments, rates and taxes; and to do all and every thing they shall judge to be for the good and welfare of the State, and for the government and ordering thereof; provided nevertheless, they shall not have any power to add to, alter, abolish, or infringe any part of this constitution. And the enacting style in making laws shall be "by the Senate and House of Representatives in General Court assembled and by the authority of the same."

XIV.—THE Senate and House of Representatives shall be two separate and distinct bodies, each to appoint its own officers, and settle its own rules of proceedings; and each shall have an equal right to originate or reject any bill, resolve or order, or to propose amendments to the same, excepting bills and resolves levying and granting money or other property of the State, which shall origniate in the House of Representatives only, and be concurred or non-concurred in whole by the Senate.

XV.—NOT less than sixty members shall constitute or make a quorum of the House of Representatives; and not less than nine shall make a quorum of the Senate.

XVI.—THE Senate and House of Representatives shall have power to adjourn themselves respectively; provided such adjournment shall not exceed two days at any one time.

XVII.—THE Governor shall be President of the Senate. He shall be General and Commander in Chief of the Militia, and Admiral of the Navy of this State; and empowered to embody the militia and cause them to be marched to any part of the State for the public safety, when he shall think necessary; and in the recess of the General Court, to march the militia, by advice of the Senate, out of the State, for the defence of this, or any other of the United States; provided always, that the Governor shall exercise the power given by this constitution, over the militia and navy of the State, according to the laws thereof, or the resolves of the General Court. He shall, with the advice of the Senate, in the recess of the General Court, have power to prorogue the same from time to time, not exceeding forty days in any one recess of said Court: and, in the sitting of said Court, to adjourn or prorogue the said Court to any time they shall desire, or to dissolve the same at their request, or to call said Court together sooner than the time to which it may be adjourned or prorogued, if the welfare of the State should require the same. He shall have power, at his discretion, to grant reprieves to condemned criminals for a term or terms of time, not exceeding six months. It shall be the duty of the Governor to inform the legislature, at every session of the General Court, of the condition of the State; and, from time to time, to recommend such matters to their consideration, as shall appear to him to concern its good government, welfare and prosperity.

XVIII.—WHENEVER the person, who may be chosen Governor, shall decline the trust to which he is thereby elected, or shall resign or die, or remove out of the State, or be otherwise disqualified, the Lieutenant Governor shall have the like power during the vacancy in the office of Governor, as the Governor is by this Constitution vested with; and, in the case of a vacancy in the office of Governor and Lieutenant Governor, the major part of the Senate shall have authority to exercise all the powers of a Governor during such vacancy; and, in case both the Governor and the Lieutenant Governor be absent from the Senate, the senior or first Senator then present shall preside.

XIX.—ALL civil officers annually chosen, with salaries annually granted for their services, shall be appointed by the General Court by ballot; each branch to have a right to originate or negative the choice. All other civil officers, and also all general, field and staff officers, both of the militia and of the troops which may be raised by, and be in the pay of this State, shall be appointed by the Governor and Senate; captains and subalterns of troops raised by, and in the pay of the State, to be also appointed by the Governor and Senate.

XX.—THE Governor and Senate shall be a Court for the trial of all impeachments of any officers of this State, provided, that if any impeachment shall be prosecuted against the Governor, Lieutenant Governor, or any one of the Senate; in such case, the person impeached shall not continue one of the Court for that trial. Previous to the trial of any impeachment, the members of the court shall be respectively sworn, truly and impartially to try and determine the charge in question, according to evidence; which oath shall be administered to the members by the President, and to him by any one of the Senate. And no judgment of said Court shall be valid, unless it be assented to by two thirds of the members of said Court present at such trial; nor shall judgment extend further than to removal of the person tried from office, and disqualification to hold or enjoy any place of honor, trust or profit under the State: the party so convicted shall nevertheless be liable and subject to indictment, trial, judgment and punishment, according to the laws of the State: and the power of impeaching all officers of the State for malconduct in their respective offices shall be vested in the House of Representatives.

XXI.—THE Governor may with the advice of the Senate, in the recess of the General Court, lay an embargo, or prohibit the exportation of any commodity for any term of time, not exceeding forty days in any one recess of said Court.

XXII.—THE Governor shall have no negative, as Governor, in any matter pointed out by this Constitution to be done by the Governor and Senate, but shall have an equal voice with any Senator on any question before them; provided that the Governor, or, in his absence out of State, the Lieutenant Governor, shall be present in Senate to enable them to proceed on the business assigned them by this Constitution, as Governor and Senate.

XXIII.—THE power of granting pardons shall be vested in the Governor, Lieutenant Governor and Speaker of the House of Representatives, for the time being, or in either two of them.

XXIV.—THE Justices of the Superior Court, the Justices of the Inferior Courts of Common Pleas, Judges of Probate of Wills, Judges of the Maritime Courts, and Justices of the Peace, shall hold their respective places during good behavior.

XXV.—THE Secretary, Treasurer General, and Commissary General shall be appointed annually.

XXVI.—The Attorney-General, Sheriffs, Registers of the Courts of Probate, Coroners, Notaries Public, and Naval Officers, shall be appointed and hold their offices during pleasure.

XXVII.—THE Justices of the Superior Court, Justices of the Inferior Courts, Courts of the General Sessions of the Peace, and Judges of the Maritime Courts, shall appoint their respective Clerks.

XXVIII.—THE Delegates for this State to the Continental Congress shall be chosen annually by joint ballot of the Senate and House of Representatives, and may be superseded, in the mean time, in the same manner. If any person holding the office of Governor, Lieutenant Governor, Senator, Judge of the Superior Court, Secretary, Attorney-General, Treasurer-General, or Commissary-General, shall be chosen a member of Congress, and accept the trust, the place, which he so held as aforesaid, shall be considered as vacated thereby, and some other person chosen to succeed him therein. And if any person, serving for this State at said Congress, shall be appointed to either of the aforesaid offices, and accept thereof, he shall be considered as resigning his seat in Congress, and some other person shall be chosen in his stead.

XXIX.—No person unless of the Protestant Religion shall be Governor, Lieutenant Governor, a member of the Senate or of the House of Representatives, or hold any judiciary employment within this State.

XXX.—All commissions shall run in the name of the State of Massachusetts Bay, bear test and be signed by the Governor or Commander in Chief of the State, for the time being, and have the seal of the State thereunto affixed, and be attested by the Secretary or his Deputy.

XXXI.—ALL writs issuing out of the clerk's office of any of the Courts of law within this State shall be in the name of the State of Massachusetts Bay, under the seal of the Court from which they issue, bear test of the Chief Justice, or senior or first Justice of the Court, where such writ is returnable, and be signed by the Clerk of such Court. Indictments shall conclude "against the peace and dignity of the State."

XXXII.—ALL the statute laws of this State, the common law, and all such parts of the English and British statute laws, as have been adopted and usually practised in the Courts of Law in this State, shall still remain and be in full force until altered or repealed by a future law or laws of the legislature; and shall be accordingly observed and obeyed by the people of this State; such parts only excepted as are repugnant to the rights and privileges contained in this Constitution: and all parts of such laws as refer to and mention the council shall be construed to extend to the Senate. And the inestimable right of trial by jury shall remain confirmed as part of this Constitution forever.

XXXIII.—ALL monies shall be issued out of the Treasury of this State, and disposed of by warrants under the hand of the Governor for the time being, with the advice and consent of the Senate, for the necessary defence and support of the government, and the protection and preservation of the inhabitants thereof, agreeably to the acts and resolves of the General Court.

XXXIV.—THE free exercise and enjoyment of religious profession and worship shall forever be allowed to every denomination of Protestants within this State.

XXXV.—THE following oath shall be taken by every person appointed to any office in this State before his entering on the execution of his office; viz. *I, A.B. do swear* (*or affirm, as the case may be*) *that I will bear faith and true allegiance to the State of Massachusetts; and that I will faithfully execute the business of the office of agreeably to the laws of this State, according to my best skill and judgment, without fear, favor, affection or partiality.*

XXXVI.—And whereas it may not be practicable to conform to this Constitution in the election of Governor, Lieutenant Governor, Senators and Representatives for the first year; therefore,

THE present Convention, if in being, or the next General Assembly, which shall be chosen upon the present Constitution, shall determine the time and manner, in which the people shall choose said officers for the first year, and upon said choice the General Assembly then in being shall be dissolved and give place to the free execution of this Constitution.

By order of the Convention,
JEREMIAH POWELL, President

Attest. SAMUEL FREEMAN, Clerk

21

Returns of the Towns on the Constitution of 1778

The towns overwhelmingly rejected the Constitution of 1778 and gave the reasons why in reporting the results of their voting. The citizens in their meetings criticized the proposed structure of the government, the plan for representation, the lack of a Bill of Rights, the manner in which the militia was to be controlled, and the exclusion of Negroes from the suffrage. Whatever the theory, it was difficult in fact to emerge from a state of nature. Most of the returns of the towns are found in MA 156/304–427; 160/1–31. The returns for Sandwich and Salisbury were transcribed by Professor Samuel E. Morison and are in the Massachusetts Historical Society, Boston. Acton, for which no return is available, voted against the Constitution, 51 to 18 (James Fletcher, *Acton in History* [Philadelphia, 1890], 253).

York (156/304)

At a meeting of the Free, and twenty one Year old Male Inhabitants of York, regularly assembled to the Number of one hundred and forty seven on Monday the 11th of March 1778

Joseph Simpson Esquire Moderator

The Proposed Constitution and form of Government for the State of Massachusetts Bay was Read and Considered, and thereupon,

Voted a Unanimous Disapprobation thereof.

A true Copy Att Daniel Moulton Town Clerk

Halifax (156/304)

Hallifax March 11th 1778

The Town being assembled to Consider of the forme of Government Sent to us from the General Court of the State of the Massachusetts Bay and the vote was put whether they approved or Disapproved Said Plan and none approved it, forty Six Disapproved it being the number of voters present——

Moses Inglee
John Waterman Selectmen of Hallifax
Jacob Tomson

Wilbraham (156/305)

At a Lawfull Town Meeting of the Freeholders and other Inhabitants of the Town of Wilbraham Duly Qualified and Legally warned in public town meeting assembled at the meeting house in said town on Tuesday the Second Day of april: anno: Domini. 1778:——at one: o:Clock afternoon to take into Consideration a Constitution and form of Government for the State of Massachusetts Bay agreed upon by the Convention of Said State February. 28. 1778 to be Laid before the Several towns and plantations in said State for their approbation or Disapprobation the Constitution and form of Government was Largely Debated upon then the following votes was past (viz) 24 in favour of the Constitution and: 51: against the Constitution——

24
51
75

a true Coppy from the Records——

attest James Warriner Town Clerk

Great Barrington (156/305)

At a Meeting of the Inhabitants of the Town of Great Barrington Legally Warned and assembled on the Second Day of April AD 1778 for the Purpose of Taking into Consideration the Constitution or form of Government Lately Sent out by the General Court of this State for that purpose, there being present forty Eight Voters the Said Constitution or form of Government Was Distinctly Read To them and the Question being Put the Said forty Eight Voters Unanimously approved of the Same

No. for the Constitution 48 against it—None

attest Wm Whiting
Jona [Nash?] Selectmen of Said Gt
Ehud Hopkins Barrington

South Hadley (156/305)

At a Legal Meeting of the Inhabitants of the Town of South Hadley on Thursday the Seventh day of April 1778 at one oClock Afternoon then met and after Considering the Constitution voted as follows
viz. Against 58 for it 4

David Nash Town Clark

Northfield (156/305)

At a Legal Meeting of the Freeholders and Other Inhabitants of the Town of Northfield April 9th 1778. To Consider approve or Disapprove of the Constitution or form of Government for State of Massachusetts Bay agreed upon by the Council and House of Representatives of said State on February 28th 1778.——

Voted and Chose Deacon Samuel Smith Moderator——

Voted To adjourn this Meeting for further Consideration untill Thursday the Sixteenth Day of April Instant at Sun Two Hours high in the Afternoon——Meet according to adjournment;——Present 43. Voters——After Due Consideration, On Motion made it was proposed and the Question put whether we approve of the Constitution or form of Government for the State of the Massachusetts Bay, agreed upon by the Council and House of Representatives in Convention on February 28th 1778. On counting Votes, it appeared there was Twenty Seven Votes for the Constitution and Sixteen against it.

A true Copy of Records Examined
Per Seth Field Town Clerk

Pursuant to the Orders of the great and General Court, We the Subscribers hereby make a Return of the doings of the Town of Northfield with Reference to the Proposed Constitution and form Government for the State of Massachusetts Bay as is above Certified by the Town Clerk and as it Stands Recorded on Northfield Town Book.

Northfield May 26th 1778.

Jonathan Belding
Seth Lyman Selectmen of
Eliphaz Wright Northfield

Royalston (156/306)

At a legal Town-Meeting held in Royalston, in the County of Worcester, on Thursday the ninth day of April, and continued by Adjournment to Monday the fourth Day of May, 1778, to take into Consideration the Constitution and form of Government for the State of the Massachusetts

Bay, as recommended by the Convention of said State, after a second reading of said proposed Constitution and form of Government, The Question was put, Whether the town approve of said Constitution and Form of Government, as it now stands, and passed in the negative unanimously. The number of Voters being *fifty four*

The town then proceded to chuse a Committee to take into Consideration said Form of Government, and make such Alterations, as they judge most conducive to the public Good. The town then voted to adjourn the 27th day of May, to hear the Report of their Committee. On that Day the Town met according to Adjournment and the Committee reported the following Constitution and form of Government for the State of Massachusetts Bay: Viz.

[The proposed Constitution, see above, No. 20, is here written out (156/306–317).]

After twice reading said Report, and full Deliberation thereon, the Question was put, Whether the Town approve of the proposed Constitution and Form of Government, reported by their Committee; and it passed in the *Affirmative unanimously*——The number of Voters being seventy six. It was then voted, That the Town Clerk be directed to make out an attested Copy of the above proposed form of Government, and transmit the same to the Secretary's office or President of the Convention, which they pray them to consider as truly expressive of the sense of this Town, respecting Government, which they are desirous may be established as soon as possible.

A True Copy Test John Fry Town Clerk

Athol (156/317)

In obervance an order of the General Court the Town of Athol assembled on the ninth day of April AD 1778 to take into Consideration the plan of Goverment sent to the Respective Towns in this State by the General Court for their Inspection and approbation and the Question Being put wheither Said Plan of Goverment was agreable to their mind and the Town unanimously voted to the number of one Hundred and one against it

Athol May the 20: 1778

George [Kilten]
James Stratton Selectmen of Athol
Josiah Goddard

Norwich (156/318)

Norwich April 13, 1778

At a Legal Meeting of the Inhabitants of Norwich Assembled for the Purpose of Considering and acting upon a New Constitution for this State held by Adjornment to the 18th of May, the Voters Present 41
those Voting for——00
those Voting against Said Constitution as it now Stand——41

Samuel Knight
Daniel Kirtland Selectmen of Norwich
James [Fairman]

Northborough (156/318)

At a meeting of the Free-holders and inhabitants of the Town of Northborough being duly Warned and Convened on the 13th of April 1778. For the purpose of takeing into Consideration a form of Government as it was Settled by the Convention of this State. There was Forty and four Legal Voters present at Said meeting——It was then put to vote by the moderator to see if the Town would accept of the Said form of Government and a unamous vote passed in the negative——

Northborough
September 12. 1778

By order of the Selectmen
Jethro Peters Town Clerk

Mendon (156/319)

State of Massachusetts-Bay
To the Honorable Council, and Honorable the House of Representatives, in General Court assembled.

Pursuant to a Resolve of the General Assembly of the State of the Massachusetts Bay, bearing Date March 4th. 1778, We the Subscribers issued a

Warrant appointing a Meeting of the Male Inhabitants of the Town of Mendon, being free and twenty one Years of Age—and said Inhabitants being accordingly warned and Convened on the 13th. of April last, The Constitution and Form of Government for the State of Massachusetts Bay, agreed upon by the Convention of Said State February 28th. 1778. was by the Selectmen, laid before said Inhabitants for their Consideration ——said Constitution being distinctly read to the Inhabitants, the Meeting was adjourned, to take the same into further Consideration——The Inhabitants being reassembled pursuant to said Adjournment May 21, The Number of Voters present in said Meeting was taken, and the Vote on the Constitution called for; when it appeared that there were two Voters for the Constitution, and fifty seven against it—fifty nine being the whole Number of Voters present in said Meeting.

Mendon May 31th., 1778

Joseph Dorr
John Chapin Selectmen of Mendon
John Penniman

Granby (156/320)

In Pursuant to a resolve of Court february 28th 1778: we Issud our Warrant for a Meeting April the 13th 1778 the Number of Voters Present at Said meeting was 55. And the Question being put whether the Meeting would approbate that form of government or Constitution and it Passed in the Neggative by the Number of 55.

Granby May the 20 1778

Witness our hands
Josiah Montague
Stephen Warnar
Asahel Smith Select Men
[Jesh] Chapin of Granby
John Moody

To the Secretarys
Office for the State
of Massichusetts Bay

Southampton (156/320)

At a Meeting of the Male Inhabitants of Southampton of the Age of Twenty one Years and upwards Assembled by Warrant from the Subscribers for the purpose of Considering the Constitution sent to said

Town by the General Court and holden by Adjournment upon Monday the Thirteenth Day of April A.D. 1778.

After Said Constitution had been read Several Times and largely Discoused upon by the Voters then present which were Seventy Three The Question was put whether they were for Adopting the said Constitution and upon a Division there Appeared to be Seventeen Voters for Adopting it and Fifty Six against it.——

The Following Question was then purposed Viz. Whether the Town approve the Constitution for this State sent to the Select Men by the General Court now read. Except in the appointing Civil Officers, Field Officers of the Militia and Field Officers and Captains Subalterns of troops in pay of this State, and the Continuance of Civil Officers in Office. Which passed in the Affirmative——

Attest John Lyman
Samuel Pom[eroy] Select Men of Southampton
Sylvester Woodbridge

Sheffield (156/321)

At a legal Meeting of the Inhabitants of the Town of Sheffield on the 15th day of April 1778.—present who voted in said Meeting 78. of which said Number 71 showed their Aprobation and 7 their Disaprobation of the Constitution of Government for the State of Massachusetts-Bay then laid before them as directed by the Honorable Council and House of Representatives of said State

Attest——
Leml. Barnard
William Bacon Select Men of Sheffield
Samuel Bush

To The Honorable Samuel Addam, Esqr Secretary of the State of Massachusetts Bay. Boston

Townsend (156/321)

At a legal Meeting of the Inhabitants of the Town of Townshend Assembled at the publick Meeting in Said Town on Wenesday the 15th day of April 1778. The Town took into consideration the Constitution or form of Government agreed upon by Honorable Convention and after debate thereon the farther consideration of the same was refforred to May Meeting

At a meeting of the Inhabitants of the Town on May 20 1778 the Town again assumed the Constitution and adjourned the same to the 25th Instant.

The Town being met according to adjournment and reasumed the consideration of the Constiution and voted as follow (viz)

Present 55 voters

In the Affirmative 53

In the Negative 2

A true Coppy attest James Hosley Town Cler

Greenfield (156/322)

Agreabel to the orders of the General Cort of the State of the Massachusetts Bay a meeting of the inhabitants of this Town was Convened By a Lawfull warning on April the 16 1778 and Continued by Adjurnment to the Second Tuesday in May 1778 for the Purpose of Considering and approving or Disapproving of a Constitution and form of Govornment for this State there was Seventy three Voters Present and voting Sixty Eight disapproved and five approved of Said Constitution.

Greenfield May the 12 1778 Attest. Samuel Wells Clark

Winthrop (156/322)

At a Town meeting of the Inhabitants of the Town of Winthrop on Munday the 20th of April 1778 present 21 Voters the Question was put whether the Town would Exept of a form of Goverment Sent to this town and the Town Voted Unamausly not to Exept of Said Form of Goverment.

Josiah Hall
Gideon Lam[bert?] Selectmen of Winthrop

Winthrop April 20th 1778

Stockbridge (156/323)

At a Town meeting of the Inhabitants of the Town of Stockbridge legally warned and held on the fourteenth Day of April 1778 and continued by Adjounment to the twenty first of the same Month, for the Purpose of taking under Consideration and acting upon a Constitution and Form of Government composed by a Convention of both Houses of the Great and General Court of the State of Massachusetts Bay and sent out to the People for their approbation, there appearing to be seventy Voters present, 39 voted to accept the said Constitution, 31 voted against it.

Certified by . . . . [Jo]nathan Curtis
Asa Bement
Elisha Bradley
Elias Gilbert
David Bixley
Select Men of the Town. of Stockbridge

Stockbridge April 21. 1778

Dunstable (156/323)

At a meting of the Inhabitance of the Town of Dunstable Being Free and Twenty one upon Aprill the 23: 1778 To Take under Consideration the Form of government or Constitution agreed on by the Convention of this State when said Constitution was Destinctly Red and Considred Voted to pospone the Resolve To the anual meting of said Town in May at Which the Constitution was again Red and Considred and voted to adjorn the meting untill the Second Day of June Next for further Considiration on which Day the meting was Held according to adjornment the Constitution being again Red and the Question Being put passed in the Nogative without one Dicinting vote,

The nomber that [aet.?] was 48——

Dunstable June 2, 1778

Josiah Blodget Jur.
Joel Parkurst
Selectmen of Dunstable

Lanesborough (156/325)

At a Regular Meeting of the Male Inhabitants of the Town of Lanesborough held on the Twenty third day of April 1778 in pursuance of a Resolve of the great and General Court of the State of Massachusetts bay, made and passed on the fourth day of March 1778 Respecting a Return of the Doings of the people of said State, in Respect to their approving or Disapproving of the form of the new Constitution——And there being one Hundred and Eleven persons in said Meeting that were free and Twenty one years of age, and voted unanimously against said form of Constitution——

Given under our hands at Lanesborough afd. the 24th day of April in the year of our Lord 1778

Jonathan Smith
James Harris — Selectmen
Jedidiah Hubbell

Kittery (156/325)

We the Subscribers agreeable to a Resolve of the General Court of the State of the Massachusetts Bay, have this day assembled the Male Inhabitants of said Town of Kittery, and have laid before them at a regular Meeting of said Inhabitants called for that purpose a Constitution of Government agreed on by the said General Court, and there appeared at said Meeting sixty four of said Inhabitants, and unanimously Voted that they DISAPPROVED of said form of Government.

Kittery April 27th. 1778

Nathal. Remick
Nicholas Spinney — Select Men of Kittery
Samuel Leighton
William Lewis

Tyringham (156/326)

State of Massachusetts Bay

The male Inhabitants of the Town of Tyringham in Said State being Duely warned meet at the meeting House in Said Town on Wednesday the 29th day of April 1778 To take into Consideration the Constitution and form of Government agreed upon by the Honorable Counsel and Representetives of the people of said State in Convention assembled the 28th of February 1778—and the said Constitution of Government was Destinctly reed over in said meeting by the moderator and after Consideration and Debate thereon the Question was put to know the minds of said Inhabitants wheather they approved of said Constitution of Government—and said Inhabitants voted unanimusly that they did not approve of it—and the Number of said Inhabitants that did appear to vote in said meeting (being Free and Twenty one years of age) was Seventy Seven

Dated at Tyringham may 23rd. 1778
Joshua Warrin
Benja. Warrin   Select men of Tyringham
Benja. Joslin

To the Honerable Secretary
of the State of Massachusetts
Bay———

Greenwich (156/327)

To the Honourable the Councel and House of Representatives of the State of the Massachusetts Bay Assembled,—Gentlemen—

The Select Men of Greenwich, (on Receipt of a Pamphlet Intituled a Constitution and Form of Government for the State of Massachusetts Bay, etc.) Issued their Warrant for Calling a Town-meeting, for the Purpose of Considering said Form of Government,

The Inhabitants being Assembled Agreable to said Warrant, said Form of Government was then Read and Considered, the Vote being Put, whether they approved of said Form of Government, it passed in the Negative.

Number of Voters at said Meeting.................................111
Number of Voters for said Constitution..........................
Number of Voters AGAINST said Constitution.......................111

The said Town of Greenwich at said Meeting Voted The following as a Reason for their not Approving of the said Form of Government (viz) Because said Constitution and Form of Government (if Established) Intirely Divests the good People of this State of Many of the Priviledges which God and Nature had Given them, and which has been so much Contended for, and Giving away that Power to a few Individuals, which ought forever to Remain with the People inviolate, who stile themselves free and Independant—

Also Resolved——

That they will not approve of a Governor, Lieut. Governor, or Senate——

That they will approve of a General Court Consisting of One Representative Body, with a President Presiding over the same, Annually Chosen by the People——

That they approve of all Officers, both Civil and Military to be Chosen by the People——

That they approve of One General and Comander in Chief Over the Militia of this State, to be Chosen by the People of this State—also One Admiral of the Navy——

That they approve of One Court Only held in and for Each County the Officers of which to be annually Chosen by the People of said County,——

That they approve of One or more Justice of the Peace in Each Town annually Chosen by said Town——

That all Officers thus Chosen as above be Commissionated by the General Court afore said——

That there be a Court of Probate of Wills etc. be held in and for Each Town, the Officers of which to be annually Chosen by said Town

That there be a Register of Deeds for and in Each Town Annually Chosen by said Town etc. with many Other Articles, which would be Necessary In Order to the Forming a Constitution, that might lay a foundation for Peace and harmony thro: this State, and forever Secure the Right and Priviledges to the People Inviolate, to Latest Posterity, which may be more fully Pointed out to a Representative by way of Instruction that may be Chosen for that Purpose.

by order and in behalf of said town

Greenwich May 5, 1778

Isaac Powers
Abijah Powers Selectmen of Greenwich
Simon Stone Jr.

New Providence (156/327)

At a Meeting Legally Warned at New Providence on May 1778 Elder Peter Worden Moderator in order to give their voice respecting the adopting the Constitution sent out by the General Court 39 Men Present a vote was called and put for adopting the same and not one man voted for it, 38 voted against it.

Joab Stafford Cheram Comet

Templeton (156/328)

Att a Legal Town Meeting of the inhabitants of Templeton on may the 6th Day 1778 Choose a moderator, and he Read the Consitution and form of government and after Consideration there was a vote Put and Past as follows vizt. Twenty Two for and Fifty one against said form Templeton the 22d Day of May 1778

Attest Ebenr Wright Town Clerk
Ebenr. Wright, Silas Cutler, Ezekiel Knowlton — Selectmen of Templeton

New Ashford (156/328)

At a Meeting legally warned at New Ashford May 7th, 1778. A vote was proposed whither the Inhabitants would adopt the Constitution sent out by the General Court 28 Men was at said Meeting and Unanimously voted against said Constitution.
By Order of the Comtt

Abraham Kirby Clerk

Mansfield (156/328)

At a meeting of the freeholders and other male Inhabitants of the Town of Mansfield being Free and 21 years of age; holden on the Eleventh day of May 1778 being duly worned and called by the selectmen of said Town for the purpose of taking into consideration a Constitution and forme of Goverment for the State of the Massechusetts Bay agreed upon by the convention of said state the 28th of February 1778, the said Forme of Goverment was then Read before said Town and was debated upon by parrigrafts——
The Town then adjorned their meeting to the 20th of May Instant at 3 of the clock afternoon for a further consideration on the subject; and then mett in as full meting as usual; and the question being put whether said Town do approve of the said Forme or not—the select men Desired the Town to mannifest their approbation or disapprobation of said forme

by bringing in their ayes and noes; when don it appeared to stand thus
Ayes for said forme................00
Noes against it....................92
Mansfield the 25th of May 1778
A True Returne of the proceedings of the above said meeting Certified by us the subscribers the above said 25th of May——

Isaac Dean Selectmen of Mansfield
Micah Allen
Isaac Dean Town Clerk

Hardwick (156/329, 331)

To the Whole Court of the State of the Massachusetts Bay in New England Now Assembled the Selectmen of the Town of Hardwick Having Received from the Late Convention a Form of a New Constitution, and Having at a Town meeting legally Warned Read the Same to the Inhabitants Who Having fully Considered the same Disaproved of said Constitution, and as said Constitution Points out that there shall be a Governor Lieut. Governor, a Senate and House of Representatives and that the Governor shall be Invested with such Power which may be to the Hurt and Damage of the good People of this State, we Humbly Conceive that one Branch of Legislature, a House of Representatives alone is sufficient to make good and wholesome laws to Rule and Govern the good People of this State
Number of Voters at said Meeting 156
Number of Voters for said Constitution 16
Number of Voters against said Constitution 140
The said Town of Hardwick at said meeting voted the following as a Reason for their Not approving said Form of goverment as their Constitution 1t. Because in article 15 it is said sixty members shall Constitute or make a Quorum of the House whereas not less than two thirds of the Members ought to make a Quorum Together with article 5th: 19th: 24th. 26th: 36th which articles are Diametrically opposite to the Libertyes and Privilidges of the good People of this State But as we are Desireous of Having a Constitution Formed on a good Basis we would propose the Following method——
1t:ly that the General of the State Militia be Chosen Annually by the People who shall Receive his orders from the General Court to march

the Militia to any Part of this State in time of the Recess of the General Court

2dly that all officers Civil and Military be Chosen by the People annually

3dly the President or Speaker of the House be Impowered to sign Warrants for the Drawing moneys that mey be voted by the assembly out of the Treasury of this State——

4thly that there be a Register, and Probate in Each Town in this State annually Chosen——

5thly that no man sustaining any Post of Profit or Honour shall be Exempted from Bearing his Proportionable Part of the Burdens of the People of this State——

6thly that whereas a Number of Negroes that are Now slaves have from time to time Humbly Petitioned to the General Court for their Liberty and Freedom and as yet have Not obtained it, But are Still Held in Slavery, which is very Contrary to the Law of god and Liberty that we Profess, and as we view this among many other, to be a Crying Sin which has Brought Gods Judgments upon the Land as you may see in Jeremiah Chapter 34th: v: 17th viz——

Therefore thus Saith the Lord ye Have not Hearkened to me in Proclaiming Liberty, Every one to his Brother and Every man to his Neighbour, Behold I Proclaim Liberty for you Saith the Lord, to the Sword to the Pestilence and to the Famin and I will [?] Removed into all the Kingdoms of the Earth——

and many other articles mentioned

and as we Conceive that the Constitution sent out for the Approbation of the People will not be Established, we therefore Request that the general Court will Issue out orders, to the Several Towns in this State, to send Delegates to convene in Congress to Form a New Goverment or Constitution for this State and Lay it Before the People for approbation, and that if two thirds of the People approve of the same it shall stand or be Established.

The Town of Hardwick at a Town meeting Legally Warned on the Eleventh Day of may 1778 voted the fore going Articles

Sylv: Washburn Town Clerk of Hardwick

To the Honorable the Council and House of Representatives in General Court assembled———

In Obedience to the Requisissions Contained in a Constitution and form of Govermen agreed upon by the Convention for that Purpos——We

Immediately Notifyed the Inhabitants of our town as therein Directed and after several Adjournments of said Meeting and on Repeated Reading and Maturely Considdering the Matters therein Contained, The Inhabitants of the Town to the Number of one hundred and fifty six on the 11th. of May Instant being Assembled for said Purpas Voted as Follows (viz)

Nomber of Voters for said Constitution sixteen against said Constitution one hundred and forty.

Dated Hardwick 20th of May 1778

signed William Paige
Timothy Paige Selectmen of Hardwick
John Hastings

Charlemont (156/332)

In Compliance with a Resolve of the General Court bearing Date March 4th. 1778—Directing the several Towns in this State To Meet together, to Cosider of the Constitution, in Order for Their Approbation, or disapprobation.——The Town of Charlemont May 12th. 1778—at a General Meeting for that Purpose, after some debating upon the Constitution, passed The following Votes.——

The Question was put whether the Town approve of the Constitution as it now stands,—it passed in the Negative By the whole House, which Consisted of fifty persons—The Town then agreed to Read by paragraphs and Make Amendments upon such, as were disagreable which amendments are as follows——

The First paragraph, is Refered to after amendments

In the 6th. paragraph the amendment is that those persons, Qualified to vote for a Representative, shall be Qualified to Vote for Governor Lieutenant Governor and Senators,—and That the words, Indians, Negroes, and Molattoes, be left out

The 9th. and 10th. Articles, are Refered to the amendment in The 5th ——In the 15th paragraph the amendment is as follows, Viz. That a Majority of the Representatives, as also of the Senators, shall make a Quorum——In the 19th paragraph, the following amendment—That the people Nominate both Civil and Militia officers.

In the 32d. paragraph, this amendment Namely That such parts, of them, be Excluded, which lay a Foundation for needless and burdensom offices, as Lawyers, Deputy sheriffs, probate office, Registers office, fees For Licence, for houses of Entertainment, the manner and Expence of Recovering Debt, the unreasonable Length, and Expence of cases at Court Unnecessary fees, or the Extravagancy of necessary Ones, etc. The Charge and trouble, arising From the above mentioned offices, might we aprihend, be in a great measure avoided, by Impowering proper persons in each Town to Do such business——

The Question was then put whether the Town Approve of the Constitution with the above Amendments——it passed in the affirmative By a majority of forty five, against five——

In the 6th. Article this amendment namely that the Representatives be paid out of the publick Treasury——

Charlemont May 12th. 1778——

Aaron Price
Oth Taylor Selectmen

Brunswick (156/333)

At a Legal meeting of the male Inhabitants of Brunswick, Being free and twenty one years of age on May 12. 1778 to Know their minds Conserning the proposed form of Goverment

It appeared by their Votes that there was
3 for said form
75 against said form

attest Nathaniel Larrabee town Clerk

Ashburnham (156/333)

Ashburnham, May 13, 1778

At a Legal meeting of the Freeholders and Other Inhabitants of said Town forty six of the Inhabitants present the form of the Intended constitution being publicly read the Question was put whether they would accept the same and forty five voted to accept the same and one against it

John Conn
Oliver Willard
William Benjamin

Belchertown (156/334)

To the General Assembly of the State of Massachusetts Bay

The Inhabitants of Belcherstown make the following Return—we have taken the Plan for a Constitution for this State agreed on in Convention Feb. 28, 1778—into our serious Consideration, deliberated on it, and as we are directed to approve or disapprove—we hereby manifest our Disapprobation of said Plan for a Constitution etc.

The Number for it were but four

Number Voting against it were one Hundred and thirty four.

We are desirous of a Constitution that shall be just and permanent—— we approve of great Part of the proposed Plan,—but can not admit of some Parts of it—we object Particularly against the nineteenth Article. Matters of this sort ought to be expressed plainly. Soldiers in the militia ought to have the Privilege of Chusing their own officers, captains, and subalterns of chusing their Field officers, each to be commissioned as in the 30th Article, if no objection be made, if made to be given into the secretary's office or where the Returns are ordered to be made, and the Governor and senate to judge whether weighty or not——We Conceive that the Secretary, Treasurer, General and Commissary General ought to be chosen by the same Persons in the same Manner as the Senate. ——We conceive it more agreable to the spirit of Liberty that the Justices of the Peace should be chosen by the freeholders of the respective Towns. Two thirds of the said Freeholders present and voting in a Town meeting for that Purpose making a choise be commissioned as in the 30th Article and their commissions annually renewed; if any objection be made against their first being commissioned or their commission being renewed, the governor and senate to judge whether said objection be valid or not, unless two thirds of the Freeholders in the Town where said Justice resides object, which ought to bar the renewal of his Commission, until he is rechosen——

——Captains and subalterns of Troops raised by and in the Pay of the State we apprehend ought to be recommended for their commissions by inlisting a sufficient number of men to serve under them, or to be appointed from the Militia officers in the country or Regement where the troops to serve under them are to be raised.

——With Regard to the 5th. Article, though at present there may be no great Inconvenience in that Plan, yet we fear that in Process of Time, it will make way for Corruption and Venality. and would query whether there ought not to be something as a qualification for a voter for a Representative which will more strongly influence him to seek the publick good, especially as it is highly Probable that the state will be thronged with foreigners.

——With Regard to the 6th Article,—Though we wish for a free and fair Representation, yet we fear that this Plan will make the House Bulky and unwieldy—and query whether the former Mode in this Province with only the addition of Liberty to each incorporated Town to send one—is not preferable.

——with Regard to the 28th Article we would Query whether the Delegate for Continental Congress ought not to be Chosen by the same Persons and in the same Manner as the governor and senate annually, and be accountable to the General Court.

——with Regard to the 31st Article—we think the Method in Connecticutt with Regard to writs preferable to this—and that it would be more expeditious and less costly to have writs run in the name of the state of Massachusetts-Bay and be signed by any Justice of the Peace in the County where the writ is returnable.

Belchertown May 13th 1778

Joseph Smith
Selectmen
Israel Cowls

Rochester (156/336)

At a Town Meeting in Rochester Duly Notifyed and Regularly Assembled on the 14th of May 1778: and by Adjournment to the 22nd. Currant Mr. Melatiah White Moderator——said Town Took into Consideration the form of Government Published for the Inspection and perusal of the Inhabitants of this State after mature Deliberation thereon: said Town Voted said form saveing only the following Objections. The Ninth Article in said Form seems to be attended with some Dificulty: as to Vote for Senators in the farthest part of the State, when we Cannot be acquainted with their Quallifications. Said Town Thinks it may be best for Each District to choose their own Senators and no more. And said Town thinks that the concent of the Senate be first Obtained

Before the militia are Embodied or marched And It appears to said Town that it will be most advantagious to the State, that Judges of Probate of Wills, their Registers, and Registers of Deeds, be appointed in Each Town—and that all County officers both Civil and Military be annually Chosen by their respective Counties: and that no person whatsoever hold no more than one office under the State at one and the Same Time——Militia officers to be annually Chosen by their respective Companies—and the Militia officers in Each Rigament to Choose the Field officers of said Rigament Annually:—The Persons then present and Voteing on above were 53 for and Two against said Form of Government.

a True Copey Attest David Wing T: Cler.

Pittsfield (156/337)

Pittsfield, May 14, 1778

At a meeting of the Freeholders and other inhabitants of the Town Pittsfield held for the purposes of considering of the Constitution sent to said Town for their approbation or disapprobation meet to the number of forty seven and unanimously Voted to axcept of the same except the 19th. 24th. and 26 Articles. Their Reason for so doing are expressed in our Instructions to our Representatives.

Attestr. William Williams Moderator
Caleb Stanley T Clerk

Egremont (156/337)

At a Meeting of the Inhabitants of Egremont in the County of Berkshire Convened and Held the 14th day of May 1778 for the Purpose of Considering and approving or Disapproving of the Bill of Constitution and form of Goverment Exhibited to the Town for their consideration.

Voters Presant 44
Votes in affirmative 14
Votes in Negative 30

Original Minits Examined

Timothy Kellog
Hooker Hubbard Select men of Egremont

Amherst (156/338)

To the Secretary of the Massachusetts State——

In Pursuance of Directions received from the Convention, Concerning the Constitution or Form of Goverment for the State aforesaid——

At a Legal Meeting of the Inhabitance of the Town of Amherst, Holden on friday the fifteenth day of May 1778——

After Taking into Serious and Mature Consideration of the Form of Goverment——

voted unanimously that they Disapproved of the Same——

Number of Voters Present Fifty three——

Amherst May 15th 1778

John Billing
Elijah Baker — Selectmen of Amherst
Reuben Dickinson

Pelham (156/338)

Pelham May the 15th 1778

At a regular Meeting of the Male Inhabitants of the Town of Pelham being free and twenty one Years of Age to consider and approve or disapprove of the form of government proposed for this State after mature deliberation and hearing the Report of their committee in was unanimously voted by all Present (the Vote being Stated approve or disapprove of the proposed Constitution) disapprove of the proposed Constitution the Number present being forty three A second Vote being proposed to return with this Account the Report of their Committee it was likewise unanimously voted return the Report of the Committee with the above Vote——

Attested by

Joseph Packad
Daniel Gray
James Taylor — Selectmen of Pelham
Jonathan Hood
Abr Livermore

Franklin (156/339)

At a Publick town meeting of the Freeholders and other Inhabitants of the town of Franklin including all the male inhabitants thereof free and 21 years of age) Duly warned and Regularly assembled at the Publick meeting House in said town on monday the 18th Day of may 1778 a moderator being Chosen the Constitution or new form of Government agreed upon by the Late Convention was taken under Consideration and after being read and Considerable Debate thereon—The Question was put whether the same was approved as a form of Government for this State in future untill the same shall be altered in manner as is Expressed by a Resolve of the general court of the fifth Day of may 1777 the whole Number of voters Presant 82, the Number voters approving 54 against 28

Franklin May 18 1778

Samuel Lethbridg
Joseph Hawes — Selectmen of Franklin
Asa Whiting

Northbridge (156/339)

In obedance to a resolve of the General Cort Past March the 4 AD 1778 We have Laid the Constitution or form of Goverment Before the inhabitance of the Town of Northbridge and thair was non voted to Except it and twenty three Negevetived the same which was all that was in said meeting at that time

Northbridge May the 18 AD 1778

Josiah Wood
Nathanel Adams — Selectmen of
James Fletcher — Northbridge

Wells (156/340)

Pursuant to a Resolve of the great and general Court of this State. We have laid before the Town of Wells the Constitution and Form of Government agreed upon by the Council and House of Representatives in Convention assembled at a Regular Meeting of the Male Inhabitants of said Town being free and Twenty one years of Age called for that purpose Who having Examined the said Constitution etc. and maturely considered the same unanimously Voted their Disapprobation thereof One Hundred and Eighteen of the Inhabitants aforesaid being present in said Meeting.

Wells May 18th 1778

John Wheelwright
Nathaniel Wells — Select Men
Stephen Titcomb — of Wells
Jonathan Hatch

Lancaster (156/340)

Lancaster May 18, 1778

Then the town of Lancaster assembled to gather upon ajurnment of a meting holden for the purpors of Receving of the Constitucion or form of Goverment—and their were assembeled the freeholders and others of the inhabitents of Sad town 152] Voted to Receve Sed Constitucion or form of Goverment 111 Voted not to Receive Said Constitucion——41

By order of the Selectmen — Cyrus Fairbank Town Clerk

Marlborough (156/341)

At a Meeting of the Male Inhabitants being Free and Twenty one years of age in the Town of Marlborough Regularly assembled May the 18th 1778.

To hear and act upon the Constitution and Form of Government, agreed upon by the Council and Representatives of the People of this State in Convention assembled after hearing and Duly Considering of Said Form of government. 76 Present at Said Meeting. 34 Voted to approve of Said Form of Government and 42 Voted to Disapprove thereof.——

Attest Wins. Brigham T. Clerk

Medfield (156/341)

Medfield May 11th 1778 Then the Inhabitants of said Town, agreeable to a Resolve of the General Court, March–4–1778 Assembled, and their being 60 Voters Present, their being 27 Votes, for the form of Government, and 33 Votes against it——

Medfield May–18–1778– By order of the Select Men

Eleazr. Wheelock Town Clerk

To the Secretary's office of this State———

Stoughtonham (156/342)

At a Meeting of the freeholders, and other Inhabitants of the Town of Stoughtonham Legaly Assembled, and Held at the Meeting House in said Town, on Monday the Eighteenth day of May 1778. Said Meeting Being Called for the Purpose of Laying Before the Town a Constitution and form of Government for the State of Massachusetts-by.
to be approved, or Disapproved by the town
Mr. Daniel Richards Moderator——
The Said form of Government Having Been Laid Before the Town, was Distinctly and Repeatedly Read and Maturely Considered. The Town then (Being Seventy Seven Persons in Number, who were free and Twenty one years of Age, and Present in Said Meeting.) Proceeded and voted unanimously, their Disapprobation of the Said Constitution, and form of Government for the State of Massachusetts-bay and Instructed their Representative upon this Subject—

Benja. Hewins
Israel Smith Selectmen of Stoughtonham
William Billing

Chatham (156/342)

At a Town meeting held by ajurnment May the 18th 1778 Deacon Paul Corwel mordarator then proceeded agreable to warrant and Read the Resolves of the Genaral Court concerning the form of government and after some debate said mordarator called a vote by dividing the House and all that was for said form of government to draw into the mens seats and all that was aginst it to draw into the women seats and it appeared when counted to be twenty one for said form and thirty three against it A true coppy taken of off the Book of Records for the town of Chatham and examined and Compaired

Attest Nathan Basset Town Clerk

Chesterfield (156/343, 420)

Chesterfield, May 30 1778

Mr. Mathew Buck Sr. The town of Chesterfield having chosen us the subscribers a Committee to form some Instructions for their Representative respecting the Constitution agreable to a Recommendation of the General Court of March the 4th 1778, and give some Reasons why it was disapproved of by the Town, would inform you, that the greates part of the articles in said Constitution were approved of by the Town as highly conducive to the Peace, good order and welfare of the State, but others (in the opinion of the Town) were rather Prejuditial, and likely to be hurtfull if not ruinous in their opperation to a free and independent People. The first Paragraft objected to is in the 5 Article where People are restrained from voting for governor etc. unless qualified with an Interest of Sixty pounds, the Reason of this objection is, because we apprehend the same Persons who are qualified to vote for a representative are also qualified to vote for Governor, Lieut. Governor and Senators——Upon the Sixth Article it is the opinion of the Town that every Town is fairly and sufficiently represented by one man, and that he ought to be paid by the State.

upon the eight Article it is the opinion of the Town that eighteen Counsellors are sufficient to be proportioned as the said article directs—— upon the eleventh article, it is the opinion of the Town that no free mans qualification should be disputed who votes for any member of the General Court who is twenty one years of age upon the fifteenth Article it is the opinion of the Town that one half at least of the whole Legislative Body ought to be together when any Law of the State is enacted—— upon the nineteenth Article we apprehend it to be the opinion of the Town that the Justices of the Superior Court be appointed by the General Court, and that the Justices of the inferior Court and Justices of the Peace be nominated by the Representatives of the County, that General officers be appointed by the General Court, Field and Staff officers be nominated either by the Representatives of the Regiment to which they belong, the Captains and Subalterns, or the People at large in the Regiment, and that Captains and Subalterns to be raised by and be in the pay of this State be chosen by the Soldiers that are to Serve under them——

Upon the twentieth article we apprehend it is the mind of the Town that county officers be tryed by officers of their own county, that field officers be tryed by the officers of their own Brigade, and Captains and Subalterns by the officers of their own Regiment, in all cases a right of appeal to the Governer and Senate

The twenty sixth and the first paragraft of the thirty second article are objected against by the Town.

Benja Bonney	Committee to give
Benj Mills	Instructions to the
John Wilde	Represent [ ] of the Town
Joseph Burnell	of Chesterfield appointed
Robart Webster	by the Town——

Present in the Town Meeting when the Constitution was considered fifty Inhabitants of the Town and unanimously disapproved of the Constitution.

	Benj Mills	
	Benja Bonney	
	Ephraim Patch	
To the Secretary of	Roger Sprague	Selectmen of
the State	Robart Weebster	Chesterfield

Williamstown (156/344)

To the Honorable Council and House of Representatives of the State of the Massachusetts Bay——

Agreable to a Resolve of the General Court passed the 4th Day of March —1778 the Costitution or form of Government has been laid before the Inhabitants of this Town at a legal meeting warned for that purpose on the 18th of May Instant after a Deliberate Consideration of the Several articles therein Contained it was put to vote whether the town will accept of the Constitution as a form of government for this State and was Disapproved by Seventy Seven and approved of by one a Committee was then Chose to give the reasons why the town Disapproves said Constitution and the meeting was adjourned to the 20th and then met and the Committee reported to the town as follows that we object against the 5th, 6th, 19th, 22d, 24th, 26th, and 28th articles and the following amendment or alteration was proposed in the report viz. that the fifth have this addition that every voter be under oath to act his own judgment in voting for any member of the General Court and that the town may admit any person to vote who is of good Conversation if they see cause though not worth 60 pounds and that the 6th article have this alteration that no town be allowed to send more than two Representatives to the General Court and to be paid for their Services out of the State Treasury—19th article have this alteration that the house of Representatives shall have a voice in the Choice of all officers mentioned in said article 22 article that the Governor shall be allowed to have two votes in the Senate 24 article that the several officers therein mentioned be appointed annually also that the several officers mentioned in the 26th article be appointed annually 28 article that the Delegates for the Congress be Chosen by the people at the same time and in the same manner that the Senators are Chosen only to be Chosen at large in the State—the above report being laid before the town and duly Considered was put to vote and was unanimously accepted by the Town. A true Copy of the vote of the town attested by me.

Isaac Stratton Town Clerk of Williamstown

Weston (156/345)

May the 18th. 1778 Agreeable to a Resolve of the House of Representatives of this State of the Massachusetts Bay March 4th. 1778. The Town of Weston in Consequence of a Warrent issued to that purpose, assembled in order duely to consider the form of Goverment sent to this Town proposed to be adopted by this State aforesaid. A Moderator being Chosen, then the said form was read over in the hearing of said town and then said meeting was ajourned to the [*blotted*]th of June when the said Town meet and further considered the same Sixty three of the Inhabitants being present then the Moderator desired the assembly to express their minds, upon the subject before them, and at length proceeded to call for a vote by yeas and nays (said yeas to approve, and nay to disapprove) and the votes being carefully looked over by us the Selectmen of said Town, found Six yeas, and fifty seven nays, and do accordingly return this as the sense of this Town, into the Secretary office of this State. agreeable to the direction of said Resolve

Josiah Smith
Isaac Jones Selectmen of Weston
Israel Whittemore
Samel Fri[*about 2 letters blotted*]

Wellfleet (156/345)

These certify That——
At a Meeting of the Male Inhabitants of the Town of Wellfleet who were free and twenty one years of age—duely Notified. Assembled and met in order to consider of and either approve or disapprove of the Constitution and form of Government. agreed upon by the late Convention of this State——

The number present at said Meeting was 57—who unanimously voted their approbation of the said Constitution and form of government

Hezekiah Doane
Samuel Smith — Selectmen of Wellfleet
Elisha Cobb

Sunderland (156/346)

Sunderland May the 18th. 1778. at a Town Meeting Legally warned and asembled In pursuance of a Resolve of the house of Representatives of the State of Massachusetts Bay in March the 4th. 1778 for the purpose of Considering and approveing or disapproving of a Certain form of a Constitution passed in said House of Representatives: then this meeting judged that said form of a Constitution, is not Calculated for the best, to promote the happiness of this State by their unanimous Vote the Number of voters present were 64 Certified by us.

To the Secretary of the State of the Massachusetts Bay

Simon Cooley
Joseph Field
Israel Hubbard
Asa Strong
Elisha Smith
Select men for the Town of Sunderland

Bridgewater (156/346)

To the Honorable the Secretary of the Massachusetts Bay.

In Obedience to a Late Resolve of the Great and General Court, Respecting the Form of Government Proposed to the Several Towns within this

State; the town of Bridgwater (Having been Previously and Duly notified of the Same) Met on the 18 Instant and having Deliberated on the Several Articles Contained in Said Form, and a Vote Being Called of the male Inhabitants (agreeable to Said Resolve,) there appeared to be Said Inhabitants, then Present and Voting, in all 246 Persons (viz)

For the Said Form of Government 6.
Against Said form................ 240.

Bridgewater May 18, 1778

Josiah Richards
Eleazer Cary
Josiah Hayden
Selectmen of Bridgewater

Sutton (156/347–358, 406)

We the subscribers the committee appointed by the Inhabitants of the Town of Sutton at their Meeting, on the 13th day of April last; to draw up the sense of the Town, as it appeared on said Day, respecting the new form of Government, presented to the Town for their Approbation or disapprobation; to shew the objections the Town have against said Form of Government, and what the Town think would be proper, in Lieu of the Things objected against; and to make Report to the May Meeting; in order for the Town to give it as Instructions to their Representatives; at the next General Court. We the said Committee having taken said Matter into serious and deliberate consideration report as follows

1. That there is a general objection, against said *Constitution and Form of Government;* because of its haveing no Article or clause against corruption or Bribery; purchasing of seats in the Legislature; or executive offices, places or Posts of Profit; or buying Pardons etc. But in all those Articles, which respect things of that nature; they appear to us to be wholly adapted to such Corruption and Bribery, as will more fully appear in the discussion of the several Articles. We are therefore of the opinion, that there ought to be an article of the following purport viz. that no Person be admitted, to vote for any Member of the Legislature; without first taking an Oath, that he will not vote for any person, in any measure, upon consideration of having received, or in hopes of receiving any Reward therefor, by way of Treat, loan or gratuity; directly or indirectly; from such person to be voted for or from any other Person, to procure Votes for him. But all his votes or suffrages for any Person to any

Place or Office to vote for such as he in his conscience judges best qualified for the Place and will best serve the publick.

And every Member of the Legislature, shall likewise previous to his entering upon the Business, he is elected to; make oath that he has not by any ways or means, directly nor indirectly, made Interest for his Place, either by flattery, threats, reward or promise of Reward. And if it can ever be made to appear that any Person in either case; has gone contrary to such Oath, being thereof presented by the grand jury, and convicted before the Superior Court; such Person shall forever be hold disqualified from holding any seat in the Legislature; or any office of Profit or voteing for any person into any of those seats or offices.

The four first Articles we don't object against.

But the V Article appears to us to wear a very gross complextion of slavery; and is diametrically repugnant to the grand and Fundamental maxim of Humane Rights; viz. *"That Law to boind all must be assented to by all."* which this Article by no means admits of, when it excludes free men, and men of property from a voice in the Elections of Representatives; Negroes etc. are excluded even tho they are free and men of property. This is manifestly ading to the already acumulated Load of guilt lying upon the Land in supporting the slave trade when the poor innocent Affricans who never hurt or offered any Injury or Insult to this country have been so unjustly assaulted inhumanely Murdered many of them; to make way for stealing others, and then cruelly brought from their native Land, and sold here like Beasts and yet now by this constitution, if by any good Providence they or any of their Posterity, obtain their Freedom and a handsome estate yet they must excluded the Privileges of Men! this must be the *bringing or incurring more Wrath upon us*. And it must be thought more insulting tho not so cruel, to deprive the original Natives of the Land the Privileges of Men. We also cant but observe that by this Article the Convention had in contemplation of having many more slaves beside the Poor Africans, when they say of others beside; being *Free* and 21 years old

We therefore think that we ought to have an Article expressive of what the State is to consist of. And to say in express Terms that every person within the State 21 years of Age shall have a sole absolute Property in himself and all his earnings having an exclusive Right to make all manner contracts, and shall so Remain until they are rendered *non compos Mentis* by lawful Authority, or have forfeited their Freedom by misdemeanour and so adjudged by Authority proper to try the same; or their service legally disposed of for the discharge of some Debt Damage or Trespass. And then that every Male Inhabitant free as afforesaid etc. Provided that Men who lie a Burden upon the publick or have little or no Property ought not to have a full or equal Vote with those that have an estate, in voting for a Representative, for then a Representative may be chosen without any property, and as the proposed Constitution stands there is all the chance that could be wished, for designing mischevious Men to purchase themselves seats in the House; for poor, shiftless spend-thrifty men and inconsiderate youngsters that have no property are cheap bought (that is) their votes easily procured Choose a Representative to go to court, to vote away the Money of those that have Estates; and the Representative with all his constitutents or Voters not pay so much Taxes as one poor *Negro, Indian or Molatto* that is not allowed to put in a single vote. Perhaps if all under what used to be voters for Representatives; were reconed each Vote equal to half one of the old voters it might be about a just and proper Medium. It is farther to be observed that this Article is grossly inconsistant with the XIV which provides that all Money Bills or Acts for levying and granting Money shall originate solely in the House and not be subject to any amendment, by the Senate; when the Representatives are chosen by Persons of no Property, and there must be sixty Pounds clear Estate to vote for a Governor or Senator. If men of no Property might vote for any part of the Legislature and not the whole; it ought to be that part of the Legislature which are under the greatest Restraints as to Money Bills Acts or Resolves.

Art. VI We wholly disapprove as it would make such an unweildy House if all were to send: and would by no Means be an equal Representation. But it is well known that all cannot and will not send, at least to attend steadily and so there is an unequal Representation, the House constantly shifting which grossly retards Business, and makes what is done broken incoherent and uninteligible and for each Town to pay its own Representatives, is a plan essentially to prevent small Towns or even large ones, at a distance from sending any at all, and is as unjust as it would be for the Massachusetts State to pay all the cost of their soulders and stores going so far to the Army over and above what those states pay who are near to it, and is just the same thing: but the soulders are doing the service of the continent and ought to be paid out of the publick chest, and so the Representatives from the remotest part of the state are doing the publick service of the state and ought to be paid out of the publick chest of the State; and not fling such an unequal Burden upon some Towns because they happen to be at a distance from where the court sits. And we are confident that we shall never have a court to the satisfaction of the People, till this Matter is Remedied about the Representation, and there be a Rational Number concluded upon for the House, and the whole State divided into so many Representative Districts: as near as may be according to the Numbers, Freehold and Invoice at large, and let those District consisting of sundery Towns and Parishes meet and choose by rotation in the several Towns or Parishes of which they consist, according to their Age and proportion as near as may be always choosing a Representative of the Town or Parish where they meet; and these Representatives shall be paid for Travel and Tendance out of the publick Chest and shall constantly attend, or if they or any one of them leaves the court attall except in case of sickness or Death of himself or Family, his district shall have right immediatly to superceed him by sending another Man or if a Representative dies or moves out of his district or is sick for the space of one month, so that he cant attend his District shall have Right to send another, these Districts to be new modled once every seven years or as oft as a general Invoice is Taken.

No objections against the VII article

Article VIII It is thought that the new apportioning of the senators to the Districts ought to be ofterner than there proposed

No objections against the IX and X Articles. But the XI Article was unanimously rejected because it puts Men to swear in their own case in Matters of fact that are as natural or lay as open to be proved by proper evidence as any Thing whatever lays a gross and needless Temptation upon to Persons to perjure themselves, and is a trifling with Oaths makeing them familiar and thus taking off the solemnity of them upon Peoples Minds.

No objection against the XII Article

Article XIII Objected against because an unlimited power is reposed in the general Court. Whereas we think that now they receive their Authority from the People, as they formerly did from the King so the People ought to reserve the same power of seting aside Laws that the King did in his Charter. And whereas it is provided that the General Court shall have no Power to add to, alter, abolish or infringe any part of the Constitution, so we think there ought here to be another Proviso that they shall not have any Power to grant any Donations or Gratuities of Lands, or to draw any Money out of the Treasury or Levy any Taxes upon the People in any ca[se] unless where the state receive a just valuable and equal consideration for the Thing so granted. provided this is not to be understood to hinder the Court from granting and engaging Bounties to encourage men to go into the War when needed; or to encourage Manufactures the giving such Wages to Officers and soulder in actual service of the War as shall be a proper Encouragment to each one in their respective Rank or Station, or the settleing reasonable Pensions upon such as are disabled in the war during their disability for their proper domestick caling

No objection against the XIV Article

Article XV Unanimously rejected because it makes so small a proportion of the House and Senate a Quorum. We consider it a Universal Rule that there should be at least one half of the Body to make a Quorum to do Business.

No objection against the XVI Article

Article XVII Unanimously rejected because it gives the Court a Power to dissolve themselves. They are the servants of the publick and when they are chosen and have accepted they have no right to dismiss themselves out of the service any more than any man that is hired by his neighbour to do any service. or to dissolve themselves (as they Term it) any more than the Army have Right to dissolve themselves before the Term is out for which they engaged, and with much better Face Might the select men of a Town dissolve themselves before the year is out since they are not ordinarily paid for their service. What the Convention or the designing men in it should ever propose this for, is not easily concieved, unless that when there should be a court upon this modle they might early in the year make an Act or Resolve to give the Governor and Senate a discretionary power to draw what Money they pleased out of the Treasury for what purpose they pleased and then dissolve; there is no way by the constitution to raise a new House before the year comes around, those that vote this dissolution may by the Resolve be amply rewarded for their viliny in dissolving: the Governor and Senate no doubt will faithfully take care of themselves while they have the whole State Purse in their Hand, and thus the State is defrauded of service: and plundered and no constitutional method to help themselves

Another thing we object against this Article is that one Man should have it in his Power to grant Reprieves for so long a Time to bring such horred expence upon the county, and it is no Iniquity by the Constitution to hire the Governor to do this, nor for the Governor to take such a Reward and so the county must bear half a years expence with the care of the prisoner; to put money in that Form into the Governors pocket, one Man alone so may no doubt be asily bought, especially when the Constitution justifys him in it. We therefore think that the Power of granting Reprieves ought not to be in any thing short of the Governor and senate, and they not longer than one Week into the siting of the next general Court.

No Objection against the XVIII Article

Article XIX Unanimously rejected because it places such an exclucive right or power in so small a number of men to appoint almost all Officers civil and military; which gives an Opportunity for purchasing Offices, and so the most worthless Fellows may obtain very important places, to the great damage of the State. We think it highly rational for a People who pretend to be free, that all Officers be nominated by the Bodies they are most immediatly to serve, and that all Offices of Profit be renewed annually, and then that the State may be uniform, and no part should act seperately, so but that there is a controul upon their publick Acts, let their Nominations pass the sanction of the General Assembly, and Commissions issue out from the Governor for such Offices as are proper for Commissions; And for Officers in the Army to be appointed as proposed in this Article; we have not yet surmounted the immense Burden and cost it was to us; the Continental Officers being appointed similar to this. We are fully perswaded that if the whole State had been districted out for raising a Rigiment each District, and then those Districts subdivided into Districts for raising a company each District, and then the select men and committees of each company District, to nominate men for the commission officers to the company of their District to inlist the Men and when they had inlisted or nearly inlisted their Quota let those that had inlisted the Men in the Rigimental District nominate their Field Officers for the District. If such a method had been taken there is no Doubt the Continental Army would have been raised filled up and compleated with a Quarter of the Time, Expence, and Trouble. And now we are labouring under the same or a worse difficulty about raising the Recruits for the Army. Therefore we can by no means consent to the constitution in this Article.

Article XX Unanimously disapproved of Because it places in the Governor and five or six other of the Senators to destroy a Man's Character and Usefulness without Law. and as this constitution lays so open to corruption; honest men are liable to be destryed by Pique, Prejudice or bribery; as, also Dishonest men in the same manner to go clear, if we can understand this article a man is to be impeached for some supposed or feigned fault or pretend mal-administation, not for the Breach of any of the particular Law or Branch of the Constitution and the Governor and Senate to say whither what he had done shall be [*blurred and torn; about 4 words*] without any Law to guide them, and also what the penalty shall be to him for breaking no Law! If he has broken any Law, why is he not to be tryed by a jury as expressed in Article XXXII, but if he has broken any Law he is to be indited tried and punished beside! so that a Man is to have two trials and two punishments for one crime; the one without Law and another according to Law; shocking to humane Nature! we never know when we are safe, when we are transgressors; or when we have done recieving punishment for a fault or pretended one! This article seems to be designed for Officers and for the removal of them: But we are of the opinion as we have heretofore said that all Offices of profit should be renewed annually and then if any thing should appear against a Man he may be droped without all this cost and sluring a Man's Character and as the case may be by another Year Things of themselves may be cleared up so that the man may be introduced to usefulness again and we should not think it amiss if in immitation of the Congress no Person should be a Governor Lieutenant Governor or Senator more than three years in six.

Articles XXI and XXII no objection against

Article XXIII unanimously disapproved of. That when the State have been at great charge to make Laws, and particular counties to convict criminals; that then, two Men should dispence with the Laws and judicial proceedings of the whole State, and let dangrous vilains go free of all punishment. it is no Transgression of this Constitution for a Malefactor if he can obtain friends to raise money and to layin with either two of those three Men. that can be bought cheapest and thus purchase a Pardon neither is it any Transgression of the Constitution for them to grant a Pardon to the worst vilain for Money. There ought to be no such Thing as Pardons when a Man is justly condemned to die or any other punishment by the Law he ought to suffer it. But if there should be any mistake or oversight, prejudice or new Evidence come to light afterward. The general Court may upon having any of these things made to appear before them, grant the Person convicted a rehearing so that no man may suffer without having all just and reasonable opportunity to save his Life and Character.

Article XXIV We disapprove because those Officers ought to be new appointed annually as we have here to fore said, and we know that *Good Behaviour* will be judged of according to disaffection on the one Hand; or Favour on the other.

Article XXV Unanimously disapproved because though it says the Secretary, Treasurer etc. shall be appointed annually yet don't say who is to appoint them The Treasurer who is the purse keeper for the whole State of all men ought to be chosen by the People at large, and he and the Secretary are so chosen in Connecticut where they have had a free Constitution.

Article XXVI Unanimously disapproved because those officers ought to hold their places against the caprice, Prejudice or corruption of any set of Men and not make Room as in this Art. when one Man is in Business to be flung out for nothing only because another Man will give more Money for the place, or is some particular Favourite; and these officers ought to be renewed annually as indeed all executive offices ought to be since the Legislature from which they derive their Being is new every year.

Articles XXVII and XXVIII no objection against

Article XXIX disapproved because notwithstanding this Persons of such pernicious Principles as deny the Right of Defending the Community by Force of Arms when assaulted by Force of Arms, may have the highest seats in Government to the great Damage or even Reuen of the State. We therefore think it highly necessary that in addition to this Article it should say that no Person holding to any pretended Principles Religious or whatever denying the Right or propriety of defending by Force of Arms all Assaults that are so made, shall hold any Office Place or Imployment whatsoever in the State; during his holding such pernicious Principles. Finally considering the imperfection of Humane Nature and the unfore seen Changes of Humane Affairs. We highly approve of Mr. Gordens proposal for a Convention chosen once in a few years in the same Manner that the Senators are to be double the Number of Senators in each District who shall be a Body absolutly distinct from the General Court not consisting of any of the same Persons who shall make such Revisals in the Constitution as they think proper and whose Business withal shall be to new apportion the Senators to the Districts. We think that Mr. Gordens Term of 20 years is too long between the haveing these Conventions We rather choose it should be as often as there is a new General Invoice taken and then that they shall new district the State for Representatives; Whatever revisals such conventions shall make beside the new apportioning and Districting as above shall be sent out to the several Towns in the State for their Approbation of Disapprobation and upon being approved by two thirds of the people at large or so far as it shall be approved of by them shall become a part of the Constitution and not otherwise.

Sutton May 18, 1778

John Sibley
Ebenr. Pierce Committee
Asa Waters

In Town Meeting for Choosing Representatives May 18th, 1778 the above and within Report was distinctly read to the Town and unanimously approved of and ordered that it be given to the Representative as the Instructions of Town to him upon said Constitution or Form of Government and that the Select Men sign a Copy of it and deliver it to him for that purpose.

Attest

Tarrant Putnam Selectmen
Jacob Commings of
Daniel Greenwood Sutton
John Jacobs
Solomon Leland

In obedince to a Resolve of the Genereal assembly of the State of the Massachuset Bay we the Subscribers Have assembled the inhabitants of the Town of Sutton agreable to the above Resolve in order to hear consider and act upon a Constitution and form of goverment for the State of the Massachuset Bay and said Constitution was duly considered artecel by artecel and the Vote was put to see if the Town would except of said constution and not one Voted to aprove of it but two Hundred and twenty voted to Disaprove of said Constution.

Sutton May 25th: 1778

Jacob Commings
Tarrant Putnam
Daniel Greenwood Select Men of Sutton
John Jacobs
Solomon Leland

Littleton (156/359)

At a Meeting of the Inhabitants of the town of Littleton Leagully Assembled at the Meeting House in Said Town on Monday the Eighteenth of May 1778 and continnued by Adjournmend to Monday June the first then Meet there being fifty eight of the Inhabitants Present fifty four Voated Not to Accept of the Constitution as formed by the Convention and four in favor of it.

Littleton June the 2—1778 A true Copy Att. per William Hy. Prentice
Town Clerk

Medway (156/359)

Agreable to a Resolve of the General Court Directing the Selectmen of the Saveral Towns in this State to Lay Before their Respective Towns the Preposed Constitution of forme of Goverment. In Obediance of the above Said Resolve we the Subscribers have Caused the inhabitance of the Town of Medway that are free and Twenty one years of Age to Assemble on the 18 Day of May 1778 Then the meeting Being opned and the forme of Goverment Read and after Some Debate the meeting was adjurned till the first Day of June and then meet. Then the Select Proceeded and numbred the People Present at Said meting and their was Sixty Voters.

Then the house was Divided and their Appeared two for Approving of the Said Constitution and fifty Eight Disapproving of the Same.

Medway June the 10: 1778

Jonathan Adams Jr.
Joseph Lovell
Simon Fisher
Henry Ellis
Selectmen

Monson (156/360)

At a meeting held on May the Eighteenth by the inhabitence of Monson to se if thay would appruve or Disappruve of the Constitution or form of government after many Debates the meeting was agurned to the twenty fifth for further Considerration whan but thirty eight appered and it was Considered article by article and voted to a man not to receve it on account of saverrel articles (viz)

the 5
the 6
the 8 and 9
the 15 and 19

the 24 and 26
and the 38th

Abijah Newell
Nathaniel Sikes
Select men

Topsfield (156/361)

At a Legal Towne meeting of the Inhabitants of the Town of Topsfield held by ajournment the Nineteenth Day of May AD 1778——
In obedience to a Resolve of the Generel Court of the State of Massachusetts Bay the said Town taking into Consideration a Constitution and form of Goverment agreed upon by the Convention of Said State February 28th 1778—to be Laid before the Several Towns and plantations in Said State for their approbation or Disapprobation
The question being put whither the Town approved off said Constitution and form of Government, it appeared by a Division that there was four for said Constitution and form of Goverment and thirty three against it——
Dated Topsfield June 26th AD 1778

Zaccheus Gould
Joseph Cummings Juner
Joseph Gould
Isaac Averell
Daniel Bixby
Selectmen of Topsfield

Amesbury (156/361)

At a legal meeting of the male Inhabitants of the Town of Almesbury [Amesbury] being free and twenty one years of age Warned for Consideration of the New Constitution or form of Government Held in Said Town May Nineteenth 1778 the Said form of Government was Laid before the Inhabitants of said town and Duely Considered and acted upon when thirty Nine Voated for the said form and none against it.

Simeon Bartlet
Ezra Worthen
Selectmen of Almesbury

Worcester (156/362)

At a Meeting of the Male Inhabitants of the Town of Worcester, above the age of twenty one years and free at the public Meeting House in said Town, being duly Warned, and there held on Tuesday the nineteenth Day of May A.D. 1778 at one O'clock in the afternoon By several adjournments from Monday the 13th Day of April A.D. 1778——Dr. John Green being Moderator——
The Town Proceeded to act on the Second Article in the Warrant——Viz: To see if the Inhabitants of said Town above described *approve* or *Disapprove* of the Constitution, or form of government lately agreed on by the Convention of this State, and to act thereon as is directed by the Late Resolve Authorizing the calling the Inhabitants together for this purpose.
There being 58 voters present. The Question was put: whether the Town approve of Said Constitution and Nine of said Inhabitants voted, in the *affirmative* and *forty nine,* voted not to accept of the said Constitution or form of government——
Then dissolved said Meeting——
A True Return of the Doings of said Inhabitants on said Article, as appears of Record——

Attest William Stearns Town Clerk

Worcester June 12th 1778

Harwich (156/362)

At a Town Meating Leaglely Notified and assembled ate Harwich May the 19 Day 1778—After Reading and Considering The New Form of Govermente a voate Bing Called and was unanimos in Faver of Said Forme Number of voaters Presente ate Said Meating was Sixty Eighte

James Pain Selecte men of
Date Harwich May th 20: 1778 Joseph Nye Harwich

Stoughton (156/363)

To the Honorable the Council and House of Representitives of the State of the Massachusetts bay

These may Sertify that at a Town meeting Legally assembled at Stoughton on the 18th Day of May 1778 of the mail inhabitants of Said Town being free and Twenty one years of age Called for the purpose of Considering and acting on the Constitution or form of Goverment Sent by the Convention of this State to the Towns for their approbation or Disapprobation——Thomas Crane Esquire moderator——There Being two hundred and thirty five voters present at Said meeting The Town voted uannimously to Reject Said Constitution or form of Goverment.

Stoughton May the 19th 1778.

Benja Gill	
Robert Swan	Selectmen
James Endicott	of
Christr. Wadsworth	Stoughton
Asahel Smith	

Ware (156/364)

State of Massachusetts Bay May 19—1778

The proceeding of the Town of Ware with Regard to the Constitution sent to us at a Meeting of the Inhabitants of said town of Ware Leagaly warned, and fifty one Voters being Present the said Constitution being Read and Deliberated it was Unanimously voted to Disapprove of the same

Alexandrew Magune	Selectmen
Oliver Coney	

Dartmouth (156/364)

Pursuant to a Resolve of the General Assembly of the State of Massachusetts Bay the inhabitants of the Town of Dartmouth at a Legal meeting warned for that purpose and held on the 19th of May AD 1778 by adjournment from the 21st of April preceeding, the inhabitants of said Town took into Consideration the forms of Government published by said General Assembly for the approbation or Rejection of the inhabitants of this State; and after duly Weighing and Considering the Contents of said form, were unanimously of opinion that the said form of government ought to be Rejected the Number present and Voting at said Meeting were one hundred and forty four.

William Davis
Thomas Kempton
Job [Almy]
Richard [Keivly]
Benja. Russell
} Selectmen of Dartmo.

[Jireb?] Willis
Thomas Smith
Jereh. Mayhow
Benja. Brownel
Gaml Bryant
} Commttee of Dartmo.

Leverett (156/365)

Agreable to the Derictions given us from the General Court we caused the In Habitance of Leverett to be warned and they meet att a Leagal meeting to act upon the constitution or form of Goverment and forty one voaters being in the meeting one voat for said form of Goverment and forty against said form of Goverment

Test

Leverett May 19, 1778 Moses Graves Select men of Leverett
[Stephan?] Ashley

Falmouth (156/365)

Falmouth May 19th 1778

At a meeting of the Male Inhabitants of the Town of Falmouth being free and Twenty one years of Age called agreeable to a Resolve of the General Court passed the 4th of March to Consider the Constitution of Government lately formed by the two Houses in Convention Assembled The Town Considered the same accordingly and on the question being put it appeared that the number who voted against it was sixty eight ——For it none——

A true Copy from Falmouth Records

Att [Nat Green?] Moody Town Clerk

New Salem (156/366)

To the Honorable House of Representatives of the State of Massechusetts Bay Gentlemen Agreeable to your Resolve We have meet and carfully Examiand the New form for a constetution and unanimasly Disaproved of it. The Number Present at said meeting, 74——Because we conceive that there are some things contained in it that are Injures to the Rights of a free People——

1ly Because there is two Branches Proposed to make the Legaslative authority When we conceive that one Branch will answer all the Porposes of good goverment much Better than two

2ly Because in said consteution mens worth of money seems to be Pointed out as qualifications But we think where the great Author of Natur hath furnished a man to the satisfaction of the Electors and he Legaly chosen he ought to have a seat and voice in any socity of men or to serve in any office whatever

3ly Because said Constetution as we conceive admitts of three times too Numeras a house since one third part the Number would dispatch Buisness with greater Briefness and be Less Burdensome to the State

4ly Because the Eases method for the People setteling their one civel Cases is Not Pointed out in this Constetution we conceive that it would be more for the well being of the People to have authority in each town to settel their own civel affairs——

5ly Because said Constetution Deprives the People of their just Rights of chusing their civel and military officers (viz) Justices Captains and Subboltons etc.——

6ly Because said Constetution maks no Provision against extravagences in Sallarys Pencions and fees we conceive that No Sallary ought to be granted Nor Pencion given or fee seet with a Less Majority then four to one——

Benjamin Southwick Jur
Uze. Putnam Selectmen
John King

Palmer (156/367)

At a meeting of the freeholders and other inhabitents of the town of Palmer Legley Convend at the Publick meeting house in said Palmer

May the 20 1778 at one of the Clock in the after noon of said Day the meeting Being opned and the modrater chson it was Put to Vote whether the town would exept of the new Constitution exebited to the town By our Representive from the Genrel Cort and the aforsaid Inhabitents Voted Not to Exept of it Everey man to the Nomber of fifty Eight.

Palmer June the 13th: 1778

Etest Per Robert Hunter town Clerk

Penobscot (156/367)

State of the Massachusetts Bay———

Penobscut May the 20th 1778———

At a Meeting of the inhabatance of a Plantation on the East Side of Penobscut River uper setelment Leaguley wornd By the Commetey of Sade Plantation to Consider the Constitution [or?] and form of Goverment Set forth By the General Cort of Sade State and Sent out for the Peoples apprabation or Disapprabation.

Preasant at Sade Meeting Thirty three Parsons Voted for the Constitution Thirty two Parsons Voted against the Constitution one Parson

To the Secretary of the State of Massachusetts Bay

John Emory
Samul [K?]enney
James Budge

Boothbay (156/368–373)

At a legal meeting of the inhabitants of the Town of Boothbay held at the meeting house by adjournment May 20th 1778 for the sole purpose of considering the constitution and form of Government for the State of Massachusetts bay, agreed on by the convention of Said State on the 28th of February last, and now laid before the Town for the approbation or disapprobation, voted unanimously that the following return be made by the Selectmen and Sent to the Secretary's office by the 15th day of June next, as a true account of the Sentiments and doings of the inhabitants of this Town upon that Subject. Viz.

This Town deeply impressed with a Sense of the importance of having a Constitution of government that might Secure the rights of individuals,

Establish the most equal distribution of Power, and provide for the most faithful exercise of it, and at the Same time possess firmness and permanancy within itself did early enter upon the Serious consideration of the Resolve that passed the General assembly of this State, on the 5th of May 1777, on which the formation of the present constitution was founded; and after mature deliberation, could not See it *their* duty to practice on the directions therein offered and therefore did neither instruct nor Send any representatives to the General Court during that year——
1st. because they were humbly of opinion that the hurry of war did not permit that calm deliberation necessary to form a constitution for a government of perpetual duration,
2dly because they hoped that, when, by the blessing of Heaven, the American arms had effectually Secured our invaded rights, vanquished the unnatural usurpers of them, and put a period to this distressful War, the Congress would be impowered and instructed to abolish all distinction of Separate States, and perfect and Secure the union of America, by reducing the whole into one great *Republick;* and therefore they thought it would have been best to have continued for the present, to act upon the former constitution with Such Temporary amendments as might be found expedient for the more easy and convenient dispatch of public business. Such as by impowering the president of the Council to Sign all papers instead of the fifteen whose Signature was heretofore required, and often not to be obtained without great delays and inconvenience.
3dly Because they apprehended that the important concerns of war, in addition to the common business of internal regulation, would be Sufficient to employ the whole time, and engross the whole care of the General Court, and therefore they concluded that, to impose on that Honorable body the additional Task of forming a constitution at the Same time, would necessitate a dangerous neglect of the Exigencies of the army on the one hand,——or an hasty immature plan of Government on the other; and hence, without intending the least disparagement of the abilities or integrity of the General Assembly (for whom they ever entertained the highest respect,) this town was humbly of opinion that a convention of delegates, who held no Seats in either house was the *only* body competent for this work.

However, being disposed, as becomes good members of Society, duly to regard every act of the Government over them the Inhabitants of this Town did, at a former meeting called for this purpose, Solemnly discuss the constitution laid before them by the Honorable Court, together with the resolve accompanying the Same; and that their judgments might be the better ripened on a matter of So much importance, they adjourned to this day and having now resumed the consideration thereof it was, Voted unanimously, that, altho it does not appear by the letter of Said resolve that anything is left to the Town but only to *approve or disapprove* Simply and in bulk, the form as it now Stands, yet it is the right of the inhabitants of this Town, as *freemen,* to express their Sentiments on every public measure of Government, and it is their duty *as honest men,* to do So on this occasion: and they cannot believe the Honourable Court intended to oblige them to approve the *whole,* while there was *one* article contained in it to which they could not consent; nor to constrain them to vote a disapprobation in universal terms, while they found any articles in the plan which they would earnestly desire to adopt; therefore this Town will give its Judgment on each article Separately; and if the whole may be ratified by a vote of Two thirds of the voters, in the State, it cannot be conceived that any Separate article might not be ratified in the Same Manner

And knowing that the Honorable Court openly disclaims all pretences to infallibility, it cannot be Supposed that they will refuse to alter, correct, or rescind every article where they See Sufficient reasons for So doing: therefore this Town is of opinion that it is their duty to the public to express the reasons of their judgment concerning every article which they cannot approve: and therefore it was

Voted unanimously that their Said judgment be expressed as follows Article 1 disapproved first because we can see no good reason why the civil year, Should have *one* beginning, and the political year *another,* that one year in office Should comprehend nearly one half of Two distinct years, whereby confusion in acts of office, and in the dates of Such acts is greatly occasioned.——

Secondly because we cannot consent to the Setting up any branch of Legislative authority, under the name of *Senate* or *Council,* that shall be able to controul the representatives of the people——

thirdly because, if Such a body were formed they could be of no other uses than the exercise of such controul would comprize, except meerly for allowing a reconsideration of matters to be enacted and fourthly because our reason Suggests that, for either of these purposes, the correcting body Should be composed of a greater (never of a Smaller) number then the body to be corrected, which otherwise ought to be Supposed to contain a greater Share of the wisdom of the community:——fifthly because all the advantages of reconsideration may be Sufficiently Secured by causing all matters to pass the Scrutiny of one or more committees of the House of Representatives previous to their coming before the house: and by ordering the three readings, usually necessary to the passing of bills to be observed also in passing resolves, and each reading to be *assigned* and each Second and third reading to be at the distance of Several days from the reading next preceeding it,

Article II disapproved first because these offices are needless in a free State; and with all their Limitations, may become dangerous to the liberties of the People. Seccondly because the powers vested in these officers by this plan, are Such as we cannot consent to lodge in any deputations Save the representatives of the people: and will never willingly See deposited in the hands of one man. Thirdly, because, without these powers, a Governor can be of no other use, than to authenticate the acts of the legislature, which may as well be done by a Speaker of the assembly. 4thly because, without necessity, we deem it no good policy to erect officers which, cannot be Supported *with dignity,* without Such expence to the State as in its present weakness, and debts, it is very ill able to defray:——especially as these offices are objects of ambition, and very naturally become the apple of discord in a State, affording a fruitful occasion to party, to envy—to jealousy—to discontent—to bribery and every corruption of heart and manners. Art III *disapproved* first because we are humbly of opinion that there are qualifications *of the person* that ought much rather to be deemed indispensible, and Should be Sought for before the quantum of his *estate*

Secondly because there are but few freeholders in the State but might according to this plan, be qualified for a governor, especially in these times when Small estates bear great nominal value—thirdly because the time of residence required for either of the orders therin Specified is too short; and leaves too much room for our enemies to qualify themselves, or their tools, for holding the reigns of Government over this people.

Article IV approved.

Article V *disapproved,* first because the time of residence is too short, as mentioned reason 3d on art 3d. Secondly because the poor, who have not sixty pounds, have as much interest in the election of Governor etc. as in that of Representatives; and ought, we apprehend, to have a voice herein as well as their rich neighbours: Thirdly, and especially, because we know of no reason in nature, or in revelation, to justify our depriving the Africans and their descendants (whose long continued Shameful and unchristian Slavery reflects dishonour and Endangers the curse of heaven on our public Struggles for our own rights) of a natural privilege of all men: and much less can we consent thus injuriously to treat the original Lords and proprietors of the land.

Article VI approved.

Article VII disapproved, first because we see not why representatives and all other officers of State Should not be elected in the beginning of the year, Secondly because we judge every town has a natural right to Send a representative to the General assembly *at any time of the year:* and to recall one and Send another at pleasure, So as not to exceed the number assigned it, and therefore ought not to be deprived of that right meerly because their Selectmen neglected to make return before the last wednesday in May.

Article VIII disapproved, first because we cannot approve the creating Such an order at all: for the reasons given under art. 1. Secondly because, if appointed, the Senate Should consist of a greater number of members, —thirdly because we humbly concieve that to determine the number to be elected, by each district, by the numbers of its respective inhabitants *only,* is not the most equitable Scale; in as much as, by this means, real property, which is the only Solid basis of a State, has the *least* influence in the election; and a Single town, with a very Small proportion of real estate, may outweigh whole counties; fourthly *because* the right of Election, *in this case,* ought to be in a compound Ratio of the numbers and real property in each district respectively;

Art IX disapproved, first because we think all officers Should be elected at the beginning of the year: Secondly because we think *one* election is Sufficient for *one* man; and the multiplying Town meetings for that purpose is laying a needless burden on the people: and therefore where any man appears to have been chosen once by the greatest number of voters, in the district, he ought to be deemed legally elected: thirdly because no Town ought to be confined to a nomination list: they may have Seen cause, before *that time,* to alter their judgment concerning the man, *themselves* had elected—and, in that case, ought not to be obliged to vote for him again, and much less for a man they had not chosen, and cannot approve, merely because he was chosen by a number of others. fourthly because this article of the constitution we humbly concieve, Should have restricted the *Same men* from holding the place of Senators in perpetuum, as it would be highly dangerous to the liberty of the people that any man Should be capable of filling So important a trust all his life, we judge no man should be Eligible more then *two years in ten:*——

Article X disapproved for reasons in Articles I: II: and IX, and especially because we think the election Should be entirely left to the people, and, in case of any election failing, Should be remitted to them at large, for a new choice:—and we cannot See why they who formerly possessed the Seats now vacant might not continue therein till the new choice is perfected; but we cannot consent that the power of election Should be left with the General Assembly in any case whatsoever:

Article XI disapproved because the qualification itself is in our opinion, quite insufficient, if never So well certified; Secondly because this mode of certifying it may open the door to many perjuries: thirdly because we Suppose an attested copy of the rate-roll from the clerk's office of the Town, where Such questioned party dwells, might much better answer the purpose of certification, and Not be liable to Such abuses.

Article XII disapproved for the reasons mentioned in Article IXth and X

Article XIII approved, excepting the word Senate in the enacting Style of laws

Article XIV approved

Article XV approved—with the exceptions of what concerns the Senate

Article XVI approved as above

Article XVII disapproved, first because we disapprove the office: Secondly because we cannot Consent to the embodying marching or ordering of the Militia by any other authority than a particular act of the General Assembly: thirdly because no persons Should, in our humble Opinion, have power to prorogue, adjourn, or dissolve the General assembly So much as *for one hour,* Except themselves or their constitutents: much less could we consent to impower any other than the General Court, to Suspend the Execution of any Law of the State, *civil* or *criminal.*

Article XVIII approved, with the exceptions above Mentioned.

Article XIX disapproved, because all appointments Should, in our judgment, be made *only* by the House of Representatives.

Article XX disapproved, because no person should be punished but for breach of the Laws of the State, nor tried by any other court then a jury of his Peers, but if *impeachment* is admitted in the constitution of this State, we cannot consent to any court for trial thereof but the house of Representitives; and do think any member of the house or any inhabitant of the State, has a right to impeach as well as present to a grand jury.

Article XXI approved with the amendment of *Speaker and Committee of the Court,* instead of Governor and Senate.

Article XXII disapproved, because we approve not the orders therein

Mentioned; much less can we consent to annihiliate the powers of a Senate, whenever it shall please a Governor to withdraw or absent himself; or give him, when present any other power than that of a Moderator without a Vote:

Article XXIII utterly disapproved, for reasons mentioned under article XVII.

Article XXIV disapproved, because we think no man should hold any office in the State longer than *one* year, without a new election.

Article XXV approved

Article XXVI disapproved for the reasons mentioned in art XXIV.

Article XXVII approved.

Article XXVIII disapproved, because we apprehend it of more importance to every individual than the delegates to Congress be men of the best qualifications than any other officer already mentioned; and therefore we judge that the election of delegates, should be left with the people at large.

Seccondly because, though we highly approve of the restrictive clause in Said article, So far as it extends; yet we judge that it ought to have prohibited any delegate from being chosen for more then two years out of ten.

Article XXIX approved

Article XXX approved, with the amendment of *Speaker of the assembly* instead of *Governor and Commander in chief:*

Article XXXI approved

Article XXXII disapproved, because we see no more reason for adopting the Statutes of Brittain than of Rome, and are not willing that a Constitution, which opens a *new* era in the State, Should bring with it any *old* laws, except the Law of God, natural and revealed; nor give Sanction to any Statutes, except those of Congress, and such as *shall* be enacted by the assembly of this state *after the constitution itself is ratified and in force.*

Article XXXIII disapproved because no money should be drawn from the treasury, in our opinion without a special vote of the Representatives of the people for that purpose; a copy whereof, attested by the Speaker we Should think Sufficient Warrant to the treasurer for delivering the Sum Contained in it:

Article XXXIV disapproved 1st because we judge that every denomination of Religion whatsoever, that gives Security to the State for a peaceable obedience to the Laws thereof, Should be equally free and equally established and supported by the constitution in all aspects whatsoever:

2d that no person should be obliged to Contribute anything to the maintainance of any form of religion to which he cannot give his conscientious attendance: and thirdly, because we judge this article ought to have stated in the clearest terms what is meant by the *free exercise* and *enjoyment* it allows.

Article XXXV approved

Article XXXVI approved with the restrictions already expressed. This may certify that the Town Meeting herein Mentioned Consisted of Sixty three Voters. that in all the Votes therein passed they were unanimous and that in Such articles as are voted approved it was expressly intended to be understood with exception of anything that might Seem to Countenance the creation of Governors, Lieutenant Governors or Senators

Given at Boothbay May 20th 1778

WmW. Cobb
Edward Emerson — Select Men

A True Coppy from the Record
Attest John Beath, Town Clerk

Shrewsbury (156/374)

To the Honorable Samuel Adams Esqr. Secretary for the State of the Masachusitts Bay

Att a Town Meeting Regularly Assembled on the Twentieth Day of May 1778 in the first Precinct in Shrewsbury for the Purpose of Hearing and Duly Considering the form of Goverment Sent out by the Great and General Court of the State of Masachusetts Bay to Approve or Disapprove the Same and the Number to Approve was four and to Disapprove was One Hundred

Shrewsbury May 20 1778

Job Cushing
Amariah Biglow
Daniel Hemen[way]
Charles Bouker
John Hastings — Selectmen of Shrewsbury

Elisha [Huges]
Ephraim Beaman
Isaac Harrington — Commee of Safety Shrewsbury

Lenox (156/375–382)

Whereas the General Court of this State have formed a Constitution of Government and ordered same to be layed before the several Towns and Plantations in this State to be considered and approved or disapproved of by them.

Agreeable to said resolve all the Male Inhabitants of the Town of Lenox being free and twenty one years of age, were legally assembled in Town Meeting on Wednesday the 20th Day of May 1778, to take into Consideration the said Form of a Constitution and approbate or disapprobate the same

The said Form of a Constitution being read and duly considered The question was put Whether said Form of a Constitution be agreeable to the Minds of this Meeting; passed in the Negative Yeas——Nays 86

Josiah Lee } Select
Attest. Lemuel Collens } Men

And whereas the People of this County have been stigmatized as being a Lawless and disobedient part of this State and averse to all Righteous Government; which is as false as it is Scandalous, for we hearty wish to have a Basis of Government firmly established upon the pure Principles of Liberty, by which the Rights and Priviledges of the People may be secured and handed down unsull'd to Posterity; But when we take into our serious Consideration the said Form of a Constitution, we humbly conceive it is not calculated to answer the valuable Purposes above mentioned, but Contrawise, for the following Reasons.

Objections against Article 1st will be found in the sequel

Objections against Article the 3d. Money ought not to be made a necessary Qualification of a Senator or Representative; which countenances averice and rejects Merit.

There appears a Contradictory Sense in the Words General Court in the first Article and the same words in the fourth, by the fourth Article it appears, that Judges of the Superior Court, Secretary, Treasurer General, Commissary General and Settled Ministers of the Gospel while in office, are not disqualified for a Seat in the Senate, tho, they are for a Seat in the General Court, and that the Judges and Registers of Probate, are disqualified for a Seat in the Senate, tho, they are not for a Seat in the General Court, when the first Article declares that the Senate and House of Representatives shall constitute the General Court. In the fourth Article the Senate and General Court appears two distinct Bodies, but in the first the Senate is comprehended in the General Court. All Fundamental Rules or Laws ought to be plain and explicit and intirely free from ambiguties and not give the Attornies a propriety in drinking their former Toast 'The Glorious uncertainty of Law' or Constitution.

Objections against Article the 5th All Men were born equally free and independent, having certain natural and inherent and unalienable Rights, among which are the enjoying and defending Life and Liberty and acquiring, possessing and protecting Property of which Rights they cannot be deprived but by injustice, except they first forfit them by commiting Crimes against the Public. We conceive this Article declares Honest Poverty a Crime for which a large Number of the true and faithfull Subjects of the State, who perhaps have fought and bled in their Countrys Cause are deprived of the above mentioned Rights (which is Tyranny) for how can a Man be said to [be] free and independent, enjoying and defending Life and Liberty and protecting property, when he has not a voice allowed him in the choice of the most important officers in the Legislature, which can make laws to bind him and appoint Judges to try him in all cases as well of Life and Liberty as of Property—No Person ought to be allowed to vote for any Officer of the Community except he has taken an Oath of Allegiance to the said Community—An Oath is the bond of society and if ever necessary it is necessary in the present case.

Reasons against Article the 6th. The charges of Representation ought to be equal as well as representation, no part of the State can justly be put to an unequal or disproportionable Cost to defray the necessary expences of Government mearly because they are remote from the Seat of Government, it has a tendency to induce the Remote parts of the State (if not necessitate them) to neglect keeping a Representative at the General Court. In a word it is making Representation unequal, all the Necessary Charges of Government ought to [be] equally assessed upon and paid by the Community.

Reasons against Article the 8th Each County ought to have its just proportion of Senators as well as Representatives otherwise Representation will still remain unequal, for according to this Article the largest County in each district containing the Majority of Voters in said District (which may be the case if it is not now) will have it in its Power to represent the whole District—it is not to be supposed that representation can be exactly equal, but it ought to be as equal as possible——

Reasons against Article the 9th. According to this Article the Senate are to be the Sole Judges of the legality or illegality of the choice of Senators for an ensuing year likewise of the Qualifications or disqualifications for said office. If they judge the Person or Persons not duly elected or not legally qualified, they still hold the Power in their own hands, and if impeached by the House of Representatives for their Conduct in so doing, there is no Court to try them agreeable to this Form of a Constitution except their own Body, for which reason it will be in the Power of the Senate to perpetuate themselves in that office to the end of Life, if they can only agree among themselves, which perhaps they may, as all may be equally anxious to continue their Political existance, in which case there can no legal redress be had, except the People fired with a just Resentment, rise like a whirlwind and spurn them from the Earth and take the Power again into their own hands, which they may neglect to do, by being lulled asleep by the influence and popolarity of the many Court Tools which this form of a Constitution enables the Senate to make both in the Civil and Military Department. In which case we may bid farewell to Liberty and expect nothing but the Roman Triumviri, with their bloody proscriptions. But the General Court or the whole Legislative body ought to be the judges, the danger is not so great when Power is lodged in a large Number of Mens hands as it is when lodged in a fue.

Reasons against Article 11th The Selectmen and Assessors of a Town are sufficient to determin by their Lists whether a Person be a legal Voter or not, without puting a Person under a Temptation to take a false Oath——Oaths ought not to be administred except where they are absolutely necessary, because by their frequency they loose their Sacredness

Reasons against Article 15th Not less than a Majority of the Senate or House of Representatives ought to make a Quorum for the business of the State cannot be safe in the hands of any Number inferior to that, especially as those nigh the Seat of Government will always have the advantage in their hands and by watching their opportunities be enabled to carry into execution their own private views, any Number short of a Majority is not the State assembled in General Court; consequently have no just right to act for the State.

Reasons against Article 19th. By this Article the Senate have the sole Right of appointing all Civil Officers (except those annually chosen, with Salaries annually granted) likewise all General, Field and Staff officers both of the Militia and Troops, likewise Captains and Subalterns of Troops which we humbly conceive is more power than can be safe in the hands of one Branch of the Legislature, it give them too great an opportunity to provide for their Connections to the injury of the Public, and which puts the Military Power in a State of dependency upon them, which power we conceive cannot be safe but immediately in the hands of the People or in the hands of the General Court according to the sense of those words in the first Article.

Reasons against Article 20th Every officer of the State ought to be liable to impeachment by any Member of the House of Representatives for male-conduct in his office otherwise it may prove very difficult if not impossible many Times to bring such offenders to justice. The People ought not to be put under such embarrisments in bringing to justice those who may wantonly abuse the Power they have intrusted them with, All Trial of Senators ought to be before the General Court, Trial by their own Body appears very pertial.

Reasons against Article 23d The Power of Granting Pardons ought not to be vested in the Governor, Lieutenant Governor and Speaker of the House, such a small number may be bribed by money or connections, by which the Criminal may escape with impunity to the prejudice of the State and Contempt of the Laws, but that Power ought to be vested in the Legislative Body——

Reasons against Article 24th. According to which the officers therein enumerated are rendered independent both of the People and Legislature, which is making the delegated Power greater than the Constituent and independent of it, or in other words, the Creature greater than the Creator. The People have an undoubted right to be pleased with those officers who are to be their judge in all cases both of Life and property, if they are not pleased with them, the wheels of Government must move very heavily and the laudable ends of the Legislature rendered abortive.

Reasons against Article 26th. The Officers therin mentioned are rendered very obnoxious to Court influence and it is to be supposed they will act accordingly, and always be ready to execute and defend the Measures which may be persued by the Senate be they ever so bad. The Senate ought not to have the Power of appointing Civil or Military officers as that will create too great a Dependency upon one Branch of the Legislature. No officer ought to be dependent but upon the People or the Legislature, not a part, but the whole.

Reasons against Article 28th Members of Congress ought to be chosen annually by the People as the Governor is directed to be in this Form of a Constitution, admiting the emendations implied in the objections against Article 5th—we conceive that if they are appointed agreeable to this Article, it is puting the delegated Power one degree further out of the hands of the Constituent, which is one step towards Tyranny and ought not to be done, but where it would be inconvenient or impossible to be otherwise, especially in cases of such Importance to the State, Members of Congress as well as all other officers of the State ought not to hold a plurality of offices, the execution of which requires them to be at different Places at the same time and different requisite Talants in which case one or the other of their Duties must unavoidably be neglected, which supposes the State must be injured or that there was no need of such Offices——Addition proposed to Article 29th. we suppose no person ought to be a Member of Congress unless he is of the Protestant Religion.

Reasons against Article 32d. It is very reasonable to suppose that many of those Laws which were fraimed and enacted under the direct influence of the Crown of Great Britain (in the Governor) labouring to suppress the groth of this State and fix us for the Chain, tho not repugnant to this Form of a Constitution, are very improper to be adopted in a Free State and would prove oppressive to the People, Witness the Law which oblidged a poor Debtor to go through a course of Law and pay the extravigant Costs, when he was willing to confess Judgment and submit to justice, which is an oppressive and Tyrannical Law and beneficial to none but Attornies Pettifoggers and those connected with them. And notwithstanding the repeated efforts of every free and unbiased Representative, heretofore, to have that Law repealed and another passed in its stead, enabling the Poor Debtor to confess Judgement and save the costs, it never could be effected, because the Majority found their account in it; And what has been may be again, especially when those whoes interest it is to have it continued, are not disqualified for being Representatives. This Article declares those Streems sweet which issued from a Bitter Fountain, which is contrary to reason as well as Scripture——But the last Clause with regard to trial by Jury, appears unexceptionable, if it may be construed to be by the Peers of the Vicinage.

We furthermore suppose there ought to be a Bill of Rights, annexed to a Constitution and declared part of it, which might serve as a Clue to lead the Legislature through the otherwise intricate parts of the Constitution, Likewise we suppose that all entailments of Estates ought to be provided against in a Constitution, which is a distructive thing in a free State and like swelled Legs and an emaciated Body Symptons of a Disolution. We further Suppose that by a Constitution the printing presses ought to be declared free for any Person who might undertake to examin the proceedings of the Legislature or any part of Government.

We likewise suppose the fifth Article of this Form of a Constitution where it prohibits a Person from having a voice in the choice of Governor or Lieutenant Governor and Senators if not worth sixty Pounds, is a violation of that clause of fourth Article of the Confederation of the United States of America, which declares that the free Inhabitants of each of the States, paupers, vagabonds, and fugatives from Justice excepted, shall be intitled to all priviledges and immunities of Free Citizens.

In offering the aforesaid Objections and reasons we suppose we have exercised the undoubted Right of Freemen, and most humbly submit them, with all their inaccuracies to your perusal——

Attest Samuel Wright T Clerk

Lenox, May 28th 1778

Dedham (156/382)

Dedham 20th May 1778

Agreeable to a resolve of the great and general Court of this State. The Inhabitants of the Town of dedham assembled this day, and having deliberately considered the proposed Constitution and Form of Government. The Question being put whether it was agreeable to the minds of the Town.

There appeared
For the Constitution 98
Against it 31

By Order of the Selectmen
Ebenr. Battelle Town Clerk

Charlton (156/382)

In obediance to a Late Resolved in a form of Constitution for the State of the Massachusetts Bay We have agreeable thareto Assambled the inhabitants of Charlton and Taken the Numbers of Voters which was Ninty Sav[en] whareof three was in favor of it; and Ninety four against it——

May the 20d 1778

Attest. Stephen Fay
John Coburn
Salem Town
Nathal Jones
Selectmen of Charlton

Caleb Ammidown
Ezra McIntire
Committee of the Same

Gloucester [New Gloucester, Maine] (156/383)

At a Meeting of the Town of Glouster May the 20th 1778 The question was put whether This Town will approve of the proposed Constitution of Government—109 voters present

Voted in the negative unanimously
attest
James Porter Town Clerk

Cape Elizabeth (156/383)

At a legal meeting of the Male Inhabitants of the Town of Cape Elizabeth being free and twenty one Years of Age called for the purpose of seeing wether they would approve of the Constatution or form of Goverment proposed by the General Court of the State of the Massachusetts Bay. The Number present at said Meeting were Thirty One. A Vote being called to see if they would approve said Constatution or Form of Goverment no person Voted for said Form of Goverment A Vote being called against said Form of Goverment Twenty Eight persons Voted

May the 20th. 1778

Daniel Strout
Benjamin Jordan
Selectmen of Cape [Elizabeth]

Worthington (156/384)

At a Meeting of the Inhabitants of the Town of Worthington Legally warned and held in said Worthington on the Eleventh Day of April 1778 the Constitution and form of Government Agreed upon by the Convention of the State of Massachusetts Bay on the 28th Day of February 1778 was taken into Consideration by said Meeting and Disapproved of by the whole of Said Meeting the Number being one Hundred and Eleven.

Worthington May the 20 day 1778

Certifyed per Jonath Brewster
Timothy Meech Select men
John Skiff

To the Secrety of the abovesaid State

Paxton, 1778 (156/385)

At a Legal Meeting of the Inhabitants of Paxton who were free and twenty one years of age May 20th 1778

article 1. Captain Adam Maynard was Chosen Moderator

2d. The Proposed form of Government for the State of Massachusetts Bay having been distinctly read and debated upon in said meeting and the question being Put Whether to Approve or Disapprove of the same it was Voted Unanimously to disapprove thereof The number present and that Voted at said Meeting were twenty nine

A true Copy from the Records
attest Abel Brown Town-Clerk

Paxton May 21 1778

Yarmouth (156/385)

At a Legal Meeting of the Inhabitants of the town of yarmouth on May the 20: 1778 amongst other things there was Taken into Consideration The form of Goverment for the State of Massachusetts Bay as Lately

agreed upon by the Conventition of Said State etc: Number Present at Said Meeting That Voted fourty Nine
Thirty one for the Form of goverment
Eighteen against the form of Goverment

Yarmouth May 21: 1778

David Thatcher
[Samuel?] Eldrige
John Chapman
Select men of Yarmouth

Pepperell (156/386)

In observance to a resolve of the Honorable General Court of this State of this State of Massachusetts Bay Dated March 4th. 1778

We the Select men of Pepperell Do Signify and assert that on the Twentieth day of May 1778 the Inhabitents of this Town in Town meeting Legally assembled for that purpose:
After Reading and Deliberating again on the form of Government sent oute by the General Court of this State for the Consideration of the People and to Express their minds, either for or against the Same.
Present in said meeting, of the Inhabitents having a Right to act, Sixty five——Fifty six Voted for the Establishment of said form: and only Two against it: the other seven refused to act, either way but stood neuters.——

Pepperrell May the 21st 1778

[Nehh?] Hobart
Jedidiah Jewett
John Shattuck Jr.
John White
Selectmen for Pepperell

The Honl. the Secretary
of Said State

Sturbridge (156/387)

At a regular Meeting in Sturbridge on the 20th of May Instant, of the male Inhabitants thereof, being free and twenty-one years of age, Called to Consider of, and approve or disapprove of a new Form of Government, present at said Meeting Fifty two and Voted Unanimously against said Form of Government.

Sturbridge 26th. of May 1778

Henry Fisk
Moses Weld
John Holbrook
Samuel Hamant
Ralph Wheelock

Selectmen for Sturbridge

Uxbridge (156/388)

To the Secretary of the State of Massachusetts Bay——

Sir, at a Legall meeting of the Inhabitants of the Town of Uxbridge being Legally warned and Duly Assembled at the Town's meeting House in said Uxbridge on Wednesday the 28th of May 1778 and Continued by Adjournment to the 8th Day of June Currant to take into Consideration the late Form of Government adobted by the General Court Number of Voters Present Quallified as Directed to Consider said form of Government—45 for Accepting said form as it now Stands none——for not Accepting Unanimous——

Uxbridge June 8th 1778

Abner Rawson
Nathanil [Meh?]
Edward Seagrave
Samuel Taft

Selectmen of Uxbridge

Nicholas Baylies
Robart Taft
Timothy Rawson

Committee of Corrispondence.

Upton (156/389)

We the inhabitants of the Town of Upton assembled in Legal Town meeting on Wednesday the 20th of May 1778

To take under consideration the Plan for a Constitution of Government for this State, prepared by the late convention, and presented to us for our approbation or disapprobation by the Council and House of Representatives of this State, after careful examination of the same. We are of opinion that a Plan or Constitution of Government, ought to be formed and established as soon as possible, on the broad bottom of universal and as near as may be equal and equally supported representation, both in the House of Senators, and that of Representatives, so that the privilege, and burden, as well as obligation and subjection might be extended to and equally enjoyed by the whole State, through which liberty may be secured to ourselves and Posterity.

We also are of opinion that both Houses of assembly ought to be fixed as to their numbers, and equally proportioned through the whole State by districts either by the valuation or polls, once in twenty years, to preserve this equality to the latest period. It likewise appears to us that one branch of the legislative Assembly ought not to be chosen and supported by Towns, which are so unequal and numerous in this large increasing State, either to increase the number to an unwealdy bulk, or lead many parts of the State to neglect their privilege, and lose their freedom to save their money.

And as freedom in a State Consists in being governed by its own will it appears to us that either the whole State ought to meet, in their persons or Representatives, for the public business, or one part will lose its freedom and the other exercise tyranny, and bear an unjust burden in support of that Government which is for the benefit of the whole.

We also apprehend that a Legislative Assembly universally and equally elected, with equal and just support, from the public chest, laid under equal obligation to attend the public business, would be more permanent, not waxing and waining so often, by which opportunities for evil are offered, and also diffuse their influence more universally thereby, giving strength to Government, and removing heart-burnings and jealousies from one part of the State against the other, which are become so dangerous and hurtful at this time.

It likewise appears to us that every freeman twenty one years of age possessed of suitable property ought to enjoy full right of electing officers of State with other freemen, without regard to Nation or Colour, seeing all Nations are made of one blood

We are of opinion that all Salary men in the State, and all whose fees of office are worth annually eighty pounds should be uneligible into either House of Assembly. And that every county should have the right of electing its Sheriff, Register or Registers of deeds and Coroners, and that each of these be uneligible for either House of Assembly. That no person be allowed to take a seat as Governor, Lieutenant Governor,

Senator or Representative, or in any of the judiciary departments, before he has first openly declared that he believes a defencive war for the preservation of the State is Lawful. Also it appears to us that Legislative, Judiciary and Executive departments ought to be preserved more distinct than is provided for in the proposed Constitution of Government.

It therefore appears to us that the Constitution, under our consideration, is not formed with all the essentials of a wise, good, and free Constitution of Government, for this State. We therefore as constrained, in point of duty to ourselves, and Posterity, Declare our *Disapprobation* of the Constitution of Government offered to us by the General Assembly of this State, and the members as follow.

(Viz) Seventy Six against it. and None for it.

Ephraim Whitney Selectmen of Upton
Thomas Nelson
James Torrey

Wrentham (156/390)

At a town meeting Regularly Warned and Held at Wrentham on the twentieth Day of May instant, agreeable to a Resolve of this grate and General Court of this State, of March the 4, 1778, for the Purpose of acting upon the Constitution and form of goverment Proposed by the Court of this State the Number Present in said meeting of male inhabitents being free and twenty one years of age was one Hundred and forty eight,—the number voting for the said form of goverment was one Hundred and eighteen and the number voting against the said form of goverment was thirty.

Wrentham May the 25, 1778

Jno Hall
Jeremiah Day
Timo Guild Selectmen
Jesse Everett
David Fisher

Petersham (156/390)

This may Certify that the Inhabitants of the Town of Petersham being assembled in Town meeting on the 20th of May A.D. 1778 To take into

Consideration the forme of Constitution presented to them by the Convention of this State for their approbation or Disapprobation were unanimus To the number of Seventy Seven voters for the Rejection of said Constitution of Goverment and none for it.

Petersham May 20th 1778

Ephraim Doolittle	
Daniel Hastings	Select men
John Wilder	of
Edward Powers	Petersham

Whately (156/391)

At a legal meeting in Whately May the 21th 1778 warned to take in to consideration the forme of Goverment agread upon by the Convention apented for that porpos to be laid before the several towns and plantations in thies State for thear approbation or disapprobation the above form being red aftor examining the same it was moved Whether the meating then present would give thear apropation to the form of Govermen agread apon by the above convention put to vote and it passed in the Negative the Number in the meating being seventeen. Sixteen Disaprovd one aprovd of the above form

May 20 1778

Thomas Sanderson	Select men of Whately
Salmon White	

Dudley (156/391)

At a meeting of the inhabitants of the Town of Dudley Regularly assembled at our meeting House in said Dudley on Thursday the 21st Day of May anno domini 1778 to act upon the form of government or Constitution of the State of Massachusetts Bay and voted unanimusly to Disapproave of said form of government there being Sixty voters present at said meeting that acted——

Dudley May the 22nd 1778

Jedidiah Marcy	
Edward Davis	Selectmen of
Nathaniel Healy	Dudley

Warwick (156/392)

At a meetting of the freeholders and other Inhabitants of the town of Warwick Duly warned and Regularly Assembled May the 21: 1778 then a Qustion was put whether the town would approve or Disapprove of the form or Constitution of goverment formed by the Last General Court yeas Voting for three (and Nays Voting against twenty four) this a true coppy of said Vote.

Amos Marsh
Thomas Rich Selectmen of Warwick
Caleb Mayo

Grafton (156/392)

In Compliance with a Late order of Court for hearing and Considering the new Constitution and form of Government—We the Subscribers have Caused a Town-meeting to be regularly warned and assembled and have laid the same before the Town and after Due Consideration on said form of Government when the vote was put there were Sixty-Seven voters present at said meeting and there was one voted to approve of said form and Sixty-Six for Disapproving there of
Grafton May 21: 1778

Elisha Brigham
Benja Goddard Select men of Grafton
Perley Batcheller
William Brigham

Mendon (156/393)

To the Inhabitants of the Town of Mendon in Town meeting Assembled May 21: 1778

Gentlemen

We Your Committee Chosen and Appointed for the purpose of Considering the plan or form of Goverment offered to the people of the State of Massachusetts Bay for their Approbation or disapprobation, have mett perused and Considered the Same and are of oppinion that the Said plan (in Some Articles) is not so well fraimed and made as it might and——ought to have been, for the good, well being, and Safety, of the natural Rights of the people——Article 5th we find by said plan that no persons shall have the privilidges of giving their votes for the Choice of Governor, Lieutenant Governor, nor Senators unless they are worth £60 it appears to us unreasonable that Men Should be Governed by Laws made by a Legislature and they debared from giving their votes in the Choise of such Legislature

article 11 it appears to us that it is very unreasonable that no person shall be allowed to give his vote for Governor Lieutenant Governor or Senators (if his Qualifications is Questioned) unless he makes oath that he is Qualefied viz that he is worth £60 = Should 1 - 2 - 3 or more be Question in that Respect is it not Likely that Every Member of the Meeting would be Qestioned and so of Conseiquence Every Member must bee put upon Oath before the Election or votes can be given in and so great Confusion may arise

Article 15th we find that 9 Senators will Make a Corum and that 5 will be a Major part, and that they will have power to Negative the house, in all Cases and so business of the Utmost Importance may be detarded untill a greater number of Senators be present

article 17th we find that the Governor is Invested with power to Imbody the Militia of this State and Cause them to be marched to any part of the State for the publick Safety when he shall think Necessary; Should it be the Misfortune of this State to Chuse a Governor that was Enemical to the people; Could not he Imbody the Militia and Cause them to be marched to one End of the State when a most vigerous asault was planed to attack the other end by a powerful Enemy and so the State fall a prey to an Enemy—was not our Publick Stoars Seized in the year 1774 and the people Alarmed and Marched for Securing the Remainder but before the people arived at the Metropilus where they were marching the posts were Sent out to Stop them because it was Law that the Governor Should have the Care of the Military Stors and Remove them at his pleasure—— would it not be much Safer that the Governors power Should be Limited that he Should not have power to Imbody the militia and Cause them to be marched unless upon Some Sudden Danger of an Invasion and that then they Should not be held no longer than untill the Senat Could be assembled and their Concurance——

article 32 we find that all the Statute Laws of this State, the Common Laws and all Such part of the English and British Statute Laws as have been Adopted and usually practised in the Courts of Law in this State Shall Still Remain and be in full force untill altered or Repealed by a future Law or Laws of the Legislature it appears to us that Notwithstanding the 34 article which is (the free Exercises and Enjoyment of Religious profession and worship shall forever be allowed to Every Denomination of Protestants within this State)—that the Same Laws are Still in force as formaly and that people who are not of the Congregation perswasion are as Liable to be Taxed for the Support and maintainance of Congregational Ministers as formaly they were and that the Assessors cannot but Tax them unless they bring in their Certificates as in Times past and it appears to us that there is no man in this world would think that he is used with Christian usage if Compelled by Laws made by man To Support a worship that is not agreeable to the Dictates of his own Conscience and way of thinking in matters of Religion: and that the said plan ought not to be approved.

James Sumner Clerk of
Said Committee

Mendon May 21st 1778. The foregoing Report of the Towns Committee upon the Constitution, being made, and read in the Meeting,—it was thereupon

Voted, That the same should be attested by the Town Clerk, and be transmitted by the Representative to the General Assembly, to the End that it might be known, for what particular Reasons the Town did not approve of the Constitution and Form of Government for the State of Massachusetts - Bay, agreed upon by the Convention of said State,

Joseph Dorr,
Town Clerk

Gorham (156/394)

Pursuant To orders of the General Court to us Directed of the 4th of March Last We The Subscribers Selectmen of The Town of Gorham have Called a Meeting of The Male inhabitants of Said Town and have Laid before Them The form of goverment which was Transmitted To us by order of Court for Said Towns approbation or Disapprobation The Numbers present at Said Meeting Consisted of fifty five and unanamosly voted To Disapprove of Said form of Goverment

To the Secretary of the State of the Massachusetts Bay
Gorham May the 21 day 1778

Andrew Crocket Selectmen
Samuel Harding of Gorham

Brookline (156/395)

At a legal meeting of the Inhabitants of the town of Brookline on Thursday May 21. 1778

Upon reading and considering the proposed new Form of Government; Voted, that the same is not calculated and adapted, to promote and secure in the best manner attainable, the true and lasting Happiness and Freedom of the People of this State; that it is essential to a Constitution designed for that most important and desireable End, that a full and express Declaration of the Rights of the People, be made a part thereof, and that the powers of Rulers should be accurately defined and properly limited, that as the Form proposed is almost totally deficient in those Respects and imperfect and intricate in many parts, it ought therefore to be Rejected, and this Meeting consisting of forty five persons do unanimously and absolutely reject the same.

A true Copy attest Stephen Shorp Town Clerk

Northampton (156/395)

At a Legal Town meeting Held at Northampton one Friday the 22d Day of May 1778 by adjournment

The Constitution and Form of Government proposed for the State of Massachusetts Bay agreed upon by the Convention of the said State February 28th 1778 was read and considered, and the question was put Whether the Town did approve of the afore said Constitution and Form of Government—and upon a Division it appeared that 36 were for it and 17 against it—Present 53 Voters

A true Copy Attest Elijah Hunt Town Clerk

Northampton May 23d 1778

Norton (156/396)

Att a Town meeting Legally warned and held at Norton in the County of Bristol on Fryday the 22 Day of May A.D. 1778 The plan of a Constitution and form of Government as perposed by the Convention of the State of the Massachusetts Bay was read and fully Debated. The number of Voters present was one hunderd and ten when the vote was put it appeared that Eight wore for it, and one hunderd and two against it.

William Cobb
William Homey Selectmen of Norton

To the Hone the Secretary of this State of the Massachusetts Bay
Norton June 3d 1778

Needham (156/396)

At a Meeting of the Inhabitants of the town of Needham Legaly Assembled on the 22d Day of May 1778 and continued by Ajornments to Wedensday the 10th. Day of June Following and then meet and acted on the form of Government to Approve or Disapprove of the Same there being 58 present at said meeting and 2 Approved and 56 Disapproved of Said form of goverment

Needham June the 11th. 1778

Robert Fuller
William Mc Intosh Select men
Nathanael Fisher
William Fuller

Hatfield (156/397)

Hatfield May 22d 1778

This may Certify that the Inhabitants of the Town of Hatfield being free and twenty one years of age in Town meeting Assembled for the Purpose of Considering the form of a Constitution after maturely considering the Same 51 Voters being Present in Said Meeting 17 Voted in favour of the Constitution and 34 Voted against it.

John Dickinson
Elijah Morton
David Morton Selectmen of Hatfield
Elihu White
John Hastings

Westborough (156/397)

To the Honorable Assembly of the State of Massachusetts Bay——
Gentlemen——

At a leagel Town meeting of the Inhabitants of the Town of Westborough on the 22d: May: 1778——
after duly considering of the form of the Constitution which was latly Sent to Said Town: for their Approbation or Disapprobation—Sixty five Voters being Present the Disapprobation: of Said Constitution or form of Goverment was Unanamusly voted

Westborough June 15th: 1778

Ebenr. Maynard
Abijah Gale
Jonathan Grout
Joseph Harrington
Barnabas Newton

Selectmen of Westboro:

Eastham (156/398)

In Pursuance to a Resolve of the General Court March 4th 1778 the Select Men and Committee of the Town of Eastham having warned a meeting of the Inhabitants of Said Town on the 22d Day of May 1778 to hear and Consider of a Constitution and Form of Goverment for the State of Massachusetts-Bay—and the Inhabitants of said town being Assembled on the said 22d Day of May And after Reading Considering and Debating upon the above said Form Did all Vote Against said Form and the Number Voting in said Meeting was fifty four Persons the town did Also Chuse a Committee to Instruct our Representative upon this Subject——

Eastham May 22d 1778

William Myrick Jur.
Amos Knowles
Barnabas Freeman
Job Crocker

Select Men and Committee of Eastham

Elisha Smith
Josiah Rogers

Committee

Sandisfield (156/398)

Att a Meeting of the Inhabitants of the Town of Sandisfield Legally Assembled on the 22d Day of May 1778 to take into Consideration the Constitution or form of Government the following Votes were pased viz——These may Certifie that Sixty four Voters were present att said Meeting and Sixty three Voted against it as it Stands and one Voter Voted for it

Samuel Smith 2d
Benjamin Smith — Select men of
Gideon Wright — Sandisfield

New Marlborough (156/399)

To the Honorable, the Secretary of the State of the Massechusetts Bay ——At a Legal meeting of the Inhabitants of the Town of New marlborough on the Nineteenth day of May 1778 and continued by adjurnment to the twenty second day of said May, the Inhabitants of said Town being assembeled to the Number of seventy two——The Constitution and form of government for the State of the Massechusitts Bay was Repeatedly read and Largely Debated on, and the vote being Put to see if the Said Town would accept of Said Constitution, and the whole of the above Seventy two Inhabitants voted that they would not accept of said Constitution, and also directed their Representative to use his Influence that said Constitution should not be Establised.

New marlborough
May the 22 1778

Jabez Ward — Select
Daniel Taylor — men of
New marlbro

Plympton (156/400)

At a Town Meeting of the Inhabitants of the Town of Plimpton Regularly assembled May 22 1778 to Consider of a Plan of Goverment For The State of the Massachusetts Bay to Approve or Disapprove of the

Same Which After Due Consideration Voted To approve of Said Constitution 17 and Voted to Disapprove of the Same 55.

Plimpton May 23, 1778 John Bryant
Isaiah Cushman Select men of Plimpton

Sandwich (156/400)

To the Secretary of the State of Massachusetts Bay

This certifies That at a Legall Meeting of the Town of Sandwich May 22d, 1778 notified for that Purpose. The constitution or Form of Government agreed upon by the late convention of this State on February 24th 1778. was Read and The Question Put Whether The Town woud agree to adopt said Form and Voted by Yeas and Nays when there were Eighty Six Votes for it and Thirteen Votes against it.

Att Micah Blackwell
Seth Freeman Select Men

Hadley (156/401)

The Town of Hadley having duly considered the Form of Government for the State of Massachusetts Bay, sent them by the General Court do approve of the same.—forty three present in the Meeting, forty voted for the said Form of Government, two voted against it.

John Cooke
Charles Phelps
Hadley 23rd May 1778 Enos Nash Select Men of Hadley
Phineus Lyman

Montague (156/401)

Montague May 23 1778

At a Meeting of the Inhabitants of the Town of Montague qualified to vote for a New Constitution duly assembled May 18th. 1778 the votes were as follows Viz.

For the Constitution 3
Against it 52

A True return, signed by order and in behalf of the Select Men

Mos. Gunn

Bellingham (156/402)

At Publik Town Meeting in Bellingham May 25. 1778. on due notice for that End all that are twenty one years old and free being notified to consider and act on the forme of Government according to a Resolve of the General Court of the State of the Massachusetts Bay in New England Dated the fourth of March last. for the Towns to approve or disapprove said form. The Said Inhabitants of Bellingham at Said Town Meeting Voted Unanimously to Disapprove Said form the number that voted was Seventy three

Laban Bates
Joseph Holbrook Select Men of Bellingham
Aaron Holbrook

Stow (156/402)

At a Town Meeting legally warned and assembled at Stow on the 25 Day of May A D 1778 by adjournment from the 30th Day of April to consider of and act upon the Report of the Convention respecting a Constitution or Form of Government.

The above affair was taken into Consideration by the Town at which Meeting where were 49 Voters of which Number 47 were against the Same and two only in Favour of said Report

Jona Wood
Charles Whitman Selectmen
Jona Hapgood

Silas Wetherbee
Luke Brooke
Daniel Whitney Committee
Jacob Hale

Stow June 15 1778

Chelmsford (156/403)

At a Publick Town Meeting of the Freeholders and other Inhabitants of the Town of Chelmsford Legally warned and Regererly Assembled at the Meating house in said Town on the twenty fifth Day of May 1778 on Purpos for the Taking into Consideration the New perposed form of Goverment Sent out for the Inspection of the People of this State the Inhabitants of Said Town taking the same into Consideration Adjorned said meating To the tenth Day of June following then the Said Town met and Considered of the Same and Passed the following Vote their being Present at said meating twenty of the Inhabitants qualified to Vote.

Unanimously Voted that it was their opinion that the said New perposed form of Goverment was not Calcolated and adapted to the True Happiness and Intrest of the People of this State, and give their Disaprobation to the same, being Established as a form of Goverment.

Chelmsford June the 10th 1778

Oliver Barron
Samuel Stevens Jr.
Zebulun Spaulding — Selectmen and
Benjamin Fletcher — Committee
Benjamin Parker — Chelmsford
Aaron Chamberlin

Hancock (156/404)

At a regular Meeting of the Male Inhabitance of the Town of Hancock in Berkshire County and State of Massechusetts bay, being free and Twenty one year of age, on the 25. Day of May AD 1778——In pursuance to a Resolve of the General Court of said State made and passed on the 4 Day of March 1778, Respecting the Return of the Doings of the people of said State, in Respect to their approving or Disapproving of the form of the New Constitution——

and there being 55 persons in said Meeting, whereof 50 persons voted against said form of Constitution, and 5 persons voted for said form of Constitution etc.——

Given under our hands at Hancock aforesaid the 25 Day of May in the year of our Lord 1778———

Benjamin Baker
Noah Ely — Selectmen
Amos Hammond

Brookfield (156/404)

To the Honorable Secretarey of the State of the Masechusets Bay or his Deputie———

Acording to a Resolve of the general Court march the fourth 1778 upon a Reguler meetting of the town of Brookfield Assembled together for the purpos of aproving or Disapproving the late forme of goverment and upon the Reading of the Constitution several times before the town the moderater put the vote

we find for the Constitution 20
against it 84

Brookfield May 25 1778

Moses Jennings
William Ayres
Abijah Cutler

Selectmen of Brookfield

Barre (156/405)

Barre May the 25th

to the Honarable Counsel and House of Representitives in generel Cort Assembled this town at Barre met on a Legal meetting warned for the purpos of Deliberating on a pamphelet Called a Constitution and after a Deliberate Hearing at Different times the whole that Etended said meetting was 87 and the Number Voting for said Constitution was Eleven and the Number Voting against said Constitution is Seventy Six

a treu Return Timothy [Nims?]

William Henry
Ralph Rice
Josiah Whiting
Benja Nye

Select men for the town of Barre

Marshfield (156/406)

At a Legal Town Meeting held by adjournment at the South Meeting-house in Marshfield the 25th day of May A.D. 1778—a Constitution and form of Government for the State of Massachusetts-Bay, was the Second time Read and Laid before the Town for their Consideration, and after Consulting and Debating thereon, they Proceeded and voted and there was ten votes for approving and accepting of Said form of Government; and there was Forty one votes for Disapproving and Rejecting it.

A true Copy attest Neh. Thomas Town Clerk

Samuel Oakman
Asa Waterman — Selectmen of Marshfield
Daniel Lewis

Georgetown (156/407)

Georgetown May 25th 1778

In Town Meeting legally Assembled for the Purpose of considering the Form of Constitution—Forty five Voters Present—after hearing read destinckty and then by Parigrafts, Debated on every Articel and Rejected by a Unanimous Vote the Fifth, Sixth, Ninth, and Nineteenth Articles, also the Thirty forteth Article by a Majority of forty one, for the following Reasons. because in the Fifth a Man being born in Afraca, India or ancient American or even being much Sun burnt deprived him of having a Vote for Representative—and by the Sixth the Inhabitants of this State will not be Eaquelly Represented—and by the Ninth the Small Destricts will have nex to no Voice in Choice of Senators and the Multiplicity of Town Meetings will be attended with great and needles Trouble to the scatered Inhabitants——and by the Nineteenth Civel and Feild Offiers are not Nominated by the Corporttion in which they are to Serve——and by the Thirty fourth a foundation is laid for Persecution and the rights of Concience Destroyed——

William Butler — Select Men of
Jordan Parker — Georgetown

York (156/407)

Honorable. Sir,

In pursuance of the Resolve of the General Court of this State respecting the Proposed Constitution and form of Government we called a meeting. The account of their proceedings therein you have here Inclosed by,

Your most
Huml. Servants

York May 25th 1778

Dan. Moulton
Joseph Sewall Select Men of York
Joseph Simpson

To the Secretary of the State
of Massachusetts Bay.

Cambridge (156/408)

At a meeting of the Male Inhabitants of the Town of Cambridge who are free and Twenty one years of Age Legally Assembled May 25th 1778.

Abraham Watson Esquire moderator.

The plan of a Constitution and form of Government for the State of the Massachusetts Bay, as proposed by the Convention, was read and fully debated on, the number of Voters present was seventy nine, all of them being freemen more than twenty one years of age,

The question was determined by yeas and nays, when there appeared for the proposed form None and against it seventy nine.

Aaron Hill
Jonas Wyeth
Tho. Farrington
Benja Lock Select Men
Benja Cooper
Edward Jackson
Benja. Baker

Pembroke (156/409)

At a Leagual Town meeting Held at Pembrokes on Monday the 25th Day of May A.D. 1778 for the Purpose of Takeing into Consideration the New form of Government for the State of Massachusetts Bay the vote was put and it appeared against it 151 for it 5

a true Coppey
Attest Jno. Turner Town Clerk

New Bristol (156/409)

New Bristol N 2 in Frenchmans Bay at a Legal Town meeting held at the meeting House the 25th of may 1778——after being Read and Due attention 42 Voter being assembled Uanomously Voted to Receive and except the New form of goverment proposed by the Honourable assembly of this State

By order of the Committee

William Gatcomb Town Clerk

Weymouth (156/410)

Weymouth May 25th 1778

Agreable to a Resolve of the General Court of March 4th 1778—the Inhabitants of the Town of Weymouth met on adjourment and took the Form of Government therein mentioned under Consideration and the Number present in said meeting that voted for said Form was Twenty Seven and the Number that voted against it was Thirty Four

James Humphrey
Cotton Tufts
Nathel Bayley
John Vinson
Asa White

Selectmen of the Town of Weymouth

Oxford (156/410)

At a Legal Town Meeting in Oxford on May the 25th 1778 after Reading the Constitution or form of Government formed by the General Assembly of the State of the Massachusetts-Bay; it was put to vote, whether the Town approve of the Form of government as therein proposed, and not one voted in the affirmative: in the Negative 38: the above is a true Extract from the Minutes of said Meeting.

Oxford, May 26.th Test Samuel Harris Town Clerk

To the Secretary
of the State of the
Massachusetts Bay

Washington (156/411)

To the Secretary of the State of the the Massachusetts. Sir

according to order We had a Meeting of the Freeholders and Lawfull Voters in the Town of Washington in the County of Birkshure in the State afore said Held by adjornment to the 11 Day of May instant and their the House was Divided and four for the Constitution and twenty five ware against Said Constitution. as Witness our Hands

Washington May the 26th: 1778 David Ensign Moderator
George Sloan Jr. Clerk

Ludlow (156/411)

At a Town Meeting legally warned and Assembled
The Vote being Called for Relative to the Constitution. There appeared Eighteen for and Nineteen against The said Constitution

Test per me Jeremiah Dutton Clerk
Dated at Ludlow this 26th day of May AD 1778

Pownalborough (156/412)

Pownalboro May 26, 1778

Sir

Agreeable to a Resolve of the General Court the constitution recommended, was laid before this Town, there were Forty two present, and unanimously disapproved of the same.

Thomas Price
Michael Sevey — Select Men of Pownalborough
Daniel Scott

To the Secretary of the State Massachusetts Bay

East Hoosac (156/413)

At a Meeting of the Inhabitants of East Hoosuck in the County of Berkshire Regularly Conveind May the 27th A D 1778——
The presant Constitution not Adopted——
Number of Votes Thirty one——

The Following Amindmint Desired by Said Meeting
paragraph th6 The Representatives paid out of the publick Treasure
paragraph th9 the Election and Qualification of Senators the General Coat to Judge
paragraph th9 General Officers and all Officers in pay of the State Appointed by the General Coart——
Field Officers of the Militia Shosin by the Commission officers of Each Battalion.——

A True Coppy
Test Jeremiah F. Greene Clerk

Blandford (156/414)

The Inhabitants of the town of Blanford in a Legal town meeting Called for the Purpose of Considering the Constitution and form of Government Sent to the Several Towns in the State of Massachusetts Bay for their Approbation Alteration or Amendment—and after Considering the Several Articles Contained in Said Constitution They Agreed to

Accept the Same—Provided the Articles hereafter mentioned are Altered According to what is hereafter Written on each Article (viz)——

Article 5th we humbly think that no person above twenty one years of Age within this State Ought to be Debarred from giving in his Vote for Representatives—because of Difference in Complexion unless their Polls are exempted from publick Taxes—Also that all Slaves should be Sett Free—and no Slaves Suffered in future to be Imported into this State——

Article 6th That the Traveling Expences of all the Representatives in this State Should be paid out of the publick Treasury of Said State and the expence of Attendance in court should be paid by the town that each Member Belongs to——

Article 19th That Captains and Subaltorns of troops to be Raised by—— and in the pay of this State—be appointed in the following manner— That Inlisting Orders be given out by the Governor and Senate to persons Recommended by the General Court to be men Qualified for those Offices and that Commissions be given to each man According to the Number of men he Shall Inlist or cause to be Inlisted——

This method having by Experience Proved to be the most effectual and Speedy way to Raise men without being Obliged to Draft any men——

Article 32nd That the Law or Rather Custom heretofore Practiced of takeing Seven Shillings for a Court writ be properly Regulated also fees of all Denominations be Regulated and not suffered to be Left to the Discretion or Rather Indiscretion of the Lawyers and others——Also—— That persons owing Small debts Should have the Benefit of Confessing Judgment Before a Justice of the Peace and thereby save unnecessary Charges——

NB The number Present in Town Meeting that voted Concerning the Constitution was forty six

The number voteing to accept the Constitution Provided the foregoing Alteration should be allowed to take Place—is Thirty Eight——

The number voting against the Constitution was Eight——

Blanford May 27th, 1778

[*Blurred or erased*]
William Boies
John Ferguson
Solomon Stewart
Isaac Gibbs
Samuel Sloper
Select men of Blanford

Harvard (156/415)

Harvard May 27th 1778

At a Legal Meeting of the Freeholders and other Inhabitants of said Town eighty nine being present the form of the Intended Constitution being Read publickly the question was put whether they would accept the same and not one Voted to accept it and eighty five Voted against accepting it.

Richard Harris
Caleb Sawyer Selectmen
William Burt

Loudon (156/415)

Att a Meeting Convined and Held in Loudon in the county of Berkshire the 27th day of May 1778 for the Purpose of Approving or Disapproving the Bill of Constitution or Mode of goverment exhibited the Town for their consideration.

Voters Presant 12
11 in the affirmative
1 in the Negative oringinal Minits Examined

Att Jonth Norton
Smith Marcy Select men of Loudon
Joel [Clarke?]

West Springfield (156/416)

To the Honourable Councel and house of Representatives of the State of the Massachusetts Bay in General Court assembled these may Certifie that agreeable to a Resolve of the Great and General Court of the State of the Massachusetts-Bay March 4: 1778 We the Select men of the Town of West Springfield have by a warrant under our hand, and seals Directed to the Constables of said town to warn all the Male Inhabitants of said town from twenty one years of age and upward to meet and assemble themselves together for the porpass of Considering on the Constatution and form of Goverment for the State of the Massachusetts Bay for the future which form was sent to said town to be laid before the Inhabitants by the Great and General Court of this State by them to be approved or Disapproved and the Inhabitants of said town accordingly assembled themselves together at time and places as Directed in the warrant and had the aforesaid form of Goverment Read to them for there Consideration and it Being of so waitty Consern they Adjourned there meeting to a future Day who meet again according to adjournment and Considered farther upon it and they not being fully satisfied they adjourned said meeting again to the 27 of this Instant may where they Duly Considered the afore said Constatution and there being 55 voters in said Meeting Exclusive of the Modarator the Moderator put the question for the accepting of the afore said form of Goverment and there was three persons voted for it and fifty two voters that was against said form of Goverment as it now stands.

West Springfield May 27: 1778

Benjamin Day
Jona White
Selectmen of West Springfield

Pearsontown (156/417)

Pearsontown May the 27th 1778

Pursuant to a late resolve of the General Court of the State of the Massachusetts Bay for Ascertaining the number of Votes of the Male inhabitants being Free and twenty one Years of Age in the Plantation of Pearsontown for or against the Constitution and Form of Government Passed May the 5th 1777 [1778] by the General Court of said State. We this Day met and Voted

for None
against Twenty One

Geo. Freeman
John Sanborn
Dominicus Mitchell
Peter Moulton
Daniel Harty
Committee of Corresponden[ce?] inspection and [*illegible*] for Pearsontown

Bluehill Bay (156/418)

Bluehill Bay May 27th 1778

Agreable to the ordor of the Great and General Court of the State of Massachusetts Bay we the Inhabitants of Bluehill Bay twenty six in Number——Being assembled according to Warning have voted unanimusly to receive the form of Government.

John Roundey
Nathan Parker Committee
John Peters

Bluehill Bay May 28th 1778

Sur I Do in the Behalf of the Committ of Bluehill Bay send these few lines to You for to Lett you know that the Committe Desires that you Would forward this Return into the Seceterys Offis as Soon as you Can and You will Ablige Yours to serve

John Roundey

PS Sur and if there is Aney thing that we have Ommetted in the Return I Would have you Let us know by Captain Haskell for we Are so as it ware Out of the Wourld that we Dont hardley know Wither we Do Rite or Rong But we mean to Do as Well as We Can.

Shelburne (156/419)

In Pursuance of a Resolve of the General Court of the State of the Massachusetts Bay; We have had a Town Meeting which was Legally warned and held in Shelburn on Thirsday the 14th Day of May A D—1778, and so Continued by Ajournment to the 27th—to hear: take into Consideration and Determine upon the Constitution Where one hundred and two of the Inhabitants were present being Voters—Who Unanimously Voted against it as it now stands for these several Reasons following Viz.

Article—1st—because the Last Clause Refers to the 5th and some following articles.

Article 3rd The Reason why Do not except this article is because we look upon it that the People of Each Town are the most Sutable judges of the Qualifycations of the Persons to Represent them to the Great and General Court.

Article 5th The Reason why we Do not Except this article is because the qualifycation for Voters: for Governor Lieutenant Governor and Senators, is not agreeable to our minds: for we think that Every free and Holsome Inhabitant has as good a Right to put in his Vote for the above officers as he has for a Representative.

Article 6th The Reason why this article is not agreeable to our minds is: we look upon it that the Representative ought to be paid out of the Publick Chest as it appears it will be for the welfare of the State.

Article 9th The Reason why we Do not Except this article is because the first Clause Refers to the 5th article Respecting the qualifycation of Voters.

Article 11th The same objections against this article as against the 9th

Article 19th The Reason why we Don't Except this article is because we look upon it that the People Ought to put in all the officers included in said article = Exclusive of the judges of the Superior Court and judges of the Inferior Court and General Officers.

Articles 24th and 26th: The Reason why we Do not Except these articles is because we think al the Officers Contained in them Ough to be Chosen Annually.

Article 32nd: we object against this article because of that Sentence that mentions the Old Usages and Customs which we Look upon Oppressive.

The above Reasons were Laid before the Town in the abovesaid meeting by a Committee Chosen for that Purpose and Unanimously Voted to Except of them by the Number of Voters above Certifyed.

To be Directed to the Secretary of the
State of the Massachusetts Bay
Shelburn May the 28th—1778 Per Order of us

John Wells
John Long Select men for
Aaron Skinner Shelburn

Bristol (156/420)

Sir

Agreable to a Resolve of the Honourable Council and Hous of Representatives for the State of Massachusetts Bay of the 4th of March 1778, we have assembled the Inhabitance of our Town and laied before them the printed copy of the Form of Government for this said State of Massachusetts-Bay, and duly considered the same, one Hundred and three Voters was present at said meeting and Voted unanimously against said form of Government; Sum Artickels ware well aproved of, others disaproved of in a particuler manner to have a Governor and Lieutenant Governor vested with such larg powers this Town highly Disaproves of: and likwise for Every Town to pay their own Representatives appers to this Town to lay the Cost and burden of the Court too much on the Distant Towns which was the Cheiff objections in this Town and in as much as there was no provesion made for us to aprove of the artickels we like and Disapprove and vote against the artickels we Disliked, it is for these Reasons this Town Voted against the Whol Form of Government——

To the Honourable
John Avery Dept. Secr.
Bristol May 29th 1778

James Husten
Thomas Johnston
Samuel Boyd
Select Men of Bristol

Barnstable (156/421)

Barnstable May 30th 1778

To the Secretary of the State of the Massachusetts Bay

Sir. agreable to a late Resolve of the General Court we the Subscribers, Selectmen of the Town of Barnstable have notifyed said Town to meet together on the 28th day of May currant for the purpose of approveing or Disproving the proposed form of goverment agreed on by the Convention agreable to a Late Resolve of the General Court and the Town being met on said day after debating on said form of goverment voted as follows. viz the Number voting for Said form of Goverment was Ten the Number voting against said form of goverment was fifty nine.

Nymphas Marston
Ebenezer Jenkins

Swansey (156/422)

We the Subscribors In pursuance of a Late Resolve of the State of Massachusetts Bay etc. have on the first Day of June 1778 laid the Constitution and form of Goverment transmitted to us before a legal meeting regularly assembled in the Town of Swanzey for that purpose where the Number of persons Voted for said form Goverment were four and Number of persons Voting against the same were fifty six from yours to serve

4
56

Andrew Cole Select men of
Seth Wood Swanzey

To the Honorable Secretary
of the State of Massachusetts
Bay

Berwick (156/422)

At a Legall town meeting of the male Inhabitants of the town of Berwick being free and more than 21 years of age June 1st: 1778 at which meeting we the Subscribers Selectmen of Said town Laid before the town the Constitution and Form of Government for the State of the Massachusetts Bay agreed upon by the Convention of Said State February 28th 1778 Said meeting Being called for that purpose in order that the Inhabitants of Said town might duly consider upon Said Form of Government and either approve or Disapprove of the Same. Present in Said meeting 148 and after matuer Consideration thereon voted Unanimously to Disaprove of the Same.

Berwick June 10 1778

James Warren Jr.
John Hill
Jedidiah Goodwin Selectmen of Berwick
James Brackett

Scarborough (156/423)

Scarborough June 1t 1778 The Inhabitants of said Town according to the Resolve of the Great and General Court of this State were Legally Assembled to the Number of thirty nine who were sutably quallified to

vote and unanimously Voted to Approve of the Form of Government proposed to them Excepting the following Articles
Viz

Fifth Article with regard to choice of Senators
Sixth Article we wholly disapprove of
Nineth Dito——
Tenth Article we disapprove of with regard to Senators as above.
Twelvth Dito——
Ninetheenth Article we wholly disapprove of
In regard to Senators the Town are humbly of opinion that they ought to be chosen by the Representitives.
To his Honor the Secretary of the State of the Massachusetts Bay——

Reuben [Figg]
Amos Andrews — Selectmen of
John A. Milliken — Scarborough

Newton (156/425)

At a meeting of the Male Inhabitants of the Town of Newton, who are free and twenty One years of Age. On the first Day of June 1778.—— The Plan of the Constitution and form of Government for the Massachusetts Bay, (as proposed by the Convention February 28th 1778,) having been Read was fully debated, the Number of Voters present being Eighty. 5 of said voters Approved of said Constitution; and 75 Disapproved of it.

John King
Aaron Richardson — Selectmen of Newton
Nathan Fuller
William Hoogs
John Stone

Shirley (156/425)

Agreeable to a Resolve of the General Court, the Inhabitants of the Town of Shirley being duly warned, and assembled, at the public meeting-house in said Town on Monday the first Day of June Instant, to take under Consideration a Constitution and form of Government as Drawn up by the Convention of this State February 28th 1778——Voted unanimusly not to approve of said Constitution and form of Government, there being nineteen voters Present at said meeting.

Shirley June 1st 1778

By order of the Select Men
John Ivory Town Clerk

Plymouth (156/426)

At a Meeting of the Town of Plimouth Legally assembled and held at the Court house in Plimouth, June 1st AD 1778——
by Adjournment from the 18th of May Last,
The Report of the Committe appointed to take into Consideration the Form of Goverment lately Drawn up by the Convention of this State, was read which is as follows Viz.

The Committee Appointed to take into Consideration the Constitution lately drawn up by the Convention of this State and to consider the Advantages and Disadvantages arriseing therefrom——Beg leave to report——That they have repeatedly perused said Constitution with great candor and deliberation and are of opinion, that many parts of it are bottomed on Principalls of Equal liberty, and calculated to secure the Governed, from the Encroachments of Ambition and the artifices of Designing rulers, such more Especially, is the Establishment, of Annual Elections in the Severall branches of the Legislature, Fundementual in Every free Goverment, and the best barrier against Corruption, and the restless passions of Mankind.

Your Committe would be happy,
if they could Speak with the Same applause, of Every Articall in the Constitution, but Justice to themselves and Posterity, Oblige them to point out Severall Things, which they apprehend are Meterial Defects, and above all the inequallity of the representation prescribed in the Sixth articul an inequallity, that may opperate to the disadvantage of the Towns bordering on the Sea Coast whenever any Commerciall question may be agitated in the Generall Assembly——The Erecting of a Court of Probate is also in the judgment of your Committe, an useless burthen

on Society, as it often unnecessarily subjects the widdow, and Fatherless to the Expence of Travilling twenty or thirty miles, for the settlement of—Very Small Estates, which may as well be done by two or three honest men in Each Town——The mode of impeachment and the Tenure, by which many Subordinate civil officers, hold their Commissions, appears Verry Exceptionable, and are Capable of amendment, much for the benefit of the Community——The necessity of a Rotation in the office of Governor, Lieutenant Governor and Senators will be Evident to Every body who Reflects that the appointment of many Civil, and all millitary officers is vested in the Governor and Senate, which power of appointing, may Enable a sett of Enterpriseing intrigueing Men, to Establish and intrist and influance through the State, that may be Daingerous, to the liberties, of the people——The want of a Rotation, therefore of these officers in the Constitution under Consideration, is a Very Capitall omission——Your Committee are further of opinion, that a bill, Clearly Ascerting the rights of the people, as Men, Christians, and Subjects, aught to have Preceeded the Constitution, and these rights should be Expressed in the fullest and most unequivocall terms——Upon the whole as this Constitution, is in so many parts Defective, and as when once Established, it will probably remain unalterable, Except by Coercion and Violence, Your Committe think that it aught to be rejected——

Joshua Thomas
Thomas Mayhew
Zacheus Bartlett
Elkanah Watson

After Debating the matter some Considerable time The Vote was Called Whether the town would accept said form of Goverment or not, Their being One hundred and Thirty Voters Present one hundred and twenty two were against said form of Goverment and Eight were in favour of it.

Attest. Ephm Spooner Town Clerk

Sherborn (156/427)

At a meeting of the male inhabitants of the town of Sherburn being Free twenty one years of age to take into Consideration a Constitution or Form of Government Formed by the Convention of this State to be laid before the Several Towns for their approbation or Disapprobation and after mature Deliberation their on. a vote was passed by yeas and nays: and it appeared that their was Five in favour of Said Constitution and Forty five against it.

Sherburn the 1st June 1778
By Order of the Select men Daniel Whitney Town Clerk

Methuen (156/428)

Methuen June 1, 1778

The Town meet and Took under Considerration the Constitution or Form of Goverment and after a mature Dleberation it was putt to Vote and none for it and eighty against it.

Cutting Marsh
John Sargent Jr. Select men of Methuen

Beverly (156/424, 429–432)

These May Certify to the Honorable Great and General Court of the State of the Massachusetts Bay——

That at a regular assembled meeting of the male Inhabitants of the Town of Beverly being free and Twenty one years of age on the first day of June 1778——The Constitution and form of Goverment for the State of Massachusetts Bay agreed upon by the Convention of said State February 28th 1778 was Laid before said Town and after the Most Canded and Deliberate Exammination thereof thay unanimously voted their Disapprobation of the Same. The Number of Voters Present was fifty Eight.

Isaac Thorndike
Thomas Stephens Select Men of Beverly
William Langdell
Joseph Wood

To Captain Josiah Batchelder junior. Representative of the town of Beverly for the present year.

Sir

We the inhabitants of this town, having considered the Constitution and Form of Government recommended to us by the Convention of this State, and adopted such a mode of disquisition as might best ascertain its merits or demerits, after the most candid and deliberate examination are of opinion that it is not well calculated to promote the general welfare, and that it is not the best that could reasonably be devised and would readily be adopted by the people.——That without searching for the reasons that induced the exclusion in the 5th Article, so inconsonant to that extensive liberality of sentiment which ought to prevail in a Free State, we find ourselves more nearly affected by considering the 6th. This, from the point on which it treats, ought to have secured to us the most inestimable privilege as a people; but we are surprized to find a great proportion of us stripped of it, and in the main that Representation, which is the very basis and support of freedom in a large society, is the most exceptionable article in this Constitution. This most important point, *The forming of a Body to represent the People,* as it must be a miniature of the whole, so it ought to be, in justice and good policy *too,* an exact one: and the difficulty of making it so, however great, must be surmounted, For if the Representation be *unequal,* the Government will not long continue *equal,* and the time would soon arrive, when the *majority* of *this Body,* really representing but *a small part of the State,* might advance their own and their constituents' private interest, to the great injury and oppression of the rest of the people. The power thus placed in their hands, combined with the almost irresistible allurements of interest will offer such a violent temptation to them to do wrong, as members of political Bodies have scarcely ever resisted with success. But, on the other hand, if that Body be a fair and exact Epitome of the whole People, or in other words, if the Representation be equal, it will be invariably for their interest to do strict justice; whatever is for the interest of the people at large will be for theirs too, so that the general good will be their object. In the one case, we have nothing on our side, while power and interest may co-operate against us; in the other, right, power, and interest combine in our favor, to make duty and inclination, in the servants of the public, go hand in hand. With such security and not otherwise, the Powers of Government may be trusted to the *few* for the benefit of the *many.*

If it should be said, on the plan of representation by towns, which we have been used to, or as pointed out in the Constitution and Form of Government before us, an equal representation according to numbers would make the Body unwieldy, and therefore inadmissible, we grant that the house would be much too large; but at the same time we also add, that notwithstanding the unequal retrenchment proposed by the late Convention, the numbers allowed of would even now be far too many, and half a century hence, should this State continue to populate, they would be increased beyond all decent bounds. This we think proves incontestably that the measure taken to prevent the house from being too numerous is inadequate, and that it is unjust is obvious, as no one can justify the exclusion of a large body of Freemen from the rights of representation, while others are in full possession of them, merely because their local situations are different. The injustice must further appear, if it be considered, that as all contribute alike to the formation of Government, by parting with an equal share of those rights which all equally possessed so all are equally entitled to the benefits which arise from it. In a word the equal right of representation ought ever to be contended for and insisted on by every individual as a matter of right, and of the highest importance, whenever he is called upon to give his consent to any form of Government.

Were we to point out a mode of representation which we think right and best, we should place all on an equal footing, yet so circumscribe the numbers of the house, that they should never exceed what are absolutely necessary to the proper knowledge of the State, and transacting the public business of it. And we cannot but think that the best method to secure an equal representation, and at the same time prevent the evil of having an unwieldy house, would be to lay aside the distinction of towns, and take up in its stead a representation by counties. Each county may be divided into districts and every district throughout the State contain an equal number of Freemen. The number of Freemen necessary to compose a district may be so determined that, though each district have one representative, yet the entire number of districts shall not exceed such number as it is thought best that the whole house should consist of. By this mode all would be put upon the like footing, and none would have reason of complaint. This plan we conceive to be easy if we have but virtue enough to listen to what is honest and just.

We might say much on the impropriety of the mode of electing Senators, as men at one extremity of the State must determine upon the qualifications of men at the other, to serve in that important Body, with whose true character, few of them, from their local situation, can become acquainted. This will unavoidably give the Representatives in some parts a great influence, from year to year to introduce those to be voted for by their constituents, whom they themselves chuse to have elected. In this way a great part of the Senators may in fact be chosen by the house, to the subversion of that distinction and independence of the two branches, so necessary to good government. We cannot but think that if each county or district was to elect its own member or members for the Senate, that important part of the Legislature would be much more equally chosen than upon the plan of the late Convention. But, conceiving, as we do, that the inequality of the Representation is enough to ensure a disapprobation of the proposed Constitution, we forbear entering minutely into this particular. The same reason prevents our remarks on several other articles which we think exceptionable.

But we cannot dismiss it without observing the want of an article which we think any constitution that is confirmed and ratified by the people ought to contain. We mean one, by which it shall be provided, that on a certain day in the year 1798 or such time as may be judged best, a Convention chosen by the people at large, distinct from the General Court, shall be held, to determine on such amendment, alteration, addition, or erasement, as should be found just; such innovations to have the sanction of the people; and that, after other twenty years, the constitution shall again be taken up in the same manner, and so on successively. This, if any human method can, might in time perfect a constitution and secure it inviolate——

These being the sentiments of the town, in conformity thereto, you are hereby instructed to oppose the ratification of the Plan proposed by the State Convention, and should it be voted in, when it appears a considerable part of the People are not in favor of it, to enter your Protest explicitly against it. But, should the same be set aside, we expect that some other Body, distinct from the General Court, be delegated from among the people for the sole and entire purpose of forming a Bill of Rights and Constitution of Government; the 1st of which, we conceive, ought to describe the Natural Rights of Man pure as he inherits them from the Great Parent of Nature, distinguishing those, the Controul of which he may part with to Society for Social Benefits, from those He cannot: and the 2nd Mark out, with perspicuity and plainness what portion of them, and on what Conditions, they are parted with, clearly defining all the Restrictions and Limitations of Government, so as to admit of no Prevarication. It should also contain a full and fixed assurance of the Equivalent to be received in return.

We mean not to dictate how all these matters should be particularly conducted, but expect a candid reception of these general hints as originating from a sincere desire to secure the invaluable liberties of the people. For the *reasons mentioned* we reject the Constitution, and not from a disposition to prevent good order and encourage anarchy, and oppostition to equal government. Good government, we are sensible, is essential to the happiness of a community; and this we ardently wish to take place, and shall sincerely endeavour to encourage and promote.

But if any form is offered to us, which we in our consciences think does tend to the public welfare, but in its consequences is destructive of it, to oppose it with a decent but manly and zealous freedom and firmness, is a duty we owe to ourselves and posterity, and we shall ever esteem ourselves bound to attend to its calls.

At a reguler meeting of the Male Inhabitents of the Town of Beverly being Free and Twenty one years of age on June the first 1778

Voted the foregoing Instructions to their representative to the Great and General Court

attest Joseph Wood T. Clerk

Scituate (160/1)

To the Honorable the Secretary of the State of the Massachusetts Bay

Sir agreable to a resolve of the General Court of the State of the Massachusetts Bay. Past in March the 4th: 1778: We the Subscribers transmeet to your Honor a copy of the vots and proseedings of the Town of Scituate on the Subject of approving or Disaproving of the Constitution of government—Recommended by the General Court of said State. At a meeting of the freeholders and other Inhabitents of the Town of Scituat, legly warned in Public Town Meeting assambled at the North Precinct meeting house in said Town on Monday the 1 Day of June 1778 on a motion made it wase put whether said Town ware for having the Said Constitution of Government established as it Now Stands—Past in the Negative in the following manner. Viz. for having the said Constitution established 2 against it 134

James Briggs
Calvin Peirce Selectmen of
Scituate, June the 5th, 1778 Joshua Jacobs Jun. Scituate

Westfield (160/1)

In observence of a proposed Constitution for the State of Massachusetts Bay agreed upon by Convention in February 1778:—

We the subscriber hereby Certify that at a Legal meeting of the Inhabitants of Westfield being regularly Assembled on the Second Day of June 1778 for to take into Consideration the Proposed Constitution and to approve or Disapprove of the Same and upon due Consideration thereon had there being Seventy two Voters in said meeting the Question being put in favour of said Constitution there is six for it: and sixty-six voting against it——

fore 6
agt 66
72

John Ingersoll
John Kellogg
Daniel Fowler
David Wellar

Selectmen of Westfield

To the Secretary of the State of Massachusetts Bay

Edgecomb (160/2)

At a Meeting of the Freeholders and other Inhabitants of the Town of Edgecumb duly Qualified and Legally warned in publick town meeting assembled at the Dwelling house of Mr. William Cleford Inholder in said Town—on Tuesday the Second Day of June Anno Domini 1778—at Ten o Clock in the forenoon—after a Moderator was Chosen—the Question was put to see if the Town would approve of the form of Government which then Laid before them, agreeable to a Resolve of the General Court the members then present Voted in the Negative—Unanimously.——the Number of Voters was fifteen present at said Meeting——the Reason of so few in Number being at said meeting—it was an Extream Rainy Day and very Difficult Traveling as many had some distance to Travel they did not attend said Meeting
Given under our hands at Edgecumbe this Second Day of June A.D. 1778

Moses Davis
Joseph Decker
John Cunningham
Solomon Trask
N. Herrondon
Will Cuningham

Selectmen and Committee of Edgecumbe

Newbury (160/2)

These certify that att a Legall Meeting of the Town of Newbury Held June 2, 1778 by Adjournment The Votes against the Constitution and form of Government for the State of the Massachusetts Bay ware Fifty-Six, for the Same One

Joshua Ordway
Silas Adams — Selectmen of
Newbury June 3, 1778 — John Atkinson — Newbury

Taunton (160/3)

Bristol County Taunton June 2nd 1778 At a meeting Legally warned and held at Taunton on the Eleventh Day of May A.D. 1778 and continued by several adjournments to this Day the form of Constitution of Government was Read number of voters present ninety the number for approving of said form Eighteen for Disapproving Seventy-Two

Simeon Williams
Elizah Lincoln — Selectmen of
Apollos Leonard — Taunton
Solomon Dean

To be Left at the
Secretarys office of the State of Massachusetts Bay

Hingham (160/3)

At a Town Meeting held at Hingham on the third Day of June Instant for the purpose of Approving or Rejecting the plan proposed for a form of Government or Constitution when the same was Rejected by Fifty Six Votes Nem: Con:

N.B. Two of the Select Men are under the Opperation of the Small Pox

Charles Cushing } Select Men of Hingham
Jacob Leavitt } Comit. of Safty
Thomas Burr

Western (160/4)

Western June 3. 1778

We The subscribers and Select men of Western: According to the orders of the Great and General Court; have Called a Town Meeting of the Inhabitants of Said Town; in order to see what Said Town would do with Regard to A Constitution and Form of Goverment for the State of Massachusetts Bay; agreed upon by the Convention of Said State February 28: 1778: to be laid before the Several towns and Plantations in Said State, for their approbation or disapprobation: This may Certify that the number present in Said Meeting was Forty Seven; and the number Voting for said Constitution was two: And the number Voting against said Constitution was Forty five.

Deuty Partridge
[Samuel Bascom?] Select Men of
William Blair Western

Ipswich (160/4)

At a Legal Meeting of the Male Inhabitants of the Town of Ipswich being free and twenty one years of age held by adjournemnt on thursday the 4th day of June 1778, to hear and Consider the Proposed Constitution, after maturely Considering the same.——

The Vote Being put whether the Town did approve of the Constitution and form of Government proposed, it passed in Negative Unanimously One hundred and ninety one voters present at said meeting the Vote being put whether the Town did disapprove of the Constitution and form of Government it passed in the Affirmative excepting one person

Copy on file Examined Attest John Baker To. Clerk

Walpole (160/5)

Agreable to a Resolve of the General Court of the 4th of March 1778 the Inhabitants of this town met being warned for the Purpose of taking under their Consideration the Preposed form for a Constitution and on adjournment from time to time to the 4th of June Instant they came to the following Vote 33 Voted for the Constitution and 14 against the same.

Walpole June the 6th 1778 George Payson town Clerk

Dorchester (160/5)

Dorchester June 5th. 1778——

These may Certify that at a Meeting of the Freeholders and other Inhabitants of the Town of Dorchester that were free and Twenty one years of age June 5th 1778 by adjournment from the eleventh day of May last the number voting against the Constitution and Form of Goverment lately agreed on by the Convention of this State was Twenty Three, being the whole number present at the meeting that Voted

Noah Clap
Samuel Topliff Selectmen of
Ezekiel Tolman Dorchester

Fitchburg (160/5)

At a Legal meeting of the Town of Fitchburgh Quallified By Law to Voat in Town meeting Assembled May the 22 1778

Present at said meeting 26

ly 1 Voted and Chose Deacon Goodridge Moderator

ly 2 the Voat Being Put by the Moderator for the Approbation or Disapprobation of the Form of Goverment or Constituon and the Voat was as follows For the Constitution 22

Against the Constitution——4

David Goodridge
Phinehas Hartwell Selectmen
Abraham Gibson for
Elijah Carter Fitchburgh

Fitchburgh June the 8th 1778
To the secretaries Office

Andover (160/6)

At a Regular meeting of the Male Inhabitants of the Town of Andover being free and Twenty one Years of Age, who Assembled on the first Monday of June instant, in order to consider upon the late form of Goverment when the Number of Voters where as followeth—Viz——

For said form of Government....................33
against the Same..............................32

Andover June 8th, 1778

Benja. Stevens
John Inguls
Selectmen of Andover

Leominster (160/6)

This may Certify that at a Legal Meeting of the inhabitants of the town of Leominster on the 8th of June Instant in order to Consult on and approve or Disapprove of a Constitution and form of Government for the State of the Massachusetts Bay There was twenty one voted to Axcept of the same and ten voted to Reject it

Leominster June 8th, 1778
By order of the Selectmen

Timo. Boutell Town Clerk

Spencer (160/7, 9)

The State of Massachusetts Bay.

To the Honorable General Court Assembled, may it please your Honors

The petition and Remonstance of the Town and the Inhabitants of Spencer Humbly Sheweth

That having taken into their Serious Consideration A Constitution and form of Government for the State of Massachusetts Bay, Agreed upon by the Convention of Said State for their Approbation Or Disapprobation,—and as the General Court have not Expressly Given Liberty to their Constituents to Object to any Article Seperately, yet we have taken upon us to give Our Reasons for Our Non Acceptance and hope it will be Cordially Recieved,—and as Government is of the utmost Importance to any people, So it Behoves us of this State at this time of taking upon us a Mode or form of Government, to be Carefull of any Inovations upon the Rights of the people or Any Infringements upon them as free men,—And as Government is Absolutely Necessary for the well Being of any People, it Concerns us to Establish that of the Best kind, and to avoid Every Inconvenience which may in any wise Obstruct the free Exercise thereof,—And as we Concieve that there are Some parts of this Constitution that are Injurious to the Rights of a free and generous people, we Shall with Submission and Modesty, Endeavour to lay them Before your Honours for your Censure Or Approbation, and if we should be so happy as to give any light upon the matter of Government it would be a Great Consolation to us, that Our Mite has been of any Service to the Erecting this Grand Fabrick.——

Therefore we Concieve that the Depriving of any men or Set of men for the Sole Cause of Colour from giving there votes for a Representative, to be an Infringment upon the Rights of Mankind, if so be they are freed by Law and pay there full proportion of taxes, and it is Our Fundamental Principle that taxation and Reprsentation Cannot be Seperated,—that the Great Secret of Government is Governing all By all,—that the House of Representatives has a Right to their voice in Military, as well as Civil Officers to Originate Or Negative a Choice,—It is of the Utmost Importance to the Safety of the State that the power of Granting Pardons be not Vested in Governor, Lieutenant Governor and Speaker of the House But that the joint Voice of the three Branches of the Legislature be joined therein—it Seemeth Inconsistent to Reason that the Creature Should Continue Longer than his Creator,—we look upon it as the Right of freemen that all Commissioners to be Chosen Once a Year,—And as there is no provision made in the Articles of this Constitution of the Right of Petitioning the General Court when Agreived, Or as Cases may Require, we think it Highly Necessary that there Should be an Article Expressive of that Invaluable Right which is justly Due to all free People,—Or Otherwise Set forth in a Bill of Rights to the Same Affect, and we Look upon it most Expedient to have a Convention Chosen for the Intent of Forming a Constitution Separate from the General Court,—and this we submit to your Honours, not as factious or seditious but

Lovers of Good Order and Government, and your Petitioners in Duty Bound Shall Ever Pray

Spencer June 8th 1778

William Frink
John Parker — Committee
John Muzzy
Ebenr Mason

A true copy Attest Wm White T. Clerk

To the President of the Convention of Massachusetts Bay for forming a Constitution for said state

Sir:

Agreeable to the order of the Convention we have called a meeting of the Inhabitants of the town of Spencer who are free and twenty one years of age, to take into consideration the form of a constitution which we received from the Convention, and to give their votes either for or against it. Present 102 members, unanimously rejected the same

Spencer June the 8th 1778

William Bennis
John White — Selectmen of Spencer
Aaron Hunt
Elizah How
John Bisco

Holliston (160/8)

At a Legal meeting of the Freeholders and other In Habitents of The Town of Holliston that are Free and Twenty one years old as ordered by the General Cort of the State Being Duly warned and in Town Meeting assembled on Monday the 8 day of June A.D. 1778 Then the Plan of a Constitution and form of government for the State of Massachusetts Bay as Proposed By the Convention was read and fully Debated on: the Number of Voters Present ware Sixty-Seven the Question was put Whether they would set up Said plan their appeared for the Proposed Form five and against it Sixty-two——

Attest

Staples Chamberlin
Abner Perry — Selectmen of Holliston
Samuel Whiting
Joseph Biglow

Holliston June the 13:1778

Attleborough (160/8)

At a town meeting Lawfully warned and held by adjournment at the meeting House in the first precinct in the Town of attleborough on the 8th day of June 1778 to consider of the form or Plan of government Sent to us by the General Court for our approbation or Disapprobation the number of inhabitants Present at said meeting were 127 whereof 51 members Did Signify their approbation of said form of government and 76 members Voted against it

Witness
June 13th., 1778

Elisha May
Jonathan Stanley
Jonathan Wilkinson
Selectmen of Attleboro

Wheelerborough, (160/10)

Wheelerborough. 8th June 1778

By Virtue of a Warrant issued from the House of Representitives of the State of the Massachusetts Bay, the 4th day of March ultimo, Directing the Selectmen and Committees of the several Towns and Plantations in this State, to take the Votes for and against the Form of a Constitution now abroad.—Agreeable to and in compliance of which Warrant, We the Select men and Committee of this Township (Tho under the great Disadvantage of having no Book of said Form sent us, by which we were not Able to Act till we could Borrow one, which happening very late involved us in the extreme Busy Season of Fishing and Planting; whereby a Majority of the Inhabitants were prevented from Meeting at all. Wherefore the votes obtained were Seventeen for the said form of Constitution

Three——against said Form

one——Neuter

N.B.: By inquireing of those who did not meet we find the Inhabitants who did not meet are generally in Favour of the Constitution as far as they could judge from the verbal Account given them

Benjamin Wheeler
Andrew Grant
Ephrm. Grant

Dracut (160/10)

Agreable to a Resolve of the Great and General Court of the State of Massachusetts Bay The town of Dracutt at a Meeting Appointed for the Consideration of the Constitution or Form of Government at Which Meeting there Were Fifty two voters Present all Which Unanimously Voted to Reject the said Form of Government.

Dracutt June the 8: 1778	Thomas Hovey Jo. B. Varnum	Selectmen of Dracutt

Lincoln (160/11)

Agreeable to a resolve of the great and general court of the 4th of March 1778 we have assembled the inhabitants of the town of Lincoln in order to know the mind of said inhabitants whether they would approve of the constitution and form of government agreed upon by the convention of the state of Massachusetts by February 28th 1778 thirty nine Voters present at said meeting the Vote being put by the moderator and there was one that approved of said Constitution and thirty eight that Disapproved of the same

Lincoln June 8th 1778

Samuel Farrar Abijah Peirce Josiah Nelson Benjn. Munroe Jacob Baker	Selectmen of Lincoln

Rutland (160/12)

At a meeting Legally warned and assembled April the 20th, 1778 agreeable to a Resolve in Convention for State of Massachusetts Bay February the 28th, 1778, to form a Constitution and Mode of Goverment for said State, after hearing said Constitution and form of Goverment Read at the said Meeting on the twentieth Day of April and at the adjournment on the Eighth Day of June A.D. 1778 Sixty nine Voters Present——Voted not to adopt said Constitution and form of Goverment for the State of Massachusetts Bay agreed upon by the Convention of said State February 28th, 1778

Nemen: Contra:

John Frink
Phinehas Walker — Select Men of Rutland
Simon Heald

Rutland June the 8th. 1778

Douglas (160/12)

To the General Assembly of the State of Massachusetts Bay

At a meeting of the Inhabitants of the Town of Douglass after one warning given to take under Consideration the Constitution or Form of Government for said State, the number of male inhabitants being free and Twenty one years of age present at said meeting were Thirty six. Twenty seven of whom voted not to accept said Form, the other nine did not vote Either in the affirmative or Negative

Douglass June 8, 1778

Caleb Whiting
Benja Wares — Selectmen of Douglass
Elijah Moore

Tewksbury (160/13)

To the Honorable John Avery Dept. Secretary This may Certify your Honour that at a general town meeting being Duly and Legally warned and assembled of the Freeholders and other inhabitance of the town of Tewksbury on June the 8: 1778 to Consider the Constitution or forme of Government and to act upon the same

Number of votes for the Constitution or form of government	00
Number against the Constitution or form of government	22

A true copy of the votes attest Newman Scarlett Town Clark

Tewksbury June the 12: 1778

Boston (160/14)

Agreable to a Resolve of the General Assembly of this State passed March 4, 1778—the Inhabitants of the town of Boston being free and twenty one years of age, at a regular meeting called for that purpose, met in Faneuil Hall on Monday the 25th day of May 1778 from whence they adjourned to the Old Brick Meeting House in this town; when the *Constitution* or *Form of* Government as agreed upon by the convention of said *State* February 28, 1778— was distinctly read and duly considered—and the question being put. Viz.—Whether the Inhabitants do approve of the same; it passed in the negative unanimously; nine hundred and sixty eight Persons being present and Voting on the Question——

John Scollay
Gustavus Fellows
Harbottle Dorr
Thos Greenough — Selectmen of Boston
Jona. Williams
Jno. Preston
Nathan Frazier
Ezekl Price

Boston: June 8 1778

[A fuller account from *A Report of the Record Commissioners of the City of Boston, Containing the Boston Town Records, 1778 to 1783* (Boston, 1895), 21–24 is reprinted here.]

At a Meeting of the Inhabitants of the Town of Boston, being free, and Twenty One Years of age, duely qualified and legally warned, in public Town Meeting assembled at Faneuil Hall, on Monday 25th. Day of May Anno Domini 1778.

Warrant for Calling the Meeting.............................read

The Honorable Thomas Cushing Esq. was chosen Moderator of this Meeting by a Hand Vote.

A Motion being made for an Adjournment on Account of the Small Number of Inhabitants at this Meeting, when Business of so much Moment, as the accepting or rejecting of the Form of Government agreed on by the late Convention, was to be transacted——It was previously Voted, that at the Adjournment moved for, all the Bells be rung for ½ an hour, before the time of Meeting, and that the Constables be desired to go through their several Wards and desire the Inhabitants to shut up their Shops, that all qualified might attend the Meeting.

Voted, that this Meeting be adjourned to ½ past 3 O'Clock in the Afternoon, then to attend at the old Brick Meeting House.

3 O'Clock Afternoon, met according to Adjournment

A *Constitution and Form of Government* for the *State* of *Massachusett's Bay,* as agreed on by the *Convention* of said *State* February 28th. 1778, to be laid before the several Towns and Plantations, in said *State,* for their Approbation or Disapprobation, was distinctly read and duely considered——And the Question being put, Viz: ——Whether the Inhabitants do *approve,* or disapprove of said Form of Government, Nine hundred and Sixty eight Persons being present, and voting on the Question.

On a Motion Voted, that

Mr. John Winthrop
Mr. Joseph Barrel
Perez Morton Esq.
Mr. Ezekiel Price
Mr. Nathaniel Appleton

Be a Committee to draw up Instructions relative to a Form of Government for this State, to report at the Adjournment.

Voted, that this Meeting be adjourned to Monday next, 3 O'Clock P.M. to meet at Faneuil Hall.

June 1t. 1778, 3 O'Clock P.M. next according to Adjournment.

The Honorable Thomas Cushing Esq. Moderator of this Meeting being absent, occasioned by Sickness,

Jonathan Williams Esq.

was chosen Moderator Pro. Temp. by a Hand Vote.

The Committee appointed to draw up Instructions for our Representatives, relative to a Constitution or Form of Government—Reported the following Draught, Viz.

To the Representatives of the Town of Boston——

Gentlemen,

You are hereby instructed by the Town of Boston to inform the Honorable General Court, that after *mature Deliberation,* in a very full Meeting, consisting of Nine hundred and Sixty eight, we voted unanimously, to Reject the Form sent out by the Convention, and proposed by them for the Government of this State in future, and to assure them, that a full

Conviction of the Impropriety of this Matter's Originating with the General Court, was the Reason which induced us, the last Year, to instruct our Representatives, *on no Terms to consent to any Proposals for this Purpose;* and we are free to declare, the Specimen we now have, in the *Form proposed,* has confirmed us fully, even to *Demonstration,* that we were right in our Conjectures of that Honorable Body's being improper for this Business: —A Convention for this, and *this alone,* whose Existence is known No Longer than the Constitution is forming, can have no Prepossessions in their own Favor, while it is hard for the General Court, upon a Matter of this Kind, to divest themselves of the Idea of their being *Members;* and the probability that they may continue such, may induce them to form the Government with peculiar Reference to themselves: ——To this we suppose it is owing, that the Legislative and Executive Branches are so blended, and that nothing appears, but that the Members of the Court may monopolize to themselves a Variety of Offices, which we are fully persuaded, the best Form of Government will ever keep these Branches intirely distinct, and the Members confined to their particular Duties, without Incumbrance.

'Tis needless to particularize the many Objections which we could offer to the Form——It is defective in its Foundation; for it's surely of Importance, that all Forms of Government should be prefaced by a Bill of Rights; in this we find no Mention of any:—But, was it unexceptionable in all its Parts, except that of Representation, that alone would be Sufficient with every one possessed of the least Idea of Justice, or the smallest Knowledge of the *Rights* of Human Nature, to reject with Disdain, a Proposal so diametrically opposite to both.—Representation ought to be conformable to some Rule, either *Property* or *Numbers, or both;* but in the Present no Regard is had to either, and *Reason, Justice, and Common Sense,* must be tortured to a great Degree, to accept that Representation, as equal, which may be as *Ten* or *Twenty* to *One:* "For every incorporated Town, without ascertaining the Number of Voters, may send one Member, while no Town, having any Number under three hundred, shall send more." If this is equal, if this is just, all the Rules of Arithmetic, which have been in use since the Formation of Figures, must be done away; but until this *new Rule* of Calculation receives the Stamp of Authority, we cannot Consent to it; for we are possessed of that *antiquated Notion,* that two and two are always equal to four, and it appears to *us* absolutely impossible to prove the contrary.

We were, and still are of Opinion, that a *time* of War is not the time to form Constitutions; we feel the ill Consequence of this Matter, having taken up the time of the General Court, while the Army was neglected—We wish the present may profit by the Errors of the last.—Should it be declared, that this Form is adopted by two thirds of the State, you will be careful that exact Scrutiny be made, as to the Numbers, and at all Events *enter your solemn Protest against the Glaring Injustice of Representation;* but should it meet the Fate we hope and expect, of a total Rejection, and a new one is proposed, you are by no Means to give your Consent, but protest against and oppose it in every Stage of its Progress, and thereby do what is in your power, to prevent unnecessary Expences of public Money.

The present Form of Government we look upon equal to the Exigencies of the Times, and hold ourselves bound to support it with our Lives and Fortunes.

At a proper Time your Constituents wish ardently a new form, and perhaps in a Day of Tranquility, such an One may be adopted as shall please all good Men, and save us from the Dissentions which we find attending the present Time.

The foregoing Draught of Instructions to our Representatives having been read and considered, the Question was put—Whether the same shall be accepted, and given to our Representatives as their Instructions—Passed in the Affirmative.

On a Motion Voted, that those Instructions be printed in the News Papers.

Then the Meeting was dissolved.

Reading (160/15)

To the Honorable the Secretary of the State of Massachusetts Bay

The Inhabitants of Reading being this Day met in Town-Meeting to consider the Constitution sent out by the Honorable the General Court—there appeared to be present 76 Voters—

1 approved of the Constitution

75 disapproved

Benja Brown Moderator

Attest. Jacob Emerson Town Clerk

Reading June 8th 1778

Watertown (160/15) *

At a Publick Town Meeting of the male Inhabitants of Watertown that were twenty one years of age and upwards being regularly assembled on the 8th day of June AD 1778. They took into Consideration The Form of Government agreed upon by the Convention of this State to be laid before the Several Towns for their Approbation or Disapprobation and after the same was Read and a Debate thereon. The Question was put whether it is your minds to approve of the Same and it passed in the Negative unanimously there being Sixty Voters present

Attest. Jona. Brown Town Clerk

Salem (160/16)

At a Meeting of the Freeholders and other inhabitants of Salem, lawfully qualified to vote in town affairs at the town house on Monday the eighth day of June instant to take into consideration and Act upon the Constitution and Form of Government, proposed for the State of Massachusetts Bay——

Voted—That this town disapprove of the Constitution and Form of Government sent out by the Convention of this State to the people at large for reasons assigned in the votes of the Convention of Delegates who met at Ipswich the 29th April 1778——There were one hundred and eight voters at the meeting the whole of which number Voted against said Constitution——

Salem 9th June 1778

Ebenr. Beckford
John Gardner 3d
William Pickman
Jona. Peele Jun.

Select Men of Salem

Westminster (160/17–19)

To the Honorable the Greate and General Court Assembled att Boston May the 15. 1778——

Agreeable to the Resolve of the Late General Assembly the Town of Westminister; att a Legall meeting Called for the purpose of Takeing

* The town records contain the following note: "Voted that the Representative endavor to prevent any thing being don Relating to a New Constitution at present." (*Watertown Records* [Boston, 1928], VI, 182.)

into their Consideration; the Constitution formed by their Convention, and approved of by the Whole Legislative Body: and Sent out for Exceptence or Rejection. Haveing appointd a Committee to Consider and Report theiron: Which Committee after Duely Weighing the Contents theirof; Have Reported as follows viz That it is the opinion of the Committee that no Constitution Whatsoever ought to be Established, till previous theirto the bill of Rights be Set forth, and the Constitution formed theirfrom: That So the Lowest Capacity may be able to Determine his Natural Rights, and judge of the acquiteableness of the Constitution theirby——as to the Constitution the following articles appears to us Exceptionable viz——

Article the 5th Which Deprives a part of the humane Race of their Natural Rights, mearly on account of their Couler—Which in our opinion no power on Earth has a Just Right to Doe: therefore ought to be Expunged the Constitution——

The 9th article that part Which Respects the method of Chusing the Councile or Sennet, appears to us to be Justly Exceptionable inasmuch as the greatest part of the Sennet must be appointed Without the perticuler Knoledge of the Electers; as to their Qualification or fittness, for their high and Importent office—but as to their being appointed from Seperate Districts We have no Special objections against it—further We are of opinion that the Sennet may be Elected from and out of the house of Representitives, with much Greater Safty, then from any other body of men w[hat]ever——10th article approved so far as it Respects The [Go]vernour and Leut Governor—The 12th article approved of Confining the Choice of the Sennet to the house of Representitives—the 13th article approved of With this Reserve that no other Courts be Established but Such as have been yousually Established within the State——

The above Report being Distinctly Read, and on the first parrigraft with Regard to Establishing a bill of Rights previous to any Constitution being Established—voted to Except said Report forty Nine against Said Constitution being Excepted and not one in favour theirof——The Remainder part of the Report being Read and Voted to Except theirof—and the Ninteenth article being Refered by the above Said Committee to the Town for their Consideration and Determination theiron: on a motion made Voted that Said article was Dissagreeable to the Town for Reasons following Because it Deprives the people att Large of appointing their own Rulers and officers and places the power where it may (and no

Doubt) Will be greately abuised; for once Establish a power in the hands of a Selected Number of men, and authorise them to Establish officers over the people over Whome they have no power: is a Daring Step to Despotism; Even an attempt to Doe it is an appugnation of the peoples authority, and those that Doe it, Deserve the Resentment of the people att Large: the oftener power Returnes into the hands of the people the better and when for the good of the whole power is Delegated, it ought to be Done by the whole; and no officer Whatsoever from the highest to the Lowest, ought to be putt in Trust, but by the Sufferiges of the people; a Neglect hear Will Enevitabley prove fatal to the Liberties of Amarica. We find by awefull Experience that a Neglect hearin hes proved the almost Intire Loss of the Inglish Constitution: England after all her bosted privelidges (by meanes of their own Supine Neglect) Stand but one Step higher in the Scale of Liberty—then almost any power in Europ——Where can the power be Layed So Safe as in the hands of the people? and Who can Delegate it So well as they? or Who hes the Boldness—Without blushing? to Say the people are Not Suiteable to putt in their own officers—if so Why Doe we wast our blood and Treasure to obtaine that which When obtained We are not fitt to Enjoy —if but a Selected few only are fitt to appoint our Rulers—Why Ware We uneasie under George—againe if the General Court must be authorised to Elect all officers Will they not monopolise all places of Honour and prophit to themselves to the Exclusion of many others perhaps as capeable as themselves——and further When they have made a band of officers perhapps Verry Dissagreeable to the people, no power is Left in the people to Dissband them; Saveing only a Long Worrey to obtaine an Impeachment, Which When obtained is brought before those Verry beings Who gave them existance; Who always may, and We bleave will have to Greate a Degree of mercy on the works of their own hands.—— and Leave the people to Sweet under their heavie burthens——

Then The Vote being putt Whether the above Reasons Ware agreeable and in passed in the afarmetive and Voted that They be Sent to our Representative

A true coppy attested

Abner Holden Town Clerk

Westminister June the 9th 1778

To Deacon Joseph Miller Representitive for the town of Westminister
To be layed in the secreterries office

Leicester (160/20)

In Consiquence of a Resolve past the General Court March the 4: 1778 to be trainsmited to the Selectmen of the Several towns in this State with a form of Government anexed theirto to be approved or Disapproved by Said towns and plaintations agreable to Said Resolve the Selectmen have called a town meeting and Said town Duly Considering of Said form of Government and acted there on as follow viz Seventy five Voters present at Said meeting Seventy four of Said Number voted against Said form of Government and one of Said Voters Voted in favor of Said form of Government

Leicester June the 11th: 1778

James Baldwin
Thomas Newhall
Henry King
Hez. Ward
Selectmen of Leicester

Princeton (160/21)

Agreable to a Resolve of the General Court directing the Select Men of the Several Towns etc. to call a Meeting of the Inhabitants that are free and twenty one years of age to consider and approve or disapprove of the new form of Government transmitted to the Select Men; Accordingly we the Subscribers have, agreeable to Said Directions, called a meeting and after a Consideration of Said form of Government the vote was taken thereon and upon Counting, there appeared to be twenty approveing; and seventeen, disapproveing of said form of Government

Ephm Woolson
Joseph Sargent
Samuel Hustings
Selectmen for Princeton

Princeton, June 11, 1778

Wilmington (160/21)

At a Legal Meeting of the Freeholders and other Inhabitants of said Town of Wilmington being free and 21 years of age upon due warning given assembled and met together at the Meeting House in said Town on Fryday the 12th. Day of June 1778—To Consider of the Form of Government and Constitution Drawn up for the State of Massachusetts Bay——and Continued by adjornment to the 29th day of June 1778—— After Reading Said form of Government over and over and Debateing thereon—upon mature Deliberation the Vote was put to see if the freeholders and other Inhabitants of said Town would accept of Said Form of Government and Constitution—and it past in the Negative by a Unanimous Vote there being 73 Voters present at said meeting voting against it and not one for it.

A true extract from the records

Attest Cadwallader Ford Jnr.
T. Clerk

Wilmington June 29, 1778
To the Honorable John Avery Dept Secry. Boston

Boxford (160/22)

Boxford June 17th 1778

Sir
Agreable to the Direction of the General Court we would inform that this Town having met divers Times to consider of the proposed form of Goverment, have at Length at their last meeting (forty one Voters being present) unanimously disapproved of the Same

We are with due Respect
Your most Obedient Humble Servants
Asa Perley
John Cushing — Selectmen of Boxford
Benjamin Perley
Asa Merril

Concord (160/23)

At a meeting of the Inhabitents of the Town of Concord being free and twenty one years of age upon an adjournment on the fourteenth Day of June 1778 after Reading the form of Goverment Sent to Said Town by the General assembley of this State, for our approving, or Disapproving the same there being in number present at said meeting one hundred and Eleven, which number voted unanimously to Disapprove of the Same for Reasons heretofore Given by the Town on that important affair——

Concord June the 25th. 1778

By order and in the name of the
Selectmen Ephraim Wood Jnr. Town Clerk

Milton (160/23)

Forty eight Freemen (of twenty one years of age) of the Inhabitants of the Town of Milton in legal Town Meeting assembled on the 15th Day of June 1778 to deliberate and determine upon a Form of Government for the State of Massachusetts Bay as sent forth by a late Honorable Convention for the approbation or rejection of the People are of opinion, That the said Form of Government ought to be rejected——And they Do therefore *unanimously* vote to reject the same

Attested Ebenezer Tucker Selectmen for the Town
Ralph Houghton of
William Badcock Milton

Lexington (160/24–27)

At a legal Meeting of the Freemen of the Town of Lexington, by adjournment, on June 15, 1778. The Committee appointed by the Town to assign Reasons, why the Constitution and Form of Government, draughted and sent out by the late Honorable Convention to the Inhabitants of this State, for their Approbation or Disapprobation, is not approved and accepted by them, as also to prepare Instructions for the Representative of said Town, upon that Subject, Agreeable to a Resolve of the General Court, of said State, dated March 4 1778. reported the following Draught. Viz———

The Freemen of the Town of Lexington, having, upon mature Consideration voted, that they do not approve of the Constitution and Form of government, sent out by the late Honorable Convention, to the Inhabitants of this State, for their Approbation or Disapprobation, cannot look upon it improper to Suggest some Reasons, why they could not chearfully accept of said Constitution and Form of Government, as calculated to answer the important Ends proposed.

Accordingly, it may be observed that it appears to Us, 'That, in emerging from a State of Nature into a State of well regulated Society, Mankind give up some of their natural Rights, in order that others, of greater Importance, to their Well-being, safety and Happiness, both as Societies and Individuals, might be the better enjoyed, secured and defended:———

'That a civil Constitution or Form of Government is of the Nature of a most sacred Covenant, or Contract, entred into by the Individuals, which form the Society, for which such Constitution, or Form of Government is intended, whereby they mutually and solemnly engage to support and defend each other, in the Enjoyment of those Rights, which they mean to retain———

'That the great End of establishing any Constitution or Form of Government among a People or in Society, is to maintain secure and defend those retained Rights inviolate: And, Consequently 'that it is of the hightest importance both to the Public Peace and Utility, and to the safety and security of Individuals, that said Rights intended to be retained (at least those that are fundamental to the well-being of Society and the Liberty and safety of Individuals) should be, in the most explicit Terms, declared.———And that, not only that Government, and Persons in Authority, might know their stated Limits and Bounds; but also the Subjects, and all Members of Such Societies, might know when their Rights and Liberties are infringed or violated; and have some known and established Standard to which they might, with becoming Confidence, appeal, for the Redress of Greivances and Oppressions, whether real or supposed. And we must readily acknowledge, That the total Omission of a Declaration of Rights, of this Kind, is no small Objection to the Constitution before Us.

Next to a Declaration of Rights, it is humbly conceived, That Equality of Representation, is of the greatest Importance to the Preservation of the Liberties of the Subject, and the Peace and Safety of Society. But we cannot think that the Provision made in this form of Government, is adequate to this Purpose. And we are of Opinion, That it is not without Grounds, to be feared, that through the Imperfections of Mankind, in some future Times, small Towns may become an easy Prey to the corrupt Influence of designing Men, to the no small Danger of the public Tranquility, as well as the Liberties of the People: As hath been frequently, and *Notoriously* the Fact, in England, and many other States

A Rotation, in the Members of the supreme Council of a Nation and the Legislative Body of a State (even where such are Elective) hath been frequently suggested, and earnestly recommended, by the best Writers on Policy and Government,—and by Practice and Experience found, to be a powerful Check, to the Arts and Schemes of Ambitious and designing Men, and a Means under Providence of prolonging the Liberty, Safety and Tranquility of such States and Commonwealths, as have adopted it. Of This the Commonwealth of Rome was a striking Instance; where no Citizen could be legally elected to the Consulship, which was the Office of the Supreme Magistrate, but once in Ten Years.——and we could have wished, that the Example of the Honorable Congress, in the Articles of Confederation, had been adopted in this matter:——And that no Citizen of this State had been Eligible to the Office of Supreme Magistrate, or as a Member of the General Court, more than Two Years in Five, Three Years in Seven, or, at least for some limited Term

We have complained of it, in Times past, under the Charter, and still look upon it of dangerous Tendency, to have the Legislative and Executive Powers blended in the same Persons. And the Wise and judicious in all ages have spoken of it as a very great Greivance to have, in the Supreme Council, or Legislative Body of a State, Placemen and Pensioners; or which amounts almost to the same Thing. Persons who hold Lucretive Posts, in the Gift of that Court, or are dependent thereupon for their Offices, and the Salaries or Perquisites annexed thereunto. And we cannot persuade ourselves, that the Provision made, in this Constitution, would be an adequate Remedy. Canvassing for Elections, corrupt Influence and open Bribery, have had the most baleful effects, to the Subversion of Liberty and the Destruction of good Government in Free States; and that in almost all ages: and yet we cannot find anything in this Constitution, to give the least Check to Practices of this Kind.

We could have wished, That "the inestimable Right of Trial by Jury" had been more explicitly defined.

We don't find any sufficient Provision for any Alteration, or Amendment of this Constitution, but by the General Court, or by instructing our Representatives. Whereas, it appears to Us, at least, of the highest Importance, That a Door should be left open for the People to move in this Matter; and a Way explicitly pointed out, wherein They might Legally and Constitutionally, propose, seek and Effect, any such alterations or amendments, in any future Time, as might appear to them advantageous or necessary.——And the rather, as this might give Satisfaction to the People; and be an happy Means, under Providence, of preventing popular Commotions, Mobs, Bloodshed, and Civil War; which too frequently, have been the Consequences of the want of such an Opening, which They might have legally and Constitutionally improved.

These, in General, are a Sketch of the Reasons that have induced us to withhold our approbation of the Constitution and Form of Government transmitted to Us, by the late Honorable Convention.

Wherefore, as the late General Court have explicitly recommended it, to the Several Towns in this State to instruct their Representatives upon this Subject:——The Representative of this Town is accordingly, hereby instructed and directed, to lay the proceedings of said Town, hereupon, with these Reasons, why this Constitution and Form of Government was not approved, before the General Court. And in Case the Establishment of this Constitution and Form of Government should be proposed in said general Court, in the Name of his Constituents, to give his Voice in the Negative.

If this Form of Government should not be established (as we have some Grounds to believe it will not) and it should be proposed in Court, to form another——We would say,——that, Nothwithstanding this Town instructed and impowered their Representative for this Purpose last Year; and Notwithstanding we earnestly hope to have a good Constitution in due Time, established, in this State; yet for various reasons which to Us, at least, appear of Weight, we could wish to have it waved for the Present—Not only because the Form of Government, We are now under, as it hath done, may still answer all the Purposes of Government; —But also because it may interrupt the Deliberations of the Court upon affairs of more immediate Concernment to the Well-being, and perhaps to the very Existence of the State, which may demand all their Time, and all their attention:—and especially, because our Brethren, absent in the War and foremost in Toils and Danger, in the Great Contest, in which we are engaged, may think themselves not well treated in being deprived of having a Voice in so interesting an Affair.—The Representative of this Town is, therefore, for these and other obvious Reasons, hereby, further instructed, to use his Influence to have the Matter waved, at least, for the Present.——But, in Case the Court should determine to have the Matter further attempted at present, The Representative is further instructed to use his Influence, that it may be done by a Convention, freely chosen by the People, for that Purpose, and that only.——

All which is submitted by the Said Committee

Thaddeus Boweman
John Chandler
John Bridge — Committee
Joshua Reed

The above Draught, being repeatedly read, was voted Nem. Con.
A True Coppy Attested Joseph Mason Town Clerk

Newburyport (160/28) *

At a Legal Meeting of the Male Inhabitants of the Town of Newbury Port, being free and twenty one years of age, held June 15th 1778 agreably to the Resolve of the General Court of March 4th. 1778——

Voted Nathl. Carter Esq. Moderator——

Two hundred and eighteen Male Inhabitants, being free and twenty one years of Age, present.

There were two hundred eighteen Votes for rejecting the form of Government, lately recommended by the General Court, of this State——
And none in favor of it.

Abel Greenleaf
Samuel Tufts
Jona. Titcomb
Select Men of the Town of Newbury Port

Deer Island (160/29)

At a Leagal meeting of the Inhabitance of Deer island in order to Recive theire vots for or against the Constitution of goverment fordmd by the

* On March 26, the town had voted that "the mode of representation contained in the constitution lately proposed by the convention of this state, is unequal and unjust, as thereby all the inhabitants of this state are not equally represented, and that some other parts of the same constitution are not founded on the true principles of government; and that a convention of the several towns of this county by their delegates, will have a probable tendency to reform the same agreeably to the natural rights of mankind and the true principles of government." It therefore directed the selectmen "to write circular letters to the several towns within the county, proposing a convention of those towns, by their delegates to be holden at such time and place as the selectmen shall think proper; in said circular letters to propose to each of the towns aforesaid, to send the like number of delegates to said convention, as the same towns have by law right to send representatives to the general court." See Joshua Coffin, *A Sketch of the History of Newbury, Newburyport, and West Newbury from 1635 to 1845* (Boston, 1845), 254–255. The product was the *Essex Result* (see below, No. 22).

Convention of the State of Massachusitts bay——Said meeting holden at the usual place of meeting on Said Island and for the porpose aforesaid agreeible to the Resolve of Said Covention on this first Day of July 1778 there aperd to be at said meeting

	..........46 Votters
for the Constitution	46
against said Constitution	...00

a true list of the whole votters as also those for and those against said Constitution

Taken by us the Commitee of Said Island

Nathan Clesson
Thomas Sanders
John Raynes

Pelham (160/30)

The Committee having maturely considered the proposed Constitution report that tis their Opinion the Qualification required by the third Article of one to be chosen a representative is not necessary one may be equally fit if not fitter to represent any Place if not posessed of two hundered Pence as he who is posessed of two hundred Pounds.

That to vote on all Elections even that of the Governour not excepted should be allowed to all freemen in the State of whatever Denomination without the Limitations contained in the fifth Article even if they be not worth sixty Pounds clear of all Charges thereon.

That the House of Representative which when too numerous is only a charge without any real Advantage to the Country be reduced to a moderate Number—the voters for each increased—and a more equal Representation if possible attained than what seems to be pointed out by the sixth Article.

That in Place of the Oath required by the eleventh Article of a Representative that he is qualified as required by the Constitution a Certificate from the Selectmen who must be allowed to have the best Opportunity to know the truth in these Matters shall determine the Affair.

That the civil officers in each County annualy chosen or holding their Places during good Beheaviour be chosen by the freemen in each County, that military Officers either in the Militia or in the Pay of this State be chosen by their respective Companies Regiments and Brigads not as appointed by the niententh article.

That the thirtieth and second Article is so very large and general the Committee are affraid if admitted it will leave the honourable Judges of the Superiour and Justices of the inferiour Courts to excercise their Patience at the Mercy of the Lawyers and the Juries who are less knowing in these Maters to be missed in some Cases and therefore are of Opinion it would be best to point out some Laws that would suit the greatest Number of Cases and in the present Circumstances leave the Rest to the Rules of Equity untill the State could reform their Laws and settle a more perfect Order as many wise People have of late done—

Upon the whole as the Constitution proposed seems to contain in it many Things truely valuable yet labours under several material Defects seems in some Particulars too favourable to some Classes of Men while it excludes others—and contains in it several Things which appear not agreeable to the genuine Dictates of Reason and those generous Principles of Freedom which glows in the Breast of every true Son of Liberty—— therefore the Commitee are of Opinion that tis best the Town should at present disapprove of the proposed Constitution untill it be narrowly reviewed have its Defects supplyed be formed upon more generous Principles and attain a greater Measure of Perfection——

North Yarmouth (160/31)

At a regular meeting of the Male Inhabitants of the town of North Yarmouth free and twenty one years, called for the purpose of laying before them the Form of Government, drawn up by the late Convention, for this State—for their Consideration, and approbation or disapprobation there of——Said Form of Government having been Read, and Article by Article, particularly debated, a vote was called to know the Minds of the Town whether they approve, or disapprove of the same—when Sixty four voted their Approbation, and twenty their disapprobation thereof——

Certified by Us	Paul Prince	Selectmen of said Town
	Samuel Merrill	

Sandwich *

At a Legal meeting of the Town of Sandwich May 22d 1778——Then the Constitution or Form of Govenment agreed upon by the Convention of this State on February 28th 1778 was distinctly read and Debated after which the Question was put whether the Town approved of Said Form and Voted by Yeas and Nay
86 Yeas and 13 Nays.——
To Nathaniel Freeman and Joseph Nye Esquires Gentlemen you being this Day elected to represent this Town——
And the constitution or Form of Government agreed upon by the late Convention of this State and sent to this Town being read in meeting and duly considered and a major part of the male Inhabitants being free and twenty one years of age present having voted to adopt the said constitution and form of Government the Town of Sandwich do hereby instruct you to give your vote for enacting the same which was read and voted.

Salisbury †

At a meeting of the freeholders and other inhabitants of the town of Salisbury assembled at the West meeting house in said town May the 20th 1778 Dr. Samuel Nye Chosen Moderator. Voted that the meeting be adjournd to Tuesday the ninth Day of June next at one o'clock afternoon at this place——upon adjournment of said meeting June the ninth 1778 it was Put to Vote whether the town would approve of the proposd Constitution for the State of the Massachusetts Bay. it was unanimously Voted in the Negative. number of Voters present at said meeting ninty

* Town records, Massachusetts Historical Society.
† Town records, Massachusetts Historical Society.

22

The Essex Result, 1778

The towns of Essex County met in convention to consider the proposed Constitution of 1778. The carefully considered and detailed criticisms given in the Essex Result were probably composed by the conservative Newburyport lawyer Theophilus Parsons. But when it came to proposing alternatives the document was as unrealistic as some of the less literate responses. The Essex Result is reprinted from *Result of the Convention of Delegates Holden at Ipswich in the County of Essex, Who Were Deputed to Take into Consideration the Constitution and Form of Government, Proposed by the Convention of the State of Massachusetts-Bay* (Newbury-Port: Printed and Sold by John Mycall, 1778).

In Convention of Delegates from the several towns of Lynn, Salem, Danvers, Wenham, Manchester, Gloucester, Ipswich, Newbury-Port, Salisbury, Methuen, Boxford, and Topsfield, holden by adjournment at Ipswich, on the twenty-ninth day of April, one thousand seven hundred and seventy-eight.

Peter Coffin Esq; in the Chair.

The Constitution and form of Government framed by the Convention of this State, was read paragraph by paragraph, and after debate, the following votes were passed.

1. That the present situation of this State renders it best, that the framing of a Constitution therefor, should be postponed 'till the public affairs are in a more peaceable and settled condition.

2. That a bill of rights, clearly ascertaining and defining the rights of conscience, and that security of person and property, which every member in the State hath a right to expect from the supreme power thereof, ought to be settled and established, previous to the ratification of any constitution for the State.

3. That the executive power in any State, ought not to have any share or voice in the legislative power in framing the laws, and therefore, that the second article of the Constitution is liable to exception.

4. That any man who is chosen Governor, ought to be properly qualified in point of property—that the qualification therefor, mentioned in the third article of the Constitution, is not sufficient—nor is the same

qualification directed to be ascertained on fixed principles, as it ought to be, on account of the fluctuation of the nominal value of money, and of property.

5. That in every free Republican Government, where the legislative power is rested in an house or houses of representatives, all the members of the State ought to be equally represented.

6. That the mode of representation proposed in the sixth article of the constitution, is not so equal a representation as can reasonably be devised.

7. That therefore the mode of representation in said sixth article is exceptionable.

8. That the representation proposed in said article is also exceptionable, as it will produce an unwieldy assembly.

9. That the mode of election of Senators pointed out in the Constitution is exceptionable.

10. That the rights of conscience, and the security of person and property each member of the State is entitled to, are not ascertained and defined in the Constitution, with a precision sufficient to limit the legislative power—and therefore, that the thirteenth article of the constitution is exceptionable.

11. That the fifteenth article is exceptionable, because the numbers that constitute a quorum in the House of Representatives and Senate, are too small.

12. That the seventeenth article of the constitution is exceptionable, because the supreme executive officer is not vested with proper authority —and because an independence between the executive and legislative body is not preserved.

13. That the nineteenth article is exceptionable, because a due independence is not kept up between the supreme legislative, judicial, and executive powers, nor between any two of them.

14. That the twentieth article is exceptionable, because the supreme executive officer hath a voice, and must be present in that Court, which alone hath authority to try impeachments.

15. That the twenty second article is exceptionable, because the supreme executive power is not preserved distinct from, and independent of, the supreme legislative power.

16. That the twenty third article is exceptionable, because the power of granting pardons is not solely vested in the supreme executive power of the State.

17. That the twenty eighth article is exceptionable, because the dele-

gates for the Continental Congress may be elected by the House of Representatives, when all the Senators may vote against the election of those who are delegated.

18. That the thirty fourth article is exceptionable, because the rights of conscience are not therein clearly defined and ascertained; and further, because the free exercise and enjoyment of religious worship is there said to be *allowed* to all the protestants in the State, when in fact, that free exercise and enjoyment is the natural and uncontroulable right of every member of the State.

A committee was then appointed to attempt the ascertaining of the true principles of government, applicable to the territory of the Massachusetts-Bay; to state the non-conformity of the constitution proposed by the Convention of this State to those principles, and to delineate the general outlines of a constitution conformable thereto; and to report the same to this Body.

This Convention was then adjourned to the twelfth day of May next, to be holden at Ipswich.

The Convention met pursuant to adjournment, and their committee presented the following report.

The committee appointed by this Convention at their last adjournment, have proceeded upon the service assigned them. With diffidence have they undertaken the several parts of their duty, and the manner in which they have executed them, they submit to the candor of this Body. When they considered of what vast consequence, the forming of a Constitution is to the members of this State, the length of time that is necessary to canvass and digest any proposed plan of government, before the establishment of it, and the consummate coolness, and solemn deliberation which should attend, not only those gentlemen who have, reposed in them, the important trust of delineating the several lines in which the various powers of government are to move, but also all those, who are to form an opinion of the execution of that trust, your committee must be excused when they express a surprise and regret, that so short a time is allowed the freemen inhabiting the territory of the Massachusetts-Bay, to revise and comprehend the form of government proposed to them by the convention of this State, to compare it with those principles on which every free government ought to be founded, and to ascertain it's conformity or non-conformity thereto. All this is necessary to be done, before a true opinion of it's merit or demerit can be formed. This opinion is to be certified within a time which, in our apprehension, is much too short for this purpose, and to be certified by a people, who, during that time, have had and will have their minds perplexed and oppressed with a variety of public cares. The committee also beg leave to observe, that the constitution proposed for public approbation, was formed by gentlemen, who, at the same time, had a large share in conducting an important war, and who were employed in carrying into execution almost all the various powers of government.

The committee however proceeded in attempting the task assigned them, and the success of that attempt is now reported.

The reason and understanding of mankind, as well as the experience of all ages, confirm the truth of this proposition, that the benefits resulting to individuals from a free government, conduce much more to their happiness, than the retaining of all their natural rights in a state of nature. These benefits are greater or less, as the form of government, and the mode of exercising the supreme power of the State, are more or less conformable to those principles of equal impartial liberty, which is the property of all men from their birth as the gift of their Creator, compared with the manners and genius of the people, their occupations, customs, modes of thinking, situation, extent of country, and numbers. If the constitution and form of government are wholly repugnant to those principles, wretched are the subjects of that State. They have surrendered a portion of their natural rights, the enjoyment of which was in some degree a blessing, and the consequence is, they find themselves stripped of the remainder. As an anodyne to compose the spirits of these slaves, and to lull them into a passively obedient state, they are told, that tyranny is preferable to no government at all; a proposition which is to be doubted, unless considered under some limitation. Surely a state of nature is more excellent than that, in which men are meanly submissive to the haughty will of an imperious tyrant, whose savage passions are not bounded by the laws of reason, religion, honor, or a regard to his subjects, and the point to which all his movements center, is the gratification of a brutal appetite. As in a state of nature much happiness cannot be enjoyed by individuals, so it has been conformable to the inclinations of almost all men, to enter into a political society so constituted, as to remove the inconveniences they were obliged to submit to in their former state, and, at the same time, to retain all those natural rights, the enjoyment of which would be consistent with the nature of a free government, and the necessary subordination to the supreme power of the state.

To determine what form of government, in any given case, will produce the greatest possible happiness to the subject, is an arduous task, not to be compassed perhaps by any human powers. Some of the greatest geniuses and most learned philosophers of all ages, impelled by their sollicitude to promote the happiness of mankind, have nobly dared to attempt it: and their labours have crowned them with immortality. A Solon, a Lycurgus of Greece, a Numa of Rome are remembered with honor, when the wide extended empires of succeeding tyrants, are hardly important enough to be faintly sketched out on the map, while their superb thrones have long since crumbled into dust. The man who alone undertakes to form a constitution, ought to be an unimpassioned being; one enlightened mind; biassed neither by the lust of power, the allurements of pleasure, nor the glitter of wealth; perfectly acquainted with all the alienable and unalienable rights of mankind; possessed of this grand truth, that all men are born equally free, and that no man ought to surrender any part of his natural rights, without receiving the greatest possible equivalent; and influenced by the impartial principles of rectitude and justice, without partiality for, or prejudice against the interest or professions of any individuals or class of men. He ought also to be master of the histories of all the empires and states which are now existing, and all those which have figured in antiquity, and thereby able to collect and blend their respective excellencies, and avoid those defects which experience hath pointed out. Rousseau, a learned foreigner, a citizen of Geneva, sensible of the importance and difficulty of the subject, thought it impossible for any body of people, to form a free and equal constitution for themselves, in which, every individual should have equal justice done him, and be permitted to enjoy a share of power in the state, equal to what should be enjoyed by any other. Each individual, said he, will struggle, not only to retain all his own natural rights, but to acquire a controul over those of others. Fraud, circumvention, and an union of interest of some classes of people, combined with an inattention to the rights of posterity, will prevail over the principles of equity, justice, and good policy. The Genevans, perhaps the most virtuous republicans now existing, thought like Rousseau. They called the celebrated Calvin to their assistance. He came, and, by their gratitude, have they embalmed his memory.

The freemen inhabiting the territory of the Massachusetts-Bay are now forming a political society for themselves. Perhaps their situation is more favorable in some respects, for erecting a free government, than any other people were ever favored with. That attachment to old forms, which usually embarrasses, has not place amongst them. They have the history and experience of all States before them. Mankind have been toiling through ages for their information; and the philosophers and learned men of antiquity have trimmed their midnight lamps, to transmit to them instruction. We live also in an age, when the principles of political liberty, and the foundation of governments, have been freely canvassed, and fairly settled. Yet some difficulties we have to encounter. Not content with removing our attachment to the old government, perhaps we have contracted a prejudice against some part of it without foundation. The idea of liberty has been held up in so dazzling colours, that some of us may not be willing to submit to that subordination necessary in the freest States. Perhaps we may say further, that we do not consider ourselves united as brothers, with an united interest, but have fancied a clashing of interests amongst the various classes of men, and have acquired a thirst of power, and a wish of domination, over some of the community. We are contending for freedom——Let us all be equally free——It is possible, and it is just. Our interests when candidly considered are one. Let us have a constitution founded, not upon party or prejudice—not one for to-day or to-morrow—but for posterity. Let *Esto perpetua* be it's motto. If it is founded in good policy; it will be founded in justice and honesty. Let all ambitious and interested views be discarded, and let regard be had only to the good of the whole, in which the situation and rights of posterity must be considered: and let equal justice be done to all the members of the community; and we thereby imitate our common father, who at our births, dispersed his favors, not only with a liberal, but with an equal hand.

Was it asked, what is the best form of government for the people of the Massachusetts-Bay? we confess it would be a question of infinite importance: and the man who could truly answer it, would merit a statue of gold to his memory, and his fame would be recorded in the annals of late posterity, with unrivalled lustre. The question, however, must be answered, and let it have the best answer we can possibly give it. Was a man to mention a despotic government, his life would be a just forfeit to the resentments of an affronted people. Was he to hint monarchy, he would deservedly be hissed off the stage, and consigned to infamy. A republican form is the only one consonant to the feelings of the generous and brave Americans. Let us now attend to those principles, upon which all republican governments, who boast any degree of political liberty, are founded, and which must enter into the spirit of a FREE republican constitution. For all republics are not FREE.

All men are born equally free. The rights they possess at their births are equal, and of the same kind. Some of those rights are alienable, and may be parted with for an equivalent. Others are unalienable and inherent, and of that importance, that no equivalent can be received in exchange. Sometimes we shall mention the surrendering of a power to controul our natural rights, which perhaps is speaking with more precision, than when we use the expression of parting with natural rights—but the same thing is intended. Those rights which are unalienable, and of that importance, are called the rights of conscience. We have duties, for the discharge of which we are accountable to our Creator and benefactor, which no human power can cancel. What those duties are, is determinable by right reason, which may be, and is called, a well informed conscience. What this conscience dictates as our duty, is so; and that power which assumes a controul over it, is an usurper; for no consent can be pleaded to justify the controul, as any consent in this case is void. The alienation of some rights, in themselves alienable, may be also void, if the bargain is of that nature, that no equivalent can be received. Thus, if a man surrender all his alienable rights, without reserving a controul over the supreme power, or a right to resume in certain cases, the surrender is void, for he becomes a slave; and a slave can receive no equivalent. Common equity would set aside this bargain.

When men form themselves into society, and erect a body politic or State, they are to be considered as one moral whole, which is in possession of the supreme power of the State. This supreme power is composed of the powers of each individual collected together, and VOLUNTARILY parted with by him. No individual, in this case, parts with his unalienable rights, the supreme power therefore cannot controul them. Each individual also surrenders the power of controuling his natural alienable rights, ONLY

WHEN THE GOOD OF THE WHOLE REQUIRES it. The supreme power therefore can do nothing but what is for the good of the whole; and when it goes beyond this line, it is a power usurped. If the individual receives an equivalent for the right of controul he has parted with, the surrender of that right is valid; if he receives no equivalent, the surrender is void, and the supreme power as it respects him is an usurper. If the supreme power is so directed and executed that he does not enjoy political liberty, it is an illegal power, and he is not bound to obey. Political liberty is by some defined, a liberty of doing whatever is not prohibited by law. The definition is erroneous. A tyrant may govern by laws. The republic's of Venice and Holland govern by laws, yet those republic's have degenerated into insupportable tyrannies. Let it be thus defined; political liberty is the right every man in the state has, to do whatever is not prohibited by laws, TO WHICH HE HAS GIVEN HIS CONSENT. This definition is in unison with the feelings of a free people. But to return—If a fundamental principle on which each individual enters into society is, that he shall be bound by no laws but those to which he has consented, he cannot be considered as consenting to any law enacted by a minority: for he parts with the power of controuling his natural rights, only when the good of the whole requires it; and of this there can be but one absolute judge in the State. If the minority can assume the right of judging, there may then be two judges; for however large the minority may be, there must be another body still larger, who have the same claim, if not a better, to the right of absolute determination. If therefore the supreme power should be so modelled and exerted, that a law may be enacted by a minority, the inforcing of that law upon an individual who is opposed to it, is an act of tyranny. Further, as every individual, in entering into the society, parted with a power of controuling his natural rights equal to that parted with by any other, or in other words, as all the members of the society contributed an equal portion of their natural rights, towards the forming of the supreme power, so every member ought to receive equal benefit from, have equal influence in forming, and retain an equal controul over, the supreme power.

It has been observed, that each individual parts with the power of controuling his natural alienable rights, only when the good of the whole requires it, he therefore has remaining, after entering into political society, all his unalienable natural rights, and a part also of his alienable natural rights, provided the good of the whole does not require the sacrifice of them. Over the class of unalienable rights the supreme power hath no controul, and they ought to be clearly defined and ascertained in a BILL OF RIGHTS, previous to the ratification of any constitution. The bill of rights should also contain the equivalent every man receives, as a consideration for the rights he has surrendered. This equivalent consists principally in the security of his person and property, and is also unassailable by the supreme power: for if the equivalent is taken back, those natural rights which were parted with to purchase it, return to the original proprietor, as nothing is more true, than that ALLEGIANCE AND PROTECTION ARE RECIPROCAL.

The committee also proceeded to consider upon what principles, and in what manner, the supreme power of the state thus composed of the powers of the several individuals thereof, may be formed, modelled, and exerted in a republic, so that every member of the state may enjoy political liberty. This is called by some, *the ascertaining of the political law of the state.* Let it now be called *the forming of a constitution.*

The reason why the supreme governor of the world is a rightful and just governor, and entitled to the allegiance of the universe is, because he is infinitely good, wise, and powerful. His goodness prompts him to the best measures, his wisdom qualifies him to discern them, and his power to effect them. In a state likewise, the supreme power is best disposed of, when it is so modelled and balanced, and rested in such hands, that it has the greatest share of goodness, wisdom, and power, which is consistent with the lot of humanity.

That state, (other things being equal) which has reposed the supreme power in the hands of one or a small number of persons, is the most powerful state. An union, expedition, secrecy and dispatch are to be found only here. Where power is to be executed by a large number, there will not probably be either of the requisites just mentioned. Many men have various opinions: and each one will be tenacious of his own, as he thinks it preferable to any other; for when he thinks otherwise, it will cease to be his opinion. From this diversity of opinions results disunion; from disunion, a want of expedition and dispatch. And the larger the number to whom a secret is entrusted, the greater is the probability of it's disclosure. This inconvenience more fully strikes us when we consider that want of secrecy may prevent the successful execution of any measures, however excellently formed and digested.

But from a single person, or a very small number, we are not to expect that political honesty, and upright regard to the interest of the body of the people, and the civil rights of each individual, which are essential to a good and free constitution. For these qualities we are to go to the body of the people. The voice of the people is said to be the voice of God. No man will be so hardy and presumptuous, as to affirm the truth of that proposition in it's fullest extent. But if this is considered as the intent of it, that the people have always a disposition to promote their own happiness, and that when they have time to be informed, and the necessary means of information given them, they will be able to determine upon the necessary measures therefor, no man, of a tolerable acquaintance with mankind, will deny the truth of it. The inconvenience and difficulty in forming any free permanent constitution are, that such is the lot of humanity, the bulk of the people, whose happiness is principally to be consulted in forming a constitution, and in legislation, (as they include the majority) are so situated in life, and such are their laudable occupations, that they cannot have time for, nor the means of furnishing themselves with proper information, but must be indebted to some of their fellow subjects for the communication. Happy is the man, and blessings will attend his memory, who shall improve his leisure, and those abilities which heaven has indulged him with, in communicating that true information, and impartial knowledge, to his fellow subjects, which will insure their happiness. But the artful demagogue, who to gratify his ambition or avarice, shall, with the gloss of false patriotism, mislead his countrymen, and meanly snatch from them the golden glorious opportunity of forming a system of political and civil liberty, fraught with blessings for themselves, and remote posterity, what language can paint his demerit? The execrations of ages will be a punishment inadequate; and his name, though ever blackening as it rolls down the stream of time, will not catch its proper hue.

Yet, when we are forming a Constitution, by deductions that follow from established principles, (which is the only good method of forming one for futurity,) we are to look further than to the bulk of the people, for the greatest wisdom, firmness, consistency, and perseverance. These qualities will most probably be found amongst men of education and fortune. From such men we are to expect genius cultivated by reading, and all the various advantages and assistances, which art, and a liberal education aided by wealth, can furnish. From these result learning, a thorough knowledge of the interests of their country, when considered abstractedly, when compared with the neighbouring States, and when with those more remote, and an acquaintance with it's produce and manufacture, and it's exports and imports. All these are necessary to be known, in order to determine what is the true interest of any state; and without that interest is ascertained, impossible will it be to discover, whether a variety of certain laws may be beneficial or hurtful. From gentlemen whose private affairs compel them to take care of their own household, and deprive them of leisure, these qualifications are not to be generally expected, whatever class of men they are enrolled in.

Let all these respective excellencies be united. Let the supreme power be so disposed and ballanced, that the laws may have in view the interest of the whole; let them be wisely and consistently framed for that end, and firmly adhered to; and let them be executed with vigour and dispatch.

Before we proceed further, it must be again considered, and kept always in view, that we are not attempting to form a temporary constitution, one adjusted only to our present circumstances. We wish for one founded upon such principles as will secure to us freedom and happiness, however our circumstances may vary. One that will smile amidst the declensions of European and Asiatic empires, and survive the rude storms of time. It is not therefore to be understood, that all the men of fortune of the present day, are men of wisdom and learning, or that they are not. Nor that the bulk of the people, the farmers, the merchants, the tradesmen, and labourers, are all honest and upright, with single views to the public good, or that they are not. In each of the classes there are undoubtedly exceptions, as the rules laid down are general. The proposition is only this. That among gentlemen of education, fortune and leisure, we shall find the largest number of men, possessed of wisdom, learning, and a firmness and consistency of character. That among the bulk of the people, we shall find the greatest share of political honesty, probity, and a regard to the interest of the whole, of which they compose the majority. That wisdom and firmness are not sufficient without good intentions, nor the latter without the former. The conclusion is, let the legislative body unite them all. The former are called the excellencies that result from an aristocracy; the latter, those that result from a democracy.

The supreme power is considered as including the legislative, judicial, and executive powers. The nature and employment of these several powers deserve a distinct attention.

The legislative power is employed in making laws, or prescribing such rules of action to every individual in the state, as the good of the whole requires, to be conformed to by him in his conduct to the governors and governed, with respect both to their persons and property, according to the several relations he stands in. What rules of action the good of the whole requires, can be ascertained only by the majority, for a reason formerly mentioned. Therefore the legislative power must be so formed and exerted, that in prescribing any rule of action, or, in other words, enacting any law, the majority must consent. This may be more evident, when the fundamental condition on which every man enters into society, is considered. No man consented that his natural alienable rights should be wantonly controuled: they were controulable, only when that controul should be subservient to the good of the whole; and that subserviency, from the very nature of government, can be determined but by one absolute judge. The minority cannot be that judge, because then there may be two judges opposed to each other, so that this subserviency remains undetermined. Now the enacting of a law, is only the exercise of this controul over the natural alienable rights of each member of the state; and therefore this law must have the consent of the majority, or be invalid, as being contrary to the fundamental condition of the original social contract. In a state of nature, every man had the sovereign controul over his own person. He might also have, in that state, a qualified property. Whatever lands or chattels he had acquired the peaceable possession of, were exclusively his, by right of occupancy or possession. For while they were unpossessed he had a right to them equally with any other man, and therefore could not be disturbed in his possession, without being injured; for no man could lawfully dispossess him, without having a better right, which no man had. Over this qualified property every man in a state of nature had also a sovereign controul. And in entering into political society, he surrendered this right of controul over his person and property, (with an exception to the rights of conscience) to the supreme legislative power, to be exercised by that power, *when the good of the whole demanded it.* This was all the right he could surrender, being all the alienable right of which he was possessed. The only objects of legislation therefore, are the person and property of the individuals which compose the state. If the law affects only the persons of the members, the consent of a majority of any members is sufficient. If the law affects the property only, the consent of those who hold a majority of the property is enough. If it affects, (as it will very frequently, if not always,) both the person and property, the consent of a majority of the members, and of those members also, who hold a majority of the property is necessary. If the consent of the latter is not obtained, their interest is taken from them against their consent, and their boasted security of property is vanished. Those who make the law, in this case give and grant what is not theirs. The law, in it's principles, becomes a second stamp act. Lord Chatham very finely ridiculed the British house of commons upon that principle. "You can give and grant, said he, only your own. Here you give and grant, what? The property of the Americans." The people of the Massachusetts-Bay then thought his Lordship's ridicule well pointed. And would they be willing to merit the same? Certainly they will agree in the principle, should they mistake the application. The laws of the province of Massachusetts-Bay adopted the same principle, and very happily applied it. As the votes of proprietors of common and undivided lands in their meetings, can affect only their property, therefore it is enacted, that in ascertaining the majority, the votes shall be collected according to the respective interests of the proprietors. If each member, without regard to his property, has equal influence in legislation with any other, it follows, that some members enjoy greater benefits and powers in legislation than others, when these benefits and powers are compared with the rights parted with to purchase them. For the property-holder parts with the controul over his person, as well as he who hath no property, and the former also parts with the controul over his property, of which the latter is destitute. Therefore to constitute a perfect law in a free state, affecting the persons and property of the members, it is necessary that the law be for the good of the whole, which is to be determined by a majority of the members, and that majority should include those, who possess a major part of the property in the state.

The judicial power follows next after the legislative power; for it cannot act, until after laws are prescribed. Every wise legislator annexes a sanction to his laws, which is most commonly penal, (that is) a punishment either corporal or pecuniary, to be inflicted on the member who shall infringe them. It is the part of the judicial power (which in this territory has always been, and always ought to be, a court and jury) to ascertain the member who hath broken the law. Every man is to be presumed innocent, until the judicial power hath determined him guilty. When that decision is known, the law annexes the punishment, and the offender is turned over to the executive arm, by whom it is inflicted on him. The judicial power hath also to determine what legal contracts have been broken, and what member hath been injured by a violation of the law, to consider the damages that have been sustained, and to ascertain the recompense. The executive power takes care that this recompense is paid.

The executive power is sometimes divided into the external executive, and internal executive. The former comprehends war, peace, the sending and receiving ambassadors, and whatever concerns the transactions of the state with any other independent state. The confederation of the United States of America hath lopped off this branch of the executive, and placed it in Congress. We have therefore only to consider the internal executive power, which is employed in the peace, security and protection of the subject and his property, and in the defence of the state. The executive power is to marshal and command her militia and armies for her defence, to enforce the law, and to carry into execution all the orders of the legislative powers.

A little attention to the subject will convince us, that these three powers ought to be in different hands, and independent of one another, and so ballanced, and each having that check upon the other, that their independence shall be preserved—If the three powers are united, the government will be absolute, *whether these powers are in the hands of one or a large number*. The same party will be the legislator, accuser, judge and executioner; and what probability will an accused person have of an acquittal, however innocent he may be, when his judge will be also a party.

If the legislative and judicial powers are united, the maker of the law will also interpret it; and the law may then speak a language, dictated by the whims, the caprice, or the prejudice of the judge, with impunity to him—And what people are so unhappy as those, whose laws are uncertain. It will also be in the breast of the judge, when grasping after his prey, to make a retrospective law, which shall bring the unhappy offender within it; and this also he can do with impunity—The subject can have no peaceable remedy—The judge will try himself, and an acquittal is the certain consequence. He has it also in his power to enact any law, which may shelter him from deserved vengeance.

Should the executive and legislative powers be united, mischiefs the most terrible would follow. The executive would enact those laws it pleased to execute, and no others—The judicial power would be set aside as inconvenient and tardy—The security and protection of the subject would be a shadow—The executive power would make itself absolute, and the government end in a tyranny——Lewis the eleventh of France, by cunning and treachery compleated the union of the executive and legislative powers of that kingdom, and upon that union established a system of tyranny. France was formerly under a free government.

The assembly or representatives of the united states of Holland, exercise the executive and legislative powers, and the government there is absolute.

Should the executive and judicial powers be united, the subject would then have no permanent security of his person and property. The executive power would interpret the laws and bend them to his will; and, as he is the judge, he may leap over them by artful constructions, and gratify, with impunity, the most rapacious passions. Perhaps no cause in any state has contributed more to promote internal convulsions, and to stain the scaffold with it's best blood, than this unhappy union. And it is an union which the executive power in all states, hath attempted to form: if that could not be compassed, to make the judicial power dependent upon it. Indeed the dependence of any of these powers upon either of the others, which in all states has always been attempted by one or the other of them, has so often been productive of such calamities, and of the shedding of such oceans of blood, that the page of history seems to be one continued tale of human wretchedness.

The following principles now seem to be established.

1. That the supreme power is limited, and cannot controul the unalienable rights of mankind, nor resume the equivalent (that is, the security of person and property) which each individual receives, as a consideration for the alienable rights he parted with in entering into political society.

2. That these unalienable rights, and this equivalent, are to be clearly defined and ascertained in a BILL OF RIGHTS, previous to the ratification of any constitution.

3. That the supreme power should be so formed and modelled, as to exert the greatest possible power, wisdom, and goodness.

4. That the legislative, judicial, and executive powers, are to be lodged in different hands, that each branch is to be independent, and further, to be so ballanced, and be able to exert such checks upon the others, as will preserve it from a dependence on, or an union with them.

5. That government can exert the greatest power when it's supreme authority is vested in the hands of one or a few.

6. That the laws will be made with the greatest wisdom, and best intentions, when men, of all the several classes in the state concur in the enacting of them.

7. That a government which is so constituted, that it cannot afford a degree of political liberty nearly equal to all it's members, is not founded upon principles of freedom and justice, and where any member enjoys no degree of political liberty, the government, so far as it respects him, is a tyranny, for he is controuled by laws to which he has never consented.

8. That the legislative power of a state hath no authority to controul the natural rights of any of it's members, unless the good of the whole requires it.

9. That a majority of the state is the only judge when the general good does require it.

10. That where the legislative power of the state is so formed, that a law may be enacted by the minority, each member of the state does not enjoy political liberty. And

11. That in a free government, a law affecting the person and property of it's members, is not valid, unless it has the consent of a majority of the members, which majority should include those, who hold a major part of the property in the state.

It may be necessary to proceed further, and notice some particular principles, which should be attended to in forming the three several powers in a free republican government.

The first important branch that comes under our consideration, is the legislative body. Was the number of the people so small, that the whole could meet together without inconvenience, the opinion of the majority would be more easily known. But, besides the inconvenience of assembling such numbers, no great advantages could follow. Sixty thousand people could not discuss with candor, and determine with deliberation. Tumults, riots, and murder would be the result. But the impracticability of forming such an assembly, renders it needless to make any further observations. The opinions and consent of the majority must be collected from persons, delegated by every freeman of the state for that purpose. Every freeman, who hath sufficient discretion, should have a voice in the election of his legislators. To speak with precision, in every free state where the power of legislation is lodged in the hands of one or more bodies of representatives elected for that purpose, the person of every member of the state, and all the property in it, ought to be represented, because they are objects of legislation. All the members of the state are qualified to make the election, unless they have not sufficient discretion, or are so situated as to have no wills of their own. Persons not twenty one years old are deemed of the former class, from their want of years and experience. The municipal law of this country will not trust them with the disposition of their lands, and consigns them to the care of their parents or guardians. Women what age soever they are of, are also considered as not having a sufficient acquired discretion; not from a deficiency in their mental powers, but from the natural tenderness and delicacy of their minds, their retired mode of life, and various domestic duties. These concurring, prevent that promiscuous intercourse with the world, which is necessary to qualify them for electors. Slaves are of the latter class and have no wills. But are slaves members of a free government? We feel the absurdity, and would to God, the situation of America and the tempers of it's inhabitants were such, that the slave-holder could not be found in the land.

The rights of representation should be so equally and impartially distributed, that the representatives should have the same views, and interests with the people at large. They should think, feel, and act like them, and in fine, should be an exact miniature of their constituents. They should be (if we may use the expression) the whole body politic, with all it's property, rights, and priviledges, reduced to a smaller scale, every part being diminished in just proportion. To pursue the metaphor. If in adjusting the representation of freeman, any ten are reduced into one, all the other tens should be alike reduced: or if any hundred should be reduced to one, all the other hundreds should have just the same reduction. The representation ought also to be so adjusted, that it should be the interest of the representatives at all times, to do justice, therefore equal interest among the people, should have equal interest among the body of representatives. The majority of the representatives should also represent a majority of the people, and the legislative body should be so constructed, that every law affecting property, should have the consent of those who hold a majority of the property. The law would then be determined to be for the good of the whole by the proper judge, the majority, and the necessary consent thereto would be obtained: and all the members of the State would enjoy political liberty, and an equal degree of it. If the scale to which the body politic is to be reduced, is but a little smaller than the original, or, in other words, if a small number of freemen should be reduced to one, that is, send one representative, the number of representatives would be too large for the public good. The expences of government would be enormous. The body would be too unwieldy to deliberate with candor and coolness. The variety of opinions and oppositions would irritate the passions. Parties would be formed and factions engendered. The members would list under the banners of their respective leaders: address and intrigue would conduct the debates, and the result would tend only to promote the ambition or interest of a particular party. Such has always been in some degree, the course and event of debates instituted and managed by a large multitude.

For these reasons, some foreign politicians have laid it down as a rule, that no body of men larger than an hundred, would transact business well: and Lord Chesterfield called the British house of commons a mere mob, because of the number of men which composed it.

Elections ought also to be free. No bribery, corruption, or undue influence should have place. They stifle the free voice of the people, corrupt their morals, and introduce a degeneracy of manners, a supineness of temper, and an inattention to their liberties, which pave the road for the approach of tyranny, in all it's frightful forms.

The man who buys an elector by his bribes, will sell him again, and reap a profit from the bargain; and he thereby becomes a dangerous member of society. The legislative body will hold the purse strings, and men will struggle for a place in that body to acquire a share of the public wealth. It has always been the case. Bribery will be attempted, and the laws will not prevent it. All states have enacted severe laws against it, and they have been ineffectual. The defect was in their forms of government. They were not so contrived, as to prevent the practicability of it. If a small corporation can place a man in the legislative body, to bribe will be easy and cheap. To bribe a large corporation would be difficult and expensive, if practicable. In Great-Britain, the representatives of their counties and great cities are freely elected. To bribe the electors there, is impracticable: and their representatives are the most upright and able statesmen in parliament. The small boroughs are bought by the ministry and opulent men; and their representatives are the mere tools of administration or faction. Let us take warning.

A further check upon bribery is, when the corrupter of a people knows not the electors. If delegates were first appointed by a number of corporations, who at a short day were to elect their representatives, these bloodhounds in a state would be at fault. They would not scent their game. Besides, the representatives would probably be much better men—they would be double refined.

But it may be said, the virtuous American would blast with indignation the man, who should proffer him a bribe. Let it now be admitted as a fact. We ask, will that always be the case? The most virtuous states have become vicious. The morals of all people, in all ages, have been shockingly corrupted. The rigidly virtuous Spartans, who banished the use of gold and silver, who gloried in their poverty for centuries, at last fell a prey to luxury and corruption. The Romans, whose intense love to their country, astonishes a modern patriot, who fought the battles of the republic for three hundred years without pay, and who, as volunteers, extended her empire over Italy, were at last dissolved in luxury, courted the hand of bribery, and finally sold themselves as slaves, and prostrated their country to tyrants the most ignominious and brutal. Shall we alone boast an exemption from the general fate of mankind? Are our private and political virtues to be transmitted untainted from generation to generation, through a course of ages? Have we not already degenerated from the pure morals and disinterested patriotism of our ancestors? And are not our manners becoming soft and luxurious, and have not our vices began to shoot? Would one venture to prophecy, that in a century from this period, we shall be a corrupt luxurious people, perhaps the close of that century would stamp this prophecy with the title of history.

The rights of representation should also be held sacred and inviolable, and for this purpose, representation should be fixed upon known and easy principles; and the constitution should make provision, that recourse should constantly be had to those principles within a very small period of years, to rectify the errors that will creep in through lapse of time, or alteration of situations. The want of fixed principles of government, and a stated regular recourse to them, have produced the dissolution of all states, whose constitutions have been transmitted to us by history.

But the legislative power must not be trusted with one assembly. A single assembly is frequently influenced by the vices, follies, passions, and prejudices of an individual. It is liable to be avaricious, and to exempt itself from the burdens it lays upon it's constituents. It is subject to ambition, and after a series of years, will be prompted to vote itself perpetual. The long parliament in England voted itself perpetual, and thereby, for a time, destroyed the political liberty of the subject. Holland was governed by one representative assembly annually elected. They afterwards voted themselves from annual to septennial; then for life; and finally exerted the power of filling up all vacancies, without application to their constituents. The government of Holland is now a tyranny *though a republic.*

The result of a single assembly will be hasty and indigested, and their judgments frequently absurd and inconsistent. There must be a second body to revise with coolness and wisdom, and to controul with firmness, independent upon the first, either for their creation, or existence. Yet the first must retain a right to a similar revision and controul over the second.

Let us now ascertain some particular principles which should be attended to, in forming the executive power.

When we recollect the nature and employment of this power, we find that it ought to be conducted with vigour and dispatch. It should be able to execute the laws without opposition, and to controul all the turbulent spirits in the state, who should infringe them. If the laws are not obeyed, the legislative power is vain, and the judicial is mere pageantry. As these laws, with their several sanctions, are the only securities of person and property, the members of the state can confide in, if they lay dormant through failure of execution, violence and oppression will erect their heads, and stalk unmolested through the land. The judicial power ought to discriminate the offender, as soon after the commission of the offence, as an impartial trial will admit; and the executive arm to inflict the punishment immediately after the criminal is ascertained. This would have an happy tendency to prevent crimes, as the commission of them would awaken the attendant idea of punishment; and the hope of an escape, which is often an inducement, would be cut off. The executive power ought therefore in these cases, to be exerted with union, vigour, and dispatch. Another duty of that power is to arrest offenders, to bring them to trial. This cannot often be done, unless secrecy and expedition are used. The want of these two requisites, will be more especially inconvenient in repressing treasons, and those more enormous offences which strike at the happiness, if not existence of the whole. Offenders of these classes do not act alone. Some number is necessary to the compleating of the crime. Cabals are formed with art, and secrecy presides over their councils; while measures the most fatal are the result, to be executed by desperation. On these men the thunder of the state should be hurled with rapidity; for if they hear it roll at a distance, their danger is over. When they gain intelligence of the process, they abscond, and wait a more favourable opportunity. If that is attended with difficulty, they destroy all the evidence of their guilt, brave government, and deride the justice and power of the state.

It has been observed likewise, that the executive power is to act as Captain-General, to marshal the militia and armies of the state, and, for her defence, to lead them on to battle. These armies should always be composed of the militia or body of the people. Standing armies are a tremendous curse to a state. In all periods in which they have existed, they have been the scourge of mankind. In this department, union, vigour, secrecy, and dispatch are more peculiarly necessary. Was one to propose a body of militia, over which two Generals, with equal authority, should have the command, he would be laughed at. Should one pretend, that the General should have no controul over his subordinate officers, either to remove them or to supply their posts, he would be pitied for his ignorance of the subject he was discussing. It is obviously necessary, that the man who calls the militia to action, and assumes the military controul over them in the field, should previously know the number of his men, their equipments and residence, and the talents and tempers of the several ranks of officers, and their respective departments in the state, that he may wisely determine to whom the necessary orders are to be issued. Regular and particular returns of these requisites should be frequently made. Let it be enquired, are these returns to be made only to the legislative body, or a branch of it, which necessarily moves slow?—Is the General to go to them for information? intreat them to remove an improper officer, and give him another they shall chuse? and in fine is he to supplicate his orders from them, and constantly walk where their leading-strings shall direct his steps? If so, where are the power and force of the militia—where the union—where the dispatch and profound secrecy? Or shall these returns be made to him?—when he may see with his own eyes—be his own judge of the merit, or demerit of his officers—discern their various talents and qualifications, and employ them as the service and defence of his country demand. Besides, the legislative body or a branch of it is local—they cannot therefore personally inform themselves of these facts, but must judge upon trust. The General's opinion will be founded upon his own observations—the officers and privates of the militia will act under his eye: and, if he has it in his power immediately to promote or disgrace them, they will be induced to noble exertions. It may further be observed here, that if the subordinate civil or military executive officers are appointed by the legislative body or a branch of it, the former will become dependent upon the latter, and the necessary independence of either the legislative or executive powers upon the other is wanting. The legislative power will have that undue influence over the executive which will amount to a controul, for the latter will be their creatures, and will fear their creators.

One further observation may be pertinent. Such is the temper of mankind, that each man will be too liable to introduce his own friends and connexions into office, without regarding the public interest. If one man or a small number appoint, their connexions will probably be introduced. If a large number appoint, all their connexions will receive the same favour. The smaller the number appointing, the more contracted are their connexions, and for that reason, there will be a greater probability of better officers, as the connexions of one man or a very small number can fill but a very few of the offices. When a small number of men have the power of appointment, or the management in any particular department, their conduct is accurately noticed. On any miscarriage or imprudence the public resentment lies with weight. All the eyes of the people are converted to a point, and produce that attention to their censure, and that fear of misbehaviour, which are the greatest security the state can have, of the wisdom and prudence of its servants. This observation will strike us, when we recollect that many a man will zealously promote an affair in a public assembly, of which he is but one of a large number, yet, at the same time, he would blush to be thought the sole author of it. For all these reasons, the supreme executive power should be rested in the hands of one or of a small number, who should have the appointment of all subordinate executive officers. Should the supreme executive officer be elected by the legislative body, there would be a dependence of the executive power upon the legislative. Should he be elected by the judicial body, there also would be a dependence. The people at large must therefore designate the person, to whom they will delegate this power. And upon the people, there ought to be a dependence of all the powers in government, for all the officers in the state are but the servants of the people.

We have not noticed the navy-department. The conducting of that department is indisputably in the supreme executive power: and we suppose, that all the observations respecting the Captain-General, apply to the Admiral.

We are next to fix upon some general rules which should govern us in forming the judicial power. This power is to be independent upon the executive and legislative. The judicial power should be a court and jury, or as they are commonly called, the Judges and jury. The jury are the peers or equals of every man, and are to try all facts. The province of the Judges is to preside in and regulate all trials, and ascertain the law. We shall only consider the appointment of the Judges. The same power which appoints them, ought not to have the power of removing them, not even for misbehavior. That conduct only would then be deemed misbehavior which was opposed to the will of the power removing. A removal in this case for proper reasons, would not be often attainable: for to remove a man from an office, because he is not properly qualified to discharge the duties of it, is a severe censure upon that man or body of men who appointed him—and mankind do not love to censure themselves. Whoever appoints the judges, they ought not to be removable at pleasure, for they will then feel a dependence upon that man or body of men who hath the power of removal. Nor ought they to be dependent upon either the executive or legislative power for their sallaries; for if they are, that power on whom they are thus dependent, can starve them into a compliance. One of these two powers should appoint, and the other remove. The legislative will not probably appoint so good men as the executive, for reasons formerly mentioned. The former are composed of a large body of men who have a numerous train of friends and connexions, and they do not hazard their reputations, which the executive will. It has often been mentioned that where a large body of men are responsible for any measures, a regard to their reputations, and to the public opinion, will not prompt them to use that care and precaution, which such regard will prompt one or a few to make use of. Let one more observation be now introduced to confirm it. Every man has some friends and dependents who will endeavor to snatch him from the public hatred. One man has but a few comparatively, they are not numerous enough to protect him, and he falls a victim to his own misconduct. When measures are conducted by a large number, their friends and connexions are numerous and noisy—they are dispersed through the State—their clamors stifle the execrations of the people, whose groans cannot even be heard. But to resume, neither will the executive body be the most proper judge when to remove. If this body is judge, it must also be the accuser, or the legislative body, or a branch of it, must be—If the executive body complains, it will be both accuser and judge—If the complaint is preferred by the legislative body, or a branch of it, when the judges are appointed by the legislative body, then a body of men who were concerned in the appointment, must in most cases complain of the impropriety of their own appointment. Let therefore the judges be appointed by the executive body—let their salaries be independent—and let them hold their places during good behaviour—Let their misbehaviour be determinable by the legislative body—Let one branch thereof impeach, and the other judge. Upon these principles the judicial body will be independent so long as they behave well and a proper court is appointed to ascertain their mal-conduct.

The Committee afterwards proceeded to consider the Constitution framed by the Convention of this State. They have examined that Constitution with all the care the shortness of the time would admit. And they are compelled, though reluctantly to say, that some of the principles upon which it is founded, appeared to them inconsonant, not only to the natural rights of mankind, but to the fundamental condition of the original social contract, and the principles of a free republican government. In that form of government the governor appears to be the supreme executive officer, and the legislative power is in an house of representatives and senate. It may be necessary to descend to a more particular consideration of the several articles of that constitution.

The second article thereof appears exceptionable upon the principles we have already attempted to establish, because the supreme executive officer hath a seat and voice in one branch of the legislative body, and is assisting in originating and framing the laws, the Governor being entitled to a seat and voice in the Senate, and to preside in it, and may thereby have that influence in the legislative body, which the supreme executive officer ought not to have.

The third article among other things, ascertains the qualifications of the Governor, Lieutenant Governor, Senators and Representatives respecting property—The estate sufficient to qualify a man for Governor is so small, it is hardly any qualification at all. Further, the method of ascertaining the value of the estates of the officers aforesaid is vague and uncertain as it depends upon the nature and quantity of the currency, and the encrease of property, and not upon any fixed principles. This article therefore appears to be exceptionable.

The sixth article regulates the election of representatives. So many objections present themselves to this article, we are at a loss which first to mention. The representation is grossly unequal, and it is flagrantly unjust. It violates the fundamental principle of the original social contract, and introduces an unweildy and expensive house. Representation ought to be equal upon the principles formerly mentioned. By this article any corporation, however small, may send one representative, while no corporation can send more than one, unless it has three hundred freemen. Twenty corporations (of three hundred freemen in each) containing in the whole six thousand freemen, may send forty representatives, when one corporation, which shall contain six thousand two hundred and twenty, can send but nineteen. One third of the state may send a majority of the representatives, and all the laws may be enacted by a minority— Do all the members of the state then, enjoy political liberty? Will they not be controuled by laws enacted against their consent? When we go further and find, that sixty members make an house, and that the concurrence of thirty one (which is about one twelfth of what may be the present number of representatives) is sufficient to bind the persons and properties of the members of the State, we stand amazed, and are sorry that any well disposed Americans were so inattentive to the consequences of such an arrangement.

The number of representatives is too large to debate with coolness and deliberation, the public business will be protracted to an undue length and the pay of the house is enormous. As the number of freemen in the State encreases, these inconveniences will encrease; and in a century, the house of representatives will, from their numbers, be a mere mob. Observations upon this article croud upon us, but we will dismiss it, with wishing that the mode of representation there proposed, may be candidly compared with the principles which have been already mentioned in the course of our observations upon the legislative power, and upon representation in a free republic.

The ninth article regulates the election of Senators, which we think exceptionable. As the Senators for each district will be elected by all the freemen in the state properly qualified, a trust is reposed in the people which they are unequal to. The freemen in the late province of Main, are to give in their votes for senators in the western district, and so, on the contrary. Is it supposeable that the freemen in the county of Lincoln can judge of the political merits of a senator in Berkshire? Must not the several corporations in the state, in a great measure depend upon their representatives for information? And will not the house of representatives in fact chuse the senators? That independence of the senate upon the house, which the constitution seems to have intended, is visionary, and the benefits which were expected to result from a senate, as one distinct branch of the legislative body, will not be discoverable.

The tenth article prescribes the method in which the Governor is to be elected. This method is open to, and will introduce bribery and corruption, and also originate parties and factions in the state. The Governor of Rhode-Island was formerly elected in this manner, and we all know how long a late Governor there, procured his re-election by methods the most unjustifiable. Bribery was attempted in an open and flagrant manner.

The thirteenth article ascertains the authority of the general court, and by that article we find their power is limited only by the several articles of the constitution. We do not find that the rights of conscience are ascertained and defined, unless they may be thought to be in the thirty fourth article. That article we conceive to be expressed in very loose and uncertain terms. What is a *religious* profession and worship of God, has been disputed for sixteen hundred years, and the various sects of christians have not yet settled the dispute. What is a free exercise and enjoyment of religious worship has been, and still is, a subject of much altercation. And this free exercise and enjoyment is said to be *allowed* to the protestants of this state by the constitution, when we suppose it to be an unalienable right of all mankind, which no human power can wrest from them. We do not find any bill of rights either accompanying the constitution, or interwoven with it, and no attempt is made to define and secure that protection of the person and property of the members of the state, which the legislative and executive bodies cannot withhold, unless the general words *of confirming the right to trial by jury,* should be considered as such definition and security. We think a bill of rights ascertaining and clearly describing the rights of conscience, and that security of person and property, the supreme power of the state is bound to afford to all the members thereof, ought to be fully ratified, before, or at the same time with, the establishment of any constitution.

The fifteenth article fixes the number which shall constitute a quorum in the senate and house of representatives—We think these numbers much too small—This constitution will immediately introduce about three hundred and sixty mumbers into the house. If sixty make a quorum, the house may totally change its members six different times; and it probably will very often in the course of a long session, be composed of such a variety of members, as will retard the public business, and introduce confusion in the debates, and inconsistency in the result. Besides the number of members, whose concurrence is necessary to enact a law, is so small, that the subjects of the state will have no security, that the laws which are to controul their natural rights, have the consent of a majority of the freemen. The same reasoning applies to the senate, though not so strikingly, as a quorum of that body must consist of nearly a third of the senators.

The eighteenth article describes the several powers of the Governor or the supreme executive officer. We find in comparing the several articles of the constitution, that the senate are the only court to try impeachments. We also conceive that every officer in the state ought to be amenable to such court. We think therefore that the members of that court ought never to be advisory to any officer in the state. If their advice is the result of inattention or corruption, they cannot be brought to punishment by impeachment, as they will be their own judges. Neither will the officer who pursues their advice be often, if ever, punishable, for a similar reason. To condemn this officer will be to reprobate their own advice—consequently a proper body is not formed to advise the Governor, when a sudden emergency may render advice expedient: for the senate advise, and are the court to try impeachments. We would now make one further observation, that we cannot discover in this article or in any part of the constitution that the executive power is entrusted with a check upon the legislative power, sufficient to prevent the encroachment of the latter upon the former—Without this check the legislative power will exercise the executive, and in a series of years the government will be as absolute as that of Holland.

The nineteenth article regulates the appointment of the several classes of officers. And we find that almost all the officers are appointed by the Governor and Senate. An objection formerly made occurs here. The Senate with the Governor are the court to remove these officers for misbehaviour. Those officers, in general, who are guilty of male-conduct in the execution of their office, were improper men to be appointed. Sufficient care was not taken in ascertaining their political military or moral qualifications. Will the senators therefore if they appoint, be a proper court to remove. Will not a regard to their own characters have an undue bias upon them. This objection will grow stronger, if we may suppose that the time will come when a man may procure his appointment to office by bribery. The members of that court therefore who alone can remove for misbehaviour, should not be concerned in the appointment. Besides, if one branch of the legislative body appoint the executive officers, and the same branch alone can remove them, the legislative power will acquire an undue influence over the executive.

The twenty second article describes the authority the Governor shall have in all business to be transacted by him and the Senate. The Governor by this article must be present in conducting an impeachment. He has it therefore in his power to rescue a favourite from impeachment, so long as he is Governor, by absenting himself from the Senate, whenever the impeachment is to be brought forwards.

We cannot conceive upon what principles the twenty third article ascertains the speaker of the house to be one of the three, the majority of whom have the power of granting pardons. The speaker is an officer of one branch of the legislative body, and hourly depends upon them for his existence in that character—he therefore would not probably be disposed to offend any leading party in the house, by consenting to, or denying a pardon. An undue influence might prevail and the power of pardoning be improperly exercised.—When the speaker is guilty of this improper exercise, he cannot be punished but by impeachment, and as he is commonly a favourite of a considerable party in the house, it will be difficult to procure the accusation; for his party will support him.

The judges by the twenty fourth article are to hold their places during good behaviour, but we do not find that their salaries are any where directed to be fixed. The house of representatives may therefore starve them into a state of dependence.

The twenty-eighth article determines the mode of electing and removing the delegates for Congress. It is by joint ballot of the house and Senate. These delegates should be some of the best men in the State. Their abilities and characters should be thoroughly investigated. This will be more effectually done, if they are elected by the legislative body, each branch having a right to originate or negative the choice, and removal. And we cannot conceive why they should not be elected in this manner, as well as all officers who are annually appointed with annual grants of their sallaries, as is directed in the nineteenth article. By the mode of election now excepted against, the house may choose their delegates, altho' every Senator should vote against their choice.

The thirty-fourth article respecting liberty of conscience, we think exceptionable, but the observations necessary to be made thereon, were introduced in animadverting upon the thirteenth article.

The Committee have purposely been as concise as possible in their observations upon the Constitution proposed by the Convention of this State—Where they thought it was nonconformable to the principles of a free republican government, they have ventured to point out the nonconformity—Where they thought it was repugnant to the original social contract, they have taken the liberty to suggest that repugnance—And where they were persuaded it was founded in political injustice, they have dared to assert it.

The Committee, in obedience to the direction of this body, afterwards proceeded to delineate the general outlines of a Constitution, conformable to what have been already reported by them, as the principles of a free republican government, and as the natural rights of mankind.

They first attempted to delineate the legislative body. It has already been premised, that the legislative power is to be lodged in two bodies, composed of the representatives of the people. That representation ought to be equal. And that no law affecting the person and property of the members of the state ought to be enacted, without the consent of a majority of the members, and of those also who hold a major part of the property.

In forming the first body of legislators, let regard be had only to the representation of persons, not of property. This body we call the house of representatives. Ascertain the number of representatives. It ought not to be so large as will induce an enormous expence to government, nor too unwieldy to deliberate with coolness and attention; nor so small as to be unacquainted with the situation and circumstances of the state. One hundred will be large enough, and perhaps it may be too large. We are persuaded that any number of men exceeding that, cannot do business with such expedition and propriety a smaller number could. However let that at present be considered as the number. Let us have the number of freemen in the several counties in the state; and let these representatives be apportioned among the respective counties, in proportion to their number of freemen. The representation yet remains equal. Let the representatives for the several counties be elected in this manner. Let the several towns in the respective counties, the first wednesday in May annually, choose delegates to meet in county convention on the thursday next after the second wednesday in May annually, and there elect the representatives for the county—Let the number of delegates each town shall send to the county convention be regulated in this manner. Ascertain that town which hath the smallest number of freemen; and let that town send one. Suppose the smallest town contains fifty. All the other towns shall then send as many members as they have fifties. If after the fifties are deducted, there remains an odd number, and that number is twenty five, or more, let them send another, if less, let no notice be taken of it. We have taken a certain for an uncertain number. Here the representation is as equal as the situation of a large political society will admit. No qualification should be necessary for a representative, except residence in the county the two years preceeding his election, and the payment of taxes those years. Any freeman may be an elector who hath resided in the county the year preceeding. The same qualification is requisite for a delegate, that is required of a representative. The representatives are designed to represent the persons of the members, and therefore we do not consider a qualification in point of property necessary for them.

These representatives shall be returned from the several parts of the county in this manner—Each county convention shall divide the county into as many districts as they send representatives, by the following rule—As we have the number of freemen in the county, and the number of county representatives, by dividing the greater by the less we have the number of freemen entitled to send one representative. Then add as many adjoining towns together as contain that number of freemen, or as near as may be, and let those towns form one district, and proceed in this manner through the county. Let a representative be chosen out of each district, and let all the representatives be elected out of the members who compose the county convention. In this house we find a proportionate representation of persons. If a law passes this house it hath the consent of a majority of the freemen; and here we may look for political honesty, probity and upright intentions to the good of the whole. Let this house therefore originate money-bills, as they will not have that inducement to extravagant liberality which an house composed of opulent men would, as the former would feel more sensibly the consequences. This county convention hath other business to do, which shall be mentioned hereafter. We shall now only observe, that this convention, upon a proper summons, is to meet again, to supply all vacancies in it's representation, by electing other representatives out of the district in which the vacancy falls. The formation of the second body of legislators next came under consideration, which may be called the senate. In electing the members for this body, let the representation of property be attended to. The senators may be chosen most easily in a county convention, which may be called the senatorial convention. Ascertain the number of senators. Perhaps thirty three will be neither too large nor too small. Let seven more be added to the thirty three which will make forty—these seven will be wanted for another purpose to be mentioned hereafter—Apportion the whole number upon the several counties, in proportion to the state-tax each county pays. Each freeman of the state, who is possessed of a certain quantity of property, may be an elector of the senators. To ascertain the value of a man's estate by a valuation is exceedingly difficult if possible, unless he voluntarily returns a valuation—To ascertain it by oath would be laying snares for a man's conscience, and would be a needless multiplication of oaths if another method could be devised—To fix his property at any certain sum, would be vague and uncertain, such is the fluctuation of even the best currency, and such the continual alteration of the nominal value of property—Let the state-tax assessed on each freeman's estate decide it—That tax will generally bear a very just proportion to the nominal value of a currency, and of property. Let every freeman whose estate pays such a proportion of the state-tax that had been last assessed previous to his electing, as three pounds is to an hundred thousand pounds, be an elector—The senatorial convention may be composed of delegates from the several towns elected in this manner. Ascertain the town which contains the smallest number of freemen whose estates pay such tax, and ascertain that number. Suppose it to be thirty. Let that town send one, and let all the other towns in the county send as many delegates as they have thirties. If after the thirties are deducted, there remains an odd number, and that number is fifteen, or more, let them send another, if it is less than fifteen let no notice be taken of it. Let the delegates for the senatorial convention be chosen at the same time with the county delegates, and meet in convention the second wednesday in May annually, which is the day before the county convention is to meet—and let no county delegate be a senatorial delegate the same year—We have here a senate (deducting seven in the manner and for the purpose hereafter to be mentioned) which more peculiarly represents the property of the state; and no act will pass both branches of the legislative body, without having the consent of those members who hold a major part of the property of the state. In electing the senate in this manner, the representation will be as equal as the fluctuation of property will admit of, and it is an equal representation of property so far as the number of senators are proportioned among the several counties. Such is the distribution of intestate estates in this country, the inequality between the estates of the bulk of the property holders is so inconsiderable, and the tax necessary to qualify a man to be an elector of a senator is so moderate, it may be demonstrated, that a law which passes both branches will have the consent of those persons who hold a majority of the property in the state. No freeman should be a delegate for the senatorial convention unless his estate pays the same tax which was necessary to qualify him to elect delegates for that convention; and no freeman shall be an elector of a delegate for that convention, nor a delegate therefor, unless he has been an inhabitant of the county for the two years next preceeding. No person shall be capable of an election into the senate unless he has been an inhabitant of the county for three years next preceeding his election—His qualification in point of estate is also to be considered. Let the state tax which was assessed upon his estate for the three years next preceeding his election be upon an average, at the rate of six pounds in an hundred thousand annually.

This will be all the duty of the senatorial convention unless there should be a vacancy in the senate when it will be again convened to fill up the vacancy. These two bodies will have the execution of the legislative power; and they are composed of the necessary members to make a just proportion of taxes among the several counties. This is all the discretionary power they will have in apportioning the taxes.

Once in five years at least, the legislative body shall make a valuation for the several counties in the State, and at the same time each county shall make a county valuation, by a county convention chosen for that purpose only, by the same rules which the legislative body observed in making the State valuation—and whenever a State valuation is made, let the several county valuations be also made. The legislative body after they have proportioned the State tax among the several counties, shall also proportion the tax among the several plantations and towns, agreeably to the county valuation, to be filed in the records of the General Court for that purpose. It may be observed that this county valuation will be taken and adjusted in county convention, in which persons only are to be equally represented: and it may also be objected that property ought also to be represented for this purpose. It is answered that each man in the county will pay at least a poll tax, and therefore ought to be represented in this convention—that it is impracticable in one convention to have persons and property both represented, with any degree of equality, without great intricacy—and that, where both cannot be represented without great intricacy, the representation of property should yield the preference to that of persons. The counties ought not to be compelled to pay their own representatives—if so, the counties remote from the seat of government would be at a greater charge than the other counties, which would be unjust—for they have only an equal influence in legislation with the other counties, yet they cannot use that influence but at a greater expence——They therefore labor under greater disadvantages in the enjoyment of their political liberties, than the other counties. If the remote counties enjoyed a larger proportional influence in legislation than the other counties, it would be just they should pay their own members, for the enhanced expence would tend to check this inequality of representation.

All the representatives should attend the house, if possible, and all the senators the senate. A change of faces in the course of a session retards and perplexes the public business. No man should accept of a seat in the legislative body without he intends a constant attendance upon his duty. Unavoidable accidents, necessary private business, sickness and death may, and will prevent a general attendance: but the numbers requisite to constitute a quorum of the house and senate should be so large as to admit of the absence of members, only for the reasons aforesaid. If members declined to attend their duty they should be expelled, and others chosen who would do better. Let seventy five constitute a quorum of the house, and twenty four of the senate. However no law ought to be enacted at any time, unless it has the concurrence of fifty one representatives, and seventeen senators.

We have now the legislative body (deducting seven of the senators.) Each branch hath a negative upon the other—and either branch may originate any bill or propose any amendment, except a money bill, which should be concurred or nonconcurred by the senate in the whole. The legislative body is so formed and ballanced that the laws will be made with the greatest wisdom and the best intentions; and the proper consent thereto is obtained. Each man enjoys political liberty, and his civil rights will be taken care of. And all orders of men are interested in government, will put confidence in it, and struggle for it's support. As the county and senatorial delegates are chosen the same day throughout the State, as all the county conventions are held at the same time, and all the senatorial conventions on one day, and as these delegates are formed into conventions on a short day after their election, elections will be free, bribery will be impracticable, and party and factions will not be formed. As the senatorial conventions are held the day before the county conventions, the latter will have notice of the persons elected senators, and will not return them as representatives—The senatorial convention should after it's first election of senators be adjourned without day, but not dissolved, and to be occasionally called together by the supreme executive officer to keep the senate full, should a senator elected decline the office, or afterwards resign, be expelled, or die. The county convention in the same way are to keep the representation full, and also supply all vacancies in the offices they will be authorised to appoint to and elect as will be presently mentioned. By making provision in the constitution that recourse be had to these principles of representation every twenty years, by taking new lists of the freemen for that purpose, and by a new distribution of the number of representatives agreeably thereto, and of the senators in proportion to the State tax, representation will be always free and equal. These principles easily accommodate themselves to the erection of new counties and towns. Crude and hasty determinations of the house will be revised or controuled by the senate; and those views of the senate which may arise from ambition or a disregard to civil liberty will be frustrated. Government will acquire a dignity and firmness, which is the greatest security of the subject: while the people look on, and observe the conduct of their servants, and continue or withdraw their favour annually, according to their merit or demerit.

The forming of the executive power came next in course. Every freeman in the State should have a voice in this formation; for as the executive power hath no controul over property, but in pursuance of established laws, the consent of the property-holders need not be considered as necessary. Let the head of the executive power be a Governor (or in his absence, or on his death, a Lieutenant Governor) and let him be elected in the several county conventions by ballot, on the same day the representatives are chosen. Let a return be made by each man fixed upon by the several conventions, and the man who is returned by any county shall be considered as having as many votes, as that county sends representatives. Therefore the whole number of votes will be one hundred. He who hath fifty one or more votes is Governor. Let the Lieutenant-Governor be designated in the same way. This head of the supreme executive power should have a privy council, or a small select number (suppose seven) to advise with. Let him not chuse them himself—for he might then, if wickedly disposed, elect no persons who had integrity enough to controul him by their advice. Let the legislative body elect them in this manner. The house shall chuse by ballot seven out of the senate. These shall be a privy council, four of whom shall constitute a quorum. Let the Governor alone marshal the militia, and regulate the same, together with the navy, and appoint all their officers, and remove them at pleasure. The temper, use, and end of a militia and navy require it. He should likewise command the navy and militia, and have power to march the latter any where within the state. Was this territory so situated, that the militia could not be marched out of it, without entering an enemy's country, he should have no power to march them out of the state. But the late province of Main militia must march through New-Hampshire to enter Massachusetts, and so, on the contrary. The neighbouring states are all friends and allies, united by a perpetual confederacy. Should Providence or Portsmouth be attacked suddenly, a day's delay might be of most pernicious consequence. Was the consent of the legislative body, or a branch of it, necessary, a longer delay would be unavoidable. Still the Governor should be under a controul. Let him march the militia without the state with the advice of his privy council, and his authority be continued for ten days and no longer, unless the legislative body in the mean time prolong it. In these ten days he may convene the legislative body, and take their opinion. If his authority is not continued, the legislative body may controul him, and order the militia back. If his conduct is disapproved, his reputation, and that of his advisers is ruined. He will never venture on the measure, unless the general good requires it, and then he will be applauded. Remember the election of Governor and council is annual. But the legislative body must have a check upon the Captain General. He is best qualified to appoint his subordinate officers, but he may appoint improper ones—He has the sword, and may wish to form cabals amongst his officers to perpetuate his power—The legislative body should therefore have a power of removing any militia officer at pleasure—Each branch should have this power. The Captain General will then be effectually controuled. The Governor with his privy council may also appoint the following executive officers, viz The attorney General and the justices of the peace, who shall hold their places during good behaviour—This misbehaviour shall be determined by the senate on impeachment of the house. On this scheme a mutual check is thus far preserved in both the powers. The supreme executive officer as he is annually removeable by the people, will for that, and the other reasons formerly mentioned, probably appoint the best officers: and when he does otherwise the legislative power will remove them. The militia officers which are solely appointed, and removeable at pleasure, by the Governor, are removeable at pleasure by either branch of the legislative. Those executive officers which are removeable only for misbehaviour, the consent of the privy council, chosen by the legislative body, is first necessary to their appointment, and afterwards they are removeable by the senate, on impeachment of the house. We now want only to give the executive power a check upon the legislative, to prevent the latter from encroaching on the former, and stripping it of all it's rights. The legislative in all states hath attempted it where this check was wanting, and have prevailed, and the freedom of the state was thereby destroyed. This attempt hath resulted from that lust of domination, which in some degree influences all men, and all bodies of men. The Governor therefore with the consent of the privy council, may negative any law, proposed to be enacted by the legislative body. The advantages which will attend the due use of this negative are, that thereby the executive power will be preserved entire—the encroachments of the legislative will be repelled, and the powers of both be properly balanced. All the business of the legislative body will be brought into one point, and subject to an impartial consideration on a regular consistent plan. As the Governor will have it in charge to state the situation of the government to the legislative body at the opening of every session, as far as his information will qualify him therefor, he will now know officially, all that has been done, with what design the laws were enacted, how far they have answered the proposed end, and what still remains to compleat the intention of the legislative body. The reasons why he will not make an improper use of his negative are—his annual election—the annual election of the privy council, by and out of the legislative body—His political character and honour are at stake—If he makes a proper use of his negative by preserving the executive powers entire, by pointing out any mistake in the laws which may escape any body of men through inattention, he will have the smiles of the people. If on the contrary, he makes an improper use of his negative, and wantonly opposes a law that is for the public good, his reputation, and that of his privy council are forfeited, and they are disgracefully tumbled from their seats. This Governor is not appointed by a King, or his ministry, nor does he receive instructions from a party of men, who are pursuing an interest diametrically opposite to the good of the state. His interest is the same with that of every man in the state; and he knows he must soon return, and sink to a level with the rest of the community.

The danger is, he will be too cautious of using his negative for the interest of the state. His fear of offending may prompt him, if he is a timid man, to yield up some parts of the executive power. The Governor should be thus qualified for his office—He shall have been an inhabitant of the state for four years next preceeding his election, and paid public taxes those years—Let the state tax assessed upon his estate those years be, upon an average, at the rate of sixteen pounds in an hundred thousand annually.

The Lieutenant Governor should have the same qualifications that are required from the Governor. In the absence out of the state of the Governor and Lieutenant Governor, or on their deaths, or while an impeachment is pending against them, or in case neither should be chosen at the annual election, let the executive power devolve upon the privy council until the office is again filled. By ascertaining in this way the qualification required from the Governor in point of property, and from the other servants of the state of whom a qualification in point of property is required, that ambition which prompts a man to aspire to any of these offices or places will benefit the state as the public tax he pays will be one criterion of his qualification. By electing the Governor in this manner, he hath the major voice of the people, and bribery or undue influence is impracticable. The privy council have also the major voice of the people, as they are chosen by a majority of the representatives: they are also selected from the senate, which it is to be presumed, will be composed of some of the best men in the state. As a further security against any inconveniency resulting from the length of time a Governor may hold the chair, no man ought to be a Governor more than three years in any six. There ought also, as soon as the circumstances of the state will admit of it, to be a gradation of officers, to qualify men for their respective departments—a rotation also of the senators will prevent any undue influence a man may acquire, by the long possession of an important office. After a period of six years let the following rules be observed. Let no man be eligible as Governor, (or Lieutenant Governor) unless he has had a seat in the senate or privy council for two years, or hath formerly been Governor or Lieutenant Governor. Let no man be eligible as senator, unless he had a seat in the house, senate, or privy council, the preceeding year—And let one fourth of the senate (which for this purpose is to include the privy council) be annually made ineligible to that rank, for two years; and let this fourth part be ascertained by lot. This lot, together with the provisions just mentioned, will introduce a rotation in the chair, privy council, senate and house: and the state will have a sufficient number of it's members qualified for these important offices, by the gradation established. These servants of the state should have competent and honourable stipends; not so large, as will enable them to raise a fortune at the expence of the industrious classes of the people; nor so small, that a man must injure his estate by serving the public. An inadequate salary would exclude from service, all but the vainly ambitious; and the ambitious man will endeavour to repay himself by attempting measures which will hazard the constitution. These stipends should be paid out of the public treasury, and the Governor's should be made certain upon fixed principles, otherwise the legislative body could starve him into a state of dependance.

There still remain some other officers to be elected—Let the legislative body choose the delegates for Congress, and the Receiver General and Commissary General, and let each branch have a right to originate or negative the choice.

Let the following officers, who may be considered as county officers, be thus elected—Let each county convention every three years choose the Sheriff, Coroners, and county Registers; and let that convention annually choose a county Treasurer, and a deputy Attorney General, to prosecute on behalf of the state at the court of sessions, in the absence of the Attorney General.

Let us also consider in whose hands the power of pardoning should be lodged. If the legislative body or a branch of it are entrusted with it, the same body which made or were concerned in making the law, will excuse the breach of it. This body is so numerous that most offenders will have some relation or connexion with some of it's members, undue influence for that reason may take place, and if a pardon should be issued improperly, the public blame will fall upon such members, it would not have the weight of a feather; and no conviction upon an impeachment could follow—The house would not impeach themselves, and the senators would not condemn the senate. If this power of pardoning is lodged with the Governor and privy council, the number is so small, that all can personally inform themselves of the facts, and misinformation will be detected. Their own reputation would guard them against undue influence, for the censure of the people will hang on their necks with the weight of a mill-stone—And impeachments will stare them in the face, and conviction strike them with terror. Let the power of pardoning be therefore lodged with the Governor and privy council.

The right of convening, adjourning, proroguing, and dissolving the legislative body deserves consideration. The constitution will make provision for their convention on the last wednesday in May annually. Let each branch of the legislative, have power to adjourn itself for two days —Let the legislative body have power to adjourn or prorogue itself to any time within the year. Let the Governor and privy council have authority to convene them at pleasure, when the public business calls for it, for the assembling of the legislative body may often be necessary, previous to the day to which that body had adjourned or prorogued itself, as the legislative body when dispersed cannot assemble itself. And to prevent any attempts of their voting a continuance of their political existence, let the constitution make provision, that some time in every year, on or before the wednesday preceeding the last wednesday in May, the Governor shall dissolve them. Before that day, he shall not have power to do it, without their consent.

As the principles which should govern in forming the judicial power have been already mentioned, a few observations only, are necessary to apply those principles.

Let the judges of the common law courts, of the admiralty, and probate, and the register of probate, be appointed by the Governor and privy council; let the stipends of these judges be fixed; and let all those officers be removeable only for misbehaviour. Let the senate be the judge of that misbehaviour, on impeachment of the house.

The committee have now compleated the general out lines of a constitution, which they suppose may be conformable to the principles of a free republican government—They have not attempted the description of the less important parts of a constitution, as they naturally and obviously are determinable by attention to those principles—Neither do they exhibit these general out lines, as the only ones which can be consonant to the natural rights of mankind, to the fundamental terms of the original social contract, and to the principles of political justice; for they do not assume to themselves infallibility. To compleat the task assigned them by this body, this constitution is held up in a general view, to convince us of the practicability of enjoying a free republican government, in which our natural rights are attended to, in which the original social contract is observed, and in which political justice governs; and also to justify us in our objections to the constitution proposed by the convention of this state, which we have taken the liberty to say is, in our apprehension, in some degree deficient in those respects.

To balance a large society on republican or general laws, is a work of so great difficulty, that no human genius, however comprehensive, is perhaps able, by the mere dint of reason and reflection, to effect it. The penetrating and dispassionate judgments of many must unite in this work: experience must guide their labour: time must bring it to perfection: and the feeling of inconveniencies must correct the mistakes which they will probably fall into, in their first trials and experiments.

The plan which the preceeding observations were intended to exhibit in a general view, is now compleated. The principles of a free republican form of government have been attempted, some reasons in support of them have been mentioned, the out lines of a constitution have been delineated in conformity to them, and the objections to the form of government proposed by the general convention have been stated.

This was at least the task enjoined upon the committee, and whether it has been successfully executed, they presume not to determine. They aimed at modelling the three branches of the supreme power in such a manner, that the government might act with the greatest vigour and wisdom, and with the best intentions—They aimed that each of those branches should retain a check upon the others, sufficient to preserve it's independence—They aimed that no member of the state should be controuled by any law, or be deprived of his property, against his consent—They aimed that all the members of the state should enjoy political liberty, and that their civil liberties should have equal care taken of them—and in fine, that they should be a free and an happy people—The committee are sensible, that the spirit of a free republican constitution, or the moving power which should give it action, ought to be political virtue, patriotism, and a just regard to the natural rights of mankind. This spirit, if wanting, can be obtained only from that Being, who infused the breath of Life into our first parent.

The committee have only further to report, that the inhabitants of the several towns who deputed delegates for this convention, be seriously advised, and solemnly exhorted, as they value the political freedom and happiness of themselves and of their posterity, to convene all the freemen of their several towns in town meeting, for this purpose regularly notified, and that they do unanimously vote their disapprobation of the constitution and form of government, framed by the convention of this state; that a regular return of the same be made to the secretary's office, that it may there remain a grateful monument to our posterity of that consistent, impartial and persevering attachment to political, religious, and civil liberty, which actuated their fathers, and in defence of which, they bravely fought, chearfully bled, and gloriously died.

The above report being read was accepted.

Attest, PETER COFFIN, *Chairman.*

23

Berkshire County Remonstrance, August 26, 1778

The towns in Berkshire County again defended themselves against charges of lawlessness and disloyalty in closing the courts. They insisted that unless the General Court immediately called a constitutional convention, the courts would remain closed, and the county would seek other means of redress. The remonstrance is found in MA 220/462. See also *Acts and Resolves Public and Private of the Province of the Massachusetts Bay* (Boston, 1869–86), V, 1028–1029.

"State of Massachusetts Bay—} To the Honorable the Council and the Honorable House of Representatives in General Court Assembled—

Pittsfield August 26th, 1778,

We the subscribers Delegates from the several Towns in the County of Berkshire, chosen and appointed for the Special purpose of Petitioning the Great and General Court to call a special convention of Delegates from each Town in this State, for the purpose of forming a Bill of Rights and a Constitution or Form of Government—

Humbly shew—

That your Memorialists have from the time of the Stamp Act to this present Day, manifested a constant and uniform Abhorrence and Detestation (not only in Sentiment but overt actions) of all the Unconstitutional Measures taken by the British Parliment to tax, depauperate and Subjugate these now United and Independent States of America—

That they can Vie with any County in this State not only in Voluntarily appearing in arms upon the least notice, when their Brethren in Distress needed their Assistance as at the Massacre at Lexington, the Fight at Bunkers Hill etc. etc.; But also in filling up their Quotas of Men from time to time, demanded either by this State or the Commanding Officer in these Parts: although our Situation has been such, as might have justified the General Court had they called upon Us for no such supplies, over and above which our Zeal in the Common Cause has carried Us beyond our Ability in the frequent Excursions against the

Common Enemy, as in the Battle of Bennington, in assisting Colonel Brown in the Capture of so many Hundreds at the Carrying place at Tyconderoga, in the quelling the Tories at divers times in a Neighbouring State, which otherwise, might have suffered amazingly, and in instances of the like Nature too many to enumerate—

Notwithstanding this Our Fidelity to the State and our exertions for the Common Cauze. We have by designing and disaffected Men been represented as a Mobbish, Ungovernable refractory, licentious and dissolute People, by means whereof have been threatned with Dismemberment; more especially, as we conceive, on Account of our not admitting the Course of common Law—

It is true we were the first County that put a Stop to Courts, and were soon followed by many others, Nay in effect by the whole State—And we are not certain but that it might have been as well (if not better) had they continued so, rather than to have Law dealt out by piece meal as it is this Day, without any Foundation to support it, for We doubt not we should before this time have had a Bill of rights, and a Constitution which are the only things, We at this time are empowered to pray for— And We do now with the greatest Deference Petition your Honors, that you would issue your Precepts to all the Towns and places within this State (called upon to pay public Taxes) requiring them to choose Delegates to set as soon as may be in some suitable place to form a Bill of Rights and a Constitution for this State, without which We shall retain the aforesaid Character, if grounded upon the Non-admission Law, as abundantly appears to Us this Day by the Yeas and Nays, brought in from the respective Towns We represent, taken in Town Meeting, especially called for that purpose, there being four fifths of the Inhabitants of said County against supporting the Courts of Law, untill a Constitution be formed and Accepted by the people—

If this our request is rejected, We shall endeavour by addressing the first Committee of Safety etc. in this State and others, that there be a State Convention formed for the purpose aforesaid—And if this Honorable Court are for dismembing there are other States, which have Constitutions who will We doubt not, as bad as we are, gladly receive us; And We shall to the utmost of our Ability support and defend authority and Law as we should with greater Cheerfulness in this State to which We belong was there any proper Foundation for it—

We are with all Submission your Honors youngest Child and are determined to the utmost of our Power to protect and secure our just

Inheritance, and hope our parent, will graciously concur and assist by granting this our request.

And as in Duty bound will every pray—

Ezra Fellows—Sheffield
William Whiting—G. Barrington
Joseph Chaffee, Daniel Kinne—Partridgefield
Elisha Baker—Williamston
Jabez Ward, Caleb Wright—N. Marlboro'
Jona. Smith, James Harris—Lanesborough
William Williams, Valentine Rathbone, Enoch Root—Pittsfield
Caleb Hyde, William Walker—Lenox
Asa Bement—Stockbridge
Jabez Holden—Sandisfield
Joseph Pierce, John Burrows—Gageboro'
William Douglas—Hancock
Benjamin Pierson—Richmond
Smith Marcy—Loudon
Eusebius Bushnell, George Sloan—Washington
Joseph Gilbert—Alfred
Jesse Bradley—Lee
Benjamin Taylor—New Ashford

24

Response of the Worcester Committee of Correspondence, October 8, 1778

The Committee of Correspondence for the town of Pittsfield had written to Worcester and Hampshire counties for support in behalf of Berkshire's demand for a constitutional convention (see No. 23). The Worcester Committee of Correspondence, far from approving Berkshire's actions in closing the courts, emphasized the necessity for law and order while the constitution was being formed. The response is found in the William Williams Collection, 376–379, Berkshire Athenaeum, Pittsfield, Massachusetts.

To the Committee of Correspondence etc. for the town of Pittsfield in the County of Berkshire,
Gentlemen:

William Young Esqr delivered us a Letter for our Consideration from you, by which we are informed that a Convention of the Several Committees of that County sat there on the 12th of August last, in order to know and determine, whether that County was for opening and supporting the Courts of Quarter Sessions and Common Pleas, untill a new Constitution should be formed and accepted by the people: and that you were by them appointed to write to the Committees in Hampshire and this County.

We are told that by the reccommendation of that Convention, the Several towns in your County met and determined the Question by Yeas and Nays, and that four fifths were against supporting the Courts under the present Constitution. Likewise, that the several towns, at the same time chose delegates, who met there on the 26th of the same month, and petitioned the General Court, that they would issue their precepts to all the towns and places, within this State (called upon to pay public taxes) requireing them to chuse delegates to set as soon as may be, in some convenient place, to form a bill of Rights and a Constitution for this State; assuring them that if this request should be rejected, they should endeavour by advising the first Commissioner of Safety in this State and others, that there be a State Convention formed for that purpose etc. The import of which appears to us to be of such Consequence to the

Public, that we think it our duty to write you our sentiments upon it, which we request you to communicate to your next County Convention. As Corporate parts of the same Community, or as individuals, we consider ourselves entitled to no preheminence, as an "elder Brother," but as having at all times an equal and common right to offer each other our opinions; we shall, therefore, speek with the freedom of independent Americans. We cannot agree with you, Gentlemen, with respect to the non-admission of the Courts of Quarter Sessions and Common Pleas, untill the formation and acceptance of a new Constitution. Our opinion, we hope will appear to be founded in reason, and consistant with the interest of America and the liberties of Mankind. That Power, which declared these States independent, by whose wisdom, patriotism and prudence we find ourselves in a situation, which perhaps no people on earth were ever in before, that of forming for ourselves a Constitution from the formation, recommended it to this State to adhere, as near as possible to their antient forms and Constitution, untill a new one should be formed and established. In consequence of which reccommendation, the authority of this State immediately restored the Several executive Courts of Justice, which by law were before appointed to be held in it. The people sanctified the measure by their consent, it therefor is constitutional so long as such consent shall continue, as the Consent of a Majority of the State: For it is a principal laid down by some of the best political writers, that what ever, in government, is publicly allowed at any perticular period, has been regularly and openly introduced and established by the approbation of the majority of those who have the power of establishing it is constitutional at that period. Now that so small a minority as four fifths of one County in this State which cannot possibly be supposed to be more than one fourteenth of the whole, should not only oppose such a great majority of a State, but act directly contrary to the sense and reccommendation of the whole Continent, in our opinion is acting like persons that do not understand the true principals of Liberty and are durating from the end this Country had in view in commencing the Contest with Great Britain. The reason that is given for stoping the Courts of Quarter Sessions and Common Pleas, will be equally conclusive for stoping the Superior Courts, the consequence of which will be, that, untill the formation and acceptance and establishment of a new Constitution which will require time and ought not to be done in a hurry without due consideration all treasons and misprisions of treasons, murders and felons of what kind soever, committed in your County, cannot be tried; for the Law makes it necessary that these Crimes shall be tried in the same County they were Committed. Every member of Society must dread the consequence of suffering such offences to pass with impunity; our Lives, liberties and Estates would become insecure, and we should soon be in a situation worse than that of a State of nature; and such criminal offences cannot be supposed to be less frequent in your County or in any other, but rather increase in proportion as the operation of the laws are suspended; for it is absolutely necessary that punishment should be held forth as motives to restrain and counter ballance the effects of the passions of many individuals in all societies. It is our opinion, that the operation of the executive Courts, rather than be an abstraction, will be an assistance and of great advantage to us, while we are forming a Constitution it will tend to establish that order and regularity among the people which is necessary for that cool dispassionate deliberation which such important a matter requires. And we are apprehensive, that the powers of Government in the meantime, should be suffered by stoping the Courts of Justice, the concursion of jarring these ties would throw the State into anarchy and confusion, it is the wish and endeavour of our internal enemies, those canker worms among us, who desparing of devouring our liberties by open force, are secretly and subtlely seeking the opportunity of knawing assunder the Cords of our Union [on] which alone our political salvation depends, The idea of Committees forming County Conventions, and these County Conventions advising State Conventions to act in opposition to, or in conformity with the General Court, the supreme authority of the State, seems to us at present to involve in it the greatest absurdity and to be intirely inconsistant with the best and most established maxims of government. The supposition of two different powers in a State assuming the right of controling the people, whose doings are liable to interfere with each other, forms that great political solecism imperium in imperio, a head within a head, and the State in which a monster of this nature exists, will soon be brought under that fatal denomination of a kingdom divided against itself, which cannot stand.

When the talons of Slavery were about to fasten upon us, when tyranny was shaking over us his iron rod, and those in power were assisting and endeavouring to reduce us to absolute subjection, it was necessary for the people to bestir themselves and invent some method to prevent the fatal catastrophe; the Committees of the several towns in each County did then assemble together and form County Conventions, which were at that time very favourable, and tended greatly to the Salvation of America. But when we had repelled the fatal blow . . . . their places those in power that were endeavouring our distruction, and; agreeable to the reccommendation of the Continental Congress, assumed the forms and execution of legislative, and executive government the reason and necessity of the Convention ceased.

At this day, it appears to us, they can do no good, but may be productive of great and lasting mischief and for Committees to take to themselves such power is, we conseive, without the line of their duty; they are made by the Law, and the Law has limited and defined their power and jurisdiction, every step beyond which is an illegal arrogation. Our government is now placed in an assembly, that is annually and freely chosen by the people, and if they find any, to whom it was intrusted, exert it to the prejudice of their constituents, they have it in their power, in the short revolution of one year, to remedy the evil by leaving out such and chusing others. In such an assembly where their own and the peoples interest is so interwoven, that if they act for themselves, they must act for the common interest of the whole, we can have no fear of placing our influence in these, we conceive, are the proper persons to point out a method of forming a bill of rights and a Constitution, and of obtaining the consent and approbation of the people. In the petition of your Convention to the General Court, an extract of which we have in your letter, you say that you assured them that if your request was rejected "You should endeavor, by advising the first Committee of safety in this State and others, that there be a State Convention formed for that purpose." who this first Committee is, we acknowledge we cannot determine, but it appears to us that the convention take upon themselves, by this to controll the doings of the General Court, they put them under duress and obliged them to grant their request, or they will put their designs in execution themselves, which is in fact governing the Court and not being governed by them.

If we set up in this way to controll the established authority of the State, we cannot but think we should act contrary to the principles and motives that first induced us to oppose the authority of Great Britain—and "will give just occassion to our adversaries to reproach us, as being men of turbulent dispositions and licentious principles, that cannot bear to be restrained by good and wholesome Laws, even tho they are of our own making, nor submit to rulers of our own chusing." And in truth such intestine divisions and opposition to legal government will give more advantage to our enemy than all their fleets and armies, It was not the laws, then in being, we complained of as the motive of our resistance, but the executors of the laws, who instead of using them for the end they were designed, prostituted them to flaginous purposes. The executive authority is now deposited in those that have the confidence of the people men of virtue and knowledge, whose doings and decisions meet with universal approbation. We in this County, and we will venture to say those of other counties in this State, that have had the experience, are perfectly satisfied, and well pleased, that the laws are once more regularly executed. We feel the good effects of it. We know how and where to apply for the redress of injuries. We cannot be deprived of our personal liberty or our property, by the capricious and arbital decision of a body of men who are guided by no rule, are not bound even with the tie of an oath, but judge and determine just as their passions and prejudices lead them but among us "the laws bear sway." These, Gentlemen, are our sentiments, which we submit to your consideration. We hope they will be received with all that candor and impartiality, which our good intention may claim. We wish not to inflame and excite passions but to promote and cement Union and harmony among us, which at present we conceive necessary to save the States from ruin.

We are, Gentlemen, with all due respect yours etc. Daniel Bigelow, Nathaniel Heywood, William Dana, Joseph Barber, Jonathan Rice. Committee of Correspondence, Inspection and Safety for town of Worcester

Worcester, October 8th 1778.

25

Statement of Berkshire County Representatives, November 17, 1778

After receipt of the Berkshire County remonstrance (above, No. 23), the General Court dispatched a committee which met at Pittsfield with representatives of the Berkshire towns on November 17, 1778. The statement quoted here was reported back to the legislature on January 14, 1779. It is found in MA 220/456–462. See also MA 220/134, 452–456; *Acts and Resolves, V,* 1029–1032.

To the Honorable Committee from the General Court of Massachusetts Bay now convened at Pittsfield—

Mr. Chairman, Sir

We whose Names are underwriten indulging some Apprehensions of the Importance of Civil and religious Liberty, the destructive Nature of Tyranny and lawless power, and the absolute necessity of legal Government, to prevent Anarchy and Confusion; have taken this method to indulge our own Feelings and Sentiments respecting the important matters that have for some Time been the Subject of debate in this present Meeting—Political Disquisitions, if managed with Decency, Moderation and Candor are a good preservative against Ignorance and Servility and such a state of perfect Quietude as would endanger the Rights of Mankind united in the Bands of Society. We wish to preserve this Character in what we have now to offer in the Defence of our Constituents in opposing, in times past, the executive Courts of Justice in this County.

We wish with the least Delay to come to the Merits of the cause, and shall now proceed to make those observations on the Nature of Government which are necessary to bring into view the Apprehensions we indulge respecting the present Condition of this state, whether we have a fundamental Constitution or not; and how far we have Government duly organized and how far not: In free States the people are to be considered as the fountain of power. And the social Tie as founded in Compact. The people at large are endowed with alienable and unalienable Rights. Those which are unalienable, are those which belong to Conscience respecting the worship of God and the practice of the Christian Religion, and that of being determined or governed by the Majority in the Institution or formation of Government. The alienable are those which may be delegated for the Common good, or those which are for the common good to be parted with. It is of the unalienable Rights, particularly that of being determined or governed by the Majority in the Institution or formation of Government of which something further is necessary to be considered at this Time. That the Majority should be governed by the Minority in the first Institution of Government is not only contrary to the common apprehensions of Mankind in general, but it contradicts the common Law of Justice and benevolence.

Mankind being in a state of nature equal, the larger Number (Cæteris paribus) is of more worth than the lesser, and the common happiness is to be preferred to that of Individuals. When Men form the social Compact, for the Majority to consent to be governed by the Minority is down right popery in politicks, as submission to him who claims Infallibility, and of being the only Judge of Right and rong, is popery in Religion. In all free Governments duly organized there is an essential Distinction to be observed between the fundamental Constitution, and Legislation. The fundamental Constitution is the Basis and ground work of Legislation, and asscertains the Rights Franchises, Immunities and Liberties of the people, Howr and how often officers Civil and military shall be elected by the people, and circumscribing and defining the powers of the Rulers, and so affoarding a sacred Barrier against Tyranny and Despotism. This in antient and corrupt Kingdoms when they have woke out of Slavery to some happy dawnings of Liberty, has been called a Bill of Rights, Magna Charta etc. which must be considered as imperfect Emblems of the Securities of the present grand period. Legislators stand on this foundation, and enact Laws agreeably to it. They cannot give Life to the Constitution: it is the approbation of the Majority of the people at large that gives Life and being to it. This is the foundation of Legislation that is agreeable to true Liberty, it is above the whole Legislature of a free state, it being the foundation upon which the Legislature stands. A Representative Body may form but cannot impose said Constitution upon a free people. The giving Existence to the fundamental Constitution of a free state is a Trust that cannot be delegated. For any rational person to give his vote for another person to aid and assist in forming said Constitution with a view of imposing it on the people without reserving to himself a Right of Inspection Approbation rejection or Amendment, imports, if not impiety, yet real popery in politicks. We could bring many Vouchers for this Doctrine sufficient for our present purpose is the following Extract from a Noted Writer. in answer to that assertion of another respectable writer that 'The bare Idea of a State without a power some where vested to alter every part of its Laws is the height of political Absurdity.' [Introduction to Blackstone's *Commentaries,* p. 97; note by the editor of *Acts and Resolves*] He remarks upon it, 'A position, which I apprehend, ought to be, in some Measure limited and explained. For if it refers to those particular Regulations, which take place in Consequence of Immemorial Custom, or are enacted by positive Statue, and at the same Time, are subordinate to the fundamental Constitution from which the Legislature itself derives its Authority; it is admitted to be within the power or Trust vested in the Legislature to alter these, pro, Re nata, as the good of Society may require. But this power or Authority of the Legislature to make Alterations cannot be supposed to extend to the Infringement of those essentials Rights and previleges, which are reserved to the Members of a free state at large, as their undoubted Birthright and unalienable property. I say, in every free State there are some Liberties and previleges, which the Society has not given out of their own Hands to their Governors, not even to the Legislature: and to suppose the contrary would be the height of political absurdity; for it is saying that a state is free and not free at the same Time; or which is the same thing, that its Members are possessed of Liberties, of all which they may be divested at the will of the Legislature; that is, they enjoy them during pleasure, but can claim no property in them

In a word nothing is more certain than that Government in the general nature of it is a Trust in behalf of the people. And there cannot be a Maxim, in my opinion, more ill grounded, than that there must be an arbitrary power lodged somewhere in every Government. If this were true, the different kinds of Government in the world would be more alike, and on a level, than they are generally supposed to be. In our own Government in particular, tho' no one thinks with more respect of the powers which the Constitution hath vested in every branch of the Legislature; yet I must be excused in saying what is strictly true, that the whole Legislature is so far from having an absolute power, that it hath not power in several Cases that might be mentioned. For instance, their Authority does not extend to making the house of Commons perpetual, or giving that house a power to fill up their own vacancies: the house of Commons being the representatives of all the Commons of England and in that Capassity only a branch of the Legislature; and if they concur in destroying the foundation on which they themselves stand; and if they annihilate the Rights of their Constituents and claim a share in the Legislature upon any other footing than that upon which the Constitution hath given it to them; they subvert the very Trust under which alone they act, and thereby forfeit all their Authority. In short they cannot dispence with any of those essential Rights of the people which it ought to be the great object of Government as it is of our Constitution in particular to preserve.'—

These reasonings tend abundantly to evince, that the whole Legislature of any state is insufficient to give Life to the fundamental Constitution of such state, it being the foundation on which they themselves stand and from which alone the Legislature derives its Authority—

May it be considered, further, that to suppose the Representative Body capable of forming and imposing this Compact or Constitution without the Inspection and Approbation Rejection or Amendment of the people at large would involve in it the greatest Absurdity. This would make them greater than the people who send them, this supposes them their own Creators, formers of the foundation upon which they themselve stand. This imports uncontroulable Dominion over their Constituents for what should hinder them from making such a Constitution as invests them and their successors in office with unlimited Authority, if it be admitted that the Representatives are the people as to forming and imposing the fundamental Constitution of the state upon them without their Approbation and perhaps in opposition to their united sense—In this the very essence of true Liberty consists, viz in every free state the Constitution is adopted by the Majority.

It is needful to be observed that we are not to Judge of true Liberty by other Nations of the Earth, darkness has overspread the Earth, Tyranny Triumps thro' the world. The Day light of Liberty, only begins to dawn upon these Ends of the Earth. To measure the freedom, the Rights and previleges of the American Empire by those enjoyed by other Nations would be folly

It is now both easy and natural to apply these reasonings to the present State of Massachusetts Bay. We think it undeniably follows from the preceeding Reasonings that the Compact in this state is not yet formed: when did the Majority of the people at large assent to such Constitution, and what is it? if the Majority of the people of this state have adopted any such fundamental Constitution it is unknown to us and we shall submit to it as we always mean to be governed by the Majority—

Nor will any of those consequences follow on this supposition, that we have no Law, or that the Honorable Council and House of Representatives are Usurpers and Tyrants. Far from it. We consider our case as very Extraordinary. We do not consider this state in all Respects as in a state of Nature tho' destitute of such fundamental Constitution. When the powers of Government were totally dissolved in this state, we esteemed the State Congress as a necessary and useful body of Men suited to our Exigencies and sufficiently authorized to levy Taxes, raise an Army and do what was necessary for our common defence and it is Sir in this Light that we view our present Honorable Court and for these and other reasons *have inculcated* a careful Adherence to their orders. Time will not permit to argue this Matter any longer, for your Honors patience must have been tryed already. These have been some of the reasons we have indulged, and Sentiments we have cultivated respecting Constitution, and for these Reasons we have been looking forward towards a new Constitution—But we must further add

That a fear of being finally deprived of a Constitution and of being thrown into confusion and divisions by delaying the formation of a new Constitution, has caused our Constituents so early and invariably to oppose the executive Courts—We have feared, we now realize those fears, that upon our submission we shall sink down into a dead Calm and never transmit to posterity a single Right nor leave them the least Knowledge of so fair an Inheritance, as we may now convey to them.—

We and our Constituents have also indulged some fears respecting some of the particular persons appointed for our Rulers least in the future Execution of Law they should execute their own private Resentments, we are willing to hope the best—

We have been ready to consider some of them as indulging an unnatural temper in vilifying and reproaching their own County but we hope they will do better for the future, and that we shall do better, and we wish to give them our confidence.—We are determined to cultivate a spirit of meekness forbearance and Love and to study the Things that shall make for peace and order.

It has appeared to us and those we are appointed to represent that in an early opposition to the executive Courts, such opposition would become general thro' the state, which in our opinion would bring on a new Constitution without Delay. Our hope of which is now very much weakened, and such are the Dissentions of this state that we are now ready to fear we shall never obtain any other than what is called our present Constitution our Apprehensions of which have been already explained—

It is with Gratitude we reflect on the Appointment of this Honorable Committee by the General Court for the purpose of peace Reconciliation and order thro' this County, and their impartial and faithful Execution of their Commission. We are persuaded by the Temper and Moderation exhibited that they will not embibe any prejudices against this County, by what they have seen and heared, and that they will make a Just Representation of our state to the General Court.—

To evince to your Honors our Love of peace Reconciliation and legal Government, and that we have been actuated not by personal Prejudices or Motives of Ambition, notwithstanding the powerful Reasons we have had for a Suspension of the Executive Courts we are willing to forego our own opinions and if it shall be thought best by our Constituents to submit to the establishment of the Executive Courts in this County—

Pittsfield Valentine Rathbone
Josiah Wright
James Noble

[The following, which is disintegrated in MA 220/462, is taken from *Acts and Resolves,* V, 1032, and completes the above document.]

We the Subscribers Delagates from the Several Towns in the County of Berksheir Approveing of and consenting to the foregoing letter have hereunto Set our hands

Town	
Hancock	Reuben Ely
	Asa Douglas
New Providence	Joab Stafford
Lanesborough	James Barker
Partridgefield	Ebenr. Peirce
	Daniel Kinne
Windsor	Arnold Lewes
Washington	Esebius Bushnell
	Jonathan Smith

III

Formation of the Constitution of 1780

February 1779—March 1780

26

Resolve on the Question of a Constitution, February 20, 1779

To determine the sentiments of the people, the House of Representatives queried them as to whether they wanted a new constitution made and whether they would empower their representatives for the next year to vote for a constitutional convention. The resolve is found in MA 160/32.

STATE OF MASSACHUSETTS-BAY

IN THE HOUSE OF REPRESENTATIVES, FEBRUARY 19, 1779

Whereas the Constitution or Form of Civil Government, which was proposed by the late Convention of this State to the People thereof, hath been disapproved by a majority of the Inhabitants of said State:

And whereas it is doubtful, from the Representations made to this Court what are the Sentiments of the major part of the good People of this State as to the Expediency of now proceeding to form a new Constitution of Government:

Therefore, *Resolved,* That the Selectmen of the several Towns within this State cause the Freeholders, and other Inhabitants in their respective Towns duly qualified to vote for Representatives, to be lawfully warned to meet together in some convenient Place therein, on or before the last Wednesday of May next, to consider of and determine upon the following Questions.

First, Whether they chuse at this Time to have a new Constitution of Form of Government made.

Secondly, Whether they will impower their Representatives for the next Year to vote for the calling a State Convention, for the sole Purpose of forming a new Constitution, provided it will appear to them, on examination, that a major Part of the People present and voting at the Meetings called in the Manner and for the Purpose aforsaid, shall have answered the first Question in the Affirmative.

And in Order that the Sense of the People may be Known thereon: Be is further *Resolved,* That the Selectmen of each Town be and hereby are directed to return into the Secretary's Office, on or before the first Wednesday in *June* next, the Doings of their respective Towns on the first Question above mentioned, certifying the Numbers voting in the Affirmative, and the Numbers voting in the Negative, on said Question.

Sent up for Concurrence,
John Pickering, Speaker

In Council, February 20, 1779
Read and concurred, John Avery, Dep. Secretary
Consented to by the Major Part of the Council.
A true Copy, Attest,

John Avery, Dep. Secretary

27

Opinions of Hampshire County Towns, March 30, 1779

Shortly after the House's Resolve on the Question of a Constitution (No. 26), a gathering of towns in western Hampshire County reiterated the demand for immediate action on a Bill of Rights and Constitution. It called for a county-wide convention to meet and consider the kind of government that was desirable. The document is found in Joseph Hawley Papers, Box 1, New York Public Library.

Opinions of a Meeting of Committees of a Number of Towns in Western Hampshire County, March 30, 1779

1. It is the Opinion of this Convention That all men are Born Equally Free and Independent, and that no man Can be bound by a Law that he has not Given his Consent to, Either by his Person, or Legal Representative.
2. We are of Opinion that the Power is originally in the People and that no select Body of men can Lawfully Legislate for them, unless the People have by Some mode or form Delegated their Power to them as their Representatives, which form of Government we call a Constitution of a state or kingdom; by which there should be Proper Bounds set to the Legislative and Executive Authority, without which the People Cannot be saf, Free or Happy.
3. We are of Opinion, That us the People at Large in this County and state Authorized the Congress to Declare us Independant to Great Britain, and as we have under God maintained our Independance with our Blood and Treasure to this Day: It is our opinion we are free from any Charter Law, or Laws Derived from Britain, and that we know of no Constitution in this state Consented too by the People at Large.
4. We are of opinion that a Legal Representative is a Creature of the Constitution of a state, or Kingdom; but we Desire to know how such a Creature can Exist in a Legal Sense Prior to that Constitution on which his being and Existance Depends.
5. We are of Opinion that by Delaying and Putting off the Forming a Bill of Rights and a free Constitution for this state, we are Deprived of a Great Blessing viz Civil Goverment and Good wholesom Laws

——Founded thereon, whereby the Virtuous may be Protected in their Liberty and Property, and Transgressors brought to proper Punishment.

6. We are not without Fear that there is Designing men in this state that Intends by Delaying the Forming a Bill of Rights and a free Constitution to Lull People to sleep, or Fatigue them other ways so as to obtain a Constitution to their minds Calculated to answer their own Ends and wicked Purposes, By which mean the People will Loose the Benefit of their Independance, and may Rather be said to have Changed Masters than Measures [?].
7. We are of opinion that it is the Duty of Virtuous Leaders to Preserve the Liberty of the People over whome they Preside, and whenever from a desire to agrandize Themselves they Enddeaver to Persuade the People to submit to Arbitrary Infringments of their Rights, they not only forfeit their Title to the Respect which is Due to a virtuous Member of Society, but Deserve to be Treated with the severity Due to a Traitor.
8. Whereas there is a General uneasiness in the People in the western Part of this state with Regard to the Execution of Law Derived from the old Constitution (so called) and to Prevent the Difficulties we fear will arrise by Intestine Broils and mobs, we think it Expedient without Loss of Time to Call upon the Committees of the several Towns in this County in a Convention that they may Give their opinion with us on such matters as shall be Laid before them for the General Good of the state at Large, in writing and forming a Bill of Rights and Constitution, and Bear Testimony against a Constitution without a Name and Legislation without Law.

Therefore Resolved

That a Coppy of the foregoing Votes be sent to the selectmen or Committees of the several Towns in this County: and they are hereby Desired to Assemble by their Respective Committees at the Court House at Northampton on Tuesday the twentieth Day of April Next at Ten oclock A.M. then and there to act upon any matter or matters of Importance Relative to the state that may be Laid before them.

Also Resolved that the Chairman be, and he is hereby Directed to send attested coppies of the forgoing votes to the several Towns in the County as aforesaid.

Capt. Thomas Weeks chairman
Capt. William White, clerk.

28

Berkshire County Address, May 3, 1779

Berkshire maintained the position expressed in earlier statements; it was aware of the necessity of law, but opposed the sitting of the courts until a new constitution was formed. The government then in operation, based as it was upon the old charter, was unacceptable. The address is found in MA 201/6–8.

County of Berkshire, State of Massachusetts-Bay

To the Honorable the Judges of the superior Court appointed to sit at Great Barrington on Tuesday the fourth of May 1779—

May it please your Honors

We being a Convention formed by Delegates from the several Towns in the County of Berkshire, beg leave to lay before your Honors the sense of our Constituents, which is as follows viz. that it is creating a dangerous President to admit or consent to the operation of Law untill there is a Constitution or Form of Government with a Bill of Rights explicitly approved of and firmly established by a Majority of the Freemen of this State, for which reason the good People of this County are oposed to the seting of Courts at this or any future time untill a Constitution be formed and approved of by the People of this State—And here we beg leave to give some account of ourselves, and the reasons of our Conduct and in the first place would premise That we always had a sense of the Necessity of Law, especially in time of War, that we feel the Want of a due Exercise of it, and in many instances the sad effects of not enjoying of it, and as we have heretofore observed to a former Assembly, will do all in our power to uphold Authority and Law when settled upon a good foundation—But to our supprise in the seting of the first general Assembly in 1775 contrary to any Charter that we ever yet saw, The Members of each County were called upon to nomenate suitable persons in the civil and Military Line which were chosen by the House and commissioned by the Councill, in which effectual care was taken that those then present should be in the Nomenation, which procedure aroused our attention that such persons should nomenate and vote for themselves or be elected in a form that the Charter knew nothing of—We have further reasons for the non admission of Law on the present foundation, we keep our Eye on the Origin of the present mode of

Government, which as it is acknowledged by our Oponents, stands on the advice of the Continental Congress in 1775, which advice as may be seen had a special reference to a reconciliation to the Crown of Great Britain and in the exercise of such a mode mode of Government all our Officers civil and military were appointed and still hold their Authority, but when the Revolution took place by the subsequent Declaration of Independence that advice certainly ceased, and although there was a Proclamation from the general Court dated January 23d. 1776 congratulating the People on a new form of Government, yet this was before the declaration of Independence, every Law therefore exercised at that time must have the Crown for its Index, yet the general Plea is by our Oponents that we hold our Authority and Government consequent upon said Advice from Congress, it is a Truth too well known to be denied, that since the Declaration of Independence there has been no social Compact or fundamental Constitution formed and adopted by the great Majority of the People of this State therefore the Basis and foundation of the present mode of Government is what we dislike, together with the Spirit and Principle which actuates many of the men who would inforce it—And considering all those Reasons (which appear to us of weight) we are fearfull of the Consequences should the operation of Law take place upon the present Foundation, especially if it should be attempted to be enforced by Violence, as some have intimated, which intimations we hope will appear to be groundless, as they have very much exasperated the People; We must therefore in Duty to ourselves to our Country and Constituents earnestly desire that your Honors would desist from attempting to set in this County untill the explicit voice of the great Majority of the Freemen of this State may be taken by Yeas and Nays respecting the Validity of the present Form of Government, by whoes Determination when explicitly and regularly known we are determined chearfully and religiously to abide by—

The above being read and duly considered was unanimously approved of

signed per Order of said Convention

Stockbridge May 3d. 1779 Jonathan Younglove, Chairman

Great Barrington May 4th. 1779 A true Copy of the original paper sent to the Court.

And. Henshaw, Cler.

29

Returns of the Towns on Resolves of February 20, 1779, May 1779

Over two-thirds of the towns voted on whether they desired a new Constitution and on whether they would empower their representatives to call a state convention to frame one. The response seemed positive. The table below has been constructed from returns in MA 160/32–125. The first return reproduced, from Wellfleet, is a sample of what most of the others were like. In addition, returns of special interest, signaled by an asterisk in the table, are reproduced.

Page Archive Vol. 160	Town	Number present	Whether choose to have a Constitution at this time		Whether will empower representatives to call state convention	
			Yes	No	Yes	No
	Barnstable Co.					
32	Wellfleet *	. .	23	1	. .	. .
33	Barnstable	. .	2	56	. .	No instructions
34	Yarmouth	. .	. .	Unanimous	. .	. .
35	Truro	. .	Unanimous	. .	Unanimous	. .
	Berkshire Co.					
36	Tyringham	. .	46	0	. .	. .
36	Richmond	. .	67	0	Yes	. .
37	Stockbridge	. .	130	0	. .	. .
37	Alford	. .	22	0	. .	. .
37	Partridgefield	. .	63	0	. .	. .
38	Sandisfield	. .	61	0	. .	. .
38	Pittsfield	. .	74	0	. .	. .
39	Hancock	. .	18	0	Yes	. .
39	New Providence Plantation	. .	98	0	. .	. .
40	Great Barrington	. .	55	0	. .	. .
41	Williamstown	. .	118	1	Yes	. .
41	Sheffield	. .	100	2	. .	. .

Page Archive Vol. 160	Town	Number present	Whether choose to have a Constitution at this time		Whether will empower representatives to call state convention	
			Yes	No	Yes	No
	Bristol Co.					
42	Berkley	40	0	40	. .	. .
42	Dighton	. .	92	10	Yes	. .
43	Freetown	35	6	29	. .	. .
44	Attleborough	. .	121	0	121	0
44	Mansfield	. .	31	0	. .	. .
	Cumberland Co.					
45	Falmouth	. .	10	33	. .	. .
46	Gorham	32	0	32	. .	. .
46	Fryeburg [*York*]	. .	8	9	. .	. .
	Essex Co.					
48	Rowley	. .	2	Vote neg.	. .	. .
49	Salem *	. .	1	25	If majority of towns have answered in affirmative	. .
50	Marblehead	. .	. .	. .	Yes	. .
50	Bradford	48	0	48	. .	. .
51	Ipswich	. .	41	68	. .	. .
51	Salisbury	. .	22	1	Yes	. .
52	Newburyport	42	0	42	. .	. .
53	Lynn	. .	26	12	Yes	. .
53	Methuen	. .	0	50	. .	. .
54	Boxford	. .	0	31	. .	. .
55	Topsfield	. .	4	36	. .	. .
55	Beverly	. .	0	25	. .	. .
	Hampshire Co.					
56	Palmer	36	36	0	. .	. .
57	South Brimfield	69	69	0	. .	. .
58	Southwick	66	66	0	Yes	. .
58	Granby	. .	27	5	. .	. .
59	Granville	. .	66	3	. .	. .
60	Amherst	67	67	0	Yes	. .
60	Norwich	26	26	0	26	0
61	Warwick	. .	43	42	. .	. .
62	New Salem *	102	102	0	. .	. .
63	Leverett	. .	37	1	37	1

Page Archive Vol. 160	Town	Number present	Whether choose to have a Constitution at this time		Whether will empower representatives to call state convention	
			Yes	No	Yes	No
64	Brimfield	. .	40	9	. .	. .
64	West Springfield	60	40	20	. .	. .
65	Whately	13	13	0	. .	. .
65	Hatfield	61	61	0	Yes	. .
66	Belchertown *	. .	67	1	Unanimous	. .
66	Hadley	27	27	0	. .	. .
67	Deerfield	. .	15	3	. .	. .
67	Worthington *	. .	84	0	. .	. .
68	Westfield	76	75	1	. .	. .
68	Conway	. .	. .	. .	Unanimous	. .
69	Sunderland	. .	60	0	Unanimous	. .
70	Southampton *	58	58	0	Yes	. .
	Middlesex Co.					
71	Marlborough	. .	100	0	Yes	. .
71	Cambridge	106	0	106	. .	. .
72	Townsend	. .	40	0	Yes	. .
72	Medford	. .	22	15	. .	. .
73	Lincoln	21	2	19	. .	. .
74	Groton	. .	67	15	67	15
75	Chelmsford	38	16	22	. .	. .
75?	Stoneham	. .	[24?]	. .	. .	. .
76	Littleton	. .	4	44	. .	. .
77	Tewksbury	. .	20	2	. .	. .
78	Watertown	. .	3	20	. .	. .
79	Malden	. .	26	5	. .	. .
79	Westford *	70	70	0	. .	. .
80	Ashby	35	35	0	. .	. .
81	Framingham	. .	22	67	. .	. .
82	Sherborn	. .	41	5	. .	. .
82	Holliston	. .	39	6	. .	. .
83	Acton	. .	0	50	. .	. .
83	Weston	. .	3	59	. .	. .
84	Newton	. .	41	5	. .	. .
85	Sudbury	. .	59	10	Yes	. .
	Plymouth Co.					
86	Pembroke	. .	0	40	. .	. .
86a	Middleborough *	. .	116	25	. .	141

Page Archive Vol. 160	Town	Number present	Whether choose to have a Constitution at this time		Whether will empower representatives to call state convention	
			Yes	No	Yes	No
87	Bridgewater	. .	137	75	. .	. .
87	Rochester *	41	1	40	. .	. .
88	Scituate	. .	72	4	. .	. .
89	Marshfield	. .	20	2	20	2
89	Plympton	. .	0	115	. .	. .
	Suffolk Co.					
90	Boston *	. .	351	0	Yes	. .
91	Stoughtonham	37	23	14	0	37
92	Weymouth	. .	29	22	. .	. .
93	Milton	. .	42	2	. .	. .
94	Medfield	. .	19	20	. .	. .
94	Dorchester	. .	9	24	. .	. .
95	Medway	. .	0	24	. .	. .
95	Walpole	. .	59	4	. .	. .
96	Stoughton	. .	49	7	. .	. .
96	Wrentham	. .	92	0	. .	. .
97	Dedham	. .	29	3	Yes	. .
	Worcester Co.					
97	Oakham *	. .	Yes	1	Yes	1
99	Upton	. .	32	9	. .	. .
99	Hardwick	. .	81	0	81	0
100	Western	68	68	0	Yes	. .
100	Sutton *	. .	83	0	Yes	. .
101	Lancaster *	98	84	14	Yes	. .
102	Royalston	. .	Yes	0	Yes	. .
102	Grafton	. .	44	8	. .	. .
102	Oxford	. .	0	No	Unanimous	. .
103	Barre	. .	70	0	Unanimous	. .
103	Petersham	. .	80	1	. .	. .
104	Athol	61	61	0	Yes	. .
104	Rutland	. .	16	37	. .	. .
105	Uxbridge	. .	48	0	Yes	. .
106	Leicester	. .	67	0	. .	. .
106	Spencer	57	43	14	. .	. .
107	Shrewsbury *	57	56	1	. .	No
108	Brookfield	. .	104	4	. .	. .
109	Mendon	. .	79	67	Yes	. .

Page Archive Vol. 160	Town	Number present	Whether choose to have a Constitution at this time: Yes	No	Whether will empower representatives to call state convention: Yes	No
110	Leominster	..	43	3	..	..
110	Winchendon	..	18	7	..	..
111	Westminster	..	1	74	..	..
112	Dudley	..	76	0	..	..
113	Ashburnham	..	49	0	Yes	..
113	Lunenburg	52	11	41	..	..
114	Northbridge	..	28	0	Yes	..
115	Harvard	..	51	0	Yes	..
116	Westborough	..	84	0	Unanimous	..
117	Paxton	..	23	12	..	..
117	Templeton	66	66	0	..	..
118	Southborough *	71	71	0	..	..
119	Ward *	..	32	0	Yes	..
120	Fitchburg	..	45	0	Unanimous	0
	York Co.					
121	Berwick	82	0	82	..	..
122	Wells	..	15	47	..	..
123	York	70	0	70	..	..
123	Kittery	..	0	42	..	..

Wellfleet (160/32)

At a Meeting of the Freeholders and other inhabitants of the town of Wellfleet legally warned and duly qualifyed (as within Mentioned) assembled and meet at the Meeting house in said Wellfleet on Monday the 10 May Current for the purpose within mentioned upon the Question being put Whether they chuse at this Time to have a New Constitution or form of Government made it passed in the Affirmative—
Number Voteing in the Affirmative Twenty Three
Number Voteing in the Negative One—

Jonathan Young

Wellfleet May 11, 1779 Selectmen of Wellfleet

Barnabas Young

Salem (160/49)

At a Meeting of the Freeholders and other inhabitants of Salem lawfully qualified to Vote in the Choice of Representatives Voted——
That this town do not agree to have a New Constitution or Form of Government Made at this time
26 voters—25 against said Constitution and one for it——
That this town impower their Representatives chosen for the next year to Vote for calling a State Convention for the Sole purpose of forming a new Constitution provided it shall appear to them in examination that a major part of the people present and voting at the Meetings called in the manner and for the purpose aforesaid shall have answered the first Question in the Affirmative

Attest Edward Norris
Town Clerk

Salem 13th. May, 1779

New Salem (160/62)

To the Honourable General Assembly of this State.
Gentlemen—

Agreeable to the act of the General Court, We caused the free holder and other Inhabitant of this Town Quallified by Law to vote in Town affairs, to meet together on the 18th. Instant for the Purpose of knowing their opinions, on the Expediency of haveing a New Constitution, or Form of Government——Present, 102, Voted too a man; that they Consent to have a new Form of Government made; with this Proviso—that the same, if made, be laid before the several Towns in this State, for their approbation or dislike;——

We Beg leave, Likewise, to inform the Honourable Court, that it is for want of abillity; and not from any Disrespect, that we have not sent a Representative this Present year——

New Salem May 19th. 1779

Amos Foster — Select Men
Benjamin Southick — of
Uzziel Putnam — New Salem

Belchertown, May 21, 1779 (160/66)

Belcherstown May 21, 1779

At a meeting of the Freeholders and other Inhabitants of Belcherstown Qualifyed by Law to vote for a Representative it was Put to vote whether they would send a Representative to the General Court this year and it Passed in the Negative——

2ly it was Put to vote and the Question asked wheather they chuse at this time to have a new Constitution or form of Goverment made and there was Sixty Seven men voted for it and but one man voted against it

and 3ly they Unanimusly vote that there may be a State Convention Called for that Purpos—the meeting was Disolved

Nathaniel Dwight
Samuel Howe
Daniel Smith
Elijah Chapin
Selectmen of Belcherstown

To the Secretary of the State of the Massachusetts

Worthington (160/67)

At a Meeting of the Freeholders and Other Inhabitants of the Town of Worthington Legally Warned and held in said Town of Worthington On Thursday the Twentieth Day of May Instant———And Agreeable to a resolve of the General Court at Boston the 20th of February 1779 and in Answer to the first Question Therein contained Voted Unanimously that it be their Minds to have a new Constitution or form of goverment made with as much Expediency as may be Consistant with its nature and Importance

Votes in the Affirmative No. 84
in the Negative—o—

Dated at Worthington
May the 22th 1779

Jonathan Brewster
Moses Porter
William Barr
Selectmen of Worthington

Westford (160/79)

Agreeable to a Resolve of the Great and General court of February 11, 1779 the inhabitants of the Town of Westford qualified to vote for a Representative were assembled on May the 21, 1779 to Consider of and determine upon the question Contained in said Resolve, there being present and voting seventy voters; and on the first question, viz. Whether they Chuse at this time to have a new Constitution and form of government made" Voted unanimously in the affirmative on the following Condition, viz. that the freeholders and other Inhabitants in this State at large exercise (being Called upon therefore) the right of chusing a State Convention for that purpose otherwise voted unanimously that no Constitution and form of government be made for the present.

Westford May 24, 1779
Copy examined by Nathaniel Boynton Town Clerk

Middleborough (160/86a)

To the Honorable the Great and General Court for the State of the Massahusetts Bay. Gentleman: The following is an account of the Proseedings of the Town of Middleborough at a Town Meting Regularly Warned to Hear and answer the Several Questions Sent out by the Great and General Court of this state as Spissefyed in the within Resolves———(viz)

In answering the first Question there was one Hundred and Sixteen voted in the affermative and Twenty five voted in the negetive——

In answering the Second Question their was none voted in the affermative But their was one hundred forty and one voted in the Negetive———

But the Town With all due Submission Humbly offer their Sentements as followeth (viz)———

That it is the oppinion of the Town Considering the Multipliscety of Business Devolvid on the General Court at this diffecult day that it is Best that they do not Take it upon them to Chuse a State Convention to form a new Constitution or form of government: But that the Good People of said state Be allowed the Priviledg to form County Conventions and that they (after Consultation) appoint delegates from the said Countye Conventions to meet neer the Senter of the State for the Purpose of forming a Constitution and when formed that it be Sent for the People to approve or to disapprove or to amend and that the County and State convention Shall (if Possable) Compleat their Buisness By the first day of October next insuing this date.———

Dated at Middleboro.
the 17d of May AD 1779

John Alden
Edmond Wood
Thomas Nelson Selectmen
Isaac Tonyon

Rochester (160/87)

To the Secretary of the State of the Massachusettes Bay—

This may Certify, the legal voters of the town of Rochester had legal warning and mett at the Townhouse in Said Town on the 20th day of May to consider wheather they would have a forme of Goverment at this time Sett up, or not, forty one was all the voters present, one voted for Setting up Goverment at this time, and forty for Continuing the present moode as yett.

Rochester May 20, 1779 AD.

Enoch Hammond Selectmen
Melatiah White of
David Wing Rochester

Boston (160/90)

Agreable to a Resolve of the General Assembly of this State passed February 19, 1779 The Freeholders and other Inhabitants of the town of Boston duly qualified to vote for Representatives legally warned in publick Town Meeting assembled at Faneuil Hall on Wednesday the 5th Day of May 1779———

The aforesaid *Resolve* was read and duly considered, it was then moved and carried, that the First question in said Resolve Viz. "Whether the Town choose at this time to have a new Constitution or Form of Government made" be determined by Yeas and Nays—And the Inhabitants being directed to withdraw and bring in their Votes accordingly, the same were brought in, when the number was found to be three hundred and fifty one, and all yeas——The Town have given Instructions to their Representatives relative to the 2d Question in said Resolve

J. Scollay
M. Greenough
Harbottle Dorr
Ezekiel Price
Nathan Frazier

Selectmen of Boston

Boston May 11, 1779

Oakham (160/97)

Worcester County—Oakham May 17th. 1779

Agreeable to a Resolve of General Court of February last the voters for a Representative were legally warned

I to meet to see if they were desirous there should be a new form of Goverment at this Time made

Voted in the affirmative

II To See if they would vote to Instruct the Representatives to Call a Convention solely for that Purpose

Voted unanimously in the affirmative except one person who is an old insignifant Torey, and never ought to vote in any Case

Jesse Allen
Thomas White
William Green
Isaiah Parmenter

Select Men of Oakham

Sutton (160/100)

At a Legal Town meeting of the Town of Sutton at the meeting House in the first parrish in Sutton on monday the 17: Day of May 1779 The two following votes was passed

The first Question put (viz.)

Whether the Town Chuse at this Time to have a new Constitution or form of Goverment mad it past in the affirmative

The Second Question was put (viz.)

Whether this Town will impower thier Reprsentive "for this present year to vote for the Calling a State convention for the sole purpose of

forming a new Constitution and it passed in the affirmative with this proviso (viz)
[Pro?] vided that when said Convention shall have formed a Constitution [a co?]py thierof shall be sent to Each own in this State to the people at Larg for thier approbation or Disapprobation or amendment.
N:B in answer to the first Question——
Eighty three voted for it and not one against it.

A True Copy attest

Follansbe Chase
Town Clerk

Lancaster (160/101)

Lancaster May 17th 1779

At a legall meeting of the freeholders and other Inhabitants of the town of Lancaster Regularly assembled to Vote in town affairs, agreable to an Order of the Great and General Court of February 19, 1779 to the Selectmen directed The town being meet Voted Accordingly (Viz)——

1st—Voted to have a new Constitution and form of Government made
Present at the above meeting voting 98: 84 yeas and 14 Nays:

2dly—Voted and accepted of the Second Article on the Court orders as above concerning a new Constitution with this addition, we do impower our Representative to give his Vote for Chusing a Convention for the purpose mentioned, with this proviso that said Constitution shall Return into the hands of the people when made For there approbation or Disapprobation

The above is a true Copy of the proceedings

William Greenleaf	Selectmen
Nathaniel Beaman	of
Ephm Wilder	Lancaster
Manh. Sawyer	

Shrewsbury (160/107)

At a Legal Town meeting Holden at Shrewsbury on Wednesday the 19th day of May 1779 in consequence of a Resolve of the Great and General Court of the State of the Massachusetts Bay, of February 19th 1779 Respecting a New Constitution or Form of Government, and after takeing into Serious Consideration the first Question therein proposed Viz. Whether they Chuse, at this time to have a New Constitution or Form of Government made, which passed in the Affirmative; Provided the People at Large may Choose the Convention for Forming said Constitution or Form of Government, according to the Constitution of Choosing Representatives before the year 1775 and not otherwise. And Mr. Ephraim Beaman whome the Town of Shrewsbury have chosen to Represent them in the Great and General Court the Ensuing year is Directed and Impowered, In this respect, to Govern himself accordingly. Present at, and acting in said meeting Fifty seven Votable Inhabitants of said Town; Fifty six of which number, Voted in the Affirmative, one only in the Negative———

Edward Flint
Robert Andrews
Ezra Beaman
Select men of Shrewsbury

Shrewsbury
May 19th. 1779
To be Lodged in the secretary's
Office Immediately
p. favour of Mr. Ephraim Beaman
Representative for Shrewsbury

Southborough (160/118)

To the Honorable General Court of the State of the Massachusetts Bay

In Pursuance of a hand Bill directed to the Selectmen of the Several Towns in this State bearing date. February 19th a:d. 1779 upon the Establishing a new form of Goverment in Compliance of the Same the Inhabitants of the Town of Southborough being duly warned for that Purpose meet the 20th of May A.D. 1779 the number of Voters present att said meeting was Seventy one and all Voted for a new form of Goverment without a dissenter

Southboro. May 24th 1779

Joshua Smith
Seth Newton
Elijah Brigham
Ezra Taylor
Selectmen for Southborough

Ward (160/119)

In obedience to the Directions of the General Court latly sent to the Several Towns in this State Requiring the Select men to tack the voice and determination of the people Resecting of forming a new Constitution of government We Do hereby Certifie that at a legal Town meeting of the Inhbitants of the Town of Ward on the 19th of this instant the first question proposed Concerning the matter being put to vote it passed in the affirmative the Number voting for it being thirty two and none in the negative.

upon the Second Question voted (altho we send no Representative of our own) that the Representatives of the State Should vote if they see Cause for the Calling a State Convention for the sole purpose of forming a new Constitution upon Condition that the same be Chosen by the peple at large.——

Ward May 28th. 1779

Charles Richardson
Samuel Eddy
John Hart
Jonahan Cutlar
Jacob Hewens

Select Men of Ward

30

The Call for a Convention, June 1779

The House of Representatives, after collating the town returns on the desirability of a new constitution, called for a convention and outlined procedures for ratification of the document there to be drafted. The House acted on June 15, the Council on June 21. The document is found in MA 160/125.

State of Massachusetts-Bay.
In the House of Representatives, June 15, 1779.

Whereas by the Returns made into the Secretary's Office from more than two thirds of the Towns belonging to this State, agreeably to a Resolve of the General Court of the 20th of February last, it appears that a large majority of the inhabitants of such Towns, as have made return as aforesaid, think it proper to have a new Constitution or Form of Government, and are of opinion that the same ought to be formed by a Convention of Delegates who should be specially authorized to meet for this Purpose: Therefore,

Resolved, That it be and it hereby is recommended to the several Inhabitants of the several towns in this State to form a Convention for the sole purpose of framing a new Constitution, consisting of such Number of Delegates from each town throughout the State, as every different town is intitled to send Representatives to the General Court, to meet at Cambridge, in the county of Middlesex, on the first day of September next.

And the Selectmen of the several towns and places in this State, impowered by the laws thereof to send Members to the General Assembly, are hereby authorized and directed to call a Meeting of their respective towns at least fourteen days before the meeting of the said Convention, to elect one or more Delegates to represent them in said Convention, at which Meeting for the election of such Delegate or Delegates, every Freeman, inhabitant of such town, who is twenty one years of age, shall have a right to vote.

Be it also Resolved, That it be and hereby is recommended to the inhabitants of the several towns in this State to instruct their respective Delegates to cause a printed copy of the Form of a Constitution they may agree upon in Convention, to be transmitted to the Selectmen of each town, and the Committee of each plantation, and the said Selectmen and Committees are hereby impowered and directed to lay the same before their respective towns and plantations at a regular meeting of the Male inhabitants thereof, being free and twenty one years of age, to be called for that purpose, in order to its being duly considered and approved or disapproved by said towns and plantations; and it is also recommended to the several towns within this State to instruct their respective Representatives to establish the said Form of a Constitution as the Constitution and Form of Government of the State of Massachusetts-Bay, if upon a fair Examination it shall appear that it is approved of by at least two thirds of those who are free and twenty one years of age, belonging to this State, and present in the several Meetings.

Sent up for Concurrence,
John Hancock, Speaker
In Council, June 21, 1779. Read and concurred.
John Avery, Dep. Secretary
Consented to by the Major Part of the Council.

31

Votes of Towns in Choosing Delegates, July–October 1779

The towns dispatched their delegates to the convention with notice of their election. For the most part, these documents merely indicated that the individual named had been chosen to act for the town. Some, however, included instructions and statements of the interests that the members of the convention were to keep in mind. Returns of special interest are reproduced below and are signaled by a dagger (†) in the table. Unless otherwise indicated, the returns are found in MA 160/124–293.

Page, Archive Vol. 160	Town	Date
124	Winchendon	July 5, 1779
	Northfield	July 7, 1779
	Pembroke	July 12, 1779
125	Rowley	July 7, 1779
126	Medford	July 8, 1779
	Pittsfield †	July 8, 1779
	Woburn	July 8, 1779
127	Bellingham †	July 9, 1779
	Dorchester	July 12, 1779
128	Methuen	July 12, 1779
	Wilmington	July 12, 1779
	Northbridge	July 12, 1779
129	Topsfield †	July 12, 1779
	Chelmsford	July 12, 1779
130	Cambridge	July 12, 1779
131	Littleton	July 12, 1779
132	Concord	July 13, 1779
133	Lanesborough	July 14, 1779
	Tyringham	July 15, 1779
134	Natick	July 15, 1779
135	Stockbridge	July 15, 1779

Page, Archive Vol. 160	Town	Date
136	Hopkinton	Aug. 16, 1779
137	Windsor	July 19, 1779
	Lenox	July 20, 1779
	Easton	July 26, 1779
	Hingham	July 26, 1779
138	New Providence	July 26, 1779
	Halifax	July 26, 1779
139	Williamstown †	July 27, 1779
140	Lincoln	July 28, 1779
141	Princeton	July 28, 1779
	Andover	July 2, 1779
142	Acton	July 30, 1779
143	Harvard	July 30, 1779
	Weymouth	July 22, 1779
144	Southampton	July 30, 1779
	Palmer	July 30, 1779
145	Westford	Aug. 2, 1779
	Greenwich	Aug. 2, 1779
146	Danvers	Aug. 2, 1779
147	Newburyport	Aug. 2, 1779
	Fitchburg	Aug. 2, 1779
	Taunton	Aug. 2, 1779
148	Lynn	Aug. 2, 1779
	Plympton	Aug. 2, 1779
149	Lexington	Aug. 2, 1779
149	Charlestown	Aug. 2, 1779
150	Weston	Aug. 2, 1779
151	Chelsea	Aug. 2, 1779
	Wrentham	Aug. 2, 1779
152	Roxbury	[Aug. 2, 1779]
153	Abington	Aug. 2, 1779
154	Dartmouth	Aug. 2, 1779
155	Attleborough	Aug. 2, 1779
156	Franklin	Aug. 2, 1779
157	Newton	Aug. 2, 1779
158	Uxbridge	Aug. 2, 1779

Page, Archive Vol. 160	Town	Date
	Kittery	Aug. 2, 1779
159	Dunstable	Aug. 3, 1779
160	Brookline	Aug. 3, 1779
	Egremont	Aug. 3, 1779
161	Beverly	Aug. 3, 1779
162	Middleborough	Aug. 3, 1779
	Plymouth	Aug. 4, 1779
163	Gloucester	Aug. 4, 1779
164	Bradford	Aug. 4, 1779
165	Bedford	Aug. 4, 1779
	Newbury	Aug. 4, 1179
166	Stoughtonham	Aug. 4, 1779
167	Amesbury	Aug. 5, 1779
168	Salisbury	Aug. 5, 1779
169	Haverhill	Aug. 5, 1779
170	Sheffield	Aug. 5, 1779
170–171	Medway	Aug. 6, 1779
172	Freetown	Aug. 6, 1779
173	Norwich	Aug. 7, 1779
174	Bolton	Aug. 9, 1779
175	Grafton	Aug. 9, 1779
176	Ipswich	Aug. 9, 1779
	Townsend	July 9, 1779
	Belchertown	Aug. 9, 1779
177	Marlborough	Aug. 9, 1779
	Lunenburg	Aug. 9, 1779
178	Sherborn	Aug. 9, 1779
179	Stow	Aug. 9, 1779
180	Chesterfield	Aug. 9, 1779
	Lancaster	Aug. 9, 1779
181	Dracut	Aug. 9, 1779
182	West Stockbridge	Aug. 9, 1779
183	Holliston	Aug. 9, 1779
184	Great Barrington	Aug. 9, 1779
	Scarborough	Aug. 9, 1779
185	Stoughton	Aug. 9, 1779
	Medfield	Aug. 9, 1779

Page, Archive Vol. 160	Town	Date
186	Milton	Aug. 9, 1779
	Bridgewater	Aug. 9, 1779
187	Lunenburg †	Aug. 9, 1779
188	Berwick	Aug. 9, 1779
189	Wells	Aug. 9, 1779
190	Braintree	Aug. 9, 1779
191	York	Aug. 9, 1779
192	Oakham	Aug. 10, 1779
193	Upton	Aug. 10, 1779
194	Sunderland	Aug. 10, 1779
195	Charlemont	Aug. 10, 1779
	Paxton	Aug. 10, 1779
196	Winthrop	Aug. 10, 1779
197	New Marlborough	Aug. 10, 1779
197	The Gore	Aug. 11, 1779
198	Alford	Aug. 11, 1779
	Westhampton	Aug. 11, 1779
199	Sandwich	Aug. 11, 1779
200	Leominster	Aug. 11, 1779
200–201, 203	Boston	Aug. 12, 1779
202	Tewksbury	Aug. 12, 1779
	Pepperell	Aug. 12, 1779
204	Billerica	Aug. 12, 1779
205	Warwick	Aug. 12, 1779
	Richmond	Aug. 12, 1779
206	Becket	Aug. 12, 1779
207	Hatfield	Aug. 12, 1779
	Colrain	Aug. 13, 1779
208	Mansfield	Aug. 13, 1779
	Pelham	Aug. 13, 1779
209	Mendon	Aug. 14, 1779
210	Yarmouth	Aug. 14, 1779
211	Hancock †	Aug. 15, 1779
212	Westfield	Aug. 16, 1779
213	South Hadley	Aug. 16, 1779
214	Greenfield	Aug. 16, 1779

Page, Archive Vol. 160	Town	Date
215	South Brimfield	Aug. 16, 1779
216	Kingston	Aug. 16, 1779
	New Braintree	Aug. 16, 1779
217	Groton	Aug. 16, 1779
218	Worcester	Aug. 16, 1779
219	Shrewsbury	Aug. 16, 1779
220	Petersham	Aug. 16, 1779
221	Hardwick	Aug. 16, 1779
222	Hubbardston	Aug. 16, 1779
223	Northampton	Aug. 16, 1779
224	Wilbraham	Aug. 16, 1779
	Shelburne	Aug. 16, 1779
225	Douglas †	Aug. 16, 1779
226	Sturbridge	Aug. 16, 1779
	Ashfield	Aug. 16, 1779
227	Westborough	Aug. 16, 1779
228	Leicester	Aug. 16, 1779
229	Brookfield	Aug. 16, 1779
	Gorham	Aug. 16, 1779
231	Partridgefield	Aug. 16, 1779
232	Reading	Aug. 16, 1779
233	Sudbury	Aug. 16, 1779
234	Groton	Aug. 16, 1779
235	Malden	Aug. 16, 1779
	Rutland	Aug. 16, 1779
236	Foxborough	Aug. 16, 1779
237	Scituate	Aug. 16, 1779
	Royalston	Aug. 16, 1779
238	Dighton	Aug. 16, 1779
	Rehoboth	Aug. 16, 1779
	Norton	Aug. 16, 1779
239	Granville	Aug. 17, 1779
240	Sutton	Aug. 17, 1779
241	Shutesbury	Aug. 17, 1779
	Worthington	Aug. 17, 1779
242	Spencer	Aug. 17, 1779
	Dudley	Aug. 17, 1779

Page Archive Vol. 160	Town	Date
243	Southborough	Aug. 17, 1779
244	Monson	Aug. 17, 1779
245	Athol	Aug. 17, 1779
	Amherst	Aug. 17, 1779
	Westminster	Aug. 17, 1779
246	Framingham	Aug. 18, 1779
247	Uxbridge	Aug. 18, 1779
	Charlton	Aug. 18, 1779
248	Waltham	Aug. 18, 1779
249	Northborough	Aug. 18, 1779
	Rochester	Aug. 19, 1779
250	Leverett	Aug. 19, 1779
251	Barre	Aug. 23, 1779
252	Oxford	Aug. 23, 1779
253	Watertown	Aug. 23, 1779
254	Southwick	Aug. 23, 1779
	Marshfield	Aug. 23, 1779
230, 255–265	Sandisfield †	Aug. 16, ?, 1779
266–277	Stoughton †	?
278	Hanover	? 1779
279	Berkley	Aug. 23, 1779
280	West Springfield	Aug. 24, 1779
281	Brimfield	Aug. 24, 1779
282	Springfield	Aug. 24, 1779
283	Dudley †	Aug 18, 24, 1779
284	Dedham	Aug. 29, 1779
285	Salem	Aug. 29, 1779
286	Bristol	Aug. 29, 1779
	Swansey †	Aug. 30, 1779
287	Templeton	Aug 30, 1779
	Middleton	Aug. 30, 1779
288	Gorham †	? 1779
289	Western †	Aug. 30, 1779
290	Raynham	Aug. 30, 1779
	Williamsburg	Aug. 31, 1779
	Walpole	Aug. 31, 1779

Page, Archive Vol. 160	Town	Date
291	Ahsby	Sept. 27, 1779
	Adams	Oct. 4, 1779
	Buckland	Oct. 18, 1779
292	Needham	Oct. 19, 1779
	Marblehead	Sept 20, 1779
	New Salem	Oct. 20, 1779
293	Holden	Oct. 25, 1779
	Sunderland	[June ?] 1779

Pittsfield *

Report of the Committee appointed by the Town to draw up Instructions for their Representatives in State Convention is as follows:——

To Col. Williams.

Sir,—As you have been duly elected by the town of Pittsfield their representative to meet in a convention of this State at Cambridge, the 1st of September next, for the purpose of forming a new Constitution for the people of this State, which we view as a matter of the greatest consequence to the present and future generations, it will doubtless be agreeable to you to understand their sentiments for the government of your deportment. You are therefore hereby instructed to unite with said convention in drawing up a Bill of Rights and in forming a new Constitution for the people of this State. We wish you to oppose all unnecessary delay in this great work, and to proceed in it with the utmost wisdom and caution.

In the Bill of Rights, you will endeavor that all those unalienable and important rights which are essential to true liberty, and form the basis of government in a free State, shall be inserted: particularly, that this people have a right to adopt that form of government which appears to us most eligible, and best calculated to promote the happiness of ourselves and posterity; that as all men by nature are free, and have no dominion one over another, and all power originates in the people, so, in a state of civil society, all power is founded in compact; that every man has an unalienable right to enjoy his own opinion in matters of

* Smith, *History of Pittsfield,* 366–367.

religion, and to worship God in that manner that is agreeable to his own sentiments without any control whatsoever, and that no particular mode or sect of religion ought to be established, but that every one be protected in the peaceable enjoyment of his religious persuasion and way of worship; that no man can be deprived of liberty, and subjected to perpetual bondage and servitude, unless he has forfeited his liberty as a malefactor; that the people have a right peaceably to assemble, consider of their grievances, and petition for redress; that, as civil rulers derive their authority from the people, so they are accountable to them for the use of it; that elections ought to be free, equal, and annual; that, as all men are equal by nature, so, when they enter into a state of civil government, they are entitled precisely to the same rights and privileges, or to an equal degree of political happiness; that the right of trial by jury ought to be perpetual; that no man's property of right can be taken from him without his consent, given either in person or by his representative; that no laws are obligatory on the people but those that have obtained a like consent, nor are such laws of any force, if, proceeding from a corrupt majority of the legislature, they are incompatible with the fundamental principles of government, and tend to subvert it; that the freedom of speech and debates and proceedings in the House of Representatives ought not to be questioned or impeached in any court, or place out of the General Court; that excessive bail shall not be required, nor excessive fines imposed, nor cruel and unjust punishments inflicted; that jurors ought to be duly impanelled and returned, and all jurors ought to be freeholders. These, and all other liberties which you find essential to true liberty, you will claim, demand, and insist upon, as the birthrights of this people.

In respect to the Constitution, you will use your best endeavors that the following things may be inserted in it amongst others: That the election of the representative body be annual; that no representative on any occasion shall absent himself from said House without leave first had from said body, but shall constantly attend on the business during the sessions. All taxes shall be levied with the utmost equality on polls, faculty, and property. You may consent to government by a Governor, Council, and House of Representatives. The Governor and Council shall have no negative voice upon the House of Representatives; but all disputed points shall be settled by the majority of the whole legislative body. The supreme judges of the executive courts shall be elected by the suffrages of the people at large, and be commissioned by the Governor.

That all grants of money shall originate in the House of Representatives. The judges of the maritime courts, the attorney-general, and high sheriffs of each county, are to be appointed by the suffrages of people at large, and commissioned by the Governor. The justices of the Common Pleas and Quarter Sessions of the Peace in each county be elected by the suffrages of the people of said counties. That no person, unless of the Protestant religion, shall be Governor, Lieutenant-governor, or member of the Council or the House of Representatives.

The said Bill of Rights and Constitution you will move may be printed, and sent abroad for the approbation of the people of this State at large, and that each town be requested by said convention to show their approbation or disapprobation of every paragraph in said Bill of Rights and Constitution, and that it be not sent abroad for their approbation or disapprobation in the lump; and that the objectionable parts, if any such shall be, shall be pointed out by each town.

You are not to dissolve the convention, but to adjourn from time to time, as you shall find necessary, till said form of government is approved by the majority of the people.

On the whole, we empower you to act agreeable to the dictates of your own judgment after you have heard all the reasonings upon the various subjects of disquisition, having an invariable respect to the true liberty and real happiness of this State throughout all generations, any instructions herein contained to the contrary notwithstanding.

THOMAS ALLEN,
ELI ROOT,
JAMES NOBLE,
LEBBEUS BACKUS. } *Committee.*

Accepted. Attest:

Eli Root, *Moderator*

Bellingham *

Aug 6 1779 to Mr. Noah Alden Sir you being chosen By the Inhabitants of this Town to Represent them in a convention at Cambridge

* George F. Partridge, *History of the Town of Bellingham, Massachusetts, 1719–1919* (Bellingham, Mass., 1919), 133–134. The delegate wrote to his adviser and friend, Isaac Backus, minister in Middleborough, as follows: "Our town have chosen me as thare Delegate to go to Cambridge for the Sole purpose of forming a New Constitution or forme of

next September for the sole Purpose of forming a Constitution for the Massachusetts we your Constituants Claim it as Our Inherent right at all times to Instruct those that Represent us But more necessary on such an Important Object which not only so Nearly Concerns ourselves But our Posterity. we Do in the first place instruct you Previous to your Entering upon the framing of a form of Government you See that Each part of the State have Properly Deligated their Power for Such a Purpose and that a Bill of Rights Be formed where in the Natural Rites of Individuals Be Clearly ascertained that is all Such Rights as the Supream Power of the State Shall [have] no authority to Controal, to be a part of the Constitution that you use your Influence that the Legislative Power consist of a Senate and House of Representatives, the Representatives to Be Annually Chosen from the Towns as they were in the year 1776. that the Constitution be so framed that Elections be free and frequent, most likely to Prevent bribery Corruption and Influance that the Executive Power be So Lodged as to Execute the Laws with Dispatch . . . the Senators to be annually Chosen by the people That the holding the Court of probate . . . in but one town in the County as hereto fore . . . has been a grievous burden to us . . . that Each Incorporated Town may have power to hold a Court of Probate . . . and record Deeds in the same Town. We further Instruct you that when you have Drawn a form of government you cause a fair Coppy thereof to be Printed . . . that the Convention Adjourn to some futer Day and the Coppy be laid before your several Towns for their Consideration and Amendment to be returned to the Convention. That the Juditial be So established that Justice may be impartially Demonstrated without Enormous Expense that the Right of Trial by Jury be kept Sacred and Close . . . that Statutes of Old England nor any foreign Law be adopted . . . that a County Assemble be Established to Grant County Taxes in each county and settle all the county Matters.

Government for this State the waitest affair of a temporal nature I humbly conceive that Ever this state tuck in hand the vue I have of the matter is that it is Essentially nessary that in the first place thare should be a bill of Rights assertaining what are the natural sivel and Religious Rights of the people and a form of government predecated upon said bill of rights perfectly agreabel thare to and Never Know laws afterwards made Repugnant to said Bill of Rights but as I am sensabel that the delegates will not be all of my mind and the work is grate and my gifts Small and I am inexperienced in a work of this sort Dear brother I pray you to favour me with your mind on the subject Expesualy what are the Rights of the people and how that Bill of Rights ought to be Drawn. I hope my dear brethren will not forgit me in thare prayers to God that I may be Enabled to Contend Earnestly bouldly and wisely for the libertys of the people in general and for the libertys of the Lords people in purticklure." *Ibid.*, 132.

Topsfield (160/129)

At a Legal Meeting of the Freeholders and other Inhabitants of Topsfield on the 12th day of July 1779.

Mr. Israel Clarke [Freeman?] and Mr. Abraham Hobbs was Elected delegates to represent the Town in a Convention to be held at Cambridge on the first day of September next for the sole purpose of framing a new Constitution agreable to a resolve of the General Court of the State of Massachusetts Bay of June 15th. 1779

The Town voted that their delegates be instructed to Cause a printed Copy of the form of a Constitution they may agree upon in Convention to be transmitted to the Selectmen of Each Town and the Committees of each plantation, in order to its being duly Considred and approved or Disapproved by said Towns and plantations agreable to a resolve of the General Court of June 15th: 1779.

Attest Stephen Perkins Town Clerk

Williamstown (160/139)

agreable to a Resolve of the General Court of this State Passed June 21, 1779

The Inhabitants of this Town have been warned and met on the 27th. of July 1779 after the moderator was Chosen the Resolve of Court being Read and Considered the Town made Choice by Ballot of Captain Stephen Davis and Mr. Elisha Baker for their Delegates to Represent them in a State Convention to be Conveened at Cambridge on the 1st. of September next for the purpose of forming a Constitution and the following Instructions were unanimously voted by the Town (viz)——

that the Convention form a Constitution with a Bill of Rights for this State and cause the same to be printed and sent to the several Towns and plantations in this State for their Consideration and that they adjourn and require each Town and plantation to make Returns to them at their next meeting of their approbation or Disapprobation and the numbers voting for or against Said Constitution and also to Direct each Town and plantation to Specify in their Returns what articles are Disagreable and propose Such amendments or alterations as the major part of the voters then present Shall agree to and the State Convention when met according to their own adjournment Shall Examine the returns of the Several Towns and plantations in this State and if it shall appear that the Constitution and Bill of Rights is approved by two thirds of the people in this State present in their Several meetings then the Same to be Established. if not approved as aforsaid then the Convention to Consider the objections and proposed amendments and make such alterations as shall appear Necessary to make it agreable to the people and Send it out again as aforsaid and so proceed from time to time till they shall have made such a Constitution that shall meet with the approbation of two thirds of the people in this State——also to Insist upon the Electing of Civil and Military Officers to be allowed to the people at large and also the Electing of Legislative and Executive authority to be in the people——

A true copy attest
Isaac Stratton Town Clerk of Williamstown

Lunenburg (160/187)

To Cap George Kimball

Sir

You being chosen to represent this town at a State Convention to be held at Cambridge the 1st September next, for the sole purpose of framing a new Constitution of Government——

As we have delagated you to act in this important matter. We the inhabitants of the town of Lunenberg think it proper to give you some instructions for your conduct in said Assembly——

1st As it is of the greatest importance that all forms of Goverment should be preceeded and accompanyed with a bill of rights. That the rights of the people at large may be ascertained and fixed as well as those of the rulers we would have you use your utmost endeavour that the new constitution of Goverment be prefaced by a bill of rights——

2d. We would have you use your endeavour that representation may be as free and equal as the nature of the thing will admit——

3d As we apprehend it is inconsistent with a free goverment that one branch of the legislature should be dependent on the other for their Election. We would have you exert Your influence. that the Council or Senate be proportioned through the different counties in the State. And that the people of each county chuse the number allowed to their respective county——

4. As it is of the last importance that the inestimable right of trials by jury be preserved. We would have you endeavour that said right be confirmed, and if any alterations are proposed to be made, by which said right will be made more secure to the people, we would have you consent thereto——

5. When the Convention have agreed upon a form of Goverment we would have you give your consent to have it printed and a coppy thereof sent to each town and plantation in this State, that it may be considered and approved or disapproved by said towns and plantations——

As these are all the matters upon which we think it necessary to give you any instructions. we shall leave you to act on the other parts of the constitution as your wisdom and prudence may dictate, hoping the Convention will be directed by the great ruler of all things to form such a Constitution as will be for the happyness of this and all succeeding Generations——

The Town Voted that if the third article in the above instructions Cannot be obtained then Delegate be Directed to use his influence that the Council or Senate be Chosen by the house of representatives.

At a Legal Meeting of the inhabitants of the Town of Lunenburg August 9th 1779

the foregoing instructions ware Voted for a Rule of Conduct for their Deligate

test Jedidiah Bailey
Town Clerk

Hancock (160/211)

August the 15 1779

This is to sartafi that the in habatans of handcock bein legolly wornd and met and chose a modarater and Clark the Clark bein absent made Choys of [*illegible*] Asa Douglas to represent this town in Congres at Cambrig the furst day of Septem bar for form in a Constitushan for the mase cusets bay and voted to give the foloin instrucshons when they shold form and send out to the Peopel and two thurds of the Peopel shold exsept of it—that thay shold order and [Direct?] ho and hou it shold be en nacted in to a law and other wise to set and make a mendments til the Peopel suted provided it may be don in one year from the furst setin of said Congres

Bennagah Maccol
Clark for the Day

Douglas (160/225)

Douglass August the 16: 1779

The inhabitants of the Town of Douglass met at the meeting house; being Legally warnd For to Chuse a Deligate or Deligates to Represent them: in a State Convention; to be held at Cambridge on the first Day of September Next for the Sole purpose of fraiming a New Constitution of Civil goverment

Said meeting was ajourd to the 23d. of this Instant Then the Town meet according to adjournment——at Nine of the o'Clock in the fore noon and uninamously Choose, Mr. Eliphazi Stearns For their Deligate to Represent them at the——a bove said Convention
and then voted: that the said Deligate is Hereby instructed to give his vote in favour of such a form of gover ment: or Simelar to that: that is in use in the State of Connectticuts.——provide such a constitution shall be in nomination So far as the Circumstace of this State will admit
And Likewise that a printed copy of the form of a constitution they may agree up on in convention be transmitted to the Selectmen—of Each Town——

A true Coppy
attest William Dudley town Clerk

Sandisfield (160/230, 255–265)

The Committee of the Town of Sandisfield to whom was Refered the forming of Instructions for their Delegates to meet in convention with the Delegates from the other Towns and Districts in this State at Cambridge on the first Day of September Next for the purpose of framing the form of a Constitution to be presented to the several Towns and Districts in this state to be by them Adopted, if they shall see Cause, as a System of Government, for the same, Beg Leave to report the following

Draught as proper for them to observe in their Consultations of said Constitution and in framing of the same—

To Messrs. James Ayrault David Deming—

We having Delegated you as our Representatives to meet in Convention at Cambridge for the purposes Abovementioned, Doubt not but what you will make use of your well known and Approved Abilities, and which we Expect you will endeavour, the following Instructions from your Constituents be the rule of your procedure in that important affair——

In Emerging from a State of nature into a Governmental form in Order that each one retain their rights which are Unalienable, each one Should place himself on the broad Basis of Equality, wherein Benevolence hath its Genuine Flow, that [hence?] the System be so formed, that it shall be peculiarly out of the Power of Designing men to Encroach on the Inherent and Unalienable rights of the People, for the People as such, are less Disposed to incroach on their own Liberties than Individuals are, they are so far from it, that they are in one sense their only Guardians, therefore in forming a Constitution Especialy as it is for Generations to Come, and which they are nearly interested, such Lines ought to be Drawn as rules of Government, that the Servants of the People ought to be as much as may be in the Possession of the People, and when the People through Mystakes or the Wiley Designs of Art and Cunning—have made an Improper Choice, or Injudiciously reposed a Trust they ought to have early Opportunity of Remediing the evil, which is to be secured in the forming of a Constitution, and it being of the greatest importance, that a people in the Circumstances that this State are in, Should as soon as may be, have a System of Government formed, The Convention for that purpose, should be so modeled, as that such a Desired end may be the soonest obtained——We therefore instruct you that in the early part of Convention you make use of your Abilities and Influence, that the General Court of this State, be addressed and petitioned to impower this said Convention, when they shall have Draughted the Form of a Constitution to adjourn themselves to a Certain time in which the several Towns and Districts shall have Oppertunity of perusal and aprobation or Disaprobation of Said Form, and that the Several Towns etc. be requested to make Amendments where they shall judge proper, and send the said Form with said Amendments, if any such there be with Aprobation or Disaprobation as the Case shall be to the Said Adjourned Convention, and then the whole Convention being possesed of the minds of the People at Large Relative to such a Form as may be Acceptable to the People, as such will the more readily Adopt such a system as shall be Agreable to their Constituents, and that the Convention be impowered to Adjourn themselves from time to time untill such a Constitution be finished and finally Accepted, Trusting that while the Convention Considers the Exigencies of the state and the importance of the Considerations before them, that nothing Unecesary will Retard their Business, or Protract their sesions to improper Periods of time——you will have a Due regard to the Aforementioned Considerations, and Let the following particulars have that weight in your minds, as the sense of your Constituents ought Always to have,——you will Endeavour in the forming of the Constitution that the free Exercise of religious Principles, or Profesion worship and Liberty of Conscience shall be for ever Secured to all Denominations of Protestants—and Protestant Disenters of all Denominations within this State, without any Compulsion whatever. Always Allowing the Legislative Body of this State the Power of Toleration to other Denominations of Christians from time to time as they Shall see Cause, at the same time, Reserving to our Selves, the Right of Instructions to our Representatives Respecting Said Toleration as well as in other Cases——there ought to be Annualy held and Convened A General Court of Said State, on the Last Thursday of May, and on the Second Thursday of October, and at other times as that Honorable Body shall Direct and Judge Necesary, Consisting of a Senate or Council, and house of Representatives——For the Dignity and Benefit of the State there ought to be a Governor and Lieutenant Governor annualy Elected, the Governor should have a Seat and Voice in the Senate, the Lieutenant Governor shall have a seat in the Senate but not a Voice, only when he shall preside in the Chair, and as Equality in Honorary Titles in the Several States seems to be somewhat Necesary and some stile of Distinction very proper to the office, the State and Title of the Governor shall be that of his Exelency, and that of the Lieutenant Governor His Honour——

In point of Qualification for any person to be Elected Governor Lieutenant Governor Senator or a Representative we Suppose that it be Sufficient, that he be possessed of a Freehold Estate, in the State Town or District, for which he shall be Elected, and that he be an inhabitant of the same, a Convenient time, not Less than one year before his Election to Office, the Judges of the Superiour Court Secretary Treasurer General Commisary General Setled Ministers while in Office, Military Officers while in pay of this or the United States and Judges and Registers of Probate ought to be Considered as Disqualifyed from having a seat in the General Court—and the Judge of Probate ought not to hear and Determine an Appeal from his own judgment——

Each Voter for Governor Lieutenant Governor Senator and Representative ought to be under Solemn Oath for the faithful Discharge of his Trust—his Qualification to Vote for each one ought to be equal the Particulars of qualification to be Determined by the wisdom of the Convention—Priviledge and Interest ought to be Peculiarly the great Basis on which representation ought to be founded, as one great Business of representation, and which makes it the most necessary is the Preventing the several Bodies Corporate of which the great whole is formed, from Encroaching on the Priveledges and Interests of each other, therefore it is necessary, that each Body Corporate within this State, shall be authorised to send one representative to the General Court Excepting the Town of Boston, which shall be authorised to send Two, and the Charge of Said Representation shall be borne at Large and paid out of the Tresury of said State, and since Numbers are not to be wholly Excluded, but in some Degree brought into Consideration in Representation, in addition to the above Number set to the several Bodies Corporate, each town may send Double that number if they see Cause, provided that the Number Added be paid out of the Treasury of the several Bodies Corporate—The several Bodies Corporate or Towns within this State ought to be Convened within their Several Towns in the Months of April and September annually for the purpose of Choosing a Representative or Representatives to serve them in General Court in this State.

The Number of Senators ought to be Twenty and that said Senators be Divided into Districts and the Largeness of Each District and the Proportion of said Number proper to each District to be Determined as the Convention shall think best——

The Senators ought to be annualy Chosen by the People and in such manner as the wisdom of the Convention shall Direct——

That on the Day in the month of April in which the Towns shall be assembled for the Choice of a representative or Representatives the Voters shall give in their Votes for a Governor Lieutenant Governor and Senators and Said Votes to be transmited as Convention Shall Direct——

The General Court ought to be the Supreme Legislative Authority of this State and shall have full Power to Constitute and Erect judicatories and Courts of record and other Courts and make and pass from time to time all good and wholsome Laws for said State and to do all such acts and things proper for such a body for the well Ordering Said State——

The Senate and house of representatives are to be Considered as two Distinct Bodies each to Apoint its own Oficers and to Setle their own rules of proceeding and all bills shall originate from the representatives in General Court and be Concured or nonconcured by the Senate

The Governor and in his Absence the Lieutenant Governor shall be President of the Senate and be posesed of such powers as the Convention in their wisdom shall think Proper, saving always the rights of the People, saving also the power of Negativing the Senate——

All Officers who are Annualy Chosen and have Salaries annualy paid them and all General Officers Should be Chosen by Joint Ballot of both houses of the General Court——

All other Civil and field Officers should be Nominated by the representatives of the County in which they are to be Chosen and then approved of by the house of Representatives and to be Concured with by the Governor and Senate——

And all General and other Officers of the Troops in the pay of this State Should be Apointed by Joint Ballot of both houses——All Staff officers to be nominated by the representatives of the County in which they are to be appointed and aproved of by the house of representatives and Concured to by Governor and Senate——

The Power of granting Pardons ought to be Vested in the Governor and Senate and in the Absence of the Governor in the Lieutenant Governor and Senate and in the absence of the Governor and Lieutenant Governor, in the Senate, Justics of the Superiour Court the Justices of the Inferiour of Comon Pleas Judges of Probate of Wills Judges of the Maritime Courts Justices of the Peace the Secretary Treasurer General Commisary General Attorney General Sheriffs Registers of the Court of Probates Coroners Notaries Public and Naval Officers ought to be Annualy Appointed.——The Delegates of Congress as the People are so nearly Concerned in their results and their Staitions so important they ought to be Elected by the People in the same maner as the Governor and Lieutenant Governor are or shall be appointed which ought to be at Large in the State and a Certain given Number that shall have the greatest Number of Votes Shall be Delegates in the Congress—all Writs and Indictments ought to be signed by a Senator or Justice of the peace, the Writs and or indictments signed by a Senator, ought to Extend through any County in this State, although he liveth not in said County or District, and shall bear the Seal of the State—and all Writs and Indictments Signed by a Justice of the Peace Shall Extend through the County in which such Justice Dwells and shall bear the seal of the Court in Said County, and such Writs of Indictments ought not to bear Test, the Chief or Senior Justice or first Justice in said Court, as in this Line of proceeding, there will be great Expence Saved by the people—no person unless he be of the Protestant religion ought to have a Seat in the Congress of the United States of America or possess any Legislative or Judiciary Trust within this State——The Inestimable right of trial by juries shall be Inviolably maintained by a Constitution to be framed and secured to the Latest generations,—in this State—The Laws which have been Enacted in this state ought to be revised by a Committee Apointed for that purpose, and such as are found to have a Tendency to Abridge the Liberties of the People, especially all such as were made in Connection with Great Britain—and found to be Incompatible with this State in its present being and Connexions Should be repealed or Altered so as to establish the rights of the People in their present Independant State in a Consistent maner——

That by rights of Constitution Originating from the Convienence and profit of the People there ought to be a Register of Deeds in every Town in this State——and for the same reasons there ought to be a Judge of Probate in at Least every Four Towns in Said State—as there will hence arise Less Cost to those who are Concerned therin and the Validity of their Inheritance or Titles more easily known——

The Power of the Peoples money ought to be as much as may be in the Power or Controul of the People—Therefore all monies ought to be Isued out of the Tresury and Disposed of Agreable to the Acts and Resolves of the General Court by a Warrant from a Committee of pay Table Annualy Appointed for that purpose by Joint Ballot of both houses of the General Court——The Rights of the People forming the Militia of this State to Choose their several Captains of the Militia and Subalterns and other Inferiour Officers thereof, ought to be Considered as part of the Constitutional rights of the People, and ought to be Considered and Confirmed as such in the Constitution to be framed.

Stoughton (160/266–277)

The Committee appointed by the town to prepare Instructions to Give thire Delagate elected for the Sole purpose of assisting in framing a

Constitution of Goverment for the State;—exhibit and Report the following Draught——

To the Reverend Mr. Jedidiah Adams

Sir.

The town of Stoughton having by a Unanimous choice Delegated you to Sitt in a State Convention to be held at Cambridg on the first Day of September next for the Sole Purpose of Fraiming a Constitution of Goverment for the State of Massachusetts bay. And you having by free Consent be Come the Servant of the people by accepting said Delegation—Therefore the town think proper to Exercise their Right of instructing you on this Subject.——

As the Great End and design of all goverment ought to be the Safety and Happiness of the people or for the Security and Protection of the Community as Such and to enable individuals Equally to Enjoy all the Blessings and benfits resulting there from;——

you are therefore instructed to make this Fundamental Principle the Grand Object of your Studies and the Ultimate end of your Exertion, thus far in general but to be more perticular——

You are directed to use and employ your most assiduous Endeavours as Soon as the Convention Meets that a Bill of Rights be in the first place compiled, wherin the inherent and unaleinable Rights of Conscience and all those aleinable rights ar not necessary to be given up in to the hands of goverment together with the equivalent individuals ought undoubtedly to Recive from Goverment for their relinquishing a part of their natural and alienable rights for the nesessary Support of the Same; shall be clearly, fully and unequivocally ascertained defined and explained, the following Mode or plan for Collecting the wisdom of the State in framing the Constitution, appearing to your Constituents the most Eligible; You are to endeavour that the Same be adopted by the Convention, viz.

Let the whole Convention be divided into as many parts as there are Counties; and Let the Delegats of Each county Choose a Commitee to frame a Constitution; and when framed let them meet in County convention with in the limits of each County at time and place agreed on to Consider alter or amend their respective forms and when so done as to be approved by a majority Let them be published for the considerations of the people Then let the Smallest County choose one Commitee Man from a mong their own number of Delegates, to Carry in their form of Goverment to be Compared with the Rest;—and let each County that have not Double the number of inhabitants do Likwise;——those that have double to Choose two, and so on in the Same proportion with all;——

Let a sufficient lenght of time be allowed to Effect the Purposes afore Said——then let the Commitee Choosen to carry in and Compair their Draughts together meet in one grand Commitee at time and place agreed on and then let them proceed to frame out of the above Meterials the best Constitution of Goverment in the world.——

As Soon as the Grand Commitee have Compleated this task let all the delegates in the State Reassemble in one Convention to Consider alter or amend or otherwise approve of the Same;

Then transmitt it to the town agreeable to a Resolve of the General Court for their approbation in whole or in part, and that returns be made to the Convention for examination and ratification if the towns Direct the Same For it is apparent to your Constituents that the mode recommended by the General Court for the Establishment of the Constitution will institue a president dangerous to the liberties of the people.——

As you must be fully Satisfyed that a republican form of goverment is the most agreeable to the genius of the people; therefore you are Directed Carefully to investigate the true principles of such a form

And where as their are various opinions in the world respecting these principles, it must be agreeable to you to know the Sentiments of your Constituents on these important points, therefore they will attempt to enumerate and adjust some of them and Leave the rest to the exercise of your Superiour Talants

1t. That man in a State of Nature, unconected with society Cannot justly be Contrould by any Earthly power what ever but when united to Society he is under the Controul of the Supreame power there of in a Certain limited degree——

2d. That the Design of man in entering into society and Submitting him self to Controul of the Supreme Power of the State is to obtain greater benefitts and advantages than he Could possiblely enjoy by being out of it that is he expects, lays claim and is justly entitled to the Protection and Security of his person and property together with the enjoyment of all those natural Rights whether alieanble or unalienable that he has not explicitly given up to the Controul of the Supreme power in the Social Contract

3d. That in the Social Contract every individual is bound with each other to the Supreme Power to Submit to its Controul where the good

of the whole Requirest it; and also to contribute his full and equal propotion of power according to his best abilities for the Support and Defenc of that Power——And the Supreame power is Likewise bound to every individual that is a Good Subject and peacefull Member of Society to protect his Person Secure his property and defend his in Defeasable Rights and liberties against the violence and oppression of the wicked
4th. That the Supreme Power of the State is Composed of the power of individuals united together and Exercised by the Consent of the Majority of the Members of the State for the good of the Whole.
5th. That the Supreme power is limited and can not Controul the unalienable Rights of mankind; or those that are alienable, if not expressly Given up the Social Contract, nor resume the equivalent that is the Security of the person and property which each individual Receives as a Consideration for those alienable Rights he parted with in entering into political society;——
6th. That the Supreme power Should be so ajusted and ballanced as to exert the greatest possible energy wisdom and goodness;——
7th That the Supreme power is divisible into Several Deparments, viz the legislative judicial and executive; and that the powers particular to each may and ought to be delegated to certain Distinct and Seperate Bodies of men in such manner that the powers beloging to all or either two of the branches may not be exercised by any one of them.——
8th. That the Majority of the people wherein the Supreme power is vested has a Controul over all the delegated Powers of the State; or other words, that all persons entrusted with any of the Delegated powers of the State are Servants of the people and as Such are elective by them and accountable to them and removeable for breach of Trust incapacity or misbehavior——
9th. That all the Delegated Powers of the State are to be Considered as so many Streams issuing out or flowing from the grand fountain of Supreme power and that the people ought with care, jealousey and circumspection to prevent these Streams from flowing too copious and rapid least in time the grand fountain be exhausted and their Liberties Deluged in a flood of Tyranny; or other wise that every Degree or portion of power is or ought to be instituted and delegated by the people to promote their Safty and happyness; and that no grater degree or portion of power, ought to be given to any man or Body of men in any Deparment than what is absolutely necessary to promote and Secure there Safty and happyness;——

10th. That the legislative department ought to be restricted and confind wholly to the Business and duty of making just and equal laws agreeable to the Constitution and in passing just and equal Taxes to be appropriated by them for the good of the whole, and that the Subjects of Legislation and taxation are person and property and that where Polittical and republican Liberty fully Subsists no law can be enacted or tax imposed that shall be binding on any person whether property holder or not with out his consent;—therefore the Consequence is this; that in order that political Liberty should fully Subsist, and the freeman give his consent to the Making a Law or the imposing a tax;——every free man and all the property in the State Should be Equally Represented as nearly as the nature of the thing will admitt and that the Legeslature Should Consist of two Branches the one to Represent persons the other the property of the State

These, Sir. appear to your Constituents to be Some of the essential leading principles of a free Goverment and you are directed to Endeavour that no article in the Constitution be repugnant to them;—but the general use and improvment that ought to be made of the foregoing and the other Principles of a free Goverment not here mentioned your Constituents refer to your wisdom and Discretion. yet not with standing there are Some Rights and Priviledges that the Towns as Such are justly intitled to which they are not allowed to enjoy under the old Constitution and your are instructed to do your best Endeavours to have them inserted in the Proposed new Constitution (viz) That Courts of equity be established in each Town for trial of civil causes to prevent the unecessary expences attending the usual Course and process of Common Law in County Courts also that the probate businss and Recording of Deeds be done in Each town. Likwise that each Town Choose their own Magistrates and other officers Requisite to effect the purposes affore said and that the Statute and Common Laws of England as they have usually been practiced in the Court of Law be excluded from any part of the Constitution;——

And you are further enjoind to Spare no pain to have the following articles inserted in the Constitution in order that the freedom of the State may be preserved in violate for Ever and that the Majority of the People wherein the supreme power exist may retain their inherent controul over the Legislative judicial and executive Powers of the State (viz). That their shall be Chosen by ballet, and every freeman to be a voter one person in the Smallest County two Persons in each County that have Double the number of inhabitants to the Smallest and so on in the same proportion, to sitt in State Congress to be Stiled the Council of Censors and Controul;—who Shall meet together for the first time in three years after the establishment of the Constitution and that said Council be Chosen and Set once in three years for ever after the majority of whom shall be a quorum in every case ecept as to Caling a Convention, in which two thirds of the whole Number elected Shall agree and all Persons belonging to the legislative, judicial or executive departments to be disqualifyed for sitting in Said Council,—And the Duty and business of Said Council shall be, in the behalf of the people to enquire whether the Constitution has been preserved inviolate, and whether the legislative juditical and executive branches of Goverment have performed their duty as guardians of the people or rasumed to themselves or exercised other or greater powers than they are intitled to by the Constitution they are also to Enquire whether the publick taxes have been justly Laid and collected in all parts of the State in what Manner the publick monies have been Disposed of and whether the Laws have been Duely executed; for these purposes they Shall have power to Send for Persons papers and records they Shall have authority to pass publick Censures to order impeachments and negative Laws enacted contrary to the principles of the Constitution: these powers they Shall Continue to have for and during the Space of one year from the Day of their election and no Longer——

The Said Council of Censors and Controul Shall also have power to Call a Convention, to meet with in two years after their Sitting if their appear to them an absolute necessity of amending any article of the Constitution which may be Defective Explaining Such as may be though not clearly Expressed or ading Such as are necessary for the Preservation of the Rights and happiness of the people but the article to be amended and the amendments proposed and such Articles as are proposed to be added or abolished Shall be promulgated at Least Six months before the Day appointed for the Election of Such Convention for the previous Consideration of the people That they may have an oppertunity of in Structing their Delegats on the Subject,——

George Crossman Town Clerk

a True Copy from Stoughton Record
Attest George Crossman Town Clerk

Dudley (160/283)

Dudley August 18: 1779

at a meeting of the freeholders and other Inhabitants of the Town of Dudley Regular Assembled for the purpose of Choosing a Delegate for the Convention to be held at Cambridge on the first of September next in order to form a Constitution. and at Said meeting made Choice of Mr. Joseph Upham Delegate for Said Convention and we the Subscribers being Choosed as a Commitee to Draw a draught of Instructions for Said Delegate beg leave to Report as follows viz.

Sir.

that you use your Endeavour that a Bill of Rights be first formed and in General with others that you will Endeavour to form such a Constitution as will not only Secure to us our Liberties and Priviledges but will be the Security of the Rights Liberties and Privilidges of the Succeeding Generations down to the Latest Posterity and among the many Articles that may be in the plan we Earnestly Request that a few which we hint at may be in the plan

1 Govenour and Lieutenant Govenour and Senate be Choosen by the people anually the Govenour to have a Casting vote in the Sennate

2) that Every Town have a Right to Choose their Justice of the Peace annually

3) that no Sallery men nor none of the Executive Authority Shall have a Seat in the Assembly

4) that Each County have a right to Choose high Sheriff and Judges of probates

5) that our Deeds be Recorded by the Town Clark

Jacob Warner
Joseph Sabin Comnitee
Jonathan Day

Dudley August the 24th 1779 the within written Instructions was brought before the Town and accepted

Attest

Edward Davis Town Clerk

Swansey (160/286)

To the Honorable Gentlemens of the Convention Convened and held at Cambridge on the first Day of September Next This is to Certify that at a meeting of the Freemen of the Town of Swanzey Legally Warned and Assembled at the Meeting House in said Town on Monday the 30th Day of August A.D 1779 the Town Voted and made Choice of Captain Philip Slead and Mr. John Masons Delegates to Represent them at Said Conventions for the Sole purpose of Fraiming a New Constitution——

Tis with Regret we have Occation to Observe to your Honors that we had the Resolves of Court for that purpose in Season and that by some Accident they was mislaid Lost or otherwise taken by some Disaffected person and Concealed from us which was the sole reason we were so late in Warning our Meeting for the above purpose which time Limitted for calling Said Meeting Escaped our Memmory which we hope will be a Sufficient apology and not Debarr us from the priviledge of Freemen in an Affair of so great Importance——

From your Most Obedient Humble Servants

Andrew Cole
Seth Wood — Selectmen
David Peirce — of Swanzey

Gorham (160/288)

as God hath made of one blood all the Nations That dwell on the Earth all men that come into the world are in a state of Equality no one higher or lower but all upon a par, this gives Rome [room?] and stimulates the benevolent social passions of the soul to exercise and inclines individuals to form into civil societies as the savest way, to their protection and mutual happiness, and as Civil Society, without Rulers is like a body without a head, it is necessary that there be a first magistrate vested with so much power and no more as is necessary for the Due execution of the Laws and the Protection and good of the people under his charge, which is the sole end of his Choice. The Legislative Body to Consist of a President and representatives of the People without Governour and without Council as not only unnessessary but inconvenient, and perhaps dangerous, there are so many objection against both that might be offered, that it is hoped they will never exist in this state, one Assembly as a Legislator is thought to be much the best to dispatch publick business and the affairs of State the Jewish Synedrem approved by heaven was an Excellent Institution of Goverment and the Jews happy under that Goverment while wise and good men constituted the same the Roman Senate was a happy Constitution of goverment and the Romans a happy People while the Patricians considered their interest the same with that of the Plebiens but when the Patriciens made their interest distinct from the Plebiens confusion and misery insued

The President in his Legislative capacity to be speaker of the House and to have voice with the Rest, considered as Primus inter pares—In his Executive Capacity to sign all Commissions of Persons chosen into office, and in the recess of the House of Representatives, To conduct the weighty affairs of the Goverment, with the aid and assistance of a privy Council of five or seven of the best men of the State To command the Militia

The Assembly of Representatives to chuse the Generals of the Army Brigadiers etc. and also the superiour Judges etc.

The several counties in the State to chuse their field officer viz colonals, majors etc. and the Justices of the Court, Justices of the Peace, Coroners etc.

Every Town to chuse their Captains Lieutenants and Ensigns

That no qualification be required of any officer or Ruler but merit viz a sufficient knowledge and understanding in matters relative to the office, and fidelity and firmness in the cause of Liberty. Pecuniary Qalifications can never give a good understanding or good Heart

That no Restriction be laide on any Profession of Christianity or denomination of Christians, but all Equally intiteled to protection of the Laws

The sense of Gorham relative to to a mode of goverment the more simple, the less Danger of the loss of Liberty and most tending to happiness with the least expence

Humbly addressed to the Honorable Committy on the mode of goverment.

Western (160/289)

Western August 30th 1779——

To the Convention to be held at Cambridge the first Day of September next in order to form a Constitution

This may Certify that the inhabitants of said Town of Western have this 30th of August as above written have ben Legally assembled in order to Choose a Member to join the said Convention at Cambridge accordingly made Choice of Colo. Danforth Keyes to Attend on said Buisiness as soon as may be

N. B that we have not Received a precept for to Choose a member for said Convention and hearing of the preecept, miscarrying have Proceeded as above

Attested to by Deuty Partridge Moderator of said Meeting——

32

Proceedings of the Convention, March 2, 1780

The constitutional convention convened on September 1, 1779 and labored for seven months before it completed a draft for submittal to the towns. On March 2, 1780 the constitution was sent to the towns which were to report their opinions to the convention by June 7, 1780. The reconvened convention would then make any changes that two-thirds of the constituents favored. The proceedings for March 2, 1780 are reprinted from *Journal of the Convention*, 168–169.

Resolved, That this Convention be adjourned to the first Wednesday in June next, to meet at Boston; and that eighteen hundred copies of the Form of Government, which shall be agreed upon, be printed; and including such as shall be ordered to each Member of the Convention, be sent to the Selectmen of each Town, and the Committees of each Plantation, under the direction of a Committee to be appointed for the purpose: And that they be requested, as soon as may be, to lay them before the Inhabitants of their respective Towns and Plantations. And if the major part of the Inhabitants of the said Towns and Plantations disapprove of any particular part of the same, that they be desired to state their objections distinctly, and the reasons therefor: And the Selectmen and Committees aforesaid are desired to transmit the same to the Secretary of the Convention, on the first Wednesday in June, or if may be, on the last Wednesday in May, in order to his laying the same before a Committee, to be appointed for the purpose of examining and arranging them for the revision and consideration of the Convention at the adjournment; with the number of voters in the said town and plantation meetings, on each side of every question; in order that the said Convention, at the adjournment, may collect the general sense of their constituents on the several parts of the proposed Constitution: And if there doth not appear to be two thirds of their constituents in favour thereof, that the Convention may alter it in such a manner as that it may be agreeable to the sentiments of two thirds of the voters throughout the State.

Resolved, That it be recommended to the Inhabitants of the several towns and plantations in this State, to empower their Delegates, at the next Session of this Convention, to agree upon a time when this Form of

Government shall take place, without returning the same again to the people: *Provided,* That two thirds of the male Inhabitants of the age of twenty one years and upwards, voting in the several town and plantation meetings, shall agree to the same, or the Convention shall conform it to the sentiments of two thirds of the People as aforesaid.

Resolved, That the Towns and Plantations through this State have a right to choose other Delegates, instead of the present members, to meet in Convention on the first Wednesday in June next, if they see fit.

A true Copy, Attest.

SAMUEL BARRETT, *Secretary.*

33

Address of the Convention, March 1780

In presenting the Constitution for ratification the convention explained the proposed plan. It expressed the hope that individuals would yield "particular and even favorite Opinions of smaller moment, to essential Principles." The address is reprinted from *Journal of the Convention,* 216–221.

AN ADDRESS OF THE CONVENTION, for Framing a New Constitution of Government, *for the STATE OF MASSACHUSETTS-BAY, to their CONSTITUENTS.*

FRIENDS AND COUNTRYMEN,—

HAVING had your Appointment and Instruction, we have undertaken the arduous Task of preparing a civil Constitution for the People of the Massachusetts-Bay; and we now submit it to your candid Consideration. It is your *Interest* to revise it with the greatest Care and Circumspection, and it is your undoubted *Right,* either to propose such Alterations and Amendments as you shall judge proper, or, to give it your own Sanction in its present Form, or, totally to reject it.

IN framing a Constitution, to be adapted as far as possible to the Circumstances of Posterity yet unborn, you will conceive it to be exceedingly difficult, if not impracticable, to succeed in every part of it, to the full Satisfaction of all. Could the *whole Body* of the People have Convened for the same Purpose, there might have been equal Reason to conclude, that a perfect Unanimity of Sentiments would have been an Object not to be obtained. In a Business so universally interesting, we have endeavored to act as became the Representatives of a wise, understanding and free People; and, as we have Reason to believe you would *yourselves* have done, we have opened our Sentiments to each other with Candor, and made such mutual Concessions as we could consistently, and without marring the only Plan, which in our most mature Judgment we can at present offer to you.

THE Interest of the Society is common to all its Members. The great Enquiry is, wherein this Common Interest consists. In determining this

Question, an Advantage may arise from a Variety of Sentiments offered to public Examination concerning it. But wise Men are not apt to be obstinately tenacious of their own Opinions: They will always pay a due Regard to those of other Men and keep their minds open to Conviction. We conceive, that in the present instance, by accommodating ourselves to each other, and individually yielding particular and even favorite Opinions of smaller moment, to essential Principles, and Considerations of general Utility, the public Opinion of the Plan now before you may be consolidated.—But without such mutual Condescension in unimportant Matters, we may almost venture to predict, that we shall not soon, if ever, be blessed with such a Constitution as those are intitled to, who have struggled hard for Freedom and Independence. You will permit us on this Occasion, just to hint to you our own Apprehension, that there may be amongst us, some Persons disaffected to that great Cause for which we are contending, who may be secretly instructed by our common Enemy to divide and distract us; in hopes of preventing our Union in any Form of Government whatever, and by this Means of depriving us of the most honorable Testimony, as well as the greatest Security of our Freedom and Independence.—If there be such Men, it is our Wisdom to mark them, and guard ourselves against their Designs.

We may not expect to agree in a perfect System of Government: This is not the Lot of Mankind. The great End of Government, is, to promote the Supreme Good of human Society: Every social affection should therefore be interested in the Forming of a Government and in judging of one when it is Formed. Would it not be prudent for Individuals to cast out of the Scale smaller considerations, and fall in with an evident Majority, unless in Matters in which their Consciences shall constrain them to determine otherwise? Such a Sacrifice, made for the sake of Union, would afford a strong Evidence of public Affection; and Union strengthened by the social Feeling, would promise a greater Stability to any Constitution, and, in its operation, a greater Degree of Happiness to the Society. It is here to be remembered, that on the Expiration of Fifteen Years a new Convention may be held, in order that such Amendments may be made in the plan you may now agree to, as Experience, that best Instructor, shall then point out to be expedient or necessary.

A government without Power to exert itself, is at best, but an useless Piece of Machinery. It is probable, that for the want of Energy, it would speedily lose even the Appearance of Government, and sink into Anarchy. Unless a due Proportion of Weight is given to each of the Powers of Government, there will soon be a Confusion of the whole. An Overbearing of any one of its Parts on the rest, would destroy the Balance and accelerate its Dissolution and Ruin: And, a Power without *any* Restraint is Tyranny. The Powers of Government must then be balanced: To do this accurately requires the highest Skill in political Architecture. Those who are to be invested with the Administration, should have such Powers given to them, as are requisite to render them useful in their respective Places; and such *checks* should be added to every Branch of Power as may be sufficient to prevent its becoming formidable and injurious to the Commonwealth. If we have been so fortunate as to succeed in this point of the greatest Importance, our Happiness will be complete, in the Prospect of having laid a good Foundation for many Generations. *You* are the judges how far we have succeeded; and whether we have raised our Superstructure, agreeably to our professed Design, upon the Principles of a *Free Commonwealth.*

In order to assist your Judgments, we have thought it necessary, briefly to explain to you the Grounds and Reasons upon which we have formed our Plan. In the third article of the Declaration of Rights, we have, with as much Precision as we were capable of, provided for the free exercise of the *Rights of Conscience:* We are very sensible that our Constituents hold those Rights infinitely more valuable than all others; and we flatter ourselves, that while we have considered Morality and the Public Worship of GOD, as important to the happiness of Society, we have sufficiently guarded the rights of Conscience from every possible infringement. This Article underwent long debates, and took Time in proportion to its importance; and we feel ourselves peculiarly happy in being able to inform you, that though the debates were managed by persons of various denominations, it was finally agreed upon with much more Unanimity than usually takes place in disquisitions of this Nature. We wish you to consider the Subject with Candor, and Attention. Surely it would be an affront to the People of Massachusetts-Bay to labour to convince them, that the Honor and Happiness of a People depend upon Morality; and that the Public Worship of GOD has a tendency to inculcate the Principles thereof, as well as to preserve a People from forsaking Civilization, and falling into a state of Savage barbarity.

In the form now presented to you, there are no more Departments of Government than are absolutely necessary for the free and full Exercise of the Powers thereof. The House of Representatives is intended as the Representative of the Persons, and the Senate of the property of the Commonwealth. These are to be annually chosen and to sit in separate Bodies, each having a Negative upon the Acts of [the] other. This Power of a Negative in each must ever be necessary; for all Bodies of Men, assembled upon the same occasion and united by one common Interest of Rank, Honor, or Estate, are liable, like an individual, to mistake, bias and prejudice. These two Houses are vested with the Powers of Legislation, and are to be chosen by the Male Inhabitants who are Twenty one Years of age, and have a Freehold of the small annual Income of Three Pounds, or Sixty Pounds in any Estate. Your Delegates considered that Persons who are Twenty one Years of age, and have no Property, are either those who live upon a part of a Paternal estate, expecting the Fee thereof, who are but just entering into business, or those whose Idleness of Life and profligacy of manners will forever bar them from acquiring and possessing Property. And we will submit it to the former class, whether they would not think it safer for them to have their right of Voting for a Representative suspended for [a] small space of Time, than forever hereafter to have their Privileges liable to the control of Men, who will pay less regard to the Rights of Property because they have nothing to lose.

The Power of Revising, and stating objections to any Bill or Resolve that shall be passed by the two Houses, we were of opinion ought to be lodged in the hands of some *one* person; not only to preserve the Laws from being unsystematical and inaccurate, but that a due balance may be preserved in the three capital powers of Government. The Legislative, the Judicial and Executive Powers naturally exist in every Government: And the History of the rise and fall of the Empires of the World affords us ample proof, that when the same Man or Body of Men enact, interpret and execute the Laws, property becomes too precarious to be valuable, and a People are finally borne down with the force of corruption resulting from the Union of those Powers. The Governor is emphatically the Representative of the whole People, being chosen not by one Town or County, but by the People at large. We have therefore thought it safest to rest this Power in his hands; and as the Safety of the Commonwealth requires, that there should be one Commander in Chief over the Militia, we have given the Governor that Command for the same reason, that we thought him the only proper Person that could be trusted with the power of revising the Bills and Resolves of the General Assembly; but the People may if they please choose their own Officers.

You will observe that we have resolved, that Representation ought to be founded on the Principle of equality; but it cannot be understood thereby that each Town in the Commonwealth shall have Weight and importance in a just proportion to its Numbers and property. An exact Representation would be unpracticable even in a System of Government arising from the State of Nature, and much more so in a state already divided into nearly three hundred Corporations. But we have agreed that each Town having One hundred and fifty Rateable Polls shall be entitled to send one Member, and to prevent an advantage arising to the greater towns by their numbers, have agreed that no Town shall send two unless it hath three hundred and seventy-five Rateable Polls, and then the still larger Towns are to send one Member for every two hundred and twenty-five Rateable Polls over and above Three hundred and seventy-five. This method of calculation will give a more exact Representation, when applied to all the Towns in the State, than any that we could fix upon.

We have however digressed from this rule in admitting the small Towns now incorporated to send Members. There are but a few of them which will not, from their continual increase, be able to send one upon the above plan in a very little Time. And the few who will never probably have that number have been heretofore in the exercise of this privilege, and will now be very unwilling to relinquish it.

To prevent the governor from abusing the Power which is necessary to be put into his hands, we have provided that he shall have a Council to advise him at all Times and upon all important Occasions, and he with the advice of his Council is to have the Appointment of Civil Officers. This was very readily agreed to by your Delegates, and will undoubtedly be agreeable to their Constituents; for if those Officers who are to interpret and execute the Laws are to be dependent upon the Election of the people, it must forever keep them under the Control of ambitious, artful and interested men, who can obtain most Votes for them.—If they were to be Appointed by the Two Houses or either of them, the persons appointing them would be too numerous to be accountable for putting weak or wicked Men into Office. Besides the House is designed as the Grand Inquest of the Commonwealth, and are to impeach Officers for malconduct; the Senate are to try the Merits of such impeachments; it would be therefore unfit that they should have the Creation of those Officers which the one may impeach and the other remove: but we conceive there is the greatest propriety in Vesting the Governor with this Power, he being, as we have before observed, the complete representative of all the People, and at all Times liable to be impeached by the House before the Senate for maladministration. And we would here observe that all the Powers which we have given the Governor are necessary to be lodged in the hands of one Man, as the General of the Army and first Magistrate, and none can be entitled to it but he who has the Annual and United Suffrages of the whole Commonwealth.

You will readily conceive it to be necessary for your own Safety, that your Judges should hold their Offices during good behaviour; for Men who hold their places upon so precarious a Tenure as annual or other frequent Appointments will never so assiduously apply themselves to study as will be necessary to the filling their places with dignity. Judges should at all Times feel themselves independent and free.

Your Delegates have further provided that the Supreme Judicial Department, by fixed and ample Salaries, may be enabled to devote themselves wholly to the Duties of their important Office. And for this reason, as well as to keep this Department separate from the others in Government, have excluded them from a Seat in the Legislature; and when our Constituents consider that the final Decision of their Lives and Property must be had in this Court, we conceive they will universally approve the measure. The Judges of Probate, and those other officers whose presence is always necessary in their respective Counties, are also excluded.

We have attended to the inconveniencies suggested to have arisen from having but one Judge of Probate in each County; but the erecting and altering Courts of Justice being a mere matter of Legislation, we have left it with your future Legislature to make such Alterations as the Circumstances of the several Counties may require.

Your Delegates did not conceive themselves to be vested with Power to set up one Denomination of Christians above another; for Religion must at all Times be a matter between God and individuals: But we have nevertheless, found ourselves obliged by a Solemn Test, to provide for the exclusion of those from Offices who will not disclaim those Principles of Spiritual Jurisdiction which Roman Catholicks *in some Countries* have held, and which are subversive of a free Government established by the People. We find it necessary to continue the former Laws, and Modes of proceeding in Courts of Justice, until a future Legislature shall alter them: For, unless this is done, the title to Estates will become precarious, Law-suits will be multiplied, and universal Confusion must take place. And least the Commonwealth, for want of a due Administration of Civil Justice, should be involved in Anarchy, we have proposed to continue the present Magistrates and Officers until new Appointments shall take place.

Thus we have, with plainness and sincerity, given you the Reasons upon which we founded the principal parts of the System laid before you, which appeared to us as most necessary to be explained: And we do most humbly beseech the Great Disposer of all Events, that we and our Posterity may be established in, and long enjoy the Blessings of a well-ordered and free Government.

In the Name, and pursuant to a Resolution of the Convention,

JAMES BOWDOIN, *President.*

Attest.

SAMUEL BARRETT, *Secretary.*

34

The Constitution of 1780

The Constitution of 1780 was a product not only of seven months of work by the convention, but also of years of agitation of the issues, of commonly held assumptions about the polity, of colonial precedent, and of immediate problems in the use of power. The Constitution is reprinted from *Journal of the Convention,* 222–249.

A CONSTITUTION OR FRAME OF GOVERNMENT, Agreed upon by the Delegates of the People of the STATE OF MASSACHUSETTS-BAY,—In Convention,—*Begun and held at* Cambridge, *on the First of* September, *1779, and continued by Adjournments to the Second of* March, *1780.*

PREAMBLE.

THE end of the institution, maintenance and administration of government, is to secure the existence of the body-politic; to protect it; and to furnish the individuals who compose it, with the power of enjoying, in safety and tranquillity, their natural rights, and the blessings of life: And whenever these great objects are not obtained, the people have a right to alter the government, and to take measures necessary for their safety, prosperity and happiness.

THE body-politic is formed by a voluntary association of individuals: It is a social compact, by which the whole people covenants with each citizen, and each citizen with the whole people, that all shall be governed by certain laws for the common good. It is the duty of the people, therefore, in framing a Constitution of Government, to provide for an equitable mode of making laws, as well as for an impartial interpretation, and a faithful execution of them; that every man may, at all times, find his security in them.

WE, therefore, the people of Massachusetts, acknowledging, with grateful hearts, the goodness of the Great Legislator of the Universe, in affording us, in the course of His providence, an opportunity, deliberately and peaceably, without fraud, violence or surprise, of entering into an original, explicit, and solemn compact with each other; and of forming a new Constitution of Civil Government, for ourselves and posterity; and devoutly imploring His direction in so interesting a design, DO agree upon, ordain and establish, the following *Declaration of Rights, and Frame of Government,* as the CONSTITUTION of the COMMONWEALTH of MASSACHUSETTS.

PART THE FIRST.

A Declaration of the Rights of the Inhabitants of the Commonwealth of Massachusetts.

ART. I.—ALL men are born free and equal, and have certain natural, essential, and unalienable rights; among which may be reckoned the right of enjoying and defending their lives and liberties; that of acquiring, possessing, and protecting property; in fine, that of seeking and obtaining their safety and happiness.

II.—IT is the right as well as the duty of all men in society, publicly, and at stated seasons, to worship the SUPREME BEING, the great creator and preserver of the universe. And no subject shall be hurt, molested, or restrained, in his person, liberty, or estate, for worshipping GOD in the manner and season most agreeable to the dictates of his own conscience; or for his religious profession or sentiments; provided he doth not disturb the public peace, or obstruct others in their religious worship.

III.—As the happiness of a people, and the good order and preservation of civil government, essentially depend upon piety, religion and morality; and as these cannot be generally diffused through a community, but by the institution of the public worship of GOD, and of public instructions in piety, religion and morality: Therefore, to promote their happiness and to secure the good order and preservation of their government, the people of this Commonwealth have a right to invest their legislature with power to authorize and require, and the legislature shall, from time to time, authorize and require, the several towns, parishes, precincts, and other bodies-politic, or religious societies, to make suitable provision, at their own expense, for the institution of the public worship of GOD, and for the support and maintenance of public protestant teachers of piety, religion and morality, in all cases where such provision shall not be made voluntarily.

AND the people of this Commonwealth have also a right to, and do, invest their legislature with authority to enjoin upon all the subjects an attendance upon the instructions of the public teachers aforesaid, at stated times and seasons, if there be any on whose instructions they can conscientiously and conveniently attend.

PROVIDED notwithstanding, that the several towns, parishes, precincts, and other bodies-politic, or religious societies, shall, at all times, have the exclusive right of electing their public teachers, and of contracting with them for their support and maintenance.

AND all monies paid by the subject to the support of public worship, and of the public teachers aforesaid, shall, if he require it, be uniformly applied to the support of the public teacher or teachers of his own religious sect or denomination, provided there be any on whose instructions he attends: otherwise it may be paid towards the support of the teacher or teachers of the parish or precinct in which the said monies are raised.

AND every denomination of christians, demeaning themselves peaceably, and as good subjects of the Commonwealth, shall be equally under the protection of the law: And no subordination of any one sect or denomination to another shall ever be established by law.

IV.—THE people of this Commonwealth have the sole and exclusive right of governing themselves as a free, sovereign, and independent state; and do, and forever hereafter shall, exercise and enjoy every power, jurisdiction, and right, which is not, or may not hereafter, be by them expressly delegated to the United States of America, in Congress assembled.

V.—ALL power residing originally in the people, and being derived from them, the several magistrates and officers of government, vested with authority, whether legislative, executive, or judicial, are their substitutes and agents, and are at all times accountable to them.

VI.—No man, nor corporation, or association of men, have any other title to obtain advantages, or particular and exclusive privileges, distinct from those of the community, than what arises from the consideration of services rendered to the public; and this title being in nature neither hereditary, nor transmissible to children, or descendants, or relations by blood, the idea of a man born a magistrate, lawgiver, or judge, is absurd and unnatural.

VII.—Government is instituted for the common good; for the protection, safety, prosperity and happiness of the people; and not for the profit, honor, or private interest of any one man, family, or class of men: Therefore the people alone have an incontestible, unalienable, and indefeasible right to institute government; and to reform, alter, or totally change the same, when their protection, safety, prosperity and happiness require it.

VIII.—In order to prevent those, who are vested with authority, from becoming oppressors, the people have a right, at such periods and in such manner as they shall establish by their frame of government, to cause their public officers to return to private life; and to fill up vacant places by certain and regular elections and appointments.

IX.—All elections ought to be free; and all the inhabitants of this Commonwealth, having such qualifications as they shall establish by their frame of government, have an equal right to elect officers, and to be elected, for public employments.

X.—Each individual of the society has a right to be protected by it in the enjoyment of his life, liberty and property, according to standing laws. He is obliged, consequently, to contribute his share to the expense of this protection; to give his personal service, or an equivalent, when necessary: But no part of the property of any individual, can, with justice, be taken from him, or applied to public uses without his own consent, or that of the representative body of the people: In fine, the people of this Commonwealth are not controlable by any other laws, than those to which their constitutional representative body have given their consent. And whenever the public exigencies require, that the property of any individual should be appropriated to public uses, he shall receive a reasonable compensation therefor.

XI.—Every subject of the Commonwealth ought to find a certain remedy, by having recourse to the laws, for all injuries or wrongs which he may receive in his person, property, or character. He ought to obtain right and justice freely, and without being obliged to purchase it; completely, and without any denial; promptly, and without delay; conformably to the laws.

XII.—No subject shall be held to answer for any crime or offence, until the same is fully and plainly, substantially and formally, described to him; or be compelled to accuse, or furnish evidence against himself. And every subject shall have a right to produce all proofs, that may be favorable to him; to meet the witnesses against him face to face, and to be fully heard in his defence by himself, or his council, at his election. And no subject shall be arrested, imprisoned, despoiled, or deprived of his property, immunities, or privileges, put out of the protection of the law, exiled, or deprived of his life, liberty, or estate; but by the judgment of his peers, or the law of the land.

And the legislature shall not make any law, that shall subject any person to a capital or infamous punishment, excepting for the government of the army and navy, without trial by jury.

XIII.—In criminal prosecutions, the verification of facts in the vicinity where they happen, is one of the greatest securities of the life, liberty, and property of the citizen.

XIV.—Every subject has a right to be secure from all unreasonable searches, and seizures of his person, his houses, his papers, and all his possessions. All warrants, therefore, are contrary to this right, if the cause or foundation of them be not previously supported by oath or affirmation; and if the order in the warrant to a civil officer, to make search in suspected places, or to arrest one or more suspected persons, or to seize their property, be not accompanied with a special designation of the persons or objects of search, arrest, or seizure: and no warrant ought to be issued but in cases, and with the formalities, prescribed by the laws.

XV.—In all controversies concerning property, and in all suits between two or more persons, except in cases in which it has heretofore been otherways used and practised, the parties have a right to a trial by jury; and this method of procedure shall be held sacred, unless, in causes arising on the high-seas, and such as relate to mariners wages, the legislature shall hereafter find it necessary to alter it.

XVI.—The liberty of the press is essential to the security of freedom in a state: it ought not, therefore, to be restrained in this Commonwealth.

XVII.—The people have a right to keep and to bear arms for the common defence. And as in time of peace armies are dangerous to liberty, they ought not to be maintained without the consent of the legislature; and the military power shall always be held in an exact subordination to the civil authority, and be governed by it.

XVIII.—A Frequent recurrence to the fundamental principles of the constitution, and a constant adherence to those of piety, justice, moderation, temperance, industry, and frugality, are absolutely necessary to preserve the advantages of liberty, and to maintain a free government: The people ought, consequently, to have a particular attention to all those principles, in the choice of their officers and representatives: And they have a right to require of their law-givers and magistrates, an exact and constant observance of them, in the formation and execution of the laws necessary for the good administration of the Commonwealth.

XIX.—The people have a right, in an orderly and peaceable manner, to assemble to consult upon the common good; give instructions to their representatives; and to request of the legislative body, by the way of addresses, petitions, or remonstrances, redress of the wrongs done them, and of the grievances they suffer.

XX.—The power of suspending the laws, or the execution of the laws, ought never to be exercised but by the legislature, or by authority derived from it, to be exercised in such particular cases only as the legislature shall expressly provide for.

XXI.—The freedom of deliberation, speech and debate, in either house of the legislature, is so essential to the rights of the people, that it cannot be the foundation of any accusation or prosecution, action or complaint, in any other court or place whatsoever.

XXII.—The legislature ought frequently to assemble for the redress of grievances, for correcting, strengthening, and confirming the laws, and for making new laws, as the common good may require.

XXIII.—No subsidy, charge, tax, impost, or duties, ought to be established, fixed, laid, or levied, under any pretext whatsoever, without the consent of the people, or their representatives in the legislature.

XXIV.—Laws made to punish for actions done before the existence of such laws, and which have not been declared crimes by preceding laws, are unjust, oppressive, and inconsistent with the fundamental principles of a free government.

XXV.—No subject ought, in any case, or in any time, to be declared guilty of treason or felony by the legislature.

XXVI.—No magistrate or court of law shall demand excessive bail or sureties, impose excessive fines, or inflict cruel or unusual punishments.

XXVII.—In time of peace no soldier ought to be quartered in any house without the consent of the owner; and in time of war such quarters ought not to be made but by the civil magistrate, in a manner ordained by the legislature.

XXVIII.—No person can in any case be subjected to law-martial, or to any penalties or pains, by virtue of that law, except those employed in the army or navy, and except the militia in actual service, but by authority of the legislature.

XXIX.—It is essential to the preservation of the rights of every individual, his life, liberty, property and character, that there be an impartial interpretation of the laws, and administration of justice. It is the right of every citizen to be tried by judges as free, impartial and independent as the lot of humanity will admit. It is therefore not only the best policy, but for the security of the rights of the people, and of every citizen, that the judges of the supreme judicial court should hold their offices as long as they behave themselves well; and that they should have honorable salaries ascertained and established by standing laws.

XXX.—In the government of this Commonwealth, the legislative department shall never exercise the executive and judicial powers, or either of them: The executive shall never exercise the legislative and judicial powers, or either of them: The judicial shall never exercise the legislative and executive powers, or either of them: to the end it may be a government of laws and not of men.

PART THE SECOND.

The Frame of Government.

THE people, inhabiting the territory formerly called the Province of Massachusetts-Bay, do hereby solemnly and mutually agree with each other, to form themselves into a free, sovereign, and independent body-politic or state, by the name of THE COMMONWEALTH OF MASSACHUSETTS.

CHAPTER I.

The Legislative Power.

SECTION I.

The General Court.

ART. I.—THE department of legislation shall be formed by two branches, *a Senate* and *House of Representatives:* each of which shall have a negative on the other.

THE legislative body shall assemble every year, on the last Wednesday in May, and at such other times as they shall judge necessary; and shall dissolve and be dissolved on the day next preceding the said last Wednesday in May; and shall be styled, THE GENERAL COURT OF MASSACHUSETTS.

II.—No bill or resolve of the Senate or House of Representatives shall become a law, and have force as such, until it shall have been laid before the Governor for his revisal: And if he, upon such revision, approve thereof, he shall signify his approbation by signing the same. But if he have any objection to the passing of such bill or resolve, he shall return the same, together with his objections thereto, in writing, to the Senate or House of Representatives, in which soever the same shall have originated; who shall enter the objections sent down by the Governor, at large, on their records, and proceed to reconsider the said bill or resolve: But if, after such reconsideration, two thirds of the said Senate or House of Representatives, shall, notwithstanding the said objections, agree to pass the same, it shall, together with the objections, be sent to the other branch of the legislature, where it shall also be reconsidered, and if approved by two thirds of the members present, shall have the force of a law: But in all such cases the votes of both houses shall be determined by yeas and nays; and the names of the persons voting for, or against, the said bill or resolve, shall be entered upon the public records of the Commonwealth.

And in order to prevent unnecessary delays, if any bill or resolve shall not be returned by the Governor within five days after it shall have been presented, the same shall have the force of a law.

III.—The General Court shall forever have full power and authority to erect and constitute judicatories and courts of record, or other courts, to be held in the name of the Commonwealth, for the hearing, trying, and determining of all manner of crimes, offences, pleas, processes, plaints, actions, matters, causes and things, whatsoever, arising or happening within the Commonwealth, or between or concerning persons inhabiting, or residing, or brought within the same; whether the same be criminal or civil, or whether the said crimes be capital or not capital, and whether the said pleas be real, personal, or mixt; and for the awarding and making out of execution thereupon: To which courts and judicatories are hereby given and granted full power and authority, from time to time, to administer oaths or affirmations, for the better discovery of truth in any matter in controversy or depending before them.

IV.—And further, full power and authority are hereby given and granted to the said General Court, from time to time, to make, ordain, and establish, all manner of wholesome and reasonable orders, laws, statutes, and ordinances, directions and instructions, either with penalties or without; so as the same be not repugnant or contrary to this Constitution, as they shall judge to be for the good and welfare of this Commonwealth, and for the government and ordering thereof, and of the subjects of the same, and for the necessary support and defence of the government thereof; and to name and settle annually, or provide by fixed laws, for the naming and settling all civil officers within the said Commonwealth, the election and constitution of whom are not hereafter in this Form of Government otherwise provided for; and to set forth the several duties, powers and limits; of the several civil and military officers of this Commonwealth, and the forms of such oaths or affirmations as shall be respectively administered unto them for the execution of their several offices and places, so as the same be not repugnant or contrary to this Constitution; and to impose and levy proportional and reasonable assessments, rates, and taxes, upon all the inhabitants of, and persons resident, and estates lying, within the said Commonwealth; and also to impose, and levy reasonable duties and excises, upon any produce, goods, wares, merchandize, and commodities whatsoever, brought into, produced, manufactured, or being within the same; to be issued and disposed of by warrant, under the hand of the Governor of this Commonwealth for the time being, with the advice and consent of the Council, for the public service, in the necessary defence and support of the government of the said Commonwealth, and the protection and preservation of the subjects thereof, according to such acts as are or shall be in force within the same.

AND while the public charges of government, or any part thereof, shall be assessed on polls and estates, in the manner that has hitherto been practised, in order that such assessments may be made with equality, there shall be a valuation of estates within the Commonwealth taken anew once in every ten years at least, and as much oftener as the General Court shall order.

CHAPTER I.

SECTION II.

Senate.

ART. I—THERE shall be annually elected by the freeholders and other inhabitants of this Commonwealth, qualified as in this Constitution is provided, forty persons to be Counsellors and Senators for the year ensuing their election; to be chosen by the inhabitants of the districts, into which the Commonwealth may from time to time be divided by the General Court for that purpose: And the General Court, in assigning the numbers to be elected by the respective districts, shall govern themselves by the proportion of the public taxes paid by the said districts; and timely make known to the inhabitants of the Commonwealth, the limits of each district, and the number of Counsellors and Senators to be chosen therein; provided, that the number of such districts shall never be less than thirteen; and that no district be so large as to entitle the same to choose more than six Senators.

And the several counties in this Commonwealth shall, until the General Court shall determine it necessary to alter the said districts, be districts for the choice of Counsellors and Senators, (except that the counties of Dukes County and Nantucket shall form one district for that purpose) and shall elect the following number for Counsellors and Senators, viz:

Suffolk	Six	York	Two
Essex	Six	Dukes County and Nantucket	One
Middlesex	Five		
Hampshire	Four	Worcester	Five
Plymouth	Three	Cumberland	One
Barnstable	One	Lincoln	One
Bristol	Three	Berkshire	Two.

II.—The Senate shall be the first branch of the legislature; and the Senators shall be chosen in the following manner, viz: There shall be a meeting on the first Monday in April annually, forever, of the inhabitants of each town in the several counties of this Commonwealth; to be called by the Selectmen, and warned in due course of law, at least seven days before the first Monday in April, for the purpose of electing persons to be Senators and Counsellors: And at such meetings every male inhabitant of twenty-one years of age and upwards, having a freehold estate within the Commonwealth, of the annual income of three pounds, or any estate of the value of sixty pounds, shall have a right to give in his vote for the Senators for the district of which he is an inhabitant. And to remove all doubts concerning the meaning of the word "inhabitant" in this constitution, every person shall be considered as an inhabitant, for the purpose of electing and being elected into any office, or place within this State, in that town, district, or plantation, where he dwelleth, or hath his home.

The Selectmen of the several towns shall preside at such meetings impartially; and shall receive the votes of all the inhabitants of such towns present and qualified to vote for Senators, and shall sort and count them in open town meeting, and in presence of the Town Clerk, who shall make a fair record in presence of the Selectmen, and in open town meeting, of the name of every person voted for, and of the number of votes against his name; and a fair copy of this record shall be attested by the Selectmen and the Town-Clerk, and shall be sealed up, directed to the Secretary of the Commonwealth for the time being, with a superscription, expressing the purport of the contents thereof, and delivered by the Town-Clerk of such towns, to the Sheriff of the county in which such town lies, thirty days at least before the last Wednesday in May annually; or it shall be delivered into the Secretary's office seventeen days at least before the said last Wednesday in May; and the Sheriff of each county shall deliver all such certificates by him received, into the Secretary's office seventeen days before the said last Wednesday in May.

And the inhabitants of plantations unincorporated, qualified as this Constitution provides, who are or shall be empowered and required to assess taxes upon themselves toward the support of government, shall have the same privilege of voting for Counsellors and Senators, in the plantations where they reside, as town inhabitants have in their respective towns; and the plantation-meetings for that purpose shall be held annually on the same first Monday in April, at such place in the plantations respectively, as the Assessors thereof shall direct; which Assessors shall have like authority for notifying the electors, collecting and returning the votes, as the Selectmen and Town-Clerks have in their several towns, by this Constitution. And all other persons living in places unincorporated (qualified as aforesaid) who shall be assessed to the support of government by the Assessors of an adjacent town, shall have the privilege of giving in their votes for Counsellors and Senators, in the town where they shall be assessed, and be notified of the place of meeting by the Selectmen of the town where they shall be assessed, for that purpose, accordingly.

III.—And that there may be a due convention of Senators on the last Wednesday in May annually, the Governor, with five of the Council, for the time being, shall, as soon as may be, examine the returned copies of such records; and fourteen days before the said day he shall issue his summons to such persons as shall appear to be chosen by a majority of voters, to attend on that day, and take their seats accordingly: Provided nevertheless, that for the first year the said returned copies shall be examined by the President and five of the Council of the former Constitution of Government; and the said President shall, in like manner, issue his summons to the persons so elected, that they may take their seats as aforesaid.

IV.—The Senate shall be the final judge of the elections, returns and qualifications of their own members, as pointed out in the Constitution; and shall, on the said last Wednesday in May annually, determine and declare who are elected by each district, to be Senators, by a majority of votes: And in case there shall not appear to be the full number of Senators returned elected by a majority of votes for any district, the deficiency shall be supplied in the following manner, viz. The members of the House of Representatives, and such Senators as shall be declared elected, shall take the names of such persons as shall be found to have the highest number of votes in such district, and not elected, amounting to twice the number of Senators wanting, if there be so many voted for; and, out of these, shall elect by ballot a number of Senators sufficient to fill up the vacancies in such district: And in this manner all such vacancies shall be filled up in every district of the Commonwealth; and in like manner all vacancies in the Senate, arising by death, removal out of the State, or otherwise, shall be supplied as soon as may be after such vacancies shall happen.

V.—Provided nevertheless, that no person shall be capable of being elected as a Senator, who is not seized in his own right of a freehold within this Commonwealth, of the value of three hundred pounds at least, or possessed of personal estate to the value of six hundred pounds at least, or of both to the amount of the same sum, and who has not been an inhabitant of this Commonwealth for the space of five years immediately preceding his election, and, at the time of his election, he shall be an inhabitant in the district, for which he shall be chosen.

VI.—The Senate shall have power to adjourn themselves, provided such adjournments do not exceed two days at a time.

VII.—The Senate shall choose its own President, appoint its own officers, and determine its own rules of proceeding.

VIII.—The Senate shall be a court with full authority to hear and determine all impeachments made by the House of Representatives, against any officer or officers of the Commonwealth, for misconduct and mal-administration in their offices. But, previous to the trial of every impeachment, the members of the Senate shall respectively be sworn, truly and impartially to try and determine the charge in question, according to evidence. Their judgment, however, shall not extend further than to removal from office and disqualification to hold or enjoy any place of honor, trust, or profit, under this Commonwealth: But the party, so convicted, shall be, nevertheless, liable to indictment, trial, judgment, and punishment, according to the laws of the land.

IX.—Not less than sixteen members of the Senate shall constitute a quorum for doing business.

CHAPTER I.

SECTION III.

House of Representatives.

Art. I.—There shall be in the Legislature of this Commonwealth, a representation of the people, annually elected, and founded upon the principle of equality.

II.—And in order to provide for a representation of the citizens of this Commonwealth, founded upon the principle of equality, every corporate town, containing one hundred and fifty rateable polls, may elect one Representative: Every corporate town, containing three hundred and seventy-five rateable polls, may elect two Representatives: Every corporate town, containing six hundred rateable polls, may elect three Representatives; and proceeding in that manner, making two hundred and twenty-five rateable polls the mean increasing number for every additional Representative.

Provided nevertheless, that each town now incorporated, not having one hundred and fifty rateable polls, may elect one Representative: but no place shall hereafter be incorporated with the privilege of electing a Representative, unless there are within the same one hundred and fifty rateable polls.

And the House of Representatives shall have power, from time to time, to impose fines upon such towns as shall neglect to choose and return members to the same, agreeably to this Constitution.

The expenses of travelling to the General Assembly, and returning home, once in every session, and no more, shall be paid by the government, out of the public treasury, to every member who shall attend as seasonably as he can, in the judgment of the House, and does not depart without leave.

III.—Every member of the House of Representatives shall be chosen by written votes; and for one year at least next preceding his election shall have been an inhabitant of, and have been seized in his own right of a freehold of the value of one hundred pounds within the town he shall be chosen to represent, or any rateable estate to the value of two hundred pounds; and he shall cease to represent the said town immediately on his ceasing to be qualified as aforesaid.

IV.—Every male person, being twenty-one years of age, and resident in any particular town in this Commonwealth for the space of one year next preceding, having a freehold estate within the same town, of the annual income of three pounds, or any estate of the value of sixty pounds, shall have a right to vote in the choice of a Representative or Representatives for the said town.

V.—The members of the House of Representatives shall be chosen annually in the month of May, ten days at least before the last Wednesday of that month.

VI.—The House of Representatives shall be the Grand Inquest of this Commonwealth; and all impeachments made by them shall be heard and tried by the Senate.

VII.—All money-bills shall originate in the House of Representatives; but the Senate may propose or concur with amendments, as on other bills.

VIII.—The House of Representatives shall have power to adjourn themselves; provided such adjournment shall not exceed two days at a time.

IX.—Not less than sixty members of the House of Representatives shall constitute a quorum for doing business.

X.—The House of Representatives shall be the judge of the returns, elections, and qualifications of its own members, as pointed out in the constitution; shall choose their own Speaker; appoint their own officers, and settle the rules and orders of proceeding in their own house: They shall have authority to punish by imprisonment, every person, not a member, who shall be guilty of disrespect to the House, by any disorderly, or contemptuous behaviour, in its presence; or who, in the town where the General Court is sitting, and during the time of its sitting, shall threaten harm to the body or estate of any of its members, for any thing said or done in the House; or who shall assault any of them therefor; or who shall assault, or arrest, any witness, or other person, ordered to attend the House, in his way in going, or returning; or who shall rescue any person arrested by the order of the House.

And no member of the House of Representatives shall be arrested, or held to bail on mean process, during his going unto, returning from, or his attending, the General Assembly.

XI.—The Senate shall have the same powers in the like cases; and the Governor and Council shall have the same authority to punish in like cases. Provided, that no imprisonment on the warrant or order of the Governor, Council, Senate, or House of Representatives, for either of the above described offences, be for a term exceeding thirty days.

And the Senate and House of Representatives may try, and determine, all cases where their rights and privileges are concerned, and which, by the Constitution, they have authority to try and determine, by committees of their own members, or in such other way as they may respectively think best.

CHAPTER II.

Executive Power.

SECTION I.

Governor.

Art. I.—There shall be a Supreme Executive Magistrate, who shall be styled, THE GOVERNOR OF THE COMMONWEALTH OF MASSACHUSETTS; and whose title shall be—HIS EXCELLENCY.

II.—The Governor shall be chosen annually: And no person shall be eligible to this office, unless at the time of his election, he shall have been an inhabitant of this Commonwealth for seven years next preceding; and unless he shall, at the same time, be seized in his own right, of a freehold within the Commonwealth, of the value of one thousand pounds; and unless he shall declare himself to be of the christian religion.

III.—Those persons who shall be qualified to vote for Senators and Representatives within the several towns of this Commonwealth, shall, at a meeting, to be called for that purpose, on the first Monday of April annually, give in their votes for a Governor, to the Selectmen, who shall preside at such meetings; and the Town Clerk, in the presence and with the assistance of the Selectmen, shall, in open town meeting, sort and count the votes, and form a list of the persons voted for, with the number of votes for each person against his name; and shall make a fair record of the same in the town books, and a public declaration thereof in the said meeting; and shall, in the presence of the inhabitants, seal up copies of the said list, attested by him and the Selectmen, and transmit the same to the Sheriff of the county, thirty days at least before the last Wednesday in May; and the Sheriff shall transmit the same to the Secretary's office seventeen days at least before the said last Wednesday in May; or the Selectmen may cause returns of the same to be made to the office of the Secretary of the Commonwealth seventeen days at least before the said day; and the Secretary shall lay the same before the Senate and the House of Representatives, on the last Wednesday in May, to be by them examined: And in case of an election by a majority of all the votes returned, the choice shall be by them declared and published: But if no person shall have a majority of votes, the House of Representatives shall, by ballot, elect two out of four persons who had the highest number of votes, if so many shall have been voted for; but, if otherwise, out of the number voted for; and make return to the Senate of the two persons so elected; on which, the Senate shall proceed, by ballot, to elect one, who shall be declared Governor.

IV.—The Governor shall have authority, from time to time, at his discretion, to assemble and call together the Counsellors of this Commonwealth for the time being; and the Governor, with the said Counsellors, or five of them at least, shall, and may, from time to time, hold and keep a Council, for the ordering and directing the affairs of the Commonwealth, agreeably to the Constitution and the laws of the land.

V.—The Governor, with advice of Council, shall have full power and authority, during the session of the General Court, to adjourn or prorogue the same to any time the two Houses shall desire; and to dissolve the same on the day next preceding the last Wednesday in May; and, in the recess of the said Court, to prorogue the same from time to time, not exceeding ninety days in any one recess; and to call it together sooner than the time to which it may be adjourned or prorogued, if the welfare of the Commonwealth shall require the same: And in case of any infectious distemper prevailing in the place where the said Court is next at any time to convene, or any other cause happening whereby danger may arise to the health or lives of the members from their attendance, he may direct the session to be held at some other the most convenient place within the State.

And the Governor shall dissolve the said General Court on the day next preceding the last Wednesday in May.

VI.—In cases of disagreement between the two Houses, with regard to the necessity, expediency or time of adjournment, or prorogation, the Governor, with advice of the Council, shall have a right to adjourn or prorogue the General Court, not exceeding ninety days, as he shall determine the public good shall require.

VII.—The Governor of this Commonwealth, for the time being, shall be the commander-in-chief of the army and navy, and of all the military forces of the State, by sea and land; and shall have full power, by himself, or by any commander, or other officer or officers, from time to time, to train, instruct, exercise and govern the militia and navy; and, for the special defence and safety of the Commonwealth, to assemble in martial array, and put in warlike posture, the inhabitants thereof, and to lead and conduct them, and with them, to encounter, repel, resist, expel and pursue, by force of arms, as well as by sea as by land, within or without the limits of this Commonwealth, and also to kill, slay and destroy, if necessary, and conquer, by all fitting ways, enterprizes and means whatsoever, all and every such person and persons as shall, at any time hereafter, in a hostile manner, attempt or enterprize the destruction, invasion, detriment, or annoyance of this Commonwealth; and to use and exercise, over the army and navy, and over the militia in actual service, the law martial, in time of war or invasion, and also in time of rebellion, declared by the legislature to exist, as occasion shall necessarily require; and to take and surprise by all ways and means whatsoever, all and every such person or persons, with their ships, arms, ammunition and other goods, as shall, in a hostile manner, invade, or attempt the invading, conquering, or annoying this Commonwealth; and that the Governor be intrusted with all these and other powers, incident to the offices of Captain-General and Commander-in-Chief, and Admiral, to be exercised agreeably to the rules and regulations of the Constitution, and the laws of the land, and not otherwise.

Provided, that the said Governor shall not, at any time hereafter, by virtue of any power by this Constitution granted, or hereafter to be granted to him by the legislature, transport any of the inhabitants of this Commonwealth, or oblige them to march out of the limits of the same, without their free and voluntary consent, or the consent of the General Court; except so far as may be necessary to march or transport them by land or water, for the defence of such part of the State, to which they cannot otherwise conveniently have access.

VIII.—The power of pardoning offences, except such as persons may be convicted of before the Senate by an impeachment of the House, shall be in the Governor, by and with the advice of Council: But no charter of pardon, granted by the Governor, with advice of the Council, before conviction, shall avail the party pleading the same, notwithstanding any general or particular expressions contained therein, descriptive of the offence, or offences intended to be pardoned.

IX.—All judicial officers, the Attorney-General, the Solicitor-General, all Sheriffs, Coroners, and Registers of Probate, shall be nominated and appointed by the Governor, by and with the advice and consent of the Council; and every such nomination shall be made by the Governor, and made at least seven days prior to such appointment.

X.—The Captains and subalterns of the militia shall be elected by the written votes of the train-band and alarm list of their respective companies, of twenty-one years of age and upwards: The field-officers of Regiments shall be elected by the written votes of the captains and subalterns of their respective regiments: The Brigadiers shall be elected in like manner, by the field officers of their respective brigades: And such officers, so elected, shall be commissioned by the Governor, who shall determine their rank.

The Legislature shall, by standing laws, direct the time and manner of convening the electors, and of collecting votes, and of certifying to the Governor the officers elected.

The Major-Generals shall be appointed by the Senate and House of Representatives, each having a negative upon the other; and be commissioned by the Governor.

And if the electors of Brigadiers, field-officers, captains or subalterns, shall neglect or refuse to make such elections, after being duly notified, according to the laws for the time being, then the Governor, with advice of Council, shall appoint suitable persons to fill such offices.

And no officer, duly commissioned to command in the militia, shall be removed from his office, but by the address of both houses to the Governor, or by fair trial in court martial, pursuant to the laws of the Commonwealth for the time being.

The commanding officers of regiments shall appoint their Adjutants and Quarter-masters; the Brigadiers their Brigade-Majors; and the Major-Generals their Aids: and the Governor shall appoint the Adjutant General.

The Governor, with advice of Council, shall appoint all officers of the continental army, whom by the confederation of the United States it is provided that this Commonwealth shall appoint,—as also all officers of forts and garrisons.

The divisions of the militia into brigades, regiments and companies, made in pursuance of the militia laws now in force, shall be considered as the proper divisions of the militia of this Commonwealth, until the same shall be altered in pursuance of some future law.

XI.—No monies shall be issued out of the treasury of this Commonwealth, and disposed of (except such sums as may be appropriated for the redemption of bills of credit or Treasurer's notes, or for the payment of interest arising thereon) but by warrant under the hand of the Governor for the time being, with the advice and consent of the Council, for the necessary defence and support of the Commonwealth; and for the protection and preservation of the inhabitants thereof, agreeably to the acts and resolves of the General Court.

XII.—All public boards, the Commissary-General, all superintending officers of public magazines and stores, belonging to this Commonwealth, and all commanding officers of forts and garrisons within the same, shall, once in every three months, officially and without requisition, and at other times, when required by the Governor, deliver to him an account of all goods, stores, provisions, ammunition, cannon with their appendages, and small arms with their accoutrements, and of all other public property whatever under their care respectively; distinguishing the quantity, number, quality and kind of each, as particularly as may be; together with the condition of such forts and garrisons: And the said commanding officer shall exhibit to the Governor, when required by him, true and exact plans of such forts, and of the land and sea, or harbour or harbours adjacent.

AND the said boards, and all public officers, shall communicate to the Governor, as soon as may be after receiving the same, all letters, dispatches, and intelligences of a public nature, which shall be directed to them respectively.

XIII.—As the public good requires that the Governor should not be under the undue influence of any of the members of the General Court, by a dependence on them for his support—that he should, in all cases, act with freedom for the benefit of the public—that he should not have his attention necessarily diverted from that object to his private concerns —and that he should maintain the dignity of the Commonwealth in the character of its chief magistrate—it is necessary that he should have an honorable stated salary, of a fixed and permanent value, amply sufficient for those purposes, and established by standing laws: And it shall be among the first acts of the General Court, after the Commencement of this Constitution, to establish such salary by law accordingly.

PERMANENT and honorable salaries shall also be established by law for the Justices of the Supreme Judicial Court.

AND if it shall be found, that any of the salaries aforesaid, so established, are insufficient, they shall, from time to time, be enlarged, as the General Court shall judge proper.

CHAPTER II.

SECTION II.

Lieutenant-Governor.

ART. I.—THERE shall be annually elected a Lieutenant-Governor of the Commonwealth of Massachusetts, whose title shall be HIS HONOR— and who shall be qualified, in point of religion, property, and residence in the Commonwealth, in the same manner with the Governor: And the day and manner of his election, and the qualifications of the electors, shall be the same as are required in the election of a Governor. The return of the votes for this officer, and the declaration of his election, shall be in the same manner: And if no one person shall be found to have a majority of all the votes returned, the vacancy shall be filled by the

Senate and House of Representatives, in the same manner as the Governor is to be elected, in case no one person shall have a majority of the votes of the people to be Governor.

II.—The Governor, and in his absence the Lieutenant-Governor, shall be President of the Council, but shall have no vote in Council: And the Lieutenant-Governor shall always be a member of the Council, except when the chair of the Governor shall be vacant.

III.—Whenever the chair of the Governor shall be vacant, by reason of his death, or absence from the Commonwealth, or otherwise, the Lieutenant-Governor, for the time being, shall, during such vacancy, perform all the duties incumbent upon the Governor, and shall have and exercise all the powers and authorities, which by this Constitution the Governor is vested with, when personally present.

CHAPTER II.

SECTION III.

Council, and the Manner of Settling Elections by the Legislature.

Art. I.—There shall be a Council for advising the Governor in the executive part of government, to consist of nine persons besides the Lieutenant-Governor, whom the Governor, for the time being, shall have full power and authority, from time to time, at his discretion, to assemble and call together. And the Governor, with the said Counsellors, or five of them at least, shall and may, from time to time, hold and keep a council, for the ordering and directing the affairs of the Commonwealth, according to the laws of the land.

II.—Nine Counsellors shall be annually chosen from among the persons returned for Counsellors and Senators, on the last Wednesday in May, by the joint ballot of the Senators and Representatives assembled in one room: And in case there shall not be found, upon the first choice, the whole number of nine persons who will accept a seat in the Council, the deficiency shall be made up by the electors aforesaid from among the people at large; and the number of Senators left shall constitute the Senate for the year. The seats of the persons thus elected from the Senate, and accepting the trust, shall be vacated in the Senate.

III.—The Counsellors, in the civil arrangements of the Commonwealth, shall have rank next after the Lieutenant-Governor.

IV.—Not more than two Counsellors shall be chosen out of any one district of this Commonwealth.

V.—The resolutions and advice of the Council shall be recorded in a register, and signed by the members present; and this record may be called for at any time by either House of the Legislature; and any member of the Council may insert his opinion contrary to the resolution of the majority.

VI.—Whenever the office of the Governor and Lieutenant-Governor shall be vacant, by reason of death, absence, or otherwise, then the Council or the major part of them, shall, during such vacancy, have full power and authority, to do, and execute, all and every such acts, matters and things, as the Governor or the Lieutenant-Governor might or could, by virtue of this Constitution, do or execute, if they, or either of them, were personally present.

VII.—And whereas the elections appointed to be made by this Constitution, on the last Wednesday in May annually, by the two Houses of the Legislature, may not be completed on that day, the said elections may be adjourned from day to day until the same shall be completed. And the order of elections shall be as follows; the vacancies in the Senate, if any, shall first be filled up; the Governor and Lieutenant-Governor shall then be elected, provided there should be no choice of them by the people: And afterwards the two Houses shall proceed to the election of the Council.

CHAPTER II.

SECTION IV.

Secretary, Treasurer, Commissary, etc.

Art. I.—The Secretary, Treasurer and Receiver-General, and the Commissary-General, Notaries-Public, and Naval-Officers, shall be chosen annually, by joint ballot of the Senators and Representatives in one room. And that the citizens of this Commonwealth may be assured, from time to time, that the monies remaining in the public Treasury, upon the settlement and liquidation of the public accounts, are their property, no man shall be eligible as Treasurer and Receiver-General more than five years successively.

II.—The records of the Commonwealth shall be kept in the office of the Secretary, who may appoint his Deputies, for whose conduct he shall be accountable, and he shall attend the Governor and Council, the Senate and House of Representatives, in person, or by his deputies, as they shall respectively require.

CHAPTER III.

Judiciary Power.

Art. I—The tenure that all commission officers shall by law have in their offices, shall be expressed in their respective commissions. All judicial officers, duly appointed, commissioned and sworn, shall hold their offices during good behaviour, excepting such concerning whom there is different provision made in this Constitution: Provided, nevertheless, the Governor, with consent of the Council, may remove them upon the address of both Houses of the Legislature.

II.—Each branch of the Legislature, as well as the Governor and Council, shall have authority to require the opinions of the Justices of the Supreme Judicial Court, upon important questions of law, and upon solemn occasions.

III.—In order that the people may not suffer from the long continuance in place of any Justice of the Peace, who shall fail of discharging the important duties of his office with ability or fidelity, all commissions of Justices of the Peace shall expire and become void, in the term of seven years from their respective dates; and, upon the expiration of any commission, the same may, if necessary, be renewed, or another person appointed, as shall most conduce to the well being of the Commonwealth.

IV.—The Judges of Probate of Wills, and for granting letters of administration, shall hold their courts at such place or places, on fixed days, as the convenience of the people shall require. And the Legislature shall, from time to time, hereafter appoint such times and places; until which appointments, the said Courts shall be holden at the times and places which the respective Judges shall direct.

V.—All causes of marriage, divorce and alimony, and all appeals from the Judges of Probate, shall be heard and determined by the Governor and Council until the Legislature shall, by law, make other provision.

CHAPTER IV.

Delegates to Congress.

The delegates of this Commonwealth to the Congress of the United States, shall, sometime in the month of June annually, be elected by the joint ballot of the Senate and House of Representatives, assembled together in one room; to serve in Congress for one year, to commence on the first Monday in November then next ensuing. They shall have commissions under the hand of the Governor, and the great seal of the Commonwealth; but may be recalled at any time within the year, and others chosen and commissioned, in the same manner, in their stead.

CHAPTER V.

The University at Cambridge, and Encouragement of Literature, etc.

SECTION I.

The University.

Art. I.—Whereas our wise and pious ancestors, so early as the year one thousand six hundred and thirty six, laid the foundation of Harvard-College, in which University many persons of great eminence have, by the blessing of god, been initiated in those arts and sciences, which qualified them for public employments, both in Church and State: And whereas the encouragement of Arts and Sciences, and all good literature, tends to the honor of god, the advantage of the christian religion, and the great benefit of this, and the other United States of America—It is declared, That the president and fellows of harvard-college, in their corporate capacity, and their successors in that capacity, their officers and servants, shall have, hold, use, exercise and enjoy, all the powers, authorities, rights, liberties, privileges, immunities and franchises, which they now have, or are entitled to have, hold, use, exercise and enjoy: And the same are hereby ratified and confirmed unto them, the said President and Fellows of Harvard-College, and to their successors, and to their officers and servants, respectively, forever.

II.—And whereas there have been at sundry times, by divers persons, gifts, grants, devises of houses, lands, tenements, goods, chattels, legacies and conveyances, heretofore made, either to Harvard-College in Cambridge, in New-England, or to the President and Fellows of Harvard-College, or to the said College, by some other description, under several charters successively: IT IS DECLARED, That all the said gifts, grants, devises, legacies and conveyances, are hereby forever confirmed unto the President and Fellows of Harvard-College, and to their successors, in the capacity aforesaid, according to the true intent and meaning of the donor or donors, grantor or grantors, devisor or devisors.

III.—And whereas by an act of the General Court of the Colony of Massachusetts-Bay, passed in the year one thousand six hundred and forty-two, the Governor and Deputy-Governor, for the time being, and all the magistrates of that jurisdiction, were, with the President, and a number of the clergy in the said act described, constituted the Overseers of Harvard-College: And it being necessary, in this new Constitution of Government, to ascertain who shall be deemed successors to the said Governor, Deputy-Governor and Magistrates: IT IS DECLARED, That the Governor, Lieutenant-Governor, Council and Senate of this Commonwealth, are, and shall be deemed, their successors; who, with the President of Harvard-College, for the time being, together with the ministers of the congregational churches in the towns of Cambridge, Watertown, Charlestown, Boston, Roxbury, and Dorchester, mentioned in the said act, shall be, and hereby are, vested with all the powers and authority belonging, or in any way appertaining to the Overseers of Harvard-College; PROVIDED, that nothing herein shall be construed to prevent the Legislature of this Commonwealth from making such alterations in the government of the said university, as shall be conducive to its advantage, and the interest of the republic of letters, in as full a manner as might have been done by the Legislature of the late Province of the Massachusetts-Bay.

CHAPTER V.

SECTION II.

The Encouragement of Literature, etc.

Wisdom, and knowledge, as well as virtue, diffused generally among the body of the people, being necessary for the preservation of their rights and liberties; and as these depend on spreading the opportunities and advantages of education in the various parts of the country, and among the different orders of the people, it shall be the duty of legislators and magistrates, in all future periods of this Commonwealth, to cherish the interests of literature and the sciences, and all seminaries of them; especially the university at Cambridge, public schools, and grammar schools in the towns; to encourage private societies and public institutions, rewards and immunities, for the promotion of agriculture, arts, sciences, commerce, trades, manufactures, and a natural history of the country; to countenance and inculcate the principles of humanity and general benevolence, public and private charity, industry and frugality, honesty and punctuality in their dealings; sincerity, good humour, and all social affections, and generous sentiments among the people.

CHAPTER VI.

Oaths and Subscriptions; Incompatibility of and Exclusion from Offices; Pecuniary Qualifications; Commissions; Writs; Confirmation of Laws; Habeas Corpus; The Enacting Style; Continuance of Officers; Provision for a future Revisal of the Constitution, etc.

Art. I.—Any person chosen Governor, Lieutenant-Governor, Counsellor, Senator, or Representative, and accepting the trust, shall, before he proceed to execute the duties of his place or office, make and subscribe the following declaration, viz.—

"I, A. B. do declare, that I believe the christian religion, and have a firm persuasion of its truth; and that I am seized and possessed, in my own right, of the property required by the Constitution as one qualification for the office or place to which I am elected."

And the Governor, Lieutenant-Governor, and Counsellors, shall make and subscribe the said declaration, in the presence of the two Houses of Assembly; and the Senators and Representatives first elected under this Constitution, before the President and five of the Council of the former Constitution, and, forever afterwards, before the Governor and Council for the time being.

And every person chosen to either of the places or offices aforesaid, as also any person appointed or commissioned to any judicial, executive, military, or other office under the government, shall, before he enters on the discharge of the business of his place or office, take and subscribe the following declaration, and oaths or affirmations, viz.—

"I, A. B. do truly and sincerely acknowledge, profess, testify and declare, that the Commonwealth of Massachusetts is, and of right ought to be, a free, sovereign and independent State; and I do swear, that I will bear true faith and allegiance to the said Commonwealth, and that I will defend the same against traitorous conspiracies and all hostile attempts whatsoever: And that I do renounce and adjure all allegiance, subjection and obedience to the King, Queen or Government of Great Britain, (as the case may be) and every other foreign power whatsoever: And that no foreign Prince, Person, Prelate, State or Potentate, hath, or ought to have, any jurisdiction, superiority, pre-eminence, authority, dispensing or other power, in any matter, civil, ecclesiastical or spiritual, within this Commonwealth; except the authority and power which is or may be vested by their Constituents in the Congress of the United States: And I do further testify and declare, that no man or body of men hath or can have any right to absolve or discharge me from the obligation of this oath, declaration or affirmation; and that I do make this acknowledgment, profession, testimony, declaration, denial, renunciation and abjuration, heartily and truly, according to the common meaning and acceptation of the foregoing words, without any equivocation, mental evasion, or secret reservation whatsoever. So help me GOD."

"I, A. B. do solemnly swear and affirm, that I will faithfully and impartially discharge and perform all the duties incumbent on me as ; according to the best of my abilities and understanding, agreeably to the rules and regulations of the Constitution, and the laws of this Commonwealth." "So help me GOD."

Provided always, that when any person, chosen or appointed as aforesaid, shall be of the denomination of the people called Quakers, and shall decline taking the said oaths, he shall make his affirmation in the foregoing form, and subscribe the same, omitting the words *"I do swear," "and adjure," "oath or," "and abjuration,"* in the first oath; and in the second oath, the words *"swear and;"* and in each of them the words *"So help me* GOD;" subjoining instead thereof, *"This I do under the pains and penalties of perjury."*

AND the said oaths or affirmations shall be taken and subscribed by the Governor, Lieutenant Governor, and Counsellors, before the President of the Senate, in the presence of the two Houses of Assembly; and by the Senators and Representatives first elected under this Constitution, before the President and five of the Council of the former Constitution; and forever afterwards before the Governor and Council for the time being: And by the residue of the officers aforesaid, before such persons and in such manner as from time to time shall be prescribed by the Legislature.

II.—No Governor, Lieutenant Governor, or Judge of the Supreme Judicial Court, shall hold any other office or place, under the authority of this Commonwealth, except such as by this Constitution they are admitted to hold, saving that the Judges of the said Court may hold the offices of Justices of the Peace through the State; nor shall they hold any other place or office, or receive any pension or salary from any other State or Government or Power whatever.

No person shall be capable of holding or exercising at the same time, within this State, more than one of the following offices, viz:—Judge of Probate—Sheriff—Register of Probate—or Register of Deeds—and never more than any two offices which are to be held by appointment of the Governor, or the Governor and Council, or the Senate, or the House of Representatives, or by the election of the people of the State at large, or of the people of any county, military offices and the offices of Justices of the Peace excepted, shall be held by one person.

No person holding the office of Judge of the Supreme Judicial Court—Secretary—Attorney General—Solicitor General—Treasurer or Receiver General—Judge of Probate—Commissary General—President, Professor, or Instructor of Harvard College—Sheriff—Clerk of the House of Representatives—Register of Probate—Register of Deeds—Clerk of the Supreme Judicial Court—Clerk of the Inferior Court of Common Pleas—or Officer of the Customs, including in this description Naval Officers—shall at the same time have a seat in the Senate or House of Representatives; but their being chosen or appointed to, and accepting the same, shall operate as a resignation of their seat in the Senate or House of Representatives; and the place so vacated shall be filled up.

And the same rule shall take place in case any judge of the said Supreme Judicial Court, or Judge of Probate, shall accept a seat in Council; or any Counsellor shall accept of either of those offices or places.

And no person shall ever be admitted to hold a seat in the Legislature, or any office of trust or importance under the Government of this Commonwealth, who shall, in the due course of law, have been convicted of bribery or corruption in obtaining an election or appointment.

III.—In all cases where sums of money are mentioned in this Constitution, the value thereof shall be computed in silver at six shillings and eight pence per ounce: And it shall be in the power of the Legislature from time to time to increase such qualifications, as to property, of the persons to be elected to offices, as the circumstances of the Commonwealth shall require.

IV.—All commissions shall be in the name of the Commonwealth of Massachusetts, signed by the Governor, and attested by the Secretary or his Deputy, and have the great seal of the Commonwealth affixed thereto.

V.—All writs, issuing out of the clerk's office in any of the Courts of law, shall be in the name of the Commonwealth of Massachusetts: They shall be under the seal of the Court from whence they issue: They shall bear test of the first Justice of the Court to which they shall be returnable, who is not a party, and be signed by the clerk of such court.

VI.—All the laws which have heretofore been adopted, used and approved in the Province, Colony or State of Massachusetts Bay, and usually practiced on in the Courts of law, shall still remain and be in full force, until altered or repealed by the Legislature; such parts only excepted as are repugnant to the rights and liberties contained in this Constitution.

VII.—The privilege and benefit of the writ of *habeas corpus* shall be enjoyed in this Commonwealth in the most free, easy, cheap, expeditious and ample manner; and shall not be suspended by the Legislature, except upon the most urgent and pressing occasions, and for a limited time not exceeding twelve months.

VIII.—The enacting style, in making and passing all acts, statutes and laws, shall be—"Be it enacted by the Senate and House of Representatives, in General Court assembled, and by the authority of the same."

IX.—To the end there may be no failure of justice or danger arise to the Commonwealth from a change of the Form of Government—all officers, civil and military, holding commissions under the government and people of Massachusetts Bay in New-England, and all other officers of the said government and people, at the time this Constitution shall take effect, shall have, hold, use, exercise and enjoy all the powers and authority to them granted or committed, until other persons shall be appointed in their stead: And all courts of law shall proceed in the execution of the business of their respective departments; and all the executive and legislative officers, bodies and powers shall continue in full force, in the enjoyment and exercise of all their trusts, employments and authority; until the General Court and the supreme and executive officers under this Constitution are designated and invested with their respective trusts, powers and authority.

X.—In order the more effectually to adhere to the principles of the Constitution, and to correct those violations which by any means may be made therein, as well as to form such alterations as from experience shall be found necessary—the General Court, which shall be in the year of our Lord one thousand seven hundred and ninety-five, shall issue precepts to the Selectmen of the several towns, and to the Assessors of the unincorporated plantations, directing them to convene the qualified voters of their respective towns and plantations for the purpose of collecting their sentiments on the necessity or expediency of revising the Constitution, in order to amendments.

And if it shall appear by the returns made, that two thirds of the qualified voters throughout the State, who shall assemble and vote in consequence of the said precepts, are in favor of such revision or amendment, the General Court shall issue precepts, or direct them to be issued from the Secretary's office to the several towns, to elect Delegates to meet in Convention for the purpose aforesaid.

The said Delegates to be chosen in the same manner and proportion as their Representatives in the second branch of the Legislature are by this Constitution to be chosen.

XI.—This form of government shall be enrolled on parchment, and deposited in the Secretary's office, and be a part of the laws of the land—and printed copies thereof shall be prefixed to the book containing the laws of this Commonwealth, in all future editions of the said laws.

JAMES BOWDOIN, *President.*

Attest. SAMUEL BARRETT, *Secretary.*

IV

Ratification

May 1780—June 1780

35

Returns of the Towns on the Constitution of 1780

The town returns reveal the extent to which the proposed constitution was discussed. Community action varied from place to place. Some votes were perfunctory. Some towns considered each clause in great detail. Some meetings simply reported a numerical result; others sent in substantial disquisitions on political theory. No clear-cut statistical conclusion was possible from an examination of the returns. But when the convention tabulated the reports in June, it proclaimed the Constitution ratified. Most of the returns are found in MA 276/10–77; 277/1–124. Returns not in the archives have been inserted from the collection in the Massachusetts Historical Society gathered by Samuel Eliot Morison and from local sources as indicated.

BERKSHIRE COUNTY

Adams (276/10)

State of the Massachusetts Bay

To the Honourable Convention Seting at Boston

Whereas the Town of Adams Being Leagally Conveind to take In to Consideration the Constitution or form of Government Being Present at said meeting Sixty Voters

Firstly: Proseeded and made Choice of Captain Enos Parker Moderator

Secondly Proseeded to Consider the Bill of Rights: and (on the third Articule Voted in the Negative Unanimusly—But that No person or persons on Any pretence whatsoever Shall be Compeled to Attend on Any Public Worship or to Contribute to the supoart or Maintainance of Any Public Teacher Contrary to his or their sentiments) 60 Votes in the Negative of this 3 Articule

---

29 Articule in the Bill of Rights Voted in the Negative and Voted that the Judges Mentined in said Articule Be not Continued During good Behaviour But that they be Annually Elected and Sworn

---

Articule tenth of the Executive Power
Unanimusly Voted in the Negative

Voted that Every individyal Bairing Arms or Doing Duty ought of Right to have a Voice in Electing of his Own officer

---

Judiciary Power

Articule First Unanimusly Voted in the Negative But that No Civiel Whatsoever be Alowed to hold their Commissions More than one year at a time and that they be Annualy Chosen and Commissioned

---

Page 44 Chapter 6

Articule 2nd Past the Vote with this Addition that the Justices of the peace be Debard from holding any seat in the General Coart

---

True Extracts from the Minutes of Said Meeting

Test Giles Burns Town Clark
Enos Parker Moderator

Becket (276/11)

Becket May 4th. 1780

at a Town Meeting Regularly assembled on the Day above said and Continued by several adjurnments Convened for Purpose of taking in to Consideration the Proposed Constitution or form of government sent out by the Late Convention for the approbation or disaprobation of the People at large after taking the same in to Serious Consideration The Whole Passed unanimous accept the articles here after Mentioned Present thirty four———

The 3d article in the Bill of Rights their appeared ten in the affirmative and ten in the Negative The objectors to said article are of the opinion that Every Person ought to have Liberty to Support or Maintain the Gosple in such way or Manner as is agreed on by the Religious Society where he attends Public Worship which—they apprehend is Not allowed in said article as it now stands and are desirous such Liberty should be fully granted and clearly expressed———

Chapter the 1st. Section 2d Senate—article 1th Twenty in the affirmative three in the Negative The objectors are of opinion the Number of Senators is two Large that it will make Needless Charge to the Common Welth———

on the 5th. article in the same Chapter their was fourteen in the affirmative and Eleven in the Negative——The objectors are of the opinion that the Estate Requiset to Quallify a Person for a seat in that House is two much and that it may Prevent some Person otherwise well Quallified from serving the Public in that station

Chapter 2d Executive Power Section 1th. the Governor——article 2d Ninteen in the affirmative and six in the Negative the objections the same as in the above or 5th. article——on the 10th. article in the same Chapter in the affirmative twelve and Nine in the Negative the objectors are of the opinion that all above the age of sixteen years ought to have their Vote in Choice of Captain and subalterns——on the 13th article of the same Chapter one in the afirmative and Twenty Eight in the Negative—The objectors are of the opinion that annual sallaries would be Preferable for those Important officers than sallaries Established by Law as Money may appreciate and there by become Burdensom to the Common Welth——

Beckett May 27th, 1780.

Nathaniel Kingsley
Elisha Carpenter
Ebenr. Walden

Selectmen of Becket

Hancock (276/12)

To the Honnourable Convention of Delegates Elected by the Good People of the Massachusetts Bay for the Purpose of forming a Constitution of Government for Said State to be Convened at Boston on Wednesday the Seventh Day of June in the year of our Lord one thousand Seven hundred and Eighty

The Subscribers hereunto beg leave to Certify to your Honnours that the Freeholders and other Inhabitants of the Town of Hancock Quallified as this State Directs upon due Warning given Assembled and met together on the twenty ninth Day of May and took into their consideration the form of a Constitution for Said State and Unanimously Voted that the Same be Established and Setled as the Constitution of Government for this State with the Amendment Anext to the following Articles.

Viz that Such an amendment take place in the 9th Article that all Justices of the peace shall be Elected by the Voters quallified to Vote for representatives in each Town for said Amendment 20 against it one and all Judges of the Inferiour County Court be annually Elected by the House of Representatives

---

That Such an amendment take place in the tenth Article that all Captains and Subalterns be Chosen by the whole Trainband and Alarum List for the amendment thirty five none against it

---

That such an amendment take place Relative to the Governor that he shall Declare himself to be of the Protestant Christian Relegion
Dated in Hancock the twenty ninth Day of May in the Year of our Lord one thousand Seven hundred and Eighty and in the fourth year of the Independance of America.

William Borman — Select Men
John Boardman — of the Town
Daniel Goodrich — [afor]said
Wait Palmer — Town Clark

Lanesborough (276/13)

That in the Article of Representation we think that allowing such a large number of Representitives as is allowed in the Constitution will be very expensive, and unequal, and that the Town of Boston ought not to send more than four, and that the Six next largest Towns send but two, and no other Town be allowed to send more that one Representitive, and that not less than one Third part of the number of Representitives Shall make a Quorum———
That in the Choice of Captains and Subbalterns by Persons of twenty one years of age and upwards, and no other, is unjust, for every Soldier as soon as he is called to Duty ought to be allowed to vote in the Choice aforesaid as well as others
That the Justices of the Inferiour Courts and Justices of the Peace ought to be chosen by the Freemen in the County and Towns where they belong and that they continue in Office not more than three years———
That there be a Register of Deeds in every Town put in by the People
That there be a Court of Probate in every Rigiment———
That there be a Confession Bill established by the Constitution———
That no person who is a Member of any Religious Society or denomina-

tion or that does Steadily attend at any publick place of worship Shall be Taxed toward the Support of any other Minister or Society whatsoever

At a Town meeting Continued by Adjurnement to Fryday the 26th of May 1780—
the above was voted without a disenting vote
Lanesborough May 26th 1780

Wolcott Hubbell Town Clark
Jedediah Hubbell moderater

Lee (276/14)

At a Meeting of the Male Inhabitants of the Town of Lee being free and Twenty one Years of age Leagally Warned and holden on thursday the 11 day of May AD 1780 and Continued by adjornment to Wensday the 31st of May for the Purpose of Acting upon the Constitution and Form of Government Composed by a Convention of Deligats from the Serverl Towns in this State Convened at Cambridge September 1st 1779 and Continued by Adjornments to March the furst 1780———
The third articul in this Bill of Rights Being red about Duly Considered passed in the Negative by 13 Aganst 5 for this Reasons, Viz———
(Because it is our opinion that the Sevil Law ought not to have any Power to Oblige any one to Soporte the Gospel)———
Chapter fust Second Section and Second Part Second Article the Nomber Aganst this Articul Objected is 21 one [sic] and 8 for it this articul is objected for this Reason that we think it unreasnabul that any shud be taxed With out a vorse in Electing———
the fifth Articul is Objected to for this Reason that we think it Right for the Electors to Electe Whome they will———
Chapter fust Section Third Articul 3 is objected for this reason that we think it Right for the Electors to Electe whome they will———
Dito 4 is objected to for this Reason that we think it Unreasnabul that any Shud be taxed with out a vours in Electing———
The Remainder of this Constitution is accepted by the Hall wich is twenty nine voters

The Votes of the town of Lee upon the Several Articles contained in the Bill of Rights and Constitution of [Govern]ment agreed upon by the Deligates of the People of the State of Massachusett Bay taken at a Legal twon Meeting with the Number of Voters for and against each article of the Same———

Bill of Rightes Numebers of Voters for Each Article of the Same		Bill of Rights Number of Voters against Each Article of the same
Article the first	19	0
2 Ditto	19	0
3 Ditto	5	13
4 Ditto	29	0

The Same Number Continued and without objecttion Accepted all to the first Chapter Second Section and Second Part Second Articles

2 Ditto	8	21
3 Ditto	29	0
4 Ditto	29	0
5 Ditto	8	21
6 Ditto	29	0
7 Ditto	29	0
8 Ditto	29	0
9 Ditto	29	0
Chapter first Section third		
Art. 1	29	0
2 Ditto	29	0
3 Ditto	8	21
4 Ditto	8	21

the Remainder of this Constitution is accepted by the Hold which is twenty nine Voters

Oliver West Slet
Josiah Yale men

Lenox *

2. To have the constitution read, and determine by yeas and nays whether we approve of it or not, and the numbers for and against it to be precisely ascertained.

At a town meeting legally held in Lenox on the first day of May A.D. 1780

2ly. The constitution was read over in said meeting.

3ly. Voted yeas 45. Nays 2.

* Town records, Massachusetts Historical Society.

3ly. To take into consideration the form of government with the bill of rights proposed by the state convention and act thereon.

3ly. To reconsider the vote taken at the last town meeting respecting the constitution and take the same under consideration a second time and determine on yeas and nays whether we approve or disapprove of the same that returns of our votes respecting said constitution may be made to the convention at Boston on the first Wednesday in June next, and to do any other necessary business.

At a town meeting legally held in Lenox the 25th day of May 1780

10ly. Voted that the delegate from this town to the state convention be, and he is hereby empowered and directed to agree to and establish the constitution with the declaration of rights proposed by said convention, provided two thirds of the votes in the state approve the same, and further agree when it shall have force and operation agreeable to the recommendation of said convention.

New Marlborough (276/15)

At a Legal Town meeting of the Inhabitants of New Marlborough on May the 11th 1780 warned in Pursuance of a Resolve of the Convention of this State dated March 2 1780. for Laying before the Inhabitants of the several Towns and Districts of this State the Constitution or Frame of Government Purposed to be adopted in said State——The inhabitants Present Taking the Constitution into their Serious Consideration, Passed upon the whole with the following objections (viz)
In Chapter first Section Second article second, and section third article fourth, all that is contained in the above articles making money an Essential Qualification for a Voter was objected to by 54. In favor of the above said articls 4—as being Contrary to the first article in the Bill of Rights which we agree with The next objection in Chapter 1st Section 2d. the Senate. Chapter 1 Section 3 House of Representatives. Chapt. 2d Section 1 Governor and in Chapter 2. Section 2d Lieutenant governor, all the Last mentioned articles are objected to for that such Large Sums of money is made a Nessesary Qualification for the above said offices as Renders it inconvenient in many Respects and Dangerous in Some, the Last mentioned articles yeas 8 Nays 29

Objt. 3d In Chapter 2 Section 1th—Article 9th for that the remotest Part of the State by the Governor and Council cannot be fairly and justly represented without the Suffrages of the People by their Representatives or the officors of the County in Geneal—yeas 1 Nays 42——
Objt. Chapter 6 article 3; Nays 57. this article objected to for that the Legislative have Power to alter the Qualification to office as they shall see fit. which we think amounts to afull Power to make the Qualifications such that thire Cannot be more than one, and Prehaps no Representative in some Countys——
ob. 5 no yeas Nays 53 in Chapter 6 articl 10th—this article objected to for that the Time Perfixed for altering or Revising the Constitution ought not to be more than five years——In Chapter 6 article 2 after mention of the officers of Harvard Colledge, all Settled ministers of the Gospel of all Denominations, ought to be Inserted in addation there to ——The Question being Put upon the whole of the Declaration of Rights and Frame of Government with the foregoing objections it Passed Yeas 63 Nays 1
Our Deligate instructed to agree with the Convention upon a time when the Constitution Shall Take Place

Zenas Wheeler Selectmen of
Elijah Shelden N. Marlborough

New Salem (276/17)

The Inhabitants of the Town of New Salem being Lawfully assembled in Town Meeting on the 22d of May 1780; To take into Consideration the Form of Government lately presented to us, past the following votes, (viz).
(1st, Voted that the 3d Article in the Declaration of Rights be Vacated or Cast out; there appearing 43 against the article and 35 for it. The Reasons for Rejecting this article are these;—That we look upon it that the Rights of Conscience are better Secured in the preceeding article without it than with it; it being in our Opinion Repugnant to the two first articles in said Declaration. Besides if it is as our Convention tell us, (to which we agree) ie, that Religion must at all Times be a matter between GOD and individuals, then we see not the least propriety or fitness, in the Peoples Investing their Legislature with any spiritual

Jurisdiction Over the Subject; which this article does evidently in some sort provide for.)

2ly Voted that the Constitution be Revised in the Year 1787, in Stead of the Year 1795, there being 78 in favour of this Amendment, and none against it.

3ly That every Man being a proper Town Inhabitant, who pays Taxes, be allowed the Right and Priviledge of Voting in Common with his fellow Citizens; there being 32 for it and but one against it. We view it both unfair and unjust, to Tax Men without their Consent.

4ly That the House of Representatives Consist of nomore than 200 Members, Dividing the State into somany Districts for that purpose as Equally as may be, and them to be paid wholly out of the State Treasury. There appearing 32 for it and 2 against it. By this plan we might have a full and an equal Representation and persivere therein. which could not be in the Plan Proposed by the Convention.

5ly Voted against the 1st article in Chapter 5th Section 1st 35 appearing against said Article and none for it We think it Unreasonable for Men to Enjoy every priviledge of free Citizens without bearing a part of the Burdens of the Community.

New Salem May 22, 1780

Daniel Shaw — Select Men
John Chamberlin — of
Theo. Crocker — New Salem

The Honorable The Convention for
for Forming a New Plan of
Govert. to be held in Boston on Wednesday 7th June 1780.

Pittsfield (276/18)

At a Legal Meeting of the Inhabitants of the Town of Pittsfield duly Qualified on Monday the Eighth Day of May 1780 for the purpose of Considering, approving or disapproving the Constitution sent out to them by the Convention. The number of Voters being Eighty, the Address, Declaration of Rights and Constitution being read to them at large.

Voted. To take the Same into Consideration Article by Article

And every Article in the Declaration of Rights was unanimously accepted Except one Disentunt to Article 3d. And one to Article 10th.

As was the Constitution also, Except 15 Discentunts to the 4th Article in the first Section in the first Chapter. And 4 to the 2d. Article in the Second Section in Said Chapter. And one to the 2d. Article in the First Section of the 2d. Chapter.

And being Called upon by the Moderator to Exhibit their reasons, some of them desired time, upon which the Meeting was adjourned to the 17th of Said Month.

And met according to adjournment at which time no reasons were offered, and not one Disentunt appeared

Att Caleb Stanley Town Clerk

These Certify that in a Legal Meeting of the Inhabitants of the Town of Pittsfield Qulified to Vote in Town affairs on the 17th Day of May 1780. it was voted that the Within be the Instructions for the Deligate appointed to meet and Sit in State Convention to be holden at Boston on the first Wednesday in June Next

Att Caleb Stanley T. Clerk

Pittsfield, May 17th 1780——

To Colonel James Easton,

Sir

As you are chosen a Delegate to represent us in State Convention to be holden at Boston on the 8th Day of June next ensuing to receive and examine the Returns of the several Towns and places within this State relative to the Constitution sent forth for their approbation or Disapprobation in which we expect you'll meet with little Difficulty as we apprehend more than two Thirds of the State will approve of the same. Such being the Case, as the Reigns of Government are so relaxed and this County in particular so long deprived of all Law you are strictly required to endeavor that the Constitution take place as soon as possible which we hope will not exceed the Month of August next.——

If we are disappointed in our Expectations and there is great Variance in the Returns made from the several Towns within the State to that Degree that you shall be obliged to send it out for a Revision we expect that you do not dissolve yourselves till such Time as one is formed and accepted.

Thomas Allen
William Williams Committee
Jno Brown

Richmond (276/19)

At an adjourned Town Meeting of the Inhabitants of Richmont on Monday the 29th of May 1780 at 9 O.Clock AM. the said Inhabitants took into Consideration the Constitution or frame of Government made and proposed by the Honorable Convention convened for that purpose at Cambridge on the first of Sept 1779 and expressed their minds on it by yeas and nays as follows Viz

On the Bill of Rights

		Yeas	Nays			Yeas	Nays
Article	1	17	—	Article	26	20	
	2	17	—		27	20	
	3	11	43		28	20	
	4	20	—		29	—	25
	5	20			30	24	
	6	20		Frame of Government			
	7	20		Chapter 1st			
	8	20		Section 1			
	9	20		Article	1	24	
	10	20			2	1	27
	11	20			3	31	
	12	21			4	31	
	13	21		Section 2			
	14	20		Article	1	31	
	15	20			2	3	27
	16	20			3	33	
	17	20			4	33	
	18	20			5	33	
	19	20			6	33	
	20	20			7	33	
	21	20			8	32	
	22	20			9	33	
	23	20		Section 3d			
	24	20		Article	1	33	
	25	20			2	31	1

		Yeas	*Nays*
Article	3	6	26
	4	2	30
	5	31	
	6	32	
	7	32	
	8	32	
	9	32	
	10	32	
	11	32	
Chapter	2		
Section	1		
Article	1	18	
	2	23	
	3	35	
	4	35	
	5	35	
	6	41	1
	7	40	
	8	39	
	9	39	
	10	3	40
	11	43	1
	12	44	
	13	45	
Section	2nd		
Article	1	5	38
	2	40	
	3	42	

		Yeas	*Nays*
Section	3d		
Article	1	43	
	2	44	
Chapter	3		
Article	1	5	39
	2	46	
	3		47
	4	47	
	5	47	
Chapter	4th	45	1
Chapter	5		
Section	1		
Article	1	49	
	2	49	
	3	49	
Section	2nd		
Article		49	
Chapter	6th		
Article	1	—	43
	2	48	
	3	12	36
	4	38	
	5	3	39
	6	31	15
	7	47	
	8	47	
	9	47	
	10	47	
	11	47	

After the Articles of the frame of government had been put to vote separately the said frame of government was put to vote without amendment and on a Trial it was voted unanimously in the Negative

The Town of Richmond having shewn their disapprobation of a Number of Articles in the Frame of Government Voted the following Objections Reasons and Amendments viz

(Bill of Rights Article 3rd Objection. This Article is an infringement of the Right of Conscience

Amendment that this Article be erased from the Bill of Rights)

Article 29th Objection The Term of the Continuance of the Judges of the supreme judicial Court in their offices is impolitic Reasons. Persons may be appointed to said Offices which upon Trial do not answer the Expectation of their Constituants and yet can not be displaced by any charge of actual Misbehaviour but by continuing in their offices deprive the Commonwealth of the Benefit of Persons better Qualified

Amendment—That the said Officers by appointed annually

Constitution

Chapter 1 Section 1 Article 2nd Objection The undue Controul which the Governor has on the Legislative Body

Reasons. We think the Senate and House of Representatives a sufficient Legislative Body—That this Power by partiale influence may prevent the Enacting of Laws which are calculated for the general Benefit of the Common Wealth for as much as the Governor and Elevin of the Council as the Case may be may controul the whole Legislative Body—and this Power in the Governor is a manifest infringement of those excellent Principles laid down in the 30th Article of the Bill of Rights

Section 2nd Article 2 Objection. The Qualifications of Voters for senators

Reasons. Excluding Persons from a share in Representation for want of pecuniary Qualifications is an infringement on the Natural Rights of the Subject and will exclude many good members of Society and the bad Members of Society may be better excluded in another Line.

Amendment That no Persons be admitted to vote for a Governor Lieut Governor Senators or Representatives until they shall obtain Certificates from the Select men of the Towns in which they live that they are good members of Society and of sober Life and Conversation and then take an Oath of Fidelity to the Common Wealth and that they will act conscienciously in voting in any matter which concerns the State and be inrolled in the Corporation to which they belong as possessed of these Privileges and ever after allowed the above privileges till forfeited by misbehaviour.

Section 3rd Article 3d Objection. The pecuniary Qualifications of Members may cease to exist by Reason of fire or some other Providential calamity and thereby the use of a valuable member of society be lost to the Community

Article 4th Objected to for Reasons mentioned in our Objections to the 2nd Article of the preceeding Section

Chapter 2nd Section 1 Article 9 Objection the Nomination of the Officers mentioned in this Article being made by the Governor and Council

Reasons the disadvantage the Governor and Council will be under of knowing Characters in remote parts of the State

Amendment. That the above named Officers be nominated by the Senate and House of Representatives

Article 10th Objection 1st The field Officers and Brigadiers nominated by their inferior officers

2nd The nomination of Officers in the Militia Line being made by the Governor and Council

3rd The Officers in the Continental army being nominated as above

4th the Exclusion of Persons under 21 years of age from voting for their Respective Officers

Reasons 1st. This mode of nomination will tend to exclude every Character however qualified which are not of the Line from these offices and will tend to destroy that dependence of the Military Power on the Civil Authority and that exact subordination to it which is necessary

2nd The Governor and Council will not have the advantage of knowing the most suitable Characters for Officers in the Militia and Continental Lines which the Senate and House of Representatives will have.

3d We think it impolitic and injurious to deprive young men from voting for those officers under whose immediate Command they are bound to do actual service as it will weaken the springs of their Emulation and although at that time of Life they may be subject to [torn] yet they will never be free from Corruption

Amendments 1st. That the officers mentioned in the Militia and Continental Service be nominated by the Senate and House of Representatives

That all Persons who are subject to do duty in the Militia have a voice in the nomination of their Respective Captains and Subalterns

Article 13 Objection The Salaries proposed for the officers mentioned in the Article are not subject to Diminution

Reasons. The Governor and other Officers mentioned may at some favourable Crisis by their influence make those salaries enormous and burthensome to the people

Amendment That the General Court have Power to add to or diminish from these salaries as they shall judge proper

Chapter 3rd Article 1st Objection The Term which the officers mentioned in this Article are to continue in office

Reason. The Continuance of Persons in Office for a long or unlimited Term makes them too independent of their Constituents exposes them to negligince and haughtiness and endangers the Rights of the People and may deprive the State of the benefit of persons better Qualified.

Amendment—That these Officers be appointed annually

Chapter 6th Article 1st Objection. The omission of specifying the Protestant Religion particularly

Reason. the Religious Liberties of the People may be greatly endangered by that Omission

Article 5th We desire this amendment may be made to this Article That Justices of the Peace be impowered to grant out Writs in Cases to be tried before the inferiour Courts

Article 3 of the above Chapters

Objection. The Legislature by having power of increasing the Qualifications relating to money is dangerous to the Liberties of the poorer class of people and therefore inadmissible

Voted that it is the opinion of the Inhabitants of this Town that the pecuniary Qualifications of the Governor and Lieutenant Governor are too high and that they be stated as low as five hundred pounds also that it is necessary to Confine the Choice to one of the Protestant Profession

Attest Nat. Bishop T. Clerk

To the Honble Convention of Delegates
for the State of Massachusetts Bay at Boston

Sandisfield (276/20)

Att a Meeting of the Inhabitants of the Town of Sandisfield Legaly Assembled on the 28th of April 1780 the following Votes were passed Continued by adjournment to the First Day of June viz.

Number Men present Acting on the bill of Rights 54 every Article Aproved of Except the 3d 34 aprovd 20 desaprovd

---

Constitution Chapter: 1 Article 1st Aprovd Article 2d is Contrary to the bill of rights as Expresd in Article: 30th and we suppose that the people are Compleetly represented in the Legislative body and that body Compleat in power of Legislation. with[?] the voice of the Governor and that it be rather inconsistant to attempt the making a power of Legislation Superior to a Compleat and supreme power of Legislation which we Consider is the Case if the Governor hath a Controuling power over that Body and we Conceive that such a power would have a Tendency to Bias the minds of the Legislators and the Course of Legislation Retarded and that such a Body is Capable of revising their own Acts and refutting theron without the Least Controul in a Single person or any Body Distinct from them and further that the method in the article proposed would be an infringement of the rights of that body 19 Disaprove 4 Aprove

Article 3d Aprovd. The whole of Art: 4th stands aprovd excepting where it grants certain Liberties to the Legislature of apointing Civil officers it ought to be aded all Judicial officers, Atorney General Solicitor General Sheriffs Coroner Register of probate Secretary Tresurer and Receiver General Comisary General Notaries Public and Naval Officers ought and should be appointed by the Legislature and all the monies of the Comon Wealth ought to be isued out of the Tresury from Commission of pay Table appointed for that purpose by Joint Ballot of both houses in one room anualy and Controulable by the house of representatives and answerable to them for their Conduct in said office. The monies of the Comon Wealth are peculiarly the property of the people and ought to be imediatly used under their Controul—Judges of the Supreme Court of Judicature ought to be Chosen by joint Ballot of both houses and ought to hold their places During good behaviour. Judges of the Inferior Court of Common pleas and Judges of probate ought to be Chosen by Joint Ballot of both houses of Legislature and in one room and Justices of the peace shall be anualy Elected in the following manner, Nominated by the representatives of the County in which they are to be apointed and aproved of by 2d branch of Legislature and concured to by the first and Comissioned by the Governor. They being of a Judicial Department are by the bill of rights Article 30th forbid a seat in Legislature —25 Disaprove 5 Aprove

---

Chapter 1st Section 2d Article 1st 26 Senators we think are a number large enough for the first branch of Legislation and each District ought to have one Senator and the remaining number apointed in the same proportion as assigned in the proposed Constitution. The Burdens of the people ought to be as Light as may be—13 Disaprove 3 aprove. Article 2d 27 Disaprove 6 Aprove Article 3d. The word Council ought to be erased and the word Senate inserted 20 Disaprove 2 Aprove——Article 4th Aproved——Article 5th 23 Disaprovd 11 Aprove——Articles 7, 8, and 9 Aproved

---

Chapter 1st Section 3d. Article 1st Aproved—Article 2d. here is Danger from Various reasons that the 2d Legislative Body will be too Large and representation Unequal therefore in Article 2d. the third and succeeding number ought not to be less than 500 20 Disaprove 3 aprove. Article 3d. 28 Disaprove 4 aprove Article 4th 18 Disaprove 6 aprove Article 5th if the representatives were Chosen on the Day that the Senators are it would save Cost and trouble to the people and would be a known time of election and all voters might atend their Duty—28 Disaprove 3 aprove—Articles 6th 7 and 8 Aproved—Articles 9 and 10 Aprovd —Article 11th what respects the government and Council ought to be Left out for reasons herafter mentioned—25 Disaprove and 3 aprove——

Chapter 2d. Section 1st. Article 1st Aproved. Article 2d. The proposed frame of Government make provision that the Governor shall be of the Christian religion but sais not of what Denomination and since it is a Community of Protestants that are Covenanting and emerging from a State of nature and for their posterity it is necessary to say that not only the Governor but all executive Legislative Judicial and Military officers shall be of the Protestant Christian religion 11 Disaprove 2 aprove— Article 3d Disaproved because the voice of the people ought to be had jointly in the Choice of the supreme Executive Magistrate either by themselves or Representatives 21 Disaprove 2 Approve—Article 4th. is suposed needless and otherwise provided for in the proposed amendment 10 Disaprove 2 Approve Article 5th The words with Advice of Council ought to be Left out for the above reasons 20 Disaprove 2 approve———Article 6th the two houses ought to Agree as to the time of Adjournment Therfore the article ought to be Left out as it stands 20 Disaprove 2 Approve Article 7th. Aproved Article 8th The word senate ought to be inserted in the room of Council 22 Disaprove 2 Approve—Article 9th otherwise provided for in this Amendment 12 Disaprove 3 Approve—Article 10th 22 Disaprove 12 Approve—Article 11th otherwise provided for in the proposed Amendment———15 Disaprove 2 Approve———Article 12th. At the end of this article it ought to be aded in order that they may be Laid before the Legislative Body 20 Disaprove 6 Aprove———Article 13th Aproved———

Chapter 2d Section 2d Article 1st Aproved Article 2d Expunged as needless if the proposed Amendment be adopted, 18 Disaprove 3 Aprove Article 3 Aproved

---

Chapter 2d Section 3d Articles 1st 2d 3d 4th, 5th, 6 and 7th Such a body of men Distinct from others and Constantly paid out of the Treasury will be burdensome to the people and as proposed in the Constitution a Tendency to Create a formidable power against the Legislative body which ought to feel it self free 14 Disaprove 2 Aprove

---

Chapter 2d Section 4th Article 1st Aproved. Article 2d. The word Council ought to be Left out—18 Disaprove 2 Approve Chapter 3d Article 1st. after the word Sworn Substitute as is provided for in the Constitution nevertheless, the Governor shall remove them on joint advice of both houses of Legislature 12 Disaprove 3 approve———Article 2d. The word Council ought to be Left out for reasons above given 21 Disaprove 3 Approve Article 3d otherwise provided for in this Amendment. 9 Disaprove 3 Approve Article 4th aproved Article 5th Disaproved of as inconsistent with the bill of rights Article 30th and also with the Convenience of the people and all causes of the Marriage Divorce and Alimony and Appeals from the Judge of probate ought to be heard and determined by the Judges of the Supreme Court of Judicature 17 Disaprove 2 Aprove

---

Chapter 4th The Delegates to Congress being the grand representation of the whole Confederation ought to be Chosen by the people out of a Nomination List formed for that purpose who shall Declare themselves Protestant Christians on their Acceptance of that Trust. 19 Disaprove 2 Aprove

---

Chapter: 5th Approved

Chapter 6th Article 1st after the word believe the word Protestant ought to inserted 17 Disaprove 2 aprove Article 2d Aproved Article: 3d 15 Disaprove 2 Aprove: Article 4th Aproved. Article 5th all writs Returnable to the Superiour or Inferiour Court Shall be signed by a Justice of the peace or Senator and the Senators writ to extend through any county in the State but that signed by the Justice to be Confined to that County in which he liveth and each writ bear the Seal of the State We suppose this mode would be more free and easy and Cheap for the people and the above should stand as a substitute to the 5th article 19 Disaprove 3 aprove

Articles 6th 7th 8th 9th 10th and 11th aproved

for a Council to the Governor the senate in time of the session seem to be the most natural Council for the Govenor and in their recess the Governor shall in matters of importance Call for a Number of the Senate nighest to the place of his residence who shall advise the Governor. theron and Said Number Shall not be more than nine nor less than five. After the Amendment by this Convention if such Amendment should be the people ought to have a Revision therof—the Convention ought to be Considered as Impowred to apoint a time when this Constitution Shall take place in its full Latitude

Chapter 6th Article 3d. The Legislature have no right to make Alteration in Respect of Property Stated in this Constitution

The foregoing a Coppy of the proceedings of the Town of Sandisfield on the System of Government

Test David Deming Moderator

Sheffield *

Town Warrant April 17, 1780. "2nd, To take Into Consideration the doings of the Convention for forming a Constitution."

Warrant, October 7, 1780. 4th "To see if the town will Allow Deacon Kellogg Reasonable Expenses in Attending the Convention to form a Constitution."

At an adjourned Meeting, Monday, October 30, 1780. "Voted to allow Deacon Silas Kellogg nine pounds in full for his Service in attending on the Convention for forming a Constitution for this State."

Stockbridge (276/21)

Stockbridge June 1st, 1780

Sir

The freemen of this Town have made choise of their Representatives, Mr. John Bacon and Jahliel Woodbridge Esquire, for their Delegates to Convention———We shall herewith send you the Returns of the votes, of the Male Inhabitants of this Town from 21 years old and upwards, upon the Several Articles Contained in the Bill of Rights and Constitution or Frame of Government, with the Number of Votes for and against Each article—Together with the Instructions of the Town to you their Delegate to Represent them in the Convention to meet at Boston on the [first?] Wednesday Instant June.———

Voted that our Delegate or Delegates in Convention Endeavour to Effect an alteration in the Several Articles of the Declaration of Rights, and Frame of Government, against which the Major Part of the Voters in this Town have Voted agreeable to amendments proposed by us, and hereunto Annexed—But if there should not appear to be two thirds of the people of this State who may have Voted on the Article, in Favor of such amendments, or the printed Declaration of Rights and Frame of Government now proposed to the people of this State, In such Case our Delegates in Convention assembled be invested with Power to make such alterations as may be agreeable to the Sentiments of two thirds of the Votes of the People throughout this State, and to agree upon a Time

* Town records, Massachusetts Historical Society.

when this Form of Government Shall take Place without Returning the Same again to the People

Test Asa Bement Moderator

To Jahl. Woodbridge Esquire.
P S your Family is well

The votes of the town of Stockbridge, upon the Several Articles Conained in the Bill of Rights and Constitution or Frame of Government agreed upon by the Delegates of the People of the State of Massachusetts-Bay, Taken at a Legal Town Meeting with the Number of Voters for, and against, each Article of the Same———

Bill of Rights Number of Voters for Each Article of the Same		Bill of Rights Number of Voters Against Each Article of the Same
Article the First	111	0
2 Ditto	111	0
3 Ditto	19	98
4 Ditto	117	0
5 Ditto	116	0
6 Ditto	114	0
7 Ditto	114	0
8 Ditto	112	0
9 Ditto	112	1
10 Ditto	112	0
11 Ditto	115	0
12 Ditto	111	0
13 Ditto	113	0
14 Ditto	109	0
15 Ditto	92	1
16 Ditto	100	0
17 Ditto	102	0
18 Ditto	102	0
19 Ditto	107	0
20 Ditto	99	0
21 Ditto	92	0
22 Ditto	91	0
23 Ditto	92	0
24 Ditto	94	00
25 Ditto	95	0
26 Ditto	96	0
27 Ditto	95	1

	Article	*For*	*Against*
28	Ditto	94	0
29	Ditto	75	7
30	Ditto	89	0

The Constitution or Frame of Government

	The Number of Voters For Each Article of the Constitution		The Number of Voters Against Each Article of the Constitution	
	Chapter first, Section First		Chapter first, Section first	
	Article first	43	Article first	0
2	Ditto	37		11
3	Ditto	48		0
4	Ditto	57		0
	Senate Chapter 1st Section 2nd		Senate Chapter 1st Section 2d	
	Article First	50	Article First	0
2	Ditto	50		11
3	Ditto	46		0
4	Ditto	58		7
5	Ditto	42		27
6	Ditto	60		0
7	Ditto	60		0
8	Ditto	60		0
9	Ditto	60		0
	Section 3rd House of Representatives		Section 3d House of Representatives	
	Article First	64	Article First	1
2	Ditto	68		5
3	Ditto	66		3
4	Ditto			
5	Ditto	39		0
6	Ditto	39		0
7	Ditto	39		0
8	Ditto	39		0
9	Ditto	39		0
10	Ditto	39		0
11	Ditto	39		0
	Chapter Second Executive Power Section First		Chapter Second Executive Power Section First	
	Article First	37		
2	Ditto			

3 Ditto	39	2
Article fourth	46	0
5 Ditto	46	0
6 Ditto	46	0
7 Ditto	46	0
8 Ditto	46	0
9 Ditto, as amended	49	0
10	1	20
That the Governor and Council approve the Major and Brigadier General and Field Officers	31	1
That the Companys Choose Captains and Subalterns	30	8
11	31	0
12	31	0
13	31	0
Chapter 2nd Section Second		Chapter Second Section 2d
Article First,	25	0
2 Ditto	25	0
3 Ditto	25	0
Chapter 2d Section 3rd		Chapter 2d Section 3
Article First	24	0
2 Ditto	24	0
3 Ditto	24	0
4 Ditto	24	0
5 Ditto	24	0
6 Ditto	24	0
7 Ditto	24	0
Chapter 2d Section 4th		Chapter 2d Section 4th
Article First	26	0
2 Ditto	26	0
Chapter 3rd Judiciary Power		Chapter 3rd Judiciary Power
Article First	9	8
2 Ditto	17	0
3 Ditto	16	1
4 Ditto	17	0
5 Ditto	17	0
Chapter 4th Delegates to Congress		Chapter 4th Delegates to Congress
Article First	23	2

Chapter 5th Section 1st University	Chapter 5th Section 1st University	
	[For]	[Against]
Article First	20	0
2 Ditto	20	0
3 Ditto	20	0
Chapter 5 Section 2nd Encouragement of Literature	Chapter 5 Section 2nd Encouragement of Literature	
	26	0
Chapter 6th Oaths etc.	Chapter 6th Oaths etc.	
Article First (Exclude ordained Ministers	26	0
2 Ditto	26	0
3 Ditto	26	Qualifications not to be altered by the Legislature
5 Ditto	26	
6 Ditto	26	0
7 Ditto	26	0
8 Ditto	26	0
9 Ditto	26	0
10 Ditto	26	0
11 Ditto	26	0

Asa Bement Select Men
Josiah Jones of Stockbridge

Tyringham (276/22)

Tyringham 30th of May AD 1780——

The Inhabitants of the Town of Tyringham Legally assembled in Public Town meeting on the 30th of May Instant for the purpose of taking into consideration the New Constitution or Mode of Government passed these Several votes as follows (viz) After reading the Bill of Rights and the Constitution, The question was put Whether the Town will accept of the Same for their Rule or Mode of Government——The Vote passed one in the affirmative and fifty seven in the Negative——

The afore mentioned number of 57 voted and agreed that they will accept of the fore mentioned Bill of Rights and Constitution to be the rule or Mode of Government for this State provided these [*1 word torn*] amendments may be made as follows—viz

1st That all Superior Judges and all other Officers appointed by the Government and Counsel Ought to be annually appointed as we make no doubt of their being continued in office during good Behavour——

2dly We are very sensible that a very large Number of the Good Inhabitants of this State that pay a very considerable part of the Taxes of the Same are by the frame of Constitution Debard of the priviledge of freemen——It is our oppinion that Every male Inhabitant that is free and twenty one years of age shall have free Liberty to Vote in all matters in the Town he Belongs to unless by some Vicious Conduct he has forfeited the Same as they have hitherto been called upon to Vote themselves Independent of Great Britain and to stand forth in the defence of their darling Right and priviledges and have nobly done the Same. We immagine they will not now give up so dear a priviledge as that of Representation which they have a right to provided they are Taxed to pay their full proportion of money or service to the support and defence of the Community——

3dly It is our oppinion that the setting of a convention for the Revisal and amendment of the Constitution shall be asserted in the Bill of Rights and shall be perpetually once in fifteen years——

4thly It is our oppinion that no specified sum of money should be Absolutely a Nessessary qualification in any person appointed to Office by the people

5thly. We are of oppinion that the members of the house of Representatives shall be paid for their service out of the Public treasury of the State.

6thly That an Article ought to be Inserted in the Bill of Rights that persons in cases of Debt may be allowed the priviledge of confessing Judgement previous to any Action theiron——

7thly That every town shall have the priviledge of a Register of Deeds within the town——

8thly. We are of an Oppinion that the Appointment of Justices of the peace be by Nomination of the General Voice of the Inhabitants of the Town where such Justice is appointed——

9thly That all trainband Soldiers shall have the priviledge of having a Vote in the choice of officers in the militia viz Captains and Subalterns

N. B. That the Last or Ninth Article in the amendment had 34 in favour of it as it stands in the amendment and 23 as it stands in the Constitution or form of government.

Extract from the Minutes Attest— Japheth Chapin, Solomon Jackson, Eliezar Fielde } Selectmen of Tyringham

Elisha Garfield, Town Clerk

Washington (276/23)

At a meeting of the Freeholders and other Inhabitants of the Town of Washington Legaly Warned and Meet at the Meetinghouse on Monday the 29th day of May 1780 to Take into Consideration the Late Constitution sent out for the Approbation or Disapprobation of the Saim by a Convention Convened at Cambridge in September the 1st 1779; And the Town Voted to Chuse a Committee of twelve to Perruse the Saim and Make Returns to the Town and General Assembly———
Which Committee Convened on the above Said Day at the Meetinghouse and Made Choice of Lieutenant Jabez Cornish Chairman and George Sloan Scribe and perceeded as Follows viz———

Chapter first Section first the Legeslative Power———
Article first———yey Number 12 Voted for———
2———yey———12 Ditto———
3———yey———12 Ditto———
4———Nay———12 Against it. The Committee eunanimously agreed against the fourth Article and Voted that no Body of men whatsoever has a Rite to Lay any Duty or Excise on the Produce of the Country or Manefactory of the Country Whatsoever———

Chapter first Section Seacond Senet———
Article 1st———yey Number 12 Voted for———
2 ———yey Ditto 12 Voted for———
3 ———yey Ditto 12 Ditto———
4 ———yey Ditto 12 Ditto———
5 ———yey Ditto 12 Ditto———
6 ———yey Ditto 12 Ditto———
7 ———yey Ditto 12 Ditto———
8 ———yey Ditto 12 Ditto———
9 ———yey Ditto 12 Ditto———

Chapter first Section third House of Representatives———
Article 1st———yey Number 12 voted for it
2 ———Ney ——— 12 voted against it
3 ———yey Ditto 12 Ditto———
4 ———yey Ditto 12 Ditto———
5 ———yey Ditto 12 Ditto———
6 ———yey Ditto 12 Ditto———
7 ———yey Ditto 12 Ditto———

8 ——yey Ditto 12 Ditto——
9 ——yey Ditto 12 Ditto——
10 ——yey Ditto 12 Ditto——
11 ——yey Ditto 12 Ditto——

The Commitee Eunanimously agreed against the Second article and Voted that Each Town has an undeniable Rite to Equel Representation in the General Assembly——and Whereas there is a large Number of Deligates from the Marchantile Towns and but Small Numbers from the Inland Towns We have Laid in our objection——

Chapter Seacond Section first Executive Power——
Article 1st——yey——Number 12 for it——
2 ——yey——Ditto 12 Ditto——
3 ——yey——Ditto 12 Ditto——
4 ——yey——Ditto 12 Ditto——
5 ——yey——Ditto 12 Ditto——
6 ——yey——Ditto 12 Ditto——
7 ——yey——Ditto 12 Ditto——
8 ——yey——Ditto 12 Ditto——
9 ——yey——Ditto 12 Ditto——
10 ——yey——Ditto 12 Ditto——
11 ——yey——Ditto 12 Ditto——
12 ——yey——Ditto 12 Ditto——
13 ——yey——Ditto 12 Ditto——

Chapter Seacond Section Seacond Lieutenant Governor——
Article 1st——yey——Number——12 for it——
2 ——yey——Ditto—— 12 Ditto——
3 ——yey——Ditto—— 12 Ditto——

Chapter Seacond Section third, Counsel and Manner of setling elections by the legislature——
Article 1st——yey——Number 12 for it
2 ——yey——Ditto 12 Ditto
3 ——yey——Ditto 12 Ditto
4 ——yey——Ditto 12 Ditto
5 ——yey——Ditto 12 Ditto
6 ——yey——Ditto 12 Ditto
7 ——yey——Ditto 12 Ditto

Chapter Seacond Section fourth Sectretory Treasurery Commissary
Article 1st——yey——Number 12 for it
2 ——yey——Ditto 12 Ditto

Chapter third Judicatory Power———
Article 1st———yey———Number 12 for it
2 ———yey———Ditto 12 Ditto
3 ———yey———Number 12 For it
4 ———yey———Ditto 12 Ditto
5 ———yey———Ditto 12 Ditto

Chapter fourth Deligates to Congress———
Article 1st———yey———Number 12 for it.

Chapter fifth Section first the University———
Article 1st———yey———Number 12 for it
2 ———yey———Ditto 12 Ditto
3 ———yey———Ditto 12 Ditto

Chapter fifth Section Seacond the Encurridgemt of Literature
Article 1st———yey———Number 12—for it———
Chapter Sixth Oaths and subscriptions Incompatibility of and Exclusion from Officers———
Article 1st———yey———Number———12———for it
2 ———yey———Ditto——— 12———Ditto
3 ———yey———Ditto——— 12———Ditto
4 ———yey———Ditto——— 12———Ditto
5 ———yey———Ditto——— 12———Ditto
6 ———yey———Ditto——— 12———Ditto
7 ———yey———Ditto——— 12———Ditto
8 ———yey———Ditto——— 12———Ditto
9 ———yey———Ditto——— 12———Ditto
10 ———yey———Ditto——— 12———Ditto

We whose Names are Under Written Being Chosen at a Publick Town Meeting and being Convened at the Meetinghouse and after Deliberately Debateing on the Constitution Parrigraff by Parigraff We have Passed all the Constitution Except the two aforesaid Articles and made Return to the Town Meeting and Said Meeting Ecquiest in the Return the Number thirty Eight being No More Preasant at Said Meeting

Leiut. Jabez Cornish Chairman
George Sloan Scribe

Names of the Comtee
Daniel Olds
Phillip Mattoon
Ahimaaz Easton
Liet. Jabez Cornish

Jesse Ladd
Seth Jillit
Jeames McKnight
Samuel Smith
George Sloan
Azariah Ashley
Daniel Francklin
David Martin

in [obedience?] to the Resolves of the Convention held att Cambridge for the Purpose of forming a new Constitution we have taken approbation of the inhabitants which is as above—

Jabez Cornish
William Bill
Sam Smith

Selectmen for the town of Washington

West Stockbridge (276/24)

At a Meeting of the Inhabitants of West Stockbridge on the Eleventh Day of May Legally Assembled for that purpose the Constitution or Frame of Governmnet as Agreed upon by the Convention of The State of the Massachusetts Bay was laid before the Said Town and a Vote taken whether they approved of the same as it then stoot, which Vote passed. Unanimously in the Negative

The following which were objected to Viz Article 2nd of the House of Representatives by which Every Corperated town containing one Hundred and fifty ratable polls may elect one Representative and Every town encreasing thier number of ratible polls by the mean number of two Hundred and twenty five may in the same preportion increase the number of Representatives.

The amendment proposed on this article was that no Town be allowed to elect more than four Representatives and that Every incorperated town be allowed to elect one

The next article Objected to was the qualification of the Governor where it is provided that no person shall be eligable to that Office unless he Declare himself to be of the Christian Religion it was proposed to Dele Christian and insert Protestant it was further Objected to the Governor having the sole Nomination of Judicial Offices and proposed that any one of the Council Should have a right to nominate to Civil Offices And that the Representatives of Each County should have a right to nominate the Justices of thier Respective Counties. It was thought unreasonable to Deprive any one enroled in the trainband list the privilige of voting for *His own* Offices and therefore that the Captain and Subalterns should be elected not by the vote of such as are twenty one years of age and upwards only but by the whole list These amendments being made and the vote again put it passed in the affirmative Eighteen being for this Constitution with the Amendments Proposed and two against it: the Town consists of one-hundred-fourteen Rateable Polls of men of twenty one years of age The town then voted to impower the Delegates at the next session of Convention to agree upon a time when this form of Government shall take Place

West Stock. May 11th AD 1780 Test Amos Fowler
Town Clerke

Williamstown (276/25)

At a legal meeting of the Inhabitants of Williamstown called for that purpose present 98 voters after reading and considering the Bill of Rights and Constitution the following articles were Objected to as follows (viz) in the Bill of Rights article 3d—12 voted against it Ditto article 29th 24 voted against it—in the Frame of Government Chapter 1st Section 2 article 1st—11 voted against it Chapter 2—Section 1st article 3d 10 voted against it and proposed that all voters for any part of the Legislative or Executive power shall be under oath as a necessary Qualification for voting—Ditto [on?] article 9th. 14 voted against it Ditto article 10th 15 voted against it Chapter 3d. article 1st 17 voted against it—Then voted to have the Constitution take place as soon as may be provided it shall be found by the Returns to be agreable to two thirds of the People of this state or the Convention Shall Conform it to the sentiments of two thirds of the people of this State

attested

Williamstown Nehemiah Woodcock
May 3d. 1780 Isaac Stratton Selectmen

At a meeting of the inhabitance of Williamtown on the 4 Day of May 1780 to Consider the Constiution and Bill of Rights after Reading the same it was put to vote in the [gross?] 51 voted for it and 47 against it

James Meacham Moderator
Stephen Davis—Select man

Windsor (276/26)

Aarticles Objected against in the Costitution

1ly The 3d Article in the Bill of Right is all bad exceping the Last claus, for the following reasons first it gives the legislature Power to make Laws to oblidge the Inhabitants of the Several Towns Preceints etc. to provide for Gospel Teachers with this reserve that every man if he Desire it, may have his money paid to the Teacher of his own Denomination otherways it may be paid to the Town or parish to which he belongs. Being thus stated it oblidges every Quacor and Baptist to pay Ministor rates as effectually [*1 word torn*] there was a Law of the State that Obliged every man of every Denomination to pay them that lived within the Bounds of a Town, or parish.———

2ly it is as much against the Quacors and Baptists Principles to Request any money to be paid to their own Teachers as to pay it to another therefore it lays them under an absolute necessity of Doing that, that is against their Conscince or to Suffer their money to be paid to the Town or parish to which they belong———

The 9th Article of the Second Chapter Section the first where the Governor hath the Power of Nominating all Juditial Officers Sherifes Corriners etc. which Power ought to be left with the People at large or with the Representatives of the Several Counties for the following Reasons first, if we should be so unhappy as to make choice of a Govenor who is badly dissposed he may (By having this Power) Secure to himself his futer Election and may other points By Disposing of Commisions to his favorites———

2ly If he should be ever so well Disposed tis impossible that [?] should have a personal acquaintence with every Officer nesesary to be apointed in this State. as the people at Large have who are Daly Conversing with them daly.

3ly it is not safor to put any more athority into one Mans hand, than what is of absolute necessity.———and if the Govenor should give himself so much Time as would be nesesary for that purpose he neglect other business of more importance———

Chapter 2d. Article 13th Last clase ought to be mendid thus if the Salaries are found too Large they Should be Lessened. by the General

Cort———Chapter 6th Article 2d is good with these words rased out Military Officers and Justices of the Peace excepted—should be holden by one man for the following reason two Commissions of profit or honour is as much as is safe to be granted to one man———Chapter 6th Article 6th where all the old Laws are Confirmed without Day which ought to have bin limited to Some Sertain time Sufficient to propose others in their room———Chapter 6th Article 9th all Civil and Military Officers are to hold their Commisions without Day which ought to be limited to some Sertain Period. for the following reasons, their is many men in this State who have got Commissions without the consent of the people which is directly contrary to the spirit and meaning of this Constitution.

Chapter 6 artal 3 it ort Not to Be in the Powr of the General Cort to incres the soms to Qualifi any Members

Thirty Eight yeas to Exsept of the Frame of Government with the above oldaration.

A Trew Coppy Att John Brown
Town Clark

Dated at Windsor May 19. 1780

At a Town meting Legally Worned and Held in Windsor for the Following Purpos viz to take into Consideration the Present Constitution etc.———

A motion being made whether the Bill of Rites Shall Stand as it is Exsepting the 4th Claws in the 3rd Article Past by 70 yeas———

Twenty Seven nays against the frame of Goverment as it now Stands

A Trew Coppy Att John Brown
Town Clark

BRISTOL COUNTY

Attleborough (276/27)

At a Town meeting Lawfully warned and held in Attleborough on the Second Day of May 1780 that meeting then held was to Consider of the Constitution or Frame of Government as reported by the Convention. The frame of government was then Read and a committee Chosen Consisting of 13 to Consider the same and the meeting was then ajourned to the 22d Day of May then the Plan or Frame of Government was Taken up and the Town Voted it should be Read Article by article the First article in the Dicleration of Rights was read and Unanimously accepted the number of voters then Present were 227 the Second article received unanimously the 3d article underwent Long Debates, the Question being put the number in favour of the article were 154 against it 89 offering for reason that the Civel authority have no Legal right to interfere in matters of Religion. The Remainder of the articles in the Dicleration of Rights Passed unanimously the number being as above 227 The remainder of the Constitution was unanimously voted in Except the second article in the Second Chapter the Town unanimously Voted that any Person Elected to be Govenor whould Declare himself to be of the Protestant Religion in stead of the words Christian Religion also the fifth article in the same Chapter where it is said the Govenor may in case of any Infection Remove the Court to some other Place, it was voted that the Governor should be obliged to do it then, voted that the Legeslature Shall not be impowed to Increase the Qualification of any officer Respecting the Sum they may be worth at the time of their Election in the Legeslative Body in this State. Also voted that the Judge of Probate and Regester of Deeds be appointed in Each Town said appointment to be by the Governor and Councel then Voted that the Convention be impowered to Establish a Form of Government without sending it back to the People—

Voted that the new Constitution Take place as soon as Conveniently may be also voted that any Person on whom an oath may be imposed may if he choose it swear by the Ever Living God in stead of swearing by the form as Reported by the Convention.

Attleborough May 22 1780 Stephen Richardson, Jonathan Stanley, Selectmen of Attleborough

Berkley (276/28)

At a Legal Town Meeting held in the Town Berkley on Monday the fifteenth Day of May Currant, for taking into Consideration the Constitution or frame of Goverment agreable to a Resolve accompanying the Same.———

When a motion was made that the Said Constitution or Frame of Goverment might be Read and it passed in the affirmative and it was Read accordingly,———

2d Motion was made for the ajornment of Said Meeting in order to give further time for the Purusal and Consideration of Said Constituon, and it Passed in the affermitive for the ajornment to Thursday the twenty fifth Day of Said May, and Said Meeting was ajorned accordingly———

Atest Samuel Tobey Jr. Town Clerk

May 25th 1780 Meet agreable To the above ajornment When A motion was Made for Reading the Declaration of Rights, and the frame of Goverment parragraft by Parragraft, and to Pass upon Each Paragraft as we go along, and it Passed in the affirmative———

2d the Preamble was Read, as allso the Declaration of Rights, Paragraft by Paragraft, and Unanimously voted without any amendment by the hole Number present at Said Meeting, which was 45———

Then Proceded To Read the Remainder of Said Constitution Through Paragraft by Paragraft, and Each Paragraft Unanously Voted Except the Ninth Paragraft respecting the Governors appointment of the Sherifs of Each County, as allso the tenth Paragraft respecting The term the Militia officers are to hold their Commissions as Likewise the Second Paragraft where the Governer, in order to Qullify himself for that office, is obliged to Declare himself to be of the Christian Religion, as allso the first Paragraft where it Respects the Oath to be taken by the Govener, Lieutenant

Govenor, Senator, or Representative in Each of the afore Said Paragrafts the amendments were as follows. Viz———

9 Paragraft where it Respects the appointment and Continuence in office [of?] Sheriffs, there was 17 in favour of the hole Paragraft as it was reported without any amendment and 17 in favour of the following amendment Namely that the Sheriff of each County Should be Chosen by the Legal Voters in said County in the same Manner as the County Regesters were Chosen under the old Constitution, Except that the Said Sheriff Shall be Elected anew once in three year or some other person as the Electors Shall Determine by their votes———

[torn] Paragraft where it Says the Govener Shall be of The Christian Religeon there was 37 for Dela the word Christian, and in the Rome put in the word Protestant and 5 in favour of the Paragraft without any amendment———

The 10th paragraft there was 28 for the Militia officers That are to be Chosen by the People in stead of their Holding their Commissions During good behavour, that they Shoul be Chosen a New once in three year, and 21 in favour of the paragraft without any amendment———

The above are the procedings of the Town of Berkley on the Constitution or frame of government.

Atest Samuel Tobey Jur. Town Clerk

Dartmouth (276/29)

At a Town Meeting Legally Warned and held at the Town house in Dartmouth the Tenth day of May 1780. Abraham Smith Chosen Moderator for said Meeting. the Town took into Consideration this Form of Government, and after Reading it and Debating theron. Chose Edward Pope Esquire, John Chaffee, William Tallman, John Smith, Benja. Russell, Job Almy, and Jonathan Taber a Committee to Take into Consideration the Form of Government and to make report to the Adjornment of this meeting:———this meeting is Adjourned to the 22d day of this Instant May at 12 O'Clock on said day.———The Town met according to Adjournment and the Gentlemen of the Committee being Called upon made the following report (viz)—

Dartmouth May 22, 1780.———

Your Committee who were chosen to take under consideration the Constitution or Form of Government and report to the Town what alteration (if any) ought to be made have with Due attention attended that Business, and report as follows: That our Deligates who shall be chosen to meet in Convention be instructed and directed to accept of said Constitution or Form of Government with the amendments here after pointed out and that they be injoined to use their endeavours in Convention that the same be obtained. And As it was recommended to the Several Towns in this State by the last Convention to impower their Dilegates at the next Session of Convention to fix upon a time when this Form of Government shall take place the Wisdom and Prudence of Convention can best judge what time will be best; therefore we would advise that, that matter be wholly left to them.——

The amendments proposed, with our reasons, agreeable to the request of Convention, are those following. viz.

[That in the 3rd Article in the Declaration of Rights there be this Addition that any Subject or Subjects professing and attending Publick worship and who are willing to support it be exemted from being obliged to pay or make any provision to any Minister or Teacher not of his or their profession: For the following reason: It appears doubtfull in said articles whether the Rights of Conscience are sufficiently secured or not to those who are really desirious to, and do attend publick Worship and who are not limited to any perticular outward Teacher or such as have a legal support, for we have reason to fear (according to the tenor of that Article) that a subject or subjects professing such Principals will be obliged to support a Publick Minister or Teacher, which will be directly opposite to his or their religious principals; for in this Case we humbly conceive it intirely out of the power of the legislature to establish a way of Worship that shall be agreable to the Conceptions and Convictions of the minds of individals, as it is a matter that solely relates to and stands between God and the Soul before whose Tribunial all must account each one for himself.]

That in the 4th Artical in the 25th Page the words and that pays a Poll Tax except such who from their respective offices and age are exemted by Law. Sui juris be added after the words, every male Person and to Exspunge the following clame in Said Article, viz. having a freehold Estate within the same Town of the annual income of three pound, or any Estate of the value of Sixty pounds, For the following Resons Such quallification appears to your Committee to be inconsistant with the Liberty we are contending for So long especialy as any Subject who is not a quallified voter is obliged to pay a pool Tax.——That the word *Defend,* in the Proviso made in the 46th Page omitting certain words in the Oath required to be taken by any judicial executive military, or other officers, be likewise omitted and such other word or words substituted in room thereof as the Convention shall think proper, that are not inconsistant with the Religious principals of that Denomination of People called Quakers, as that word is exceptionable to them——That the whole of the Last clause in the 3d article page 48 be erased viz. *And it shall be in the power of the Legislature from time to time to increase such Quallifications as to property, of the Persons to be elected to offices as the circumstances of the Common Wealth shall require*——For the following reason, That it will be in the power of the legislature to increase the Quallification of persons to be elected to office as to property, in such a manner as may be dangerious to the Liberties of the people.——

We would further recommend that our Dilegates be required and Instructed to use their influence in Convention that the same alterations take place in the 16th article of the Declaration of Rights: And the Article that respects the Writ of habeas Corpus as are proposed in the Instructions given to the Delegates of the Town of Boston, for the same reasons, as Published in Boston News Papers.——

The foregoing Report of the Committee was Excepted by a unanimous vote of one Hundred and Fifty Two persons present and the Reverend Samuel West and the Honorable Walter Spooner Esquire Were Unanimously Chosen Delagtes, for the Town of Dartmouth to represent them in Convention Convened at Boston the first Wednesday in June Next.

A true copy Attest, Benj. Akin Town Clar

William Davis
Alden Spooner
Benja. Russell
Richard Kerby — Select men of Dartmouth

Dighton (276/30)

at a town meeting Legalaly Warned and held in Dighton May the 22th 1780 the afore Going Decleration of Rights and form of Goverment was Laid Before the town and Pased agreable to the Entrys made In the Margins of Each Article; and those articles that was Rejected and the town has Given there Reasons for We have Sent By our Delegate

James Dean
Rufus Whitmarsh
Elijah Walker — Selectmen
Simeon Williams

[Notes in margin of printed Constitution]

Preamble	approved unanimus 104 Voters
Part I	
Article I	104 Voters and approved unanimus
Article II	approved by 88 disapproved by 16
Article III	Disapprovd by 99 approved by 5
Article IV	approved unanimus
Article V	approved Ditto
Article VI	approved Ditto
Article VII	approved Ditto
Article VIII	approved unanimus
Article IX	approved Ditto
Article X	approved by all But one
Article XI	approved unanimus
Article XII	approved unanimus
Article XIII	approved Ditto
Article XIV	approved Ditto
Article XV	approved Unan.
Article XVI	approved Unan.
Article XVII	approved Ditto
Article XVIII	approved Ditto
Article XIX	approved Ditto
Article XX	approved Ditto
Article XXI	approved Ditto
Article XXII	approved Ditto
Article XXIII	approved Ditto
Article XXIV	approved Ditto
Article XXV	approved Ditto
Article XXVI	approved unanimus
Article XXVII	approved Ditto
Article XXVIII	approved Ditto
Article XXIX	approved Ditto
Article XXX	approved Ditto

Part the Second
The Frame of Government—approved unanimus

Chapter I Section 1

Article I	approved Ditto
Article II	approved Ditto
Article III	approved Unanimus
Article IV	approved Unanimus

Chapter I Section 2

Article I	approved unanimus
Article II	This article was approved by 46 and disaproved by 54—
Article III	100 Voters approved Unanimous
Article IV	Approved Ditto
Article V	Approved Ditto
Article VI	Approved Ditto

Article VII	Approved Ditto
Article VIII	Approved Ditto
Article IX	Approved Ditto

Constitution
Chapter I
Section III

Article I	approved unananimus
Article II	approved Ditto
Article III	approved Ditto
Article IV	approved by 46 Disaproved by 54
Article V	approved unanimus
Article VI	approved Ditto
Article VII	approved Ditto
Article VIII	approved Ditto
Article IX	approved Ditto
Article X	approved Ditto
Article XI	approved Ditto

Chapter II
Section I

Article I	approved Ditto
Article II	approved by all But 1
Article III	approved unanimous
Article IV	approved Ditto
Article V	approved Ditto
Article VI	approved Ditto
Article VII	approved unanimus
Article VIII	approved Ditto
Article IX	Disapproved by all But two
Article X	approved unanimus
Article XI	approved Ditto
Article XII	approved Ditto
Article XIII	approved by all But one

Section II

Article I	approved unanimous
Article II	approved Ditto
Article III	approved Ditto

Section III

Article I	approved unanimus
Article II	approved Ditto
Article III	approved Ditto
Article IV	approved Ditto
Article V	approved Ditto
Article VI	approved unanimus
Article VII	approved Ditto

Section IV

Article I	approved unanimus
Article II	approved Ditto

Chapter III

Article I	approved Ditto
Article II	approved Ditto
Article III	approved by 30 and Disaproved by 70
Article IV	approved unanimus
Article V	approved unanimus
Chapter IV	approved Ditto

Chapter V		Article III	approved unanimus
Section I		Article IV	approved Ditto
Article I	approved Ditto	Article V	approved Ditto
Article II	approved unanimus	Article VI	approved Ditto
Article III	approved Ditto	Article VII	approved Ditto
Section II	Approved Ditto	Article VIII	approved Ditto
Chapter VI		Article IX	Approved unanimus
Article I	approved unanimus	Article X	Approved Ditto
Article II	approved unanimus	Article XI	approved Ditto

[Note on back of Constitution]

Dighton the 3rd. art. in the Bill of Rights at Mr. Pearses house near the Orange Tree

Easton (276/31)

Att a Town Meeting of the inhabitants of the Town of Easton on the 15th Day of May AD 1780 and Continued by Agurnment to the 26th of May then the Town toock under Concederation and acted on the several articels in the Proposed Plan of Goverment Composed by the Convention of the State of Macechuset Bay as followeth (Viz)——

Decklaration of the Rites of the inhabitants

	Yeas	Nays
Articel 1.	51	
2.	53	
3.	00	71

in Stead of Said third articel as Proposed by the Convention it is the minds of the town that it should be insarted as followeth (viz) that Each Perticular Religus Society ought to have full and free liberty to Agree with and Pay their Religous teachers in such a way and Method as they shall agree on, and that No Person shall be taxed for the soport of any Minister of a Differant Denomination than that of his Own Religious Profession and Every Denomination of Christians Demeaning themselves Peacably and as good Subjects of the Common Welth Shall be Equally under the Protection of the law. and Subordenation of any Own sect or Denomination to another shall Ever bee Established by law. in favour of the articel as Proposed by the town

Yeas	*Nays*
88	00

[Article]		
4—	54	00
5—	51	00
6—	41	
7—	60	
8—	56	
9—	75	
10—	81	
11—	81	
12—	76	
13—	54	
14—	69	
15—	59	
16—	67	
17—	63	
18—	58	
19—	70	
20—	42	
21—	62	
22—	58	
23—	65	
24—	66	
25—	65	
26—	55	
27—	50	
28—	68	
29—	33—	14
30—	52	

Frame of government

Chapter first

Section 1

Articel	Yeas	Nays
1—	51	00
2—	47	

Article	*Yeas*	*Nays*
3—	57	
4—	35	

Section 2nd

1—	28	
2—	28	
3—	22	
4—	22	
5—	27	
6—	24	
7—	26	
8—	40	
9—	10	

Section 3

1—	54	
2—	37	
3—	39	
4—	15—	59
5—	51	
6—	26	
7—	12	
8—	13	
9—	9	
10—	24	
11—	28	

Chapter 2nd

Section [1]

Articel	Yeas	Nays
1—	25—	19
2—	00—	48

the alteration proposed in the second articel to have the Words Christian Religion Dealed and the words Protestant Religion insarted in favour of the articel With the Proposed amendment—57

Article Yeas Nays

3— 25— 11
4 17
5 13
6 13
7— 00— 26 The Proposed amendment is the governer with the advice of the Council etc. in favour of the articel with the Proposed amendment

———24
8— 8
9— 4— 11
10— 21
11— 11
12— 15
13— 00— 25 the amendment Proposed is that if it shall be found that any of the saleries afore said so established are insoficiant or more than soficient they shall from time to time be inlarged or deminished as the General Court shall Judge Proper. In favour of the articel with the amendment: 31

Section 2nd

Articel Yeas Nays

1 16
2 11
3 17

Section the 3

1 11 8
2 13 7
3 9
4 19

Article Yeas Nays

5 23
6 17
7 18

Section 4th

1 22
2 17

Chapter 3

[Article]

1 18
2 23
3 18
4 00 it is the Opinion of the Town that there ought to be a Probate office and Judge of Probate to be appointed in Each and Every incorporate Town within this State in favour of the articel with the Proposed amendment

36

5 27

Chapter 5

[Article]

1 13
2 14
3 11

Section 2nd

18

Chapter 6th

[Article]

1 00 23 The amendment Proposed is that the Word Christian be Dealed and the Word Protestant be insarted with the amendment

24 —

Article	*Yeas*	*Nays*	
2	00	20	The amendment Proposed is that Setteled or Ordained ministers of the Gospel be aded to the Number of those that are Excluded from a seat in the Senate and house of Representatives With the amendment
	21		
3	7	11	
4	17		
5	16		
6	17		
7	12		

Article	*Yeas*	*Nays*	
8	7		
9	18		
10	00	23	The amendment Proposed that in-stead of the General Court that shall be in the year of our lord 1795. it should be the General Court that shall be in the year of our lord 1787, in favour of the articel With the Proposed amendment——
	22		
11	19		

Easton June the 5th 1780

Seth Pratt	Select
Elijah Howard	men of
Jonathan Pratt	Easton

Freetown (276/32)

To the Honorable Samuel Barrett Esqr. Secretary of the Convention——

These certify that upon previs warning the Town of Freetown meet on the 22nd instant and took into consideration the form of government then chose a committee who on the 27th instant brought in to the aj'onme't of said meeting as folloeth Wee the Committee being chose by the town of Freetown at a publick town meeting held on the 22nd instant to inspect into the form of government that was laid Before us have meet to gether This 27th day of May instant and do conclude and make our report To this Town meeting that Stands ajorned from the 22d instant To This present day the 27th instant as follows viz (Taking the form of Government into our Serious consideration Do find many articles that apear inconsistant to that Liberty that we think we have been so Long Contending for (viz) the third article of the Declaration of Rights for one) the power invested in the Governer for the 2d the power invested into the house of representatives for the 3d and the manner of Laying Exceises or duties on Manufactoris Lastly, and we do finally give it as our opinion that it is better for ous to remain under the same form of Government as we have held to Ever sence the Commencement of this war untill this present and unhapy Contest is decided——the above report after being debated was put to vote and Their apeared Thirty for the report and Sixteen against it.

A trew Copy from the minits atest
for and by order of the Selectmen and Committee
Freetown May the 27th 1870 Samuel Barnaby Town Clerk

Mansfield (276/33)

The proceedings of the Town of Mansfield on the proposed Constitution or forme of Government for the Common Welth of Massachusetts at a Meeting duly Worned, and holden on Munday the 1st day of May 1780, and Continued by Adjournment to friday the 26th of the same.——

The Said Constitution being publickly read, and maturely considered, and Debated upon, the question was first put whether the said Town will accept of the said Constitution in Groce without any amendment or alteration passed in the Negative unannimously

Then 2dly. the Town proceeded to Signify their Sentiments, on seperate parts of the Constitution by their votes as followeth (viz)

		in favor of	aganst
	On Preamble		
The question put and passed		34	1
	On Declaration of Rights		
	Article		
	1	passed 53	
	2	passed 52	5
	3	passed 43	12
	4—to the 9th Inclucively	passed 51	1
	10	passed 49	5
	11—Inclucively and to the end of bill of rights	passed 40	1

Legislative Power

[Chapter]	[Section]	[Article]	[Paragraph]		[in favor of]	[against]
1	1			Passed in Groce	37	4
	2	1			34	4
		2	1	Negatived	0	50

for the following reasons (viz.)

The propperty required as a quallification for Electors of Senators this Town are humbly of oppinion is unjust; Notwithstanding in assigning the numbers, References to be had to the proportion of Taxes each District pays; and therefore in the address of this Convention page 11th are called Representitives of propperty, which we allow they are, but not of propperty only; for we conceive the Senate aught to Represent persons as well as propperty, and that the Second Branch Represents propperty as well as persons for sure both branches make but one General Court, and each Branch aught Equally to consult the safty, Prosperity, and the happiness of the Whole; and if so evry male inhabitant of the Common-Welth of the age of Twentyone years and upwards being of understanding soficient to mannage the common and ordinary affairs of life and is a good subject. we think should be a voter for Senator or Senators in the Town where they have their usual residence and are taxed (unless by law excused:) and proposed an amendment to be made to said article accordingly

[Chapter]	[Section]	[Article]	[Paragraph]		[in favor of]	[against]
			2	Inclusive and to the end of the section		
				passed in Groce	36	6
1	3	1		Passed	24	1
		2		Negatived	0	28

For this Reason, that we are of oppinion that the Incorporate Town should be deprived of the priviledge of sending a Representitive to the General Court, who finde themselves able, and pleas to improve the priviledge; Probably but fue Towns under the Number of a hundred and fifty polls will Ever send, except on some perticular Time or occasion, and the House thereby but a Trifle Inlarged; We therefore Prepose an alteration in said Article so as Evry Corporate Town may elect and returne one Representative, but not be subject to a fine or penalty for Not sending, Evry Corporate town having three hundred and seventy five Ratable Polls Exclucive of slaves, may Elect and returne Two, and so on making the mean increasing number Exclusive of slaves the same as stands in the article; or otherwise we would propose, that sutch Towns under the Number of a hundred and fifty polls which in future may be Incorporated may have a Right to associate with some Town or Towns adjoining, for the Choice or Election of Representatives in the same manner proposed in the Committees Report page 26th——
the above amendment passed 22— 1

[Chapter]	[Section]	[Article]	[Paragraph]		[in favor of]	[against]
1	3	3		passed	24—	1
		4		Negatived—		26

For here we finde the same quallification of propperty Required for a Voter for a Representative as is proposed by the Convention for the electors of the Senate; We are very sorrey to differ in oppinion from the Honorable Convention in a matter of so grate Importance as that of determining; who shall, and who shall not have a voice in the choice of a Representitive; Doubtless there are, and ever will be some in the Commonwelth who pay little regard to the Rights of propperty as is hinted at in the address Page 12th this we readily Grante, but on the other hand, how many young men Neither Profligates nor idle persons, for some years must be debar'd that priviledge? how many sensable, honest, and naturly Industerouss men, by Numberless Misfortins Never Acquire and possess propperty of the value of sixty pounds? and how many Thousands of good honest men, and Good members of society who are at this day possessed of a comfortable Interest, which before the publick debts of the common welth are discharged, will not be possessed of a soficiency to quallify them to vote for Representatives if this article takes place as it now stands; We readily allow as we said before that there are and ever will be some who pay little regard to the rights of Propperty: But shall it from thence be argued, that thousands of honest Good members of society shall be subjected to laws framed by Legislators, the Election of Whom, they could have no voice in? Shall a subject of a free Common Welth, be obbliged to contribute his share to publick Expences, to give his personal servis, or an aquivilent, where necessary; see bill of Rights Page 10th and be excluded from voting for a Representative; This appears to us in some degree, Slavery. on these Considerations, with others which might be mentioned We reject said article as it now stands: and do propose to have sutch alteration, or amendment mad to said article, whereby Evry male person being Twenty one Years of age and upwards being a Good subject of the Common-Welth, and Resident in any peticular Town for the space of one year, may in sutch Town, have a Right to vote for a representative, or Representatives for said Town. Provided also that he has paid taxes in the same Town (unless by law excused)

[Chapter]	[Section]	[Article]	[Paragraph]		[in favor of]	[aganst]
				the above amendment passed	22	2
1	3	5		and to the 8 article Inclucively passed	25	0
		9		Negatived——	4	19

We are of Oppinion that a Quorum of the house so small as that of sixty will be dangerous to the Common-Welth; and propose one hundred to be the least Number to constitute a Quorum in the house of Representatives to do Business. This amendment passed 21 1

[Chapter]	[Section]	[Article]	[Paragraph]	[in favor of]	[against]
		10	Inclucive to the End of the 1t chapter Passed in groce	24	1
2	1	1	passed	29	1
		2	Negatived	—	30

and propose that the word Christian, in the last line in said article be eraesed and the word Prodistant be substituted in stead thereof. This amendment passed 28 0

		3	Negatived	0	26

and propose the same quallification for the Electors of the Governer, as we have proposed for the Electors of Senators, and Representatives [*interlineated*: see the paper] † this past 23 0

[The symbol refers to a small slip of paper on which were written the following words:]

Part of the amendement proposed to this article; which was overlooked on the Record; viz † between the words "one who" in the last line add in these words (viz) of the Two so returned. See the Number of Votes in favor of the amendment

		4	to the 12th Inclucively passed	18	2
		13	3 Negatived—	0	22

The salleries of the Governor and of the Judges we find may be raised if found Insoficient, which we think to be reasonable; and it appears to us as reasonable that they should be lowered when circumstances will admitt, Peticularly in regard to the Governors, for in a time of war a Governors Sallery ought to be more then in a time of peace, then of Consequence, if it be Raised in time of war so high as it aught to be, in Time of peace it will be higher then needful; and propose an amendment to join Parrigraft accordingly. This proposed amendment passed 21 1

2	1		Negatived	0	18

and only propose the same quallifications for the Electors of the Lieutenant Governor which this Town propose for the quallifications of the Electors of the Governor and the quallification of the Lieutenant Governor in point of Religion to be the same which we propose for a quallification for the Governor. this amendment past 22 0

[Chapter]	[Section]	[Article]	[Paragraph]	[in favor of]	[against]
		2	and 3d. being to the End of the 2d. Section passt	21	0
	3		and so on to the End of the fifth Chapter in groce past	14	3
6		1	and 2d. passed	14	1
		3	Negatived	0	18

for the following reason viz because in the latter part of the article we finde the Legislature are impowered from Time to Time to Increase the quallifications as to the Propperty of persons to be Elected into offices as the circumstances of the Common Welth Shall require; But we are not Inclined to think Propperty to be a more assential quallification then what was hinted at in a part of an Article in the 27th Page of the Committee Report and which was sat aside by the Honorable Convention———We are not able to see any advantage which can Ever arise to the people in general by the Quallifications being increased, and for the General Court to be thus Inpowered We conceive would be dangerous; and we propose to have that part of the article Eraised

Chapter	Section	Article	Paragraph	in favour of	aganst
	the Amendment or alteration Passed			17	0
6		4	and to the end of the Constitution passed	17	1

And then passed the following Resolves unanimously viz.

1tly That it is not the Sence and meaning of this Town, in any of their Votes passed in favour of any part of the proposed Constitution or forme of Government that any part or parts thereof be accepted by this Town as a constitution or forme of Government for the state, or Common-Welth of Massachusetts; No otherwise then with this proviso (viz) that the amendments and alterations which this Town has proposed be made; or otherwise that the whole Constitution be Conformed to the minds of Two thirds of the voters voting for and against the same; if, by the returns it shall appear that Two thirds are agreed in sentiments———

2dly that Provided two thirds of the Inhabitants voting in the Several Towns and plantation meetings in this state are agreed in sentiments and so appears by the returnes; and the forme of Government be Conformed to the Sentiments of Two thirds; then the Time of its taking place be referred to the detirmanation of the Honorable Convention

Passed without a Negative vote 19 0

Lastly voted that the Town Clerk be and is hereby Instructed to furnish the deligate of this Town with a Coppy of the proceedings of this Town on the proposed Constitution or forme of Government.

A True Coppy

Certified under my hand at Mansfield this sixth day of June 1780

per Isaac Dean, T. Cle [*torn*]

P. S. Voted at the above said meeting that if it appears by the returnes that Two thirds of the voters throughout the State voting in the Towns and plantation meetings for and against the said forme of Government are agreed in sentiment, and the said Constitution be Conformed to the sentiments of Two thirds as aforesaid; the deligate from this Town is hereby Instructed and Impowered to vote in Convention for the Confirmation of the same, as the Constitution, or forme of Government for the Common Welth of Massachusetts.

passed 19 for against 0

attest. Issac Dean Town Clerk

Norton (276/34)

The proceedings of the Town of Norton with regard to the proposed Constitution or frame of Government sent to said Town att A Legal Town meeting held on Munday the Eighth Day of May 1780
The Said frame of Government Being publickly read. after Some Debates the Question was put wheather the Town approved of the said frame of government as it now stands it passed in the Negative unanimously. present 78 Voters Then the Town proceeded to Chuse a Committee to take the said frame or Constitution of Government under their further Consideration and report to the Town at a perposed Adjornment.——The Meeting was then adjourned to Thursday the 25 of May at which time the Town meat and further adjorned to Thursday the first of June next at two of the Clock in the afternoon when the Town again meat and the Committee reported as follows The Committee to whom was refered the Consideration of the New Constitution of Government perposed by the Convention for the Consideration of the Several Towns. Do report That it is their Opinion that before the Same pass to become the Constitution of this State the followin alterations and amendments should be made therein to

Part the first in the Decleration of Rights

Artical 3th that thare be added to the fourth paragraph: that no person of one Denomination shall Knowingly be Taxed towards the support of a minister of another Denomination Artical 10th we think it would be most for the Safety of the people that instead of the words Representative Body it should be the General Court

Part the Second the frame of Government

Chapter the first Section 1st artical 2 we would perpose the following alteration viz That when the governor shall return any law to Either of the two Houses and upon their reconsideration thereof a major part of both Houses Shall adhear to their former votes, it shall pass to be a law altho the Governor Refuse to sign it———

The Reason for this alteration is. That we dont think it will be Safe for the people when a majority of both Houses Shall unite in any law for the Governor to have the power to negative them

Section 2d artical 1st we object against the Number of Senators there perposed, and it is our opinion that no more then twenty Eight Senators ought to be anualy Chosen

Our Reasons for which is that Experience has Taught us that business may be well done without a Larger number. and likewise that the multiplying publick officers unless necessity Riquire it has often proved Dangerous to the Libertyes of the people

Section 2d Artical 2 We object against the Qualification of such as are to Vote for Senators and representitives and think that Every male Inhabitant of twenty one years and paying taxes should have Liberty to vote

our reason for it is this—That Every person that is Called upon to pay taxes ought to have a share in the Choice of those that tax them

Section 3 artical 2d We object against it and think some such method as follows would be more for the Common benefit of the State Viz.

That Each Incorporat town should send one Representitive and no Town unless they have one thousand Rateable poles shall be Intitled to send two, and that no Town in the State should send more then two Except the town of Boston, which Town shall be intitled to send four.

Our Reasons are—that by the method perposed the House will be so large as that it will be very Difficult if not impossible that the publick Business should be done Either with that correctness or Dispatch—as if confined to a Smaller Number and further we think the Smaller Towns will not have an Equal Representation with the larger Towns for it is

Evident that many of our towns will have one third, and some it is likely, nigh one half that will not be represented——

Chapter 2d artical 3d We object against the method perposed for the Choice of a Governor——(if not Chose by the people at large) and think the two Houses in one room ought (in that case) make Choice of one of the Two that have the most Votes of the people

our Reasons for which is—We think the people at large Quallifyed as perposed Should have a voice in said Election or at least that both Houses should Unite in said Choice.——

Chapter 2 Section 1st Artical 2 we think that Instead of the words Christian Religion ought to be protestant Religion——

Our Reason for which is—That we think it Dangerous Even to leave any the least opening for a Roman Catholick to fill the first Seat in the Government

Artical 13th We think no fixed Salary ought to be Established to the governor or any other officer or Sorvent of this State, but that it should be voted by the majorety of Both Houes yearly.

Our Reason for which is this—that we think it would be Verry Dangerous at this Time so to fix a matter of that nature so as that it would be out of the power of any future Assembly to make the least alteration——

Chapter 2d Section 3th We wholly object to Except that part of the Seventh Artical that has respect to the Compleating the Elections of officers Exclusive of Councilors therein mentioned The Reasons for our objection to the last mentioned section are as follows

We can not think it will be for the Benefitt of the people that such a body of men as privy Counellors should have an Existance in this State. and further we are of opinion that such a body of men with the powers as mentioned therein will not only be Burthensome and Expensive but Dangerous and that thay would answer no good porpose. But that Senators may answer all the Ends for which this Council was perposed.

Chapter 4th it is our opinion that the Delegates Chosen to sett in Congress should be Qullified in the same manner as before mentioned for the Qullifications of a Governor Except property which we think should be fixed at least at five hunderd pounds Each

Chapter 5 Section 1 artical 1 and 2 we think it best to add Exept grants of the general Court and not to make good former grants or Donations

Chapter 6th Section 2 we think that no Judge of the admiralty or Judge of the Inferior Court Should have a Seat in the General Court, for reasons to us as obvious and as just, as the Exclusion of many others in said Section

Chapter 6 Section 2 artical 10 [chap. 6, art. 10] we would have aded and soon as if ⅔ of the people Desire it

Artical 3 We think the Qullifycations of persons to be Elected for officers ought not to be altered by any Court here after but by the people at large

Chapter 1st Section 3 artical 9 objected against and think it would be Best we think that not less than one hundred shall Constitute a quorum for Doing Buisness

The foregoing Report was [accepted?] by the Town of Norton in the following manner the Number of Voteers was 108—on the 3d artical in the bill of Rights, for it 72—against it 36 the whole of the remaining part was [accepted?] if the amendments obtained therein expressed to wit for it with the amendments 103 against it 5—

N. B. There was a Vote upon the fourth artical in the Bill of Rights which passed in the following manner 51 for it as it stands 24 against

June 5, 1780 A true Account of the proceedings
of the Said Town

Attested By us William Cobb, William Thomas, Daniel Deane — Selectmen of Norton

Rehoboth (276/35)

At A Meeting of the Freeholdors and other Inhabitants of the Town of Rehoboth on Monday the 22nd Day of May 1780—at the New meeting House at two of the clock in the afternoone Chose Mr. Ephraim Starkweather Moderator for said meeting. Then the New form of Goverment was Proposed by the Convention was Read to the Town and the Question was Put whether the town will approve of the same as it now Stands and it Passt in the Negative 104 for it and 351 against it

Then the Town Proceeded and chose a Committe to state the objections and Report to the Town and then Ajorned said meeting to the 29th Instant at one of the clock in the afternoone

May 29th 1780 the Town Being met according to Adjournment Voted to Read the Report of the Committe on the Present form of goverment under Consideration.

then Proceeded to Read the Bill of Rights
The first and Second Article Past unanimously in the afirmative as it stands. Haveing Read the Bill of Rights through and takeing the number for and against Each Article. The town Adjourned to the 2nd. day of June at 8 of the Clock in the morning. The Town being then met Proceeded on a motion made to Read the Bill of Rights again in order that those Persons Present that Did not vote Before might then vote and the Number for and against Each Article taken at Both Adjournments is as followeth

for the 1st and 2nd Aarticle		351
for the 3rd	Ditto	104
Against the 3rd	Ditto	251
who Proposed the Amendment hereto anext were		233
against said admendment		100
then the 4th and on to the 29th Past unanimous		351
for the 29th		43
against it		71
for the 30		351
Part the 2nd. Chapter 1 Article the 1st	for it	19
against it		103
section 2nd	for it	17
against it		65

then Proceeded to chuse A committe to State the objections and Propose the amendments which were as is hereunto Anext for

which there was for it	48
and against it	12

then voted the Select men are Desired to transmit a Coppy of the Number for and against Each article with the Reasons therefor to the Secretary of the Convention.
Also Voted that the Delegates for the Convention agree to the proposels of the convention when the Form of Goverment Shall take Place without Returning the Same again to the People

Attest William Cole
Joshua Smith
Simeon Cole Selectmen of Rehoboth
Jesse Perin

A Substitute in the Roome of the Article in the Bill of Rights

The People of this Comon wealth have also a Right to and Do Invest their Legesliture with Authority to Enjoyn upon all their Subjects of this Comon Welth An attendance upon the Publick worship of God at Stated Times and Seasons (if thier be any on which they can Consciantiously and conveniantly attend) also to make and Ennact Such good and wholsom Laws as Shall tend to the Governing the morals of the People and a Due Observance of the Lords Day and other Days set apart for Publick Worship aforesaid. And Every Denomination of christians Demeaning themselves Peaceably and as good Subjects of the comonwealth shall be equally under the Protection of the Law and no Subordination of any one sect or Denomination to another shall be Ever Established By Law.———

The objections Against haveing Governor etc. as Reported and accepted. ———Your Committe Report that as the Town have Rejected [said?] Governor, Lieutenant Governor and Senate we think the whole of the Remainder is Rejected in Consequence thereof.———

We therefore give our Reasons for Rejecting A Governor Senate and etc. is from our Being of opinion that our safty and happiness Esentially consists in being governed by one house of Representitives which shall be stiled the Great and General Court of the Comonwealth of the Massachusetts to be elected Annually. Whose Rules and Regulations shall be simeler to that of the Honourable Continental Congress. And the House of Representatives to Annually Ellect all the Executive officers and all other Publick Officers Except Judges of Probates of Wills and Register of Deeds which ought forever Hereafter be Done in Each Respective Town and all military officers to be chosen Agreable to the Proposed form of Government and the Judges of the Supreme Judicial Court to hold their office During their good Behaviour and no Legislative officer to be an Judicial officer and no Judicial officer to be an Executive officer etc. all which objections and amendments we think absolutely Nesecary for Enjoying a free well Regulated Government.

Raynham (276/36)

Att A Legal Meeting of The Inhabitance of the Town of Raynham Convened on Monday the 22d Day of May Instant for the Purpos of

Considering accepting or not accepting——a new Constitution or Frame of government for the State of Massachusettsbay and after Reading the same and sum debate theron Thought best To Choose a Committe for better Consideration thereof and we the said committe (haveing Examined the said Constitution or frame of government in the most Deliberate manner, and find no material objection against any article Except the third in the Bill of Rights Which Relates To Religion and morality and Considering the said article in sum degree ambiguous or may Extend in its meaning so far as To give Power To the Legislature To subject sum of one Denomination—of Religious societies To be Taxed To the support of a Religious Teacher of an other which we intirely Disclaim Their Right To do and it is our opinion That the said Third article in the Bill of Rights aught To be more Explicit so that it may be Easily under stoot by all men. If not There will be Dainger of Different societies Quariling and Contending in the Law about Their Rights which will Tend to The Destruction of Piety Religion and morality and intirely subvert the intentions of said Third article)——Which we Humbley submit as our Real and Candid opinions and report To said Town on adjournment met This 29th Day of May A.D 1780——

Signed In behalf of said committe

Jonathan Shaw Chairman

To the Convention for forming a plan of Goverment for the State of the Massachusetts Bay etc.——

Gentlemen

These may Certefie that we subscribers having notefied the inhabitants of the Town of Raynham and they being assembled in Town meeting on the 22d Day of May instant for the purpose of accepting the declaration of Rights and plan of Goverment Exhibited to them by the Honorable Convention—and there being Sixty Six voteors present upon adjournment of said meeting on the 29th of May instant and the vote apeared to be unanimous for accepting the whole of said plan or form of Goverment and Declaration of Rights excepting the third article in the Declaration of Rights. and as there was a Committee Chosen to Consider and Report what might be propper for the Town to do on such a weighty affair—and there was Eleven men objected to the third article and fully approved of the Report of said Committee and twas said that there was ninteen by some who were present that—approved the Report and the Report is herewith Exhibited and we are with Due Respect your Humble servants etc.

Done at Raynham. May 29th 1780.

Jon. Hall
Joshua Leonard
Robert Brettun [?]
Select men of Raynham

Swansey (276/37)

The following the Report of the Committe of the Town of Swanzey who were Chosen by said Town to Consult upon the New Frame of Goverment——They accordingly made Report as follows——

(Objecting Particular against the 3d Article in the Constitution for the following Reasons——

1st. The Christian Relegion stands in no Need of the Civil power for its Support and it seems contrary to the True Spirit it that the Civil Power should at all interfear, as Christ has declared his Kingdom is not of this world.

2d. Experience inform us That Relegion has been Greatly Corrupted, by its being mixt in with civil goverments——

3d. The Legislature cannot act agreeable to such a Power as is Vested in them by the third article without Rendering individuals unhappy who have an Equal Right to the Blessings of goverments by forceing from Them their Property and applying it to the support of those whome they may think are injuring the Cause of Relegion——

We also object against Every other part of the Constitution wherein it does not very Particular—agree with the Present form of goverment as it seems more Pleaseing to the People in general and Particular to the inhabitants of the Town Swanzey——who have appeared to act upon the new Constitution) Therefore set forth our reasons as *above*

This Report Laid Before said Town the 5th of June 1780 and unanimously voted——

There was Ninety Voters

John Richmond in behalf of the Committe

[?]iel Pearc
Joshua Mason
William Brown
Selectmen of Swanzey

The Honorable Samuel Barrett Esqr.
Secratery

Taunton (276/38)

At a Town Meeting held at Taunton on the 25th Day of May A.D. 1780 for the purpose of considering the new form of government

The question being put and a vote called to se if the Town would accept of the proposed Declaration of Rights (Except the 3d. articale therein mentioned) Voted for accepting 82, against it one. Whole number present 83.

Chapter 1st Section 1st.	The Generel Court. for acceptance 82; against it one.
Chapter 1st Section 2nd.	The Senate. for acceptance 83. against it one
Chapter 1st Section 3d.	House of Representatives (except the 4th article) for acceptance 83; against one.
Chapter 2nd Section 1st.	Executive power. for acceptance 83. against it one.
Chapter 2d Section 2d.	Lieutenant Governer. for acceptance 83. against it one
Chapter 2d Section 3rd	Council etc. for acceptance 83; against it one
Chapter 2d Section 4th.	Secretary etc. for acceptance 83. against it one
Chapter 3rd	Judiciary Power. for acceptance 83. against it one
Chapter 4th	Deligates to Congress for acceptance 84. whole number
Chapter 5th Section 1st.	the University for acceptance 56. whole number present 56—
Chapter 5th Section 2nd.	Encouragement of Literature etc. for acceptance 56
Chapter 6th	Oaths etc. for accepting (Except the 3d articale) 56. whole number

The meeting was then adjurned to Tuesday next at one oclock afternoon

May 30th, 1780. The Town then met. A vote was called to se if said Town would accept of the 3d articale mentioned in the Declaration of Rights. for acceptance 97. against it 5. whole number present 112.

Chapter 1st Section 3d: Mentioning the quallification of voters for acceptance 103: against it. 9.

Voted unanimas on the 3d articale in Chapter 6th mentioning the Qualification of persons to be Elected to offices that the Legislature should not have the Power of ever increasing those quallifications as we think it a Power that may be Excercised to the great injury of the subject. whole number 112.

The vote for accepting the 10th articale in Chapter 6th is now reconsidered and now unanimasly voted that a new Convention be called within Seven years and that a major part of voters be mentioned instead of two thirds. Further voted that the Deligates for this Town agree with the other Dilegates in convention when this Form of government shall take place without Returning the same again to the Town.

Attest James Williams T. Cler——

A true copy of the procedings of the town of Taunton

Apollos Leonard
Cornelius White
Nathanael Briggs
Noah Dean
Select men of Taunton

HAMPSHIRE COUNTY

Ashfield (276/39)

At a legal Town Meetin, at the Congregational Meeting House in Ashfield on the 16th Day of May 1780 Voted to make Choice of a Committee of seven to Consider the Constitution and frame of government and make such alterations as they shall think Proper and lay the same before the adjourned Meeting.——
Voted that Captain Elisha Cronson, Jno. Bement, Aaron Lyon, Warren Green, [Chilial?] Smith, Jno Ellis, Phinv. Bartlit, be a Committe for said Purpose.
Voted to adjorn this Meeting to the 25th of May Instant at 2 O'Clock in the afternoon at this Place.

Thirsday May 25th, 1780. Met agreeable to adjournment at which Time the above Committee brought in their Report and the Town proceeded to Consider and act upon the abovesaid Constitution and Frame of Government article by article assertaining the Number voting for, and against Each article:
And where there is an amendment of any article by said Committee the Number in favor of it with the amendment is set Dowin, with the amendment and reasons for it as laid before the Town by said Committe.

Constitution etc. Part I. Decleration of Rights etc.

Article	1.	In favor of	38——	against it	none
	2.	Ditto	38	Ditto	none
	3.	Ditto	8	Ditto——	28 to the last Paragraph

Committees Reason for Rejecting said third Article. Because it is unconstitutional to human Nature and no Precept in the word of God to support it.—

4.	In favor of it	33	against it	none
5.	Ditto	18	Ditto	none
6.	Ditto	18	Ditto	none
7.	Ditto	18	Ditto	none
8.	Ditto	19	Ditto	none
9.	Ditto	20	Ditto	none

Article	[In favor of it]		[against it]	
10.	Ditto	20	Ditto	none
11.	Ditto	21	Ditto	none
12.	Ditto	20	Ditto	none
13.	Ditto	20	Ditto	none
14.	Ditto	20	Ditto	none
15.	Ditto	21	Ditto	none
16.	Ditto	21	Ditto	none
17.	Ditto	21	Ditto	none
18.	Ditto	21	Ditto	none
19.	Ditto	21	Ditto	none
20.	Ditto	21	Ditto	none
21.	Ditto	21	Ditto	none
22.	In favor of it	21	against it	none
23.	Ditto	21	Ditto	none
24.	Ditto	21	Ditto	none
25.	Ditto	21	Ditto	none
26.	Ditto	21	Ditto	none
27.	Ditto	22	Ditto	none
28.	Ditto	22	Ditto	none
29.	Ditto	3 in favor of it with amendment 24		

Amendment. The Judges of the Supreme Judicial Court shall be Chosen by the House of Representatives by ballot annually. Reason. That it is not good Policy nor for the sucurity of the Rights of the People that the Judges of the Supreme Judicial Court should hold their office for more than one year.

Article 30. In favor of it 27—Against it none

Part the Second Frame of Government

Chapter I. Section I. The General Court

Article 1. In favor of it 3. In favor of it with the Amendment 24

Amendment. The Department of Legislation shall Consist of one Branch viz. The House of Representatives and Dele the word Senate out of the whole Frame of Government whereever it is mentioned.* N.B. Wherever any article is accepted with amendment, and the amendment not set down directly under it, or specially reford to, it then refors to the amendment under the first article in the second part Chapter 1 Section 1 Reason. They that is the Senate are unnecessary and Burdensom to the Commonwilth

Adjourned to tomorrow 1 o'Clock afternoon met agreeable to adjournment

	2.	In favor of it	2	With the above amendment 27
	3.	Ditto	24	Against it none
	4.	Ditto	32	Against it none

Chapter 1 Section Second
The Senate

Article	1.	In favor of it	4	In favor of it with the Amendment	15
	2.	Ditto	2	Ditto	21
	3.	Ditto	2	Ditto	18
	4.	Ditto	4	Against it	17
	5.	Ditto	4	Ditto	21
	6.	Ditto	2	Ditto	21
	7.	Ditto	2	Ditto	22
	8.	Ditto	2	Ditto	22

Section 3d.

Article	1.	In favor of it	25	against it none
	2.	Ditto	16	Ditto none
	3.	Ditto	7	In favor of it with the amendment 19

Amendment Omit the Pecuniary Qualification

4. In favor of it 1 with the Amendment 12

Amendment. That every Male Person being 21 years of Age having the approbation of the Select Men and taken the Oath of Alligionc to the United States of America Shall have a Right to Vote in all publick Town Meetings———

Article	5.	In favor of it.	28	Against it none
	6.	Ditto	2	In favor of it with the Amendment 27
	7.	Ditto	2	Ditto 29
	8.	Ditto	28	against it none
	9.	Ditto	33	Ditto none
	10.	Ditto	31	Ditto none
	11.	Ditto	2	In favor it with the Amendment 26

Adjourned to Wednesday the last Day of May Instant
Met agreeable to adjournment and proceded to Busness

Chapter 2 Section 1 Governer

Article	1.	In favor of it	4	against it 5
	2.	In favor of it	13	Ditto 9
	3.	Ditto	2	In favor of it with the Amendment 22
	4.	Ditto	23	Against it 5
	5.	Ditto	2	In favor of it with the Amendment 26
	6.	Ditto	4	Ditto 25

7.	Ditto	19	against it none
8.	Ditto	2	With the amendment 24
9.	Ditto	3	With the amendment 26

The Amendment. The several officers mentioned in said Article to be chosen in the House of Representatives annually

10.	Ditto	2	With the amendment on the [said?] paragraph 21

That the House of Representatives act in Conjunction with the Governer and Council.

11.	Ditto	25	against it none
12.	Ditto	27	against it none
13.	Ditto	2	In favor of it with the Amendment 22

Chapter 2 Section 2 Lieutenant Governer

Article 1.	In favor of it	3	In favor of it with the Amendment 15
2.	Ditto	16	against it 1
3.	Ditto	13	Ditto 2

Section Third Council etc.

Article 1.	In favor of it	19	against it none
2.	Ditto	2	In favor of it with the Amendment 21
3.	Ditto	24	against it none
4.	Ditto	21	Ditto none
5.	Ditto	4	In favor with the Amendment 20
6.	Ditto	20	against it none
7.	Ditto	2	In favor with the Amendment 22

Adjournd till tommorrow 2 O'Clock the Afternoon Meet agreeable to Adjournment and proceded to Buisness

Chapter 2 Section 4 Secretary etc.

Article 1.	In favor of it	2	With the Amendment 27
2.	Ditto	2	Ditto 29

Chapter 3 Judiciary Power

Article 1.	In favor of it	2	With the Amendment * 9

* The Amendment (see on Page 2d under the 29 article of the Declaration of Rights

2.	Ditto	4	Against it none
3.	Ditto	1	In favor with Amendment † 10

[† See Page fourth at the Top]

† That the Justius of the Peace shall be chosen by Ballot Annually in a Legal town meeting in the Several towns in this State Called for the People and Commissioned by the Governer———

Reason that it is the Natural Right of the Commonwilth

Article 4 In favor of it 1: with the Amendment 9
Amendment that the Selectmen of the Several Townes Shall be invested with authority to Settle the Estates of the Deceast instead of Judges of Probate with a Right of an Appeal.
Reason it is not only our natural Right but advantagius to the Commonwilth and not so [oppresive to the] widdow and fatherless

5. in favor of [*illegible*] Amendment

Amendment Leave out And all appeals from the Judges of Probate

Chapter 4 the Congress

In favor of it 2 with the amendment 9

Chapter 5 University at Cambridge

Section 1 of the University

Article 1	In favor of it	5	against it	1
2	Ditto	8	Ditto	4
3	Ditto	4	In favor with the Amendment	5

Amendment Dele Congregational

Chapter 5 Section 2 Encouragment of Literature etc.

In favor of it 7 against it none

Chapter 6 Oaths and Subscriptions etc.

Article 1 In favor of it 4 with the amendment 3
The Amendment In the Oaths live out the words [Prot.?] be of the Denomination called Quaker
Reason Granting the Affirmation being sufficient for one denomination of Christian then it is taking Gods name in vain to impose it upon any other denomination

2	Ditto	9	against it	none
3	Ditto	8	Ditto	1
4	Ditto	12	Ditto	none
5	Ditto	9	Ditto	none
6	Ditto	8	Ditto	1
7	Ditto	13	Ditto	none
8	Ditto	3	In favor with the amendment	6
9	Ditto	8	Against it	1
10	Ditto	9	Ditto	none
11	Ditto	9	Ditto	none

Attest—Jacob Sherwin Town Clerk
Benjamin Phillips Select Men of
Rowland Sears Ashfield

Ashfield 2d June 1780

Belchertown (276/40)

To the Convention to meet at Boston on the first Wednesday in June AD: 1780 for framing and compleating a new Constitution of Government for the State of Massachusetts-Bay.

Respected Gentlemen: we, the Inhabitants of Belcherstown, have read your Address, Declaration of Rights and proposed Frame of Government: and we hope paid a proper Attention thereto.

And as you call for our sentiments upon the Form sent to us, and tell us it is our Right to propose such Alterations and Amendments as we judge proper or give it our sanction in its present Form. or totally reject it We chuse the former, but are unwilling to receive it as it now stands and unwilling to reject the many good things in it.

We do not Object to the Declaration of Rights; tho in another view we may object to a clause in Article 29th We approve of great Part of the proposed Frame of Government There are however some things in it to which we object, and we think with good Reason—we desire some Alterations and Amendments and some additional Insertions.—as

1 We object against the Qualifications for Voters for Governor, Lieutenant Governor or Senators councellors and Representatives (as mentioned in the sundry Passages relative thereto) in Point of Estate we imagine that upon that Plan, some will be deprived of having any share in Legislation—nay denied that Liberty and Freedom which we are at this Day Contending for.

Our Idea is that the male Inhabitants of this state who are free and twenty one years of Age have a right to Vote for Governor, Lieutenant Governor, Senators and Councellors and Representatives—except Foreigners, who ought not to have and Exercise that Right until they obtain the Freedom of some Town where they inhabit by the unanimous Approbation of the select Men of the same

There are 4 for the above passage as they stand in the Book and 83 for the above alteration.

2 Whereas (by Chapter 1 Section 3 Article 5 Page 25) Representatives are to be chosen in May—we conceive it might be done at the Annual Meeting for chusing Governor Senators etc. in April, and thereby save the trouble and expence of one meeting, and give the Representatives more time to order their Domestic affairs and prepare to

attend the service of the publick 2 for it as in Book and 81 with this altoration

3 We apprehend there is a very essential Defect in the Qualification prescribed for the Governor and Lieutenant Governor (Chapter 2 Section 1 Article 2 Page 27 and section 2 Article 1) in Point of Religion We conceive the term Christian Religion is much too lax—and if the term Protestant were substituted instead of Christian, though the Idea conveyed thereby would be proper: yet it ought not to rest solely on his Declaration—a wicked designing man would make such Declaration, and there may be a case when the contrary may be proved not withstanding such a Declaration We desire that the words *unless he shall declare him self of the Christian Religion* be erased, and these words inserted instead of them viz *unless he be of the Protestant Christian Religion.*

We desire likewise that the same words may be inserted in the Qualification for Senators and Councellors and Representatives—For we apprehend the Administration of publick affairs in this Common wealth cannot be safe in any other hands. and that this ought to be a fixed point in the Constitution and Alterations made accordingly in the Declaration—We desire also that for the same Reason it may be inserted in the Constitution that no Man shall bear any office in this Common wealth either Civil or Military unless he be of the Protestant Religion.

None for these Passages as in Book but 94 with this amendment

4 Whereas Provision is made (Chapter 1 Section 3 Article 2) for Paying the Expences of Travel only to the Representatives—we conceive this Article needs Amendment—and that the Representatives (as well as senators) ought to be supported and paid out of the publick Chest—our Reasons are

(1) Because they are Representatives not meerly of this or that particular Town (which would suppose them to have the interest of that Town only to provide for) But of the whole Body of the People—and though they are to guard the Rights of the Town where they are chosen as they are presumed to know the state of it, yet they are equally to guard the Rights of the whole, and we would have them, by the mode of support and Payment as well as other things, divest themselves of Party and Prejudice and seek and pursue the grand interest of the whole.

(2) we think it is most agreable to the Fundamental Principle of Equality on which Representation is attempted to be founded.—as they are to do the Business of the whole community, it is but equal they Should be

paid by the whole, and that each individual should contribute his proportional share which will not be the case if each Town supports its own representative—and we conceive it can only be done in this way.

3) We imagine that by this means publick Business would be better attended

2 for it as in Book and 83 for this amendment

5 With Regard to the Justices of the superior Court we should think it much preferable to the proposed Plan, that they be commissioned only for three years—at the End of which their Commission may be renewed, unless some reasonable objection be made against it—By this means a bad one may be removed with less Trouble and Observation, and (the sallery being fixed and sufficient) there is sufficient Encouragement for Men of Ability and Integrity, and a greater stimulus to good Behaviour. (this refers to Declaration 29 and Chapter 3 Article 1)

None for it as in Book but 72 with this alterration

6 It is our opinion that Justice of the Inferior Court Should be taken out of the Justices of the County and commissioned for three years only at one time for Reasons similar to those given in the preceeding articles none for as in Book but 73 with this alterration

7 For similar Reasons we apprehend that the Attorney General Sollicitor general and Judges of Probate ought not to be commissioned for longer than three years.

None for as in Book but 73 with this alterration

8 For the Reasons given Chapter 3 article 3 we are of opinion that seven years is vastly to long for a commission for a Justice of the Peace—that their Commission ought to be but for one year—and that there ought to be no more Justices in any Town than the Town has Liberty to send Representatives—and that they ought to be recommended to the Governor and Council for a Commission (annually) by a majority of the Votes in every Town of those Persons who vote for Representatives as they may be presumed: to be the best Judges of this Qualifications

none for as in Book But with 61 with this alterration

9 It is our opinion that the sherif of Each County ought to be annually elected at the time and in the manner that the Councellors and Senators are and that there is equal reason for it.

none for as in Book 61 with this alterration

10 It is our opinion that military officers ought to be annually elected—To the End that those who are unfit for their Posts may be easily dropped, and such as are Worthy as they come on the stage Elected and

that by this means that military Power may be more easily kept in a proper subordination to the Civil Authority

none for as in Book 61 with this alterration

11 It is our opinion that besides the Requisition of all publick Boards, of officers of forts etc. Chapter 2 Section 1 article 12—they ought to be obliged to render a like Account to either House of the Legislature whenever requested. This may be absolutely necessary for the publick safety (as in Case of a dispute with the Governor etc.) and is what either House has a Right to Demand by the 5th article in the Declaration of Rights

none for as in Book Chapter 2 Section 1 Article 12

But with the Amendment 56

12 We desire it may be inserted in the Constitution that the Town Clerk in each town shall be a register of Deeds for the Town This we apprehend would save much trouble and cost to the subject and be of publick utility—and may as well be inserted in the Constitution as left to the Legislature—and if done give satisfaction to many

None for this as in Book but 73 with this amendment

13 Whereas the Counties are so large that it is a great Inconvenience to many that there is but one court of Probate in a County we desire that the Counties may be divided into proper Districts for the Ease of the subjects in this Matter—we think the members of this Convention as capable of doing this as a future Legislature, and that if Provisions were made therefor in the Constitution, it would greatly Tend to the Quiet of the People.

None for as in Book but 68 with this amendment

14 Tho Trial by Peers be declared to be a Right—yet no Provision is made in the Frame of Government how grand or petit Juries shall be obtained—we desire that a proper mode for this may be pointed out and fixed in the Constitution, that we may not be liable to be in as bad or worse circumstances in this Respect then we should have been a few years ago, had Injunctions from Brittain taken Place among us.

There be 84 for having this inserted in the Constitution

15 We desire hereafter that more certain and exact Provisions be made for the future Revision of this Constitution than is Prescribed in Chapter 6 Article 10—viz That on that Day seven years from the time this Constitution takes place the Inhabitants of each Town in this Common wealth shall assemble, (and it shall be the Duty of the select Men of Each Town previously to warn them in due course of law to meet on

said Day)—and manifest their minds, whether they desire a Revision and alteration of this Constitution—and send an Account of their determination to the General Court—with the Numbers in each town voting for or against such Revision in 60 Days—and if it appears by the said Returns that two thirds of the People in the State are desirous of such Revision the General Court Shall appoint Time and Place and issue out Precepts for calling a state Convention of Delegates for the Purpose, the Same Numbers to be chosen in each Town as they may by this Constitution chuse Representatives and in the same manner who shall revise the same. and in like manner the inhabitants shall meet for said Purpose every seven years—and their Returns shall be made to the General Court who shall proceed Accordingly—But no alteration shall Ever be made in this Constitution unless it be by Consent of two thirds of the male Inhabitants of this State who are Free and twenty one years of age—Foreigners not having the freedom of any Town excepted.

All the rest of the Declaration of Rights and the Constitution is excepted and by the number of 84 as it stands in the Book

Henry Dwight Select
[Joseph] Smith Men

Belcherstown the 22th of May—1780

Bernardston (276/41)

At a Legal Meeting of the Freeholders and other Inhabitants of Bernardston holden at the house of Major John [Burk?] in Said Town May the 10th 1780 in order to consider of and act upon the Constitution
then the question was put whether they will vote for the 3d Article of the Declaration of the Rights of the Inhabitants of the Commonwelth of Massachusets and there was thirty for it and Nine against it
Then the question was put whether they will vote the qualification of voters for Governers Senat etc. and there was twenty three for it and thirteen against it and then the question was put whether they will vote the whole of the Remainder of the Constitution and there was twenty six for and three against it

Aaron Field Selectmen of
Elisha Burnham Bernardston

Brimfield (276/42)

The Doings of The Town of Brimfield in the County of Hampshire upon the Constitution published by Convention for Their Approbation March 2, 1780——

The Town Voted

1st to exapt of the Constitution as published, without Amendment

Number for the same——81

Number agaist—— 1

And the Town directed Their Deligate in Convention That if said Constitution should not be agreed upon by Two thirds of the Inhabitants of the State assembled in The Town meetings for that Purpose, to endevour the alteration thereof. So that it may be made agreeable to the said Two Thirds, and when it shall be the Convention be made conformable thereto which he is inpowered to do to agree upon a Time when the said form of Government shall take place without returning the same again to the People.

T. Danielson

The above is a State of Facts as they ly upon my Mind, am certain have not exceeded the Number present in Town Meeting, and but one in the Negative, The other Matters I can not be mistaken in, being present in The Meeting. But the Town Clerk Did not find Me the Votes and forgot to call upon him for them, I am gentlemen of the Committee your humble Servant

T. Danielson

South Brimfield, 1780 (276/43)

[Printed Constitution with marginal notes, as follows. Angle brackets indicate that notes were crossed out.]

Part the First

Article I ⟨Excepted by 18 that was present and one that rejected⟩

Article II ⟨Excepted by 30 that was present and None against⟩

Article III	⟨Excepted by 25 with the written amendment and no one religious sect or denomination of Christians shall be assessed for the support of the Publick Teachers of any other Denomination⟩
Article IV	⟨Excepted by 26⟩
Article V	⟨Excepted by 24⟩
Article VI	⟨Excepted by 26⟩
Article VII	⟨Excepted by 30⟩
Article VIII	⟨Excepted by 35⟩
Article IX	⟨Excepted by 33⟩
Article X	⟨Excepted by 30⟩
Article XI	⟨Excepted by 30⟩
Article XII	⟨Excepted by 23⟩
Article XIII	⟨Excepted by 23⟩
Article XIV	⟨Excepted by 23⟩
Article XV	⟨Excepted by 22⟩
Article XVI	⟨Excepted by 23⟩
Article XVII	⟨Excepted by 23⟩
Article XVIII	⟨Excepted by 23⟩
Article XIX	⟨Excepted by 22⟩
Article XX	⟨Excepted by 18⟩
Article XXI	⟨Excepted by 19⟩
Article XXII	⟨Excepted by 19⟩
Article XXIII	⟨Excepted by 20⟩
Article XXIV	⟨Excepted by 22⟩
Article XXV	⟨Excepted by 22⟩
Article XXVI	⟨Excepted by 19⟩
Article XXVII	⟨Excepted by 19⟩
Article XXVIII	⟨Excepted by 21⟩
Article XXIX	⟨Excepted by 31 with this Amendment [vizt?] that the Judges be annually appointed⟩
Article XXX	⟨Excepted by 36⟩

Part the Second. The Frame of Government ⟨this Excepted by 34⟩

Chapter I, Section I

Article I	⟨Excepted by 30⟩
Article II	⟨Excepted by 32⟩
Article III	⟨Excepted by 33⟩
Article IV	⟨Excepted by 18⟩

Chapter I, Section II	
Article I	⟨Excepted by 12⟩
Article II	⟨Excepted by 13⟩
Article III	⟨Excepted by 13⟩
Article IV	⟨Excepted by 13⟩
Article V	⟨Excepted by 17 with this amendment: to a [*illegible*] one halfe of the sume for that [*illegible*]⟩
Article VI	Excepted by 17
Article VII	Excepted by 17
Article VIII	⟨Excepted by 20⟩
Article IX	⟨Excepted by 20⟩
Chapter I, Section III	
Article I	⟨Excepted by 20⟩
Article II	⟨Excepted by 22⟩
Article III	⟨Excepted by 22⟩
Article IV	⟨Excepted by 22⟩
Article V	⟨Excepted by 22⟩
Article VI	⟨Excepted by 22⟩
Article VII	⟨Excepted by 22⟩
Article VIII	⟨Excepted by 22⟩
Article IX	⟨Excepted by 22⟩
Article X	⟨Excepted by 25⟩
Article XI	⟨Excepted by 25⟩
Chapter II, Section I	
Article I	⟨Excepted by 23 and rejected by 2———⟩
Article II	⟨Excepted by 27 with the writ amendment [amend] 400 Pound instead of 1000⟩
Article III	⟨Excepted by 27⟩
Article IV	⟨Excepted by 27———⟩
Article V	⟨Excepted by 26⟩
Article VI	⟨Excepted by 24⟩
Article VII	⟨Excepted by 23⟩
Article VIII	⟨Excepted by 23⟩
Article IX	⟨Excepted by 25 with the under written Reserve that the Court of Probate be Erected in Every 3 or 4 Towns as may be convenient⟩
Article X	⟨Excepted with the written amendments by 31⟩ [The written amendments are ⟨annually⟩ in-

serted after "Captains and subalterns of the militia shall be"; ⟨annually⟩ inserted after "The field-officers of regiments, shall be"; ⟨annually⟩ inserted after "the Brigadiers shall be"; and ⟨*During such appointment*⟩ inserted after "And no officer, duly commissioned to command in the militia, shall be removed from his office."]

Article XI	⟨Excepted by 31⟩
Article XII	⟨Excepted by 31⟩
Article XIII	⟨Excepted by 34⟩
Chapter II, Section II	
Article I	⟨This article Excepted by 41 with the same amendments as are made in the article for a governor⟩
Article II	⟨Excepted by 37⟩
Article III	⟨Excepted by 37⟩
Chapter II, Section III	
Article I	⟨Excepted by 38⟩
Article II	⟨Excepted by 38⟩
Article III	⟨Excepted by 37⟩
Article IV	⟨Excepted by 37⟩
Article V	⟨Excepted by 35⟩
Article VI	⟨Excepted by 36⟩
Article VII	⟨Excepted by 27⟩
Chapter II, Section IV	
Article I	⟨Excepted by 29⟩
Article II	⟨Excepted by 25⟩
Chapter III	
Article I	⟨Accepted by 23 with the within amendment Their annual apointment⟩
Article II	⟨Accepted by 26⟩
Article III	⟨Accepted by 24 with the written amendment⟩ [The written amendment is ⟨*one year*⟩, instead of seven, inserted after "all commissions of Justices of the Peace shall expire and become void, in term of."]
Article IV	⟨Accepted by 17⟩
Article V	⟨Accepted by 17⟩

Chapter IV	⟨Unanimous by 17 being all present that they be chosen by the People at Large⟩
Chapter V, Section I	
Article I	⟨Accepted by 17⟩
Article II	⟨Accepted by 17⟩
Article III	⟨Accepted by 17⟩
Chapter V, Section II	⟨Excepted by 21⟩
Chapter VI	⟨This Chapture excepted by 17⟩

[Resolution Convention, March 2, 1780, printed with Constitution, with marginal notes as follows, on page 53]

After "Resolved, That it be recommended to the Inhabitants of the Several Towns; . . . to agree upon a Time when this Form of Government shall take place" This Resolve Voted

After "Resolved, that the Towns and Plantations . . . have a Right to choose other Delegates . . ." Voted that the same Dilligat be Continud

South Brimfield May 29, 1780 pursuant to the Resolve of the Convention we have laid this Constitution and Frame of Government before our town and they have after mature consideration voted as we have inserted in the foregoing pages

atest

Jonas Blodget
Wilm Belknap — Select
Jonathan Cram — Men
Joseph Needham

Charlemont *

At a legal meeting of the freeholders and other inhabitants of the town of Charlemont held at the Meeting house in Said Town on Friday the nineteenth day of May 1780.

1st. Deacon Aaron Rice Chosen Moderator of Said Meeting.

2nd Voted not to send a representative the ensuing year—The Question being put whether the town approve of the Constitution as it now stands ——passed in the Negative.

Voted to Chuse three men as a Committee to make ammendments, Deacon Aaron Rice, Jonathan Hastings, Thomas Nichols chosen for

* Town records, Massachusetts Historical Society.

that purpose. Adjourned to friday the 26th of this Inst. May at twelve o'clock

---

Met by adjournment——
Voted to reconsider the vote respecting a representative. Deacon Aaron Rice chosen to represent the town in the Great and General Court the ensuing year.

The Question was then put whether the town would make any amendments to the Constitution or whether they would accept it as it now stands—a majority of those present voted to accept it as it now stands. Near or quite half The Voters were absent.

Aaron Rice Moderator

Chesterfield (276/44)

Report of the Committee Chosen and appointed by the Town of Chesterfield to take into Consideration the Frame of Government lately Sent out to the Several Towns in this State for their approbation or Disaprobation or amendment and for Revising the same———
Part First in the BILL OF RIGHTS

Artical 3d. Paragraph 3d. Provided notwithstanding that the Several Towns, parishes, Precincts, and other Bodies politic or Religious Societies, Shall at all Times have the Exclusive Right of Electing their public Teachers and of Contracting with them for their Support and maintainence,—be added to the Second Artical—the Rest of the artical be Expunged, Excepting the last paragraph and that to be Considered as the third Artical—yeas 25; nays 20
Artical 16 in the Bill of Rights be altered by putting the word Shall in the room of ought 25 for it none against it
Artical 29 that the Surpreem Judicial Judges Shall have Honourable Saliries voted to them annually and not Established by Standing Laws 25 for it none against it
Part Second Chapter 1 Section 2 Article 1 and 2
2 Artical 1 and 2
Artical 1 that General Court Shall not have any Right to alter any of the Districts by Dividing them 25 for it none against it———
Artical 2d that Every man that is an Inhabitant of a Town and is of the age of twenty one years Shall have a Right to vote for Senators
25 for it none against it———

Section 3 Artical 2d. that Every Member Shall be paid for his Time and Expence of Travilling to and from the General Assembly out of the Publick Chest
25 for it none against it
Artical 4th that Every male Person of the age of twenty one years and Resident in any perticular Town in this Common Wealth for the Space of one year Shall have a Right to vote for Representatives 25 for it none against it———
Artical 9th that not less then one Hundred and Sixty members of the house of Representatives shall Constitute a Corum for doing business 25 for it none against it
Chapter 2d Section 1 Artical 2d. that the word Protestant be added to the Governers Qualifications 25 for it none against it
Artical 3d but if no Person is chosen Governer the two Houses shall be booth in one Room and vote for one out of four that shall appear to have the most votes if so many have been voted for and the Person thus Chosen Shall be declared governer 25 for it none against it———
Artical 10 that Every male Person shall have a Right to vote for Military Officers as soon as he is sixteen years old and comes into the Train Band and that all Milicia Officers shall be chosen once in sevin years at least and commissioned accordingly 24 for it 4 against it
Artical 18th that the Governor shall have an Honourable Salery voted to him annually and not Established by standing Laws—22 for it none against it
Chapter 2d Section 3d Artical 2—that the nine Counsellors be Chosen out of those Persons who shall be Chosen for Senators and Counsellors and if they are not Chosen the first time they shall proceed to Choose untill they have Chosen them out of the [Forty] Senators—16 for none against it———
Artical 4 their shall not be more than one Counsellor Chosen out of one District 24 for, none against it
Chapter 6 Artical 3d it shall not be in the Power of the Legislator to increas or decreas the Qualifycations as to Property of the Persons to be Elected to Office 22 for none against it———
Artical 10 that the General Court shall issu Precepts to the Select Men of the Several Towns and to the assessors of the unincorporated Plantations Directing them to Convene at the End of Sevin years from the time of this Plan of Government takes place to revise the Constitution in order that such amendments may be made in it as the people think

Proper—and to Examine the Laws to see if they do Infringe upon the Constitution and in such case to repeal them 17 for and 3 against it

The town of Chesterfield at a Legal Meeting of the 1 of June 1780 voted to Accept of the Constitution with the foregoing amendments also that it take place the first of September next———

test. John Stephanson T. Clerk

Colrain (276/45)

To the Secretary of Convention at Boston This Certifies that at a Legal Meeting of the Inhabitants of Colrain on the Twenty Sixth day of May 1780. The Town agreed to have the following Amendments—in the Constitution to viz. Third Article of Declaration of Rights disapproved all but the Seven first Lines and the Last Clause for Amendmendment 21 Voters Against it 22 Reasons. we Judge that the Legislature have not a right to Command the Subject in matters of Religion—to protection only—also on the first Article Second Section Amendment we propose that the Number of Counselors and Senators be 30. Reason to avoid Unnesary Cost for the Amendment 37—2 against, also Second Article. we are of Opinion that Every male Inhabitant resideing in Any Town in this State being free and twenty One years of Age and a friend to the Independance of Said State and of Sober life and Conversation Certifyed by the Select men has a right to Vote for Governor Lieutenant Governor Council Senators and Representatives, Reason Taxation without Representation we Consider unreasonable for Amendment 38—4 against—Also fifth Article we disaprove one of the Qualifications of Senators to viz Six hundred pounds of Estate we consider Money not a Quallification in this Matter for Amendment 27 against none—Also Ninth Article we Judge that Eleven Senators is Sufficient to Constitute a Quorum for doing Business. Reason to prevent Unnesassary Cost for Amendment 30 Against none—Also Third Article 3 Section we disapprove one of the Qualifications of representatives viz. £ 200 of Estate. reason we Consider money no Qualification in this Matter for Amendment 27 Against none—Also 4th Article we move for the Same Amendment in this Article as for Senators and for the Same Reasons for the Amendment 34 Against none Also 2d. Article 2d. Chapter first Section we move for Two Amendments in this Article viz. we Consider money is not a Qualification for this Important office. 2dly that the

Word protestant be Substitueted Instead of Christian reason first we Could wish the Important Chair to be filled with Quallifications prefarable to that of Money 2d reason we are a protestant People for the Amendment 36—against none also 6th Article: Said Chapter we move for Amendment to viz: that in Case of disagreement Between the Two houses with respect to Adjourning the General Court that the Governor Shall not Exceed the Longest Term of Time. Reason a Longer Adjournment than is thought best by Either house may be Injurious to the State for the Amendment 33—against none Also 9th Article we disaprove of the Whole of this Article. reason A matter or Matters of this Importance ought of right to be Acted upon by Both houses of Legislature. Justices of the Peace to be Nominated by the People and Commissioned by the Governor for Amendment 32 Against none. Also Article 10th we move for Two Amendments to viz. first that the field officers of Regiments Appoint their Adjutants and Quarter Masters 2dly that the Governor and Both houses do appoint Continenetal and Garison Officers for the Amendment 27 against none Also 12 Article we move that it be Aded to this Article that those dispatches returns etc. be Laid by the Governor before Both houses as Soon as may be reason we Consider and Judge it highly reasonable that the representitives of the People Shall know the State of the Common Wealth for Amendment 36. none against—Also Chapter 3 article 3d. we move for Amendment to viz that Justices of the peace be Chosen Annualy. Reason. that they may be thereby Animated to Officiate faithfully—being dependant on the People for Continuance in Such Office for the Amendment 32. Against 2 Also Chapter 5 Section 2 we Object to the Town being oblidged to keep Gramer Schools Reason as Towns in General are not of Ability to Keep a Sufficency of English Schools for the Amendment 26 against 3. Also Chapter 6 Article first we move for Amendment to viz: that the word Protestant be substituted in place of Christian Reason—we are a Protestant people—for Amendment 25 against 4 Also Chapter 6. Article 2d. we move for an Addition to this Article to viz. that no person be suffered to hold any office in this Common Wealth who has not been friendly to the Independance of this Common Wealth reason a person who has Acted the Traitor in this Important Matter is not to be Trusted. for the Amendment 31 Against none Also Chapter 6 Article 3 Rejected for Before mentioned reasons for amentment 30 Against none—

A true coppy of the minutes

James Stewart Town Clerk

Conway (276/46–47)

At a Legal meeting of the Town of Conway Called By the Selectmen of said Town Pursuant to a Request of the Convention held at Cambridge etc. to form a Constatution for this State. Said Town Assembled the 27th of May following. and after Due Delibration on the Sevral Articuls etc. etc. the following votes ware taken (Viz) Voted Unanimously to Accept the Declaration of Rights of the Comon welth of Massachusetts Bay Proposed By the abovesaid convention—Voted Unanimously to Accept the Power and form or Meathod of proceedings repossited in the Trust of the Legislative Body of this State Contained in the first Chapter 1st, 2nd and 3rd Sections—The Question was put to see if the Town would Accept the 2nd articul of the 1st Section in the 2nd. Chapter (viz Governor) with the addition of the worde Prodistant before the words Christian Religion and also Every other articul Contained in Said Section but the 10th. Voted Unanimously in the affairmative Then the Question was Continued to see if the Town would Accept the 10th articul of the abovesaid Chapter and Section Voted 15 for it and 9 against it—Voted unanimously to Accept the 2nd. Chapter and 2nd. Section (Viz) Lieutenant Governor—also the 3rd. and 4th Section of the Same Chapter——— Voted to accept the 3rd. Chapter (Viz) Judiciary Power Excepting Nine Persons who objected against Commisian officers holding their Commisions Dureing good behavour Contained in the first articul of said Chapter—Voted Unanimously to accept the 4th Chapter (Viz) Deligates to the Congress—Voted Unanimously to Accept the 5th. Chapter 1st and 2nd Section (Viz) the University at Cambridge and Encouragement of Literature etc.—Voted Unanimously to Accept the last Chapter with the Addition of the words Prodistant before the words Christian Religon in the Governors Decliration———Voted Unanimously that it is the openion of this Town that no person that has appeared to be Enemical in this war shall not have a Seat in the Legislative Executive or Judicial Bodies dureing this Constitution———

attest. Oliver Wetmore Town Clerk

N.B. it may Be observed that there was one Unanimous Vote Taken on the 10th articul of the 2nd. Chapter and first Section (Governor) that the appointing officers for the *armey* Should be in the Power of the Governor Councill and hous of Representatives and that the Town has

Chose a Committee to give the Reasons of the above objections which Reasons are to be Transmitted to the Convention with the above—I am also to Inform the Honourable Convention that the whole Number of Voters present at the above meeting was about 40———

To the Honourable Convention to be held at Boston on the first Wednesday in June: 1780 we being appointed by the Inhabitants of Conway as a committee to form the Reasons for the Objections made in the Several Articuls in the form of Government to be in this State we offer the following such. (viz) on the first objection for adding the word Protestant to the Christian Religion: because it did not exclud parsons of the Romish faith from the Governors Seat.———On the 2nd Objection which was on the 10th articul of Chapter 2nd and Section first the Reason is because Soldiers from Sixteen years old to twenty one which make a great part of the company have no Right to Vote for their officers Objected also against the Governor and Councills appointing the officers of the Continantal Army without the Voice of the House of Representatives On the 3rd. Objection which was on the first articul in the 3rd. Chapter. Commissioned officers holding their office During good behavior because being long continued in office they may grow arbitrary or Slack in Duty and not haveing a time perficks for a new choice is not agreable to a free Constitution. The Reason for the articul to be added to the Constitution is because that parsons that have heitherto manifested great Reluctance in aidding or assisting in the cause we are ingaged in or inimical thereto may not hold Place of Power and trust in this Commonweth by this Constitution

Attest. Samuel Wells Chairman of the Committee

Conway June the 1th. 1780

Cummington (276/47)

At a Meeting of the Freeholders and other Inhabitants of the town of Cummington in the County of Hampshire May 25 on Adjournment from May 22, 1780 Voted to Approve of the Constitution or Form of Goverment (fifty five for and one against) with these alterations, viz.
Part 1st Chapter 1st Section 3 Article 9. Not less than two hundred members of the house to Constitute a Quorum for Doing Business———
Part Second, the General Court Chapter 1st Section 1st Article 2nd. No Bill or Resolve Whatever ought to become a Law unless two thirds the

Majority of the Senate and house of Representatives both Assembled in one room Each Individual (of the Senate and House) having Equal voice and to be Determined by yeas and nays

Ebenr. Colson	Select men
Joshua Shaw	of
Barnabas Packard	Cummington

Deerfield *

May 15th, [1780] a meeting was held to act on the new Constitution. The Clerk was directed to read the instrument "Paragraph by Paragraph, pausing between them." After this a committee of nine was chosen "to peruse the Constitution or Form of Government now presented to the people of this State for their Approbation or Disapprobation, and make such objections to it, as they think ought to be made, and Lay the same before the Town at an adjourned meeting." Met the 25th, when the paper was again read by the Clerk. June 1st, the operation was repeated, with another adjournment.

June 5th, voted not to have the Clerk read the Constitution again. Doubtless they had it all by heart, at this meeting. Voted, 14 to 9, "not to accept the third article in the Declaration of Rights." Voted unanimously that "in the Qualifications of the person eligible to the office of Governor Instead of his Declaring himself to be of the Christian Religion, it should be that he Declare himself of the Protestant Religion." They also objected that fifteen years was too long a period before the Constitution should be revised, and proposed eight years instead. In other respects it was satisfactory. The freeholders of Deerfield having done their duty with great deliberation the meeting dissolved. It is to be presumed from the small vote that the Tories held themselves aloof from the meeting.

Granby (276/48)

The Proceedings of the Town of Granby on the form of Constitution. Presented to us By the Convention Lately held at Cambridge——
Number of Voters present in the meeting——41

* George Sheldon, *History of Deerfield, Massachusetts* (Deerfield, Mass., 1896), II, 731.

The Whole Book or form of Constitution, Voted. Except the following articles
Viz. Article 3d in the Declaration of Rights. To this article 13 in the afirmitive and 28 in the Negative

---

Constitution Chapter first Section 2d Article 2d Passed in the Negative Number of Voters 39: and Not any in the afirmitive

---

Chapter 2d article 2d Not one in the afirmitive, and 39 in the Negative

---

Chapter 2d article 9th. Not one in the afirmitive, and 39 in the Negative

---

Chapter 2d article 10th. Not any in the afirmitive, and 39 in the Negative

---

Chapter 6 article 10th: None in the afirmitive. And 39 in the Negative

---

Whereas the Convention Have Desired that those who are Objectors to any Part of the form of Constitution, would State there objections and reasons fairly in wrighting. We therefore ofer the following Reasons to our objections in the above articles. in there order. Viz. to the first of these articles Viz. that it imples not only an Inconsistancy with it Self in its Parts and Paragrafts but that it also is Contradictory to the 2d or foregoing article. And also that whilst it Secures and Establishes to one subject the Rights and Liberties of Conscience, in making Provision for And worshiping God. agreeable to the Light of his one Conscience, It is Subversive of. and is an infringment of the Rights of others.
2d. That we do not find that the Great Law Giver of Heaven and Earth hath ever given to us a wright to Invest others with authority or to authorize them to make Laws. to Bind the Subject to make Provisions For, or to worship God, Contrary to the Light and Dictates of his owe Conscience.

Constitution Chapter 1 Article 2d Section 2d. That it is our opinion that the Sum mentioned for the qualification of Voters aught to be reduced one third Part

---

Chapter 2d article 2d that the word (christian) aught to be Dealed and the word (Protistant) Substituted in its room.

Chapter 2d Article 9th
That all Judiciel and other officers whose Power and authority Shall Extend throughout the Whole State. Shall be Chosen by joint Ballot of the Senate and House of Representatives Assembled in one Room:—and that all Judisciel and other officers whose Power and Authority is limited to the Counties In which they Dwell and For which They are Chosen and Commisioned: Shall be Chosen By the Respective Towns Contained in these Countys: And by Ballot of those who are qualified to Vote For Senators and Representatives

---

Chapter 2d article 10th
that all shall Be Considered as qulified For Voting For malitia officers from Sixteen years old and upwards
N B meening the Captains and Subalterns

Chapter 6 Article 10th—
Thatt the Term of fifteen years mentioned in this Form of Constitution: Be Reduced to the Term of Ten years

Granby May 27th 1780

Israel Clark, Samuel Moody, John Moody — Selectmen of Granby
Nathn. Smith, Town Clerk

			For it	Against
Declaration of right		Article 3	13	28
Chapter	Section	Article		
1	2	2		39
2	0	3		39
2		9		39
6		10		39

Granville (276/49)

At a legal Meeting of the Freeholders and other Inhabitants of the Town of Granville on May the 8th 1780, the Select Men of said Town laid before them the Constitution or Form of Government framed by the Convention of the State of Massachusetts Bay, they taking the same into Consideration passed the following Votes on the Several Articles in Said Constitution———

Part the first

A Declaration of the Rights of the Inhabitants of the common Wealth of the Massachusetts Bay

Article	for	against	Article	for	against
1	44	1	16	79	1
2	54	—	17	80	—
*3	6	64	18	80	—
4	72	—	19	80	—
5	72	—	20	83	—
6	72	—	21	82	1
7	72	—	22	82	1
8	72	—	23	83	—
9	74	1	24	84	—
10	74	2	25	86	—
11	76	—	26	85	—
12	77	—	27	85	—
13	78	—	28	85	—
14	80	—	29	60	19
15	76	4	30	81	—

* The objection to the third Article is as follows. The Article Asserts that the People have a Right to invest their Legislature with a Power to interfere in Matters that properly belong to the Christian Church; after the most mature Consideration we are obliged to deny that any such Right is or can be invested in the Legislature: because:———

1st Christ himself is the only Lord of Conscience and King and Law Giver in his Church. Teachers of Religion are officers in his Kingdom, qualified and sent by him, for whose Maintenance he hath made Sufficient Provision, by the Laws which belong to his own Kingdom—Therefore no Supplementary Laws of human Legislatures are necessary———

2nd. The interference of the Magistrate in Matters that belong to the Christian Church is in our View an Incroachment on the Kingly Office of Jesus Christ, who Stands in no need of the help of any civil Legislature whatever; consequently is an Affront to him.

3rd. The Interference of the Civil Magistrate in Matters that belong to Christ and Conscience, ever has been, and ever will be productive of Oppression to Mankind. There could be no persecution if the civil

Magistrate did not Support the Power and Cruelty of Men of narrow and ambitious Minds———

4th. True Religion has evidently declined and been currupted by the interference of Statesmen and Politicians. Church History proves this to have been the Case from the Days of Constantine down to our own Day———

PART THE SECOND

The Frame of Government 79 for Chapter 1st———

The Legislative Power

Section 1st.

The General Court

Article	for	against	Article	for	against
1	79		3rd	78	
2	78		4	74	

Chapter 1st Section 2nd

Article	for	against	Article	for	against
1	73	2	6	56	—
2	37	29	7	56	—
3	66	—	8	53	1
4	59	—	9	54	—
5	43	15			

Chapter 1st Section 3rd

Article	for	against	Article	for	against
1	53	—	7	44	—
2	61	—	8	48	—
3	54	6	9	48	—
4	33	32	10	51	—
5	65	—	11	51	—
6	65	—			

Executive Power

Chapter 2nd.

Section 1st

Article	for	against	article	for	against	article	for	against
1	83	—	6	66	3	11	62	—
2	47	36	7	63	4	12	58	—
3	69	4	8	77	—	13	33	19
4	74	—	9	40	15			
5	77	—	10	6	57			

Objection, to the 10th Article is because those of the Train Band under twenty one years are not allowed to vote for their Captain and Subalterns———

Reasons—All and every Member in any Society or Community liable to do duty for themselves in the same, ought to have a Voice in electing their Officers———

Chapter 2nd Section 2nd Lieutenant Governor

Article	for	against	Article	for	against	Article	for	against
1	30	5	2	60	1	3	59	—

Chapter 2nd Section 3rd—Council etc.

Article	for	against	Article	for	against	Article	for	against
1	63	1	4	66	—	7	60	—
2	61	—	5	58	1			
3	61	—	6	59	—			

Chapter 2nd Section 4th Secretary Treasurer etc.

Article	for	against	Article	for	against
1	58	—	2	31	1

Chapter 3rd. Judiciary Power

Article	for	against	Article	for	against	Article	for	against
1	41	2	3	33	2	5	47	1
2	42	—	4	38	—			

Chapter 4th Delegates to Congress 48 for 1 against

The University etc.

Chapter 5th

Section 1st

1	40	8	2	51	1	3	46	1

Encouragement of Literature etc.

Chapter 5—Section 2nd 58 for———

Chapter 6th Oaths and Subscriptions

Article	for	against	Article	for	against	Article	for	against
1	44	—	5	71	—	9	34	—
2.	—	75	6	27	15	10	42	—
3.	—	71	7	45	—	11	42	—
4	71	—	8	39	—			

Objection, to the Second Article, is because the settled Gospel Minister is not excluded

Reason—By said Article settled Gospel Ministers are eligable to a Seat in the House of Representatives, and to impose Taxes and Burdens on those they represent, when according to the present Laws, they themselves bear no part of the Burthens they impose on their Inhabitants ———Objections to this 3rd Article are because the Legislature has a Right to augment the Qualifications of Persons to be elected Reasons— It is not safe to lodge any such Power with the Legislature, but that the Qualifications ought now to be established———

A true Return of the Votes for and against each Article
Titus Fowler
Timo. Robinson Selectmen of Granville
Josiah Harvey

Greenfield (276/50)

To the Honourable Secretary of the Convention for forming of a Constitution Sir the votes of this town on the Constitution are as follows Voted to Except Every Artickel in the bill of Rights except the third By the Number of 45 the 3d Articel approved by 17 Disapproved by 28 Their objection is that the Lejeslator has nothing to do with matters of Relegion
The form of Government Chapter 1 Section 1
Every Artickel approved by the Number of 44
Chapter 1st Section 2d the Senate Every Artickel approved Except the 2d by the Number 44 the 2d Articel approved by 2 Disaproved by 42 their objections are that Every man Hath Not a Right in Legislation and Taxsation
Chapter 1 Section 3d hous of Representitive Every Articel approved Except the 4th by the Number of 34 the 4th approved by None Disaproved by 34 their objection Because every free man hath not a Voice in Legislation and Taxsation
Chapter 2th Section 4th Executive Power Every Articel approved of by the Number of 34 Chapter 2d Section 2d Approved by the Number of 36 Disaproved by None
Chapter 2d Section 3d Council Every Articel Approved
Chapter 2d Section 4th Secretary Treasurer Commissary
Every Articel Approved of By the Number of 36
Chapter 3d Judiciary Power Every Articel Approved of by the Number of 36 Chapter 4th Deligates to Congress Approved Chapter 5th Section 1 University Every Articel Approved of except the first by Number

of 36 The Objection is Because that the Studience of harvards Collage are Not Subject to taxation

Chapter 5th Section 2d Approved of by Number of 36

Chapter 6th Exepted by the Number of 36

Greenfield May 22 1780

Ebenezer Graves	Select men
Isaac Newton	of
Samel. Staughton	Grenfield

To Sacretary of the Convention at Boston

Greenwich (276/51)

To the Honorable Convention of the State of Massachusetts Bay Now Sitting in Boston for the Purpose of Framing a new Constitution or form of Government—Gentlemen—

We Humbly Lay before you the Proceedings of the Town of Greenwich on a Book Containing a New form of Government Sent out for the Consideration of the People at Large.

———Objections———

In Page 15th article 2d. the words Two thirds objected to———For reasons following (viz) Because it the Governor the Power of a Negative on the Legislative and it repugnant to article First in the Same Page it is also contrary to a plain Expression on page Eleventh in the Address to the people———In Page 24th article 2d. Mode of Representation objected to———For Reasons following (viz) Because the Landage intrest have not a Proper Weight in Scale, and the House of Representatives will be too Numerous, and their not being paid out of the Publick Chest For attendance———Page 27th Article 2d. Objected to the Words Christian Religion, Because it admits of a Roman Catholic to be the First Magistrate in this State and because we View it Necessary to the preservation of a free Government and security of the Protestant Cause that no Papist should be admitted to a Seat in the Legislative or Judicial Departments.———

In Page 31st Article 9th Objected to, because by said article we are Deprived of our Right of Electing own Civil Officors———and also it being Repugnant to the fifth article in the Declaration of Rights——— Page 33d article 10th objected to, because the two Houses of Legislation have not a voice in the choice of the officers of the Continental army and forts and garrisons

Page 50th article tenth objected to Because we think the Period assigned for the revision of the Constitution ought to be at least within the Term of seven years after it take place——

Page 40 The method of Electing Deligates to Congress objected to, Because thereby the People are Deprived of their Natural Rights, as, in our oppinion it is the Right of the People to Elect their own Delegates——

In Page 34th article 13th Objected to, where the Salary's of the Governor and Justices of the Supreme Judicial Courts are to be Established by Standing Laws—Because in our oppinion it ought always to be in the Power of the Legislative to grant, Annually, all Salarys or Wages to all Publick officers of this State——

At a legal Town meeting held at the Publick meeting house in said Greenwich on the 8th day of May 1780 and continued by adjournments to the 5th of June Instant and at said meeting Unanimously voted and agreed to the above objections and Reasons There for to the number of Seventy three voting in said meeting

Greenwich June 5, 1780 Caleb West
Abijah Powers Selectmen of Greenwich
Joseph Hinds 2d

Page 33d. Article 12th Objected to for Reasons following

Because the Governor is not Required in said article to Lodge an account of all Stores and circumstances or state of things there in mentioned in the Secretary's office for the Revisal of the Legislature

Through forgetfulness this article failed of a Proper Entry——

Hadley *

Put to vote whether the town will impower their representatives for the next year to vote for the calling a state convention for the sole purpose of forming a new constitution and passed in the affirmative unanimously 27 present.

April 27, 1780, The constitution agreed upon in convention at Cambridge, together with the address being read in the meeting Meeting adjourned to May 11, 1780 The form of government read in part

* Town records, Massachusetts Historical Society.

Voted upon the bill of rights, Article 25th, 27 for 1 against. Adjourned to May 15, 1780, The remainder of the constitution read Article by Article.

Voted upon Chapter	1, Section 2,	Article 5,	12 for	5 against.
" " "	1, Section 3,	Article 2,	9 for	9 against.
" " "	2, Section 1,	Article 7,	22 for	3 against.
" " "	2, Section 1,	Article 10,	12 for	12 against.

Adjourned to May, 17, 1780

Voted upon Chapter 6, Article 1st, five for omitting the declaration and twenty against omitting it.

Voted that where the words Christian Religion are used in the constitution it is desired the words Christian Protestant Religion may be used instead thereof, 25 for.

Voted upon Chapter 6, Article 10, that the time for revising the constitution exceed not ten years. 25 for

Voted Mr. Charles Phelps delegate for this town in convention be and he is hereby impowered at the next session to agree upon a time when this form of government shall take place, without returning the same again to the people provided that two thirds of the male inhabitants of the age of twenty one years and upwards voting in the several town and plantation meetings. Shall agree to the same or the Convention Shall confirm it to the sentiments of two thirds of the people.

Put to vote whether this town approve of this constitution excepting those articles before particularly objected against and passed in the affirmative, 17 for 1 against.

Hatfield (276/52)

At a Legal Town Meeting in Hatfield May 22d 1780 the Town took under Consideration the Constitution or Frame of Government agreed upon by the Delagates of the State of the Massachusetts Bay Met in Convention after the town had largely debated and Considered the same the Question was put whether they would agree thereto without Amendment. Eight Voted in the affirmative and 31 in the Negative an Amendment was proposed in the 3 Article of the Declaration of rights the last paragraph where every denomination of Christans are mentioned that it should be protestant Christians 27 voted for the amendment and 13 against it

In Chapter 2d. Section 1. article 2d. an amendment was proposed viz that the Governors to be Chosen Should declare them selves to be of the religion that protestants profess. 33 Voted for the Amendment and 7 against it

A further Amendment was proposed viz that no officer civil or military should hold his office more than Seven years unless by a New appointment 28 Voted for the amendment and 11 against it The Reasons In the first place the officers that may be appointed most of them will be unknown to those that appoint them and they may be misguided by rong persons that are prejudiced 2 those that appoint the officers may be biased by Connections 3. When an officer is appointed it is difficult to remove him by impeachment 4 when persons grow old they are fond of their offices though everybody (except themselves) are sensible they are unfit to Continue in office

Then the Vote was put for the Constitution with the Amendments 30 Voted in the affirmative and 4 in the Negative

Oliver Partridge
Phinehos Frary Selectmen of Hatfield
Benja. Wells

Voted that the Deligate for Hatfield at the next Session of the Convention agree when the form of Goverment shall take place without Returning the same again to the people Provided that two thirds of the Male Inhabitants of the age of twenty years [twenty-one] and upwards Voting in the Several Towns and plantation meetings shall agree to the same or the Convention shall conform it to the sentiments of two thirds of the People

Copy of Record Examined
Oliver Partridge Town Clerk of Hatfield

Leverett (276/53)

At a Meeting of the Town of Leverett for the purpose of taking into consideration the New Constitution of Government Have stated their objections with the Amendments in the following manner———Viz.

Part the Second the Frame of Government

Article 4th. the latter clause of said Article all votters out of 46 Voted that their should be no duties excises levyed on any produce, goods, wares, Marchandize or commodities whatsoever and 35 voted it as it stands in the Constitution.

Chapter 1 Section 2 Senate

Article the 2—35 Voted it as it stands in the Constitution, and 5 were for admiting all to vote of Twenty-one years of age wheither may have Estate or no estate

Section 3 House of Representatives

Article 2 This article Unanimously objected too

The amendment

Every corporate Town shall elect one Representative Every corporate town containing Four Hundred rateable polls may elect two Representatives. Every corporate Town containing Eight Hundred rateable polls may elect three Representatives Every corporate Town containing thirteen Hundred rateable polles may elect four Representatives and proceeding in that manner adding one Hundred rateable polls to the increasing number for every additional Representative. Voted Unanimously

The Ninth Article under the same section

This Article unanimously objected too

The Amendment

Not less than half of the members of the House of Representatives that are elected and returned shall constitute a quoram for doing business. thirteen Voted for the Amendment four against it

Chapter 2 The Executive Power

Section 1 the Ninth Article, The latter clause of said article—Unanimously objected too. Viz, and that every such nomination shall be made by the Governor and made at least seven days Prior to such appointment. The Amendment that every such nomination shall be made at least thirty days prior to such appointment Voted Unanimously for this amendment Part of the tenth article of the same Chapter Viz and no officer duly commissioned to command in the militia shall be removed from his office, but by the address of both houses to the Governor or by fair trial in court martial pursuant to the laws of the Commonwealth for the time being This clause objected too Unannimously———The Amendment. That all officers in the militia of all Ranks shall be chosen and commissioned Once in every three years and chosen in the manner described Ninteen for the amendment and two against it (viz) against the Governor and Counsel Commissoning the officers

The thirteenth Article of the 2d chapter voted by sixteen to stand as in the Constitution and objected too by four viz that the Governors Salary should be fixed and permanent

Chapter 2d. Section 2 Lieutenant Governer

Article the first Voted as it stands in the Constitution by Eighteen objected too by two, for its not allowing all to vote of twenty one years of age.

Chapter 3. The Judiciary Power

Article first voted as it stands by Eighteen objected too by two Article the third voted as it stands in the Constitution by 15 objected too by five their not being anually chosen

Chapter Sixth respecting Oaths etc.

Article Sixth voted too by Ninteen as it stands Objected too by one.

Article tenth of the Same chapter

The time Sett for revising the Constitution voted against Unanimously The Amendment that it shall be revised once at least in every Seven years Voted this amendment by Ninteen two objectors who were for a less term. Voted that the Form of Government Shall take place (provided that two thirds of the Male Inhabitance of the age of twenty one Years voting the same) at the first day of September next.

All the articles in the Constitution was Unanimously Voted for Excepting the above.

William Bowman Selectmen of
Moses Graves Leverett

Ludlow (276/54)

The Inhabitants of Ludlow in Compliance with the Resolve of the Convention of the 2d. March 1780. Report as their Opinion That in the Address these Words be inserted is to be held. Your Consitutents of Ludlow are of Opinion that the Words "May be held" are not explicit or that the Compilers of the Address were not full in the idea that a new Convention was to take place in 1795. The Eleventh page at the bottom these words be inserted—and are to be chosen by the Male Inhabitants who are twenty one years of age and Pay any tax. Because it is our Opinion that every Male of twenty one years of age has a right to Vote in all cases of a public nature———Page fourteenth the words be inserted———each Town shall send one member and no Town more then four except Boston which shall have a right to send six———Wee supose this method will be a more exact Representation than that pointed out by the Convention———Also we are of Opinion that one hundred and fifty Pounds for a Senator, Fifty Pounds for a Representative Five hundred for a Governor and Lieutenant Governor are sufficient qualifications as to Estate Provided they have other qualifications equal to those important Offices———Page thirty second Article tenth—Sixteen years old and upwards—it is our Opinion that every Soldier has a right to Choose his Officer—Page forty eighth Article the third these word be inserted—and the Legislature shall not increase such qualifications as to property of the Persons to be elected to Offices without the Consent of the People of the Commonwealth Because wee conceive that should the Legislature have the Power to incrase etc. it would totaly subvert the natural rights of the People———The above purposed Amendments in the New frame of Government passed Unanimous with every other Article in the said Constitution except the third Article in the Bill of rights which had fourteen for and twelve against it by the Town of Ludlow convened for the above purpose on the 25th of May 1780.

Attest Moses Wilder
Timothy Keyes Select Men of Ludlow
Jeremiah Dutton

Monson (276/55)

We the Inhabitants of the town of Monson, being legally assembled in Town Meeting; to consider the Constitution or form of goverment made and sent out for the Peoples Approbation, Disapprobation, or Amendment.———Do Propose, the amendments hereafter mentioned; and do instruct and Enjoin upon our Delegat to use his utmose endeavour to have the same effected———

Bill of Rights. (article 3d.) Voted, that Every man shall pay his money to the Parish-teacher where he belongs Provided there be any of his own denomination in said Parish.———

Chapter. 1st Section 2. Article 2. In all other places where Property is Required as a qualification for Voters. Voted that the sum be reduced one half.

Chapter 1st Section 3d. Article 2d. House of Representatives. Voted that Every Incorporated Town; be allowed to send one Representative and the largest town be allowed to send five and those between, in Proportion to the bigness.———

Chapter 1 Section 3d Article 3d Voted where Property is required as a qualification for a representative the sum be reduced one half.———

Chapter 2d. Section 1st. Article 10th. Voted that the male inhabitants from Sixteen years old and upwards be allowed to chuse their Militia officers.———

Chapter 6th. Article 3d the last clause rejected. Voted that the word Protestant be put preceding the word Christian, in the qualification for a governor; likewise in his oath

Voted to accept the Constitution with the above amendments

Number for it 36
Against it 1

Voted to accept the Constitution as it now stand in print if it can't be altered

Number for it 20
Number against 21

A true coppy attest Jese Mirrick Town Clerk
Monson May 26, 1780

Montague (276/56)

To the Secretary of the Convention Held at Boston for Frameing a New Constitution Turn to the Last Page

[Printed Constitution with marginal notes, as follows]

Part the First [Declaration of Rights]

Article I	Yeas 34	Article XVI	Yeas 50
Article II	Yeas 34	Article XVII	Yeas 50
Article III	Yeas 32	Article XVIII	Yeas 50
	Nays 17	Article XIX	Yeas 50
Article IV	Yeas 50	Article XX	Yeas 50
Article V	Yeas 50	Article XXI	Yeas 50
Article VI	Yeas 50	Article XXII	Yeas 50
Article VII	Yeas 5 [50?]	Article XXIII	Yeas 50
Article VIII	Yeas 50	Article XXIV	Yeas 50
Article IX	Yeas 50	Article XXV	Yeas 50
Article X	Yeas 50	Article XXVI	Yeas 50
Article XI	Yeas 50	Article XXVII	Yeas 50
Article XII	Yeas 50	Article XXVIII	Yeas 50
Article XIII	Yeas 50	Article XXIX	Yeas 48
Article XIV	Yeas 50		Nays 2
Article XV	Yeas 50	Article XXX	Yeas 50

Part the Second. The Frame of Government Yeas 50

Chapter I, Section I
- Article I Yeas 50
- Article II Yeas 48
- Article III Yeas 45
- Article IV Yeas 48

Chapter II, Section II
- Article I Yeas 28
- Article II Yeas 23 Nays 13
- Article III Yeas 35
- Article IV Yeas 35
- Article V Yeas 32 Nays 2
- Article VI Yeas 35
- Article VII Yeas 35
- Article VIII Yeas 35
- Article IX Yeas 35

Chapter I, Section III
- Article I Yeas 35
- Article II Yeas 19
- Article III Yeas 38
- Article IV Yeas 23 Nays 7
- Article V Yeas 30
- Article VI Yeas 30
- Article VII Yeas 30
- Article VIII Yeas 30
- Article IX Yeas 30
- Article X Yeas 30
- Article XI Yeas 30

Chapter II, Section I
- Article I Yeas 30
- Article II Yeas 30
- Article III Yeas 30
- Article IV Yeas 30
- Article V Yeas 30
- Article VI Yeas 30
- Article VII Yeas 30
- Article VIII Yeas 30
- Article IX Yeas 29 Nay 1
- Article X Nays 30 Agains the first part of this Chapter Respecting the Qualification of voters for captains and subalterns Yeas 30 [for rest of Article x]
- Article XI Yeas 30
- Article XII Yeas 30
- Article XIII Yeas 30

Chapter II, Section II
- Article I Yeas 30
- Article II Yeas 30
- Article III Yeas 30

Chapter II, Section III
- Article I Yeas 30
- Article II Yeas 30
- Article III Yeas 30
- Article IV Yeas 30
- Article V Yeas 30
- Article VI Yeas 30
- Article VII Yeas 30

Chapter II, Section IV
- Article I Yeas 30
- Article II Yeas 30

Chapter III
- Article I Yeas 30
- Article II Yeas 30
- Article III Yeas 30
- Article IV Yeas 30

Chapter IV Yeas 40

Chapter V, Section I	Yeas 40 for this Chapter [Refers to Articles I, II, III]	Article II	Yeas 40 Nays 1
		Article III	Yeas 30
		Article IV	[No marginal note]
		Article V	[No marginal note]
Chapter V, Section II	Yeas 40	Article VI	Yeas 30
		Article VII	Yeas 30
Chapter VI		Article VIII	Yeas 30
Article I	Yeas 40	Article IX	Yeas 30
		Article X	Yeas 30

Hampshire County
Montague

Murrayfield *

The town meeting held in Murrayfield to act upon the constitution was appointed to be held May 2d. 1780. The first action taken by the town was choosing a committee of three from each school district to consider the proposed Constitution and declaration of rights and report at an adjourned meeting. This committee consisted of the following persons: Samuel Jones, John Jones, Benjamin Eggleston, Deacon James Hamilton, Lieutenant William Moore, Deacon Jesse Johnson, Doctor David Shepard, Ensign Stephen Lyman, Deacon Samuel Matthews, William Bell, Lieutenant John Newton Parmenter, Aaron Bell, Ebenezer Stowe, Lieutenant James Clark, Captain James Black, Jonathan Webber, Gershom Rust, Reuben Woolworth, Benjamin Converse, Robert Proctor, and Daniel Twadwell. The meeting then adjourned to May 16th, at which eight voted for and the remainder against the proposed constitution. But another meeting was called and held May 26th, to further consider and vote upon the proposed constitution, with the following results:

"On the second article of the Constitution, Section one, Chapter two, page 17, objected against by fifteen." A proposed "alteration that the governor instead of being of the Christian Religion it should be inserted that he shall be of the Christian and Protestant Religion, voted by fifteen."

"Article ten, page 32 objected against as it stands now by twelve votes." The provision objected to was as follows: "The Captains and subalterns of the militia shall be elected by the written votes of the train-band and alarm list of their respective companies, of twenty-one years of age and

* Alfred M. Copeland, *A History of the Town of Murrayfield, 1760–1783* (Springfield, Mass., 1892), 133–134.

upwards;" etc. The town "voted for the alteration following, viz.: That all persons that are in the train-band and alarm list above the age of sixteen shall have liberty to vote for their captains and subalters,' by a vote of thirteen.

"Part second, Chapter one, Section one, Article four was voted for by ten, objected against by two." The reason offered was "that those articles that have duties and excises laid on them will come dearer to the purchaser." This article defined the power and authority of the General Court. The part of it particularly objected to reads as follows: "And also to impose, and levy reasonable duties and excises, upon any produce, goods, wares, merchandize, and commodities whatsoever, brought into, produced, manufactured, or being within the same.

"Chapter six, voted for a revision of the Constitution in ten years if the people have a mind for it.

"Voted that all the other articles in the Constitution shall stand as they be, or that we are willing that they should stand without any alteration."

Northfield (276/57)

The town of Northfield at a Legal Meeting May 2d. 1780 and Continued by Several Adjournments to the 22d Day of May Instant. Present 44 voters———

The Question being Put whether we would accept of the proposed Constitution and form of Government as it now Stands; Voted and passed in the Negative, 42 votes against it and 2 for it.———

The objections or Reasons are as follows. Vizt

Chapter 2d. Section 1st Article 2d Relative to the Qualifications of Civil Officers, We are of opinion that all Civil Officers in the State Should Previous to their Entring upon the Execution of their Office, Declare themselves to be of the Christian Protestant Religion. Reason 1. It appears to us, that the Safety of the State Calls for the Exclusion of all Roman Catholicks from holding any Civil Office therein.———

2d. We are of Opinion the Abjuration Oath Provided in the Constitution is not sufficient to Exclude all such.———Furthermore it is Objected, That Wheras by the Constitution it is Implyed that there Should be but one Register of Deeds in Each County. We are of Opinion that Every Corporate Town have a Right and ought to have a Register of Deeds in their own Towns. Therefore to have but one Register of Deeds in a

County is greatly to the Disadvantage of the Publick, as it greatly increases the Travil and Cost of the Subject, Neither is it so Safe to have the Office but in One Town as in every Town in the County. Moreover we view it Repugnant to the 7th Article in the Bill of Rights, which Declares that Government is Instituted for the Common good; etc. and not for the Profit, Honour or private Interest of any Man family or Class of Men etc. Voted to Accept of the Constitution and form of Government with the Amendments above Expressed. It was Objected to with Regard to the Qualifications of Voters Chapter 1st Section 2d Article 2d Voted, 37 for the Article as it now stands and 7 against it.——Also Chapter 6th. article 3d On the Increasing Qualifications as to Property of Persons to be Elected to Office. Voted 43 for the Article and 1 against it.——

A true copy Examd. by Seth Field
Town Clerk

Hezekiah Stratton
Samuel Mattoon
Aaron Whitney
Lemuel Holton
Selectmen of Northfield

To the Secretary of the Convention for forming a Constitution of Government for the State of the Massachusetts Bay

Northampton (276/58)

Northampton Returns to the Convention on the Constitution for the Massachusetts Bay

To the Honorable the Convention for framing a New Constitution of Government for the state of the Massachusetts Bay, to meet at Boston on the first Wednesday of June next.

In compliance with the proposal of the said convention which were sitting at Boston on the second day of March last, the inhabitants of the town of Northampton liege men of the State abovesaid of the age of twenty one years and upwards in town meeting assembled on Monday the twenty second of May A.D. 1780 do humbly object to the several articles of that frame of government agreed upon at Boston on the said Second day of March by the said Convention which was there and then assembled hereinafter specified and for the reasons hereinafter set down,

That is to say, To that part of the twelfth article of the declaration of rights wherein it is declared that "the defendant shall have right to be fully heard in his defence by himself or his Council at his election." Because we conceive that the defendant ought not only to have his election whether he will make his defence in person or by Council, but ought to have his election and be at full liberty in the choice of his council; provided he shall choose for his council no other than some liege man of this or any other of the united States——The time may come when the supreme court for the time being may like a former supreme court of the Massachusetts Bay take upon them to confine not only the defendant but the plaintiff to their bar of admitted and habitted Barristers in their choice of council; we therefore propose that the part of the article referred to, should, in conformity to the wholesome Law or act of this State run thus, "in his defence by himself, or" such other person who shall procure for his council, provided such person be a liege man of this or any other of the united States.

We also beg leave to object to the last paragraph of the same twelfth article, because we conceive that the said paragraph and the last part of the twenty eighth article of the said declaration do militate if they are not directly repugnant. We therefore propose that the said last paragraph of the said twelfth article should be wholly expunged.

We also disapprove of the first exception in the fifteenth article of the declaration etc. as too loose and uncertain to have a place in a declaration of rights which we judge ought in all its parts to be conceived in as precise, clear, and certain terms as language will admit. Besides, if by "cases in which it has heretofore been otherwise used and practised" it was intended to exempt from the trial of a jury all such matters and causes, as we are exempted from such trial by any statute or statutes of this State; we exceedingly disapprove of the substance and intent of the said exception and specially the whole power and authority given by our statutes to commissioners of Sewers—and the council on appeal to them; all which by such an interpretation of the exception is preserved whole to such commissioners, and exempts all such matters from jury trial, in great derogation of common right and the law of the land. And if no more was intended than Issues in law made by joinders in demurrer, or them and also the ordinary's or probate etc. jurisdiction, we conceive that all that should be declared fully and expressly in precise and determinate words and by no means in such terms as the said exception contains, which admit of vast litigation and various pretensions, and will leave it in the power of the ordinary legislature to take away the sacred right of the subject to trial by jury in more instances than they would venture to do, if the whole fifteenth article should be dropt, and wholly expunged from the constitution As it is therefore subject to great and various exceptions we shall not presume to propose any correction to that article, but submit it to the wisdom of the full convention to provide a much better security to the subjects of this state, of their invaluable right and privilege of a trial by a jury of the vicinage, in all their controversies and suits concerning property real and personal than can be secured to them by that article in its present dress.

We also judge that the people's right to keep and bear arms, declared in the seventeenth article of the same declaration is not expressed with that ample and manly openness and latitude which the importance of the right merits; and therefore propose that it should run in this or some such like manner, to wit, The people have a right to keep and bear arms as well for their own as the common defence. Which mode of expression we are of opinion would harmonize much better with the first article than the form of expression used in the said seventeenth article.

We except to the first article of the chapter intitled the Senate, as setting the number of that branch too low. We conceive that forty men after nine or seven shall be detached from them to constitute a Council for the Governor, will not be a sufficient ballance for the house of Representatives; a small number of men altho in no wise dependant are exposed to be borne down or worried out by a great body of men such as the house of Representatives will and ought to be. We therefore propose that the Senate consist of the number of Sixty at the least before the said draught of Counsellors. No one need be apprehensive of any great charges being caused by an augmentation of the number, for they will rarely perhaps never sit but when the whole General Assembly will be sitting. And we see no reason why the pay of a Senator ought to be more than that of a representative, they are not to come in the place of the hebdomadal council of quondam Governors. It was their sittings which created an enormous expence to the Government. We have fresh in mind that the Commons in the long parliament bore down the house of Lords chiefly by reason of the Lord's being much inferior in number to the Commons. Much might be said in favour even of a greater number than sixty in case the Council are to be drafted from that number; but we forbear lest we should be tedious.

As to the qualifications of the voters for Senators we are fully of opinion that a freehold in the State of the annual income of three pounds will attach a man to the State as much at least as two hundred pounds value in all estate. The case may be that a man may have two hundred pounds value of estate and no real estate: And personal estate, especially of some sort, is very easily transferred from place to place.

If our opinion of the number of the Senate should meet with success, it will be thought proper no doubt that the quorum of the Senate contained in the ninth article should be augmented to thirty one or twenty seven.

We propose that the paragraph of the second article of the chapter intitled "House of Representatives" which respects the power of the house to fine delinquent towns should stand in the words following, to wit. And the house of Representatives shall have power from time to time to impose a fine upon any town in the State, qualified by the constitution to send a representative or representatives to the General Court which shall be guilty of making default of chusing and returning one member at the least to the house of representatives.

We are clearly of opinion that the fore part of the fifth article of the chapter intitled "executive power" ought to be in substance as follows, to wit, The Governor *shall* during any session of the General Court adjourn or prorogue the same to any time and place the two houses shall desire; and shall dissolve the said General Court on the day next preceeding the last Wednesday in May annually if the said Court shall then be in being; and in the recess of the said court may with the advice of the Council prorogue the same from time to time not exceeding ninety days in the whole in any one recess; and may with the advice of Council call it together sooner than the time to which it may stand adjourned or prorogued if the welfare of the Commonwealth shall require the same.

And as the last paragraph of the said fifth article will be surplusage in case the above amendment should take place, we beg leave to suggest what follows to be provided in its stead; to wit, The Governor shall have power upon the request of both houses of Assembly to disolve the said General Court sooner in the year than the day next preceeding the last Wednesday in May. We propose that the sixth article of the same chapter should be varied so as to stand thus. In cases of disagreement between the two houses with regard to the necessity, expediency, time or place of adjournment, or prorogation, the Governor with advice of the

Council shall have a right to adjourn or prorogue the General Court not exceeding ninety days, as he with such advice shall determine the publick good shall require.

We except to the eighth article as defective in not providing and giving express authority to the whole legislative to enact pardons and indemnities before convictions. We conceive that such power ought to be expressly saved to them at the least, and therefore propose that the eighth article be altered so as to read as follows, to wit. But no pardon before conviction except by the legislature, shall avail the party etc. Such statute pardons possibly may be salutary in a short time.

We propose that at the end of the second paragraph of the tenth article of the same chapter these words should be added, to wit, who shall continue in office for a term not exceeding seven years from the date of their respective Commissions. and at the end of the third paragraph of the same article the words following should be added, to wit; Whose respective commissions shall expire and become void at the end of seven years at furthest from their dates. The like reasons and several more may be assigned for the expiration of military commissions at the end of seven years as are given in page 39th for the expiration of the commissions of Justices of the peace.

In the Section intitled Council and the manner of Settling Elections etc. we would propose the following alterations viz. That the Council should consist of but seven persons exclusive of the Lieutenant Governor. And that the Governor with the said counsellors or four of them at least shall and may hold and keep the Council. by this alteration expence may be saved and yet the business of the publick well performed.

In the section intitled Secretary Treasurer, Commissary etc. We could wish that the latter part of the first article, which regards the Treasurer's continuance in office, should be expressed in such manner that the people may understand the reason why the treasurer cannot with safety to the Commonwealth hold his office more than five years.

In chapter 4th we would propose the following amendments viz. That the election of Delegates to Congress be by the Senate and House of Representatives each having a negative on the other. The office of the said delegates being of the highest importance we humbly conceive the greatest deliberation ought to be used in their choice; whereas in the method proposed by the convention we apprehend that the influence of the Senate may be overborne by that of the House.

We also beg leave to propose that in the place of the tenth article of chapter 6th the following be substituted, viz, In order the more effectually to adhere to the principles of the Constitution and to correct those violations which by any means may be made therein as well as to form such alterations as from experience shall be found necessary, the General Court shall in 1787 issue precepts or direct them to be issued from the Secretary's office to the several towns and plantations to elect delegates to meet in Convention for the purpose aforesaid. The said delegates to be chosen in the same manner etc. As the Constitution will be the work of uninspired men we have much reason to expect there will be defects in it which the experience of seven years will discover and we therefore humbly conceive there can be no advantage in postponing a revision of it longer than that time.

We would also propose that the Letter S in the word Laws in the last article of the Constitution be expunged.

Also we greatly disapprove of the fourth article of the third section of the first chapter, intitled house of Representatives, as materially defective, and as rescinding the natural, essential, and unalienable rights of many persons, inhabitants of this Commonwealth, to vote in the choice of a Representative or Representatives, for the town in which they are or may be inhabitants; and we beg leave to propose that the following addition should be made to the said fourth article, to wit, and also every rateable poll being twenty one years of age, and who shall have been resident in this Commonwealth for the space of three years next preceeding, and who shall be willing to take such oath of allegiance to the Commonwealth as the Laws for the time being shall prescribe.

In order to make the first article of this chapter, expressly conformable to your elegant address to your countrymen, and also to make it consistent with the principle of personal equality (which we conceive ought to be attended to, as well as the principle of corporation equality) it ought to run thus, viz. There shall be in the legislature of this Commonwealth, a representative of the persons of the people annually elected; and in order to provide for a representation of the Citizens of this Commonwealth founded upon the said principle of personal equality, the said fourth article ought to contain the above proposed addition or something tantamount. We are obliged, Gentlemen, to believe that all along in settling the bill of rights, and constructing the frame of Government, the convention had it full in their intention, that the house of representatives should be chosen, and appointed, in such manner as that they should be as properly, and truly, a representative of the persons as the Senate of the property of the Commonwealth. We say that we are constrained to such a belief, because the convention themselves have plainly declared the same to have been their intention. And it is impossible for us to admit so black a thought as to imagine that the convention had an intention, by their address, to beguile their constituents into a supposition, that provision was made in the frame of Government, for a representative of the persons, as well as for the property of the Commonwealth, when really at the same time they were conscious that it was not so in fact; and that in truth there was not in all the frame of Government, any ground for such distinction, as is supposed in the address; for however justly and exactly the number of Senators in the frame of Government may be apportioned according to the property of each district, and provision made that they should continue forever hereafter to be so apportioned, yet that can never afford any foundation for the distinction of a representative of the persons, and a representative of the property of the Commonwealth: for altho such a provision will truly determine the share or particular part of any given whole number which every district into which the whole State may be divided, shall elect and depute; yet nothing can be more clear than that the ground of distinction between a personal and property representation, must wholly depend on the qualifications of the electors, and that if there shall be no difference made between the qualifications of the voters for the members of the house of Representatives, and for the members of the Senate, but each member of both houses shall be chosen by the same identical persons, as they must necessarily be if the voters for the members of both houses are all to have precisely the like qualifications and no part of the number of persons, having the like qualifications are to be excluded, then the distinction abovesaid is wholly out of doors and becomes an absolute nullity. Who would ever imagine that if all the male persons in this State of the age of twenty one years and of no property should by the constitution have as good a right to give their votes for the Senators, as the men in the State of the best property, and the votes of all the voters should have an equal estimation in determining the election. We say, into whose head could it ever enter to denominate a body so elected, a representative of the property of the Commonwealth however exactly and minutely the number or share of the whole Senate, which each district should be intitled to elect, might be adjusted to the property of each district, in relation to the property of the whole Commonwealth? but the case is so evident that it would be affrontive to dwell any longer upon it. We must therefore judge that this default of providing for a personal representative in the legislature, proceeded from inadvertency and forgetfulness, an infirmity which human nature is universally liable to. And we are further obliged to account for this omission, in the Constitution, in the way abovesaid, by an attention to several matters in the declaration of rights, which, when carefully reviewed, and considered by the Convention, we persuade ourselves will appear, not to harmonize with the omission which we are observing upon.

But that we may come home to the enquiry, concerning the justice of excluding such individuals, inhabitants of this State, from voting, not to say from a right to vote in the choice of a representative (for that is impossible) as come within the description of the proposed addition to the said fourth article; we beg that a recurrence may be had to the second paragraph of the preamble to the declaration of rights. There we find it declared, "that the body politick" (perhaps it might have been more properly said the constitution of the body politick) "is formed by a voluntary association of individuals, it is a social compact by" "which the whole people covenants with each citizen, and each citizen with the whole people that all shall be governed by certain Laws for the common good: it is the duty of the people therefore, in framing a constitution of Government, to provide for an equitable mode of making laws, as well" etc. Now can any one say, that the citizens of the State, who are included in the description of the proposed addition, and who do not answer the description of the said fourth article, as it now stands, have ever covenanted, consented, and agreed, or will ever covenant, consent, and agree, with the rest of the people, to be governed by Laws founded on an article of a constitution, which totally excludes them from any share or voice in appointing the legislature for the State; or will such persons ever consent, and agree, to be governed by laws, which shall be enacted by a legislature, appointed wholly without their participation; or can a constitution so framed be said to provide for an equitable mode of making laws, etc. Will any one stand forth and say, that persons who have been born within the state, and have always lived in it, till they have arrived to the age of twenty one years, perhaps much above that age, and who have always paid their poll tax, ever since they were sixteen years old, and are still rateable, and are rated and pay for their polls, the sum set on each poll, in every rate that is made for defraying either the continental State, or town charges, be the same higher or lower; we say, will any one affirm, that such persons are not citizens of the Commonwealth?

Is not the consequence then, if the said paragraph is true, that an association of many individuals, of the State, which without consent totally excludes many such adult male persons, from any participation in the appointment of the legislature, is in fact no constitution, and does not make a body politick? yea, is it not absolutely a void business? As to what may be replied, by way of answer in behalf of infants, that is, persons under the age of twenty one years, we ask leave to refer to what Mr. Locke has most judiciously said, on that head, in the sixth chapter of the second book of his treatise of Government, intitled paternal power; which is much too lengthy to be recited on this occasion, but well deserving to be resorted to. And as to the case of women, of whatever age or condition they may be, we ask leave to refer to what is very sensibly, as well as genteelly said on the Subject, in the twenty ninth page of the Essex result.

We also humbly conceive that the exclusion which we complain of, directly militates and is absolutely repugnant to the genuine sense of the first article of the declaration of Rights; unless it be true that a majority of any State have a right without any forfeiture of the minority to deprive them of what the said first article declares are the natural, essential, and unalienable rights of all men. By that article all men are declared "to be born free and equal;" this is true only with respect to the right of dominion, and jurisdiction over one another. The right of enjoying that equality, freedom, and liberty, is, in the same article, declared unalienable, Very strange it would be, if others should have a right by their superior strength, to take away a right from any individual, which he himself could not alienate by his own consent and agreement; but this will truly be the case, or the exclusion which we except to, is directly repugnant to this first article.

If it is true that all men are naturally equal with respect to a right of dominion, government, and jurisdiction, over each other, that is to say, no one has any degree or spark of such right over another, then it will follow that any given number of such equals, will, if they should all live on the earth for thirty years, and no one of them within that time should be guilty of any crime or fault whereby he should forfeit his native equality and freedom; and no one of them should consent to come under the power and dominion of one or more of the rest, or alienate his native equality and freedom, (and by the way the article declares that he has no right to alienate it,) we suppose that at the end of the thirty years, they will all be as equal and free, as they were at the first moment of their existence. We further suppose that if one hundred of such equal freemen should be at once on the earth together, of what age soever they were, and some one of the hundred, should happen to have an hundred times as much brutal strength, as all the other individuals taken singly, or, perhaps, what is an equivalent thereto, an hundred times as much natural cunning, as any individual of the rest, he would not have any rights against the will of any one of his bretheren, to assume the exercise of dominion and jurisdiction over him, however easy it might be for him to do it; and if no one of the hundred would have a right to do so, we suppose that no ten together would have any right to it, and if not ten, then ninety nine of the hundred would not have any right to domination over the remaining hundreth man; for nought to nought gives but nought; the inevitable consequence then is, that if the ninety nine should endeavour to subjugate, and exercise government, over the hundredth man, without his consent, he would have a good right to resist, and in case the ninety nine should overcome and subdue him, the hundredth man would have a good right, at any time, when any lucky moment presented, to do any thing that should be necessary, to regain his natural liberty and freedom, whereof he had been thus wrongfully deprived; full as good a right against the ninety nine as he would have had against any single one of the hundred, who by his superior brutal strength, had usurped upon him. Now Gentlemen in case the form of Government which you have sent out to the people, shall be affirmed and established, is it not intended that every rateable poll of this state, of the age of twenty one years, shall be obliged to submit, and be subject to such a legislative body, as is therein projected and described? is it not intended that all such persons shall be the subjects of their legislation? and that their persons shall be controlable by the laws of that legislature whether they ever were or shall be the owners of a freehold estate within this state of the annual income of three pounds, or of any estate of the value of sixty pounds or not? Is it not intended that they shall be obliged to contribute to the subsidies, taxes, imposts, or duties, which shall be established, fixed, and laid by such a legislative, and be liable to be restrained of their liberty by the acts of such a legislative, for such causes as they shall judge they ought to be, whether they ever were or shall be qualified, as is expressed in the said fourth article of the third section of chapter first, intitled "house of representatives" or not? then will not such persons be in a state of absolute slavery to such a legislative, while they shall continue without the quantum of property prescribed in the said article? If they are to be subject to the jurisdiction and legislation of your legislature, with regard to life, liberty, and their day wages, or whatever small property they may acquire, and yet have no voice in the appointment of that legislature, what is the difference of their condition from that of the hundredth man who without his consent had jurisdiction usurped over him, by the other ninety nine or any single one of the above mentioned hundred of superior animal strength or natural cunning? But perhaps it will be said that this subjugation of these persons unqualified to vote, and consequently excluded by the Said fourth article, is done by their own consent, as it is done by the convention in whose choice they have, or might have had, a vote; and that Mr. Locke tells us, "that the liberty of a man in society is to be under no other legislative power, but such as is established by his consent;" and that the said legislative body, to be from time to time established without their participation, will be by their consent, as it has been done by the convention, the appointment of which body they had a voice, and consequently they were their agents; and, as their agents have consented to it, it is become the act of the constituents: We answer, that the objection supposes what is not true in fact, to wit, that the convention have been impowered and authorized to agree upon and establish a model of Government for this state, it is certain that the convention have never had such a power given to them, as is evident, if we consider the proposals upon which they were elected, which were that delegates should be chosen by the several towns in this State, for the sole purpose of devising and agreeing upon a constitution or frame of Government to be communicated and laid before the people; which, if two thirds of the people capable of acting, to wit, the freemen of the state, of the age of twenty one years, should accept and affirm, it should then, and not till then, be the constitution of this state, and binding on the whole. And the same is further evident, to wit, that the Convention have no power to establish a Constitution for the State, if they themselves understand their own powers; for they themselves by clear implication acknowledge that they have no such power, in their second resolve of the second of March last, whereby they ask the people that such a power may be given them; not expressly and directly indeed, but implicitly and indirectly: And wherefore do they ask it, if they had it given them by their original appointment? So that if the people should now affirm the frame of Government which the convention have communicated to them, containing the said fourth article, whereby many adult rateable persons who are inhabitants and citizens of this state, and have never done any thing to forfeit their natural and most important rights, are excluded from voting for a representative or representatives for the towns where they dwell; it will be precisely a like case, with that above put, to wit, where the ninety nine of an hundred free and equal men conclude to usurp dominion and jurisdiction over the hundredth man against his will, that is, to deprive him of his natural liberty, which is no other than to enslave him when he has been guilty of nothing, whereby he had forfeited that natural liberty and equality. It is certain that the said section, intitled "house of representatives," supposes that the polls in the State whether they shall be owners of property or not, will always be taxed; witness the second article of the said section, and we know that they always have been the subjects of legislation in this state and have had many heavy burdens and services set on them by the legislature, expecially in time of war, and that will, no doubt, continue to be the case (though probably not in so great a degree) even if they should have a voice in the appointment of representatives.

Dont we know that whenever any mention is made of a tax act, or proposal in the legislature of taxation, it is always spoken of as a tax on polls and estates; that whenever a list is ordered for the purpose of a new valuation, an exact account is directed to be taken of the number of polls above the age of sixteen years in the several towns in this state: and that when the house or their Comittee are settling a valuation, the first business always is to fix the proportion of a single poll to a thousand pound; and dont we know that the owners of a large property, generally, upon such occasions, strive to get the polls share as high as they can; for they are fully sensible, that it is their interest, that the polls share should not be low, for the higher that is, the less will remain on the estates; and they conduct in the case accordingly. Now do we hear from these poor polls, a single objection against the persons who are owners of large property, their voting for the members of the house of representatives? they consider that such property-holders have personal interests and concerns as well as the poor day laborer; further, do they object a word against the owners of the property chusing one entire branch of the legislature, exclusive of themselves, to be guardians of such property? they feel and own the force of the argument for property's having great weight in the legislature, because property ever was, and ever will be, the subject of legislation and taxation. But pray Gentlemen, shall not the polls, the persons of the state, have some weight also, who will always be the subjects of legislation and taxation? Are life, members, and liberty of no value or consideration? Indeed Gentlemen we are shocked at the thought, that the persons of adult men should, like live stock and dead chattels, be brought to account to augment the capital whereon to draw representatives for particular towns, in the same manner as such chattels are to be brought into the property capitals to augment the number of Senators, and when they have been improved and made the most of that may be for that purpose, they should be wholly sunk and discarded not to say like villains but absolutely like brute beasts. Shall these poor adult persons who are always to be taxed as high as our men of property shall prevail to have them set, and their low pittances of day wages, be taken to lighten the burden on property, shall these poor polls who have gone for us into the greatest perils, and undergone infinite fatigues in the present war to rescue us from slavery, and had a great hand, under God, in working out the great salvation in our land, which is, in a great degree wrought out, some of them leaving at home their poor families, to endure the sufferings of hunger and nakedness, shall they now be treated by us like villains and African slaves? God forbid. What have they done to forfeit this right of participating in the choice of one branch of the two branches which are to constitute our legislative, when they are willing that your men of property should enjoy the exclusive right of chusing the first branch? have they forfeited it in the exercise which they have made of this right of participating in the choice of you Gentlemen to your important, very important trust? we hope not, and we hope that you will on further consideration verify it, that they have not, by giving them a voice in the choice and appointment of that very branch of the legislative, which you yourselves tell us is by you intended, to be the representative of the persons of the Commonwealth, and thereby remove all cause for them to regret their choice of you.

Gentlemen, we cannot yet dismiss this very affecting subject. Shall we treat these polls precisely as Britain intended and resolved to treat all the sons of America? that is to say, to bind us in all cases whatsoever, without a single vote for the legislature who were to bind and legislate for us: at which all Americans who deserved freedom, had the highest indignation, and that most justly. We say, who deserved freedom; for he who is willing to enslave his brother, is, if possible, less deserving of liberty, than he who is content to be enslaved. Shall we who hold property, when

God shall have fully secured it to us, be content to see our brethren, who have done their full share in procuring that security, shall we be content and satisfied, we say, to see these our deserving brethren on election days, standing aloof, and sneaking into corners, and ashamed to show their heads, in the meetings of freemen, because, by the constitution of the land, they are doomed intruders, if they should appear at such meetings? the thought is abhorrent to justice and too afflictive to good minds to be endured.

We beg leave also freely to declare to you that we disapprove of the third article of the first section, intitled Governor; of the second chapter intitled executive power; and apprehend, in case our last proposal shall be adopted, that it ought to stand thus, "Those persons who shall be qualified to vote for representatives, within the several towns of this Commonwealth, shall, at a meeting to be called for that purpose etc." That adult male persons inhabitants of the state, ought, and have a right to have a vote in the choice and appointment of the first executive magistrate, we think may be fairly argued from the powers, which, by the frame of Government are given to that magistrate. In the first place, the most important of his powers, is his power of nominating, and, with the advice of his council, appointing, almost all judicial and executive officers. You are pleased in your preamble to your declaration of rights to aver, that it is the duty of the people, in framing a Constitution of Government, to provide, not only for an equitable mode of making laws, but also for an impartial interpretation, and a faithful execution of them; that every man may at all times find his security in them. Now we humbly ask, whether the polls, or male persons of the age of twenty one years, are or are not a part of the people of the State, although they shall not own a freehold of three pounds per annum, or any estate to the value of sixty pounds? most certainly they are. Will not an impartial interpretation and a faithful execution of the laws affect and concern them? most certainly it will: And without such an interpretation and execution of the laws, that part of the people will find no more security in them, than the men of property. Besides, the fifth article of the declaration declares, that all power residing originally in the people, and being derived from them, the several magistrates and officers of Government, vested with authority whether legislative, executive, or judicial, are their substitutes, and agents, and [are?] etc. Now if the male adult persons of the state who have not so much property as is prescribed and required in the said third article, to intitle a man to vote in the choice of the Governor are a part of the people of the state, but shall not be admitted to vote in the choice of their first magistrate, the said fifth article of the declaration will be absolutely falsified, and ought to be expunged.

Also the Governor by the frame of Government is to be commander in chief of all the military forces of the state, by sea and land. These poor people always have been, and we believe always will be, considered as part of the military force of the State, both by sea and land, they most certainly therefore will be interested in this first magistrate considered in his military character, and consequently cannot justly be excluded from voting in his choice. As to the Governor's exercise of his civil powers, the property men will be wholly safe, for the Governor will not be able to act scarce any thing in his civil character, without the advice and consent of his council, which council are always to be of the men who shall be chosen solely by the property men, in case they will accept their choice.

Pray Gentlemen, therefore, make the experiment for one seven years, of admitting these poor persons, qualified as is specified in the proposed addition to the said fourth article, to the exercise of their natural, not to say unalienable right of participating in the choice of the representative of the persons of the Commonwealth and also of the first magistrate of the same: And if by the experience of seven years it shall be found so unsalutary, as to become absolutely necessary to deny that exercise to them, as it is in the case of infants, at the time of the first revision of the constitution they may be denied that exercise.

Thus Gentlemen we have taken the liberty to object to several of the articles in that frame of Government which has been sent out to the people, and have proposed such alterations and amendments as appeared to us to be reasonable. We have also humbly offered the reasons which induced us to propose those alterations; which we cheerfully submit to your revision and full consideration; not doubting but you will give every argument we have used in favour of the proposed alterations its full weight. And we shall be happy to find that they have the same influence upon your minds, as they have had upon ours. But if it should be otherwise after you have fully considered them, we shall submit to it as it now stands, or as the Convention shall conform to the sentiments of two thirds: We do not mean to be so tenacious of our own opinions, as not to approve of any thing that is not done exactly to our taste.

The town voted that the foregoing paragraph be added at the conclusion of the reasons offered in favour of the proposed amendments in the Constitution.

For it 79
Against it 6

73

The question was put whether the members of the meeting at the Time above specified gave their consent to the recommendation of the Convention contained in their Second Resolve of the 2d. of March last and it passed in the affirmitive.

Yeas 57. Nays 29

Ephraim Wright Moderator

Norwich (276/59)

At a Legal Meeting of the Inhabitantes of the Town Norwich Assembled for the Purpose of taking into Consederation a form of Government for the State of Massachusetts Bay on May 18: 1780———
36 Voters present———
on the third Article of the Bill of Rites 6 voted against the article as it stood
4 article in the 3 section 36 in the Negative
12 article Voted in the Negative
9 article in the 2 Chapter Voted in the Negative
the above articles Recommended for alterations our Dalegate is Persessed with the minds of the People———
the Town voted to Except of the Constitution with such alterations as the Convention shall think propper and Establish the same to take Place when they shall think Best
Norwich May 18 AD 1780

Samuel Knight
Daniel Kirkland Select men of Norwich
David Scott

Palmer (276/60)

At a Meeting of the Inhabitants of Palmer from twenty one years old and upward Legally conveined at the Publick Meeting House in said

Town on Wednesday, the 24th Day of May Anno Domini 1780 For the sole purpose of Takeing under Consideration the Constitution or form of Goverment Proposed by the Convention for the Common Welth of the Massachusetts Bay.

John Smith Moderator

The Proposed Constitution Being Red, the Town made Choice of a Committee, to Consult, Consider, and Report their oppinion there on. The Commitee Returned and made their Report, and after Reading said Constitution again; and after Due Consideration Proceeded to the following Votes and amendments.—viz

In Page 27th Chapter 2d The Executive Power

The Latter Clause of the Second article, would propose the following amendment viz. Unlese He shall Declare himself to be of the Christian, Protestant Reformed Reledgion.

The Reasons for this alteration is this: That it is our Duty to keep the Executive Power as free as Possable from such Principles of Religion as have heretofore been the Destruction of many Common welths. Again we apprehend it is No infringment on any mans Contiance, Because it Does Not oblige any Person what Ever to accept of the office, but by his own free will and Consent.———

This article with the amendment was put. there being then Fifty Seven Voters present, and it past unanimously in the Affermative——

Page 39th Chapter 3d Judiciary Power

Article first, Would Recomend an amendment in the Latter Clause of the article viz. Provided Nevertheless the Governer with the Consent of the Counsell shall Remove them upon the address of Both Houses of Legislature.—

The Reasons for this amendment is Because the Governor as a single Person may be mistaken in his judgment, and more likely then both Houses of Legislature. Therefore we are of oppinion the Removel of a Person from office Lyeth safer in the Hands of both Houses, then in one single Person; However just the intention may be.

The article with the amendment etc. was put to Vote being then 57 voters present and it unanimously past in the affirmative. Again Page 44th Chapter 6th The Form of oath etc.

Article first, It is the oppinion of this Town that any Parson being Chosen Governor, Lieutenant Governor, Senator, Counseller, or Representative, and accepting the same ought to Declare him self to be of the Christian Protestan Reformed Relegion. For the same Reasons Given for the amendment of the Quallifications for a Governor.

This article Past in the affermative being 57 Voters and the whole that ware present.

Article 10th Page 50th we strongly Recomend the following amendments viz That the General Court that shall be in the year of our Lord 1790 shall issue precepts to the Selectmen of the Several Towns, and to the assessors of uncorporated plantations: In order to chuse Deligates to meet in Convention some time in that year, and in some convenient place in the state: Which Time and place of Meeting shall be appointed by the General Court. In order to Correct such Violations as by any means may be made in this Constitution, and to form such alterations as from Experience shall be found Nessessary. The Deligates to be Chosen in the Same manner and Proportion as the Representatives in the Second branch of the Legislature of this Constitution are chosen. ——The Reasons for this alteration is this viz——that we beleave that Ten years will be a Time sufficient to Determine whether their will be a Nessessity for an alteration or amendment in this Constitution, as Experience by that time will undoubtedly Discover: and if their should be any mistakes crept in unawars: The soonner Removed the Better We are Likewise of the opinion that the safest and shortes wai is: That The General court, send Precepts to the Several Towns etc. Directing them to send members to Convention, and Not take the Long Round about way, To Collect the sense of the People first and then send Precepts again in order to form a Convention.—If there sould be no need to alter the Constitution by that Time we shall Heartiley Rejoyce and be fully satisfied to pay the Deligates at their Return without Doing any business, But that Hapiness We Do not Expect.——

This article with the Mendment past unanimously in the affermative, there being then present 57 Voters——

Then it was put to Vote on the whole form of Goverment as proposed by the Convention, Togather with the Mendments as above mentioned: There being then present 57 Voters, and it past in the afermative 56 for, and one against it——

The Town then ordered the following Instructions to Mr. Joshua Shaw deligate to said Convention, as followeth, viz Sir you are Desired to use your utmost influence to get the above mentioned alterations made in the Constitution We Do not wish to be singular in our sentiments; No farther than is for the safety of the Common welth. You will be carefull Not to Endeavour to over throw the proposed Constitution at Large; but unly Deliver the sense of this Town on such alterations as we have proposed. You are Likewise Desired to propose the addition of the following article. viz

That for the Ease, Convenience, and benefit of the Inhabitants, That all Licences for Inholders and Retailors of Speretious Liquors, may be Granted by the Select men in the Several Towns where such Licence is to be Exercised.———

Also for the same Reason that all Deeds and Conveyences of Land be Recorded in the Several Towns and Plantations where the Lands Lye. The state of Connecticut have for a Long Time, Practised on this Plan: and found it by Experience to be a Great privilidge———

A true Copey from the menits atast

Per Robert Hunter Town Clerk

John Smith
Robart Ferrell — Selectmen
John Quinten — of
Samuel Shaw — Palmer

Pelham (276/61)

To the Honourable Convention of the State of Massachusetts Bay, to be convened in the month of June, for the purpose of framing a rule of Goverment, Gentlemen, we humbly lay before you the Proceedings of the Town of Pelham; upon a Book, containing a form of Goverment, Sent out for the Consideration of the People at Large.

Objections, with the reasons therefor, and Amendments etc., 1st, in Page 19th Article 1st, said Article purports that there shall be 40 Senators Chosen Annually, it is the Opinion of this Town, that 30 would be amply Sufficient, as so Large a body seems to be unnecessary and consequently burdensom.

2d in Page 24th Article 2d. it is the opinion of this Town, that the mode of representation, will compose too Large a body, and make it unwieldy and burdensom to the People, it is our opinion, that in Large Towns, after one representative, is chosen, Persuant to the plan of 150 Poles, that the mean increasing Number, then ought to be 300, as it is reasonable that One representative, is as fully acquainted, with the separate interests and concerns of 300 Poles in Large and Populous Towns, as one representative Possibly can be, of 150 Poles in small and scattered Towns

3d. in page 25th Ditto This Town acquiesce in that clause in the above article, (to wit) in paying Traveling Expences to and from the General Assembly, with such restrictions etc., would subjoin this clause, (Viz) that the representatives shall be paid for there Attendance, while at the General Court, out of the Publick Chest, without Exemption of any Towns, that should refuse to send, upon the above plan, as it would in our opinion, injoin a strict attendance, of all its members.

4th in Page 27th Article 2d. The word, Christians, to be Expunged, and the word Protestant to be inserted as it will in our opinion, make more ample and full Exclusion, of those from office, whose Principles are subversive, of a free goverment.

5th in Page 31st, Article 9th, under this Article is comprised the Choice of County Justices of the peace, which Nomination and appointment is given to the Governer, and Council, it is the opinion of this Town, that, that is a priviledge that ought to be Lodged in the hands of the People, belonging to the Towns and Counties, where such persons dwell, (and his Excellency to Commission them) as it appears, the people must be best acquainted, with the Tallents Principles etc., of those persons, to be Chosen.

6th in Page 32d Article 10th, That Clause, that none shall have the Priviledge to give in there Vote for millitia officers, under the age of 21 years, it is our opinion that all those of 16 years, and upwards, ought to injoy that Priviledge, as a third part of our Companyes, at home and in the Army, Consists of that age. 7th Likwise it is our opinion, that the Commissions of Millitary Officers, ought to Expire and become Void, in the term of 7 years, from there respective dates, for reasons given Page 39th, respecting Justices etc.

8th Page 33d Article 10th, We acquiesce that the Governer and Council, shall appoint all Continental officers, on Condition those officers, shall fill up there Companies by Voluntary inlistment. Otherwise it is our opinion, that those that shall be Drafted, ought to have a Voice in the Choice of there own officers.

9th in Page 44th Article 1st in those Oaths and Declarations, the word Christian to be expunged. and the word Protestant to be inserted, reasons already given above etc.

10th in Page 50th Article 10th, the Period to be Contracted,—from 15 years to 7, as that term of time in our opinion, is quite sufficient to prove its beneficial affects in Practice and then to undergo a critical revision.

Unanimously voted that this Town Except the New Constitution, or frame of goverment, with the above amendment. 79 voters.

Attest

John Dick Town Clerk

Pelham May 22d. 1780 Samuel Hyde, Jacob Edson, Hugh Johnston — Select Men etc.

Shelburne (276/62)

At a town meeting Held in Shelburn the 23rd Day of May 1780. To Hear and Determine upon the Constitution. Voting for and against the same, as follows Viz

First article in Bill of Rights	51 for it 0 against	9 article	54 for 0 ———
2nd article	53 for 0 ———	10 article	61 for 0 ———
3rd article first paragraff	23 for 25 against	11 article	40 for 0 ———
2nd paragraff	38 for 4 against	12 article	44 for 0 ———
3rd paragraff	53 for 0 against	13 article	50 for 0 ———
4th paragraff	26 for 20 against	14 article	50 for 0 ———
5th paragraff	55 for 0 ———	15 article	20 for 3 against
4th article	58 for 0 ———	16 article	35 for 0 ———
5 article	62 for 0 ———	17 article	39 for 0 ———
6 article	62 for 0 ———	18 article	33 for 0 ———
7 article	62 for 0 ———	19 article	44 for 0 ———
8 article	60 for 0 ———	20 article	53 for 0 ———

21 article	56 for
	0 ———
22 article	54 for
	0 ———
23 article	56 for
	0 ———
24 article	58 for
	0 ———
25 article	59 for
	0 ———
26 article	59 for
	0 ———
27 article	59 for
	0 ———
28 article	62 for
	0 ———
29 article	0 for
	39 ———
30th article	48 for
	0 ———
Frame of Government the article for altering the title of the Massachusetts	15 for
	0 ———
The first article of the first Sexion in the first Chapter	16 for
	0 ———
2nd article	18 for
	0 ———
3rd article	17 for
	0 ———
4 article	19 for
	0 ———
Sexion 2nd article 1st	0 for
	20 against
2nd article 1st paragraff	0 for
	23 against
2nd paragraff	29 for
	0 ———
3rd paragraff	21 for
	0 ———
3rd article	29 for
	0 ———
4th article	27 for
	0 ———
5th article	22 for
	0 ———
6 article	20 for
	3 against
7 article	28 for
	0 ———
8 article	28 for
	0 ———
9th article	27 for
	2 against
Sexion 3rd article 1st	28 for
	0 ———
Article 2nd Paragraff 1st	12 for
	8 against
Paragraff 2nd	0 for
	20 against
3rd paragraff	21 for
	0 ———
4th Paragraff	18 for
	5 against
Article 3rd	26 for
	0 against
article 4th	0 for
	27 against
5th article	28 for
	0 against
6 article	29 for
	0 ———
7 article	30 for
	0 ———
8th article	27 for
	5 against
9th article	28 for
	0 ———
10 article	32 for
	0 ———
11th article	24 for
	0 ———

2nd Chapter of the first Sexion

Article 1st	21 for
	0 ——
2nd article	0 for
	26 against
3rd article	25 for
	0 against
4 article	0 for
	32 against
5 article	27 for
	0 against
6 article	22 for
	2 against
7th article	30 for
	0 ——
8 article	25 for
	0 ——
9 article	0 for
	14 against
10 Article 1st paragraff	2 for
	21 against
2nd paragraff	15 for
	0 ——
3rd paragraff	22 for
	0 ——
4 paragraff	18 for
	0 ——
5 paragraff	8 for
	6 against
6 paragraff	23 for
	0 ——
7 paragraff	2 for
	21 against
8 paragraff	22 for
	0 ——
Article 11th	23 for
	0 ——
article 12	24 for
	0 ——
13 article	23 for
	0 ——

Chapter 2nd Sexion 2nd

1st article	0 for
	24 against
2 article	24 for
	0 ——
3 article	23 for
	0 ——

Chapter 2nd Sexion 3rd

article 1st	0 for
	21 against
article 2nd	0 for
	22 against
3rd article	0 for
	22 against
4 article	0 for
	24 against
5 article	0 for
	22 against
6th article	0 for
	21 against
7 article	0 for
	23 against

Chapter 2nd Sexion 4th

1st article	24 for
	0 ——
2 article	0 for
	23 against

Chapter 3rd Judicatory Power

1st article	0 for
	10 against
2nd article	0 for
	11 against
3rd article	11 for
	0 ——
4th article	11 for
	0 ——
5 article	21 for
	0 ——
Chapter 4th	13 for
	0 ——

Chapter 5th Sexion 1st	
1st article	14 for
	0 ———
2nd article	15 for
	0 ———
3rd articel	14 for
	0 ———
Chapter 5th Sexion 2nd	18 for
	0 ———
Chapter 6th article 1st	
3 first paragraffs	0 for
	19 against
4–5–6 and 7th paragraffs	18 for
	0 —
8 paragraff	0 for
	19 against
Article 2nd 1st paragraff	23 for
	0 ———
2nd paragraff	0 for
	20 against
3rd Paragraff	21 for
	0 ———

4 Paragraff	22 for
	0 ———
5th Paragraff	22 for
	0 ———
article 3rd	0 for
	22 against
4th article	21 for
	0 ———
5 article	22 for
	0 ———
6 article	11 for
	6 against
7 article	22 for
	0 ———
8 article	0 for
	15 against
9 article	16 for
	0———
10 article 1st paragraff	0 for
	19 against
2nd and 3rd Paragraff	18 for
	1 against
11th article	19 for
	0 against

The above is a true Coppy from the Minutes
Errors Excepted Test Aaron Skinner Town Clerk

Shelburne June the 1st 1780

John Wells — Select
Aaron Skinner — men of
Jno Long — Shelburne

Objections in the Bill of Rights———
Article 3rd Paragraph 1st Reasons why we object against this Paragraph is because we think the Civil Authority ought not to have a right to oblidge any People to settle a minister or to say what salary they shall give him for his suport———29th Article Bill of Rights: Reasons we object against this article is because we think that the appointment officers mentioned in said Article ought to Ly with the Legesletive Body and ought to be appointed Anully———

Objections against Each Article in the Frame of government

1st article Sexion 2d as follows Viz the Number Chosen Senators too Large and Like wise we think that two Branches is a naugh. Viz Goveneor and Council and House of Representatives———

2d Article Sexion 2d Paragraph 1st because it appears Reasonable that Every man that is free a twenty one years of age and is liable to Taxation ought to give in his Vote in all Political affairs

Chapter 1st Sexion 3rd Article 2d. objections as follows that Every Town that Liable to taxation ought to be Represented if they hant one 150 voters that they may have Liberty of Joining with some other Town———

4th Article Sexion 3rd—Reason because Every free man ought to be a voter———

Chapter 2d. Sexion 1st Article 2d—objections we think that the word Christian ought to have the word Protestant added to it———

4th Article Sexion 1st objections we think the governor ought to have two thirds of the Council to make a Quorum———

9th Article Sexion 1st: we think the officers mentioned in Said Article ought to Ly with the Legeslative Body———

10th Article objection we think that Every soldier that is Liable to be Draughted for Sarvic ought to have his vote for his officers———

10th Article Paragraph 7th we think all Continental officers ought to be Nominated by the House of Representatives———

Chapter 2d Sexion 2d Article 1st objections against this Article the same as is asigned the Governor as to Religion

Chapter 2 Sexion 3d Article 1: 2: 3: 4: 5: 6: 7:
objections is the same that is given in the first Article with regard to the Senate

Chapter 2: Sexion 4th: objection against this Article is because *three Branches* we Dont approve of———

Chapter 3d Article 1st objections against this article is because we Dont approve of three Branches———

Article 2d. objections: why we Dont Except this article is we Dont alow of three Branches———

Chapter 6: Article 1st objection: why we Dont Except three first Paragraphs is because all officers requred by this Article to be Sworn must believe the Christian Religion and we would be glad to have the word Protestant Added

Article 1st Paragraph 8th objections why we Dont Except this Paragraph is because it mentions three Branches———

Article 2nd Paragraph 2d objections why we Dont Except this Paragraph it refers to three Branches———

Article 3rd objections why we Dont Except this Article is because we think that the Qualifications mentioned in said Article are too High already———

Article 8th objections: why we Dont Except of this Article is because we Dont a Low of three Branches———

Article 10th Paragraph 1st objections why we Dont Except of this Paragraph is because we think the time set for a revision of this Constitution too Long———

The Above is a true Coppy from the minuts Errors Excepted

Attest. Aaron Skinner Town Clark

Shelburne June 1th 1780

John Wells
Aaron Skinner
Jno Long — Selectmen of Shelburne

Shutesbury (276/63)

At a Legal Meeting of the Town of Shutesbury held May 8th 1780 Voted to Chuse a Committee of seven Carefully to Exammin the form of a Constitution agreed upon by a late Convention of the State of Massechusetts Bay and to state any objections or propose any amendment as they shall think proper and lay the same before the Town at a proposed adjourment of this Meeting———

Voted that this Meeting be adjourned to Monday May 22d

Monday May 22d 1780 Met according to adjournment.

Present and acting 47 The Committee appointed to Consider the form of a Constitution agreed upon by a late Convention. Report as follows.———

The Declaration of Rights

Article 3d This article is rejected as having no place in the Bill of Rights. for the following reasons (viz) it is a Contradiction of the 1st and 2d articles and an Infringement upon the liberties of the people.

Article 15th Delit the words. Except in cases in which it hath heretofore been otherwise used and practised. reasons. We know of no practise to Determin property between Man and Man without trial by jury.

Article 24th Delit the words. which have not been declared crimes by preceding Laws reasons we know of no law to Exist or take place before this Constitution

Article 28th Delit the words but by the authority of the Legislature reasons. we apprehend the legislature hath no power to subject the inhabitants to Law martial Except they be in actual Service.

Article 29th After the word admit to be inserted as follows. Therefore to secure the rights of the people and of every Citizen the Judges of the Supreme Judicial Court shall be Chosen by the people annually, and their good behavour will be the best recommendation to continnue them in office.——after the above noted word admit. The remainder of the Article to be Delet——

Frame of Government

Chapter 1st Section 1st Article 2d. Delet the words two thirds in two places and instead thereof insert a majority reasons two thirds is giving the Governor too much of a negative over both Houses.

Article 4th We are of opinion that whenever any tax shall be levyed upon the inhabitants of this Common wealth it ever ought to be set fourth in the Tax act what particular use or uses the same is to be apropriated to.

Section 3d Article 2d That the Representatives be paid for their attendance as well as travell out of the public treasury.

Article 9th That not less than one Hundred members be a Quorum for doing business

Chapter 2nd Section 1st Article 2 That instead of the word Christian be inserted Protestant

Article 9th That it is an Essential Right and Prerogative of the People to Elect all Judicial officers of Every Name and Rank. and we are of opinion that they ought to be elected annually.

Article 10th That all Militia officers be annually Elected.

Article 19th That the Governors sallery and that of the Justices of the Judicial Court be annually stated and settled by the General Court according to the Exigences of the State.

Chapter 6 Article 1st The Declaration to be subscribed by the Governor etc. to be that he is of the Protestant Religion.

Article 6th When this Constitution shall take place there shall be a Code of Laws formed agreable thereto but no Laws shall be Established that Existed before it had a being.

Article 10th Delet the words ninty five and substitute instead thereof Eighty seven and once Every seven years for Ever here after

per order of Comtee John Hamilton Chairman

Shutesbury May 22d 1780

Then after Reading the Form of a Constitution aforesaid article by article with the several objections Amendments Alterations and Reasons as proposed by the Towns Committee it was accepted by a unanimous vote of the Whole House. Except the third article in the Declaration of Rights which article was put as it is stated by the Convention. and after polling the House stands thus for the article three—against it 40. it was then put as proposed by the Towns Committee and after polling stands thus for the proposal 33 against it 8

signed Nathan Haskins moderator

Att. John Powers Jnr. Town Clerk
Shutesbury May 30th 1780

South Hadley *

April 27 1780. At a Legal Meeting of the inhabitants of the Town of South Hadley on Thursday the Twenty Seventh Day of April 1780 at two o Clock After noon at the Meeting House in Said South Haldey then Met and made Choise of Mr Elisha Steel Moderator of Said Meeting Voted to take into Consideration the Constitution of this State Voted that the Consitution be Red in the Meeting Voted that a Comtt be appointed to Consider the Constitution and Make Report to the Meeting Voted Mr. Nathaniel White Philip Smith Major Josiah White Lieutenant Reubin Judd Ser Joseph Moody Ser Reubin Smith Nathan Alvord be a Comtt for the above pur pus; Voted to Adjurn to Munday the Eighth Day of May next at one o Clock after noon then Met and Continued by Adjurnment to Munday the fifteenth of this Instant May at one o Clock after noon met and Continued by Adjurnment to thursday one o Clock after noon then Met and Continued by Adjurnment to thursday the Eightenth of this instant May to one o"Clock after noon then Met Voted to Chuse an other Comtt to Consider the Constitution and make Reporte to the meeting Voted Deacon David Nash Noah Goodman Esquire Nathaniel White Joseph Kellogg Ser Joseph Moody be a Comtt for the above purpus Voted to Adjurn to Thursday the 25th

* Town records, Massachusetts Historical Society.

of this Instant May at one o Clock After Noon then met; and Continued by Adjurnment to Munday the fifth of June 1780 then met Voted to Exept of the Constitution with out Amend ment by a Large majority Voted to Disolve the meeting

Southampton (276/64)

At a meeting of the Male Inhabitants of the ages of Twenty one years in the Town of Southampton called together by the Select-Men of said Town upon the Twenty fourth Day of April A.D. 1780. The Constitution sent to said Select-Men by a Convention of this State of Massachusetts Bay was read at the Meeting was Continued by Adjournments to the 22d of May. A.D. 1780, and the Number of Voters upon the Articles of said Constitution were taken if they appeared for or against said Articles of follows, Viz.——

The Declaration of Rights passed in the Affirmative without a Dissentient Voters present 57

Chapter 1	Section 1	Article 1.	70	Voters present. no Dissentient
Ditto 1	Ditto.	Ditto 2.	70	Yeas. 3 Nays——
Ditto.	Ditto.	Ditto 2.	67	Yeas. 3 Nays upon the Governors Negative Power
Ditto		3.	68.	Yeas ——
		4.	59	Yeas. 9. Nays——
	Section 2.	Article 1.	41	Yeas. 10. Nays——
		2 and 3	62.	Yeas ——
		4.	61	Yeas. 2. Nays——
		5.	60.	Yeas. 3. Nays——
		6, 7, 8, and 9	61.	Yeas 2 Nays——
	Section 3	Articles 1, 2, and 3.	62.	Yeas. 1. Nay.——
		Articles 4, 5, 6, 7, and 8	59.	Yeas. 1. Nay——
		Article 9.	65.	Yeas 1. Nay——
		Articles 10 and 11	61.	Yeas ——

Chapter 2. Section 1.

Article 1 and 2. 62. Yeas and 2. Nays

But insteed of Christian Voted to insert the Word Protestant. 63 Yeas and 2. Nays. The Reason. Because Papists who are called Christians ought to be excluded from all Offices as they consider themselves not bound by any Oath that may not be for the Benifit of the Sea of Rome——

Also 63. Yeas. 2. Nays. That no Person unless of the Protestant Religion Shall be Governor Lieutenant Governor, Member of the Councel or the Senate or the House of Representives, or hold any Judiciary Employment within this state———
And also That wherever the Word Christian is used in the Constitution that the Word Protestant be inserted in its Room———

Chapter. 2.	Section. 1.	Article. 3	53 Yeas	———	
....		Article. 4	37 Yeas.	3. Nays———	
....		Article 5 and 6	37. Yeas	3 Nays———	
....		Article 7.	40 Yeas	———	
....		Article 8.			
....		Article 9.	37. Yeas.	3. Nays———	
....		Article 10.	31. Yeas.	9. Nays———	
....		Article 11,	31. Yeas.	18. Nays———	
		12, 13.	43. Yeas.	4. Nays———	
Chapter. 2.	Section 2.	Articles 2, 3.	45. Yeas	———	
	Section 3.	Article 6.	24 Yeas.	12. Nays———	
	Section 4	....	39. Yeas.	2. Nays———	
Chapter 3	Section	....	30. Yeas	6. Nays———	
Chapter 4			34. Yeas	———	
Chapter 5	Section 1	....	35. Yeas.	1. Nays.———	
	Section 2	....	35. Yeas.	1. Nays.———	
Chapter 6		Article 1	39. Yeas.	2. Nays———	
		Article 2	41. Yeas.	1. Nays———	
		Article 3, 4, 5, 6, 7, 8	41. Yeas	———	
		Article 9.	42. Yeas.	1. Nays———	
		Article 10.	2. Yeas.	41. Nays———	

For some material objections may appear in the Course of a few years, therefore there ought to be an oppertunity of Correcting the Constitution short of that time. In a Close examination of a Constitution no one can find every Fault that may appear in it in when it shall be in exercise———

Articles 10.	35. for 10. Yeas and 6 against it
Article 11	43. Yeas.———

At this same time viz. 15th of May A.D. 1780. These said Inhabitants of Southampton aforesaid Voted. That they do impower to their Deligates to agree upon a Time when said Form of a Constitution shall take place if Two thirds of the People approve of the same or the said Convention shall conform it to the Sentiments of Two Thirds of the People——

Southampton. May 29, 1780. The above is a true
Extract from the Minutes of said Meeting

Test Benja Lyman
Douglass King
Jona Judel Junr.
Select-Men of Southampton

Westfield for Amendments in D of Rights (276/64A) *

29 at the Meeting

		Article 3	12 for it [without?]	17
Chapter 1	Section 2nd	Article 1	28	1
Ditto 2	Ditto 1	Ditto 2	16	7
		7	19	7
		10	24	3
Chapter 3		3	26	5
2	1	9	26	6
6		2	28	1
6		10	32	1

Southampton for Amendments 63 yeas and 2 nays for inserting the word Protestant in the room of the word Christian and desire that no person should be a governor or Lieutenant Governor Senator Counsellor or Representative unless he is a Protestant

57 voters present unanimous for D of rights

	Chapter	Section	Article
Senate	1	2	1
Representatives		3	1
Governor	2	1	2
Lieutenant Governor		2	1
Council		3	1
Judicial Officers		3	1

* Material on this page appears on last sheet of Southampton document (276/64). It is unclear whether this was written by the Westfield clerk, by the Southampton clerk, or by the clerk of convention. The Westfield return is below, MA 276/68.

Southwick (276/65)

At a meeting of the Freeholders and other Inhabitants of the Town of Southwick duly warned and Legally assembled on May 29th and continued by adjurnment to June 2nd, 1780; principally for the purpose of taking into consideration, receiving, rejecting, or amending the constitution or Frame of goverment agreed upon by the Delegates of the People of the State of Massachusetts Bay in Convention begun and held at Cambridge on the 1st of September 1779 and Continued by adjournment to the 2nd of March 1780——

Though the Inhabitants of the Town aforesaid greatly revere the wisdom, integrity and publick spirit that appears to govern the honorable Convention in their publick transactions, yet such is the state of human affairs that unering wisdom is not to be expected especially in matters the most difficult and yet of the greatest importance not only to the present, but generations yet unborn——And as this Constitution or frame of government is sent by said Delegates unto their Constituents for their revition and amendment, so they as a free and independent people act their Sentiments thereon, and would with deference communicate the same to their honourable Delegates in Convention: and though the greater part of said Constitution parfectly harmonizes with their opinions, yet in some instances they cannot assent unto it. without (as they imagine) giving up their natural Rights and Privilages, which they hold too dear to part with—which objections and amendments (with humility being offered) are as follows; Viz——Part 1st Article 3 Paragraph 4th 12 present on the Question whether Civil and Ecclesiastical power is not and ought not to be connected together for the support of Religion 9 yeas. 3 Nays——

Part 2nd Chapter 1st Article 4th Paragraph 2nd. On the Question whether, the Valuation of Estates ought not to be taken at least once in five years—27 present 13 yeas 6 Nays Because of the Great Disparity of Towns and their Mutability in real and parsonal Estates——

Part 2d. Chapter 1st Section 2nd Article 5th—32 present—on the Question whether any person shall be admitted to take his Seat as Senator in this Commonwealth, who does not give solem Oath that he is of the protestant Religion, 32 Nays——

Part 2nd, Chapter 1st Section 3d Article 2nd., 32 present. Voted. Nem: Con: that the town of Boston may send four Representatives to the

General Court and no other Town but two and that any incorporated Town may send one; otherwise there would be too great a Disparity of Representation; likewise that all Representatives to the General Court shall be paid out of the publick Treasury both for Travel and attendance———

Part 2nd Chapter 1st Section 3rd Article 3rd. 32 present Voted Nem: Con: that no person shall be admitted a Seat in the house of Representatives, who does not first give solem Oath that he is of the Protestant Religion———

Part 2nd, Chapter 1st Section 3d Article 9th, 32 present. Voted. Nem: Con, that not less than one hundred members of the house of Representatives shall Constitute a Quoram for doing Business———

Part 2nd Chapter 2nd Section 1st Article 2nd 32 present—voted Nem: Con: that no person shall be admitted to the Seat of Governer in this Commonwealth unless he shall first give solem Oath he is of the Protestant Religion———

Part 2nd Chapter 2nd Section 1st Article 3rd latter clause 32 present voted Nem: Con: that when no choice of a Governer is made by the people the Senate with the house of Representatives shall proceed to the choice of one by Ballot in the same manner the Senate are Directed to in the Constitution, but as it now stands in the Constitution too much power is lodged in the hands of a few men.———

Part 2nd Chapter 2nd Section 1st Article 9th 32 present voted Nem: Con: that justices of the peace and Sheriffs of the Counties ought to be Annually chosen in the same manner as the Representatives for the General Court are and Commissioned by the Governer with advice of the Council Senate and House of Representatives, but each Branch of the Legislature ought to have Negative.

Part 2nd Chapter 2nd Section 1st Article 10th 32 present. Voted Nem: Con that Captains and Subalterns of the Militia should be Elected by the written votes of their Respective Companies of sixteen years of age and upwards———Paragraph 7th the Governer shall appoint and Commission No Officers there mentioned, without consent of both houses of Assembly———

Part 2d. Chapter 2nd Section 1st Article 13th latter clause etc. 32 present —on the Question whethor the Sallaries or Wages of the Governer, Lieutenant Governer, Council Senate and house of Representatives ought not to be appointed by the people; 9 yeas 8 nays

Part 2nd Chapter 2nd Section 2nd Article 1st 11 present—voted. Nem:

Con: that the Lieutenant Governer Council and all officers in this Commonwealth whethe civil or Military shall previous to their taking any Commission whatever give solem Oath that they are of Protestant Religion———

Part 2nd Chapter 4th 13 present Voted Nem: Con: that the Delegates of this Commonwealth to the Congress of the United States, shall be Chosen in the same manner the Governer is herein appointed to be chosen and the Same Qualifications in point of Religion shall also be required———

Mathew Laflen Selectmen
George Granger of Southwick

N.B. all the Articles not objected to, were unanimously Voted by 32 Voters the Number Present in the Meeting

Abner Fowler Deligatis

Springfield (276/66)

At a Meeting of the Inhabitants of the Town of Springfield legally assembled May 29th 1780 by Adjournment from the 22d of said Month———

The Town in the said Meeting having had laid before them, the Form of a Constitution or Frame of Government agreed on by the Convention of the State, and having considered the same———voted their Approbation of the Bill of Rights prefixed to the Said Frame of Government, and of all the several Articles or Paragraphs in the said Frame, to which no special Objection is made in the following Draught; which they voted to be laid before the Convention of the State, as their Opinion and Answer thereon, and as containing their objections thereto with the reasons thereof: which vote was passed by a Majority of 178 out of 180———

They are fully persuaded of the Necessity, in this high and important affair, that the People of this State should in every Part, as far as may be, accommodate themselves to each other; and that Towns, as well as Individuals, should yield particular and even favorite Opinions of smaller Moment, to essential Principles and Considerations of Publick Utillity: and that, under the influence of such Sentiments, they have waived Objections to some Articles which they apprehended capable of Amendment, from a desire of preserving Unanimity in Matters of less Importance, and to avoid the Imputation of being obstinately tenacious of their own Opinions.—They are however constrained to express their sentiments by way of Objection to the following Articles in the said Plan for the Reasons that are shortly subjoined thereto—viz—

To the first Article in the second Section of the first Chapter, they object to the Number of which it is thereby expressly provided and designed the Senate should consist, viz. *thirty one*. They are of Opinion that a Number considerably less (if chosen with Impartiality and Wisdom) may be sufficient to constitute the second Branch of the Legislature; and if they be not thus chosen, the inlargement of the Number will make no Increase of Advantage: it may be a needless Increase of Officers, and a needless Increase of Expence. And if it should frequently happen (as probably it may) that Persons chosen Councellors from the Senate should decline such a Choice, the Number of the Senate will be then further increased and the Objection receive additional Force———

As to the sixth Article in the third Section of said first Chapter they would observe that if the Powers mentioned in that Article are considered and designed to extend to all Persons and Offences in the State, they should object to the investing the Senate with such power; apprehending the Liberty and Security of the People to depend greatly upon their Right to be tried for Offences in the ordinary Courts of Law in the Proper Counties where the Offences are supposed to have been committed, and by a jury of the Neighbourhood.

If this Power is designed to be limited to Impeachments and Trials of Officers under the Government, (as by considering the eighth Section of the foregoing Chapter they rather suppose) then they have only to object the Want of Express Restriction———

As to the second Article in the first Section of the second Chapter, they are constrained to express their disapprobation of the Clause providing that no Person shall be eligible to the Office of Governour unless he declare himself to be of the Christian Religion———As the People of this Commonwealth are generally, if not universally, of the Protestant reformed Religion, they apprehend it would be Matter of Great and General Concern that any Person might ever be elected to this Office over them or their Posterity, who should not be of the Protestant Religion, and they are of Opinion this ought to be provided for in the most express Terms; and that the same Provision, Alteration or Amendment, should be made in the Declaration to be made by the Lieutenant Governor, Councellors, Senators and Representatives, and in the Form of the Oath to be taken by all Officers under the Government———

To the second Article, in the third Section, in the same Chapter, they object———It is calculated to give the several Towns a Right of sending so many Members to the General Court as (if exercised) will at present make the House of Representatives a very unwieldly Body; to the Disadvantage of a regular Transaction, and reasonable Dispatch of business; and will be productive of heavy and needless Expence. And as in such Case the Number will be constantly increasing, this Inconvenience and Expence will be also increasing, until the one be enormous and the other insupportable.———If to avoid these Difficulties, some Towns should decline the Exercise of these Rights in their full Extent, others would Probably improve them, and the Representation would by that Means become more unequal in Fact without effectually answering the End proposed. And as it is probable, by Reason of their different situations, that many of the more distant Towns will generally omit the full Exercise of their Rights, and that those at or near the Center of Government will exercise them in their full Extent, it may always be expected, on this Plan, that the latter will have more than an equal Proportion of Influence in the Conduct of Publick Affairs in general—And as it is provided thereby, that Sixty Members shall make a Quorum of the House, they think it may be justly feared, that in some future Times, less virtuous than the present, they may avail themselves of their Advantages of Situation and Numbers, by an easy, speedy and unexpected Collection, to determine interesting and favorite Matters, not altogether to the general Satisfaction or Benefit of the State: and that the Provision made for paying out of the Publick Treasury the Expences of Travel of the Members, will not sufficiently secure against it———They are therefore of Opinion that each and every Town, even the largest, should be expressly limitted to a certain moderate Number of Representatives, which they should not exceed, that this should be so done, that the Number should be reduced, its Increase duly restrained, and the Mischiefs or Dangers aforesaid prevented———

To the eighth Article in the same Section they have also Objection ———The Power of pardoning Offences, they think to be a necessary Power in the government: They think it most properly and safely lodged in the Hands of the Governor and Council. No sufficient Reason occurs to them why this Power should be restrained from what was formerly exercised and enjoyed; however, if the Restriction of this Power of pardoning refers only to the Conviction of Officers on Impeachments for Mal-Administration etc. they should pass it over as a Matter of lesser Moment—But the later part of that Article they consider as of more Importance; Apprehending that, however this Power ought to be exercised with the greatest Caution and Prudence, yet Cases may frequently happen when a Power of pardoning Offences before Conviction may be expedient and necessary to the great Ends of Publick Justice. Instances to support this Observation are afforded by all those Cases, especially of the higher Offences, where one of a number of Offenders against the Publick Peace is selected for a Witness for the Conviction of his Accomplices: And they apprehend that such Power may therefore be lodged with the Governor and Council provided the Charter of such Pardons, when granted, contains Expressions particularly descriptive of the Offence intended to be pardoned: and that in this State, the Danger of the Abuse of such a Power is not proportioned to the Probability of Advantage.———

To the fifth Article in the third Chapter they object———It provides, "That all Causes of Marriage, Divorce, and Alimony and all Appeals from the Judges of Probate shall be heard and determined by the Governor and Council until the Legislature shall by Law make other Provision." They notice with Attention that this Authority is given to the Governor and Council only untill the Legislature shall by Law make other Provision; but they think this Power should be originally fixed where it is obvious it most naturally and properly belongs: this they conceive to be in the Superior Court: they think it altogether improper to invest the Governor and Council with this Power: their Office and Character imply no special fitness for this Business; nor do the best Qualifications for the Ordinary Duties of their Office involve it; nor will they have any Motives to require it, unless in common with other Gentlemen, and to compleat the Character of General and extensive Knowledge———On the other Hand, they presume proper Persons will be appointed Judges of that Court—well skilled in the General System of Juris-Prudence, and who will be in Duty bound, and properly encouraged to exert their utmost Endeavors for Improvement in legal Knowledge; and they think that the Knowledge of the Laws relative to these Matters, lies naturally in their Line———that they make a Part of that

General System they are indispensably obliged to study and understand —and that therefore, they will be much more able Judges therein, than any Persons in this Common Wealth, however respectable and however judiciously chosen in Regard to their Qualifications to discharge the ordinary (the important) Duties of Councellors——Furthermore from the probability of the long Continuance of the same Judges in Office in the Superior Court, and of the frequent Alterations and Changes in the Council, another obvious Reason arises for prefering the former to Execute these Powers, as this will afford the greatest Security of a happy Uniformity and Steadiness in their Decisions and Decrees.——Add to this, that being determined by that Court, the Records of them will of Course be kept with the other Records of final Judgments on Appeals etc. for the same County, which will be of some Advantage to the People.——

But what is much more, finally—as the Superior Court would hear and ordinarily determine all such Matters in the County where they arise, it would naturally make a vast saving of Expence to the Suitors, that must unavoidably be incurred by prosecuting the same before the Governor and Council in the Capital, or in any other central Place in the State; and prevent that Delay that might often be otherwise apprehended, and which would be very grievous and Detrimental to the Parties——

On this Head which they really think very important—they have to apologize if their Observations may seem to have the Air of dictating even to the least of all their Brethren, by adding to their Objections the proposed Alteration, as they are sensible it is in some sense exceeding the Line proposed to them, and have only to say in Excuse, that this appeared to them necessary to possess others of the Reasons of their Objection, and to place them in a proper Light.——

They object to the Article prescribing the Manner of Election of the Members of Congress by the joint Ballot of the Senate and House of Representatives——

They highly approve of the Provision made by this Form of Government, that the Governor, Lieutenant Governor, Council and Senate should be chosen by the People at large;—they think the important Powers granted them make it quite expedient the People should reserve the Election of these respectable and important Officers to themselves: And as the People have already invested that respectable Body the Congress with greater Powers than are now proposed to be delegated to the

Officers aforesaid, they apprehend it proportionably important for the People that they reserve the Elections of their own Members to Congress in their own Hands———

Hampshire County [to wit] Springfield May 29th, 1780
The foregoing is a True Coppy from Springfield
Town Records
Att. William Pynchon Junr Town Clerk

Sunderland (276/67)

Sunderland May 15th, 1780

These do testify and shew that the Inhabitants of Sunderland, on the 15d of May 1780 met pursuant to a Resolution of the Convention; for the Purpose of approving or disapproving the Constitution proposed——— Therefore we in Behalf of said Town, hereby report the Doings thereof in the subsequent Manner (viz) After the Number of the House was ascertained and found to be 52 in Number the Articles against which there were Objections were called for, in Order, were found to be as follows———

Part 2d———Chapter 1d Section 3d

Article 2d Objections that the Rules therin given respecting Representation are not founded on an Equality

Reason 1/ That each Town has rights, Liberties, and Priviledges peculiar to the same, and as dear to them as those to any other, and which they have as just a right as any others to have guarded and protected.

Reason 2/ If larger Towns have more to represent them and more Voices in the General Court than the smaller, they will have the Advantage of the smaller; the smaller will not have their Rights equally guarded and protected.

Reason 3/ Where there is not an Equal Representation it has a natural tendency to create Jelousies, Uneasiness, and Divisions. Therefore would propose the following Alteration and Amendments (viz). That each Town incorporated shall send one Representative, Each Town having five hundred rateable Polls send two; and no Town, excepting Boston, however large, shall send more than two. 2/ That the whole of the Cost of Representation be paid out of the Publick State Treasury

Unanimous in the Objection, Alteration and Amendments

Article 9d Objection—that the Number therein mentioned to constitute a Court is too small———

Reason/ Because it is unsafe that so small a part of the Members of the House should transack Business for so large a Body.

Amendment/ That not less than one third part of the Representatives chosen and returned to serve in the General Court, shall constitute a Quorum for doing Business

Unanimous in the aforesaid Objection and Amendment.

Chapter 2d Section 1 Article 8

Objection—that the Power of granting Pardons is refered to too small a Number:

Amendment/ therefore ought to be in the General Court, whose Right it is not only to make Laws, but to repeal them when made.

Unanimous in the Objection and Amendment

Article 9 Including Article 1 and 3d in Chapter 3d.

Objection———1/ Because frequent Appointments tends to a faithful Discharge of Duty

2/ We esteem it out undoubted Rights either personly or by Representation; to elect and appoint all the Justices of the Peace.———

Amendment/ That the Justices of the Peace be nominated by the Representatives of the County in which they reside and be annually appointed and Commissioned by the Governor, with the Consent of his Council

Unanimous in the Objection and Amendment

Article 10/ Amendment/ The Captain and Subalterns be elected by the Trainband and alarm-list of their respective Companies of Sixteen years of Age and upwards.

15 for the Amendment

Chapter 6 Article 10d:/ that ten years be the limitted time for the Revision of this Constitution.

48 of Amendment

Voted unanimously we except of the Constitution proposed with the above Amendments

Attested by

Simon Cooley Select men
Jedidiah Clark of
Phinehas Graves Sunderland

This may Certify that att a Legal meeting of the Inhabitants of the town Captain Hubbard was appointed as our Deligate to Set in the State Convention that is to be holden at the town house in Boston on the first Wednesday of June next.

Simon Cooley Select men
Jedidiah Clark of
Phinehas Graves Sunderland

Ware (276/68)

16. article in the Declaration of Rights Proposed this amendment where it Doth not hurt the innocent

frame of Goverment Chapter 1 Section 2 article 1 Preposed to take of one third of the Council and Senate.———

Chapter 1 Section 3 article 2 Proposed that no town shall send more then four Representatives———

Chapter 2 Section 1 article 2 Proposed that the Governer shall be of the Prodestant Religion———

Article 13 Proposed that the Court shall have Liberty to Lower the Salaries as well as to Raise them

Chapter 3 article 1 Proposed that the word Shall Remove them be put in insted of the word may Remove

Chapter 6 article 3 Proposed that they Shall not increase the Qualification of Property of Parsons to be elected to Office.

At a Meeting Duly Warned May 17, 1780 of the town of Ware Ajorned till thirsday the 24 Instant and Held by Ajornment to Wednesday the 31 Instant. Met according to ajornment 31 Parsons Voted to Except of the Constitution with the alterations here made Except one man against the third article of the Declaration of Rights

a true copy David Brown Town Clerk

W. Brackendridge
Thomas Jenkins } Selectmen
Abm Cummings

Ware/Hampshire
May 17, 1780

Westfield (276/68) *

At a Legal Meeting of the Inhabitants of the Town of Westfield held by adjournment May 25, 1780.———

It was moved and seconded to see if the Town would accept of the whole Constitution or Form of Government without amendment, excepting those Articles following, which are objected to by the Committee chosen for that Purpose. Voted in the Affirmative Nem. Con.———

Article 3d in the Bill of Rights objected to: the number of Voters present for accepting it without amendment was 17—and for rejecting it 12———

Chapter 1st Section 2d. Objected that the Number of Senators is too large and that a less Number would expedite Business and be less expensive to the Commonwealth———

Voted that the Senate consist of no more than twenty eight members. yeas. 28 and nays 1.———

Chapter 2 Section 1st Article 2d. Objected to: Voted that the Governour shall declare himself to be of the Christian and Protestant Religion—yeas 16 and nays 7———

Article 7th Voted that the Commander in Chief have not Power to call out the Militia of the Commonwealth without the advice of the Council———Yeas 19. Nays 7———

10th Voted that Captains and Subalterns of the Militia be elected by the written Votes of the Train Band and alarm List of Sixteen years old and upwards. yeas 24. nays 13

Voted that no Militia officers hold their Commissions for a longer Term than three years. yeas 20 nays 4

Chapter 3d Article 3d. Voted that all Commissions of Justices of the Peace shall expire in the Term of three years—yeas 26. nays 5.———

* See also above, MA 276/64A.

Voted that all Justices of the Peace be nominated by the Inhabitants of their respective towns and not by the Governor. Yeas 26. Nays 6———.

Voted that Ministers of the Gospel be excluded a Seat in the House of Representatives yeas 28. nays 1

Voted a Revision of the Constitution in ten years yeas 32. nays 1.

Voted that in Case there be a Majority of qualified Voters in Favour of a Revision, at the Expiration of ten years, the General Court shall issue precepts to elect Delegates to meet in Convention for the purpose aforesaid yeas 29 nays———

Voted that the Delegate for said Town of Westfield, be empowered to agree upon a Time when the new Form of Government shall take Place, at the next Session of the Convention, without returning the same to the People Nem. Con.———

S. Mather Town Clerk of Westfield

Warwick (276/69)

At a Meeting of the Inhabitants of the Town of Warwick begun and held at Warwick on the 17 day of May 1780—and Continued by adjournment to the 24 of the same. The following alterations and amendments were proposed to the Constitution viz:

1st: That the 3rd. article in the Bill of Rights be wholy rejected.

2ly: That the department of legislation consist of but one branch viz a House of Representatives———

3ly That a council, or Committee, be annually Chosen by the House of Representatives of the Number of 15, viz. one out of each County, and one out of the People at large, who shall be President of the Council and Chief Majestrate of the Commonwealth and all Commissions in the Civil department shall be signed by him. Said Council to set in a seperate Body from the House for the Purpose of giving advice and Council to the House, and to be invested with all the Powers which in said Constitution are given to the Governor in Chapter 1 Section 1—Article 2 and 4 and to the Senate in Chapter 1 Section 2 article 6 and 8.—and to the Governor and Council in Chapter 2 Section 1 Article 11. Not less than a Major part of said Council to be a quorom for doing Business.

4ly: That a Captain General, or Commander in Chief be appointed by the Legislature to continue in office during good behavour to be invested with all the Power given to the Governor in Chapter 2 Section 1 Article 7. 10. and 12. and said General shall make a true return of all

Millitary Matters that come under his Care and all Commissions in the Millitary department shall be signed by him.———

5ly: That all other Powers, which by said Constitution are vested in the Governor Senate or Council shall be vested in the House of Representatives———

6ly: That all Civil and Judicial officers shall have their Salleries granted annually———

7ly: That each Town have the Previledge of Chusing a Justice of the peace to hold his office During the Pleasure of the electors.———

8ly: That the probate and Registry of Wills and Settlements of Estates be kept in each Town by the Select men and town clerk, (or Town Council and Regester to be annually by the Inhabitants of each Town for that Purpose) fees to be annually agreed upon by the Electors.———

9ly: That all licences or Publick Houses etc. be granted by the Select men of each Town———

10ly. That all deeds of lands be enrolled in the Town where the land lies, by the Town Clerk, fees to be annually setled by each Town———

Voted to receive the Constitution with the above alterations and amendments yeas 41
nays 28
69

The following amendment was also Proposed at said meeting viz: That no Person shall hold any seat in the civil department of Government except he be a Proffesser of the Christian Prostettant Religion———

Voted to Receive the Constitution with the last mentioned ammendment ———Yeas 28 Nays 41

Thomas Rich
Josiah Pomeroy Selectmen of Warwick
Josiah Robb

Westhampton (276/70)

At a Legal Meeting of the freeholders and other inhabitants of the town of Westhampton Called by the Select Men of said town on a Monday the 24th Day of April 1780. for the purpose of Examining the New Constitution or form of Government Sent us by the honorable Convention held at Cambridge on the first of September 1779 etc.

The Meeting was Continued by adjournments to the 16th of May 1780 at Which time the town Passed the following votes. viz. That their be an amendment on the fourth article first Chapter third Section of the said Constitution in the following manner. viz.

That Every Male Person 21 years of age that hath a freehold Estate or any Estate to the value of thirty pounds Shall be Sufficiently qualified to vote for a representative Yeas 19 Nays 4. Reasons given for this alteration were that by the qualifycations of voters being set so high in the Constitution that it will necessaryly Exclude a Larg numbers of persons from voting who are good friends to their Country and well wishers to the Common wealth of Massachusetts and since there is generally a considerable tax laid on the pole it is our mind that the pole tax with the Small Estates above mentioned give a sufficient Right to vote for a representative

further voted that Every Person Chosen into office of whome by this Constitution it is required that he Should declare him Self to be of the Christian Religion Should likewise be required to Declare him Self a Prodestant yeas 23.

Reasons given for the addition of the word prodesant Were that Bearly for a Man to delare himself of the Christian Religion will not Exclude a Man that holds to the principles of Spiritual [Jurisdiction?] however our delegates may think that they have Sufficiently Excluded Such persons, by oaths or afarmations. Yet we humbly conceive that the addition of this word can be of no Damage, but will rather Set our rights and privileges on a Sureer foundation and make the Constatution Set much Easier on our Minde we therefore Sincerely desire it may take place

Voted that Six hundred pound be a sufficient qalofycation (with regard to Estat) for a Governor yeas 23 Reasons given were that six hundred pound is sufficient to atach him to the interest of the Common wealth. Besides it is our humble oppinion that by the Governors being obliged to have an Estate agreeable to the Constitution, that a person Every way qalified for that important office on all other account must be Excluded in this.——— further voted that whereas this Constitution impowers the Governor to appoint the officers of forts and Garrison it is our oppinion that this is not for the Safety of the Common wealth. Especially Since the said Governor is to have the Command of the officers that he appointe Because that upon the suposition that wee may at some time be so unhappy as to have a Governor who May not ame at the Good of the Common wealth and his haveing power both to appoint and Command the officers of said forts and garrisons in which probable may be reposited large quantities of warlike Stores etc. and said officers are lyable to be recalled if suspected only by impeachment and tryal which may so prolong the time as to be very hurtfull to the Commonwealth

it is therefore the minds of this town that the officers of forts and Garrisons be appointed by the house of representatives or Senate or both jointly according as the Convention shall see fit. and that said officers continue in their office During the pleasure of those that appoint them

further voted, (on the article that respects the qullifycations of Soldiers to vote for their officers.) that all persons [who?] are obligeed to bear arms have a Right to vote for their Commissioned of[ficers yeas?] 24. Reasons given were that since the persons from sixteen years to twenty one years of age are the persons that are called upon to go into the field and are obliged to trane under those officers and perhaps have born as great or greater share of the Burden of the presen[?] contest as person of any age whatever we therefore Concider them as not only haveing a just right to choose, but as haveing Sufficien knowledge of the qualifications of an officer.

further voted that the officers of the Militia be Elected once in four years 24 Reasons given were that by an officers Considering himself to haveing a Connection in a Considerrable Degree independent from his Company may be more likely to abuse his trust than if he should consider a new Election at home.

Further voted that whereas that honorable Convention has seen fit to Exclude certain Persons of Different offices and trusts from a seat in the Legislature it is the Minds of this town that the Minesters of the Gospel be likewise Excluded yeas 22 Reasons given were that a person who is proporly Elected and regarly ordained as a Minester of the Gospel must according to Scripture and reason abide in the Callong into which he is Called. Whe humbly conceive that it is no more agreable to the Scripture for a Minester of the Gospel to be come a minester of State than it were for [King Uziah?] to burn inconce at the alter. besides wee might ad that it is not consistant with freedome and Liberty for a Legislator to lay a tax on us in which he doth not tax him self which is truly the case with regard to minesters provided they pay no rates

Ebenr French
Ephraim Wright — Selectmen of the town of Westhampton

a true Coppy
Attest
Gideon Clark Jur.
town Clerk of Westhampton

West Springfield (276/71)

At a Meeting of the Freeholders and other Inhabitants of this Town begun and held on Fryday the 21. Day of April, and continued by adjournments to the 2d day of June, Abrm. Burbank, Esquire Moderator, the following Instructions to the Delegates of this Town to Convention were agreed to, Viz.

West Springfield June 2, 1780

Gentlemen.

The Town of West Springfield having convened in a legal Meeting to consider the Constitution or Frame of Government agreed upon by the Convention of this State and by them proposed to the People for their approbation, Rejection, or Amendment, having had the same repeatedly read, proceeded to a Discussion of the Several Articles therein contained, and have unanimously voted to approve of all the several articles except these following, viz. The third article in the Bill or Rights. The Question being put whether the Meeting approved it, there appeared for it 27, against [?] Meeting then voted to choose a committee to state Objections. The Committee took the mater under Consideration and reported as follows, viz.———

1st. Because we conceive Religion or the Worship of God to be an unalianable Right inherent in every Individual, that we of Right cannot invest the Legislature with Authority to institute the Worship of God at Stated Times and Seasons this being at all Times a Matter between God and Individuals and must be a Matter of our Choice. 2. Because we conceive that if the Legislature may be impowered to oblige all the Citizens to attend on the public Worship of God at stated Times and Seasons they may also prohibit the worship of God at any other time. *If the Legislature may institute publick Worship they may* and also define what that worship shall be and so the right of private Judment will be at an End. 3) Because we conceive the Religion of the Gospel was fully instituted by it's Divine Author; (it is therefore repugnant to the rules of Christianity for the legislature to interfere otherwise than to defend the Citizens in the free Exercise of their own religious Professions and Sentiments and consequently the Interposition of the Civil Authority is not necessary to the Religion of the Gospel which has always flourished most without it and therefore the Good of Society would be promoted by leaving the Christian religion to the Care of the Great Head of the Church who has promised his Presence with it to the End of the World. Instead of promoting Religion and the consequent Good of Society we fear it will produce Law-Suits, Bitterness, and Ill-Will among the Citizens of the Commonwealth.

The Town voted to accept of the above Report.

The Town voted also to adopt the following Substitute for the 3rd. Article in the Bill of Rights.

The Citizens of this Commonwealth have at all Times the exclusive Right of electing their public Teachers and of contracting with them for their Support and Maintenance. And every Denomination of Christians demeaning themselves peaceably and as good Citizens of this Commonwealth shall be equally under the Protection of the Law, and no subordination of any one Sect or Denomination to another shall ever be established by Law.

Page 16. The Meeting voted it their Opinion that the Words *voting by Yea's and Nay's* and *the Names of the persons voting for or against the said Bill or Resolve shall be entered upon the public Records of the Commonwealth,* be erased

For this reason, because we suppose Gentlemen in many instances may be cramped in acting their Opinions freely by having their Names thus held up to public View.

Page 18 The Meeting voted an Amendment in the Article that proposes a valuation once in ten years. We think it ought to be taken once in every seven years because the property of many Towns may alter much more than others in the Term of Ten years.

Page 18 Voted, that the Senate should be left out of the Constitution Because we imagine the Expence will exceed the Benefit of such a Branch of the Legislature

Voted that the Councilors be chosen in the same manner and with the same qualifications as was proposed for the Counsellors and Senators and that they be additionally impowered to revise Laws with the Governor

Page 23 Voted, for an amendment, Viz. Where it is provided that no person shall be capable of being elected as a Senator or Counsellor who is not siezed in his own right of a Freehold within this Commonwealth of the value of Three Hundred Pounds at least or possessed of a Personal Estate to the Value of six Hundred Pounds at least etc. We propose that the Word *Rateable* should be added to the Personal Estate, because we apprehend it may sometimes happen that Gentlemen may be possessed of the Value of six hundred Pounds in Household Furniture etc. not rateable, which ought not to qualify them for that Station.

Page 24 Chapter 1 Section 3 Article 2. By the Provision that is there [made?] for Representation upon the principles of Equality the Town are of Opinion that there will be Danger of the House of Representatives being too numerous for the proper Expedition of Business, as well as great Expence to the Community. We would therefore recommend that the Number capable of chusing a Representative should be much greater than One Hundred and Fifty and also the mean increasing number for more Representatives should far exceed 225, and that no Town be fined for not chusing or sending a Representative to the General Court.

Page 25 Article 4th Voted to alter the Annual Income of three Pounds to two Pounds; and Estate of the Value of sixty pounds to fourty pounds, for the Qualification of Voters for Representatives.

Page 27. We propose an amendment in the Article where it is said the Governor shall declare himself to be of the Christian Religion; We propose instead of Christian Religion, it should be the Protestant Christian Religion, this we esteem necessary to secure a Protestant Civil Government.

Page 31. Voted, after the word *State,* to add, or either of the adjoining States this we think consistent with the Rules of humanity and good Policy and in many Instances absolutely necessary to the Safety and well being of the Whole united States.

Page 31. Article 9th. Voted for the article 22. against it 17.

Page 32. Article 10. Voted against it 45, for it 18. The Reason against it assigned because all from 16 to 21 years have no vote in the Choice of their Officers.

Page 39. Voted to have the Time of Life limited beyond which Judges of the Superior Court shall not hold their places—

Page 40. Voted the Delegates of this State to Congress shall have the same Qualifications as to Estate, Residence and Religion as is required of the Governor of this State.

Page 42. Near the Bottom, voted to erase the Word *Congregational* out of the Description of the Overseers of Harvard College; For we conceive that leaving out Ministers of other Denominations will tend to create Jealousys of their Conduct hereafter toward them.

Page 43 Chapter 5 Section II. Voted to erase the Word *Grammer-Schools.* The Reason why we think that Injunction unsalutary is because many Towns in the Country are not under Circumstances to receive any considerable advantage from Grammar Schools and therefore think it a Grievance to be at so great Expence when a good English School may answer all the valuable Ends most of the Inhabitants can expect to receive from Schools.

Page 44. Voted that before the Word *Christian* in the Declaration, the word Protestant be inserted, for the same reasons we proposed an alteration in the qualification for a Governor.

Page 48. Voted that no Minister of the Gospel, Judge of the Inferior Court or Justices of the Peace shall be a Member of the Senate Council, or House of Representatives. The Reasons why we think Ministers of the Gospel should be excluded a Seat in the Senate, Council, or House of Representatives are because their Calling as Teachers of Religion is enough to employ the whole of their attention and therefore ought not to be diverted by intermedling with affairs of State: and also because (as things have been in Times past) Ministers pay no Taxes and therefore are disqualified to vote for raising taxes of which themselves bear no part. The Reason why we would have Judges of the Inferior Court and Justices of the Peace excluded is set forth in the 30th Article of the Bill of Rights. we conceive it very improper for any set of Men at the same Time to determine their own Power and ascertain their own Fees.

Page 49. Article 6th. Voted that those Laws (and those only) which have been made in this state shall be in force

Page 50. Article 10th. Voted that there be a new Convention within 7 years for the purpose set forth in said Article.

Voted, that the Delegates from this Town to Convention use their endeavor to get the above amendments granted by Convention. Voted, That if two thirds of the Inhabitants agree for the Constitution that it be left with the Convention when it shall take place

Attest A true Copy from the minutes

Jona. White Moderator pro temp.

Wilbraham (276/72)

To the Honorable President of the Convention of the
State of Massachusetts-Bay
Honorable Sir,—

Agreable to a Resolve of the Convention we have laid the Frame of Government Sent to us before the Town for their Revisal and Examination———Upon which Revision the Town have Objections to Several parts therof—which Objections with the Reasons therefor are as follows (viz) Declaration of Rights—Article 29th the words free and independent to be expunged—for as they Stand connected with other words we are of Opinion that they will admit of Absolute Despotism———Also, the words hold their office as long as they behave themselves will be Deled—and the words be annually Elected by the People be adopted in their Stead—for this Reason because in our Opinion annual Elections are a great Barrier to the Rights of the People—and as great in the Judiciary Department as Legislative or Executive

Also Part 2: Chapter: and Section 1st That the Governor shall have no power in Legislation—which we conceive he has in his Objecting to Bills and the Consequence thereof according to the Article—Reasons; Because we think it is important for the Safety of the Rights of the People that the three Branches of Government should be kept Distinct and that a union of them would be Dangerous—to this purpose you very well Express the Matter in your address in these words—that when the same man or Body of men Enact Interpret and execute the Laws Property Becomes too precarious to be valuable and the people are finally born down with the force of Corruption Resulting from the union of those Powers—we also conceive it to be repugnant to the 30: Article of the Declaration of Rights where it is Declared that the Executive shall never Exercise the Legislative and Judicial Powers or either of them—But the Governor in Consequence of his Election as Chief Executive officer has a Considerable influence in Legislation by the Article—But we are of Opinion that the Chief Executive Officer ought to be excluded a Voice in Legislation as much as the Supream Judicial Judges.———

We also object to the money Qualifications for the Electors and Elected and have voted intirely to expunge it from the Constitution—for these Reasons first because Social virtue and knowledge is the best and only necessary Qualification of the Legislator—Secondly, because that a Selvish view to private Interest is a Disqualification of the Person before us—but all Qualifications of private Intrest are of this Kind—and therefore ought not to be made a Qualification for the Legislator for so far as he is governed by those Selvish views so far he is Disqualified for a Seat in Legislation.—Thirdly, because the Legislature, by it have a Right to make or at least to encrease their own Qualification in such a manner that the People are in Danger of being deprived of their priviledges of Electing Members for that body, at least it is in the

Power of the Legislative to Deprive them of this Right which we think ought never to be———

We then passed to the Consideration of the Mode of Representation——— and Object as the Senatorial Branch is founded Solely on Property——— to this says an ingenious author "and if Representation Should be Limited by that rule, the man who owns Six times as much as another would, consequently, have Six times the Power, though their Natural Right to freedom is the Same—Nature itself abhors such a System of Civil Government, for it will make an inequality among the People and Set up a number of Lords over the rest" and as the House of Representatives are founded on the Number of Inhabitants which we think is much too unsteady and wavering to place Representation upon—therefore we think incorporation (for these and many other Reasons which might be given) the best Rule whereon to found a just Representation———Therefore propose the following alteration (viz) that each District for Senators Send three and no more, except those that have two and one, Ramain as they are,—and that the House of Representatives be formed by this rule (viz) Every Town Send one and the town that hath Sixty Families Send two, and Boston Send four———

Then Passed to the Consideration of the Judiciary Department——— and proposed the following alteration (viz) that the Judges of the Supreme Judicial Court be Annually Elected at large through the State—The Judges of the Inferiour Court and of Probate of Wills and Justices of the peace be annually Elected by each County———For this Reason it keeps each Branch more Immediately Dependent upon the People—and therefore will Serve to keep the three Branches Distinct and Independent of each other and as each Branch are the Substitutes of the People according to the Declaration of Rights. Article 5th—we think each Branch should also be Elected by the People,—but it is Said in the Address if the People Should Elect their Judicial and executive Officers, it will forever keep them under the Controul of Ambitious artful and interested Men who can obtain most votes for them———Observe, it is Said Interested men, are ambitious and will do much hurt in the Society and will make Elections Dangerous—whence then the Reason of making Interest a Qualification for either Electers or Elected, (if there is any weight in the objection, it lies equally against all Elections, and if the Inconveniencies arising therfrom are Sufficient to give all elections, then let us give them all up, otherwise let us Retain them———But we are of opinion that it is an important right and ought to be Retained for the Welfare of Generations Yet unborn—We further Considered the Religious Qualification and propose that Wherever the Christian Religion is Mentioned in this Constitution the word Protestant be substituted in the room of Christian,—We also propose that the Alarm List, and Train Band above Sixteen years of age chuse Captains and Subalterns———

After the Consideration of the above Objections the Question was put Whether the Town will accept of the Constitution with the above Alterations———

In the Affirmative 40
Negative 13

Honored Sir,—We have Stated our Objections and given our Reasons, on the Whole it appears to us that the Constitution in the Present form is Rather too Arbitrary the People are now Contending for Freedom—and we heartily wish they might not only Obtain it—but keep it in their own Hands.———

Wilbraham June 7th 1780

John Hitchcock
James Warrinner Selectmen of Wilbraham

Williamsburg (276/73)

The Town of Williamsburgh begs leave to make the following Alterations in the Constitution published for the Approbation of the inhabitants of this State.———

May 8th 1780

at A Town Meeting legally warned and met According to adjournment present Sixty five Voters. Upon reading the 17th Article in the Bill of Rights. Voted that these words their Own be inserted which makes it read thus; that the people have a right to keep and to bear Arms for their Own and the Common defence.

Voted Nemine Contradic.———

Our reasons gentleman for making this Addition Are these.

1st that we esteem it an essential priviledge to keep Arms in Our houses for Our Own Defence and while we Continue honest and Lawfull Subjects of Government we Ought Never to be deprived of them.

Reas. 2 That the legislature in some future period may Confine all the fire Arms to some publick Magazine and thereby deprive the people of the benefit of the use of them

House of Representatives Article 2 Upon reading this Article Voted that this clause and the House of Representatives shall have power from time to time to impose fines upon such Towns as shall Neglect to choose and return Members to the same Agreably to this Constitution.

Be Struck Out——Voted Nem Con——

Our reason for having this clause left Out is that Many Towns that have a Right by the Constitution to chuse and ought to have Are not Able to support A Member at court long enough to be of much service and therefore ought not to be subject to Any penalty if they do not send.——

On reading the next clause Voted that these words be Added *and likewise their wages while attending* which makes it read thus. the expences of travilling to the General Assembly and riturning home once in every session and no more, and likewise their wages while attending shall be paid by the Goverment out of the publick Treasury, Voted Nem Con——

Our resons for this Addition Are that if this should be the Case Every Member Could Attend seasonably and tarry till the Business of the Session be finished and they Cannot Otherwise; of Course An Opportunity must necessarily fall into the hands of those that live near the Seat of Goverment to pass Acts Gratly detrimental to the more distant parts of the state which we have experienced Often to have been the Case, if this Addition should take place we Are willing the preceeding clause should remain; Otherwise not.

On Reading the 3d. Article Voted that those words *One Hundred Pound* be Altered to two hundred and fifty and that those words *Two hundred pounds* be Altered to Four hundred NC.——

Our reasons for this Alteration is to prevent any persons being Elected to be A Member of that body that has not something to Influence him to Act for the publick good——

Concerning the Governors qualification

Article 2d. Voted that the word *Christian* be Erased and the word Protestant be inserted in its Room Voted N.C.

Our Reasons for this Alteration is that as it now stands without this alteration Liberty is implicitly granted for the Admission of Papists into the Chair which we Cannot by Any means Consent to And in this Case we have the Example and Authority of All Protestant reformed Nations we desire therefore that in all places in this Constitution where the term Christian is applied to the Religion of Publick civil Officers the word *Protestant* be inserted and the word Christian be Erased.——

Concerning the Number of the Privy Council——

Article 1 Voted that the word *Nine* be erased and the word *five* be inserted in its Room and that three of this Councel Constitute a quorum

Article 2 Voted that the word *Nine* be erased and the word *five* inserted.

Article 4 Voted that the word *two* be erased and the word *one* be inserted. Voted N.C.——

Our Reasons for these Alterations Are to prevent extraordinary and Unnecessary Charges to the State we suppose that five will be a sufficient number for to advise with him upon extraordinary emergencies.

Chapter 6th. Article 9th On reading this Article we do not find that any time is fixed in which the Commissions of Millitary Officers shall be renewed Or the People have liberty to Make a New choice we therefore desire that these Commissions May expire in the time of five years and the people have an Opportunity to Make a New Choice.

Bill of Rights Article 28th Voted that those words *but by the Authority of the legislature* be Erased N.C.——

Our reason for erasing that last clause is to Manifest to you Our Opinion which is that not even the legislature Ought to have Power to try by Court Martial Any One that does not belong Either to the Army or Navy, if this should be the Case who is there that would not be subject to this form of Tryal whenever the Legislature should please we Cannot therefore Consent to it.

Chapter 2 Article 10th——On reading this Article we find this Clause *that No Officer duly Commissioned to Command in the Militia shall be removed from his Office but by the Address of Both houses to the Governor*. Voted that that Clause be erased and that this be inserted that Every Officer Duly Commissioned to Command in the Militia of Lower Rank than a Major shall be liable to be Broke by his colonel whenever he shall judge there is sufficient Complaint Brought Against him and Another be Appointed in his Room——Voted N C.——

Our Reasons for this Alteration Are that it will be too tedious and expensive to go to Both Houses and from thence to the Governor to get an Officer Removed when he has deserd. [deserved?] it and we think his Colonel Ought to be a sufficient judge in this Case and therefore Ought to have this Power——

These two last Article were accidenly missed in fore part of this Copy we have therfore inserted them here.

A true coppy of the votes Attest
Josiah Dwight Town Clerke

LINCOLN COUNTY

Edgecomb (276/77)

At a meeting of the freeholders and other inhabitants of the town of Edgecumb, duly qualified and Legally warned, Assembled on Tuesday the 23d Day of May. A.D. 1780——

After a Moderator was Chosen the frame of Government was read—and after Some Debates—it was Unanimously Voted, that the Seventh Article of the Second Chapter: Section first——is Disagreeable to the minds of this Town, and that it gives the Governor more power than one man ought to have. Voted the amendment on Said Article shall be—that the Governor Shall not order the Militia or Navy, at any time; or on any occasion to any place without the Consent of the Major part of the Council—

Voted that the frame of Goverment take place with the above amendment——

Twenty Voters present all Unanimous

Nehemieh Herrondon
William Cuningham
Thomas King
Selectmen of
Edgecumb

Georgetown *

At a town Meeting Legally Warned and Held at the Meeting House on Arrowsick Island in Georgetown on Tuesday the 23rd Day of May 1780—first voted James McCobb Esquire Moderator.

Voted that Benjamin Lemont, Nathaniel Wyman and William Lithgow Junior Be a Committee to take the New form of a Constitution Proposed by the Honorable Conochtion of this State Into their Considaration and that the said Committee make their Report to the town at their Next Meeting for the purpose of considering said form. Voted that this Meeting so far as it Respects the Consideration of said

* Town records, Massachusetts Historical Society.

form be Ajourned to the 13th Day of June next at Nine of the Clock Before Noon at this Place. June 13th 1780 Agreeable to Ajournment the town met at the Meeting House on Arrowsick Island in Georgetown, and Voted Unanimosly that the frame of Govarment in General be Established, and that the word Protestant be in the stead of Christian for the Same Reasons made use of in the Address Against any Man of the Popish Religeon holding any Office—And in Chapter 5 Section 1 Article 3rd, that the Protestant Churches Be in Stead of Congregational Churches, for the Reasons that are Mentioned in the Bill of Rights, in the 3rd Article, that no Subordination of Any one Sect or Denomination to A Nother etc James McCobb Moderator——

A true copy of the Proceedings of Said town Meeting

Recorded June the 17th 1780.

William Butler town Clerk

Newcastle *

[Article 2 of the warrant dated May 9th 1780 reads thus.]

2d To see if the town will vote to accept of a Frame of Government made by a Convention chosen and appoint for that purpose Begun and held at Cambridge the first Day of September 1779

[At a meeting held May 24th 1780 the following action was taken on the article.]

2 The Frame of Government being read it was Put to Vote there being twenty seven Voters in the Meeting it was Voted by twenty five to Accept of said frame of Government.

3 Voted not to send a Representative

Pownalborough (276/77)

At a meeting of the Town of Pownalboro' duly and legally warned, on the eighteenth Day of May AD 1780, for the Purpose, among other things, of considering, approving or disapproving a Constitution or Form of Government for Massachusetts Bay recommended by a Convention,

* Town records, Massachusetts Historical Society.

after reading and considering the same, the Question was put, whether the Town do approve of the same, and will accept of the whole as it has been now read. it passed in the negative unanimously Number Voters 29

The Question was then put whether the Town do disapprove of, and will reject the said Constitution in the whole, it passed in the affirmative 23 being for it 26 against it. The Reasons of the Town for rejecting the whole were, That the present form of government the Country was used to and answered the purposes both of internal government and carrying on the War, and that the invasions of the Enemy and the Divisions among ourselves made it improper if not dangerous at this Time to introduce a new mode of government.

Besides, a Number of our Brethren, men of Property and understanding, are now from home in the War, who have a right to be consulted and to give their opinion in a matter wherein they and their children are so much interested

A True Coppy

Att David Silvester Town Clerk

Thomaston *

At a Meeting of the Freeholders and other Inhabitants of the Town of Thomaston on Wednesday the twenty fourth Day of May A D 1780 at the Dwelling House of Mr. Oliver Robins in said Town agreeable to Notification or Warrant for that Purpose viz for the Purpose of choosing a Representative, etc.

The Question being put to see if the Town would choose a Representative passed in the Negative.

On the Second Article

A Copy of "A CONSTITUTION OR FORM OF GOVERNMENT FOR THE COMMONWEALTH OF MASSACHUSETTS" being laid before the Inhabitants they declined passing any Vote thereupon: Nor on the third Article which was to choose a Delegate to meet in Convention at the Adjournment.

David Fales
Jonathan Crocket Selectmen

* Town records, Massachusetts Historical Society.

Vassalborough *

May 25th 1780

Art 2nd in the warrant reads——

To see if the town will accept of the New Constitution or form of Goverment or to object any articles as the town shall agree Voted on Art 2nd Chose Daniel Fairfield, Mathew Hastings and Flint Barton a committee to take into consideration the frame of Constitution or form of government for the Massachusetts Bay lately come into by the convention and report to the town such amendment as they shall think necessary on the last Monday in June next at nine of the clock in the forenoon to which time this meeting stands adjourned

Adjourned to the above said time

Voted to Accept the form of Government as made by the Committe chosen for that purpose as read when the town met by adjournment

Waldoborough †

the 22 Day of May 1780

At a meeting legally cowled

Voted Capt David Urial Moderator

Voted. Not to send a Representative

Voted Not to Act on the form of Government

* Town records, Massachusetts Historical Society.

† Town records, Massachusetts Historical Society.

MIDDLESEX COUNTY

Acton (277/1)

At a legal Town Meeting on the 17th day of April 1780 to take into Consideration the Declaration of Rights and frame of Government proposed by the Honorable Convention begun and held at Cambridge on the first of September 1779, and continued by adjurnments to the 2d day of March 1780, which meeting being continued by adjournments to the 29th. Day of May, 1780—The town voted

Bill of Rights		Yeas	Nays
1	Voted to accept the Declaration of Rights except the second and third Articles 53 for 6 against	53	6
2d	Voted to accept the 2d Article 54 for—4 against	54	4
3d	Voted to accept the 3d Article 50 for 6 against	50	6
4	Voted to accept the first chapter of the frame of government 55 for 3 against	55	3
5	Voted to accept the first Section of the 2d Chapter 44 for 13 against N.B. These 13 objected principally to the ninth Article of said Section, respecting the governors appointing officers.	44	13
6	Voted to accept the 2d.3d. and 4d Sections of the 2d. Chapter 55 and 3	55	3
7	Voted to accept the 3d, 4th, and 5th Chapters 44 for —3 against	44	3
8	Voted to accept the 6th. Chapter except the 2d. and 10 Article 35 and 3	35	3
9	Voted to accept the 2d. Article of the 6th Chapter 33 for—5 against	33	5
10	Voted not to accept the 2d. Article of the 6th Chapter by 38	—	38

Because they would have the Constitution revised in 7 years after it shall be established—and would have no other Qualifications required of Voters at that Revision, than have been required in forming this Constitution

		Yeas	Nays
11	Voted to empower their Delegate to join with the Convension in establishing this Constitution, according to the Resolve of Convention of March 2d. 1780, unanimously by 36	36	

Acton, May the 29th. 1780

Francis Faulkner Samuel Parlin — Selectmen of the town of Acton

Articles Objected to

Bill of Rights

Article 2d. Objected to by 4, who desire that the first part of the last Clause may be left out, viz Provided they do not desturb the publick peace

Article 3d. Objected to by 6. Because they think it gives the civil government a power to interfere in matters of Religion which in their opinion is contrary to Reason and the word of God———

Form of Government

Chapter II Executive Power

Sexion Objected to by 13. Because some of whome would have the Governor impowered to [march?] the militia out of the State in pressing Cases, and most of them would not have him allowed to appoint civil officers.———

Chapter 6 Article 2d objected to by 5 because they would have no men allowed to act in the General Court who held a Commission under the State———

Acton

Ashby (277/2–3)

To the Honorable Convention chosen to form a new Constitution or form of Government for the State of Massachusetts Bay Agreable to your Honors Resolve We have laid the Constitution before the Inhabitants of this Town Legally Assembled in Town Meeting cald for that purpose and Voted as follows (Viz)

for the first article 51 against it 0

for the second article 27 against it 12 } the objectors reasons herewith

for the third article 16 against it 25 } annext.

for each of the following articles 17 and none against
Ashby June 2d. 1780

	Isaac Gregory	
	Asa Kendall	Select men
	John Lawrence Junr.	for
	Stephen Patch	Ashby

The Objections and Reasons

We Object against those words in the second Article, (the publick piece)——

We also Object against the Whole of the third Article;——

The reasons for our exception against those words——

The publick piece) in the Second, and for our rejection of the whole of the third Article, are as follows——

Reason the 1st: that all the Liberty and security which any religeous Society can resonably desire, is granted by the Legeslature, in the Second Article, without the words (the publick piece) which are there incerted, that said second Article stands clear and intelageble without these words —the publick piece)——

Reason 2 The third Article is inconsistant with the second for the second Article alows of no restraint upon any one as to their persons, liberty, or Estates, except in those words, objected to as above——

The third Article lays a restraint: for those who cannot Concientiously or Convenantly attend upon any publick teachers are under restraint as to their Estates and so injured as to their Liberty and property——

Reason 3 Religeous Societys as such have no voice in Chusing the Legeslature, the Legeslature therefore have no right to make Laws binding on them as such; every religeous Society, as such, is intirely independant on any body politick, the Legeslature therefore have no more right to make Laws Binding on them, as such, then the Court of Great Britton have to make Laws binding on the independant states of America——

Reason 4 as religeous Societys, and bodys politick, are bodys distinct and independant of each other, they have not aright therefore to make Laws binding on each other; how amaising absurd it would be for a number of persons in a Town to form into a religeous Society and in that Capacity make Laws or authorise others to make Laws binding on the Town as a body politick——

Reason 5 that which is of greatest importance ought not to be subordinated to that which is least the well being and prosperity of religeous

Society as such, is of greater importance, then that of politick bodys as such, the reason therefore which is given in the third Article for investing the Legeslature with authority to make Laws binding on religeous Societys as such is inconsistant and against the piece and welfare of the state—

Reason 6th. The Rivers of blood which has ran from the Veins of Marters! and all the torment which they have indured in the flames! was ocationed by the authority of Legeslature over religeous Society in consequence of the authority of the Legeslature or the authority arising from the authority of the Legeslature, the Feet of Paul and Silas where made fast in the stocks, the three Children Cast into the Furnace of fire, Daniel into the Lions Den, and many other such instances might be inumerated.———

Reason 7th. the third Article says the people of this common wealth have a right to invest their Legeslature with power to make Laws that are binding on religious Society as such (as we understand them) which is as much as to say we will not have Christ to reign over us that the Laws of his Kingdom are not sufficient to govern us, that the prosperity of his Kingdom is not eaqualy important with the Kingdoms of this world and that the Ark of God stands in need of Uzza's hand to keep it from falling to the ground, butt lett us attend sereously to this importent Truth that I will build My Church upon this Rock, and the Gates of Hell shall not prevail against it, now where resides this power in Christ only? or in the Legeslature?———it may be Objected agiainst the Reasons here given that it leaves people two Louse and does not ingadge them to there duty and therby all religion will fall to the ground and this Objection indeed is very plausable because it may flow from an outward zeal for a form of Godliness without the power butt is it not founded upon this supposition that men are not sufficiently ingadged to the practice of their Duty unless they doo somthing that God never required of them———He that made us reasonable Creatures and Conferred upon us the Blessing of the Gospell has by this frame and Situation laid us under the strongest Obligation to the practice of Piety, Religeon, and Morality, that can posibly be conceived and if this wont impress our minds to doe our Duty nothing will———

Bedford (277/4)

At a general Town Meeting of the Freeholders and other votable Inhabitants of the Town of Bedford Legally assembled on the Twenty fifth day of May last—to Consider and act upon the proposed form of Goverment and after hearing the said form of goverment Red—the Town Voted to adjourn for Further Considerration till the fifth of June Instant; June the fifth the Town meet and Voted to accept of the Form of Goverment as it Now Stands by 25 Voters—one only against it—but would Chuse that the Time of the Revision might bee sooner then Fifteen years; if the Convention shall Think propper to alter it———also Voted to Leave it to the Wisdom of the Convention to appoint the Time when the said Form of Goverment shall take place: a true copy of the proceedings of said town of Bedford By order of the Selectmen

William Meriam Town Clerk

Bedford June the 6d, 1780

Billerica (277/4)

At a Legall Town meeting of the free male Inhabitants of Billerica from twenty one years of age and upward on the 15th of May 1780, and Continued by adjournments to June 5th 1780———The Town took under consideration the Form of Government sent out by the Convention and axcepted every article—Except the article Respecting the Choice of Militia officers, we have left it with our Delagate in Convention to state our objections and the amendment which we shall Chuse, he will give the numbers voting for and against every article.
The town hath given him Instructions to act agreable to the Resolves of the Convention.

Joshua Abbot
William Tompson
Ephraim Crosby
Hezekiah Crosby

Selectmen of Billerica

Cambridge (277/5)

At a meeting of the Inhabitants of the Town of Cambridge (21 years of age and upwards) 8th May 1780 and held by adjournment to 22nd of the same, to consider the proposed new Frame of Government, and to Choose other Deligates to meet in convention on the first Wednesday in June next if they see fit———

43 present—41 Voted the following instructions———

Sir By our Choice of you to represent us in the approaching convention for establishing a Constitution or form of Government you become the Medium thro which our Objections are to be made to that Form already proposed.—

We therefore instruct you to use your Endeavours to procure an Erasement of the clause, in the 4th Article of the 1st Section, of the first Chapter of the Constitution impowering the General Court to impose and levy Duties and Excises upon any Produce goods Wares Merchandize and Commodities whatsoever, brought into produced, manufactured or being within the Commonwealth.—Because we conceive such a power to be oppressive and dangerous to the Subjects of the State.—

It is oppressive as employing a great number of Persons to collect the Revenue, who will swallow up a considerable part of it, and who will have the most favourable Opportunities to carry on iniquitous Practices without being detected.—It is likewise oppressive as the money is raised upon the Consumer, and instead of being a Tax upon Trade, much more Cosiderable sums of Money are taken from the Consumers, and thrown into the Hands of the Sellers, than would otherwise be transferred, because the sellers will put their Advance upon the money they pay as Excise, in addition to the Advance upon the Articles of sale— It is also oppressive as the Officers must necessarily be trusted with a right to make a forcible entry into the most retired apartments; for if they have not this power the widest door will be opened for perjury— It is dangerous to the Liberty of the Subjects as Government must of course be trusted with unknown sums of Money and sums which from their own nature must be uncertain, and by means of this money they may secure such influence as may subvert the Liberty we have purchased at so dear a Rate.———

You are also instructed to obtain an insertion of a Clause in the 2nd Article of the 6th Chapter of the Constitution, whereby settled Teachers of morality etc. and all persons whatever, who do not pay Taxes shall be excluded from a Seat in the House of Representatives—Because those persons, who bear no part of the public burden, cannot be such competent Judges of the Ability of the People to pay Taxes, as those who might support their part—And as to the exclusion of settled Teachers of Morality etc: let it suffice to say that we think them very important officers in the State, and that the community must suffer much from having so great a number employed in Services so distinct from their particular offices, as undoubtedly will be provided the insertion be not made— At the same time we are not unwilling that Gentlemen of this Order of shining abilities, should be introduced into superior departments, by the suffrages of the People at large.——

However we do not mean to be so strenuous in our Objections as to decline receiving the whole as it stands, provided in the opinion of the Convention the Amendments ought not to be made—Accordingly we being willing to give up our own opinion in lesser matters in order to obtain a Government whose authority may not be disputed, and which we wish may soon be established, do instruct and direct you in our name and behalf to ratify and confirm the proposed Form, whether the Amendments be made or not——

Hon. Abraham Watson Esq. Deligate for Convention
A true Coppy Attest.

Tho. Farrington Town Clerk

Charlestown (277/6)

Town Meeting in Charlestorn June 9, 1780 Twenty One present——
Voted the 3d Article in the Bill of Rights 16 for it and 5 against it——
Voted Unanimously against the Ninth Article for this Reason.
No Person that dont pay Publick Taxes ought to be Chosen into the House of Representatives—or Senate
All the other Articles passed Unanimously in the affirmative.

Nath. Gorham
Timo. Tufts [?]
Samuel Swan Selectmen of Charlestown

Chelmsford (277/7)

In Compliance With the Resolve of the Honarible Convention To us Directed Wee the Subscribers the Selectmen of the town of Chelmsford Caused the Inhabitants of said Town to be assembled on the fifteenth Day of May Last for the purpos of taking into Consideration the Form of Goverment Lately Composed by said Convention——

Then said Town proceeded as followeth the said form of Goverment was then taken into Consideration and Read at said meeting and after some Debates the said Town Voted to adjorn said meeting for further Consideration. Said Meeting being adjorned To the Twenty fifth Day of said month then the Inhabitants of the Town met according to adjornment and took into Consideration the said form of Government and proceeded to hear the same Read and further Considered therof and then Voted to adjorn to the Twenty Ninth of said May———

then the Inhabitants met according to adjornment and proceded as foloweth———

Voted to take the Constitution into Consideration artical by artical then proceeded artical by artical through the whole of the Constitution and unanomisly Excepted of the same as it Came out from the Honorable Convention Excepting Eight persons by their votes objected against the third artical in the bill of Rights. But gave no Reasons for their objections and also the Town Unanomosly voted that the word Christian be Dealed and the word prodestant be Constituted in Sted theirof in all places wheir that word is yused in the qualification of officers.

Their being at said Meeting Ninety five of said Inhabitants present and acting in said meeting with the addition of Eight of said Inhabitants which was Nesesoruly Called away upon said Day which had attended the two former Meetings and heard the Constitution Red and Debated and desireed the favour that their Votes Might be taken in favour of said Constitution as it stands with the amendment proposed which is within mentioned.

With Respect to the Time when the Constitution or form of Goverment shall Take place Wee Refer to our Delegates To join with the Delegates of the Honorable Convention in establishing the same as sone as may be with Conveniance———

Chelmsford June 5th 1780

Oliver Barron
Samuel Stevens Jr. Selectmen of
Daniel Procter Chelmsford
Benja. Spaulding

To Samuel Barrit Esqr
Secretary of Said Convention

Concord (277/8)

At a Meeting of the Inhabitents of the Town of Concord of those free and twenty years of age Regurly assembled on Monday the 22d day of May Last and Continued by adjournment until the 29th. Then Met and taking under Consideration the Frame of Government for the State of Massachusetts Bay as formed by Convention a Copy of which was sent to the Town of Concord to be Laid before the Inhabitents thereof for their approving or Disapproving the same.

According the said Constitution or form of Government was Read, a motion was then Made that the Consideration of the same might be article by article which was Done accordingly, those being Present in the Meeting 147 voters———

The Declaration of the Rights Passed unanimously Except the Second and third articles, the 2d. having two only that was Contrary minded, the third Eight

The Frame of Government Passed unanimously Except a few alterations and amendments Proposed which are as follows

In the first Chapter 3d Section 2d article it is thus Proposed for an amendment that those Incorporated Town who have not 150 Ratable poles shall nevertheless have a right to associate with some other Town or Town adjoining for the Election of a Representative and in such case the voters thus united shall have a right to Elect the same Number of representatives as they would have Done were they Inhabitants of one Corporate Town, which Representatives may be elected out of Either of the associated Town Indiffrantly: and the Legislature shall from time to time Determine what Town shall thus associate, the manner of the association, and the method and manner of Calling and Conducting the meetings of the associated Towns for the Election of Representative, if this amendment Does not take place there will be many in the State not represented———

2 Chapter 1 Section: The word Christian erased and the word Protestant Incerted.———

2 Chapter 3 Section 2 article the Choice of Councelors Should be Confined to those Returned as senators; or there is Danger of the Number of Senators being two Large.

Chapter 6. 1 article the word Christian erased and the word Protestant Incerted—

The Town Leaving with their Deligates when asembled with Deligates from other Towns in Convention, in their Wisdom to agree upon a time when the form of Government which has now been under consideration shall take place, without it being Returned to the Town of Concord again. Copy of Proceeding of the Town of Concord

Concord June the 5th 1780 By order of the Selectmen

Ephraim Wood Jur Town Clerk

Dracut (277/9)

At a Meeting of the Freeholders and other Inhabitants of the Town of Dracutt Legally Assembled at the Meeting-house in said Town on the 11th day of May 1780—For the Purpose of Considering the Several Articals Set forth in the Late Purposed Fraim of Government, after Reading and duly Considering the same, Fifty voters in said Meeting thirty five of which Voted in favour of said Fraim in the Groce the other fifteen not for nor against said fraim———

Dracutt May the 11th 1780

J. Varnum
Joseph Varnum, jr. Selectmen of Dracutt

Dracutt the 11th May 1780 The town of Dracutt at a meeting Leagally Assembled on the day above Written for the porpose of Considering the late purposed Fraim of Government Made choice of the Reverend Nathan Davis (in Sted of Deacon Amos Bradley) to Represent said Town in the Convention for the Purpose of Fraiming and further Considering said Fraim with the several Return etc———to be Held at Boston on the first Wensday of June Next.

A true Coppy Attest William Hildreth
Town Clerk

Dunstable (277/10)

At a Legul Meating of the freeholders and other Inhabitan[ts] of the town of Dunstable on the 15th day of May 1780———at which time the form of goverment agreed upon by the Late Convention was Red after which said meeting was Continued by adjurnment to Tuesday 30th Instant when some objections arose to said form of government which ware these that follow:———

1st. was touching the second and third articles of the Decleration of right in the second it is said that no subject shall be hurt molested or restrained for worshiping god in the maner and season most agreable to his own conscience provided he Doth not Dissturbe the publick peace or obstruct others in there religious worship; and in the third we find that Every denomination of Christions Demening them selves peasablely and as good subjects to the Common Welth shall be Equelly under the Protection of the law to which was objected and said that these Sentances are so general as to Engage full Protection to the Idalatrous worshippers of the Church of Rome therefore they wore not Clear in their judgment to give so much Incoragement to Idol worship as to Engage any full protection in their Idolatry for if the goverment should not Disturbe such in their protended worship it would be as much as they might Expect without our being under special obligation to protect them there in by the laws of the land——The Question being put there appeared 23 for anmemnent on these article: and none against it——

2d: objection was the 16th article in said bill of rights as to the liberty of the press as there being no restraint thereon it may be made use of to the Dishoner of god by printing herasy and so forth and like wise injurious to private Charactors;—upon the Question 26 for anmenment and none for the article as it now stands——

3d Objection was to haveing so large a number Counsellors and Senators as forty whare as twenty Eight under the former Constitution they understood answered Every purpous required that body upon the Question there appeared 12 for anmenment

4th Objection was Reletive to the governers power in marching the militia to any part of the state without the advice or consent of any the amenment Purposed was that when ever the governer should judge it needful to march the militia from and about Boston more then one Hundred miles it shall be by and with the Consent of his Council and not otherwise and by the same advice and Consent shall have full powers to march them to the assistance of the Neighbering states in the recess of the general Court for the amenment [91?] appeared

5th. Objection was to the apointment of all judicial officers the attorney General the Salicitor General all Shriffs Coroners Registors of Probats Resting in the hands of the governer and council the amenment Purposed was this that as they held it as a right therefore it aught to be put into the hands of the people at large to Chuse them the Question being put there appeared 7 for the amenment and 6 against any amenment.

6th. Objection was to the Declaration to be made and subscribed by the governer Lieutenant governer Council and house of Representatives before they Proseed to Execute the Duties of their office which is to Declare themselves to be of the Christian reglion reasons offered for said objections ware these that thereby the goverment would not be confined to Protestants: upon the Question there appered 19 for an amenment and none in the Negative——

7th. Objection was to the form of the Oath Precribed the amenment Purposed was this to have the words by the living god added as is Required in his word there appeared 13 for the amenment and not one to the Contrary———

8th Objection was that the Denomination of People Called Qakers being admitted to office upon affirmation without taking the oath in manner and form as Required of others upon the Question thare appeared 10 against this article and not one in favour of it———

9th. Objection was to the time Purposed for the Revisal of the Constitution if it should take place: the mendment Purpased was that Precepts be issued for the Choyce of Delegates for that purpous by the general Cort in seven years from this time: the Question being put Unamously agread to———

The Question was then put wheather the town would approve of said form of goverment if amended by the Convention (for substance) as Pointed out in this Return when there appeared 13 in favour of it taking place and none to the contery.———

Dunstable may the 30th, 1780

Joel Parkhurst	Select men
Nathl Holdin	of
Jona Fletcher	said
John Parham	Town
Simeon Cumings	

East Sudbury (277/11)

At a Town Meeting in East Sudbury Legally Worned on May Twenty fourth 1780 and Adjorned to May the Twenty ninth; at Said Adjournment it was put to Vote to See if the Town woold accept of the Constitution agreed on by a Late Convention; Twenty Two Voters present, Thirteen of which Voted to accept of the said Constitution with the amendment, or alteration that there shoold be a Convention Certainly Called in the Teirm of Ten Years, to make Such Alterations as at that Time shoold be thought Necessary or proper by the People———

A true coppy from the files of said Meeting

By order of the Selectmen

E. Sudbury May 29th, 1780

Joseph Curtis Town Clerk

Framingham (277/12)

At a Legal Town Meeting in Framingham on the 5th Day of June 1780———Agreable to the request of the Honourable Convention the Inhabitants of the Town Voted as follows Viz. Accepted the first article of the rights of the Inhabitants of Massachusetts Bay—107 voters no nays.
101 In favor of Article 2d. 6 against it—
113 In favor of the 3d. article 18 against it 10 not acting
141 In favor of Articles 4th 5 6 7 8th no nays
121 In favor of the 9 Article 17 against it 3 not acting
138 In favor of Article 10th 3 against it 1 not acting
141 In favor of Article 11th to 30th———
138 In favor of the 1st Section on legislative power 3 against it.
68 In favor of the 2d. Section 12 against it
79 for Choosing Senators agreble to the 2d Section
79 In favor of Article 3d to the 9th.
79 Objected to the 2d Article in the 3 Section—4 in favor
68 in favor of Article 3d———
79 Objected to the 4th Article in Chapter 1st Section 3d.

Then the Meeting was adjourned till to morrow one o Clock at this Place—June 6th 1780 The Inhabitants of the Town met according to adjournment———
15 In favor of Section 5th to 11th in Chapter 1st Section 3rd.
35 In favor of Article 2d Chapter 2d Section 1st on Executive Power
33 In favor of Article 3.—Ditto 2 nays
35 In favor of Article 4th—Chapter Ditto
36 in favor of Article 5th to 13th Ditto
36 in favor of Chapter 3d on judiciary power no nays
36 in favor of Chapter 4th Delegates to Congress no nays
38 in favor of Chapter 5th the university at Cambridge
32 in favor of Chapter Encouragement of Literature 6 nays 1 not acting
32 in favor of Chapter Encouragement of Literature 6 nays 1 not acting
General Court think necessary there may be a Convention Sooner than is proposed or as soon as they think necessary

A true coppy from the minutes
Lawson Buckminster Town Clerk

To the Honorable Convention for framing a Constitution of government

We who are inhabitants of Framingham, having considered the 3d. article in the declaration of rights, are bound in conscience to reject it for the following reasons, which are contained in the Boston Gazette of May 22. 1780 [see below, pp. 645 ff.]; and express the mind of the minority in that town; with the following additions to the 5 and 7 objections. viz. To the 5 objection we add these words—[On the clipping from the *Boston Gazette* accompanying the return, the place where the additions to the 5th and 7th objections were to be made was indicated, apparently by the town clerk, by a caret.]

To which it may be added, That it may so happen that the church may be the *minority,* if so the whole power of choosing the ministers will be taken from the church, in whom it solely resides and placed in the hands of the majority, or of those men who are not members of the church and consequently have no right to control the church in the choice of its minister,—To the 5 objection

To be added to the 7th objection—Nor is that all, but they who pay no taxes themselves, will have it in their power to tax the people. Thus may they bind heavy burdens, which will be grievous to be borne, while they themselves will not touch them with one of their fingers.

Reasons of objection to the 2nd artical of the first Chapter and third Section in the Second Parte of the form of Govenment———

is that the Inhabatance Voting in the Large towns have Greater Proportion of Representation than is Just in Proportion to a small town as each town having a Seprerite Intrest or an Intrest that may Be in dispute Between a Large town and a small town it will Be unequal as the Providion is in said artical as some towns can have ten Representatives other towns but one

We would Propos an alteration viz—after the Number for the Second —Representation Dobble the Number of Pols for Every incriesing Representation.—

Reason of objection to the 4 articel of the Second Part of the form of Goverment first Chapter 3d Section———

We say that Every male Person being twenty one year of age and Resident in any Perticuler town in this Common Wealth for the space of one year and Rated in said town has an Essential Right to Vote in the Choice of a Representative or Representatives without the annual income of three Pounds or any Estate of the Value of sixty Pounds as Life Liberty and Personal Property is Conserned with and Efected by the act of the Representatives.

[From *Boston Gazette,* sent by Framingham. For variations in the text as given in the Boston town records, see below, pp. 752 ff.]

Boston, May 22

The following is the Report of the Commitee on the 3d Article of the Bills of Rights, in the late Constitution Sent out for the Revision and Correction of the Inhabitants of this State, as accepted by this Town.

3rd Article. As the happiness of a people, and the good order and preservation of civil government essentially depend upon piety, religion and morality; and as these cannot be generally diffused through a community, but by the public worship of GOD, and public instructions in piety, religion and morality: Therefore, to promote their happiness, and to secure the good order and preservation of their government, the people of this commonwealth have a right to invest their legislature with power to authorize and require, and the legislature shall, from time to time, authorise and require all the inhabitants of this commonwealth to make provision, at their own expence, for the public worship of GOD, and for the support and maintenance of public protestant teachers of piety, religion and morality, who have not made such provision voluntarily, or who have not made voluntary provision for some other public religious teacher, or for the support of some other public worship, within this common wealth.

And the several towns, parishes, precincts, and other bodies-politic, or religious societies, shall at all times, have the exclusive right of electing their public teachers, and of contracting with them for their support and maintenance: provided nevertheless, that the minority of such towns, parishes, precincts and other bodies politic or religious societies, shall not be bound by the voice of the majority in their electing their public teachers, or contracting with them for their support, but such minority may, if they see fit, elect some other public religious teacher and support him.

And all monies assessed upon the subject for the support of public worship, and of public religious teachers, shall, if he requires it, be uniformly applied to the support of the public teacher or teachers, or the public worship which he may choose.

1st Objection. The first part of the third article was objected to, which is this——"Whereas the happiness of a people and the good order and preservation of civil government essentially depend on piety, religion, and morality"——It was proved by several expressions in the article, that by *religion* we are to understand *christianity;* consequently the porposition stands thus—That the *preservation of civil government essentially depends on christianity*———This was denied for this plain reason, That civil government was in the world before the coming of Christ; and that there were excellent commonwealths among the ancient Greeks and Romans, while they were totally ignorant of christianity. If therefore civil government existed and flourished before christianity was revealed to the world, it cannot in reason be said *essentially* to depend upon it.

2d. Objection The next objection was made against the *Right* which the people of this commonwealth are said to have, to invest their Legislature with power to authorize and require the several towns———and religious societies to make suitable provision at their own expence, for the institution of the public worship of GOD, and for the maintenance of the public protestant teachers of piety religion, and morality, in all cases where such provision shall not be made voluntarily. To this paragraph it was objected, that this right is of the religious kind: it has respect to christian worship, and to the choice and maintenance of the ministers of Christ; and as such is one of those rights that is unalienable, and which no man can transfer to another. It is most certainly *a right of conscience,* and as such, not transferable to any man, or body of men whatever. A right this, which the people cannot be brought to be willing to part with, even supposing it possible to alienate it, unless they are infatuated to a great degree.

3d. Objection It was also said by way of objection that the people have no right to invest the Legislature with power to *authorize* and *require religious societies,* etc. *because by religious societies* we are to understand the *churches of Christ* which churches can receive no authority, nor be subject to any requisition of any Legislature under Heaven; seeing Christ himself is the sole head of his church, or fountain of authority in it.

To which the objectors added—that Christ as Head of his Church, had *amply furnished* it with all those laws which are necessary for its well-being and government: and among the rest for the maintenance of his ministers. If so, no new laws of mere human contrivance are wanted, but realy that we should yield a punctual obedience to the laws which Christ has given already; which laws, as they are derived from the only proper authority, so they are exactly suited to the nature of the spiritual kingdom of Christ. Here undeniable facts were mentioned; such as, that the primitive preachers of the gospel 'till the days of Constantine, were supported upon this plan—that the ministers of the dissenting churches in England, Ireland and America, have been and now are maintained without the help of the civil law. If they have been thus supported, it was said, so might the ministers of the churches of New England be maintained.

4th Objection. The second paragraph of the 3d article, empowers the legislature to enjoin upon all the subjects an attendance on the instructions of the public teachers, provided they can *conveniently and conscientiously attend*. Here it was asked, who shall be the judge, whether the subjects can conveniently and conscientiously attend? It was found that the jury were to be judges in this matter. Consequently a man for non-attendance on the public teachers, will be liable to be prosecuted at common law, and a jury to be empowered to determine not only a matter of convenience, but a matter of conscience. To this it was said, this people will not submit.

5th. Objection. The third paragraph empowers towns etc. to elect a teacher, and to contract with him for his support. By towns the *majority* of the inhabitants are intended; consequently the *majority* would have it in their power to chuse a minister for the *minority:* and oblige them to support him. This was objected to as a most barefaced oppression, ^ because every man has certainly as much right at least to chuse his religious teacher, as he has to chuse his own lawyer or physician.^

6th. Objection. The fourth paragraph obliges a man to pay his money to support a teacher from whom he consienciously dissents, provided he should be so situated that he cannot attend upon a teacher of his own denomination. This was objected to as unjust; because no man's money can of right be taken from him without his consent, or without an adequate compensation for it.

7th. Objection. It was also said that this 3d article makes the ministers of Christ dependent ultimately on the Legislature for their support, and thereby lays a foundation for a combination between the Legislature and the teachers of religion, which at some future period, may prove fatal to the liberties of the people. But what renders this matter more alarming is, that the teachers of religion are by the constitution left eligible into places of civil government. Let us suppose then that at any given period, the minister, or a large number of them, should be sent as Representatives to the General Court, they will then have it in their power as members of the Court, to superintend their own salaries as teachers of religion—^ This is a dangerous part of the constitution.

8th. Objection. The article in the general was objected against, as calculated to blend the church of Christ and the State together; which two societies are infinitely different from each other. This distinction between the church and commonwealth was proved by the words of Christ, *My kingdom is not of this world.* In support of the disctinction, Locke, Milton, and several other writers of the first character were quoted.

Groton (277/14)

The Committee appointed to Consider of the Propriety of the amendments proposed in the Form of Government by a Number of the Inhabitants of the Town of Groton beg leave to report

1. That they are of opinion that the Legislative Power of the Common Wealth ought to Consist of three Branches the Governor being one Branch thereof and vested with the power of a Negative upon all Laws and Acts of Legislation passed by the Senate and House—which power being in the hands of the Governor will have a manifest Tendency to prevent the other Branches from making dangerous encroachments upon the Executive and Judicial Departments, preserve a proper Balance in the three Capital powers of Government and make the Acts of Legislation more systematical and Coherent——and further that as the Governor is the Representative of the whole People and the first Magistrate of the Common Wealth there never can be a vigorous Execution of, and a due obedience in the People to those Laws which are passed against his Consent——

2 That it will be safer for the Government, less expensive to the People, and more conducive to the Expedition of the public business, to have the Consel chosen by the Senate and House at large; and in that Case thirty one Senators will be a Sufficient Number.

3 That there is the same reason for the Commisary Generals holding his office but five years successively, as for the Treasurers holding his no Longer.

4 that it would not be prudent or safe to suffer any Person to be commissioned and sworn to a Civil office unless he is known and reputed to be a Protestant—and that the Governor and all Civil officers by him Commissioned shall previous to their Entering upon the duties of their offices Respectively declare themselves to be of the Protestant Christian

Religion according to the Common acceptation of the words in this Country.

5 that the Power given the Legislative Body to encrease the pecuniary qualifications of their members is unnecessary because there will be frequent revisions of the Constitution by the People themselves, and dangerous, because that if at any Time the majority of the general Court should Consist of men of the first fortunes they may pass such Laws as will Exclude men of Common condition from a seat which will manifestly tend to destroy the Liberties of the People, and that therefore the Power above mentioned ought to be struck out of the Constitution.

6 that although under the new form of Government when adopted offences must be laid in Indictments and other processes to be done against the Peace of the Common Wealth if Committed after the Establishment of this Form, yet that those offences which shall have been Committed before such Establishment may thereafter be laid to have been done against the Government in being at the time when the same was Committed

7 your Committee being deeply impressed with an apprehension that the great and important Right of delivery by Habeas Corpus may be hereafter unjustly and cruelly Suspended by the Legislature and being of opinion that so great and necessary a remedy ought to be at all times as easily obtained as is consistant with the safety of Government, do report that they think that the Suspension of the Right of Habeas Corpus should not opperate against any one Subject after the Superiour Court hath Set Two Terms in the County where the offence is alledged to have been Committed if any offence is alledged—and where the Person Committed is not charged with any offence it shall not opperate against him after the same Court hath set two terms in the County where he is Committed, but that in Either Case he shall be delivered before the Second Term is over

8 that if Sixty members Should Constitute a quorum of the House of Representatives Laws affecting the Lives and Interest of the Subject might be passed by thirty one votes only—and yet if a Large number Should be made necessary there might be a delay in business of importance upon the whole therefore your Committee beg leave to propose that Eighty members at least should be necessary to make a quorum of the House

9 that as many defects may appear in the Form when it comes to be practiced upon, which are unseen at this Time therefore a Revision ought

to take place in the year one thousand seven hundred and ninety—and that the Convention make provision for future Revisions as frequently as may be for the Interest of the People

10 that Ministers of the Gospel and Persons hired and employed by Towns or Parishes as Teachers of morality ought to be excluded a seat in the Legislature because they cannot be spared from their Parishes without great inconvenience to the Persons under their Instructions and because as they pay no Taxes themselves they ought not to have a voice in Taxing other People

13
67
for 80 49 against

The question being put upon the first Article in the Declaration of Rights voted to accept the same Ninety Eight in the affirmative forty four against it.

Upon the Second Article in the Declaration of Rights passed in the affirmative Seventy seven against thirty four

the third Article passed Seventy three for and fifty three against

the fourth Article passed ninety for and forty nine against it

the other Twenty Six articles were passed Eighty for and Sixty against them

the aforegoing Report of the Committee was accepted Eighty for and forty nine against it

Voted to accept of the Form of Government with the amendments in the aforegoing Report of the Committee Ninety against Sixty-Two

Then a motion was made and Seconded that although the amendments proposed by this Town appear to them to be of importance yet as a Revision is soon to take place, this Town agrees that if two thirds of the male Inhabitants of this State qualified to vote on this Subject and who have assembled in town meeting including the Inhabitants of this town voting herefor, shall agree to accept the Form of Government as compiled by the Convention that in Such Case the Convention shall appoint the time and provide measures for carrying the same into full Exercise

passed in the affirmative sixty nine again[st]—sixty two

The aforegoing contains the doings of the Town of Groton at a Legal meeting of the male Inhabitants qualified to vote upon the subject held upon the Twenty ninth Day of May 1780 by adjournment on the Monday following

The foregoing is proceedings of the town of Groton upon the [late] form of government or Constitution

Groton June 5th, 1780 Attest. Isaac Farnsworth Town Clerk

Holliston (277/15)

At a Legal Meeting of the Male Inhabitants of the town of Holliston of the age of Twenty one years and upwards, begun and held at the Public Meeting house in said Town on Monday May the 8th 1780 and Continued by adjournments to June the 5th 1780.

1st Captain Staples Chamberlin was Unanimously Chosen Moderater

2ly The Constitution and Frame of Government agreed upon by the Delegates of the People of the State of Massachusetts Bay begun and held at Cambridge on the first of September 1779 and Continued by Adjournments to the Second of March 1780 was Read before the Town After the said Constitution and Frame of Government was Read and Maturely Deliberated The Proceedings of the Town thereon and Votes that were passed with the Number of Persons Who Voted on Each Side of Every Question are as follows——viz.

Part the first

A Declaration of Rights of the Inhabitants of the Common Wealth of Massachusetts

the 1st and 2d Articles were Read and the Question was put whether the Town do accept the said Articles. It passed in the Affirmative

61 for the 1st article

57 for the 2d article

The 3d. Article was Read and the Question was put whether the Town do accept the same——It passed in the Negative 23 for said article and 50 against it.

It was moved that a Committee be appointed to take said article into Consideration. Voted That Colonel Abner Perry Captain Samuel Bullard and Mr. Timothy Rockwood be the Committee——

who Reported as follows

As the Happiness of a People and the good order and Preservation of Civil Government Essentially Depends upon Piety Religion and Morality and as these cannot be generally Defused through a Community but by the Institution of the Public Worship of God and of Public Instruction in Piety Religion and morality therefore to promote their happiness and to secure the good order and preservation of their Government the

People of the Common Wealth have a Right to invest their Legislature with Power to authorize and require and the Legislature shall from time to time authorize and require the Several Towns Parishes Precincts and other Bodies Politic or Religious Societies to make Suitable provision at their own expence for the Institution of the Public Worship of God and for the Support and maintenance of Public protestant Teachers of Piety Religion and Morality in all Cases where such provision shall not be made Voluntarily—provided notwithstanding that the Several Towns Parishes Precincts and other Bodies Politic or Religious Societies shall at all times have the Exclusive Right of Electing their own Public Teachers and of Contracting with them for their support and maintenance and all monies paid by the subject to the support of Public Worship and of the Public Teachers aforesaid shall if he require it be uniformly applied to the support of the Public Teacher or Teachers provided there be any on whose Instructions he attends—otherwise it may be paid towards the Support of the Teacher or Teachers of the Parish or Precinct in which the said monies are raised. And Every Denomination of Christians Demeaning themselves peaceably and as good subjects of the Common Wealth shall be Equally under the protection of the Law and no Subordination of any one Sect or Denomination to another shall ever be Established by Law.———

Which Report was Read and the Question being put whether the Town do accept the same———It passed in the Negative 14 for the report and 18 for the article—without any amendment and there was 21 that rejected the article and report (The Objections of a Number of Persons were the same that are mentioned in The Boston Gazette and the Country Journal
Printed Monday May the 22d: 1780)
The 4th, 5th, 6th, 7th, 8th, 9th, 10th, 11th, 12th, 13th, 14th, 15th, 16th, 17th, 18th, 19th, 20th, 21st, 22d, 23d, 24th, 25th, 26th, 27th, and 28th Articles were Read and the Question was put whether the Town do accept the Said articles, it passed in the affirmative

44 for the 4th article
44 for the 5 article
48 for the 6 article
47 for the 7 article
50 for the 8 article
50 for the 9 article
50 for the 10 article
50 for the 11 article
51 for the 12 article
52 for the 13 article
52 for the 14 article
53 for the 15th article
53 for the 16 article
53 for the 17 article
53 for the 18 article
53 for the 19 article

53 for the 20 article
53 for the 21st article
53 for the 22d article
53 for the 23d article
52 for the 24th article
54 for the 25 article
54 for the 26 article
54 for the 27 article
55 for the 28 article

The 29th article was Read and the Question was put whether the Town do accept the same—It passed in the Negative——17 for said article and 36 against it——It was moved that a Committee be appointed to take said article into Consideration and report Voted that Captain Samuel Bullard Mr. Joshua Hemenway and Colonel Abner Perry be the Committee——

who reported as follows

The People have a natural and most Essential Right of Giving and Granting and appropriating their own property and of Judging of the Merits of their own Servants——Grants have from time to time been made to Civil Officers of this State——Salaries Ascertained by Standing Laws must therefore be very unnecessary if not Dangerous—— which Report was Read and the Question being put whether the Town do accept the same—It passed in the affirmative 32 for the Report and 2 against it——

The 30th. Article was Read and the Question was put whether the Town do accept the same it passed in the affirmative 58 for said article——

Part the Second——The Frame of Government

The People inhabiting the territory formerly called the Province of Massachusetts Bay do hereby Solemnly and mutually agree with Each other to form themselves into a free sovereign and independent body politic or State by the name of The Common Wealth of Massachusetts ——Read and accepted

---

Chapter First The Legislative Power——

Section 1st The General Court——

The articles in this Section were Read and the Question was put whether the Town do accept the said articles It passed in the Affirmative——

61 for the 1st article
61 for the 2d article
61 for the 3d article
65 for the 4th article

Chapter First Section 2d Senate——

The articles in this Section were Read and the Question was put whether the Town do accept the said articles It passed in the affirmative——

60 for the 1st article
60 for the 2d article
60 for the 3d article
60 for the 4th article
60 for the 5th article
60 for the 6th article
60 for the 7th article
60 for the 8th article
60 for the 9 article

Chapter First Section 3d House of Representatives
The 1st Article was read and the Question being put whether the Town do accept the same—It passed in the Affirmative———60 for said article———
The 2d Article was Read and the Question being put whether the Town do accept the same it passed in the Negative 10 for said Article and 27 against it———
It was moved that a Committee be appointed to take said article into Consideration and report
Voted that Lieutenant Samuel Whiting Mr. Timothy Rockwood and Mr. Robert Mellon be that Committee———

Who Reported as follows———

Having considered of the Representation etc. We find that it will be very unequal for there will be many Towns that will not have Rateable Polls to Elect three Representatives and many more than the Number proposed to Elect Two———We therefore propose that after the Two first Representatives mentioned in the said Second article the mean increasing Number for every Additional Representative may be 450 Rateable Polls that pay taxes—which Report was Read and the Question being put whether the Town do accept the same—It passed in the Affirmative—32 for the report and 2 against it———

The 3d. 4th. 5th. 6th. 7th. and 8th. Articles were Read and the Question being put whether the Town do accept the said articles. It passed in the Affirmative

38 for the 3d article
38 for the 4th article
38 for the 5 article
38 for the 6th article
38 for the 7 article
38 for the 8 article

The 9th article was Read and It was moved that the Committee who were to Consider of the 2d Article Take this article into Consideration and report
The said Committee reported as follows
Not less than Eighty members of the House of Representatives ought to Constitute a quorum for doing Business———We Being of Opinion that

60 is too small a Number to Constitute a Quorum at any time——
Which Report was Read and the Question being put whether the Town do accept the same—It passed in the Affirmative 33 for the Report and 1 against it——
The 10th and 11th Articles were Read and the Question was put whether the Town do accept the said articles—It passed in the affirmative
27 for the 10th article
27 for the 11 article

Chapter Second Executive Power Section 1st
Governor——
The 1st Article was Read and the Question being put whether the Town do accept the same It passed in the affirmative 27 for said article——
The 2d Article was Read and the Question being put whether the Town do accept the same It passed in the Negative—29 against said Article. The Question was then put whether the Town do accept said article with the amendment that the Governor Declare himself to be of the Christian protestant Religion—It passed in the Affirmative—29 for said Article with the amendment——
The 3d. 4th. 5th. 6th. 7th. and 8th articles were Read and the Question was put whether the Town do accept the said articles—It passed in the affirmative

29 for the 3d article
29 for the 4th article
29 for the 5 article
29 for the 6th article
34 for the 7 article
34 for the 8 article

The 9th article was Read and the Question was put whether the Town do accept the same It passed in the Negative 35 against said Article——
It was moved that a Committee be appointed to take said article into Consideration and report
Voted that Colonel Abner Perry Captain John Lealand Mr. Timothy Rockwood Mr. Robert Mellen Lieutenant Samuel Whiting be the Committee——
Who Reported as follows
In the Constitution Chapter Second Section first article 9th. The Governor with the Advice and Consent of the Council shall nominate and appoint all Judicial Officers——

We as a Town Claim it as our right to choose a Justice of the Peace and that the Governor and Council Cannot with so much propriety Nominate and appoint a Justice as the People Can for this Reason because they Cannot be so Suitable a judge being at a Distance as the People Can where they Live——after the People have Nominated The Governor——shall Commissionate the Justice in Like manner as he does the Militia Officers——

And Furthermore as a Town We Claim it as our Right to Choose a person to do the Probate Business for this Reason because it will be a means not only of preventing the Expence of Travelling but preventing Great Cost that many times arises by Persons being Obliged to Lye upon Charge to get their Business done or Making another Journey

Which Report being Read the Question was put whether the Town do accept the same—It passed in the Affirmative 32 for the Report and 3 against it——

The 10th, 11th, and 12th articles were Read and the Question was put whether the Town do accept said articles. It passed in the Affirmative——

12 for the 10th article
33 for the 11 article
34 for the 12 article

The 13th Article Read and the Question was put whether the Town do accept the same It passed in the Negative 4 for said article and 30 against it.——

Voted that Captain John Lealand Join with Colonal Abner Perry and Mr. Joshua Hemenway and be a Committee to take said article into Consideration and Report——The said Committee reported as follows ——The People have a Natural and most Essential Right of Giving and Granting and appropriating their own Property and of Judging of the merits of their own Servants Grants have from time to time been made to Civil Officers of this State. Salaries Ascertained by Standing Laws must be very unnecessary if not Dangerous Therefore all Civil Officers Salaries should be Granted as Usual——

Which Report being Read the Question was put whether the Town do accept the same——It passed in the Affirmative 32 for the Report and 2 against it——

Chapter Second Section Second——

Lieutenant Governor——

The articles in this Section were Read and the Question was put whether the Town do Accept the same——It passed in the Affirmative

40 for the 1st article

40 for the 2d article——
40 for the 3 article——

Chapter Second Section Third——
Council and the manner of Settling Elections by the Legislature——
The articles in this Section were Read and the Question was put whether the Town do accept the same It passed in the Affirmative——

43 for the 1st article
43 for the 2d article
43 for the 3 article
44 for the 4th article
44 for the 5 article
44 for the 6 article
45 for the 7 article

Chapter Second Section fourth
Secretary Treasurer Commissary etc.——
The articles in This Section—Read and the Question was put whether the Town do accept the same——It passed in the Affirmative——
45 for the 1st article
45 for the 2d article

Chapter third Judiciary Power——
The 1st, 2d and 3d Articles were Read and the Question was put whether the Town do accept the said articles—It passed in the Affirmative
16 for the 1st article
45 for the 2 article—
45 for the 3 article—
The 4th article was Read and the Question was put whether the Town do accept the same. It passed in the Negative 2 for the article and 32 Against it The 5th article was Read and the Question was put whether the Town do accept the same It passed in the Affirmative 45 for said Article——

Chapter Fourth Delegates to Congress
This Chapter was Read the question was put whether the Town do accept the same——It passed in the affirmative——45 for this Chapter——

Chapter Fifth. The University at Cambridge and Encouragement of Literature etc. Section first The University

This Section was read and the Question was put whether the Town do accept the same It passed in the affirmative———16 for This Section———

Chapter fifth Section Second———
The Encouragement of Literature etc.———
This Section was Read and the Question being put whether the Town do accept the same It passed in the Affirmative———35 for this Section———

Chapter Sixth Oaths and Subscriptions Incompatibility of and Exclusion from Offices Pecuniary Qualifications Commissions Writs———
Confirmation of Laws Habeas Corpus. The Enacting Stile Continuance of Officers———Provision for a Future Revisal of the Constitution etc.———
The 1st article was Read and the Question was put whether the Town do accept the same It passed in the Negative 3 for the article———and 10 against it———It was then proposed that the Word———protestant should be in the first Declaration vizt. I, A.B. do Declare that I believe the Christian protestant Religion etc.———
The Question was put Whether the town do accept said Article with that Amendment—It passed in the affirmative———
10 for the article with the Amendment and 3 for the article without any amendment and 3 that rejected the article and amendment The 2d Article was Read and the following Amendment was proposed vizt. that no Judge of the Inferior Court Minister or Justice of the Peace shall have a Seat in Senate or House of Representatives———
The question was put whether the Town do accept said article with that Amendment It passed in the affirmative———29 for said article with the Amendment
The 3d. 4th. 5th. 6th. 7th. 8th. and 9th. articles were Read and the Question was put whether the Town do accept the said articles———It passed in Affirmative———

29 for the 3d. article
29 for the 4th. article
29 for the 5 article
29 for the 6 article
28 for the 7 article and
1 against it
29 for the 8th. article
29 for the 9 article

The 10th. article was Read and the following Amendment was proposed vizt. That Delegates shall be Elected by the Several Towns within this State to meet in Convention after the Year of our Lord 1785 and before the Year of our Lord 1790 for Revising the Constitution in order to amendments The Question was then put whether the Town do accept said article with That amendment It passed in the Affirmative——29 for said Article with the amendment——

The 11th. article was Read and the Question was put Whether the Town do accept the same It passed in the Affirmative——29 for said article——

It was moved that the said Form of Government shall take place at any Time when the Convention shall think fit provided that Two thirds of the Male Inhabitants of the age of Twenty one Years and Upwards Voting in the Several Town and Plantation Meetings shall approve of the same which being put to Vote—passed in the Affirmative 31 for it and 2 against it.

It was moved that Each Town within this State shall Choose a Register of Deeds which being put to Vote passed in the affirmative 32 for it and none against it

The Meeting was then Dissolved

Attest

Abner Perry
Staples Chamberlin
Samuel Whiting
Isaac Bullard
David Johnsone

Selectmen of Holliston

Lexington (277/16)

At a Meeting of the Male Inhabitants of the Town of Lexington being free and twenty one years of age, legally assembled, on May 22 1780 and continued by adjournments to June 5th 1780. The Declaration of Rights and Frame of Government, sent out by the Convention, for the Consideration, Approbation, Rejection or Amendment of the People of this State, having been repeatedly read, and duly attended to and considered ——The 3d 16th and 27 articles, in the Declaration of Rights; and Chapter 2d Section 1st. Article 2. and 7th Chapter 5th Section 1st Article 3d.——Chapter 6th Article 1st 3d 7th and 10th in the Frame of Government, were Objected to.

The Town taking up the several Articles Objected to, passed upon them, in the following Manner.———

In the Declaration of Rights.

Article 3d. without amendment. Yeas 41. Nays 10

Article 16. For "it ought"—*it shall not.* Yeas 55. Reason of this amendment is, That as the Liberty of the Press is essential to the Preservation of the Rights of the People, the Strongest and most definite expressions should be adopted to ascertain it: and we cannot but think that the words—*It shall not,* are more full, expressive and definite, than the words "It ought not."

Article 27 For "no Soldier *ought* to be"—no Soldier *shall* be quartered etc.———and Ibid.———latter part, for "such Quarters *ought not* to be made, but by the civil Magistrate"—such Quarters *shall not* be made, etc. The Reasons for this amendment the same as in the 16 article. Yeas, 51.

In the Frame of Government.

Chapter 2d. Section 1. Article 2d. For "unless He shall declare Himself to be of the Christian Religion"—Unless He shall declare Himself to be of the Christian *Protestant* Religion. Yeas 52.

Chapter 6th. Article 1st. For "I A.B. do declare that I believe the *Christian* Religion, and have a firm Persuation of its Truth." I, AB do declare Myself to be of the *Protestant* Religion, and that I believe the Christian Revelation, and have a firm Persuasion of its Truth etc. Yeas 31.

As to the Word Protestant, We conceive it to be a Word, which took Rise from the *pious, noble* and *truly heroic Stand,* which *Luther* and the first Reformers, with the reformed Churches in Europe, made, in Conjunction with those *Electorates, States* and free-*Cities* of the *German Empire,* which entered into solemn League to support their Cause, against the Errors, Superstition, and *Hierarchy* of the *Pope* and *Church of Rome,* and the Oppression, Persecution and Tyranny of *Charles the Fifth,* Emperor of Germany, in the Beginning of the Fifteenth Century: and more immediately from the *solemn Protest* made and entered, by the *Electors* and Deputies of Nineteen States and imperial Cities of Germany, against an unjust and impious Decree, of the Diet of the Empire, for suppressing the Glorious Reformation, on the Nineteenth of April 1529.—"On that account" (Sais an eminent Historian) "They were distinguished by the *Name* of *Protestants.*" A *Term* by which the reformed Churches of all Denominations, in Europe and America, if not through the World, have ever since been known—a *Term* which our *venerable ancestors* brought with them, when they came into this Country, and held, in a Manner, sacred, as expression of their Character, as Professors of the *pure Religion* of Jesus Christ; in opposition to the *blasphemous Absurdities* of the Church of Rome: and a *Term*, which by long use (as we humbly conceive) hath been, and still is, Technically expressive of the *true Religion of the Gospel*, as justly distinguished from *Popery*.———We therefore wish to have this expressive Word inserted in the Constitution, in those Places we have pointed out, to guard against introducing Persons into Offices of Trust and Places of Power, in the Government of this State, whose *Religion itself* leads them to hold Principles, and avow Practices inimical to Liberty, subversive of Government and dangerous to the State.

Chapter 2d Section 1 Article 7th—To the Proviso, add,—and provided He do not so march or transport them, without the advice of Council.—Yeas 41. We conceived this Limitation necessary, to prevent an undue exercise of the great Powers vested in the Governour, by this article.

Chapter 5th Section 1st Article 3d—without amendment Yeas 25 Nays 3.

Chapter 6 Article 3d Leave out—The latter part—"and it shall be in the Power of the Legislature to increase such Qualifications as to Property of the Persons to be elected to Offices as the Circumstances of the Commonwealth may require."—Yeas 33—We judge this Power too unlimited to be vested in *any* Legislature, as it may easily be so improved, as to prevent the Freedom of Elections.

Article 7th. For "not exceeding Twelve Months."—Not exceeding Six Months in Time of Peace, nor Nine Months in Time of War, or Rebellion.—Yeas 45. We conceive Twelve Months longer than is necessary; and that a suspension of the Benefit of the act referred to in the Article, for so long a Term, might be of dangerous Consequence to the Liberties of the Subject.

Article 10th In order the more effecually to adhere to the Principles of the Constitution, and to correct those Violations, which, by any Means, may be made therein, as well as to form such alterations, as from experience shall be found necessary.—There *shall be a Convention for the Purpose of Revision and amendment*, in the Year of our LORD one Thousand Seven Hundred and Ninety Five; and the General Court, which shall be in said Year of Our LORD 1795 shall issue Precepts to the Selectmen of the Several Towns, and the assessors of the unincorporated Plantations, directing them to convene the qualified Voters of their respective Towns and Plantations, to elect Delegates to meet in Convention, for the Purpose aforsaid. The said Delegates to be chosen in the same Manner and Proportion, as their Representatives, in the Second branch of the Legislature are, by this Constitution, to be chosen. Yeas 45.

Whereas in this Article, as it stands in the Constitution, it is left uncertain, whether there shall be a Revision, or not in the year 1795. We think it would be much more safe for the Liberties of the People, to have such a Revision *certain:* for if that opportunity should be Slip'd or neglected, it might operate to the great Disadvantage of some Parts, if not to the whole of the State.———and the more so, as no further Provision is made for such Revision, at any given time afterwards.———

All the other Articles, in the Declaration of Rights and Frame of Government, passed Unanimously. Yeas 48.

Resolved, that the Delegate of this Town, be instructed to use His Influence, in Convention, that the above Amendments are made in the Declaration of Rights and Frame of Government.———and also That He be instructed and impowered, agreeable to a Resolve of Convention, of March 2d 1780 to agree upon a Time, when the Form of Government shall take Place without returning the same to the People: Provided that Two Thirds of the Male Inhabitants, of the age of Twenty one years and upwards, Voting in the several Town and Plantation Meetings, shall agree to the same, or the Convention shall conform it to the Sentiments of Two Thirds of the People.———

A true Copy Attest Joseph Mason Town Clerk

Benja Brown
Joshua Reed
Willi Reed
Amos Marrett
Selectmen of Lexington

May 22nd 1780

Lincoln (277/17)

At A General Meeting of the Male Inhabitants of the Town of Lincoln being free and of the age of twenty one years and upwards being Legally Warned and Regularly assembled on the 22nd Day of May AD 1780 and by several adjournments to the fifth of June following; to hear and act upon the Doings of a Convention Chosen for the [sole?] purpose of Forming a new Constitution or Frame of Goverment for the State

of Massachusetts Bay—the Honorable Brigadier Brook, chosen Moderator of said Meeting———
the Town on Considering of what lay before them passed the following Votes (viz.)
On the 2d article in the first Section of the first Chapter in the frame of Government Voted that this Town disapprove of said article for the following reasons (viz.)
1st Because we think the Legislative Executive and Judicial powers ought to be in seperate Departments and not Exercised by the same Body or Bodies of men either in part or in whole———
2ly because we Judge this article to be Repugnant to the 17th and 30th articles in the Bill of Rights as also to the first article in the frame of Government which we think to be founded in Reason for the Vote Number 46 On the second article in the 3d section of the first Chapter Voted—that the Town Disapprove of this article for the following Reasons (Viz.)

Because we think the Mode of Representation pointed out in this article is not founded upon the Principles of Equality as Provided by the preceeding article———we apprehend that all Circumstances ought to be taken into Consideration to Determine a Representation founded in Equality: and that the number of Rateable Polls nor any other Circumstance singly Considered Determins such a Representation———This State is Constituted of a great number of Distinct and very unequal Corporations which Corporations are the Immediate Constituant part of the State and the Individuals are only the Remote parts in many respects—in all acts of the Legislature which Respect particular Corporations each Corporations hath a Distinct and seperate Interest Clashing with the Interest of all the rest and so long as Humane Nature remains the same it now is Each Representative will be under an undue bias in favour of the Corporation he Represents—Therefore Large Corporations haveing a Large Number of Representatives will have a Large and undue Influence in Determining any Question in their own favour. Should the number of Rateable Polls in any particular Corporation Increase till they over ballance all the other they Could Compleately Tyraniz over all the Rest; and every Degree of Inequality given power for the same Degree of Tyranny———
Another Circumstance which Renders the mode of Representation pointed out in this article unequal is, that the Small Corporations can have no voice in Government without being at the whole Expence of a

full Representation, whereas the large Corporations by Dividing the attendance of their Representatives Can vastly lesson their Expence and yet in such Cases as respect their Particular and seperate Interests have a full Representation———

On the third Article of the Declaration of Rights the Question was put to the Town to know whether they would approve of said article voted in the affirmative Number 46———
and against said article Number 2

Voted that the Town Disapprove of the *last* Clause of the 10th Article in Chapter 1st Section 3d where it is said: and no member of the House of Representatives shall be arrested, or held to bail on mean process, during his going unto, returning from, or his attending the General Assembly.———

Voted against this Clause in said article—Number 30. and for the same Number 11

Voted unanimusly that the new Constitution be Revised within the term of Seven years—Number 40

Voted unanimusly that the Town approve of the Constitution Except the article above Excepted against—Number 41

Voted that the Town Impower their Delegate to agree upon a time when the Constitution shall take Place agreeable to the Recommendation of the Convention

Lincoln June 6th, 1780
A true Copey Attest. Samuel Hoar Town Clerk

Littleton (277/18)

Littleton May the 22: 1780.

The Town of Littleton having Convened in a Legal meeting to Consider the Constitution or form of Goverment agreed on by the Convention and by them Proposed to the People for their Approbation or Rejection or amendment and after Reading the Said Constitution the meeting was Continued by a Adjournment to Tuesday the 30d. Instant. the Town then meet according to the Adjournment.

Voted to take it up by Articles: Declaration of Rights———Fist Article 32 for and 2 against it 2d article—30 for and 6 against it 3d Article 38 for and 5 against it 4: Article 38 for and none against it. 5 article 38 for and [none against] 6: article 40 for and none against it: 7: article

40 for and none against it 8 article 40 for and none against it 9 article 40 for and none against it 10: article 40 for and none against it 11 article 40 for and none against it 12 article 41 for and none against it 13: article 41 for and none against it 14 article—41 for and none against it 15 article 43 for and none against it 16 article 43: for and none against it 17 article 43 for and none against it 18 article 42 for and none against it 19: article 42 for and none against it 20 article 42 for and none against it 21 article 44 for and none against it 22 article 44 for and none against it 23 article 44 for and none against it 24 article 44 for and none against it 25 article 44 for and none against it 26 article 44 for and none against it 27 article 44 for and none against it 28 article 44 for and none against it 29 article 44 for and none against it 30 article 44 for and none against it———

Part the 2d Chapter fist

fist article 34 for and none against it 2: article 33 for and none against it 3: article 33 for and none against it 4 article 33 for and none against it : Chapter first Section 2: 1 article—34 for and none against it 2: article 33 for and none against it [3] article 33 for and none against it 4 article 33 for and none against it 5 article 30 for and none against it 6 article 32 for and none against it 7: article 29 for and none against it 8 article 31 for and none against it 9 article 30 for and none against it—Chapter first Section 3d———first article 34 for and none against it 2 article 33 for and none against it. 3 article 33 for and none against it 4. article 33 for and none against it 5 article 33 for and none against it 6: article 33 for and none against it [7] article 33 for and none against it 8 article 33 for and none against it 9 article 34 for and none against it 10 article 34 for and none against it 11 article 35 for and none against it

Chapter 2d Section the first

fist article 35 for and none against it 2: article unless the Governor Shall Declare himself to be of the Protestant and Christian Religion 30 for and none against it 3: article 31 for and none against it 4 article 31 for and none against it 5 article 29 for and none against it 6 article 29 for and none against it 7 article 25 for and none against it 8 article—26 for and none against it 9: article 25 for and none against it 10 article 25 for and none against it 11 article 25 for and none against it 12 article 24 for and none against it 13 article 22 for and none against it.

Chapter 2d Section the 2d

first article—21 for and none against it. 2 article 22 for and none against it 3 article 22 for and none against it

Chapter 2d Section 3d——

first article—20 for and none against it. 2 article 20 for and none against it 3 article 20 for and none against it 4 article 20 for and none against it 5 article 20 for and none against it 6 article 20 for and none against it 7 article 21 for and none against it—Section 4th——

first article 21 for and none against it 2 article 21 for and none against it——Chapter 3d——

first article—20 for and none against it——2 article 20 for and none against it 3 article—20 for and none against it 4 article—20 for and none against it 5 article 20 for and none against it——

Chapter the 4th Delegats to Congress: 20 for and none against

Chapter the 5th Section first——

first article 20 for none against it 2 article 20 for none against it 3 article 20 for: none against it

Chapter the 5: Section 2d—20 for none against it

Chapter 6

first article Voted the addition of Protestant 20 for none against it—— 2 article 20 for none against it 3 article 20 for none against it 4 article 20 for none against it 5: article 20 for none against it 6 article 20 for none against it 7 article with this alterration not Exceeding six months 20 for none against it 8 article 20 for none against it 9: article 20 for none against it 10 article 20 for none against it 11 article 20 for none against it.

Voted that Ministers of the Gospel Shall be Excluded from holding a Seat in the General Assembly

Voted that their Shall be a Convention called in fifteen years to Revise the Constitution

Littleton May the 31: 1780

Jona. Reed Selectmen
Samuel Reed of
Ephraim Whetcomb Littleton

At a Legal Town Meeting in the Town of Littleton on Monday the 22d of May 1780 and Continued by adjournment to the 30th. Voted that if Two Thirds of the returns are in Favour of the Constitution that the Convention agree upon a Time when it shall Take Place: a true coppy ats.

Jona Reed Town Clerk

20 Present and none aganst it

Malden (277/19)

A true Return of the votes and proceedings of the Town of Malden, in the county of Middlesex, upon the constitution or form of government laid before them by the convention begun and held at Cambridge September 1, 1779; at a legal meeting of said town April 18, 1780 and continued by adjournment till June 5, 1780.

The whole of the preamble was accepted by 27 votes

The Bill of Rights

The first and second articles were accepted by 27 votes.

The third article was accepted by 27 votes; two persons voted against it.

The fourth, fifth, sixth, seventh and eighth were accepted by 25 votes

All the other articles of the bill of rights were accepted by 34 votes.

It was voted to accept the preamble to the frame of Government, by 34.

Chapter first Section 1

Article 1 was accepted by 34 votes

Article 2 was rejected by 34 votes

The whole of the rest of the first section was accepted by 16 votes.

The 2d section of the first chapter was accepted by 28 votes except as to the number of Senators which was voted to be 28 as formerly, by the alteration voted by 28, the convention to alter the arrangement of them agreably througth the whole: there were three votes against the pecuniary qualifications in electors.

Chapter 1 Section 3

The first article accepted by 16

the 2d article accepted by 34

For the third article, as it stands, there was one vote: but against the pecuniary qualifications there were 9 votes. The whole of the rest of the Section was accepted by 18 votes.

Chapter 2 Section 1

Article 1 accepted by 20 rejected by 2 votes

The 2d, 3d, 4th, 5th and 6th were accepted by 34 votes In the 7th article it was voted that there be an addition of the following words "with the advice of the council" after the word, governor through the whole article; the alteration was voted and with this alteration the article was accepted by 34 votes.

The 8, 9th, 10th, and 11th articles were accepted by 34 votes.

In the 12th article, it was voted that the words, and council, should be added after the word, governor, by 34 votes.
In the 13th article, the word stated was voted to be rejected and what stands after the word purposes, instead of which this addition was voted, to be granted annually by the general court by 34 votes
The paragraph relating to the judges of the Supreme court was accepted by 34 votes

Chapter 2 Section 2d

The whole of this section was accepted by 34 votes.

Chapter 2 Section 3d

The whole accepted by 34 votes.

Chapter 2 Section 4

The whole accepted by 34 votes

Chapter 3d

The whole accepted by 34 votes

Chapter 4

Was accepted with the following addition after the word ensuing; they shall be qualified as to residence, property and religion in the same manner as the governor of this commonwealth. voted by 34.

Chapter 5

Both sections were accepted by 34 votes.

Chapter 6

The first and 2d articles were accepted by 34 votes.
The third article accepted as far as the word ounce, the rest was rejected, both by 34 votes.
The 4th, 5th and 6th articles were accepted by 34 votes.
The 7th article was accepted with the alteration of three instead of twelve months by 34 votes.
The 7th, 8th and 9th articles were accepted by 34 votes.
The 10th article was accepted with the alteration of 1789 instead of 1795 by 34 votes.
Voted, To impower the delegate of the town to agree upon a time when this constitution shall take place, without returning it again to the people, with the proviso in the 53 page of the printed copy of the constitution.
Voted, That the delegate be instructed to endeavour to procure the above alterations to be made by the convention, but if he cannot procure them, then he is impowered to consent to it as it now stands or make such alterations as shall render it agreable to the sentiments of two thirds of the people of this state

A true copy of the proceedings of the town of Malden in the Constitution, attested by order of the Selectmen

Joseph Perkins Town Clerk

Samuel Barrett Esq

Marlborough (277/20)

At a Meeting of the Freeholders and other male Inhabitants in the town of Marlboro of 21 years of age and upwards May the 22d 1780
It was put to vote whether they would accept of the Constitution and Form of Government for the Common Wealth of Massachusetts Bay it Passed in the affirmative 75 for Accepting of it and 7 against it

attest. Winslow Brigham Town Clerk

Medford (277/20)

Medford, June 1, 1780

Sir.

Pursuant to the Requisition of the Honorable Convention for framing a Constitution of Government for this State, We the Select Men of the Town of Medford called a meeting of all the male Inhabitants of said Town, being free and of 21 years of age and upwards, and laid before them the Publication containing the Constitution aforesaid, transmitted as by the said Convention, which the Town (after reading) chose a Committee to examine, and to make Report thereof, at the next meeting, and then adjourned——

The Town having met according to adjournment said Committee reported as follows, viz.

We apprehend that the Governor with the advice of the Council should in the Recess of the General Court be vested with the power on special occasions in time of War and Rebellion to order the Militia out of this State to the assistance of a neighbouring State. And that the said Governor with the advice of Council shall not be impowered to continue the Militia out of this State on the aforesaid Emergencies for a longer space than Thirty Days at one time without the Consent of the General Court.

Concerning the Writ of Habeas Corpus we are of Opinion that it should not be suspended by the Legislature on any account for a longer space of time than six months

We are of opinion that no person ought to be elected a Delegate to Congress of these United States who is not possessed of property in the State of Massachusetts to the value of six hundred pounds currency according to Convention——We should be pleased if the above alterations might be made in said Constitution, but we mean not that said alterations should prevent the Establishment of said Constitution at the next session of said Convention.

The Town after examining the foregoing alterations or amendments together with the respective Articles they relate to Voted, to accept of the 1st Section of the 2nd Chapter of said Constitution stiled *Governor,* with the foregoing amendment

Votes in favour of it 49
against it 5

Concerning the Writ of Habeas Corpus in Chapter 6 article 7 Voted unanimously to accept of it with the foregoing Amendment Number of voters 39.

The Remainder of said Report was unanimously accepted by 39 voters——

The Town then began upon the Declaration of Rights in said Publication, and went through the whole of it, and of the Constitution of Government in order——

Said Declaration was unanimously accepted (except the 3d article) Number of voters 44.

The said third article being particularly discussed, a vote was called for and 28 were in favour of it and 6 against it.——

In the Constitution of government, The 1st Chapter Section 1 stiled *General Court,* was unanimously accepted by 33 Voters

The 2nd Section of the same Chapter stiled Senate, was unanimously accepted by 26 Voters——

The 3d Section of said Chapter stiled Representatives, was unanimously accepted by 23 Voters.

All the Remainder of said Publication was unanimously accepted (with the foregoing amendments) by 23 Voters (one half of the people having before withdrawn)

Benj. Hall
Joshua Simonds
Steph Hall, Jur.
Richard Hall
Eben Hall

Select Men of Medford

Samuel Barrett Esq.

Natick (277/21)

In obedience to the Directions and Advice of the Late Convention we have Caused the Inhabitants of the town of Natick to Assemble and act on the Following articles in the new Constitution or Frame of Government Viz.———

On the Declaration of Rights

Article 1 24 for
34 against
Article 2 22 for
12 against
Article 3 for it none
29 against
Article 4 26 for
none against
Article 5—26 for———
Article 6—25 for
Article 7—25 for
Article 8—26 for
Article 9—26 for
Article 10—27 for
Article 11—26 for
Article 12—23 for
Article 13—23 for
Article 14—23 for
Article 15—17 for
Article 16—17 for
Article 17—19 for
Article 18—19 for
Article 19—19 for
Article 20—19 for
Article 21—19 for
Article 22—20 for
Article 23—20 for
Article 24—20 for
Article 25—20 for
Article 26—20 for
Article 27—20 for
Article 28—20 for
Article 29—22 for
Article 30—22 for

The Frame of Government

Chapter 1st
Section 1st
Article 1—22 for
Article 2—23 for
Article 3—23 for
Article 4—23 for
Chapter 1 for
Section 2 for
Article 1—24 for
Article 2—23 for
Article 3—23 for
Article 4—23 for
Article 5—23 for
Article 6—23 for
Article 7—23 for
Article 8—23 for
Article 9—23 for

———

Chapter 1 Section 3
23 for the several articles

———

Chapter 2d Section 1st
23 for the several articles

———

Chapter 2d Section 2d
23 for the several articles

———

Chapter 2d Section 4th
23 for the several articles

———

Chapter 3d Judiciary Power
24 for the several articles

Chapter 4th Delegates to Congress
24 for the several articles

Chapter 5th Section 1st
24 for the several articles

Chapter 5th Section 2d
24 for the several articles

Chapter 6th

Oaths and subscribtions etc. 24 for the several articles Except the tenth and if the time for Revisal Could be Reduced to seven years which we think sufficient to prove the said Constitution there is 24 for the 10th article

N. B. there is no negetive vote Except in the three first

According to the desire of the Convention we do state our objections and reasons against the 3d Article in the Decleration of Rites which are as follows.

We hold the Right of Conscience to be an unaliable right which never ought to be given up to any man or body of men therefore to invest the Legislator with power in Religious matters we Look upon it absurd and Contrary to Christian liberty, provided always that no man under the pretence of Conscience prejudice his neighbour in his life or estate or do any thing destructive to or inconsistant with human society in which Case the Law is for the transgressor and justice to be administered upon all without Respect of persons

Thomas Broad
William Bodn
William Biglow Select Men
Jason Whitney
Samuel Morse Junr

Newton (277/22)

At the Adjournment of the Town meeting of the Inhabitants of Newton legally assembled June 6, 1780, wherof Doctor John King was Moderator. Then made choice of Colonel Ward to act as Clerk for the day,—and proceeded to consider the Form of Government proposed by the Convention for the State of Massachusetts. After some deliberation, voted to accept the proposed Form of Goverment, with the following Amendments. Viz. To Part the Second, and second Article, add "that in case any Act of the General Court, as aforesaid, shall be adjudged by the People to be oppressive or contrary to their Freedom or Privileges, upon the application of the Selectmen of any Seven Towns of the Commonwealth, the General Court shall issue Precepts to the Several Towns and to the Assessors or Committee of the corporated Plantations, to convene the qualified Voters in their respective Towns and Plantations for the Purpose of considering the said Law; and if it shall appear that a majority of the People so assembled, shall be against the said Law, it shall be no longer in force 37 Yeas. 12 Nays.

That to Chapter 6, the word "Protestant" be added to the Declaration of any Person who shall accept the office of Governor, Lieutenant Governor, Counsellor, Senator, or Representative. 37 Yeas 12 Nays

In Article Third, in the Declaration of Rights, leave out the word, "Public"—in the Paragraph respecting the Teachers of Religion, 60 Yeas 36 Nays

In Chapter 6, article 10, in lieu of the proposed Convention in the year 1795, Voted, "That a Convention be called for the purpose of revising the Constitution in the year 1787 Yeas 49 Nays none

John King per order the
Selectmen

Reading (277/23)

At a legal Meeting of the Male Inhabitants of the town of Reading of Twenty one years and upwards to shew their Minds respecting the Form of Government proposed by the Convention of the State of Massachusetts-Bay———The Number of Voters on the 3d Article of the Bill of Rights were 136—of which 124 approved and 12 disapproved of it——— The Number of Voters on the Form of Government in whole were 121 —all of whom Voted their Approbation excepting with Respect to Members for Congress being of Opinion They should have the Qualifications of Estate and Residence in the State equal to the highest officer in the State—for the following Reasons———They have the Right of apportioning each State's Quotas of the Continental Charges—of making Peace or War—And of entring into alliances with foreign Powers as They shall judge proper etc: But rather than the Constitution should not take Place, They voted their Approbation of the whole in the proposed Form——and have instructed their Delegate accordingly

Peter Emerson
Elijah Upton — Selectmen
Samuel Pratt — of
William Flint — Reading
John Emerson

To Samuel Barret Esquire
Secretary to the Convention
of the State of Massachusetts Bay
Reading May 24, 1780

Sherborn (277/24)

At a Meeting of the Male inhabitants of Sherburn being free and twenty one years old on the 27th Day of April A.D. 1780 and continued by adjournment to the 22nd Day of May following and then met to take into Consideration the Constitution and Form of Government, which was formed by the Convention of this state that met at Cambridge on the first Day of September A.D. 1779 etc. Voted to Proceed upon said Constitution, article by article

Then a vote was asked whether the first article in the Bill of Rights was agreable to the Town and it Passed unanimously in the affirmative Sixty two voters Present

Second Article 59 in favour of it

Third Article 28 in favour of the whole Article 42 for Rejecting all but the last Paragraph in said Article. their Reasons for Rejecting it were that it appeared to them that all that was necessary Respecting matters of Religion is included in the Second article and in the last Paragraph of the third Article of said Bill of Rights.

61 in favour articles 4th. 5th. 6th. 7th—8th—9th—10th—11th—12th—13th—14th. 15th—16th 17th and 18th articles

56 in favour of the 19th—20th—21st—22d—23d—24th
25th 26th 27th and 28

48 in favour of the 29th and 30th

The Frame of Government

Chapter 1st 35 in favour of the whole Chapter

Chapter Second Section first

35 in favour of it. 2d. 3d 4th 5th 6th 7th and 8th Articles 6 in favour of the 9th Article 3 for having this addition, where it is said all Judicial officers shall be appointed by the governer with the advice of Council and Senate

28 in favour of the Remaining Articles in said Section

38 in favour of Section Second and third

Chapter third 38 in favour of the 1st—2nd and 3rd Articles

32 in favour of the 4th article and four against it

Chapter fourth 38 in favour of said Chapter

Chapter fifth 38 in favour of the whole Chapter

Chapter sixth

45 in favour of the first Article

45 for this Addition, to the second Article that no settled minister of the Gospel or any other Person of whatever description, that are Exempt by Law from Paying Taxes towards the maintinance or support of government shall ever have a Right to Legislate in this Commonwealth The Reasons being obvious—that it is contrary to sound policy that any man should lay any burden on the Inhabitants of this Commonwealth which Burden he feels not the least weight of

46 in favour of the remaining part of this Chapter Except the 10th Article

Voted by 32 that their should be a Convention, Called at the Expiration of Seven years from the Establishment of this Constitution, for to Revise the same

Voted by 14 that their be a Revision in ten years

Voted unanimously that it be left to the wisdom of the Convention to agree upon a time when the Form of Government shall take Place

Sherburn May the 22d 1780

Samuel Sanger	
Jedh. Sanger	Selectmen
Jedh. Phipps	of
Moses Holbrook	Sherburn

Pepperell (277/25)

Pepperrell May the 1st 1780

The Inhabitants of the Town of Pepperrell being Legally Assembled in Town meeting for the Purpos of Considering the frame of Government

Proposed by Convention, unanimously Voted to hear the same which being Read the meeting was adjourned.——Monday May 22d Met according to adjournment Voted to hear said fraim of government a second Time, then Voted that the Question be Put on the whole in grose which Passed, Twenty five in favour of it and Nine against it. no objections stated.

A true coppy of the proceedings of said town

per Henry Woods Town Clerk

Shirley *

[Copy of Article 3 in warrant dated May 10, 1780.]

To know the minds of the Town respecting the new Constitution or form of government agreed upon by the late Convention held at Cambridge.

[Copy of vote at meeting held May 25, 1780.]

Voted that the Bill of Rites and sum of the most important Chapters in said Constitution be read and then that the said Constitution be taken up paragraft by paragraft which being done there appeared in favor of the Constitution seventeen, against it twelve.

Stoneham (277/25)

At a general Town meeting in Stoneham on Thursday the 11 Day of May in the year of our Lord 1780 the inhabitants of said town being Lawfully warned asembled and meet to tack under Consideration what was sent to them by the Convention Chosen for Framing a New Constitution of Goverment——Said meeting being Continued by a jornments to the 29th of this Instant: and haveing Considered Every articel then Voted not to Except of the 3 article in the 7 page Relating to the Rights of the inhabitants of the Common wulth of the Massachusetts no further then is Expresed in the Second articel there wass 20 Vots against it and non for it——the whol of the Rest ware Voted by the same number of vots: Except the fourth Chapter Relating to Delegates to

* Town records, Massachusetts Historical Society.

Congres and that with this amendment that the Delegates for Congres shall have the same qualifycations as the Govener of this State is to Have

In the name and by order of the Select men of

Stoneham

Edward Bucknum, Town Clerk

Sudbury (277/26)

The Town of Sudbury met on the ninth Day of May 1780 being Leagally warned for the purpose of hearing of and manifesting their minds on the New Constitution of Government agreed upon by a Late Convention of Delegates of the People of the State of Massachusetts-Bay: and the Constitution, being Read to the Town, it was moved and voted that the Constitution should be Left for the Consideration of the People untill the Adjurnment of this Meeting. accordingly after transacting som other business the Meeting was Adjurned to the Twenty second Day of May and being again Met, the frame of Government was again Read and considered by single Paragrafts, and the numbers of voters hereafter mentioned Desier that the following alterations may be made there——vizt.

First they think it Reasonable that Each Town in the State Should pay their own Representatives, both their travell to and from, and attendance at the General Court: for this Reason, the remote Towns in the State where most of the Expences for travell will be paid, are not Taxed so much according to their value as the Towns that are near the center of the State, and therefore Desier that Clause in the frame of Governmen Relating to their being paid the Expences of travell out of the publick Treasury may be altered

Forty-one for this alteration and Eight against it

Also desier that the word Protestant may be inserted in the room of or added to the word Christian, in the Qualifications of the Governor, and all other officers both civil and Military, for they are Desierous that none Should be in office but Such as are of the Protestant Religion

36 for this amendment and 19 against it

And although the Constitution appears to be well Composed in General, yet by Experiance we may find (and that in a much shorter time than fifteen years) that there may be alterations made therein for the beter, and therefore Desire that the time for the General Court to issue their precepts for the purpose of Collecting the Sentiments of the People on the Expediancy of Revising the Constitution may not Exceed the term of Seven years

55 for the amendment none against it

Then the Question was put to the Town whether they did approve of the Constitution, but yet desier the foregoing alterations and it passed in the afairmetive

52 voting for and one Desenting

The Town also voted to Empower their Delegate to agree on a time when the Constitution shall take place

Asher Cutler
Ajahel Wheeler — Selectmen
Thos. Walker — of
Benjamin Smith — Sudbury
Isaac Maynard

Stow (277/27)

At a Legeal meeting of the inhabetences of the town of Stow on the first Day of May AD 1780 to consider of the Constitution or Frame of government and said meeting held by adjournment to the 29 Day of May instent and then voted the articels of the Bill of Rights and Excepted by the number of 55 and one against the third articel but gave no Resons

the frame of government Excepted by the number of 56
Section first Excepted by the number of 54
Section 2 of the form of goverment Excepted by 42
Section 3 Excepted by the number of .... 39 and 8 against it with this alteration that no Town should be fined for not senden a Representive.

1 and 2 articel of Executive power as it now stands voted against the said article by the nomber of 53

The Resons ar this that the Govener and the Lieutenant Govener shall Declair them selves to be of the Christion Religion which the above numbers objected against it as it now standen in that form but have this alteration to be of the Protestant Religion and then voted to except it by the nomber of 53

3 Chapter Excepted by the number of 45

Section 4 Excepted 44
Judiciary power Excepted 44
2 Chapter Excepted 47
3 Chapter Excepted by the 49
4 Chapter Excepted by the number 47
5 Chapter Excepted 47
6 Chapter Excepted by the 52
voted to Except of the Constitution for the Term of years set in said Constitution as it now sans—23 voted by the number of voters of 29 that it should be but for the Term of five years all the other articels of the above Constitution by the number 52

Stow June the 2:1780

Jonathan Wood	Selectmen
Jonathan Hapgood	of
Charles Whitman	Stow

Tewksbury (277/28)

Tewksbury May the 29, 1780

at a General town meeting being Deuly warned of all that are free and one and twenty years of age to Consider and act upon the Constitution or form of Government and held by adjournment to June the 5th. 1780 then Entered in the following votes (viz)

Chapter 2 Executive Power objected against Section 1 the 7: articel Voted that the Governor and General Court shall not march the Militia for more then six months at any one time without their own voluntary consent.

Chapter 2 Executive Power objected against Section 1 the 2 articel Voted that the Governor shall Declare himself to be of the Christian Protestant religion

Chapter 6 articel 10 a future revisal of the Constitution objected against Voted that the Constitution shall not stand but ten years before a new Convention be Called.

Voted that the Honorable Convention set the time when the Constitution or form of Government shall take Place.

Voted to accept of the Constitution or form of Government with the above amendments to be made

Voted for it 39 against it 2———

Attest Newman Scarlett Town Clark

Tewksbury June the 6: 1780

Townsend (277/29)

The Town of Townshend being Legally Assembled in Town meeting upon Wednesday the 17: of May: 1780. Took into Consideration the Constitution or Frame of Government Agreed upon by the Deligates of the People of the State of Massachusetts Bay, in Convention, Begun and held at Camebridge on the first of September 1779. And Continued by Adjornments to the 2d of March, 1780. 29 Voters present and acting Voted Unanimously to approve of said Constitution

Thos. Warren
Richard Wyer
Isaac Farran Selectmen
Benja. Spaulding

To the secretary of the aforesaid Convention

Waltham (277/29)

Agreable to a Recommendation of the Convention for Framing a new Constitution of Government This may certify that at a Legal meeting of the Inhabitants of the Town of Waltham who are free and Twenty one years of age on the 5th day of June 1780—said Constitution of Goverment being read to the Town and Maturely considered there being Thirty six Voters present—Thirty two of whom Voted to accept of said Constitution of Goverment as it now stands.

But would however propose the following alterations and amendment vizt. that the Habeas Corpus Act be not suspended for a Longer Time than six months as in that Time they think any Person may be brought to his Tryal or admitted to Bail

June 5th. 1780

By order of the Selectmen
Jona. Dix Junr. Town Clerk

To Samuel Barret Esqr
Secretary of the Convention

Watertown (277/30)

At a Publick Town Meeting of the Male Inhabitants of Watertown who are twenty one years of age held in Said Town on the Sixth day of

June A.D. 1780—They took into Consideration The New Form of Government agreed to by the Convention held at Boston in March last. The Same being Several times Read and after Debates thereon they came to the following vote (Viz) Voted that the form of Government or Civil Constitution agreed upon by the Convention is agreable to the minds of this town and that our Delegates in Convention be and hereby are directed to adopt the same, provided it be agreable to the minds of two thirds of the Inhabitants of this State, and if not already agreable to the minds of two thirds of the Inhabitants To make Such alterations as will render the Same Conformable to two thirds of the Inhabitants of Said State———And to Agree upon a time when the Same Shall take place———Forty five voters present. forty three for it, and two against it———

A true copy taken from the Records

Attest. Jona. Brown Town-Clerk

Westford (277/31)

Westford May 11: 1780 At a town meeting of the male Inhabitants of the town of Westford aged twenty one years and upwards regurly assembled at their meeting House to take under their consideration the new form of civil Government.

Voted and chose a Committee of thirteen Men to take under their consideration the form of Government and to report at the next meeting by adjournment.———

May 25th town met according to adjournment and past the following votes Vizt———

Voted Unamiously to accept of the 1st article of the declaration of Rights

Voted to accept of the 2d. Article except the Last Clause.

After long debating on the 3 Article of the declaration of Rights it was moved and seconded to see if the town would accept of the Said 3d Article and 21 voted in the Affirmative: the negative being called by the Moderator 68 voted in the Negative.

The Reasons for rejecting the Said 3d. Article:

and the Substitute in its room as contained on the other half of this Sheet were voted by 71 men; And 22 voted in the negative—Then voted to adjourn the meeting to the 29th day of this Month.

May 29, 1780 Town met according to adjournment and took under consideration the whole remaining part of the Constitution Article by Article: the whole of which was Accepted, voting the following Amendments

Vizt. Voted that the former clause of the 16th Article of the declaration of Rights be amended as follows vizt. The Liberty of the Press and of Speech are essential to the Security of Freedom in a State.———

Voted that it be added to the last of the 2d Article of the 1st Section and 2d chapter the following words vizt. and protestant profession.

Voted that the 7th article 1st Section 2d chapter be so amended as to give power to the Governor in the recess of the General Court to march or transport the Inhabitants of this State for the relief of a Neighbouring State invaded, or threatned with immediate Danger.———

Voted to object against the 3d Article of the Declaration of Rights and that for the Following reasons Vizt.———That it is asserted and taken for granted in the premises of said Article that the "happiness of a people, and the good order and preservation of civil government, essentially depend upon piety, Religion, and Morality, and that these cannot be generally diffused through a community, but by the Institution of the publick Worship of God, and of publick instructions in piety Religion" etc. When both antient History and modern authentick information concur to evince that flourishing civil Governments have existed and do still exist without the Civil Legislature's instituting the publick Christian worship of God, and publick Instructions in piety and the Christian Religion,—but that rather wherever such institutions and fully [executed] by the civil authority have taken place among a people instead of essentially promoting their happiness and the good order and preservation of Civil Government, it has We believe invariably promoted impiety, irreligion, hypocricy, and many sore and oppressive evils.

We think the 3d Article if adopted will be likely to form Such a combination between the Court and Clergy as that thereby the Liberties of the people will be endangered.

But not to enter into, a detail of the many reasons that might be offered to justify and require our rejection of the said 3d. Article We think it Sufficient only to add that We can not conceive ourselves in any case or degree to be intitled to Such a Right as is attributed to the people of this Common Wealth in the said 3 Article of investing the Legislature with power to Authorize and require the Several towns, parishes, precincts and other bodies politick or Religious Societies to make Suitable provision at their own expence for the institution of the publick worship of God and for the Support of Christian teachers of piety and Religion: because We fully believe that the Great Head of the Church has in his Gospel made "Suitable provision" for the Said institution of his publick worship and for the support of Christian teachers of piety and Religion: and that he has never invested any Common-Wealth or Civil Legislature as such by force and penalties to carry those his Aforesaid institutions into Execution: all attempts of which we think tend to encroach on the Unalienable Rights of Conscience and to the Marring of the true principles of Civil Government which last ever ought in our opinion to be kept distinct from possitive Gospel Institutions.

Further it appears to Us, that the General principles of Civil Government as contained in the Constitution without the said 3d. Article properly attended to and acted upon, would much better secure and promote the happiness of the people and the good order and preservation of Civil Government (which We would ever zelously promote) than retaining and adopting the said 3d Article. therefore from the principle of [regard?] for the Good and happiness of the Common Wealth; and better to secure the unalienable Rights of Conscience and from a sense of duty to ourselves and posterity, We feel ourselves bound to reject the said 3d Article of the declaration of Rights; and to enter our sincere protestation against the Same. And that our Religious Freedom and the Unalienable Rights of Conscience may be better secured and established than they are in the declaration of Rights We recommend that the 3d Article thereof be Superceded by the following as Substitute, Vizt. All men have a Natural and unalienable Right to Worship God almighty according to their own Conscience and Understanding, And no Man Ought or of Right can be compelled to attend any religious Worship or erect or Support any place of Worship or maintain any ministry contrary to or against his own free will and consent: nor can any man who acknowledges the being of a God be justly deprived or abridged of any Civil Right as a Citizen on account of his Religious Sentiments or peculiar mode of religious Worship and that no Authority can or Ought to be vested in, or Assumed by any power whatever that shall in any Case interfere with or in any Manner Control the Right of Conscience in the free exercise of Religious Worship.——

Voted that the Ministers of the Gospel while they officiate as Such and are free from Taxation of the estate under their immediate improvement ought not to be eligible to a Seat in the Senate or House of Representatives.

Voted that the 7th Article in the 6th Chapter be amended as follows: vizt. instead of the words "except upon the most urgent and pressing Occations, and for a limited time not exceeding twelve months, the following be inserted except in time of War or Rebellion and for a limited time not exceeding Six Months.———

Voted that the Constitution without fail be Subject to a revisal every ensuing sixteen years.

Voted that Our Delegate in Convention be left to act according to his discretion in regard to the Convention's (at their next Session) agreeing "Upon a time when this form of Government Shall take place without returning the Same again to the people.———

Westford June 1, 1780

Attest	Nathaniel Boynton	Selectmen
	Timothy Prescott	of
	Leonard Procter	Westford

To Mr. Samuel Barrett Esq.
Secretary of the Convention to
be held at Boston on the first
Wednesday in June next.

Weston (277/32)

At a Meeting of the Inhabitants of Weston on Thursday the 15th Day of May A.D. 1780 being Legally warned in Publick Town Meeting Assembled and passed the Following Vote Viz Voted by said Inhabitants that they will accept the Constatution or Form of Goverment as it now stand but it is our opinion that it shall be revised within Ten Years and the Revisal made certain.

Voters for the above	54
Voters against it	20
	—
Majority	34

By order of the Selectmen of Weston

Joel Smith Town Clerk

NB Voted at the above said Meeting by the above said Inhabitants that the delegates shall act discresinary when the Form of Goverment shall take place.

Woburn (277/33)

Proceedings Of a General Town Meeting May the 15th 1780 in Order to Consider the Constitution or New Form of Goverment [?] Chose a moderator Then Proceeded to Reed the Constitution or Form of Goverment and Deliberate on said Form, and the Moderator Put to Voat to see if the Town would Adjourn the Meeting For Further Consideration and it Passed in the Affirmative Accordingly the Moderator Adjourned the Meeting and When Meet together Upon From Monday the Fifteenth Day of May to Monday the 29th. Currant Did Consult and Debate on the aforesaid Form and Adjourned the Meeting For Further Consideration To June the 5th. Currant and when Meet upon Adjournment Did Voat to Consider the Form of Goverment or Constitution Article by Article.

First and Second Article in the Bill of Rights Uninanimously Agreed 3d Article Objected to and After Deliberating on said 3d Article the Moderator Tried the Voat, to see if the Town would accept as it Stood and their was 52 For its Standing as it was Against 23

Section 2d Article 2d To be Amended as Follows Being Free and Twenty One Years of Age Said Amendment to be Through the Whole Form where these Words is Wanting Unanimously Agreed to with the above Amendment—

Section 3d. Article 2d Debated and Voated on 16 For said Article Against 2. Also the Moderator Put it to Voat to see if the Town would Adjourn the Meeting it Passed in the Affirmative Accordingly the Meeting was Adjourned From June the 5th to June the Seventh to Three of the Clock P.M. and when meet upon Adjournment Proceeded to Consider the Remaining Part of the Constitution or Form of Goverment———

The First Section in the Executive Power objected to and After Deliberating on Said Section Voated to have it Amend as Follows viz. the Govenor to Take the Advice of the Council on all Immergencies what so Ever Concerning the Military and Naval Movements Number For amendment 19 For not 18

Amendments Further that the Deligates Chosen for Congress be Qualified Equal to the Representatives Chosen For the Great and General Court or Councilors as required by the Constitution Also Voated that all

ordained Ministers shall be Excluded From a Seat in the General court or Assembly in this State Also Voated that all Attornies at Law be Excluded From a Seat in said Court or Assembly, Amendment Further that their be a Convention called in Seven Years From the Ratification of this Constitution in order for a Revision of the same.
Numbers for the Above Amendments 21 against 9
Also after Deliberating and Considering the whole Constitution Voated as Follows (Viz.) To Except of the Constitution or Form of Goverment Except those Articles which are Remarked For Amendment and those with the Above Amendments Number For the Above 22 against 2
Woburn June the 8th 1780 A true coppy

Attest. James Fowle Jur. Town Clerk

Wilmington (277/34)

At a Legal meeting of the Freeholders and other Inhabitants of the Town of Wilmington on Wednesday the Seventeenth Day of May A.D. 1780: To consider of the Constitution and Form of Government for this State—and Continued by Adjornments to the 5th Day of June Instant—at the Adjournment on the 24th of May after said Constitution was read and Debated thereon. The Vote was put to see if the Town would Accept of said Constitution, with the Amendments proposed and it past in the Affirmative there being 52 Voters present That Voted—at the Adjournment on the 29th of May. The Vote was put to see if the Town would have the 3rd Article in the Decleration of Rights Amended and it past in the affirmative by a Majority—Then the Amendment was called for which is as Followeth. (viz) (That it be Recommended to the Honorable Convention, That there be free Liberty of Conscience, allowed to Calvinists and Armenians and that they have full and free Liberty to pay their money towards the Support of the Gospel, to such Public Teacher or Teachers on whom they attend—and that the Majority of any Town parish or precinct in this State Shall not have it in Their Power to Settle a Public Teacher over the Consciences of the Minority and Contrary to their Sentiments; The above Amendment was Voted by a Majority) there being 24 Vot[ers] present that Voted for the amendment and 21. Voters present that Voted against it—Voted that Mr. Edward Kendal be a Delegat[e] to attend the Convention at their Next Sitting; to Ratifye and Confirm said Constitution provided Two thirds of the people in this State being free and 21 years of Age do Accept of it—And at the Adjornme[nt] on the 5th Day of June Instant; it was moved to have the Vote fo[r] the amendment on the 3rd Article in the Declaration of Rights tri[ed?] over again: accordingly it was and past in the Negative the[re] being 46 Voters present that Voted to Receive the 3rd Article as it Origenally Stands: and 43 Voters present that Voted for the Amendment on said 3rd Article———

Then Voted to Accept of the Amendment Proposed: Respecting the Power of the Governor which is as follows (viz) we apprehend with Submission, that the Governor with Advice of the Council in the Recess of the General Court, may march the forces of the State to the Releife of any State in New England that may be Invaded———

Voted That it be Recommended to the Honorable Convention, that the Number of Councellors may not Exceed five or seven at the most———

Voted That it be Recommended to the Honorable Convention That there be a Revision of the form of Government in the year Ninety———

Voted to accept of said constitution as it Origenally Stands provided they cannot obtain any amendments on the aforesaid Articles—There being Thirty one Voters present and for it

A true extract from the Records

Attest. Cadwallader Ford Junr T. Ck.

Wilmington June the 6th. 1780

PLYMOUTH COUNTY

Abington (277/35)

Abington May [?]

To Samuel Barrett Secretary of the Convention. Sir Agreable to the Direction Received We the Subscribers have Laid the Constitution before the Inhabitants of said Town of Abington and a Hundred of Voters being present it was approved off—without a Division. Excepting the following Articles viz. The third Article in the Bill of Rights with the following Amendment That the Subject Should have the priviledge if he Require it of paying his Money—wherever he is Disposed to attend Divine Worship. the Division being Twenty for it. and Fifteen against it. being at the Adjournment of the Meeting. and also the First Article 2t Chapter Sextion the 2d, Voted the Number of Counsellors and Senators Should not exceed Thirty-four the Division being Twenty four for it, and Four against it, and Colonel Jones the Delegate for the Town is empowered to agree upon a Time when this Form of Government Shall take place without Returning the Same again to the people———

Josiah Torrey
Daniel Shaw Select-Men of Abington
Jacob Smith Jur.

Bridgewater (277/35)

To Samuel Barrett Esqr. Secretary of the Convention

Proceedings of the Town of Bridgwater upon the Constitution or Form of Government Drawn up, and Committed to the Several Towns in this State, for their Consideration and approbation, By the Honorable Convention.

In Compliance with a Recommendation of the afore Said Convention, the Town (Being Duly Notified) Met the 9th Day of May, 1780, and the Said form etc. having been Distinctly Read, the Town Proceeded to Deliberate upon the Several articles therein Contained and hear the objections made against Divers of Said articles, Particularly against the 3d article in the Bill of Rights. The Remainder of the Day being spent in Debates on Said articles the meeting was adjourned to the 22d courant, the Town Having Previously made Choice of 18 Persons as a Committee to Consider and Report at the adjournment on the whole of Said articles. Monday the 22. of May the Town Met at 9 o'Clock A.M. (at their adjournment:) and having heard the Report of their Committee Proceeded to act as follows. The Several articles in the Bill of Rights (ommitting the 3d) having been Distinctly Read and Deliberated on, the Question was then Put—when there appeared in favour of Said 29 articles 359 Votes with only one Dissentient, for Reasons unknown. The Third article was then taken up, and largely Debated,———the Question being Put their appeared in favour of Said article 333———against it 60. Some of whom apprehending the Same to be an infringment on the Rights of Conscience———Others that it was not Explicit, So as to Secure the Rights and Liberties of the Different Denominations of Christians.

FRAME OF GOVERNMENT

First Chapter being Read, and the Votes taken; they appeared for the Question, without a Dissentient. Senate.———article 1 was then Read, and a Vote obtained with only 7 Dissentient.———it was Objected that the Court Contained too large a Number of Members.

House of Representatives.———Article 1 was Read, and Consented to Unanimously.———Article 2d was then Read, and Objected to by Many, as being too large a Representation, at Present: and increasing (with the People) would naturaly Grow so as to be a Real incumbrance upon Buisiness: To the Great Damage of the State.———The Report of the Committee upon this article was then Read, and on a Vote Called (Nem Con) Said Report was accepted with only one Dissentient; and is as follows (viz) "Respecting the House of Representatives, your committee were of Opinion, That upon the Plan Proposed a Representation Cannot be had in any manner So Eaqual as that of Choosing Representatives by Districts: and ascertaining the number Each District shall be intitled to send, according to the number of Electors in each District: and vesting a Power in the Legislative authority to make alterations in the Number of Representatives Each District may hereafter Send; as the number of Electors may vary in future within such Districts,———Your committee were further unanimously of Opinion, That if upon a further Revision of this article in future Convention, it should appear that a majority of the Delegates Present Should be Tenacious of this article in the manner it now Stands, That the Delegates of this Town Should assent to it as it now is."

The Remainder of the articles Respecting Representatives was Voted unanimously

Governour———Six first articles Voted Unanimously. 7th article Voted Ditto, with the following amendment (viz.) That the Governor in the Recess of the General Court, and in his absence the Lieutenant Governor —have Power to Call forth the Militia (in Case of an actual Invasion) to the Defence of the adjoining States.

9th article Voted unanimous.———article 10. Voted, with only 2 dissents, Reasons not known.

Lieutenant Governor.———Council.———Secretary.———Treasurer etc. Being Particularly Considered, were Voted without a Dissentient.

Judiciary Powers etc.———Voted Unanimous.———

Delegates of Congress,———University—

Remainder of Chapter 5 Voted without Dissentient. upon the 6th Chapter Voted to Instruct their Delegates Respecting the Suspending the Writ of Habeus Corpus, viz.———That Such Suspention be only in time of War, and Rebellion; and for a Term of 6 months only. The Remaining Part of the 6 Chapter Passed unanimous with the afore said amendment, and likewise with an amendment on the Second article, (which was Reported by the Committee) as follows.———

"It is the opinion of the Committee That all Setled Ministers of the Gospel (as their Buisiness is Parochial, and Exempted from Taxes, upon their Polls, and Such Estates as lies in the Towns where they are Resident)—Together with the Justices of the Inferiour Courts; Ought to be Excluded from Legislative Power."

A Vote Being Called on the following Paragraph (Nem Con) said Vote was Unanimous, without a Dissentient. (viz) That the Delegates for this Town be Instructed to Give their Votes for the Constitution and Frame of Government as it now Stands; (in Case the afore said amendments Cannot be Obtained) Rather than to have it Recomitted to the People: also That Said Constitution etc. may take Place, as Soon as Conveniently may be.

Bridgewater May 29, 1780 Josiah Richards
Eleazer Cary Select men
Nathaniel Edson Bridgewater

Halifax (277/36)

To the Honnable Convention of the Massachusets for framing a Constitution or plan of Government Gentelman having Received your orders we the Town of Halifax proceded as follows viz. In Chapter first Section Second article Second Relating to voters Twenty five for it and five against it.

In Chapter Second Section third article Second In Chois of Counsellors fourteen against it and Nine for it for Reasons thay took it the Council was not to be Choisen out of the Senators without thay Chois them the first time thay voted because it is Said in Case thare Shall not be found upon the first Choise etc. But was of the minds the Council to Come out of the fortey.

In Chapter Six article tenth none for it and thirty one against it for Reasons Insted of Sending out preceps to See if the people will Send a new Convention thare minde is to Send out preceps for a new Convention which will make it Certain thay Exceped all the Rest thirty two for it and none against it

Halifax May 22, 1780 These from yours

Judah Wood
John Waterman Jr. Selectmen of Halifax

Kingston (277/37, 38)

At a meeting of the Inhabitants of the Town of Kingston Legaly warned and convened on Monday 21st May 1780 The Town proceed to take under consideration a Constitution or form of Government presented to them by the convention and after hearing the same read it was motioned and voted that a committee be chosen to consider and report their opinion theron at the adjourment of said meeting which was on the 28th of May when the said committee reported that the constitution or form of Government layed before the Town for their consideration was in their opinion well calculated in all its parts to make the people happy——

The Question was then put whither the Town will accept of the Constitution or form of Government without any alteration, and upon a divition on the Question their was 45 Yeas and one Nay.

Voted that William Drew Esquire be Impowered to agree with the Honorable Convention on a time when the said constitution shall take place

Attest. William Drew Moderator of said meeting.

Att a meeting of the Male Inhabitants of the Town of Kingston of the age of Twenty one years and upwards on May 22, 1780.

Resolved that the Constitution or Form of Government laid before this Town by the Convention of Delegates from the Several Town in this State appears to be Calculated to premote the wellfare and Happeniss of the Inhabitant there of and this Town approve of the Same the Number for it was 45 against it—1—

Resolved that William Drew Esquire be and hereby is Impowered at the Next session of the Convention to agree upon a time when the Form of Government above mentioned shall Take place with out returning the Same again to the People; Provided that two Thirds of the male Inhabitants of the age of Twenty one years and upwards, voting in the Several Town and plantation meeting shall agree to the Same, or the Convention shall conform it to the Sentiments of two Thirds of The People as aforsaid the Number for it was 41 against was: 1

A true copy attest. John Faunce Town Clerk

Marshfield (277/39)

At a Town meeting Legally warned, and Held by adjournment at the South meetinghouse in Marshfield the 5th Day of June AD 1780.—The Constitution and form of Government for the State of Massachusetts-Bay; being read a Second time and taken under Consideration and Debated on; then voted Article by Article with the following Alterations and Amendments viz: the word shall insted of Ought be inserted in the 16, 17, 20, 22, 23, 25, and 27 Articles———

Chapter 1 [Sec. 1] Article 4. So as the Same be not repugnant or Contrary to this Constitution; or the Laws of God.———

Chapter 1 Section 2 Article 5, He shall be an inhabitant in the District for which he shall be Chosen and of Known Piety and Religion and born within the united States.—and also the Same amendment in Chapter Second Section Second.———

Article 7 or the Consent of the General Court, we Desire those words may be Dealed———

Chapter Sixth, Article tenth, the Term their mentioned Ninty five, we Desire may be Eighty five, and that this form of Government Shall take Place as soon as Convenintly may be—

and then the Question was Put to Know the mind of the Town whether they will approve of and adopt the Said Constitution and form of Government with the above Alterations and amendments, and it Passed in the affirmative unanimus.———

But it was Late before we Got through it, after Sunsett and many Persons gone before this Last Question was Called and but 31 that voted. But no Person appeared against it.———

a true copy attest
Neh. Thomas Town Clerk

Middleborough (277/40)

Middleborough Massachusetts State June 1780
The following is a few Remarks on some parts of the Late Bill of Rights and frame of government for this State prepared for want of Time Sufficient To Scan the whole of an affair So very intresting and important ———we have Run through it all, and made our observations upon here and there a Little, and that: perhaps: Not so intellible as we could have wished for———

on the 3d. article in the Bill of Rights
1st That is uncessessaryly Lengthy and unmeaning, or otherwise admits of Different meanings
2nd. That it is inconsistant with itself and also with other parts of the Bill of Rights.
3d That it may Encroach upon the Consciences as well as the intrests of individuals: and thereby be very hurtfull and dangerous to Society. [*torn*] Therefor———1st its Being So Exceeding Lengthy by way of Repetition or hovering about the Same thing in Different words in a Considerable part of it Strikes the minds of people: that it means any thing, or Every thing: or Really intends Nothing,
2nd. in saying that no Subordination etc. Shall ever be Established by Law: and in another part of the same article: in Saying, that all monies paid by the Subject etc; where it must be understood: if any thing can be Learnt by it: that individuals may at some Times and under Some Circumstances be obliged to pay money as aforesaid, Contrary to the Dictates of their Consciences for the Support of Teachers as aforesaid———
3d That the Legislature are Sole Judges of what provision Shall be made for the institution of the publick worship of god and for the Support of publick Teachers etc: which ought to be a matter Between the people and the Teachers only, and the Legislature Never to Concern

about it for it may Come to pass that the Teachers aforesaid shall apply to the Legislature and say that they are not sutably provided for: it will Disgust his people and they will not attend his Teaching: thus a foundation is Laid for the overthrow of Religious Societies

amendment in the 3d article in the Bill of Rights

it is the Right as well as the Duty of all men to invest their Legislature with power and authority to Require an attendence uppon the publick worship of God (agreeable to the Second article in Said Bill) and that all men or Denomination of Christian people have an Equal Right to attend the publick worship of god where it Shall be most agreeable to the Dictates of their Consciences; and also that Every man and all Bodies of men have a Right to Support the public worship of god in such a way and manner as Shall be most agreeable to their own minds and be Compleately protected by the Law in So Doing——

and that all men have an Equal Right in all Cases with Respect to the Choice of their publick Teachers provided always that where there is Church: that they lead in Such Choice: and that it is the Right as well as the Duty of all men in Society to invest their Legislature with power and authority to Require (for Equal Benefit to Each and Every Denomination of Christian people) that all men Shall give an account or by Some means Let it be publickly known what Denomination of Christian people they join with or mean to join with in attending the publick worship of god (So far as is nessasary) So that no ill conveniance take place in Consequence of ignorance therein

---

29th Article in said Bill

We accept and Like the first part as follows and Reject the Remainder ——it is essential to the preservation of the Rights of Every individual: his Life: Liberty: property and Character: that there be an impartial interpretation of the Laws and administration of Justice.

Frame of government

part 2nd. Chapter 1st Section 1st. Legislative power article 2nd. that the governor shall have Nothing to Do in the Legislative Department as he must be the Supreme Executive Magistrate for Reasons against it we appeal to the 30th article in the Bill of Rights. where no one Shall act in Two Branches of power——

article 4th. that the Legislature Shall never name or appoint any Civil officer: But that the people at Large Shall for Ever Elect all Officers which we think to be agreeable to the 5th article in the Bill of Rights—

Surely if all officers are at all times accountable to the people for their Conduct in office: the people ought to Chuse them: and if the Right and privilege of Chusing any one officer be given out of the hands of the people: by the Same Rule the people may by Degrees Loose the privilege of Chusing Every officer. and then groan under the government of a Venal and Most Wreched Set of Villains———

and also in the same article Concerning Excises we See no way that any good Can Come of it But the Contrary: therefore are against it

---

Chapter 1st Section. 2nd. The Senate

article: 1st. we think that: 20: might answer as good a purpose as 40: and with Less Expence and greater Brevity: and in the same article we find that money makes Senators and not men: The State is to be Divided into Districts. and Each District Shall have Senators according to their intrest without any Regard to the Number of men in Such District: So that while one District with :6000: men Shall Elect :6: Senators: another District worth just as much and all owned by Six men: they must all be Senators: which we think is Very unjust and Contrary to the Rights of Nature. But if this Rule Can be Right most Certainly then if one man with an Estate of £ 60 : is properly Quallified to give one vote towards a Representative another man worth £ 600: ought in justice to give ten votes towards the Same Representative. We think that if the State is Divided into Districts as above that Each District ought to Chuse an Equal Number of Senators according to the Number of Voters in Such District: Quallified as for Voters for Representatives

article 3d: we object against all that is Said about the Council in Said article (and would Every where in Said article place an Equal Number of Senators in its Stead) as they are with us till now; an unheard of Set of officers: we think they will not only be useless and unnessasary: But Even hurtfull Burthensome and Dangerous to Society

---

article 9th: we think that Eleven members of the Senate Should Constitute a Quorum for Doing Business in Case the whole Shall Consist of :20: members———

Chapter 1st Section 3d. article. 2nd.

Too many Representatives

article. 9th. Less Representatives may make a Quorum

article: 11th. we object against the Council here as well as in all other places———

Chapter 2nd. Section 1st Executive Power
article 2nd: if it Should happen that the Best and most Sutable man in the State for governor and Being fairly Chosen, Should not have a free hold worth more than £ 999:: we must Loose all our Time and Trouble in Chusing and Loose the Best man for governor—and now in this Circumstance which may take place we do not see any provision here made what we Shall Do Next Concerning governor whether he Shall be Taken from among those that had a few Scattering Votes or the old governor Shall Stand or have no governor: in fine we know not which way to Look next for a governor: unless the Quallification be altered with Respect to interest———

---

article 4th. 5th. and 6th.———
We Still object against Councillers and place an Equal Number of Senators in their Room and Stead
article 8th we object against the Council here Likwise and would place in its Stead one half of the Senate
article: 9th. and: 10th: we object against the governor and Council or any other man or order of men in any place office or power whatever as having any kind of Right by any means whatsoever to Nominate or appoint any one officer that shall have Even the Least Degree of power over the people in Common: Either Legislative Judicial Executive or any other way if Each and Every man in common have not a Right to Vote for Each and Every officer: under which they must or Shall at any Time or by any means Subject themselves: we ask how it Came to pass that any one man or Number of men Should be possessed of a Right to Chuse officers: for other men: as we Do not understand it to be Consistant with the Right of Nature: But the Reverse and Every way inconsistant with the Sense of the 5th. article in the Bill of Rights: as it is most Certain that Every part of publick Business that is Conducted out of its proper Line will produce Some publick Evil: and that as the Chusing of the greatest part of publick officers out of its proper Chanel will have a Tendancy to fill the State with the most Corrupt, Vitious, and Sordid Set of officers: therefore productive in its Consequences of the greatest Evil. we Say that Every man ought at Least to have as good a Chance in voteing for Every officer placed over him as he has by this form of government, in voteing for Captains and Subalterns———

---

article:11th. that the governor. Nor no one man Shall Ever at any Time hold the keys of the publick Treasury alone:—in Case the governor shall have the ordering of publick money agreeable to this form of government he may Refuse to Sign warrants for Drawing money out of the Treasury; till he first be fully Supplied with money for his own use: and the general Court and Senate be oblidged to grant Such money; or be without the assistance of the governor———
Therefore we Say that the governor with Respect to publick money, Shall Sign Such warrants as Shall from time to time be directed to him from the Court and Senate and no more———

---

article 13th.—this article appears to be so full of iniquity that we Cannot by any means Discover Even the Least Shadow or Distant appearance of any kind of advantage that it Can Ever be to the people in Common: —this one only Excepted That it will Effectually provide a way in which people may and must Dispose of all their money which will Save them a great Deal of Time and trouble in Disposing of it any other way———
Since a foundation Laid by Law for Extravagancy in Support of grandure and Dignity in office; is inconsistant with political prudence———we Say that all officers or publick Servants: justly intitled to publick pay Shall have the Same granted to them by the Legislature from year to year: or from time to time; as an Equitable Reward for their Services———

Chapter 2nd Section: 2nd Lieutenant Governor
we object against the whole Section, and say that a Lieutenant is an unnessasary officer: and that the first member of the Senate shall Do all the Business here assigned to the Lieutenant governor and at all other times attend the Business of Senator as usual

---

Chapter 2nd. Section 3d. the Council
we object against having any Council as here mentioned and say that they are an unnessary Set of officers and therefore Both Chargeable and hurtfull to Society and that all the advice and assistance that a governor Shall Stand in need of from a Council the Same may be granted to him from Each or Either Branch of the Legislature.

Chapter 2nd Section 4th—article. 2nd. we object against the Council only here:
Chapter 3d—in the first place we object against the Council here as in

other places: 2ndly and that all officers here or Elswhere mentioned to hold their office Dureing good Behavior: we object against and Say: that Sence the way provided to Remove any officer for ill Conduct will be attended with so much Difficulty and the Event so precarious that it will Scarcely Ever be attempted therefore those in office will Naturally Become the most insolent haughty and imperious monsters that can be Ranked among the human Species. by way of amendment we propose that no man Shall hold any office more than three years in any five years in this way a man will Look upon his opportunity of making his fortune in private Life Rather than in publick Life Therefore he will Seek to promote his interest in private Life Even while he is in office; in Doing which he will promote the interest of Every man in private life and these make the general Body of the people appeal to the Eighth article in the Bill of Rights

3d. and that all Business proper to be Done in a probate office (for the good of the people) ought forever to be Done in Each Town by one or more persons appointed within and by Such Town for that purpose who Shall be accontable for his or their conduct in Like manner as the judge of probate now is—and that Such person or persons So appointed in Each Town would be more Likly to Do justice as he or they would know the Circumstances of individuals in one Town Better than one man Could for a whole Country.

5th. article: we object and say that it is inconsistant with the 30th. article in the Bill of Rights, and that all matter contained in said article to be heard and Determined before the governor and Council ought in our opinion to be heard and Determined by the Superior Judges of Courts and without any Extraordinary Expence to those that apply to said Court for Remedy———

Chapter 4th Delegates to Congress

we object against their being Chosen by the Senate and House of Representatives and say that the people have as good a right to Chuse their Delegates to Congress: as they have to Chuse a governor or any other officer whatever; and that the Delegates to Congress shall never have any further power Delegated and perpetuated to them; But granted to them (if need be) from Time to Time and so much and for Such Time only as shall be found nessasary: and then may be taken from them again———

Chapter 5th. the university Section 1st. article 2nd—
we say that a True and perfect account of all privileges incums: profits: or advantages: of any kind whatever arising from gifts grants Legacies Conveyances or by any other name way or means whatsoever: heretofore and now Belonging to harvard College or to any or Either of the officers (for the Time Being) Belonging to said college shall for the present Time and forever hereafter be given annually to the Senate and house of Representatives in order that it may be fairly known what further privileges or grants are Really Nessasary which may be granted accordingly or not as the said Senate and Court shall see Cause from Time to Time———
Chapter 5th Section 2nd Literature
it is Such a Complicated inconsistant Flourish of Expressions that it is in our opinion impossible To Seperate the good which we Conceive to Be intended by it, from the Numerous Evils which may take place in Consequence of it: But would by all means Encourage all Nessasary Scools in the Several Towns

---

Chapter 6th oaths etc.—we object and say that the oaths here assigned for officers to take are insufficient Light and Loose and will answer But Little or no good purpose: therefore we would place in their Room and Stead the former oaths appointed for Such officers So far as our Circumstances will admit———
article: 10th—we Say that five years from this is a Sutable time to Revise the frame of government and at the End of Said five years the people be Called upon to know their minds with Respect to a Revision of the frame of government———
We also add with Respect to the place where the Senate and general Court Shall Set from time to time to Do Business: that the Same from time to time Shall be Determined by a joint vote of the Senate and house together in one Body———
we further add that the governors power Relative to his Sending Troops out of this State or Raising troops for Defending Said State be with the advice and consent of the Senate and house of Representatives

John Alden
Edward Wood
Henry Strobridg Select men of Middleboro
Thomas Nelson
Isaac Tomson

At a Leagal Town Meeting held in the Easterly Precinct Meeting house in Middleborough on the fifth Day of June 1780 Continued by adjournments from the Eighth Day of May Last to hear a Constitution or frame of Government agread uppon by the People of the State of Massachusetts Bay.

1ly Voted Not to Recive the said Constitution or frame of Government as it now Stands yeas—000—Nays 220

2ly Voted to accept of the Constitution or frame of Government by the ammendments that this town have made yeas for said Constitution with the ammendments: 173 Nays: 3

at Said Meeting Voted to Chuse three men to Serve as Deligats at a Convention to be holden at Boston Relitive to the frame of Government the Persons Chosen to serve the towns as Deligates are Mr. Zebedee Sproutt Decen Benjamin Thomas and Lieutenant William Tomson

copey attes. Abner Brown Town Clerk

The within is assented to by us the subscribors date at Middleboro this 6th of June A.D. 1780

John Alden
Edward Wood Selectmen
Henry Strobridg of
Thomas Nelson Middleboro
Isaac Tomson

Pembroke (277/41)

At a Town Meeting Warned and Held in the Town of Pembroke on the 25th Day of May 1780 for the Purpose of Taking under Consideration the Constitution and after reading the Same the meting was adjourned to the 29th Day of Said month and then met and then the Question was Put to know The Towns mind whether they would acept of the Declaration of rights and it Passed as for the whole of the Said Declaration of Rights———85———

against it———20

and then the Question was Put to know the Towns mind wether the Constitution Should be read article by article and it Passed in the affarmative———

Chapter the first Legislative power

article the first for it—	138
article the second for it	135
against it	004
article the third for it	123
against it	012
article the fourth for it	119
against it	021

Chapter the first Section the Second Senator

article the first for it	134
against it	008
x article the Second for it	016
x against it	130

x voted notwithstanding to acept all the articles of the first Chapter Second Section relating to Counslers and Senators with the erasment of the Qualification of Property in the Electors mentioned in the 2d article for it 146

article the third for it	145
against it	001
article the fourth for it	146
article the fifth for it	138
against it	008
article Sixth for it	146
article the Seventh for it	146
article the Eighth for it	146
article the ninth for it	146

Chapter the first Section the 3 House of Representatives from thence to the End of the Constitution acepted Erasing the Qualification of Property———146 in the Electors
and Enlarging the Governors Power in the Recess of the General Court to March the Militia into the adjoining States as the Case May Require. Voted that it is the opinion of Said Town that the Constitution Should Be Revised Every Ten years also Voted that the Reverend Mr. Hitchcock the Towns Delagate Be and Hereby is Instructed to use his Influence that the Constitution May Take Place as Soon as it Can Be Conveneantly Done

A true copey attest. J[.?] Turner Town Clerk

Plymouth (277/42) *

At a Meeting of the Town of Plimouth, Legally Assembled and held at the Court house in Plimouth, May 22nd A.D. 1780——A Vote was Called to know if this Town would make any Exception Against the Constitution, or form of Government, lately Drawn up by the Convention of this State, it Passed in the Negative.
Then Voted to accept said Constitution as it now Stands, by a Unanimous Vote, This being Thirty Seven Voters Present
Then Voted, and Impowered our Delegate, in said Convention to agree upon a time when said form of Goverment Shall take Place.

A true Copy of record,
Attest. Ephm. Spooner Town Clerk

Plympton (277/43)

At a Town meeting Held at Plimpton May 26th 1780 to Take into Consideration the Constitution or form of goverment and Continued by adjornment to the fifth of June instant and then mett and passed the following Votes viz.
1. Voted to accept the Constitution or form of government with the following alterations and ammendments
2nd Vote 30 Voted to Expunge the third article in the bill of Rights out of the Constitution and Ten were for Receiveing it as it now stand
3rd Voted the following amendment of the 29th article in the bill of Rights that the general Court shall state such saleries as are expressed in said article for no Longer Term at a Time than one year
4th Voted Chapter first article 4th Eight for and 4: against the proposed addition or Rather amendment that Every good and senseble subject being free Twenty one years old and appears to be a well wisher to this Common wealth may have the privilidge of voting for a Representitive

* The town acted on the basis of a report by a committee consisting of Sylvanus Bartlett, William Watson, Theophilus Cotton, Joshua Thomas, Samuel Bartlett, Nathaniel Morton, Jr., and Ephraim Spooner that the "Draft is well made and calculated for the Good Government and Peace of the Community both for the Presant and Future Generations. Therefore we think it best This Town should Receive The Same as it now Stands without any Exception or alteration whatsoever." See *Records of the Town of Plymouth* (Plymouth, 1903), III, 394.

or Representitives in the Town where in he Resides if he be not possesed of an Estate as the Constitution prescribes.

5 Vote Chapter Second Section first Article Second 35 for and none against the proposed amendment that the govenour and Lieutenant govenour shall declare themselves to be of the Protestant Religion at their Election or before their Taking their oath.

6th Vote Chapter Second Section fourth page 34 proposed the adition or amendment that the Treasurer or Receiver general of this State during his Continuance in said office shall have sufficient Bonds men 35 for said amendment and none against it

7th Voted Chapter Second Section first article 10th proposed the following amendment to Ensert the words Sixteen insteed of the words Twenty one 24 for said amendment and five against it

Elijah Bisbee Jur
Thomas Gannett Selectmen of Plimpton

Rochester (277/44)

At a Town Meeting in Rochester May 22nd 1780: Legally Warned and Regularly assembled——said Town Made Choice of Enoch Hammond Esquire Moderator——

Bill of Rights

Article 1st: Number of persons Voteing for it 121
Ditto 2 121
Ditto 3 .... 41 with amendments: and 57 against the whole article

Then Voted the Meeting be adjourned to fryday Next 8 a Clock fore noon——

At a Town Meeting in Rochester May 26th 1780: on adjournment from May 22nd. Currant Enoch Hammond Esquire Moderator——

Bill of Rights

Article 4th: Number of persons that Voted for it 52
Ditto 5 56
Ditto 6 56
Ditto 7 56
Ditto 8 56
Ditto 9 58

Ditto 10 58
Ditto 11 58
Ditto 12 62
Ditto 13 60
Ditto 14 65
Ditto 15 69
against it 1
Ditto 16 70
Ditto 17 71
Ditto 18 71
Ditto 19 73
Ditto 20 73
Ditto 21 73
Ditto 22 73
Ditto 23 73
Ditto 24 74
Ditto 25 74
Ditto 26 74
Ditto 27 75
Ditto 28 74
Ditto 29 42
against it 39
Ditto 30 85

Legislative power——The General Court

Article 1st Number of persons that Voted for it 85
Ditto 2 85
Ditto 3 .... 85 with the alteration that the General Court shall not Erect any Court or Courts prejudicial to this Common wealth
Ditto 4 52
against it 37

The Senate——

Article 1st: Number of persons that Voted for it 83
Ditto 2 .... 69 with this alteration that Every male person free and 21 years old paying a poll Tax to be a Voter: and 41 for this alteration that Every male person paying a poll Tax shall put in one Vote, and he that pays a poll Tax and a Tax on his Estate to the Vallue of a poll Tax shall put in Two Votes, and so in proportion——

Article 3rd Number of persons Voted for it ..... 110——
Ditto 4 110
Ditto 5 110
Ditto 6 109
Ditto 7 109
Ditto 8 109
Ditto 9 107

House of Representatives——

Article 1st Number of persons that Voted for it ..... 100——
Ditto 2 95
Ditto 3 95
Ditto 4 ..... 60 with the alteration that Every male poll that is free and 21 years old paying a poll Tax be a Voter: and 28 for this alteration that Every male person paying a poll Tax Shall put in one Vote: and he that pays a poll Tax and a Tax on his Estate to the Vallue of a poll Tax shall put in 2 Votes and so in proportion
Article 5th 95
Ditto 6 98
Ditto 7 98
Ditto 8 98
Ditto 9 98
Ditto 10 103
Ditto 11 103

Executive Power——Governour

Article 1st Number Voted for it— 103
Ditto 2 ..... 103 with the addition of the word protestant after the word Christian
Ditto 3 95
Ditto 4 95
Ditto 5 90
Ditto 6 90
Ditto 7 ..... 90 with this alteration that the Governour with the advice of Council in the Recess of the General Court May March or Transport the Militia out of this Common Wealth to any of the Neighbouring states if invaded——
Article 8th 90
Ditto 9 90

Ditto 10 .... 5 and 72 with the alteration that all the soldiers from 16 years old and upwards shall have a Vote in the Choice of their officers—and 26 against it——— 78 with this alteration that there be a Rotation of officers once in 3 years: and 26 against it

Article 11th Number for it 104

Ditto 12 104

Ditto 13 104

Lieutenant Governour

Article 1st Number for it 104

Ditto 2 104

Dittto 3 104

Council etc.

Article 1st Number for it 104

Ditto 2 .... 104 with this alteration: after the words the people at Large to be added: and the Senator or Senators So refuseing, Shall have their Seats Vacuate in the Senate: and the number of Senators shall never Exceed 31 after the Counsellers are Elected

Article 3 Number for it 100———

Ditto 4 100

Ditto 5 95

Ditto 6 90

Ditto 7 80

Secretary Treasurer Commissary etc.

Article 1st Number for it 70

Ditto 2 70

Judiciary Power

Article 1st Number for it— 65———

Ditto 2 60

Ditto 3 .... 60 with the alteration that there be a Judge of Probate in Each Corporate Town in this Common Wealth Chosen by Ballot by the Inhabitants of Each Town, and Commissioned by the Governour

Article 4th: Number for it 60

Ditto 5 61

Dellegates to Congress

Number for it 50———

University

Article 1st Number for it 45———

Ditto 2 . . . . 50 with this addition and allso that all other Schools and Seminaries of Learning, allso all Towns, Precincts, Parrishes, Churches or other Corporate Bodies, shall have all Legacies etc. heretofore Granted to them: Confirmed and made Sure to them their Heirs and Successors, forever, according to the True Intent and Meaning of the Doners———

Article 3rd Number for it 50———

Encouragement of Literature etc.

Number for it 50———

Oaths and Subscriptions: Commissions Writts Habeas Corpus etc. etc.

Article 1st: Number for it 50

Ditto 2 50

Ditto 3 . . . . 90 with this alteration. That the Quallification of persons to be Elected Shall not be altered: Except Done by Convention

Article 4th Number for it 90———

Ditto 5 . . . . 90———

Ditto 6 90

Ditto 7 . . . . 90 with this alteration that the Habeas Corpus act shall not be suspended at any Time: Except in Time of war Invasion or Rebellion: and then not for a Longer Time than 4 months———

Article 8th Number for it 90

Ditto 9 90

Ditto 10 90

Ditto 11 90

and unanimously Voted that this be added to the above Form of Government———That there Shall no Slaves be Born or Imported into this Common Wealth

A True Copey from the minutes

David Wing Select Men of
Melatiah White Rochester

Scituate (277/45)

Scituate May the 1st 1780

Pursuant to the orders of the State Convention we the Subscribers have Laid the Constitution before the Town of Scituate at a meeting warned for that purpose: and held by Several ajanmments to the 3d. of June: and have acted upon Each part of said Constitution: as follows

Elijah Stodder
Joshua Clap
Daniel Litchfield

Common Wealth

Declaration of Rights

Article	voters for	against	Article	voters for	against
1	92		16	74	1
2	92		17	58	
3	46	20	18	64	
4	70		19	67	
5	63		20	59	
6	63		21	60	
7	88		22	67	
8	82		23	73	
9	69		24	80	
10	66	2	25	62	
11	76		26	71	
12	73	4	27	66	
13	69		28	48 with amendment	
14	72		29	56	23
15	60		30	66	

Part 2d Frame of Government

voters for—67

Legislative Power
Section the 1st The General Court

Article	voters for	against
1	59	
2	55	
3	47 with amendment	
4	51	14

Chapter 1st Section 2d
The Senate

Article	voters for	against
1	36 with amendment	
2	64	16
3	67	
4	55 with amendment	
5	49	4
6	74	
7	69	
8	66	
9	71	

Chapter 1t. Section 3d.
House of Representatives

Article	voters for	against
1	69	
2	62	2
3	55 with amendment	
4	59	5
5	60	
6	56	
7	52	
8	55	
9	32	14
10	61	
11		23

Chapter 2d.
Executive Power
Section 1st
Governor

1t	41 with amendment	
2	23	16
3	36	
4	41	
5	45	
6	45 with amendment	
7	48	3
8	23	8
9	19	
10	23	
11	21	
12	27 with amendment	
13	32	

Chapter 2d.
Section 2d. Lieutenant Governor
with amendment

Article	voters for	against
1	9	1
2	16	
3	22	

Chapter 2d. Section 3d. Counsel and mannar of Settleing Elections by the Legislature

Article	voters for	against
1	15	
2	14	
3	17	
4	17	
5	22	
6	23	
7	18	

Chapter 2d. Section 4 Secratary Trasurer Commissary

Article	voters for	against
1	18	
2	20	

Chapter 3d Judiciary Power

Article	voters for	against
1	9	12
2	20	
3	19	
4	16 with amendment	
5	18	

Chapter 4th Deligates to Congress
21 votes for

Chapter 5th University at Cambridge and Encouragement of Literature Section 1t.
voters for 14 against [*torn*]

Chapter 5th Section 2d The Encouragement of Literature
The whole Section
voters for
11

Chapter 6th the whole put to vote with the amendments
voters for 31

The Amendments the Town of Scituate made to the [?] are as follows——
viz——

Amendment on the 29th Article of the Declaration of Rights: That the Judges of the Supreme Judicial Court are to be Chosen anew Every five years. and their Sallaries to be granted annually at the first setting of the General Court——

Amendment—Chapter 1 Section 1t. Legislative Power Article the 4th. That there ought a valuation of Estates taken Every five years

Amendment Chapter 1t Section 2d. Article 2d. That Every man that is free and Twenty one years of age being an Inhabitant of any Town that is taxed toward the support ought to have a Right to vote for Senators

Article the 5th. amendment. That any person being in the possession of Real Estate to the amount of two hundred or personal Estate and Real Estate to the amount of three hundred pounds shall admitted to serve as a Senator——

Chapter 1t Section 3d. article 4th. Amendment That Every man being free and twenty one years of age that is taxed toward the support of Government hath a right to vote for a Representative for the town that he pays his taxes——

Chapter 2d. Section 1t. article 2d. Amendment in stead of one thousand pound. five hundred is thought sufficient for a Govenors Qualification——

Chapter 2d Section 1t amendment on the 7th. article That the Govenor in the Resess of the General Court shall have power to march the militia of this Commonwealth for the Relief of a Neighbouring State or States when Suddenly Invaded as well as to any part of this State: Not to Exceed Thirty days——

Chapter 2d. Section 1t. article 13th. amendment the Govenors salary to be granted annually the 1t. session of the General Court:

Chapter 2 Section 2d. article 1t. amendment that five hundred pounds Real Estate are sufficient for to Quallify a person to be Lieutenant Govenor

Chapter the 3d. Judiciary Power article 4th. amendment That town counsels be appointed to do the duty of Judges of Probate in Cases.

Chapter 6th Article 1t amendment Instead of the Christian Religion it ought to the Protestant Religion———

Chapter 6 article 3d. amendment. It shall not be in the power of the Legesture to increase the Qualifications as to the Property of the persons to be Elected to Offices———

Chapter 6th article 10th an amendment that the General Court in the year AD 1785 shall issue their precepts to the Select of the towns through the States to Convene the inhabitants of their towns that are free and twenty one years of age and upwards for the purpose of Collecting their sentiments on the Necessity and Expediency of Revising the Constitution in order to Amendment.

[*illegible name*]

Wareham (277/46)

At a Town Meeting held in Wareham on the 22d May 1780 for the purpose of considering the form of Government of the Common Wealth of Massachusetts, as Drawn up by the Convention appointed for forming or Drafting the Same———The Town after hearing the same Duly Read adjourned their Meeting until Monday the 29th of said May in order to a further consideration of the Same—and then met and voted that the Same be allowed with the following amendments or alterations which said Town humbly propose to the said Honourable Convention at their next Session to be Considered of, Nevertheless willing to Condescend to their better Judgment and abilities and the opinions of the people at large in the Several Towns in this State. Their amendments or alterations are

1st In the Second Article of the bill of Rights—That Roman Catholicks may not Enjoy equal priviledges with Protestant Christians yet Nevertheless to enjoy a Toleration in Particular places as the Legislature shall Direct

2d. That in the Third Article of the said Bill of Rights The fourth Paragraph in said Third article be wholly Expunged.
3d. In the Second Section of the first Chapter of the form of Government—That the number of Councillors and Senators be Reduced To Twenty Eight and That Such part of them be appointed for Councellors as the Convention shall in their Judgment think most proper. and also the number of each that shall constitute a Corum———
4th. That in the Third Section of said first Chapter the Qualification of a Member of the House of Representatives be a freehold Estate of the Value of Two hundred and fifty pound or other Estate of the value of five Hundred pounds—and That the Qulification of a Councillor or Senator be a freehold of the Value of one Thousand pound or other Estate to the value Two Thousand pound———
5th. That the Qulification of a governor be a freehold Estate of the value of not less than Two Thousand pounds—and That the Governor have authority as Captain General to March the Militia into any State adjoining to this for the Defence of the Same Should Such State be Actually Invaded in the Recess of the General Court.
Lastly—That precepts Shall be Issued in the year 1795 for Delegates to be Choosen to set in Convention for Altering Amending and Rectifying the Constitution and also again in the year 1810 and so once in every 15 years Shall be Duly holden Such a Convention for ever
Number of voters present Thirty one
all unanimous————a True Copy att.

Andrew Mackie: Town Clerk

Our Reasons for the foregoing are briefly thus
1st—The Papist are generally known to be something of a Restless Disposition and Their Religious Principles are of a Persecuting nature and Tendency when ever the Power is in their hands———
2d—We think the Third article of the Bill of Rights is Compleat without the 4th paragraph and the Retaining the Same may give power to Some to Raise money on Such persons as may not be justly charged with the payment thereof, which may Cause Contentions and Endanger the Internal peace of the people of this State in Many places———
3d—We think that the number of Councillors and Senators is too large and that 28 may be sufficient for the Constituting both the Councill and Senate; and that Increasing the number is Increasing the publick Expences more than the prospect of advantage arising therefrom———
4th and 5th———That an Interest in a Community or State is a great

Attachment to fidelity and faithfullness to the same; we think no man ought to be advanced to places of Important Trust That has not a Considerable Interest to Share the fate of others in Time of War and other Such General Calamities—as a person having nothing of value to loose in a State may be Tempted for the Sake of Gain to change sides with Enemies and thereby Endanger its Safety or otherwise Betray the Liberties for his own Emolument.———

and also we think that the Defence of the United States is Equally our own; and should our Governor have no power to march the militia to their Relief in the Recess of the General Court he might possibly be obliged to be a Spectator of the Devastation of a neighbour State and See an Enemy fix and fortify themselves therein Before an order of Council Could be obtained to march to their Relief and Thereby our own Safety Endangered———

Lastly———as a State of Humanity is a State of Imperfection and as Encroachments are apt to be made in the best Devised Constitutions ever yet Enjoyed by any people. We think, it is best that Periodical Conventions be Certainly held for Supplying Defects, and Rectifying abuses, should any be found at Conventions at their Several periods———

Israel [*illegible*] Select Men
Rowland Thacher

BARNSTABLE COUNTY

Barnstable (277/47, 48)

The inhabitants of the Town of Barnstable in full Town Meeting assembled (for the purposes of takeing into Consideration and acting upon the new Constitution or form of Government for the State of Massachusetts Bay) on the third Day of May AD 1780—after Distinctly Reading and Candidly Considering the Same made Choice of a Respectable Committee further to Consider thereof and to Report their opinion thereon at an adjournment of Said Meeting for that purpose.

At the above adjournment for the aforesaid purposes on the 23d Day of May Current the Committee Reported according to order the following votes subject to alterations amendments etc.—

first: the inhabitants of this Town Return their gratefull acknowledgments to the Honorable Convention of Delages. for the indefatiguable Care and Pains must necessarily attend them in Performing the arduous Business of forming a new plan of government Designed in all its parts to preserve such a happy Ballance betwix Ruler and People as that the Peace and Safety of the State may not be Endangered By arbitrary Despots on the one hand or Licentiousness anarcy and Confusion on the other—which appears to us to have been the grand object steadealy kept in view by the Honorable Convention by the generous Spirit of freedom on the one hand and necessary Checks on the other generally Difuseing itself thro the whole Performance but as it is acknowledged by all that it is the undoubted Right of Each individual to offer his sentiments on matters so vastly important to himself and Posterity as that of fixing the invariable Rule By which they ought to be governed and forever subjected we would with modesty offer the following Proposals by way of alteration and amendment which we Doubt not will Be Candidly attended to

Voted 2d that it is the opinion of this Town founded upon the Law of nature—and Common Sense and the Reason of things that no more of the natural Rights of a free people ought to Be given up to the governing power than is absolutely and Esentially necessary for the good government of the whole—and as we Can at present see no Reason to the Contrary: it is the opinion of this Town that the Judges of the inferiour Courts and Justices of the Peace for each County ought of Right to be Elected by the free Suffrages of the people of said County in the Same way and manner (and: if that may be agreable) on the Same Day the Senators are Chosen—and on their good Behavior to Continue in office 5 or 7 years Before a new Election takes place: the number of Justices for Each town in a County to be assertained by a County meeting held for that purpose: or in Such manner as is provided for assertaining the number of Representitives which Each town may not Exceed——we have Carefully attended to the objection: in the adress Page 15—— But we apprehend: the People at Large Especially in the Remoter Countys in the State have infinitely more to fear from the Baneful influence of the ambitious and artfull men with some future governor and five Councellors who are not Likely to be acquainted with the personal accomplishment of those he may Recommend to those important offices —besides, it ought allways to be Remembered—that the Same pernitious influence may be used in favor of a governors Election and Perhaps urged by the unworthy man in order to give his Recommendations the greater weight with a governor——Consequently those offices in the Civill Department are in the greatest Danger of Being filled with persons the most unworthy which may Prove a grievious injury—Rather than a blessing to the Community and fit to answer Little or no Valluable purposes to Society. we Cant at present apprehend more need to be urged on the Subject than just to mention that it appears to us if the matter Rested with the people of a County (who generally know thire worthyest men they will be in no Danger under those Circumstances to be unduely influenced to their own apparent injury—it is allso the opinion of this Town that as in some Cases no appeal is to be had from the inferior to the Supream Court that the Justices of the inferior Courts ought not to sit as Legislatures

Voted 3d. that this Town agrees fully with the Honorable Convention that it is of the Last importance to the Verey being of a free State that an Exact Subordination be forever Preserved of the military to the Civil Department—but how Such Subordination Can ever Be Kept up or Ever more than the Shadow of it if the Civill and Military offices be not totally seperated and never to Rest at the same time in the same hands we Cannot Conceive, and therefore wish them to be kept seperate

4th it is the opinion of this Town that the Election of the field officer ought to be by the free Suffrages of the whole alaram List of Each Rigment on one and the Same Day in a method similar to the Election of Senaters and in Like manner the Brigadier General by the whole Brigade

Voted 5th as the opinion of this Town that no person ought to be Eligeble to the office of Governor within this State or to any other office Civil or Military unless he Shall Declare himself (in fact) to be of the Christian protestant Religion;—we wish to give none offence—we Cannot Conceive any will be taken—we are in no Doubt but that in most of the kingdoms of Europe Every person must be of the Establisht Religion of the State as a necessary Quallification for office.

Voted 6th that it is the Desire of this Town that the number of members of the House of Representitives sufficient to Constitute a Quorum might be Enlarged: upon the important occations of granting Lands and Large Sums of money———

Voted 7th as the Desire of this Town that any suspension of the Habeas Corpus act may not take place but in times of the greatest Danger to the State—and that—the Same may be Exactly assertained and Specified and the Term of Such Suspension Limmited to Six months at furthest but on no occation whatever in Times of peace and safety.

Voted 8th as the opinion of this Town that the Time Limmitted and set for Reviseing the new Constitution and form of Government ought not to Exceed five or Six years.

At the adjournment of Said Meeting on the 23d of May 1780 the aforegoing Report was Read Distinctly and fully Debated and Considered by the Town when the following Votes were put Viz first Whether The Town Do approve of the Constitution or form of Government agreed on by the Honorable Convention for the State of Massachusetts Bay as it now Stands in the Printed Book without any alteration or amendment which Past in the Negative seventy four against to ten in favor of its Pasing———

2d the Question being put whether The Town will agree To the Bill of Rights and The new form of Government with the Proposed alterations and amendments Past in the affirmative fifty four for it to two against it———

Voted 3d—that a committee be appointed To take the forgoing Report of the Committee thus accepted by the Town into a fair Draught in order to its being Transmitted To the Convention———

Dated at Barnstable
May 26th 1780

a true Coppy of
the proceedings attest
of the Town
Ebenezer Bacon
Town Clerk

Sir.

Agreable To the Request of the Honorable Convention The Selectmen of Barnstable herewith Return the Votes and Proceeding of Said Town Relative to the Proposed Constitution for the State of Massachusetts Bay. We wish it Safe To hand and that the Hints given by this Town for some Little alterations therein may not be Disagreable to the Honorable Convention or militate with the General Sentiment of the people at Large wishing the Divine Guidance and Direction still To attend the Honorable Convention in Compleating the arduous Business———

I subscribe my Self in the name and per order
of the Select Men of Barnstable
Your Humble Servant
Edward Bacon

Dated at Barnstable
the 27th of May 1780

Chatham *

At a Town meeting Leagually warned and held at Chatham on the 16th day of May 1780. Joseph Howes Moderator for to hear and derter-mine and to give our judgements on the frame of Government sent to us from the Convention, and after reading and debateing on some particulars the Town thought proper to adjourn said meeting to Monday the 22nd day of this instant May. At our meeting House at one o'clock in the after noon, on said day, then to meet and act further on said frame of Government. and accordingly said meeting was adjourned to the above said day of this instant May.

At the Town meeting held by adjournment the 22d day of May 1780. Joseph Howes Moderator. After reading the above said frame of Government. there being 21 of the inhabitants that attended said meeting.

* Town records, II, 288, Massachusetts Historical Society.

The Moderater called a vote to see if they would accept said frame, and there was 11 voted for, and 10 did not see, as they said their way clear to vote anyway and stood as [?] in said affair and the Selectmen thought proper not to send any returns concerning said meeting.

Eastham (277/49)

At a meeting of the male Inhabitants of the Town of Eastham from 21 Years old and upwards on May 18. 1780 and continued by adjournment to the 23rd. Instant to take into consideration a form of Government agreed upon by the Deligates of the People of the State of the Massachusetts Bay in Convention begun and held at Cambridge September 1, 1779 and continued by adjournment to the 2d of March 1780———

Part 1st on the Declaration of Rights

Article 1st.—Approved unanimous Present 48

Article 2d. Approved by 50

Article 3d. Approved by 48 Disapproved by 7 present 55

The objectors reasons are because the 3d. article is incompatible with the 2d and therefore desire the 3d. article may be left out in this Constitution.

Article 4th, 5th, 6th, 7th, 8th, 9th, 10th, 11th, 12th, 13th, 14th, and 15th approved Unanimous, present 60

Article 16th Unanimous for amendment present 63

Reasons are because the words ought not is too loose an expression in this article. Desire the words shall not to be substituted in their stead

Article 17th Unanimous for amendment present 64

Desire the word ought to be amendend as in the foregoing article for the same Reasons.

Article 18th, and 19th approved unanimous present 64

Article 20th Unanimous for amendment present 64

Desire the word ought may be amended as in the 16th article foregoing, for the same reasons.

Article 21st. 22d: Approved unanimous present 56

Article 23d. Unanimous for amendment present 56

Desire the word ought may be amended as in the aforenamed 16th article and for the same reason

Article 24th Approved unanimous present 59

Article 25th Unanimous for amendment present 62

Desire the word ought may be amended as in the 16th article foregoing and for the same reasons.

Article 26th Approved Unanimous present 69
Article 27th Unanimous for amendment present 69
Desire the word ought may be amended as in the 16th article and for the same reasons
Article 28th. Unanimous for erasement. present 67
Desire the words. But by the authority of the legislature, erased. The reasons are because we think thire can be no necessity for the legislature to have power to subject to the law martial the whole Body Politick.———
Article 29th and 30th Aproved Unanimous present 67

Part 2d The Frame of Government
Approved Unanimous present } 68

Chapter 1st Section 1st. The General Court———
Article 1st 2d 3d and 4th Approved Unanimous present 66

Chapter 1st Section 2d Senate———

Article 1st Approved Unanimous present 63
Article 2d. Approved by 16 Disapproved by 47 present 63
The objectors reasons are because it is against the 1st article in this Constitution and inconsistant with the liberties of free men.———Desire it may be amended thus. That all men (from 21 years and upwards) that pay Taxes Vote for Governor Council Senate and House of Representatives and Desire the articles relating to the qualifications of voters for Governor Council and House of Representatives may be amended accordingly
Article 3d, 4th, 5th, 6th, 7th, 8th and 9th, approved of Unanimous present 63

Chapter 1st Section 3d House of Representatives

Article 1st. 2d. and 3d Approved Unanimous present 63
Article 4th Approved by 16. Disapproved by 47 present 63
Objectors desire an amendment in the qualification of voters as in article 2d. relating to the Senate, and for the same reasons———
Article 5th. 6th. 7th. 8th. 9th. 10th. and 11th. Approved Unanimous present 63

Chapter 2d Executive Power Section 1st Governor———

Article 1st Approved Unanimous present 63
Article 2d Unanimous for an amendment, present 63
Desire the Governor may declare himself to be of the protestant Religion in stead of the Christian Religion. Reason are because we think it safest for the common wealth.———

Article 3d.*, 4th, 5th, 6th, 7th, 8th, and 9th, approved unanimous, present 63

* Article 3d. Approved by 16 Disapproved by 47.

Desire the qualifications of voters may be amended as in the 2d. Article relating the Senate and for the same reasons———

Article 10th Approved by 52 Disapproved by 11 present 63

The objectors Desire the Militia Officers may be appointed by the Governor with the advice of the Council. Reasons are because they think the Militia will be in better order.

Article 11th, 12th and 13th, Approved unanimous present 63

Chapter 2d. Section 2d. Lieutenant Governor

Article 1st. Unanimous for amendment as followeth present 63

Desire the Lieutenant Governor may declare himself of the protestant Religion. Reasons are because we think it Safest for the common wealth and the following amendment on account of the qualifications of voters stand thus 16 for the article as it stand and 47 for an amendment as in the 2d. article relating to the Senate and for the same reasons.———

Article 2d, 3d Approved. Unanimous present 63

Chapter 2d. Section 3d. Council and manner of setling Elections by the Legislature

Article 1st, 2d, 3d, 4th, 5th, 6th, and 7th

Approved Unanimous present 63

Chapter 2d Section 4th Secretary Tresourer Commissary etc.

Article 1st 2d Approved Unamious present 63

Chapter 3d. Judiciary Power

Article 1st, 2d. 3d. 4th. and 5th. Approved Unanimous present 63

Chapter 4th. Delegates to Congress Approved Unanimous present 63

Chapter 5th Section 1st, The University at Cambridge———

Article 1st. 2d and 3d. Approved Unanimous present 63

Chapter 5th Section 2d. The encouragement of Literature etc.

Approved Unanimous present 63

Chapter 6th Oaths, etc.

Article 1st. Unanimous for amendment, present 63

Desire the amendment may be viz That I believe the Protestant Christian Religion. Reasons are that we think it safest for this Common wealth———

Article 2d. Not clearly understood. 3d. 4th. 5th. 6th. 7th. 8th. 9th, 10th and 11th. Approved Unanimous present 63

A true Coppy Test. Edward Knowles Town Clerk

Falmouth *

A meeting legally held on the 24th day of May 1780 for choice of Representative, Chose moderator Esquire Smith, Chose Major Dimmick to Represent them at the General Court, The form of Government was Distinctly Read, the vote was put, If this Declaration of Rights and this form of government be so agreable to you that you are willing to have them established or declared rights and the civil constitution of the State, please to manifest it, fifteen were for it and eleven against it.

Harwich †

At a town meeting legally notified and assembled at Harwich May the 16 1780. Solomon Freeman Esq was chosen Moderator. The Town made choice of Solomon Freeman Esq and Joseph Nye Esq to represent them at the Great and General Court. Then the town proceeded to consider the new form of Government, and after consideration, it was moved and Seconded to choose a committee to consider the same and report to the town Made choice of Solomon Freeman Esq. Joseph Nye Esq. Joseph Snow, Benjamin Freeman and Kimbal Clark for a committee and then adjourned the meeting to Friday the 26 of May at four oclock in the afternoon. Then met and the Committee four out of the five reported in favor of all its parts. A vote being called and the town did not accept of the report. Then voted and choose a second Committee to consider and report The Committee chosen was the Reverand Mr Dunster, Nathaniel Downs, James Pain, Capt Benj Berry and John Freeman and then the Town adjourned the meeting to Tuesday the sixth day of June next at two oClock in the afternoon At the adjournment on the sixth day of June 1780 after the Committee reported, the Town proceeded until came to the 3rd article of declaration of rights which being debated about being called and thirty two voted for amendments and twenty six as it stood in the book Executive power Article Second after debated a vote was called and there was thirty two votes for an amendment and six as it stands in the book and a motion made as to the revising the Constitution in order to amendments should be in seven years by a unanimous vote number of 38 present then nothing further objected.

* Town records, II, 295, Massachusetts Historical Society.
† Town records, Massachusetts Historical Society.

Sandwich *

At a Legal meeting of the Town of Sandwich May 19th 1779.——— On the Question Whether the Town chuse at this time to have a new constitution or Form of Government made voted in the negative Seventy three Nays and Three yeas.

At a Legal meeting of the Town of Sandwich on August 11th. 1779——— The Proceedings of the Convention begun and held at Concord on the 14th. of July 1779 were Read whereupon the Question was put whether This Town approve and will adopt the Proceedings of said Convention Voted in the affirmative.

At a Legal Meeting of the Town of Sandwich May 12th 1780 continued by adjournment to May 26th and then met Voted that when this meeting is adjouned it be to this day three weeks and that a copy of the Constitution be lodged with some one person in each District for the Perusal of the inhabitants until that time then to be returned.

Truro †

At a meeting of the inhabitanc of the town of truro held at the meeting hous in truro on Monday the 12 day of june 1780 at fore of the clock in the aufter noon in order to se wheather the town will vot for a forme of goverment Mr. Beniaman Collings moderatore for said meeting and the town votted to adjourne the meeting until the 20 day of instant june at the meeting house in truro at nine of the clock in the fore noon voted test

Daniel Paine town clerk

At a meeting of the inhabitanc of the town of truro held at the meeting house in truro on tuseday the 20 day of june 1780 at nine of the clock in the fore noon in order to se wheather the town will vot for a forme of goverment Mr. Beniaman Collings moderatore for said meeting and the town voted to Send to the coart the diffecult surcumstancis the town is under upon the infextions that is in the town and the town

* Town records, Massachusetts Historical Society.
† Town records, Massachusetts Historical Society.

mutially agread to abid and confide with the proseedings of the onnerible coart voted test

Daniel Paine town clerk

Wellfleet *

Town Meeting held May 15 1780

The Constitution or Frame of Government togather with the adress accompanying the same was then read in the meeting by the Moderator. Voted that the meeting be adjourned till Monday next 10 o'clock A.M. then to meet at the meeting house, for further consideration of the Constitution.

Recorded by David S. Greenough Town Clerk

May 22 1780

The Inhabitants being assembled to Consider of the Constitution agreable to their last adjournment Mr. John Greenough being Moderator the Constitution was read Article, by Article, and was approved of by a very large majority, all except the 3 articles in the bill of rights which theire was a large majority against, the number of votes for and against each article was taken by the Selectmen and returns made to the convention agreable to their directions

Recorded by David S. Greenough
Town Clerk

Yarmouth (277/50)

At Two Legal meetings of the Inhabitants of the Town of yarmouth being Twenty one years of age and upwards on Thursday the 23 day of May; and on Monday The 29 of said May following To Take into Consideration the Constitution or frame of goverment and Sent out for the approbation or Disapprobation of the people of the state of Massachusetts Bay etc. at which meetings the followings Votes was passed.——

First weither The Inhabitants Present at Said meetings would Except the Constitution or frame of goverment as it now Stands it passed in the Negative.

Second Weither the Inhabitants Present as aforesaid would Except the

* Town records, Massachusetts Historical Society.

Constitution or frame of goverment with Such Amendments or Alterations as is now Reported by your Committee for the purpose of Takeing The Constitution into Consideration and to Report it passed in the affermative

Third Weither the Town will give their delegate Instructions In Case The amendments or alterations in the Constitution agreed upon and Voted for at the last Town meeting Relative thereto: cant possibly be obtained in Convention and he shall There find that a major part of the Convention are for the Constitution as it now stands Weither the Town will Except of the Same it passed in the affermative Twenty Eight in favour of it Twenty two against it———

Attest. David Thatcher Selectmen of the Town of Yarmouth
Seth Tobey
Isaac Matthews Jr.

To Enoch Hallet Esquire: Delegate for the Town of Yarmouth in the County of Barnstable for the purpose of forming a Constitution or frame of Goverment for the People of the State of Massachusetts Bay etc: agreeable to a vote of the Inhabitants of said Town passed May 29: 1780 directing you to use your Influence that if possible you obtain in Convention at their next session the following ammendments or alterations in the Constitution as voted in said meeting: but if the said ammendments Cannot be obtained: you are alike directed that if a majority are for the Constitution as it now stands the Town will Except of the Same———

First That their shall be a Clause brought into the declaration of Rights for a more speedy and Effectual promulgation or Publication of all Laws orders or Resolves of the Great and General Court whereby the Subject may be duly apprized Thereof before he is Subjected to any penalties———

Second in the 16 article in the Declaration of Rights: the freedom of the press is unlimited: we think it ought to be Limited or restrained in Certain Cases: So far as that the Subject may not be Injured thereby in property or private Character.———

Thirdly in Chapter the Second: and article Second: No person Shall be Eligible to the office of govenor unless he Shall declare Himself to be of the Christian Religion: Voted in town Meeting that he Shall declare himself to be of the protestant Religion.

Fourthly The writt of Heapeas Corpus ought not to be suspended at any time: Except in time of war Invasion or Rebellion and in that Case not for a longer Term then Six months

Fifthly and whereas the time appointed by the Convention For the revision of the Constitution stands Perfixed to the year 1795: voted in Town meeting it ought if thought proper by two thirds of the Quallified Voters in Said State to be Revised at the End of Seven years which will be in the year 1788

Attest.

David Thatcher	Select men
Seth Tobey	of the town of
Isaac Matthews Jr.	Yarmouth

YORK COUNTY

Arundel (277/51)

At a lawful [Town] Meeting held at Arundel the 22d of May 1780 to take into Consideration the form of Government the Town chose a Committee to make Report the Meeting was adjourned to the 29th at which the Committee made Report as follows and after maturely considering the several Articles therein contained do agree to report that they make no Objections to any particular Article but in general approve the same.

In the Name and behalf of the Committee
E. Thomson Scribe

Inhabitants met according to adjournment and voted to accept the Report unanimously

Arundel 29th May 1780

Jona Stone
Asa Burbank Selectmen
Asa Durrell

Berwick (277/52)

At a Legal Town Meeting held at Berwick May 29th, 1780——
1st—Voted Colonel Ichabod Goodwin Moderator——upon which they proceeded to the Business Contained in the Warrant, for Said Meeting. Vizt: To Consider and Act upon the Constitution, or Form of Government agreed upon by the Convention and by them proposed to the people for their Approbation rejection, or amendment; After the same had destinctly read and largely debated, the following articles were objected to, Vizt.

The 1st, 2d. and 3d. and 16th In the Bill of Rights——Chapter 1st Section 1st and 3d. The 4th. Article in Each. Chapter 2d. Section 1st in the 10th Article——Upon which the following persons were Chosen, and Voted to make amendments—Vizt. [Docr.?] Low Colonel Ichd. Goodwin Mr. Jona. Hamilton Mr. Wm. Frost Jr. and Captain Wm. Rogers and Report to this Meeting upon adjournment. on Thursday next 12 O. Clock at Noon to this place; to which time and place, the Meeting was accordingly Adjourned——

At a Town Meeting held at Berwick June 1st 1780. upon Adjournment from May 29th.——

The aforesaid Committee Report as follows Vizt——

Your Committee having taken the matter into Consideration, for which they were appointed agree to Report the following amendments Vizt:

That Article 2d. in the Declaration of Rights Amended may Stand as follows Vizt.——

Article 2d It is the Right, as well as Duty of all men in Society, publickly and at Stated Seasons to Worship the Supreme Being, the great Creator and preserver of the Universe. And as the free exercise of the Right of Conscience, and private Judgement in the grand affair of Spiritual Edification, are natural, essential, and unalienable Rights, it is *declared* that no Subject Shall be hurt, molested, or restrained, in his person, Liberty, or Estate, for worshiping God in the manner and Season, most agreable to the Dictates of his own Conscience; or for his Religious profession, or Sentiments, provided he doth nothing hurtful, injurious or detrimental to the civil State, nor obstructs others in their Religious worship.——That the 3d. Article in the Declaration of Rights be amended, so as to Stand as follows Vizt.——

Article 3d. As piety, Religion and Morality are of the greatest importance to the good Order of civil Government, and as these may be more generally, and conveniently difused through a Community by the Support of the publick worship of God, and of publick Instructions in piety, Religion, and Morallity: Therefore to promote their Happiness and Secure the good order of their Civil Government, the people of this Commonwealth, may invest their Legislature with power to authorize and require, and the Legislature shall, from time to time, authorize and require, such, and only such, of the Inhabitants of the several Towns, Parishes, Precincts, and other Bodies Politic as shall voluntarily consent thereto, to make provision at their own expence, for the support of the publick worship of God, and for the support and maintenance of publick Protestant Teachers of Piety, Religion, and morallity. And the people of this Common Weealh have a Right to, and do invest their Legislature with Authority to enjoin upon all the Subjects, that cannot conscientiously or conveniently attend upon any publick worship, or Instructions, at Stated times and Seasons a Confinement to their usual places of abode, or residences at Such times and Seasons, unless in cases of urgent necessity

And all the people of this Commonwealth Shall at all times have the exclusive Right of electing their public Teachers and of contracting with them for their Support and Maintenance. And every Denomination of Christians Shall be equally under the protection of the Law: And no Subordination of any one Sect or Denomination towards another Shall ever be established by Law.———

That Article 16th in the Declaration of Rights be amended as follows vizt.

Article 16th. The Liberty of the Press is assential to the Security of Freedom in a State: it Shall not therefore be restrained in this Commonwealth, unless in Cases where it is extended to the abuse, or injury of Private Characters.

In Chapter 6th Article 7th———

The following amendment is Reported———Vizt That the Writ of Habeas Corpus, Shall not be Suspended by the Legislature, except in times of War, Invasion, and Rebellion, and then for a limited time not exceeding Six Months.———

And Said Committee recommend, that the Convention be impowered to agree upon a time when this Constitution Shall take place, without returning it to the people, and Confirm the Same for the Term of ten Years and no longer, provided the above amendments Shall by them be agreed to.———

The above amendments being Several times Read, with the Recommendation, The Vote was put whither the Town would accept the Constitution, with the above amendments, it passed in the affirmative

Voters present and Voting [for] it .... 58———
against it .... 12———

Put to Vote whither Town would chuse another Deligate to Join the Convention, pass in the Negative

Put to Vote whither the above vote Should be reconsidered. Passed in the affirmative.

Then put to Vote whither they would Send a new Deligate as aforesaid passed in the Negative———

Voted the following persons be a Committee to draw up Instructions for the Deligate Vizt.

Docr. Nathel. Low
Captain Wm. Rogers
Mr. Jona. Hamilton

And report to this Meeting upon adjournment upon Saturday next 3 O'Clock P:M: to which it was Voted, this Meeting should be adjourned and accordingly was adjourned to said Time, at this place.

At a Town Meeting held at Berwick June 3d. 1780 upon adjournment from June 1st. The aforesaid Comittee Report to this Meeting the following Instructions for their Deligate Vizt.——

The above Directions, as Reported by Said Comittee were accepted, by the Town, and Voted, and that the Same be Sent to their Deligate.

Voted This meeting be desolved
for it——26 votes
against——2——
and it was accordinly desolved

The foregoing is a true copy from the Minutes.
Attest Nahum Marshall Town Clerk
Berwick June 3d 1780
The foregoing votes and orders where passed at said meeting Examined by

John Hill | Selectmen
Jacob Shorey | of
William [Huppar?] | Berwick

Biddeford (277/53)

Sir

We herewith send you Inclosed the proceedings of the Town of Biddeford respecting the new Form of Government and

The Town met the 22nd Instant and choose a Committee to make such Alterations and Amendments as they saw fit, and lay them before the Town at the Adjournment, But at the Adjournment there was but ten met who were Unanimous to accept of it with the Alterations and Amendments specified in their Proceedings. We are sorry there were so few met, but think that ought not to dishearten any, but rather to quicken to Zeal and Perseverance those who are desirous of Order, Regularity, and good Subordination.

We are Sir, with due respect
Your most obedient
Humble servants
Benja Nason
Allason Smith
Select Men of Biddeford

Biddeford May 30th 1780

To the Secretary of the Convention of the Massachusetts Bay

At a legal Meeting of the Freeholders and other Inhabitants of the Town of Biddeford duely notified and assembled on Monday the 22nd of May 1780. 2 O'Clock P.M. to see if the Town would approve alter or reject the new Form of Government made by the Convention at Cambridge March the 2nd 1780
Rishworth Jordan Esquire Moderator——
adjourned to Monday the 29th. Instant 2 O'Clock P.M.——
Monday May 29th. 1780 Met according to Adjournment
Voted To accept the Form aforementioned with the following Alterations, on the Tenth Article of the Second Chapter, All military Officers ought to be appointed and commissioned by the Governor by and with the Advice of Council——Except, All Aid de Camps ought to be appointed by their own Major Generals, Brigade Majors by their Brigadiers or Commandants of Brigades, Adjutants and Quarter Masters by their Colonel or commanding officers of Regiments and commissioned by the Governor with the advice of Council——

Reason, Because they are liable to be under control by being dependent on the Soldiers for their Commissions and therefore cannot act free and independent——

Reason, Because they are liable to be degraded or superseeded in Case of a Vacancy by the Soldiers, if they do not act in Conformity to their Wills and capricious Humors, without Reason, or against Reason——
Ten Voters present, Unanimous——

A true copy from the Records Jere: Hill Town Clerk
NB. Ten may save the [Country.]

Buxton (277/54)

Mr President and Gentlemen of the Honorable Convention

We the Inhabitants of the Town of Buxton Having been Presented with the Constitution You Propose, We conceive it to be our Indispenceble duty to examine it with the Greatest precaution, as we have not only to answer our Right to our own particular Welfare, but forever Liable to the Censure of the Latest Posterity

A constitution founded upon Justice and equity no less than a People who have struggled so hard in the Cause of Liberty as those of America well [deserve?] we should feel our Selves Happy in its Opperation.——

Agreeable to Your directions we have Assembled, and deliberately and Impartially examined your proposed Frame of Government, and Have found the 3d. Article in the declaration of Rights and a number of others in the Course of the Legislative, and Executive Part of the Constitution, to be Contrary to our Sentiments, which Caused a Majority against the Said Frame of Government as it now Stands to the Number of forty nine. Four Persons accept of the whole, only they would have every Officer in the State a protestant; And be certain of a Revisal of the Constitution at the end of fifteen years. But in Consideration of the following amendments and alterations have agreed to accept it to the Number of thirty seven.

The Declaration of Rights (the 3d. Article excepted) we Conceive to be Just and Equittable, Which 3d. Article Apears to Stand thus, That although it is to be Acknowledged that every one has an Indisputable and Uncontrolable Right to dispose of his property to the Support of his own SECT or to a public Teacher of his own Denomination if he Can give his attention, but if he Cannot, then it is to be left with the Legislative Authority to dispose of his Monies as they shall think proper, Notwithstanding any Liberty before Allowed in the 2d. article, Which we Conceive to be an Infringement upon Conscience, As Matters of Religion Apears Intirely to be between GOD and Individuals, and that the Legislative Authority Ought not to Intefere in Matters of Religion, Except it be in Cases of disturbances of the peace in Time of Worship.——

We Conceive that the Legislative Authority ought not consist of More branches thane One House, that the Inconveniency arising in Negatives and Long debates, is more Injurious to the Good People of this State than Errors which may be Committed without Such Seperate branches. Long experience has been our Schoolmaster in this Case, and therefore we Prepose the following Method of Legislation (viz) that there shall be but one house which Shall annually be Elected from the Several Towns and Plantations in this State, and they shall have the Sole Power of Government agreable to the Constitution.

In the 3d. Section and 10th. Article You Propose the house of Representatives to be the Sole Judge of the quallifications of its own Members —Agreeable to this Article we Conceive it to be in the Power of the House when formed to the Number of Sixty (which Constitutes a quorum) to expell any they please from Their Seat in Government, this we Conceive to be Unjust and Unconstitutional, and are of oppinion that every Town and Plantation Quallifyed agreeable to the Constitution, Shall be the Sole Judges of the quallification of its Own Members.

It is our Opinion that no Person Ought to hold any Civil Office in This State except he be a Professor of the Protestant Religion.

It is our Oppinion that there Shall be a Convention for the Revisal of the Constitution not to exceed ten Years Successively, as we Conceive it will have a Tendancy to promote the free Exercise of Government in its Just and equittable Design and Institution, and that the Legislative Authority shall Issue their Warrents for Deligates for that purpose and if Upon their Refusal or Neglect, the Select Men and Committees of each Town and Plantation in the State Shall Call a Meeting of their Several Towns and Plantations for that Purpose.

Thus Gentlemen we Have endeavoured to explain our Sentiments in as Short and Comprehensive a Manner as Possible, and have endeavoured to Make Such Amendments as we in Our Judgements think most Expedient we are, Gentlemen, Your

Devoted and Very Humble Servants
Jno. Woodman
Jacob Bradbury
Ebenezer Wentworth
Select Men of Buxton

Buxton May 1780
The Convention may take notice that 12 persons only reject the whole of this Constitution

Ebenezer Wentworth, Select Man

Kittery (277/55)

Whereas it appears necessary that a Constitution or form of Government should be established, the same being done in most of the Other States and the Delegates from the differant Towns, chosen for this purpose in this State having Unanimously agreed upon one which is sent forth for inspection and Consideration——

We the Inhabitants of this Town having perused the same, Do approve, and accept of the said form of Government or Constitution as Exhibited to us by the Convention of this State agreable to a Pamphlet lately Published and now before us, subjected notwithstanding to the alterations that may be made by the said Convention at their next Meeting; and that after the same Shall be ratified we will accordingly conform our selves thereto.

This may Certifie that for the above their was four persons Against the 2d. Article and seventy six for it——3d. Article—8 Against it seventy five for it——

Nine against the form of Government. Voted all Together and Seventy one for it——

Kittery 22d May 1780

A True Copy of the Vote of this Town Attested

Dennis Fernald Town Clerk

Sanford *

At a legal meeting of the Freeholders and other inhabitants of the Town of Sanford the 25th of May 1780 to examine the several articles in the new form of Government:

1. Voted James Gare moderator.
2. Voted to choose a committee to make remarks on a number of articles in said form.
3. Voted the said committee to take under consideration the articles of the Governer, Senators, and Counsillors that shall be Protestants.
4. Voted Walter Powers, Ebenezer Buzzell, Daniel Gile, Jonathan Tibbetts, and Nathaniel Conant be a committee for the above purpose and make report to the next meeting.

* Town records, Massachusetts Historical Society.

5. Voted the seven articles be taken under consideration.
6. Voted to adjourn this meeting to thursday the first day of june next at John Knights barn at three of the o'clock in the afternoon.

Caleb Emery, Town Clerk.

At a meeting of the Freeholders and other inhabitants of the town of Sanford held by adjournment from May 25th to the present first day of June.

Mr. James Gare Moderator.

1. Voted not to accept the report of the committee brought concerning the several articles, brought in against the form of Government.
2. Voted not to act anything upon the new form of Government.

Caleb Emery, Town Clerk.

At a legal meeting held in Sanford by adjournment from the 25th day of May to the first day of June Inst.

Mr. James Gare Moderator.

1. Voted not to accept the Committee Report brought in Concerning the 7th Article.
2. Voted not to act anything upon the new form of Government..

Caleb Emery, Town Clerk.

Wells (277/56)

To the Honorable Convention for forming a New Constitution for the State of the Massachusetts Bay

The Proceedings of the Freemen of the Town of Wells in Relation to the New Constitution as proposed by the Convention unanimously agreed upon by the Inhabitants of said Town at their Meeting held on the 27th. day of April and continued by Adjournment to Monday the 22nd. day of May 1780 Seventy Four Voters being present

We have considered the Declaration of Rights with the Frame of Government agreed upon by the Deligates of the People of the State of the Massachusetts Bay in Convention and our Opinion of the same is as follows Viz

The Declaration of Rights in the several Articles We approve and have no Objection to any thing therein contained.

The Frame of Government We find in the Main agreable to our Minds and are of Opinion that it might be for the Interest of the People of this State that the same be Received and confirmed in the following articles.

We are of Opinion that the important Ends of Government would be likely to be much better answered if the Governor might have a Negative on all Acts of the Legislature. We think it very necessary that the Independance of the Executive and Judicial Departments be well secured—Nor can We conceive how this can be done effectually unless there be a Power lodged somewhere of negativing such legislative Acts as tend to destroy or violate this Independancy—And We are clearly of opinion that the Governor will be the most fit person to be intrusted with this Power; he being the first Magistrate and the Sole Representative of the whole Commonwealth; The Center of Union to all the several parts and members of the political Body; who is chosen and constituted by the whole Community to be in a peculiar manner the Guardian of the Constitution and of the Rights and Interests of the whole State—All the Individuals have a like Interest in him and stand in a like Relation to him as their common Representative—We can not but think it would be extreemly dangerous and impolitick to trust an incontroulable Power of Legislation in the Hands of those who are only the Representatives of particular and smaller Districts of the Commonwealth; who may often be disposed to act upon the private narrow Views and Interests of their particular Constituents to the prejudice of the publick Welfair and the Injury of other parts of the Community—When we consider that the several Members of the Legislative Body are to be chosen only by particular Districts as their special Representatives and may not improbably be often chosen for the very purpose of serving and promoting such Views and Designs of their Constituents as would be injurious to other parts of the State. We cannot but think that the Representatives of the Whole People who can have no reason to act under the Influence of such partial Biases and Respects should be furnished with ample and Sufficient Powers to prevent effectually the pernicious Consequences of such narrow Policy, as is calculated to serve the Interest of one part to the injury of another who may happen not to have an equal Interest in the Legislature And this Precaution seems the more reasonable and necessary when We consider it is no ways incredible or improbable—it may sometimes hapen that a Thin House of Representatives and Senators in which but a small part of the Common wealth is represented and the distant parts may Scarce have a single Member to Speak and act on their Behalf may be prevailed upon to pass Bills injurious, oppressive and pernicious to a great part of the people, which if they are suffered to have the Force of Laws would not only operate to the damage of many individuals but also occasion discontents Factions and disunions dangerous to the Commonwealth—As We with divers other parts of the State are like to be always remote from the Seat of Government and can seldom if ever expect to be equally represented in the Legislature or to have an equal Interest in the same with those parts of the State that are near the Capital. We cannot think it safe that an uncontroulable power of disposing of our Persons and properties should be vested in a Legislature in which it may sometimes happen that we are not represented and by Reason of our distance are seldom likely to have an equal Interest in it with most of our fellow Citizens———But We shall always have a Representative in the Person of the Governor. we may claim an equal Interest in him with the other parts of the State. If a partial or misguided Legislature should bear hard upon us his Protection may be claimed his Justice may be appealed to his Interposition may reasonably be hoped for—We therefore think it highly reasonable and necessary that the common Representative of the people, who may sometimes be our principal or only Representative in the general Court chosen by us to act on our behalf, may have his Hand at full Liberty and may be empowered to act effectually and with strong Arm for the Protection of all and every part of his Constituents as there may be occasion———

Nor can we think there can be any danger in deligating ample powers to the common Representative for the publick Service in Superintending the Affairs of the Commonwealth—Dependant as he must be upon the Suffrage of the People for the Authority by which he is to act; it is hard to imagine what Temptation he could be likely to have to abuse his Power of Negativing wantonly to the Vexation and detriment of his Constituents and Fellow Citizens—We may well presume that he would seldom if ever refuse and disallow any Bills passed by the Legislature unless the Reasons for doing so were weighty and plain so that he could venture an appeal upon them to the Judgement and Conscience of the People in general—And We hope that a man who shall have so large a share in the Esteem and Confidence of the people as to be chosen by them to be their common Representative and the guardians of their Rights and Revisor of their Laws would seldom be found so destitute of Wisdom and virtue as to be unworthy of the trust reposed in him or however we can scarce conceive what sufficient inducement a man of any Reflection could have wantonly to disoblige his Constituents on whom his political

Existance depends and draw upon himself their just Resentments—we fear that he would rather be too cautious of interposing his Authority so often as there might be just occasion for it And We are the more confirmed in their apprehensions because we cannot learn that our governors under the late Constitution, though holding their Commissions intirely at the pleasure of the British Crown have been wont to abuse their negativing power to the injury and vexation of the subject unless when they have acted by special Instructions—We are also of Opinion that a negative power in the common Representative upon the legislative Acts would much discourage the projecting or passing iniquitous Bills calculated to serve the private Interest and narrow views of a part to the prejudice of the publick since the promoters of such Designs must have Reason to apprehend that the Governor would interpose his Authority to defeat such Attempts and have the approbation of his Constituents in general for so doing.

The Method proposed Chapter 1 Section 1 Article 2nd for preventing these Evils seems to us inadiquate and attended with manifold inconveniencies. It is no incredible Supposition that Two Thirds of those who may sometimes vote in both Houses of the Legislature may not be chosen to represent more than a Sixth part perhaps of the persons and property of the Commonwealth—That they may be drawn by Interest prejudice and the influence of designing men to favour the Views of a powerful party to the injury of others—Nor with the Methods of voting by yeas and Nays be any great Restraint upon those who may presume that the Bills however iniquitous will not be disagreable to the majority of their particular Constituents—And in Case an injurious and impolitick Bill should happen to pass in this manner though perhaps contrary to the mind of the greater part of the People no orderly and Constitutional way would be left for preventing the pernicious Effects of it—Besides We apprehend that the method of proceeding prescribed in this Article in case a Bill should be objected to by the Governor would greatly retard and Clog the Dispatch of Business which might in some cases occasion a great Expence and be otherwise very prejudicial to the publick Interest———

For these reasons with others which might be mentioned we are fully and clearly of Opinion that it would be much for the Bennefit of the Commonwealth that the governor as the common Representative might have a Negative upon all Legislative Acts—We have opened our Sentiments and Reasons more fully on this Article because We think it a point of great Importance to our Fellow Citizens in general and particularly to ourselves and others in similar Circumstances.

2. We are also of Opinion that a House of Representatives to be Chosen in the methods proposed in Chapter 1 Section 2 Article 2nd would be at present much too numerous for the convenient Dispatch of Business besides the great Expence to the publick which would be occasioned thereby And this Inconvenience will be likely to increase continually in a proportion to the increasing Numbers of the people And We apprehend that the several parts of the State will be likely to be much more unequally represented upon that plan than would be the Case if larger Districts were apportioned to each Representative—We presume not to determine what Number of Representatives would be best suited to answer the Ends of Government, but We desire they may be Reduced to a Conveniant Number which we apprehend with Submission ought not to exceed Two Hundred.

3. Whereas it is provided and declared Chapter 2nd Section 1 Article 2 that no person shall be eligible to the Office of Governor unless he shall declare himself to be of the Christian Religion we cannot but think that the safety peace and Wealfare of a protestant Commonwealth require that its Governor declare himself to be a protestant since it has been found by Experience that a protestant People cannot be happy under the government of those who are of the Roman Church. That Authority and Jurisdiction which the Bishop of Rome claims over the whole Christian World and which all who belong to that Church must be presumed to acknowledge and submit to is We apprehend contrary to a fundamental principal of the Constitution laid down in the 4rth Article of the Declaration of Rights—We apprehend that a Papist is at least as unsuitable to be Chosen and admitted to the Office of Governor in this Commonwealth, as one that makes no profession of the Christian Religion

4 We also object to and disapprove the Methods of appointing the Officers of the Militia proposed Chapter 2 Section 1 Article 10 From what we have observed and heard we are of Opinion that since the method of appointing Officers by Election has been practised, there has frequently been more dissatisfaction and discontent than has formerly been known in Consequence of which military Authority has been weakened and relaxed so that it has often been scarce possible for the Officers to execute the Order of their Superiors. We know of no inconvenience that has been found to arise from the governors having the appointment

of all military officers and it is our mind that the appointing as well as Commissioning such Officers should be by the governor as Captain general.

5 We should also think it were better if the Senators and Representatives might be at liberty annually to elect any person to the Office of Treasurer and Receiver general for as many years successively as they may think proper. And that that Clause in Chapter 2 Section 4 Article 1 which declares that No man shall be eligible to this Office more than Five years successively, may sometimes prove an inconvenient Restraint upon the Electors from continuing a person in this Office whom they may judge most proper for it. And that a better Way might be found to answer the End aimed at in this Restriction.

6 We are also of Opinion that it would be highly expedient that the Meeting of a Convention in the year 1795 for the express purpose of Revising the Constitution and forming such alterations as from Experience shall be found necessary be absolutely ordained and determined on and not left suspended upon the Vote of Two Thirds of the Voters through the State. We think it is in a manner certain that Corrections and Amendments will by Experience be found needful. That it must be the work of Time and Experience to adjust a plan of government for a Commonwealth so wisely and happily in all its parts that the important Ends of its political union may be well provided for and a proper Guard be set against those Abuses both of Liberty and Power which would be dangerous or detrimental to the Interest and happiness of the State—And that the best precautions should be taken that the way may be kept open for applying Seasonable effectual orderly and constitutional Remedies to such Disordirs and Violations of the Constitution as may be observed and for supplying whatever be found to be deficient and correcting what may be found amiss in the plan proposed.

These Objections with the grounds and reasons of them We propose with due defference to the honourable Convention for their impartial Consideration—We have no Intention or desire to obstruct the Establishment of a new Form of government in the State which we think is much needed—We are free to declare our Consent to and acceptance of the Draught and Model which has been laid before us by the honourable Convention in all the Articles of it except those which we have here particularly objected to—And if the Alterations and Amendment We have proposed should be disapproved by the Convention we consent to wave them however reasonable they may appear to us rather than the designed Settlement of Government should be prevented—provided that a future Convention for the Revisal an Correction of the Constitution as may be needful may be determined on and ascertained within a convenient Time not exceeding Fifteen years

Attest

John Wheelwright
Nathaniel Wells
John Maxell
Stephen Larrabe Jr.
Select Men of Wells

York (277/57)

At a legal Town Meeting regularly assembled in York on Monday the 22d. of May 1780.

John Swett Esquire chosen Moderator.

The Constitution or form of Government lately drawn up and agreed upon by the delegates in Convention being read and after some debate upon it, a Commitee was appointed to take the same under consideration and report thereon upon the Adjournment.

Then the Meeting was adjourned to Saterday the 27. of the same May when but thirty of the Freeholders and other Inhabitants of said Town qualified voters met, who unanimously voted to accept of the said Committee's Report as follows.

That the Governor and Council; more especially the Governor; shall be of the Protestant Religion.

That Military Officers shall be appointed by the Governor with advice and consent of Council.

That the Power Suspending the Habeas Corpus be confined to six months.

That the Revisal and amendment (if need be) of the Constitution instead of 15 years shall be done in Ten———

But if these alterations can't be agreed upon rather than the form of Government should fail, We advise to approve of the whole, and we are content it shall take place as soon as the Honorable Convention in their Wisdom shall think fit or recommend.

We approve of his Honorable Judge Sewall our present Delegate, still to continue as such; and that he Endeavour the amendments above.

A Copy Daniel Moulton Town Clerk

SUFFOLK COUNTY

Bellingham (277/60)

At a Publick Town Meeting of the Inhabitants of the town of Bellingham Duly Warned and legaly Assembred on the 24th of April A.D. 1780 and Continued by Adjourments to the 5th of June following for Considering and [ames?] Proposeing amendments in the forme of Govenment Proposed and agreed to by the Convention of Delegates of the People of the State of the Massachusetts Bay in Convention begun and held at Cambridge on the first of September 1779.

The town of Bellingham Passed the followin Votes (viz

That We Reject the whole Bill of Rights And forme of Government as it Stands Printed

But if the following amendments may take Place we accept the Remainder as Printed.

We agreed the Adress Set forth before the Bill of Rights is no Part of the forme of Government We Agreed to the first Part of the Preamble And Rejected the last Part thereof

We agreed to the first Article in the Bill of Rights.

Article 2d. agreed to with the folowing amendment viz. Reject the words (Publick Stated Seasons) and insert in the Roome thereof at all times

Article 3. We reject the 3 Article and Propose for an amendment that all men have a Naturall and Unalienable right to worship God acording to the Dictates of their own Conscience and understanding; And that no man ought or of Right can be compelled to attend any Religious Worship, or to Erect or Suport any Place of worship, or maintaine any ministery contrary to or against his own free will and consent; Nor can any man who acknowledges the being of a God Be justly abridged or Deprived of any Civill Right as a citizen on account of his Religious Sentiment or Peculiar mode of Religious Worship; And that no authority can or ought to be vested in or Assumed by any Power Whatsoever that shall in any Case interfeer with, or in any maner controule the right of conscience in the free Excercise of Religious Worship.

And that the legislature shall have Power to make laws to Prohibit Labour and unnescesary travaling and Recreations on the first Day of the Week.

Articles 5.6.7.8.9.10. and 11th. agree toe.

Article 12. agreed toe with the adition of By Juries acording to the Custome of this State.

Article 13 and 14th agreed toe.

Article 15th agreed toe only Excluding the word (unless) and ad in the Roome the word only

Article 16. agreed toe with ading the word speach

Article 17.18.19.20.21.22. and 23. agreed toe.

Article 24 Axcept with the Alteration Reject the word Preceeding and incert in the Roome thereof laws in force in this State when the Crime was Committed

Article 25.26. and 27th accepted. Article 28 Accepted with the Adition at the end of the word legislature; and not without the Speciall Instructions of their Constituants

Article 29 and 30th Rejected, and ad that as the Bill of Rights is two large, so it is two short that it ought to be aded to the Bill of Rights the Powers and Priviledges of Every Incorporate town in this State to meet Annualy in March and to chuse all town officers and to meet at other times as the Inhabitants may agree and to transact town affairs as has been Usuall in this State.

and Also that every town that shall see fitt shall have full Power and authority to have hold and Injoy and to set up in it a Court of Probate to all intents Purposes and constructions as fully as hertofore been used in Counties in this State. And to set up and have a registry to record all Deeds of Real Estates lying in the same town. and it ought to be set forth in the Bill of Rights, that there ought to be County Assemblies in Each County in this State, the members whereoff to be chosen by the Inhabitants of Each town within the same County, said Assembly or Convention to have Powers of adjournment

on the Frame of Government under the title General Court. Article (1) first Part viz. the department of legislation shall be formed by two Branches, a Senate and House of Representatives accepted the rest rejected and incert in the Room thereof the Senate shall not have Power to Negative any act of the House of Representatives.

Article 2d Reject and incert in the Roome thereof that no law shall be Established for a law for this State but Such as Shall have been agreed toe by two thirds of the Generall court in one room assembled and untill it has been Published and Sent to Each town in this State

Article 3d Axcept with the adition next after the words other Courts in the third line, add Courts that have been Used in this State for five years last Past.

Article 4 accept the first Part, and Reject the words (under the hand of the Governour of this Common Wealth with the advice and Consent of the Council) and incert in the Roome, under the hands of the major Part of the Senate, the Same being apropriated by the House of Representatives [a]

[a] in the Frame of Government under the title Generall Court Article (1) Sectshion 4th Page 18 on the words Duties and Excises; Reject the Words (Produced Manufactured or being in the Same and incert in the Roome thereof that it shall not be in the Power of the Generall Court to Impose nor levy any Duties nor Excises on any Produse nor any Particulars manufactured of nor in the State of the Massachusetts-Bay.

Under the title Senate: Article (1) Rejected and incert in the Roome thereof that there Shall be Elected by a majority of written votes of the House of Representatives thirty one Persons out of their own number for Senators for this State, not more than one in a town, to be Elected annually on the last Wensday in May, and if they canot be chosen on that Day, then as soone after as may be—And the Said Senaters shall be Stiled the uper House and that the vacant Seates in the house of Representatives by the choice of the Senators, shall be made up speedily as follows, the Remaining Representatives shall Imediately send to the Selectmen of the Towns where those Representatives were chosen that are appointed Senators, that said Towns may if they se cause fill up the said vacat Seats. And at any time in Each year when vacancies may hapen in the House of Representatives for the time being, by Death or removel etc. the House of Representatives to send to the Select men in the maner they have used for the last five years, and the Said Senators and House of Representatives shall be the Sole legislators for the State of the Massachusetts.

Article 2.3.4.5. Rejected Article 6.7.8.9th accepted on House of Representatives.

Article (1) accepted. Article 2. Rejected and incert in the Roome thereof that Every Incorporate town in this State may Elect one Representative and that Every town that has 400 Poles that has and do Pay Publick taxes may Elect two Representatives, and Every town that has 800 such Poles may Elect three Representatives, and Every town that has

1600 such Poles may Elect four Representatives and Every town that has 3200 such Poles may Elect five Representatives. And no town shall ever be allowed to send more than 5 Representatives to sit in the Generall Court at the same time And that no town shall be fined for not Electing a Representative that lies more then fifty miles from the Place where the Generall Court shall sett, that have not more than a 100 Poles that have and do Pay Publick taxes And that Every town shall pay their own Representative or Representatives.

Article 3d. Rejected and ad in the Roome thereof Every man that is and has been an Inhabitant in any town in this State one Year and has and then does Pay Public Taxes and is a freeholder in the same Town, shall be Elegeable to be Elected a Representative for said town.

Article 4 Reject and incert in the Roome thereof Every man in this State that is an Inhabitant in any town and has and then Does Pay Publick Taxes shall have a Right to vote in the same town in the Election of a Representative or Representatives. Article 5. and 6th accepted. Article 7th. those words that all money Bills origenate in the house of Representatives accepted, all the rest of the 7th Article Rejected. Article 8 accepted. Article 9th accepted with the alteration of not less than 80 members to be a Corum.

Article 10. accepted Articl. 11. accepted only reject the words and Governour and Councel.

Executive Power, under the title Governour.

Article 1.2.3.4. Rejected. Article 5th Reject the words (Governour with the advice of Council) and incert in the Roome thereof the major Part of the Senate and house of Representatives in one House and instead of he may say they may. And wholy Reject the last Paragraft.

Article 6. Rejected. Article 7 Rejected (the word Governour and incert in the Roome thereof Generall Court Rejected the words (him self) and incert them selves and Rejected the word (Governour) towards the latter end of the first Paragraft and incert in the Roome thereof the words Generall Court. the rest of this Paragraft accepted, the last Paragraft in the 7th Article Rejected.

Article 8. Rejected and incert in the Roome thereof the Power of Pardoning offences after Conviction, shall be in the Senate with the Speaker of the House of Representatives.

Article 9 rejected and incert in the Roome thereof that the Attorney Generall and Solisceter Generall shall be apointed by the Generall Court. and That all County officers shall be Elected by County Assemblies. And

That there shall be by the Generall Court Stated county Assemblies in Each County in this State to meet Annually and that in Each Town in Each County in this State the Select Men shall be impowered to call their Town Inhabitants together annually to Chuse one or more Delegates according to the Representation amendments concerning Chusing Representatives that said Delegates meet Annually on a Certain Day and in a certaine town in Each County, with Powers to Chuse a President a Clerk and all Necessary County officers, and to Grant money to Defray County Charges, to Performe all acts necessary and Suteable for Such Assemblies, to act and Performe, and to make their own Rules and orders, and to Determin Disputed Elections of their own members, with Powers of adjournments.

Article 10. the first Paragraft Accepted only instead of the word Governour Place the word Senate and insted of (21 years of age) ad 16 years of age

Article 10 the 2d Paragraft. Rejected and incert in the Roome thereof. The Legislature shall by temporary laws Direct the time and maner of conveening the Electors and of Collecting votes and certifying to the Senate the officers so Elected. the 3 Paragraft of the 10th Article Rejected and incert in the Roome thereof the Major Generals shall be apointed by the General Court and be Comishioned by the Senate.

Article 10 the 4th Paragraft accepted with incerting the words by the Senate and Rejecting the words (Governer with advice of Councel.)

Article 10th Paragraft 5th Rejected and incert in the Roome thereof that no officer Duly Commishioned to Command in the Millitia shall be removed from his office but by order of the Generall Court or by fair triall in Court matial.

Article 10 Paragraft 6th accepted only Rejected the word Governour, and incert in the Roome thereof Generall Court

Article 10 Paragraft 7th accept only Rejecting the word Governour and Councel and incerting the General Court

Article 10 Paragraft 8th. accepted.

Article 11. accepted with the Alteration Rejecting the words (Governour for the time being with the advice and consent of Councell) and incert the Senate.

Article 12th. accept with the following alterations

Reject the word (Governour) first named and ad in the Roome of it the Senate and reject the word Governour named a second time in this Article and incert in the Roome of it the General Court, and reject the word (Governour) where it is named a third time in this 12th. Article and incert in the Roome of it the Senate

Article 13th. Rejected and add in the Roome of it All Sallaries Granted by the Generall Court Shall Be Granted Annually.

Chapter 2. Page 35. under the title Lieutenant Governour.

the Whole 3 Sections Rejected

Page 36. under the title councell etc.

the whole Seven Articles Rejected

Secretary Treasurer Commissary etc. Page. 38.

Article (1st) accepted Rejecting the word Successively and add not more then five Years in Eight Years.

Article 2d. accepted only Rejecting the words (Governer and Counsel)

Judiciary Power Page 39.

Article (1) accept the first three lines Excepting the last word all. and add. all Comisshion officers Comisshoned and Sworn shall hold their offices one year unless sooner Removed for male administration.

Article 2d, and 3d. Rejected. Article 4 Rejected and add in the Roome thereof that it shall be in the Power of Each Town in this State at their annual Town Meeting in March to chuse men that Shall have the Power of a Judge of Probate of Wills and Granting letters of administration etc. and also a Register of Probate to be Invested with all the Powers that Judges of Probate and Regestors are by the Present laws in this State invested with, as to Estates and Persons Dying in the Same Town And if any town in this State Neglects the choice of a Court of Probate and Register all the month of March in any Year, It shall be in the Power of the Senate to apoint a Judge of Probate and a Register for the Same Town.

And that it shall be in the Power of Each Town in this State Annualy in the month of march to apoint a man to record the Deeds of all Reall Estates lying within the Bounds of the Same town. Article 4. [5] reject and incert all causes of mariages Divorce and allimoney and all appeales from Courts of Probate shall be determined by the Senate. Delegates to Congress Page 40. accepted only Reject the word (Governor Councel) and incert in Roome Senate.

University at Cambridge page 41.

We have litle kowledge of said University.

It out to be incerted in the form of government that the inhabitants of this State have a Right to Know the University Charters, and the Constitution, and Powers of the Corperation thereof, And all the Gifts and

Grants of the Generall Courts of this State, and of all the Gifts, Grants and Devices of Particular Persons to and for Said University and to any and all the officers thereof. And Said Inhabitants have a Right to know the Annuall Income to and for said University, and how the Same is annualy Expended. the want of which has been Gratly Complained of and untill those things aforesaid are made Plaine, we dont see how we or the Gratest Part of the Comunity are in any capacity to act upon what is Proposed by the convention concerning the University We therefore reject the first, 2, 3d articles untill those matters are made Plaine.

As to Section 2d. the Encouragement of literature is Good and we think the inhabitants of Each Town have the Sole Right and are the Properest Judges of what Schooles are the most Suteall for the inhabitants thereof as they suport and have the advantage thereof and no town has any busness with another Town about Schooles. as that is not a matter of legeslation.

Oaths etc. Page 44 article (1st) Reject the words Governour, Lieutenant Governer, Councellors, and ad in the Rome, any Person Chosen to any office in this State that is the Gift of this State shall swear or affirm before such Person or Persons as the Generall Court shall from time to time appoint for that Purpose.

And in the Declaration next after the word Christian in the first line add Protestant.

and in the 8th Paragraft next after the word Quaker add or any other Person who aledges Scruple of Conscience as his refusall to Swear.

Article 2d. Reject and ad in the Roome, no officer whose office is in the Gift of this State Shall hold more then one Such office at the Same time and ad that Every Person that shall have accepted any office aforesaid shall not be Elegeable to any other office that Year. and ad that no officer in this State whether Town County or State shall hold any office more then one Year without a new apointment and none shall hold the same office more then five Years in Eight Years. Article 3d. Page 48 Rejected

Article 4th Reject the word Governour and incert in the roome the word Senate all the rest of the 4th article acept.

Article 5th. Page 49. accepted

Article 6th. Reject the words (and usually Practiced in the Courts of law.) all the rest of Article 6th accepted,

Article 7th the first four lines accepted, Except the last word all the rest of the 7th Article rejected.

Article 8 and 9th Page 49. 50th accepted.

Article 10 Reject and incert in the Rome thereof.
That there shall be a Convention for the Purpose of forming Such alterations and amendments in the Constitution as from Experience shall be found necessary and for the Good of the Comunity which Convention shall meet at Concord on the last Wensday in September at 10 of the clock in the forenoone; in the Year 1790. (unless the Convention that are to meet in Boston on the 7th of June 1780 shall Publish in the form of Government now under Consideration some other convenient Town near the center of this State for said Proposed Convention to meet in) the members of said Proposed Convention to be Elected as follows, The Select men in Each incorperated town and the Assessors of the unincorperated Plantations shall conveene their respective inhabitants, By issuing their warants to meet 30 Dayes before the last Wensday in September aforesaid that all may meet and act in said meetings in each of the Towns and Plantations where they Dwell and are inhabitants and that have and Do there Pay Publick Taxes, The members to be Elected according to the Representation named in these Proposed Amendments concerning Electing Representatives, and said Convention when met shall Proceed by a majority of written votes to chuse their own officers Settell Disputed Eletions of their own members and make their own Rules and orders and then Proceed to alter amend and Regulate the form of Government of this State that shall then be in being acording to their own minds and adjourn for 6 months and send the form so amended to Each town and Plantation in this State for their allowance or to Propose amendments to be sent back to said Convention at their meeting after adjournment, and said Convention Consider and adjourn and send to said Towns and Plantations untill two thirds of the Inhabitants that have and then Do Pay Publick taxes have agreed to Each article in said Proposed and amended form of Government.
And at the End of Every ten Years afterwards there shall be begun and held a Convention at the same Place on the last Wensday in September the members to be chosen in the same maner and by the same Rules and for the same Purpose and with the Powers as the Convention aforesaid is to have in the Year. 1790. Except the last Convention in any ten years apoint another Convenient town to meet in and Publish it in their altered and amended form.
Voted that the Town of Bellingham instruct our Delegate to use his utmost Endeavours that the Returns of Each Town be red and Considered in Convention, And the Generall Sence of the whole be Printed

and Sent to the Severall Towns for their inspetion and to Propose amendments, and the Convention adjourn at least five months, and that the Towns Return the Same With their amedments to the Convention at their adjournment voted

Bellingham June 5, 1780 the foregoing Perticulars were voted unamously the Numbers are fifty five

Atest Laban Bates Town Clerk

Boston (277/61–62) *

Boston May 30. 1780

We herein transmit you an attested Copy of the Proceedings of this Town with respect to the Constitution or Form of Government, in conformity to a Resolve of the Convention passed the 2d. of March last for this purpose.

J. Scollay
Ezekiel Price
Gustavus Fellows Selectmen of
[Tuttle?] Hubbart Boston

At a legal Meeting of the Male Inhabitants of the Town of Boston at Faneuil Hall on Wensday the 3d. Day of May 1780 and continued by adjournment.

The consideration of the 4 Section Page 38 was taken up and passed Nem Con—also—

VOTED that it be and hereby is recomended to the Delegates wo Represent this Town in the Convention that a Clause be inserted under said Section for limiting the time of servise of the Comissary General in like manner as the time of Servise of the Treasurer and Receiver General has been limitted———

The Committee appointed to Consider and report relative to the 7th and 16th Article of the Bill of Rights—Report That instead of the 16th Article of the Bill of Rights the same should stand. Vizt. The Liberty of Speech and of the press with respect to publick Men and their publick Conduct and publick measures is essential to the Security of fredom in a

* The full context of the discussion in which this return was framed is given in the records of the Boston town meeting, reprinted below, pp. 752–764, from *Report of the Record Commissioners of the City of Boston Town Records, 1778 to 1783* (Boston, 1895), 125–135.

State, and shall not therefore be restrained in this Common Wealth.———

That instead of the 7. Article of the 6th. Chapter it should stand as follows. Vizt. The Priviledge and Benefit of the Writs of Habeas Corpus, shall be enjoyed in this Common Wealth, in the most free, easy cheap, expeditious and ample manner and shall not be supended except in time of War Invasion or a time of Rebellion declared by the Legislature to exist, nor for a longer time than Six Months.———

The forgoing Report having been read and considered—the same was accepted Nem Con—also—

Voted, Nem Con—That the Delegates who represent this Town in Convention be and hereby are Instructed to move to the Convention at their next Meeting that these alterations may be come into.———

The Article 7 relative to the Executive Power as page 31 being under consideration, it was moved and Voted, that the Delegates who Represent this Town in Convention, be and hereby are Instructed to move to the Convention, that the following Clause may be aded to the 7 article Vizt.—or for the defence of a Neighbouring State invaded or threatned with immediate Invasion. and this Power to be granted only in the Recess of the General Court.———

The several Articles in the Constitution or form of Government (except the 3d. in the Bill of Rights and the 2d Article of the first Chapter relative to the mode of Electing Senator) haveing been considered and amended Paragraph by Paragraph—the whole was put, when it was unanimously Voted to accept the same the Meeting then consisting of Eight hundred and eighty seven Voters———

The 2d. Article of the 1th Chapter relative to the mode of Electing Senators was then put, when it appeared that Eight hundrd and eighty six were for excepting the said Article and but one who was for rejecting it—The Committee to whom was refered the consideration of the 3d Article in the Declarations of Rights Reported as follows Vizt

As the happiness of a People and the good order and preservation of Civil Goverment essentially depend upon Piety Religion and Morrality, and as these cannot be generally diffused thro a Community, but by the publick Worship of God and publick Instruction in Piety religion and morality: therefore to promote their happiness and to secure the good Order and preservation of their Goverment the People of this Common Wealth have a right to invest their Legislature with power to Authorise and require and the Legislature shall from time to time authorise and require all the Inhabitants of this Common Wealth to make provision at their own expence for the publick Worship of God, and for the support and maintainance of publick Protestant Teachers of Piety Religion and Morality—who have not made such Provision voluntary or who have not made voluntary provision for some other publick Religious Teachers or for the support of some other publick worship within this Common Wealth.———

And the several Towns, Parishes, Precincts, and other Politic or Religious Societies, shall at all times have the exclusive Right of electing their public Teachers and of contracting with them for their support and maintainance provided nevertheless that the minority of such Towns Parishes Precincts and other Bodies politic or Religious Scocties, shall not be bound by the voice of the Majority in their Electing their publick Teachers or contracting with them for their support, but such Minority may if they se fit Elect some other publick Religious Teachers and support him.———

And all Monies Assessed upon the subject for the support of publick Worship and of publick religious Teachers, shall if he requires it, be uniformly applyed to the support of the publick Teacher or Teachers or the publick worship he may chuse to support; provided however that such Teacher shall bonafida receive the same to his own use, otherwise such sum shall be appropriated to the use of the poor of aney Parish or Religious Society that such subject shall chose, if he makes his Election within twelve Months, and if not it shall be applied to the support of the poor of the parish or Precinct in which said Monies were raised.———

And all religious Sects and Denominations whatsoever, demeaning themselves peaceably and as good Subjects of the Common Wealth, shall be equally under the protection of the Law. And no subordination of aney one Sect or Denomination to another shall ever be established by Law.———

The forgoing however is not to be so Construed as to nulify or Infringe aney express voluntary contract that hath been enterd into between any Person or Persons, or aney Town Parish Precinct or Body of Men on the one part and aney teacher or Minister of Religion on the other.———

The foregoing Report of the Committee on the 3d Article which had been considered and accepted paragraph by paragraph was put as it stands amended when it appeared, that Fore hundred and twenty were for accepting the Report and One hundred and forty against it.

A Motion was then made that if the Amendments proposed by the

Town cannot be obtained by their Delegates, that they then shall and hereby are Instructed to Vote for the 3d Article in the Decleration of Rights as it stands in the form laid before the People rather than the Article should be lost at the next Meeting of the Convention—And the Question being put it appeared that too hundred and seventy seven were in favor of the motion, and one hundred and forty against it.———

Mr. Morton withdrew his dessent to the passing the Article which relates to the mode of Electing Sentors.———

The Committee appointed to draw up reasons for the proposed Alterations in some Articles of the Constitution or form of Goverment laid before the Town and also Instructions to our Delegates, in the Convention Reported accordingly, and said Report haveing been duly considered the same was accepted almost unanimously.———

Voted, almost unanimously. That the Selectmen of this Town be directed to transmit to the Secretary of the Convention the doings of this Town relative to the Form of Goverment agreeable to the Resolves of the Convention, in order to the Secretary of the Convention laying the same before a Committee to be appointed for the purpose of examining and arranging them for the Revision and consideration of the Convention at the Adjournment with the numbers of Voters on each side of every question, in order that the said Convention at the Adjournment may collect the general sence of their Constituents on the several parts of the proposed Constitution.

And if it doth not appear to be too thirds of their Constituants in favour thereof, that the Convention may alter it in such a manner as that it may be agreeable to the sentiments of too thirds of the Voters throughtout the State—also———

Voted, almost unanimously that the Delegates of this Town be and hereby are impowered at the next Session of the Convention to gree upon a time when this form of Goverment shall take place without returning the same again to the People. Provided that too thirds of the Male Inhabitants of the age of Twenty one Years and upwards, Voting in the several Town and Plantation Meetings, shall gree to the same or the Convention shall conform it to the Sentiments of too thirds of the People aforesaid. Att. William Cooper Town Clerk

At a legal Meeting of the Male Inhabitants of the Town of Boston being twenty one years of age and upwards, at Faneuil Hall on Wednesday the 3 Day of May Anno Domini 1780—10. O.Clock Forenoon

The Meeting was opened with Prayer by the Reverend Dr. Cooper

Warrant for calling the Meeting read

The Inhabitants were directed by the Selectmen to withdraw and bring in their Votes for a Moderator of that Meeting, and the same having been brought in and sorted it appeared that

The Honorable Samuel Adams Esqr. was chosen

The *Address* of the Convention for framing a new Constitution of Government for the State of Massachusetts Bay to their Constituents; together with *a Constitution or Fram of Goverment.* agreed upon by the *Delagates* of the People of this State in *Convention* begun and held at Cambridge on the first of September 1779 and submitted to the Revision of their Constituents—were distinctly read to the Inhabitants by the Moderator excepting the Clause relative to Oaths etc. which was omitted. in consequence of a Motion for that purpose

On a Motion. Voted, that the Resolves of the Convention passed the second of May 1780 as in Page 53 Shall be the first matter to be taken into consideration and acted upon at the Adjournment

It was moved and Voted, that the Town Clerk signify to the Delagates who Represent this Town in the Convention; that their attendance is requested during this Meeting

Adjourned to 3. O'Clock in the Afternoon

3. O'Clock afternoon met according to Adjournment

The Article in the 6th. Chapter relative to Oaths and Subscriptions was read

The Resolve of the Convention passed the Second March 1780 as Page 53—was again read, and after debate had thereon it was moved and Voted, that the further consideration of this Matter be postponed untill it is determined to what Place this Meeting shall be Adjourned

On a Motion Voted, that a Committee be now appointed to provide a place for the Town to Meet at, when the Meeting shall be Adjourned

Voted, that Mr. Jeremiah Belknap
Nathaniel Appleton Esqr.
Thomas Daws Esqr.

be a Committee for the purpose aforesaid

Moved and Voted, that the preceeding Vote for taking up the Resolves of the Convention in the first place be reconsidered, and that the Article relative to Oaths and Subscriptons be now considered

The Town however proceeded to the consideration of the Fram of Goverment as Page 15—and after debate had thereon a Motion was made, and passed, that when this Meeting shall be Adjourned, it shall be to the old Brick Meeting house the Place provided for the Town by the Committee chosen in the Forenoon

It was then moved, and Voted, that the 2d. Chapter relative to the Executive Power Section the first—be now taken up, a former Vote, notwithstanding

The forementioned Article, having been some time under consideration it was moved and Voted, that this Meeting be Adjourned, to to Morrow Afternoon. 3 O.Clock, then to Meet at the old Brick Meeting House

And the Meeting was accordingly Adjourned

Thursday the 4th. day of May 1780. 3. O.Clock P:M: Met According to Adjournment

The Town having Voted to proceed to the consideration of the Fram of Goverment Paragraph by Paragraph

The consideration of the first Chapter the *Legislative Power, Section 1st.* The General Court Page 15 was taken up Article by Article and the whole of said Section accepted, Nem. Cond.

The consideration of *Section 2d.* Page 18—*Senate*—was taken up Article by Article, and after considerable Debate was accepted Nem: Cond: excepting the 3d Article, to which there was one Dissentient

The consideration of Section 3d. Page 24—*House of Representatives* was taken up Article by Article, and the whole Accepted Nemo. Con

The consideration of the 2d. Chapter Vizt. *Executive Power,* Section 3d. Page 27—Governor was taken up Article by Article, and the whole of said Section accepted by the Town Neme. Con.

The consideration of the 2d. Section Page 35—*Lieutenant Governor,* was taken up Article by Article, and the whole of said Section passed—Nem Cond.

The consideration of the 3d. Section Page 36—Vizt. *Council* and the Manner of settling Elections by the Legislature was taken up, Article by Article—and the whole of said Section passed Nem Cond.

The consideration of the 4th Section Page 38—Vizt.—*Secretary, Treasurer, Commissary* etc was taken up Article by Article, and the whole of said Section passed Neme. Cond.—also

Voted, that it be and hereby is Recommended to the Delagates who Represent this Town in the Convention, that a Clause be inserted under the foregoing Section for limiting the Time of Service of the Commissary General, in like manner as the Time of Service of the Treasurer and Receiver General has been Limited

The consideration of the 3d. Chapter—Vizt. *Judiciary Power* as Page

39—was taken up Article by Article—and the whole of the Chapter accepted N C

The consideration of the 4th. Chapter Vizt. Page 40—Vizt. Delagates to Congress, was taken up and accepted Neme. Cond.

The consideration of the 5th Chapter Page 41—Vizt.—The University at Cambridge, and Encouragement of Literature etc Section the 1t. was taken up Article by Article, and the whole of said Section Accepted Nem Con

The consideration of the 2d Section in Chapter 5 Page 43 Vizt.—The encouragement of Literature was taken up, and accepted Neme. Contd.

The consideration of the 6th. Chapter Page 44—Vizt. Oaths and Subscriptions, Incompatability of and exclusion from Offices; Pecuniary Qualifications; of Laws. Commissions, Writes; Confirmations of Laws; Habeas Corpus; The Enacting Continuance of Officers 1 Provision for a Future Revisal of the Constitution etc—was taken up Article by Article and all accepted N. C saving the 7th. Article Page 49—relative to the Write of Habeas Corpus, and upon a Motion

Voted that John Lowell Esqr.
Ellis Gray Esqr.
Nathaniel Appleton Esqr.

be a Committee to consider the same and Report at the Adjournment

On a Motion Voted, that the consideration of the Preamble to the Declaration of Rights, be postponed and that the 3d. Article in said Declarating Preamble thereto excepted shall be the last Article to be acted upon at this Meeting—also

Voted, that the Declaration of Rights be now considered

The Several Articles in the Declaration of Rights excepting as aforesaid was Accordingly taken up and being duly considered, were excepted, Article by Article Nem Con Saving the 16 Article, and on a Motion Made

Voted, that John Lowell Esqr.
Ellis Gray Esqr.
Nathaniel Appleton Esqr.

be a Committee to consider the propriety of Adding a Clause to said Article for Securing freedom of Speach

Moved and Voted, that when this Meeting is Adjourned it shall be to Monday Morning 9 O.Clock

On a Motion made Voted that it be recommended to the Inhabitants of this Town to attend the Town Meeting at the Adjournment next Monday Morning 9. O.Clock, and as matters of the greatest consequence, respecting the Establishment of a Constitution of Civil Government for this State, Will then be Acted upon, it is most earnestly recommended that all Buissiness be suspended by the shutting up of Stores, Shops etc that there may be a full Attendance, and it is further

Voted, that the Ministers of the Gospel be requested to remind their respective Congregations the next Lords day, of this Adjournment, and of the importance of universally withdrawing them selves for a few hours from their ordinary Engagements, and devoting their Attention to a Matter so deeply interesting to themselves and their Posterity

Voted, that a Copy of this Vote be sent to the Ministers of every Denomination

Then the Meeting was Adjourned to next Monday 9. O.Clock

Monday the 8th. Day of May. 9. O.Clock Forenoon—Met according to Adjournment

The left Quarter of the upper Galary was Assigned by the Moderator for Strangers, and Persons under twenty One years of Age

On a Motion made Voted, that twelve Persons be appointed Monitors and

Capt. Newell
Colo. Procter
Capt. Parkman
James Brewer
John Lowel
John Lucas
John R. Sigorney
Capt. John Simpkins
Adam Colson
Dr. Nathaniel Noyes
Mr. Conent
Capt. Stanton

were accordingly chosen

The Committee appointed to Consider and Report relative to the Seventh and Sixteenth Articles, of the Bill of Rights Report—That instead of the 16th. Article of the Bill of Rights, The same should Stand as follows—Vizt. The Liberty of Speach and of the Press with respect to publick men and their Publick Conduct and Publick Measures, is essential to the Security of Freedom in a State and shall not therefore be restrained in their Common Wealth"

That instead of the 7th. Article of the 6th. Chapter it should Stand as follows—Vizt.—"The Priviledge and Benefit of the Write of Habeas Corpus shall be enjoyed in this Common Wealth, in the most free, easey, cheap, expeditious and ample manner—and shall not be suspended except in time of War, Invasion or a Time of Rebellion declared by the Legislature to exist, nor for a longer Time than Six Months

The foregoing Report having been read and considered—the Question was put. Vizt. Whether the Same, shall be accepted—Passed in the Affermative Neme. Cond.—It was Also

Voted, Neme. Cond. That the Delegates who Represent this Town in the Convention be and hereby are Instructed to move to the Convention at their Next Meeting that these alterations may be come into

The Article the 7. relative to the Execleusive Power as Page 31. being under consideration it was moved and Voted,

That the Delegates who Represent this Town in Convention be and hereby are Instructed to Move to the Convention that the following Clauses may be Added to the said 7th. Article Vizt.—Or for the Defence of a Neighbouring State invaded or threatend with immediate Invasion, and their Power to be granted only in the Recess of the General Court

The Several Articles in the Constitution or Fram of Goverment—agreed on by the Convention and by them proposed to the people for their Approbation, rejection or Amendment (except the 3d. Article in the Bill of Rights and the 2d. Article of the 1t. Chapter relative to the Mode of Electing Senators) having been considered, paragraph by Paragraph and accepted, as the several Articles stand amended, Article by Article—The whole was put, when it was unanimously Voted, to accept the Same; the Meeting then consisting of Eight Hundred and Eighty Seven Voters

The 2d. Article of the 1t. Chapter relative to the Mode of Electing Senators—was then put—when it appeared that Eight hundred Eighty Six were for accepting the said Article and but one who was for rejecting it

A Motion was made to reconsider the preceeding Vote—but the Motion did not obtain

It was moved and Voted that the consideration of the 3d. Article in the Declaration of Rights, be referred to 3. OClock Afternoon

Adjourned to 3. O.Clock in the Afternoon

3 O.Clock P:M: Met according to Adjournment

The 3d. Article of the Bill of Rights was again taken into consideration, and the debates continuing till it was dark—it was moved, that the

Meeting be Adjourned to to Morrow Morning 9. OClock in the Forenoon and that the consideration of said Article be then taken up. Paragraph by Paragraph

And the Meeting was accordingly Adjourned

Tuesday May 9th.—9. O.Clock Forenoon—Met according to Adjournment

Moved that the Consideration of the 3d. Article in the Declaration of Rights, be taken up at large and that the Vote of the last Evening for considering the Same Paragraph by Paragraph be now reconsidered—and the Question being accordingly put—Passed in the Affermative

The foregoing Article having been debated at large it was Moved and Voted, that the same be now taken up Paragraph by Paragraph

The Article being again considered in distinct Paragraphs, after by debates it was moved, and Voted, that the further consideration of this whole Article be referred to a Committee to Report such alterations as they may Judge most convenient to the Sense of the Town as discovered in the present debate

Voted, that John Lowell Esqr.
Reverend Mr. Sillman
Reverend Doctor Cooper
Ellis Gray Esqr.
Perez Morton Esqr.

be a Committee for the purpose aforesaid

Adjourned to Wednesday next 9. O.Clock Forenoon

Wednesday May 10th. 9. O.Clock Forenoon—Met according to Adjournment

The Committee to whom was referred the consideration of the third Article in the Declaration of Rights—Reported the same with such alterations as they Judged most consonant to the Sense of the Town and is as follows—Vizt.

As the Happiness of a People and the Good Order; and Preservation of civil Goverment essentially depends upon Piety, religion and morality; and as these cannot be generally deffused through a Community, but by the Publick Worship of God, and Publick Instructions in Piety religion and morality, Therefore to promote their happiness and to secure the good order and preservation of their Goverment the People of this Commonwealth have a right to invest their Legislative with Power; to Authorize and require all the Inhabitants of this Commonwealth to make provision at their own expence for the Publick Worship of God and for the support and maintainance of Publick Protestant teachers of Piety, Religion and Morality who have not made such provision voluntary, or who have not made voluntary provision for some other Publick religious Teacher or for the support of some other Publick Worship within their commonwealth—And the several Towns Parishes Precincts and other Bodies politick or religious societies shall at all times have the exclusive right of electing their Publick teachers and of contracting with them for their support and maintainance; provided nevertheless that the minority of such Towns, Parishes Precincts and other Bodies Politick or religious Societies shall not be bound by the voice of the Majority in their electing their Publick Teachers or contracting with them for their support, but such Minority may if they see fit elect some other publick religious Teacher and Support him And all Monies Assessed upon the Subject for the support Of Publick Worship and of Publick religious Teachers shall if he requires it be uniformely Applied to the support of the Publick Worship which he may chuse to support: provided however that such Teachers shall bona" fide receive the same to his own Use Otherwise such sum shall be appropriated to the use of the Poor of any Parish or religious society that such Subject shall chuse if he makes his Election within twelve Months, and if not it shall be applied to the support of the Poor of the Parish or Precinct in which said Moneys were raised. And all Religious Sects and Denominations Whatsoever, demeaning themselves Peaceably and as good Subjects of the Commonwealth shall be equally under the Protection of Law—And no Subordination of any one Sect or denomination to another shall ever be established by Law

The foregoing Report having been read, it was moved, and Voted that a Question previous to the Report, being Acted upon. Vizt. Whether there shall be any thing further Added to the 2d. Article in the Declaration of Rights, which relates to Religion—And the Question being accordingly put—Passed in the Affermative, by a great Majority

The said Report being again taken up Paragraph by Paragraph—and amended the same was Accepted by the Town

It was moved and Voted that when this Meeting shall be Adjourned it be to 4. O.Clock P:M:

Moved that a Committee be appointed to bring in an Article in addition to the Article in the 43 Page—but the Motion was withdrawn

Adjourned to 4: O.Clock P:M:

4: O: Clock: P:M: Met according to Adjournment

It was moved and carried that the foregoing Clauses be added to the Report of the Committee on the 3d Article in the Declaration of Rights Vizt.—" The foregoing however is not to be so construed as to Nullify or infring any express voluntary Contract that hath been entered into between any Person or Persons, or any Town Parish, Precinct or Body of Men on the one Part and any Teacher or Minister of Religion on the other

The aforegoing Report of the Committee of the Committee on the 3d. Article, which had been accepted paragraph by paragraph—was put in the whole as amended—when it appeared that Four hundred and twenty were for accepting the Report—and one hundred and Forty against Receiving it

A Motion was then made that if the amendments proposed by the Town cannot be obtained by their Delagates, that they then shall be and hereby are Instructed to Vote for the 3d. Article in the Declaration of Rights, as it stands in the Form laid before the People—rather than the Article, should be lost at the next Meeting of the Convention—And the Question being put—it appeared that two hundred and seventy seven were in faviour of the Motion, and one hundred and forty against it

On a Motion, Voted, to appoint a Committee to draw up the reasons for the proposed Alterations in some Articles of the Frame of a Constitution presented by the Convention; and to draught Instructions to our Delagates in the said Convention

Voted, that Perez Morton Esqr.
Mr. Samuel Eliot
William Tudor Esqr.
Mr. John Sweetser
Mr. Thomas Walley

be a Committee for the Purpose aforesaid

Adjourned to Fryday next. 3 O: Clock P:M:

Fryday May 12. 3 O.Clock P:M met according to Adjournment

Mr. Morton had leave to withdraw his dissent to the passing the Article which relates to the mode of electing Senators

The Preamble to the Constitution or Form of Goverment for the Commonwealth of Massachusetts, again read—whereupon the Question was put—Vizt. Whether the Town do approve and accept of the Same—passed in the Affermative

The Committee appointed to draw up reasons for the proposed alterations in some Articles of the Constitution or Form of Goverment laid before the Town, and also to draught Instruction to our Delagates in the Convention—Report as follows—Vizt.

Gentlemen

The Town of Boston have Convened in a legal Meeting to consider the Constitution or Forms of Goverment agreed on by the Convention, and by them proposed to the People for their Approbation, rejection, or amendment, having had the same repeatedly read proposed to a discussion of the Several Articles theirein contained and having recommended amendments in the 16th. Article of the Declaration of Rights, in the 7th. Article of the 2d. Chapter in the 4th. Section of the 2d. Chapter and in the 7th. Article of the 6th. Chapter unanimously voted to accept said Constitution or Form of Goverment with the Amendments, the third Article in the Declaration of Rights excepted, provided by the most Strenious endeavours of their Delegates the said Amendments can be procured, otherwise to accept the said Articles as they were agreed to by the Convention, But the 3d. Article in the Declaration of Rights was refered to futer consideration; the meeting then consisting of eight hundred and eighty seven Voters—The Town then proceeded to consider the 3d. Article; which having been largely debated, was amended and Voted, 420 for and 51 against it. It was then moved and seconded, that if you could not obtain this Article as amended, you should be impowered to Vote for The 3d. Article as it originally stood rather than the Amendment should be the Means of postponing the establishment of the Constitution at the next Meeting of the Convention; as some Form was necessary to give Stability and force to Goverment. The Question being put the numbers were 277 for and 140 against it. Your utmost exertions are nevertheless earnestly enjoined to obtain the Amendments A principle of respect to a Body of Men of such distinguished rank and Ability as the Convention would not assuredly have led the Town to Assign the reasons for any alterations they might make in a system they had formed and recommended. But as the Convention have requested the doing it, it is now to be performed on a higher Principle. In general it may be Observed that the Amendments proposed were made upon the idea that they would more effectually subserve the excuse of Civil and Religious Liberty, that great object of our endeavours, and the point to which all our efforts ought to tend, The Amendment of 16th. April of the Declerations of Rights, was made upon the strongest persuation, that Liberty of Speech, as it respected publick Men in their publick Conduct, was an essential and darling right of every member of a free State upon which in a very emenent Degree the preservation of their other reights depends; that nothing spoken with design to give information of the State of the Publick should be ever subject to the smalest restraint; and that any Attempt to oppose such restraint ought to excite an alarm in the People as it infered a consciousness of demerit on the part of those Attempting That such restraint was more degrading and more Strongly marked the Slaves than ever the privation of the Liberty of the Press; and that the latter, so absolutely necessary, and therefore so justly dear to every free State could not be maintained in its full force and vigour without the former. But while we hold up the Liberty of the Press, as essentially necessary to general Freedom, as it respects publick Men and Measures we reject with Abhorrence the idea of its abuse to the injury of private Characters.—The next amendment gives Power to the Governor, in the recess of the General Court, to march or transport, the Inhabitants of this State for the relief of a Neighbouring State invaded or threatened with immediate invation. This was judged incumbent on the general Principles of humanity, and absolutely necessary upon the Principles of Policy, A threatned invastion may be wholly prevented by the early appearance of a respectable Military force and Invation actually begun may be easally repeled, in many Instances by an immediate Opposition. In the former case, the Lives and Property of our Friends and Neighbours may be entirely saved and Secured; and in the Latter case fewer lives may be lost In all Probability, and less Property Destroyed, Besides delay may give oppertunity to an Enemy (so disposed) to take Post, and establish himself in such a manner as would require a very great force to remove him while an early force might be adequate to his immediate expulsion. Further the withholding immediate aid, may open a passage into our own State, and to bring the War to our own doors.—It was also suggested, that the Article, of Confederation bound us to grant immediate relief, which can only be Obtained by Vesting the Governor with such power, and was therefore Voted,—The next amendements respects the time of service of the Commissary General which is proposed to be limited to the Term of Five years. This was done because it was apprehended that a change or relation of Officers was necessary, in general to the preservation of Freedom. Persons longe in Office are apt to lose that sence of Dependance upon the People, which is essential to keep them within the Line of duty to the Publick. And especially may the good of the Community be promoted by the retirements of such Persons from Office at certain fixed periods, who have been largely intrusted with Publick Money or Stores —The next Article respects that important Write of Habeas Corpus. Many Reasons might be given for the Alterations made. It was judged best to confir the Suspension of this security of personal Liberty or freedom from Imprisonments to times of War, invation and rebellion, the terms urgent and pressing occations, being too indefinite and giving scope to the most powerfull Engine of Despotism, and Slavery. It was not conceived that any cause could possibly exist in time of peace, that could justify imprisonments without allegation or charge; and the granting a Power in a season of tranquility liable to such gross abuse, and which might be attend with consequences destructive of the dearest priviledges and best interest of the Subject was deemed incompatable with every Principle of Liberty. Nay it was apprehended that it might Opperate as an incentive to Despotism; and to hold up a temtation to Tyranny while human Nature is constituted as we find it was judged to be wholly inexpedient. Confineing the suspencion won in time of War, invation and rebellion, to Six Months, was supposed a proper Limetation, as every purpose of an honest Goverment might be fully answered, in that period. A larger pereod might lead to a State of forgetfullness of the unhappy Subject of Suspission, and he might Drag on a Wretched being in the Dark abode of a Dungion, or within the gloomy walls of a Prison, without a Single Ray of hope to enlighten his cell or a single Friend to chear his Desponding spirit. Thus may his dreadfull Confinement when the Reason that operated to his Commitment have been long done away. Can a Power pregrant with such mighty Evils be too Strongly guarded; Or can we be too solicetious to confine it within the narrow limits that will comport with the Publick safety?—The only Article now to be attended to is the third in the Deceleration of Rights, which Asserts that Piety, Religion and morality are essential to the happiness, Peace and Good order of a People and that these Principles are diffused by the Publick Worship of God, and by Publick Instructions etc—and in Consequence makes provision for their support. The alterations proposed here which you will Lay before the Convention were designed to Secure the Reights of Consience and to give the fullest Scope to religious Liberty In support of the proposition it urged that if Publick Worship and Publick teaching, did certainly (as was allowed) defuse a general Sence of Duty and moral Obligations, and, so secured the safety of our Persons and Properties, we ought chearfully to pay those from whose agency we derived such Advantages. But we are Attempting to support (it is said) the Kingdom of Christ; It may as well be said we are supporting the Kingdom of God, by institution of a Civil Goverment, which Declared to be an Ordinance to the Deity, and so refuse to pay the civil magistrate. What will be the consequence of such refusal—The greatest disorders, if not a Dissolution of Society. Suspend all provision for the inculation of Morality, religion and Piety, and confusion and every evil work may be justly dreaded; for it is found that with all the Restraints of religion induced by the Preaching of Ministers, and with all the Restraints of Goverment inforced by civil Law, the World is far from being as quiet an abode as might be wished. Remove the former by ceasing to support Morality, religion and Piety and it will be soon felt that human Laws were feble barriers opposed to the uninformed lusts of Passions of Mankind. But though we are not supporting the kingdom of Christ may we not be permitted to Assist civil society by an addoption, and by the teaching of the best set of Morals that were ever offered to the World. To Object to these Morrals, or even to the Piety and Religion we aim to inculcate, because they are drawn from the Gospel, must appear very singular to an Assembly generally professing themselves Christians. Were this really our intention, no Objection ought to be made to it provided, as in fact the case that equal Liberty is granted to every religious Sect and Denomination Whatever, and it is only required that every Man should pay to the support of Publick Worship In his own way. But should any be so Conscientious that they cannot pay to the support of any of the various denominations among us they may then alott their Money to the support of the Poor—It remains only to fix the time when this Form of Goverment shall take place; But having had large experience of your Ability and Zeal in the course of the very lengthy Session of Convention, the last Winter we very Chearfully leave the Determination of this point to that prudence, Judgement and Integrity, which have so strongly marked your conduct in this Department and to the united Wisdom of the whole Body.

The foregoing Report of the Committee having been read and considered—the Question was put—Vizt. "Whether the same shall be accepted, by the Town"—Passed in the Affermative, almost unanimously

[The Resolves of the Convention, passed on March 2, 1780 were then read and considered; whereupon the votes recorded in the last three paragraphs of the return (above, pp. 749–752) were taken and passed.]

Braintree (277/63)

The Committee of the Town of Braintree *"for taking into Consideration the Form of Government"* etc., having attended that Service, Report the following alterations, and additions, as being, in their opinion, of considerable importance. They also observed several others, such as *may,* instead of *shall; judge,* instead of *justice,* etc. which being of smaller moment, are not particularly mentioned. Though the following are, in the opinion of your Committee, of great importance, and such as they wish to take place, yet, being impressed with the necessity of having a new, and better, form of Government than the present; they also Report, as their opinion, that 'tis better to accept the new Constitution, without any alteration, than to remain any longer under the present; Provided there be possitive provision made, for having another Convention within a short space of time, and so from time to time, at regular and reasonable distances from each other, for Revision of the then Constitution.

Preamble

a. instead of *"Safety and tranquility, their natural rights, and the blessings of life":* Say, *in greater Safety and tranquility, all those rights, properties, and blessings of life, for the Secure enjoyment of which, they enter into civil Society.*

The Reason. Men, when they enter into civil Society, relinquish some of their natural rights, in order to their more Secure enjoyment of the remainder.

Declaration of Rights

Article 12th #, incert, *excepting Cases of tresspass provided for by former Laws on Tresspasses.*

10, incert, and Cases heretofore triable before a Justice of the Peace.

Article 24th—add, *excepting only, manifest breaches of natural Law (which in old Countries have obtained the name of common Law) and which are not sufficiently provided against by any written Law; which Cases, if any such there shall be, shall be tried in a Court of Equity, which Court shall be established, as soon as may be, after the Establishment of this Constitution.*

Article 25th—add, *excepting only, Cases of Treason against the State, not provided for by any written Law.*

Reasons for the two last additions. All persons living under the protection of the Laws of any civil Society, are bound, by natural Law (upon which all other good Laws are built) to refrain from all things injurious to such Society, whether such Injury is, or is not, a breach of any Written Law. The inventions of wicked men have been frequently employed in devising means to evade written Laws; and in young States they have more frequently succeeded, than in old; for, as States advance in age, they, from time to time, improve their Statute Law,—providing against such mal-doers,—and transplanting (so far as human frailty will permit) into their Written Codes, the body of natural Law; but from a consciousness of the imperfection of their codes, the best Governments have provided Courts of Equity, to soften the rigour of Written Law, and to act upon such parts of natural Law, as have been rendered Sufficiently clear and plain in their Statutes.

Without such additions, as aforesaid, will not all that has been done by this State, relative to Confiscations etc., be revoked, in effect, and great confusions ensue? And how can such confiscations be justified, but *only* upon the foot of natural Law?———

Frame of Government

General Court

No duties, or excises, to be laid upon foreign trade, so as to contravene the Articles of Confederation.

Senate

4th Article: The persons having the highest number, to be declared Elected. In Cases of equality of Votes, and Vacancies by Death etc., the election to be by joint Ballot of both Houses. R. This will preserve a *choice in the People,* and will prevent those disagreeable Sensations that would, probably, take place in the breasts of such as had near a majority, and yet should find another, who had not so much of the Voice of the People, preferred to him. This might prevent Parties, and the evil consequences attending it

---

House of Representatives

<Settled Ministers of the Gospel Not to be eligible to a Seat in the House.

4th Article All Male persons, taxable, to have a right of Voting; how, otherwise, shall be applied the principle of *equality* mentioned in the 1st Article

R. Taxation and Representation, are so connected, that where taxation takes place, Representation is necessarily undersood. As we were not, nor could be represented in the Parliament of Great Britain, we fairly concluded, that their taxing us was arbitrary and unjust: And their so doing, and claiming a *right* to make Laws binding upon *us in all Cases whatsoever* was a principal cause of the present War.

5th Article The People have a right to recall their Members, and Send others.>

Governor

3d Article: The voice of the People, so far as may be, to be preserved, similar to that mentioned concerning Senators: And for similar reasons.

9th and 10th Articles All nominations to office, to be posted in public view, in the Secretaries office, 14 days previous to their being appointed. R. such postings will give opportunity for obtaining the true characters of the persons.

Lieutenant Governor

The Election of the Lieutenant Govenor to be regulated in a similar manner to that of the Govenor and for like reasons.

Council, etc.

1st and 2nd Articles:

The choice of Counsellors to be confined to the Senators. R. in order to prevent an unnecessary expence, so that the whole number, may not exceed 40.

Their election to be regulated, like to that of Senators, and for like reasons. When a Council is called, the Governor to call *all,* indiscriminately; R. This may prevent parties, for serving any particular purposes, in favor of a Governor.

Judiciary Power

3d Article to be expunged. R. because it makes Justices and Expectants, too dependent upon a Governor and Council. *"Men who hold their places upon so precarious a tenure as annual, or other frequent appointments, will never so assiduously apply themselves to study, as will be necessary to their filling their places with dignity."*

Delegates to Congress

add, Their qualifications shall be the same, as are, in this Constitution, provided for Senators and Councellors. And in case any Member of the House, Senate, or Council, shall be elected a Delegate to Congress, and accepts thereof, his former seat shall be vacated. And no Member of Congress shall be eligible to a Seat in the House, Senate or Council.

R. If pecuniary, and residentiary qualifications, with oaths, are necessary for Senators and Counsellors, they must be so for this higher, and more important office.

Oaths

6th Article add. and in order that the Code of Laws, of this Commonwealth, may be as compleat within itself, and as plain as possible, and such, that Jurors may be as good judges of *Law,* as of *Fact;* there shall, to this end, as soon as may be after the establishment of this Constitution, be a REVISION of the present Laws, and a new and compleat Code of Laws formed, and published; so that thereafter there shall no foreign authorities in Law, be admitted in any Court of Justice within this Commonwealth. And also, there shall, as soon as may be, be a Court of Equity, constituted and established, for hearing and finally determining upon all appeals thereto, in order to soften the rigour of Written Law: And also, for judging, and finally determining upon such Cases in Natural Law, as shall not then be provided for by any special Statute Law.

R. The reasons for this, stand much upon the same ground with those annexed to the 24th and 25th Articles of the Bill of Rights.

10th Article: provision to be herein made, that there *certainly shall be,* perhaps within 7, or 10 years, another Convention, for revising this Constitution: And the like at certain distances of time, perhaps 15, or 20 years, so as not to be out of the reach of Memory, other Conventions for the like purpose: And also, at such other times as the people shall appoint.

This is a point which your Committee think, ought not to be given up, if it may be avoided.

⟨Your Committee beg leave to suggest matter for another Article;

That no Slaves Shall, in any future time be imported, nor any purchases of such be held valid in Law. When we have long struggled, at the expence of much treasure and blood, to obtain liberty for ourselves and posterity, it ill becomes us to enslave others who have an equal right to liberty with ourselves.⟩

Your Committee also Report, That it be left to your Delegate in Convention if any should be chosen to act as he shall judge best, respecting the time when this Constitution shall take place, agreeable to the Resolves of Convention of March 2d. 1780.

All which is humbly submitted
J. Palmer by order

Braintree June 5th 1780.
The above report, with the new Constitution, were, this 5th Day of June 1780, accepted by the Town of Braintree

Attest. Ebenr Thayer Jun.
Town Clerk

At a meeting of the town of Braintree, on adjournment, on the 5th of June 1780. Then Voted, that the new Constitution, with the alterations and amendments made by their Committee, be accepted.—Ninety-five voted in favor of it, but none appeared against it.

Braintree June 5th 1780 David Arnold Selectmen
To the Sect. of the Convention Stephen Penniman

Brookline (277/64)

Brookline May 15th and 16th 1780. At a Meeting of the Inhabitants of 21 years of age and upwards, assembled by special Warning, the Constitution and Form of Government agreed upon by the Convention of this State was read and considered—48 Voters being present

The Preamble was read and accepted—nem con

The first and 2nd Articles in the Declaration of Rights accepted nem. con:

(3rd Article accpeted by 39 voters objected to by 8, who proposed this Amendment: That every Estate should bear a proportion of the Charge of maintaining the Congregational Minister in that Town where the Estate lays,—but in case eight Votes should be wanting to make up two thirds of the State in favor of the Article as it stands—they would be reckoned in favour of it.)

All the following Articles to the End of the 7th of Chapter 1 Section 3. (Page 26) accepted by 48 Voters—nem con.

The following Articles to the End of the 1st of Chapter 2 Section 1 (Page 27,) accepted by 43 voters—nem con.

Article 2nd. (ibid) accepted by 12 voters—objected to by 21. who propose to dele the word Christian and insert the word Protestant.

The following Articles to the end of the 9th (Page 31) accepted by 39 voters—nem con———

Articles 10.11.12. (Page 32. 33. and 34) accepted by 22 N:C:

Article 13th (page 34 assented to, by 25 provided the Salarys be not established while the present war and scarcity lasts—because it would require at least a double Sum for an honorable Support in such Times as the present, to what would be necessary in Times of Peace and plenty and no provision is made for lessening any Salarys once established, therefore till the return of Peace and plenty as before the War, the Salarys ought to be granted yearly—the Grants to be made among the first Acts of the general Court every Year———

Chapter 2 Section 2—accepted by 25 voters . . . nem con
Section 3—accepted by 25 . . . Ditto
Section 4—accepted by 31 . . . Ditto

Chapter 3 accepted by 34—nem con———

Chapter 4 accepted by 34—ditto———

Chapter 5 Section 1st and 2nd. accepted by 34—nem con

Chapter 6 Article 1 accepted by 12—objected to by 21, who propose to dele the word Christian and insert protestant

Articles 2nd to 6th inclusive, accepted by 17—nem con

Article 7th assented to by 26 provided the Term of Suspension be only three months, and that only in time of War, Rebellion or Invasion———

Article 8th and 9th accepted by 17—nem con

Article 10th accepted by 22—objected to by 4

Article 11th and last, accepted by 26 nem con

Voted that the Delegate for this Town be empowered at the next Session of the Convention, to agree upon a Time when the Form of Government shall take place, provided two thirds of the Male Inhabitants voting throughout the State shall agree to the same, or the Convention shall conform it to the Sentiments of two thirds of the Inhabitants as aforesaid.

Brookline June 5, 1780 The aforegoing is a true Copy of the proceedings of the Inhabitants of this Town respecting the Constitution and Form of Government

Attest. Stephen Sharp Town Clerk

Chelsea (277/65)

At a General town meeting in Chelsea the Inhabitants of Said town Being Lawfully Warned and Assembled met on the nineth Day of May A.D. 1780

Voted and Chose Captain Jonathan Green Moderator of said meeting and then the Constitution, or Form of goverment for the Commonwelth of Massachusetts was Read: and then the meeting was ajorned to the 23d Day of said month when the town again met and ajorned said meeting to the first Day of June instant which time the town again met and proceeded upon the Business of the warrant.

1st: Voted to Except the Declaration of Rights as formed by the Convention, Excepting only the 16th article in said Declaration of Rights But with the following addition to said article viz. But as its freedom is not such as to Exempt any printer or printers from being answerable for false Defamitory and abusive Publications

2ly Voted to Except the Frame of Goverment as formed by said convention with the following alterations Viz

1st: In the 25 page in the 3d section in the 4th article in the place of said article to be: Every male person being twenty one years of age and Resident in any perticular town in this Common welth for the space of one year next preceeding shall have a Right to Vote in the Choice of a Representitive or Representitives for said town

2dly In all Cases where the afairs are to be transacted and Done in the presence of the town Clerk

3ly Voted That in the absence of the town Clerk it may be done in the presence of the Selectmen only

3ly Section 2d in the 4th article in page 22 at the Bottom

4ly Voted to add Excepting Vacencies made by the Choice of Councelors

5ly Voted that the Clergy be Exempted from all offices in the Civil Department.

6ly Voted that these words (at the Least) in the 23d Line of the 18th Page Be Blotted out.

7ly Voted That the words order and Direct in the paragrafs Respecting the Governor and Councel be changed for the words consult[s?] and advise

8ly Voted That the Scheme of Rotation be adopted in the principal Department of Goverment.

9ly Voted That no person shall be a member of Congress for this State unless he possesses a Right in freehold double to the Sum that by this Constitution Quallifies any person to be a Senator

all the above Votes passed by Eleven yeas and one nay

10ly Voted if our Delegate Captain Jonathan Green shall not be able to procure these alterations we Leave it at his option to Vote in Convention to the best of his judgment either for or against the frame of Goverment that shall finally be obtained in the Honorable Convention without Refering it again to the people at Large.

The last mentioned Vote was passed by Eight yeas and four nays

attest a true Coppy from Chelsea Town Book of Records
Samuel Sprague Town Clerk

Cohasset (277/66)

At a Legal meeting held in the Town of Cohasset on the Twenty fifth day of this instant and Continued by adjurnmet to the twenty ninth—then Took into Consideration the Present Constitution or forme of government as Exhibited by the Convention: after Carefully Examming the Same: then voted to accept of the Said Constitution with the following amendments viz.———

1st that there be a Convention Choosen in ten years for a revision of the Constitution from the time of its Taking place 18 in favour of it.

2ly That the governor have Power to march the militia anywhere within the State in case of an alarm Provided he march them by Companys or Regiments that they shall then Properly belong to but neither the Governer nor the general Court shall have Power to force any Person by Draft or impressment either on board a man of war or any warlike vessel or to Serve as a Soldier Without his free Consent 26 in favour of it——

3ly not less than one third of the House of Representatives shall make a Court 26 in favour

Cohasset May 29th 1780 Thomas Lothrop
Abel Kent Selectmen of the town
Job Cushing of Cohasset

Dedham (277/66)

At a Meeting of the Inhabitants of the Town of Dedham on the 24th of May A.D. 178[0] legally assembled, And continued by Adjournment to the 2d of June following. They took into Consideration the Proposed Frame of Government, and Declaration of Rights in the State of Massachusetts Bay.——The votes as follows vizt.

For the first and 2d Articles in the Bill of Rights—132—

For the 3d Article in the Declaration of Rights as it stands 2

For rejecting the Article except the concluding Paragraph which was proposed to be added to the 2d Article 67

The Articles in the Declaration of Rights from the 4th to the 15th inclusively were accepted by 69 votes—none against them——

The remaining Articles in the Declaration of Rights accepted——

For the 17th Article 33 votes—For the 30th Article 37 votes.

For the 2d Article in the Frame of government as it stands .... 35 votes

For giving the governor a Negative .... 2 votes

Voted as an Amendment in Chapter I Section 2d Article 1st that not more than 2 Senators shall be chosen in any one Town. Voters 37

1 Vote for expunging the Qualification in Electors for Representatives, which require, their having Property—for accepting the whole Section as it stands. 36 votes.

In Chapter II, Section 1—Article 7th. voted as an Amendment to add. "The Governor shall have Power by Advice of Council, to transport the Militia to any part of the 4 N.E. States, in case of threatened and actual invasion—votes 37

In Page 34th voted as an Amendment that the Sallery of the Governor

and the Judges of the superior Court shall not be augmented oftner than once in 5 years——voters 37
Chapter 6th Article 3d. the word (*not*) voted to be intrduced in the 5th line from the bottom between the words *shall* and *be* voters 37——
In Chapter 6th Article 7th voted as an Amendment that the Habeas Corpus Act shall not be suspended for more than 6 Months, and that in Time of War, Rebellion, or Invasion. Votes 37——
In Chapter 6th Article 2d. Voted that setled Ministers of the Gospel be added to the Exclusion List, and be exempted from Taxes.

All the Articles, not above excepted against, or proposed to be amended, were unanimously accepted, at a Meeting in which 37 voters were present. In Reference to the Resolve of the Convention of March 2, 1780. Voted that the Convention be impowered to determine the Time and Manner in which the Form of Government shall take Place and be carried into Administration without returning it to the People provided by the Returns it appears to be agreeable to two thirds of the Inhabitants voting upon it: or, the Convention, by Alteration, accommodate it to ⅔ds.

Dedham June 2d 1780 By order of the Selectmen
Abner Ellis Town Clerk

Dorchester (277/67)

Att at Meeting of the Freeholders and other Inhabitants of the Town of Dorchester, that were free and Twenty one years of age, April Twenty Fifth. Anno Domini 1780. Legally Warned. Voted, That the Constitution and Form of Goverment agreed upon by the late Convention be read.——
Voted, to Choose a Committee to take the Constitution and Form of Goverment under Consideration and report at some future Day——
Voted, To Choose Thirteen for a Committee.——
Voted, That Ebenr. Wales Esquire, Mr. Samuel Coolidge, Mr. Benjamin Pierce, Mr. William Allen, Deacon Samuel Topliff, Deacon Abijah White, Mr. Aaron Bird, the Reverend Mr. Moses Everett, Mr. Andrew Gillespie, Colonel Samuel Pierce, Mr. Ezekiel Tolman, Captain Ebenezer Withington and Mr. John How be a Committee.——
Voted, That the Meeting be adjourned to next May Meeting.——
Att a Meeting of the Freeholders and other Inhabitants of the Town of

Dorchester, that were free and Twenty one years of age, May 16th A.D. 1780, by adjourment from the 25th Day of April last.———

Ebenezer Wales Esquire one of the Committee appointed the 25th Day of April last to take the Constitution and Form of Goverment under Consideration and Report, reported verbally that the Committee approved of the Constitution and Form of Goverment. Preamble to the Declaration of the Rights of the Inhabitants of the Commonwealth of Massachusetts Voted.———

1st. Article in the Bill of Rights Voted. Number of Voters 54

2d Voted. Number of Voters Ditto Objected against by two Persons.

3d. Voted. Number of Voters 76. Objected against by two.

4th. Voted. Number———78.

5th. 6th. 7th. 8th. 9th. and 10th Voted Number 78.

11th. 12th. 13th. 14th. 15th. 16th. 17th. and 18th. Voted Number 79.

19th. Voted Number 78

20 Voted. Number—75.

21st. 22d. 23d. 24th. 25th. and 26th. 27th. and 28th. Voted Number 75

29th. and 30th. Voted Number—77.

The Frame of Goverment

Chapter 1st. The Legislative Power

Section 1st. The General Court

1st. Article Voted. Number of Voters 77.

2d. and 3d. Voted. Number 77

4th. Voted. Number .... 74 objected against by one.

Chapter 1st Section 2d. Senate.

1st. Article Voted. Number of Voters 76.

2d voted. Number .... 79. objected against by Eight

3d., 4th. 5th. and 6th. Voted. Number 79.

7th. and 8th. Voted. Number .... 78.

9th. Voted. Number .... 79.

Chapter 1st. Section 3d. House of Representatives.

1st. Article Voted. Number of Voters 77.

2d. Voted Number .... 70. objected against by one.

3d. Voted. Number. 70

4th. about the Choice of a Representative, having been read, Voted with this Amendment That every Person that is free and Twenty one years of Age vote for a Representative having Estats or not.

Number of voters .... 65 Four against the Amendment

5th. and 6th. Voted. Number 65

7th. Voted Number 56
8th. Voted Number 55
9th. and 10th. Voted Number 55
11th. Voted. Number 54

Voted, to Choose a Committee to State the Reasons for an Amendment in the fourth Article of this Section respecting the Choice of a Representative.

Voted, That Major Stephen Badlam, Mr. Ezekiel Leeds, Mr. Ezekiel Tolman, Mr. Andrew Gillespie and Mr. Philip Withington be a Committee for the Purpose.———

Voted, That the Meeting be adjourned to the 22d. Day of this instant May, at two of the Clock in the Afternoon.———

Att a Meeting of the Freeholders and other Inhabitants of the Town of Dorchester, that were free and 21 years of Age May 22d. AD. 1780, by adjournment from the 16th. Day of this instant May.——— A Report of the Committee appointed the 16th. instant to state the Reasons for an Amendment in the 4th. article of the 3d. Section of Chapter 1st. about the Choice of a Representative read and accepted.

Chapter 2d.———Executive Power.

Section 1st. Governor.———

1st. Article Voted. Number of voters 87.———
2d. Voted. .... Number .... 88.———
3d. Voted. .... Number .... 87.———
4th. 5th. and 6th. Voted Number .... 88.———
7th. Voted with this Amendment, excepting also an Invasion or Rebellion in a neighbouring State. Number of Voters 88th. Objected against by six———
8th. Voted. Number .... 88.———
9th. Voted Number .... 89.———
10th. Voted. Number .... 85. Objected against by one
11th. Voted Number .... 85.———
12th. Voted. Number .... 81.———
13th. Voted. Number .... 79.———

Chapter 2d.

Section 2d. Lieutenant-Governor

1st., 2nd. and 3d. Articles Voted. Number of Voters 78.

Chapter 2d. Section 3d.

Council and the manner of Setting Elections by the Legislature———

1st. Article Voted. Number of voters .... 77.———
2d., 3d., 4th., and 5th Voted. Number .... 78.———

6th. and 7th. Voted. Number .... 77.———

Chapter 2d. Section 4th. Secretary etc.

1st. Article Voted. Number of Voters .... 79.———

2d. Voted. .... Number .... 77.———

Chapter 3d. Judiciary Power

1st. and 2d. Articles Voted. Number of Voters .... 77.———

3d, 4th. and 5th Voted .. Number .... 76.———

Chapter 4th. Delegates to Congress

Voted. Number of Voters .... 76.———

Chapter 5th. The University at Cambridge etc.

Section 1st. The University

1st. Article Voted. Number .... 73.———

2d. Voted. .... Number .... 75.———

3d. Voted .... Number of Voters .... 73.———

Chapter 5th. Section 2d. The Encouragement of Literature etc.

Voted. Number of Voters .... 74.

Chapter 6th. Oaths and Subscriptions, etc.———

1st. Article Voted. Number of Voters about .... 70.———

2d. and 3d. Voted. Number .... 62.———

4th. and 5th. Voted. Number .... 63.———

6th. Voted. Number .... 64.———

7th. Voted with the Amendment not more than six months, even in a time of War, Invasion or Rebellion. Number—58———

Voted, That the Reasons assigned by the Town of Boston for an Amendment in this article be adopted. For which see the Independent Chronicle and the Universal Advertiser. Thursday May 18th 1780.———

8th. and 9th. Voted. Number———58.———

10th Voted with the Amendment that there be a Convention in Ten years, and that there be the same Qualifications for Voters for Delegates as now. Number of Voters 46. Reason because we think there will be some Defects found in the present Constitution in less than fifteen years that will be dangerous to the State.———

11th. Article Voted.

Voted, That several other Reasons might be offered for the several Amendments we have made, but being Convinced of the Prudence, Integrity, and Superior Judgment, which has already marked the Conduct of the Convention, we submit the articles to the united Wisdom of that honourable Body, to establish them as they now stand, provided the Amendments cannot be obtained.

Voted, To leave it with the Delegate, at the next Session of the Convention, to agree upon a time when the Form of Government shall take place, without returning it, Provided that two thirds of the Male Inhabitants of the Age of Twenty one years and upwards, Voting in the several Town and Plantation Meetings shall agree to the same, or the Convention shall conform it to the Sentiments of two Thirds of the People.———

Voted, That Mr. Samuel Coolidge be a Delegate for this Town, to meet in Convention on the first Wednesday in June next.———

Noah Clap
Samuel Topliff   Selectmen of the Town
Ezekiel Leeds   of Dorchester
Sam. Coolidge

Dorchester May 29th. 1780
To-Samuel Barrett Esqr.
Secretary of the Convention

May the 16th 1780 The Town of Dorchester being Convened in Legal Meeting to Consider the Constitution or Form of Government, having recommended an Amendment in the 4th Article of Section 3d. Chapter 1st. are happy in giving their Reasons for it, on so high a Principal as that of a Request from the honourable Body, who agreed upon the same.———

Said Article having been read and Debated, the following Amendment was proposed and Voted viz That the Articles of Estate and Income be omitted in the Qualification of a Voter for Representatives.———This Amendment was made upon the strongest Persuation that the Article as proposed by the Convention, infringes upon the Rights and Liberties of a number of usefull and respectible members of Society; which number we believe is daily increasing and possibly may increase in such proportion, that one half the People of this Commonwealth will have no Choice in any Branch of the General Court, and who are at the same time liable (by the 4th Article of Chapter 1st. Section first) to pay such a proportion of the Publick Taxes as they shall Judge reasonable; and the members of the said Court being all men of Considerable Property, may be induced to lay too great a proportion on the Polls, and by that means ease their Estates, and bring a heavy burden on those who have no power to remove it.———

And being fully convinced that Taxation and Representation ought to be inseperable, and that the Property and Estates of the People will be sufficiently guarded by the Senate who represent the same, we see no

Reason of sufficient weight to Debar any Person Qualified as in the article amended provides, from Voting in Choice of Representatives.

By order of the Committee Stephen Badlam Chairman

Foxborough (277/68)

At a general Town Meeting of the Inhabitants of the Town of Foxborough on Monday, the Twenty second Day of May one Thousand seven Hundred and Eighty; for the purpose of the Revisal of the form of Government for the People of the Massachusetts Bay: the following Resolves were passed for the alteration of the following articles hereafter mentioned.———

Chapter 1 Section 2d. Article 1.

First to the 1t. Article in the Senate. As a multiplicity of Officers is not only a great Expence, but in our opinion often Retards publick Business; we would propose that there be thirty-five Councellors and Senators; seven of which to be of the Governor's Privy Council, and Twenty Eight to remain in the Senate.———

Chapter 1 Section 2 Article 4

Secondly. to the 4th. Article under the same Head.———If those Senators who have a Majority of Votes in their favour with the House of Representatives shall when there does not appear to be a full Number of Votes for a sufficiency of Counsellors or Senators proceed to make up the Deficiency from those who have the next highest number of Votes the Inhabitants of small Towns will suffer an inconveniency; for it is highly probable those in populous Towns will Vote for none but their own inhabitants and doubtless many of which will have a majority of votes in the election: and so many more may have the next highest number that the whole must be supplied from one perticular Town; for prevention of which inequallity we would propose no more than two Counsellors or Senators should be the inhabitants of any one Town in either District, and we would further propose that the Deficiency be supplied from the people at large by the Senate and house of Representative[s.]

Chapter 3, Article 4

Thirdly to the 3rd. Artical under judiciary powers,———We hope it will not be unseasonable to mention the burden the Fatherless and Widow have long laboured under by reason of their being but one Probate

Courte in each County.——Many small Estates have been almost totally Dissipated before a final settlement could be obtained: we would propose that there should be some one person in each Town vested with the powers of judge of probate, and that the inhabitants of each Town my annually elect the same: and that all Estates may be settled in the Towns where the Testator or Intestate was an inhabitant.——

Chapter 6 Section 3d

Fourthly to the 3d. Article under the head of pecuniary power. We do not approve of the Legislature's being impowered to augment such pecuniary qualifications for office beyond what is proposed in this Constitution; it may be perverted to very dangerous purposes. The Effects may prove baneful before fifteen Years are expired.

Chapter 6. article 10

Fifthly to the tenth article under the same head.——This Convention ought to make such absolute provision that there should be a Revisal of this Constitution in the Year one Thousand Seven Hundred and Ninty-five or in fifteen Years from the time it shall take place and sooner if necessary. And we cannot but observe to this Honorable Convention that the previledge of Registring Deeds of sale in the Town where Estates lay is a benefit the inhabitants of this commonwelth ought to be in the enjoyment of. we trust this Convention will think this a matter worthy their attention, for want of which not onley much time and Money has been spent, but great frauds have been Committed, more especially when the purchaser happens to live remote from the place of Registering we would propose that an article be inserted in the Bill of Rights for that purpose. Present at said meeting Forty one voters— The Question being put there was thirty-Eight for and three against it.

per order of the Select Men

Attest
Amariah Marsh Town Clerk

Franklin *

The vote for the State constitution of 1780 was 105.

Hingham (277/69)

At a Town meeting holden at Hingham on the fifth day of April 1780— to take into Consideration the form of Government agreable to a re-

* Mortimer Blake, *A History of the Town of Franklin, Mass.* (Franklin, Mass., 1879), 68.

solve of the Convention of this State March 1780—and Continued by adjournment to the 22d. day of May——The town resolved to accept the Declaration of Rights Number 58 for it and two of the 58 disenting in the 3d. article,——(apprehending that provision is thereby made for the support of Roman Catholic, as well as of Protestant teachers of Piety Religion and Morality.)—the 58 Voters at the same time Proposing that if the Honorable Convention should thing proper the words *within the limits of this State* Should be added immediately after the word practiced in the 15th. article.——

Then the meeting was adjourned to the 26 day of May and then Met and Resolved, unanimously to accept of the frame of Government Number of voters 30—with the following amendments (viz) in Chapter 2d. Section 1st. article 7th. that the Governor be impowered with the advice of his Council. in the Recess of the General Court, to march or transport the inhabitants of this State to the Relief of a Neighbouring State invaded or threatned with immediate invasion.——Chapter 2d. Section 4th. Article 1st. that the time of Service of the Commissary General be limited to 5 years, Except in time of war or Rebelion, for the same Reason, that the time of Service of the Treasurer is limited to that time ——Chapter 6th. Article 7th. that the privilidge and benefit of the writ of habeas Corpus, shall be enjoyed in this Common wealth in as free easy Cheap Expeditious and ample Manner as may be,——Article 10th. in the Same Chapter. Whereas it is asserted, that in the year 1795 the General Court shall issue precepts to the select men of the several Towns etc. for the purpose of Revising the Constitution: that the same method be pursued by the General Court at the Expiration of every fifteen years hereafter, Resolved unanimously that if the foregoing proposed amendments in the frame of Government Cannot be obtained that it be passed as it now stands Number of Voters 27

A true Copy Attest.
Benja. Cushing Town Clerk

Caleb Bates
Peter Cushing

Selectmen of Hingham

Medfield (277/70)

At a Legal Meeting of the Inhabitants of the Town of Medfield Began on April 20 1780. And continued by Adjournments untill June 2d Upon the Declaration of the Bill of Rights and Fraime of Government or the form of the Constitution, And Expressed their Minds as follows.

Voted And Accepted of all the Articles in the Bill of Rights, Excepting the 3d. Article, Rejected for this reason, (Viz) the 2d. Article is sufficient to Establish Every Subject in the free injoyment of his Religious Sentiments, therefore the 3d. Article appears to us to be Needless and in it self inconsistant and ambigous Number 58 against Number 1 for it, And the 29 Article with this Amendment to have the Judges Salery, Annualy granted. Number 35 for and Number 11 against——

Part 2d. Chapter 1st. Section 1st.

Voated Article 1st. Legislation shall Consist of 3 Branches. Governeur Senate and House of Representatives, Number 38 for and 9 against——

Article 2d. that no Bill or Resolve of the Senate and house of Representative shall become a Law without the approbation of the Governour and that the Rest part of the Article be Expunged—Number 37 for Number 10——

Articl 3d. Accepted Number 33 for Number 8 against——

Article 4 that their be no Duty or Exicse Layed on the Produce in this State nor upon the Manufacturies, and that there shall be a Valuation taken once every Five years. Number 37 for 10 against.——

Section 2d. on the Senate

Voted Article 1st. that the House of Reprensatives shall anually Elect twenty Eight Senators and no more, the Rest part Expunged. Number 36 for Number 11 against

Article 2d. Expunged Number 36 for 11 against

3d—Expunged Number 36 for 11 against

4th.— Ditto Ditto

5th.—Accepted Number 26 for Number 8 against

6th.—Accepted Number 25 for Number 9 against

7th. Omitt the words Choose its own Presedent Number 36 for Number 10 against

8th—The Governour and Senate Shall be a court with full Authority etc: Number 36 for Number 9 against——

9th. that twelve Senators be a Quorum to Do Business Number 36 for Number 10 against

Section 3d. of Representatives——

Voted Article 1st. Accepted, 26 for Number 8 against.

2d. that no town shall be fined for not sending a Representative and that Every town Pay their own members travel and attendance and that the

increassing Number be Cut off to the End that no town hereafter shall Send any more Representatives then they now are Qualifyed for (viz) haveing 150 Ratables Polls etc: untill this Constitution shall be Revised, provided all Unincorporated towns be Annexed to some ajacent towns Number 36 for Number 10 against.
Article 3d. Accepted Number 13 for Number 6 Nay.
4th. and 5th. Accepted. Number 17 for 4 Nay
6th All impeachments shall be heard and tryed by the Governour and Senate Number 36 for 9 Nay.
7th. 8th. 9th. 10th. Accepted Number 17 yea Number 7 Nay.
Article 11th. the Governor and Senate shall have the same Authority as given to the house in Article 10th. Number 26 yea Number 9 Nays.———

Executive Power Section 1st.

Article 1st. Accepted Number 26 yea Number 12 Nays. Article 2d that the Govounour be annually Choosen by the Senate and House of Representative and that he shall be of the Protestant Religon Number 26 yea Number 12 Nay.
3d. Expunged Number 26 yea Number 12 Nay. Article 4th the Senate and 5 of them to be a Quorum, Number 26 yea Number 12 Nay. Article 5th. 6th. 7th. 8th. 9th. 10th. 11th. 12th. 13th. Accepted that the Salery of the Govenour be annually granted by the General Court Number 24 yea Number 2 Nay

Chapter 2d. Section 2d. Lieutenant Governour

Article 1st. their shall be annually Elected a Lieutenant Governour by the Senate and house of Representatives, Who shall be Qualifyed the same as the Governour etc.———Number 15 yea Number 5 Nay.
Article 2d. 3d. Accepted Number 16 yea Number 4 Nay.———

Section 3d. Chapter 2d.

Wholly expunged Number 16 yea Number 4 Nay

Section 4th.

Article 1st. Accepted Number 16 yea Number 4 yea, Article 2d. Read attend the Governour and Senate and House of Representatives Number 16 yea—Number 3 Nay———

Chapter 3d. Judiciary Power

Article 1st. Read the Governour with Consent of the Senate may remove them upon the address of the House of Representatives Number 16 yea Number 3 Nay.
2d. Expunge the words Governour and Counsel Number 16 yea Number 4 Nay.

3d. 4th. and 5th. Accepted Number 24 yea Number 4 Nay——

Chapter 4th. Deligates to Congress Accepted with this amendment (Viz) that Each Person Elected shall be in all Respects Qalifyed Equal to that Pointed out for the Governour Number 20 yea Number 6 Nay——

Chapters 5th. and 6th. Accepted. Number 20 yea Number 6 Nay——

Chapter 7th. Oaths etc.——

Article 1st. Omitt the word Counseler in the 1st Peragraft and add the word Protistant in the 2d. Cause, in the 3d. paragraft Read in the House of Repesantatives, 4th Paragraft accepted. and so on to the Last in which Read before the Speaker, and in Presence of the house of Representatives Number 12 yea Number 10 Nay.

2d. Accepted by Excluding Ministers of the Gosple Number 20 yea Number 8 nay.

3d. 4th. 5th. 6th. 7th. 8th. Accepted Read by the Governour Senate and house of Represantatives Number 24 yea Number 4 Nay

9th. 10th. 11th. Accepted Number 24 yea Number Nay

Voted upon the Resolves that if the Constitution should be altred for to have it sent to Each town for Examiniation and to be approved or Disapproved off.—Number 24 yea Number 4 nay——

Medfield June 6th. 1780

By order of the Select Men
Eleazr. Wheelock Town Clerk

Medway (277/72)

To the Secretary of the Convention of the State of Massachusetts Bay——

The Following Declaration is the Prosceedings of the Town of Medway at a Leagal Meeting in the Month of May 1780 this Town examined the Constitution Formed by the Late Convention held at Boston March the 2d: 1780 and sent to the Towns for their Disapproveing of any Part of the same together with their Reasons etc.——

Pursuant to the Meeting of the Freeholders and Inhabitance of the Town of Medway assembled it was Put to Vote to See if the Town will Exsept of the Constitution as it now stands and it Pased Unanimosly in the Negative of 127 Votes Not to Exsept thereof, then the Town Proceeded and Made their Objections on the Following Articals together with their Reasons therefor———

The Address of the Convention Appears to us not Onely Polite but very Plosible, yet we Consider the same as being no Part of the Constitution, and nothing more than to Show the principals on which the Convention Proceeded in frameing the Several Parts thereof———

The Preambles to the Bill of Rights and form of government, we make no objections to either of them.

Declaration of Rights etc.———

Artical 1st. Exsepted—

2 and 3 Articals we think ought to be Reduced to one Artical, to be inserted in the following words viz———It is the right as well as the Duty of all men in Society Publickly to Worship the Supreem Being the great Creator and preserver of the Universe and no Subject Shall be hurt molested or Restrainde in his Person Liberty or Estate for worshiping God in the Manner and Season most agreeable to the Dictates of his own Conscience or for his Religious Profession or Sentiments, Provided he doth not disturb the Publick peace or obstruct others in their Religious worship, and Every Denomination of Christans Demeaning them selves Peaceably and as good Subjects of the Common welth shall be Equally under the Protection of the Law, and no Subordination of any one Sect or Denomination to another shall Ever be Established by Law———The Reasons we offer for this amendment is because we think Sufficient Provisions is Made in this and in the 10 Artical for the Support and Protection of Civil and Religous Societies, and that, as the rights of Conscience are matters of a Sacred Nature, we think no attempt Ever ought to be made Whereby those rights may be infringed or given up to any man or Body of Men Whatever———

Put to Vote and Pased in the affirmative.———

The Proceeding Articals Accepted to the 29 Artical———

Artical 29 Page 14 This Artical we think is Exceptionable Especially that Part there of which admits the Judges of the Supreme Judicial Court, to hold there offices so long as they behave them selves well and the assertaining their Salaries by Standing Laws. As the office of the said Judges are of such a Nature and Importance both to the State and Subjects we think that their appointment ought to be made once in seven years, and although the said Judges ought to be made as Independent on the Peopel for support as may be, Nevertheless on the Principals that the Labourer is worthy of his hire we think that the support or salaries of the said Judges ought to be granted by the General Court annually, and that those grants ought to be made in Proportion to their Honourable Charactors and Publick services———

Put to Vote and it Pased in the affirmetive of 82 Votes.

Article 30 Put to Vote as it stands in said Constitution 36 Votes For it, and 31 against its standing

Frame of Goverment General Court———

Article 4 Page 17 and 18th. this artical we think is Exceptionable, Especially that Part thereof Whereby the General Court is Impowred to Impose and Levy duties and Excises on the Produce and Manufactures of this State etc.

As we can see no Publick advantages ariseing from the Imposeing Excises or Duties on the manufactures and Produce of this State, We think that this article ought to be amended in such way and manner as that the General Court shall not be Empowred to impose or Levy any Excise or Duties on any of the Manufactures or Produce of this State Nor on any Imported Articles which may justly be Termed the Necessarys of Life———

The Reasons we offer for this amendment is because we think that the Imposeing duties on the Produce and Manufactures of this State will have a tendancy to Descourage and Prevent the increase thereof. Besides we think that no Duties ought to be Imposed on any Necessary articals whatsoever because the Consumers of these articals will then be obliged to Pay an Unequal Proportion in the Publick charges. Furthermore we think that the Last Part of this artical ought to be amended in such a manner as that a New Valuation of Rateable Estate Shall be taken once in Every Six years at Least, Insted of 10 years therein Mentioned——— The Reason we offer for this amenment is because of the Various ways and means by which Rateable Estates Property and faculties are changed Enlarged, or Diminished, that thereby the several Towns etc. in this State may be Taxed an Equal and just Proportion, as near as may be towards the Publick charges———Put to vote and Passed in the affirmetive.———

The Senate———

Article 1 Page 18 and 19th. This Article we think Exceptionable because we conceive of no Publick advantages resulting from so Large a Number of Persons to be Elected for Counsellors and Senators. We are led to think that the Number of 40 to be Elected in the Manner Proposed will

admit of 49. Therefore we are of opinnion that the said Number ought to be reduced to the Number of Twenty Eight Exclusive of the Lieutenant Governor, to be Elected for Each District in the same Proportion as near as may be that the said Number of 40 are Proposed to be Elected by the General Court in one Room to be a Council and Senate, Vested with all the Powers and authority that the Senate and Councel were vested with by this form of Government and that not less than Nine members of the Senate to constitute a Quoram to do Publick Bisyness———
Put to Vote and it Unanimously Passed in the affirmative
Chapter 2 Page 27
Artical 2—This Town Voted to have the word Protestant put in the Next Constitution, Next before the word Christan———
Chapter 2 Governer etc.
Article 5 to Page 29 We apprehend that some Danger may arise from the Power in the Govener to Poroge the General Court in the Recess thereof for so Long a term as 90 Days therefore are of opinion that the said Prorogation ought not to Exceed the term of Thirty Days. Further more we think that it ought to be the Duty of the Governer to inform the General Court at the opening of Every Session of the circumstances of the State and from time to time to recommend such matters to their consideration as shall appear to him to concern the good Goverment Safety and Prosperity of the Same———
Article 13 Page 34 Assertaining the way and manner by which the Governer and Supream Judges are to be Supported———
Although the Governer and Justices of the Supreme Judicial Court ought to be made as Independant on the Peopel for Surport as may be Nevertheless on the Principal that the Labourer is worthy of his hire we think that the Governer and Supreme Judges ought to be Honourably Supported by the Annually Grants of the General Court in Proportion to their Honourable Charactors and Publick Service———
Section 3d. Counsellors———
Artical 1 and 2 Page 36 Assertaining the annual Election of 9 Persons for the Sole Purpose of adviseing the Governer in the Execution of his office, this Election we apprehend will be alltogether Needless and attended with unnesesary Expences alltho it is Prudent and Necesary that the Governer should have good advice and council in the Execution of his office. yet we can see no reason why the Governor cannot obtain as

good advice and councel from the Senate as he can from a Number of Persons Elected solely for that Purpose, therefore we think that the four first articals in this section ought not to be Adopted———

Put to Vote and it Pased Unanimuly in the affirmetive———

Chapter 6 Oaths etc.

Article 2 Ascertaining a number of Publick officers Who for the Importance of their office are Excluded a seat in the General Court. We apprehend that the said Exclusions are Founded in Reason and in the Principal of good Policy and on the same Principal we think that the setled Ministers of the Gospel being Pastures of Churches, ought to be Excluded the Same Seat, further more we are of opinion that the office of register of Deeds ought to be Excepted in the said Exclusion, and that Provision ought to be made Whereby all Deeds and Conveyances of Land or any Real Estate Lyeing and being within any Town may be recorded in the same Town and that Regestor of Deeds may be appointed in each town for that Purpose———

Put to Vote and it was Unanimously voted in the affermitive———

Chapter 1st.

Article 2 Page 24 We think the way by Which is ascertained the Number of Representatives Each Town is to be Intitled to Elect and chose is Exceptionable for by that way and Mode we apprehend that Number May be assertained not onely by the freeholders and Inhabitance of any town but allso by those who are foreigners Miners and Servents unqualifyed to Vote for such representatives, which way appears to us not onely Unequal But an unjust Mode of Representation. Besides that Mode we apprehend will admitt of a Number of Representatives too Large to assemble together and Transact the Publick Buisness of the State in one Room with Dispach, Therefore we are of opinion that this artical ought to be amended in the following Manner viz.———

That Every Incorporated town containing one hundred Persons being Qualifyed to Vote in the choice of a representative agreable to the Directions in this Constitution may Elect one representative. Every Incorporated town containing 300 of such Voters May Elect two. Every corporated town containing 600 of such Voters may Elect three. Every such town containing 1000 such Voters may Elect Four, Every such town containing 1500 such Voters may elect five, Every such town containing 2100 such Voters may Elect six, Every such town containing 2800 such Voters may Elect Seven and no Town shall be Intitled to Elect more than Eight representatives. Put to Vote and Unanimisly Voted in the affirmetive.——

A motion Being Made and seconed by the Town Put to Vote if it be the Minds of this Town to Instruct our Deligate appointed to form said Constitution, to Use his Influance in the Convention to have the Constitution Returned to the Peopel again when the Convention have Made their Amendment thereon, for their Approbation or Disapprobation——

Put to Vote and it Pased in the affirmetive——

Medway June the 6th. 1780

The afforegoing is a true Coppy of the Doings of this Town

Simon [Fisher?] Town Clerk

Milton (277/73)

At a Legal Town Meeting Held in [the town of] Milton on the 22d day of May 1780.

The Committee appointed by the Town to take into consideration a Constitution or Frame of Government agreed upon by the Delegates of the People of the State of Massachusetts-Bay, reported as follows. Viz. Gentlemen, we your Constituents having thoroughly considered the Constitution, or Frame of Government offered by the Convention, to the People of this State; are of opinion that it is in general exceedingly well calculated to promote the Peace, Freedom, and Prosperity of this State ——Notwithstanding we would submit, a few amendments to the consideration of the Convention.

In the 16th Article in the Declaration of Rights after "the Liberty of the Press" we would have inserted those words, viz. *and the Liberty of Speech as it respects Publick men in their Publick conduct.* For unless *this* Liberty of Speech is granted, we are apprehensive it may be dangerous in some future time, even in Publick Town meetings, to speak the truth of weak, or wicked Rulers——and thus the most regular, peaceable and effectual method of calling the servants of the People to account; and of reducing them to private life, may be in a great measure prevented.

And in the 7th article in the 2d. Chapter we would have a clause inserted giving power to the Governor, in the recess of the General Court, to order the militia or Navy to the assistance of any neighbouring State invaded, or threatned with immediate invasion.

Many reasons might be offered to support this amendment, but it is sufficient to say, that the 3d Article in the Confederation oblieges us to afford such assistance, and in the recess of the General Court, it cannot be done, but by the Governor. And in the 2d Chapter, 4th. Section and 1st. article we would have the service of the Commissary General limited to five years.—

For we apprehend every person largely entrusted with Publick property, ought to be often shifted—by that means their accounts will be much likelier to be critially examined and fairly adjusted, and the property of the People be better ascertained and secured.

In the 4th Chapter we propose that no person shall be chosen a member of Congress unless he be an Inhabitant of this State, and possessed of a considerable real Property—the Estate adequate to the important trust. we mean not precisely to determine, but leave the same to be affixed by the convention as their wisdom shall dictate———

In the 7th article in the 6th Chapter we propose that the Writ of Habeas corpus shall never be suspended but in times of war, or threatned Invasion, and then for a time not exceeding six months.

for we cannot conceive of any possible advantage arising to the community by the Legislature suspending this Writ in times of publick Tranquility. But injury may accrue to individuals, by a suspension thereof———And in times of War, or threatned Invasion, six months is fully sufficient for any Legislature to ascertain the precise crime, and to procure the evidence against any Individual, in order to bring him for Trial.

Then the following Questions were put, and Voted as follows, viz.

Question. If you will accept of the said Constitution as proposed to be amended, and do direct your Delegates to move in Convention for the same, be pleased to manifest it———yeas 111 nays 0

Question. If your Delegates cannot obtain all, or any of the aforesaid alterations, will you accept of said Constitution as reported by the Convention; if you will be pleased to manifest it.———yeas 110 nays 1

Question. Should any other amendments or propositions be made, that appear agreable to two thirds of the Voters throughout the State, Do you instruct your Delegates to join in confirming the same, if you do be pleased to manifest it,———yeas 111 nays 1.

Question. Should the Constitution be made agreable to two thirds of the Voters, as aforesaid, do you impower your Delegates to use their discretion in Convention in fixing the time when this Constitution, or Frame of Government shall take place. If you do be pleased to manifest it———yeas 111 nays 0

Attest Amariah Blake
Town Clerk

Needham (277/74)

At a Town meeting Legally Assembled in Needham May the 18th, 1780 ———Agreeable to a Recommendation of the Honorable Convention Chosen to draw up a Constitution or Form of Government for the People of the Massachusetts-Bay. Their doings thereon being read in said Meeting—By votes of the Town, said Meeting being Continued by adjournments, to the Sixth Day of June—Then said Town being Meet, proceeded as Follows, Viz. Said Town Voted to accept the whole of the Declaration of the Bill of Rights and Form of Government, except the Following Rejection and Amendments—After Meturely considering the said Form of Government and have approved of it in the General, at the same Time we find ourselves obliged in faithfullness intirely to disapprove the Third Article in the Bill of Rights, and to desire an amendment in some other instances. With respect to the Third Article in the Bill of Rights, we disapprove it in the whole; being fully persuaded the Principle on which it was founded is wrong and that it cannot by any alteration be made Consistant with the Rights of Conscience—It appears to us that all that is Necessary in a Form of Civil Government respecting Religion is fully and happily exprest in the Second Article. We do not mean to enter into any Laboured discussion of this Matter, but agreeable to desire of the Honorable Convention, we would mention in few words the arguments that Satiffies us as to the impropriety of said Article, or reather the Falshood of the Principle on which it is founded: Religion is a matter with respect to which all Mankind have an equal Right to Judge and act for themselves; but it is Impossible for Civil Law to intermeddle with it without infringing that Right.

The following Articles Were Voted upon by for an Amendment by said Town as follows, First. That the Suspention of the Writ of Habeas Corpus be Confined to Times of War and Limmited to the Term of Six months

Secondly, That every Freeholder of Twenty One Years of Age, have a Right to Vote for all Branches of the legislature where in those have a

Right to Vote that have the Quallification set forth in the Frame of Government—it appearing most agreeable to the Rights of them that are free Born.

Thirdly, That every Incorperated Town within this State, have a Right to and may Chuse a Justice or Justices of the Peace in their respective Town and also each Town have a Right to and may Chuse a Register of Deeds in and for their own respective Town; it appears most proper and agreeable to the Rights of a free People——

Forthly. That the Legislature Shall not have a Right and Liberty to augment the Quallification of any Member to be Chosen in any branch of the legislature, before a Revisel of said Form shall take place——

Lastly, That said Form of Government shall be revised within seven Years from the Time of its taking place; which Time we refer to the Wisdom of the Honorable Convention——

The foregoing was put to the Vote of the Town, and it appeared that Thirty Six were for it; and none appeared against it.

Needham June the 7th. 1780

Robert Fuller
William Fuller Selectmen
Silas Alden of
Thomas Fuller Needham

Roxbury (277/75)

Sentiments of the Town of Roxbury on the Constitution of Civil Government proposed by Convention——

Increase Sumner Esquire Moderator

At a legal Meeting of the Inhabitants of the Town of Roxbury legally assembled on the 17th day of May and contined by adjournments to the 29th. of the same Month, for the purpose of considering a Constitution or Frame of civil Goverment laid before the Town by Order of Convention, it was Voted by all the Inhabitants present at said meeting, being sixty nine in number to accept of every Clause, Article and paragraph of the said Frame of Government, except the Clause and Articles hereafter mentioned which we desire may be altered in the following Manner. Viz.

Chapter 1 Section 2 Article 8 Page 23d. after the Words this Commonwealth, insert these Words, *which disqualification shall continue untill taken off by the Legislature.*

We apprehend it unreasonable that a Subject of a free Republic Government should be rendered Incapable of serving the public forever merely for Error in Judgment, or even for mistake, which might be the Case, if the Article stands in its present Form. We think the legislature ought to be vested with a power to restore a subject disqualified for either of the Causes aforesaid.

The admission of small Corporations to send a Representative to the General Assembly we think inconsistent with the fundamental principle laid down in the Constitution, viz. that Representation ought to be *founded on the principle of equality*. Such a Representation in future, we apprehend may work great Mischiefs by giving the *Minority of People, the Majority of Power and Influence*——Small corporations ought to be joined to neighbouring Towns for the purpose of giving their Votes for Representatives, and in this Way we apprehend they will enjoy the privilege of Representation in as free a manner, as their Circumstances will admit of——

Page 31 Article 7

In this Article, the Governor, in our Opinion, ought to have power to march the Militia out of the State in the Recess of the General Court in Case a neighbouring State is invaded, we think the Confederation demands this kind of assistance of us; nor can we conceive how such a power can be abused, if the Militia is subject to the Controul of the legislature at their next Session——

Page 49 Article 7th. We object to it in its present Form because we think the legislature ought not to be the Judges of the expedience of suspending a Natural Right which every Subject enjoys of having an enquiry made into the cause of his imprisonment if it is necessary at any time, we think the Constitution ought to point out when this Necessity exists—as in time of War, Invasion, and Rebellion, and then for a Term not exceeding Six Months, at any one time——

We think a Convention ought to be made certain in the Year 1795 in order that mistakes and Errors which the wisest Bodies of Men are liable to, may be then rectifyed and corrected; and if it should be then necessary that the people might recurr to first principles in a Regular Way, without hazarding a Revolution in the Government.

In every article that mentions the *Christian Religion,* we wish to have the Word Protestant, inserted before the word Christian, this seems to us necessary to secure the peace and tranquility of the State, as well as to the promotion of that Religion which our venerable Forefathers suffered everything but death, to establish———

As to the 3d Article in the Declaration of Rights—if this Article in the Declaration of Rights can be so expressed, as to give satisfaction to those who object to its present Form without sacrificing the Right of civil Government to support public Teachers, to instruct the People in the Knowledge of the divine Being, his Perfections and Government of future Rewards and Punishments of the Sacredness of Oaths and importance of good Morals, then we consent thereto, otherwise we consent to the Article as it stands———

We empower and Delegate to agree on a time for establishing said Form of Government when the same shall be conformed to the Sentiments of two Thirds of the Inhabitants in the State.

By desire of the Selectmen William Bowman
Town Clerk

Stoughton (277/76)

At a meeting of the Inhabitants of the Town of Stoughton on the 24th of May AD. 1780, and continued by adjournments to the 31st. of the same month; the proposed civil Constitution for the People of Massachusetts-bay was considered with as much candour, and revised with as great care and circumspection as the nature of the thing and the shortness of the time allowed by the honorable Convention for the purpose, would admit; which will appear by the following votes passed in the several meetings and the number of voters on each side of every question.

The Declaration of Rights was first considered and acted on

Article	1,	voters for it	140,	against it	0	
———	2,	———	135,	———	1,	who proposed some amendments.
———	3,	———	90,	———	22,	
———	4,	———	71,	———	2,	
———	5,	———	76,	———	0,	
———	6,	———	79,	———	0,	
———	7,	———	80,	———	0,	
———	8,	———	70,	———	12	who proposed some amendment.

—— 9, is proposed to be amended by a new draft; (viz) All elections ought to be free; and all the male inhabitants of this Common-wealth that are twenty one years of age and upwards, being taxed for the support of Government have an equal right to elect officers and to be elected for public employments.——

The following reasons were offered to support the objections against the original; (viz) because the right of election is not only a civil; but it is a natural right, which ought to be considered as a principle corner-stone in the foundation for the frame of government to stand on; consequently it is unsystematical and contrary to the rules of architecture to place, or make it dependent on the frame; and as taxation and representation are reciprocal and inseparably connected; therefore the aforesaid draft and the original were voted in the following manner. (viz) Voters for the new draft 37, against it 29.

Article 10,	Voters for it	81,	against it	2	who wanted there should be some amendment
—— 11,	——	87,	——	0.	
—— 12,	——	84,	——	3	who thought it was deficient——

—— 13, appears exceptionable, because deficient; for altho a truth is asserted, yet no right is declared; therefore the following addition is proposed; (viz) therefore every subject in this Commonwealth has a right to such security.——
Voters for the addition 85, against it. 0.

—— 14, appears not explicit, therefore the following addition is proposed to be made after the last word "laws" of this Commonwealth.
Voters for the addition 87, —— 0.

—— 15, appears exceptionable, because the word "heretofore" in the exception is indefinite, therefore is proposed by way of amendment that these words be added (by the laws of this State) and inserted next after the word "practiced"
Voters for the amendment 71, —— 0.

—— 16, appears deficient and unsafe, because, the liberty of speech is as "essential to the security of freedom in a State," as that "of the press," therefore it is proposed by way of amendment that they be connected in said article.
Voters for the amendment 68, —— 0.

—— 17, ——	the original 79,	—— 0	
—— 18, ——	77,	—— 0.	
—— 19, ——	80,	—— 0.	
—— 20, ——	76,	—— 0.	
—— 21, ——	79,	—— 1.	
—— 22, ——	91,	—— 0.	
—— 23, ——	84,	—— 0.	
—— 24, ——	84,	—— 0.	
—— 25, ——	93,	—— 0.	
—— 26, ——	99,	—— 2	they being desirous to have it amended.
—— 27, ——	90,	—— 0	
—— 29, ——	81,	—— 1	
—— 30, ——	78,	—— 0	

—— 28, appears deficient and unsafe; therefore the following addition is proposed as an amendment, (viz) and that only in cases of extreme necessity, where there is an actual invasion or a violent insurrection——

Voters for the amendment 84, against it 9.——

The proceedings of the Town on the frame of Government Preamble, voters for it 90, against it 0.

On motion made, in order to gain time, the following proposition or question was put to vote (viz) It is proposed, that those articles in frame of government, that require pecuniary qualifications for the electors and elected, be altered by the honorable Convention in conformity to the amendment of the 9th Article of the Declaration of Rights: because it is agreeable to the rules of Architecture to build the frame upon the foundations and also because the aforesaid Articles appear repugnant to the first and sixth Articles of the Declaration of Rights.

Voters for the above question 37, against it 29. Therefore the greater part of those Articles will have no further notice taken of them in this return.

Chapter 1, Section 1.

Articles {1, 2, 3} Voters for them 53, against them 0.

Article 4, that part of it appears exceptionable, where power and authority is given to the General Court "to impose and levy reasonable duties and excises upon any produce" etc; because should that power ever be exercised in its full latitude and extent, by the legislature, it would be so far from promoting Agriculture, Arts and manufactures, that it would have a contrary tendency; therefore not admissable in the present form of words, and the following alteration is proposed; (viz) to impose and levy reasonable duties and excises upon spiritous liquors and the superfluities and luxuries of life. Voters for the alteration 50, against it 0.

Section 2

Article	3,	Voters for it	44,	against it	0.	
——	4,	——	39,	——	2.	
——	6,	——	43,	——	0.	
——	7,	——	47,	——	1.	
——	9,	——	48,	——	0.	
——	8,	——	54			with the same amendment as mentioned upon the 6th Article in the 3d Section same Chapter

Section 3

—— 1, —— 43, —— 0.

—— 2, is exceptionable, because unincorporated Plantations are excluded from being represented;—and as taxation and representation are, and forever ought to be reciprocal and inseparable therefore the following amendment is proposed to be inserted in said Article at the close of the proviso; (viz) Yet notwithstanding two or more unincorporated Plantations having 150 rateable Polls may join together in the choice of a Representative or either of them may join with the nearest incorporated Town in such choice. Voters for the amendment 51, against it 1.

——	3,	Voters for it	3,	against it	42,	only on account of pecuniary qualifications
——	4,	——	2	——	46,	
——	5,	——	41,	——	0.	

—— 6, appears exceptionable, because the power and right of impeaching is confined to the house of Representatives; therefore it is proposed that Towns may impeach as well as their Representatives, and that the Senate try the same.——— Voters for the amendment 54, against it 0.———

—— 7, ——for it 51, against it 0.

—— 8, —— 55, —— 0.

—— 10, —— 46, —— 0.

—— 11, —— 48, —— 0.

—— 9, is exceptionable, because too small a number of the House of representatives is to constitute a quorum for doing business;—therefore it is proposed that not less than half the returned members of the house shall constitute a quorum, and that no vote or act of the house shall ever be reconsidered without as large a number of members as first passed it.

Voters for the amendment 40, against it 0.

Chapter 2 Section 1

—— 1, voters for it 46, against it 0.

—— 4, —— 31, —— 0.

—— 5, —— 32, —— 0.

—— 7, —— 34, —— 0.

—— 8, —— 33, —— 0.

—— 9, —— 27, —— 0.

—— 11, —— 41, —— 0.

—— 12, —— 40, —— 0.

—— 13, —— 40, —— 0.

The power given to the Governor in the 6th article appears exceptionable, because unnecessary; therefore the following new draft of said Articles is proposed (viz) In all cases of disagreement between the two Houses with regard to the necessity, expediency or time of adjournment or prorogation, they shall assemble in one room, and after confering on the subject, it shall be determined by a majority of the whole by yeas and nays entered upon the journals of the House——Voters for the new draft 31, against it 0.——

The mode of appointing Major Generals as in the 10th Article appears exceptionable; because the two houses having a negative upon each other; they may make many fruitless tryals to no other purpose than only to give pain to those gentlemen who may be negatived;——therefore the following amendment is proposed; that the Major General be appointed by the joint ballot of both Houses assembled in one Room;—Voters for the amendment 37, against it 0.

Section 2.

Articles {3, 2} Voters for them 38, against them 0.

Section 3.

1, 2, 3, 4, 5, 6, 7	——	39,	——	0.

Section 4.

1, 2	——	37,	——	0.

Chapter the 3d.

1, 2, 3	——	43	——	0.
5,——it		36,	——	0

4, objected to, in the following manner; (viz.) Notwithstanding the honorable Convention, (as mentioned in their address) "have attended to the inconveniencies suggested to have arisen from having but one judge of Probate in each County," and "have left it with the future legislature to make such Alterations as the Circumstances of the several Counties may require":——Yet this part of the address appears delusive because it is not left in said Article to the future legislature to establish in each Town Courts of probate as their conveniency require; but only to determine and appoint such times and places for the Judges to hold their Courts in the Counties on fixed days as the conveniency of the People or Circumstances of the several Counties may require;—therefore a new draft is proposed—(viz) Courts for the probate of Wills and granting letters of administration shall be established in each corporate Town in this Commonwealth.—Voters for the new draft 48, against it 0.——

Chapter 4.——it	30,	——	0.——

Chapter 5.

Section 1, Voters for it	41,	against it	0.
—— 2, ——	42,	——	0.

Chapter 6.

Article 2, appears deficient; therefore the following addition is proposed (viz) "And any Elector, who shall receive any Gift or reward for his vote, in meat, drink, monies or otherwise shall forfeit his right to elect for that time and suffer such other penalty as future laws shall direct.——

——for the amendment 44, against it 0.

Article 3, Voters for it 0, against it 37 } because it appears pregnant with infinite mischeif.——

——4,	——	39,	——	0
——5,	——	42,	——	0

——6, will prove burthensome, should the present jargon of Laws remain in force for a long time; therefore it is proposed that they expire within five years, and that a new Code and System of Laws be compiled and established in the mean time. Voters for the amendment 40, against it 0. ——

Article 7,	Voters for it	29,	against it	0.
8,	——	29,	——	0.
9,	——	27,	——	0.
11,	——	31,	——	0.

10, is unsatisfactory; because it is beyond all doubt, that not only one; but that periodical Conventions ought to be held to correct those violations which by any means may be made in the Constitution, as well as to form such alterations as from experience shall be found necessary; therefore it is proposed that they be established in this Article without any dependence on the General Court; the first to be held in ten years, and ever after once in fifteen years, and that all the male inhabitants being twenty one years of age and upwards, be voters for the Choice of Delegates.

Voters for the amendment 29, for the original 2.

On motion made, the following question was put to vote. (viz) Whether the Town will empower their Delegate at the next session of the Convention to agree upon a time when the form of government shall take place.

Voters for the Question 29, against it 4.

A true Extract from the Minutes
Attest George Crossman Town Clerk

Stoughtonham (277/77)

Stoughtonham May the 22d 1780.

The Inhabitants of Said Town Being Assembled in Legal Town Meeting and Having under their Consideration the Constitution or form of Government and Sixty-Seven Voters Being Present Unanimously Voted to Accept the Same Excepting the Articles Hereafter Mentioned viz.———

Objection the 1st Chapter 1st Section 2d. Article 1st. That the Number of Senators be 29 Rather than 40. See the Reasons Annexed to the 5th Objection.———

Objection 2d. Chapter 1st Section 3d. Article the 2d. as the Mean Increasing Number for Every Additional Member is Set at 225 which makes the House unweildly we Could wish that it had Been Set 450.———

Objection 3d. Chapter 1st. Section 3d Article the 9th. That 40 be a Quorum in the House to do Business———

Objection 4th Chapter 2d. Section 1st. Article 13th. that these words may be added. or Lower the Salaries, as the Case may be———

Objection 5th. Chapter 2d. Section 3d. that the 1st. 2d. 3d. 4th. 5th. and 6th. Articles be Expunged that the Counsel Contained in Said Articles, will be unnecessary and Burdensom, and that the Senate or Such part of them as the Convention Shall appoint, be Counsel for the Governor as afore said.

Objection 6th. Chapter 3d. Article 4th. be Expunged, as that office has Ever been oppressive, Being Kept in but one Place in the County.——— We could wish that it might be Kept in Each Town by the Town Clerk and Selectmen, or Such Persons as the Towns Shall appoint and like wise that Deeds may be Recorded in Each Town by men appointed as afore said. We Could wish that there were Pecunary Qualification for a member to Congress.———

Voted, to Empower their Delegate at the Next Session of Convention, to agree upon a Time when this form of Government Shall take place agreable to a Resolve of Convention in March Last.———

Per order of the Selectmen
Benja. Hewins Town Clerk

Walpole (277/78)

May 29th 1780

Assembled the Inhabitants of the Town of Walpole in Order to Consider of the Constitution or Frame of Government agreable to the Direction of the Convention Voters Present 61 Approved of the Declaration of Rights unanimously except the 3d Article which was Disapproved by 10 of the above Number, they thinking that the 1st and 2d. Articles sufficient so far as said Declaration respects Religion———

The Constitution or Frame of Government was Approved by the above Number Except the following Articles which were Unanimously Disapproved

(Viz.) 1st the Register of Deeds, as they are of Opinion that Business might be transacted in each Town in this State with Propriety and much less cost.———

2ly. the Articles respecting the Qualifications of a Governor and Lieutenant Governor where it is said that they shall be of the Christian Religion, in their opinion it ought to have been said the Protestant Religion———

3ly. they Unanimously Disapprove of the 9 Councillers and of every Clause in those Articles respecting the same, thinking that those Councillers would be rather a Burden than a benefit, they also are of Opinion that the Senate ought to be Reduced to 31 they acting nearly agreable to the former Constitution so far as it is Consistant———

4ly they Disapprove of the Article Impowering the Legislator to Appoint but one Judge of Probate of Wills etc. in each County, as that Business might be trancacted in each Town or in Smaller Destricts at least than Counties———

5ly that among those Persons rendered incapable of holding a Seat in the Senate and House of Representetives setled Ministers of the Gospel ought to have been inserted; as in their opinion they ought never to hold a seat in either———

Walpole June 4th 1780
Seth Kingsbery
Seth Bullard — Selectmen
Timothy Mann — of Walpole
Benjamin Pettee
Eliphelet Clap

Wrentham (277/79)

Wrentham May 26 1780

At a General town meeting of the freeholders and other inhabitants of this town, being warned, Quallified, and Assembled as the law directs, at the publick meeting house in this town, by adjournment from monday the eighth day of May instant———

Proposed to the town to accept of the Declaration of rights, and frame of Goverment for this State as it now Stands, and it passed in the Negative by one hundred and Eleven Voters, and not one for it———

A motion was made and Seconed that the Third Article in the Declaration of rights be expunged, and the Question being put and the house Divided their appeared fifty six against the Question and fifty five for it,———

The Committee appointed to take into Consideration the Declaration of rights and frame of Goverment, published by the Convention latly chosen for the sole purpose of framing a Constitution, reported, which being read repeatedly and maturly considered was Voted, accepted, and is as follows.

Viz the 15th. article in the declaration of rights we think is not sufficiently plain. an Article so important which respects tryal by jury or other wise ought to be so explicit as the lowest Capacity may fully understand its meaning.

Article 29th. we find the judges of the Supreme Judicial Court are to hold their offices so long as they behave themselves well and that they should have Salaries Assertained and Established by Standing laws: this we object to for we think it not only the best policy but for the Security of the rights of the people that the judges of the Supreme Judicial Court Should not hold their offices longer than five years (unless by a new Appointment) and that they should have their Salaries granted Annually———

The 30th. Article in the Declaration of rights we think it much two Strongly expressed and Absolutly Militates with Article 2d page 15th. and Article 5th, page 40th, of the frame of Goverment and we apprehend said 30th. Article ought to be amended by inserting towards the latter end of it thes words exceping so far as is expressed in this Constitution———

Chapter 1st, Section 2. Article 1st, we object to. it is our opinion that the people at large are not so Sutable persons to elect the Counsellors and Senators as the house of Representatives are, therefore we think it best for this Common welth that the house of Representatives should elect Annually forty persons for Counsellers and Senators proportioning by districts as is in said Article provided and that nine persons be chosen for Counsellers from among the persons so elected by joint ballot of the Senators and house of Representatives in one room assembled, and the Counsellers so chosen shall hold their seat in the Senate except on tryals of impeachment.

Chapter 1st, Section 2d, frame of Goverment, Exceptionable, it is our opinion that no person ought to be Considered as a Voter for a Govener, Lieutenant Govener, Counseller or Senator unless he has been an inhabitant of this Common welth one year next preceeding such election.———

Chapter 1st, Section 3d Article 1st Exceptionable in that it appears to be consistant with the principal held up in the 11th. page of the Address which Constitutes the house of Representatives as the Representatives of the persons and the Senate of the property of the Common welth which principal we utterly disclaim, we are of opinion that the representatives elected in each town ought to be the Representatives of the property as well as the persons.———

Chapter 1st. Section 3d, Article 2d, exceptionable. it is our opinion that each town already incorporated may elect one representative, and any town hereafter incorporated, having one hundred and fifty ratable pools may (slaves excepted) elect one representative, and each incorporate town having five hundred ratable pools may elect two representatives and no town except the town of Boston may send any more than two and that the said town of Boston shall not elect more than four Representatives———

Chapter 2d Section 1st. Article 9th exceptionable. it is our opinion that the Govener and Council ought not to appoint the Judges of probate and registers of probate, for we find that all appeals from the judges of probate are to the Govener and Council———

Chapter 2d., Section 1st, Article 13th, we think is exceptionable in our opinion the Governer and Judges of the Supreme Judicial Court should have their salaries granted annually by the General Court early in their first session———

Chapter 3d. Article 4th is exceptionable, it is our opinion that a Court of probate of wills and for granting letters of Administration ought to be kept and held in every incorporate town and that it shall be amongst the first acts of the General Court to make provision for said Courts in each town accordingly, and it is our opinion that the General Court should make provision for the registering of deeds in each incorporate town

Chapter 4th. page 40th respecting delagates to Congress ought to be amended, for we apprehend that the Quallification of Delagates to Congress with respect to property ought to be considered and expressly Assertained.———Page 47th. and 48th, in the paragraft excluding from office ought to be inserted. Delagates to Congress and all persons appointed by Congress to do Bisness at forein Courts———

The last resolve but one passed by the Convention March 2d, 1780 we reject for it is our opinion that if upon a fair examination it does appear that two thirds of the persons voting in each town are in favour of the Constitution without any Amendments it ought to be sent to and Confirmed by the General Court, but otherwise if amendments are made and the Constitution Conformed as near as may be to the Sentiments of two thirds of the people it ought then to be returned to the free men of each town for their Approbation or Disapprobation, the Convention might then be Dissolved and each town make return to the General Court, an affair of such importance as this which so much concerns not only this but future Generations ought not to be indefirently passed over we therefore think it improper to accept of any part thereof untill the whole is compleated———

As to the Revision menshoned in the tenth Article page 50th, we think it is left two loose and uncertain, we are of opinion that a revision of this Constitution be made Certain, and that within the term of ten years, and after that once in twenty one years———

A true copy
Attest Jno Messinger TClerk
John Hall
Lewis Whiting
Nathan Blake Selectmen
Robert Blake
Nathan Fisher

Weymouth, 1780 (277/80)

at an adjournment of a Town Meeting held in Weymouth on Monday 22d Day of May An Do: 1780 the following Votes was Past (Viz) to accept of the Plan or fraim of goverment formed by the Convention of this State and laid before this Meeting with the following amendments (viz) where personal Estate is Required in the Constitution as a qualification for Electors and Elected that it be Expresly Mentioned Ratable Estate and that at least as much Property as is Required for Senators for a quallification be Required of Members of Congres and that no person on the Board of War Shall be a Member at the Same time of the

Senate or House of Representatives that Express provision be made in the Constitution for a Congress to be held in the Year Annoque Domini 1795.

Voted to Choose no other Deligate for the next adjourment of the Meeting of Deligates on the Constitution and that the Honorable James Humphrey Esquire Deligate for this Town be and hereby is Instructed that if the Amendments Proposed be Rejected by the Convention that he nevertheless Acceed to the Plan as it now Stands, and on putting the question their was Seventy Seven in favour of it and not one Against it.

A true coppy of the votes.

Nathaniel Bayley Town Clerk

WORCESTER COUNTY

Ashburnham *

[Article in Warrant of Meeting held May 26, 1780:—]

Article 4. To see if the Town approves of the form of Government as it now stands or whether they will make any alteration in it or not or pass any vote under said article that may be necessary.

[Action at the meeting was as follows:—]

Article 4. Voted to accept the form of Government as it now stands. three articles accepted unanimously. the articles objected against are the following (viz) the third in the bill of Rights forty seven for it as it now stands and twelve against it. Chapter 2d Section first article Seventh Voted with this amendment that the Governor with the advice of his Council have power to march the militia to any one of the neighboring or adjoining States Case of invasion in the recess of the general Court.

Chapter first Section third article forth w persons against it as it now stands.

Athol (277/83)

At a Meeting of all the Freeholders, and other inhabitants of the Town of Athol Legally assembled at the meeting House in Said Athol, on Thursday the 4th Day of May, 1780 and continued by adjournments to Wednesday the 24th instant, for the purpose of taking into Consideration the, New Constitution, or Frame of Goverment, agreed upon by the Delegates of the People of the State of Massachusetts Bay, in their Late Convention, and for the purpose of accepting, or rejecting the Same,——— after Reading considering, and Debating every artical Seperatly in Said plan of Goverment, the Town proceaded to vote thereon as follows, viz. first Began with the Decleration of Rights, the yeas and Nays of Each artical, are as follows.

* Town records, Massachusetts Historical Society.

		yeas	Nays		yeas	Nays
article	1—	118	2	16—	120	0
	2—	120	0	17—	120	0
	3—	67	44	18—	120	0
	4—	120	0	19—	120	0
	5—	120	0	20—	120	0
	6—	120	0	21—	120	0
	7—	120	0	22—	120	0
	8—	120	0	23—	120	0
	9—	120	0	24—	120	0
	10—	118	2	25—	120	0
	11—	120	0	26—	120	0
	12—	120	0	27—	118	2
	13—	120	0	28—	120	0
	14—	120	0	29—	0	120
	15—	120	0	30—	120	0

the following admendment was then proposed to the 29. article viz. That the Judges of the Supreme and Judical Courts hold their office During the pleasure of the Electors and that their Salleries be annually Granted———for the above amendment, yeas 120. Nays. 0

Secondly proceaded to vote upon the frames of Goverment.

Chapter 1. Section 1.				Section 3rd.		
article	1—	0	120	article 1.—	120	0
	2—	0	120	2—	0	120
	3—	120	0	3—	0	120
	4—	0	120	4—	0	120
Section 2nd				5—	120	0
article	1—	0	120	6—	0	120
	2—	0	120	7—	0	120
	3—	0	120	8—	0	120
	4—	0	120	9—	0	120
	5—	0	120	10—	0	120
	6—	0	120	11—	0	120
	7—	0	120	Chapter 2 Section 1.		
	8—	0	120	article 1—	0	120
	9—	0	120	2—	0	120

	yeas	Nays		yeas	Nays
3—	0	120	Chapter 3rd		
4—	0	120	article 1—	0	120
5—	0	120	2—	0	120
6—	0	120	3—	0	120
7—	0	120	4—	120	0
8—	0	120	5—	0	120
9—	0	120	Chapter 4th		
10—	0	120		0 —	— 120
11—	0	120	Chapter 5th Section 1.		
12—	0	120	article 1—	120	0
13—	0	120	2—	120	0
Section 2nd			3—	0	120
article 1—	0	120	Section 2nd		
2—	0	120		120	0
3—	0	120	Chapter 6th		
Section 3rd			article 1—	118	2
article 1—	0	120	2—	0	120
2—	0	120	3—	0	120
3—	0	120	4—	0	120
4—	0	120	5—	120	0
5—	0	120	6—	120	0
6—	0	120	7—	120	0
7—	0	120	8—	120	0
Section 4th			9—	120	0
article 1—	0	120	10—	0	120
2—	0	120	11—	120	0

Thirdly, voted that the whole of the Seccond part, of Said Constitution or Frame of Goverment, is accepted by this Town provoided that the following (or Similar) amendendments be made therein. viz.———

That the Department of Legislation be formed of But one Branch viz a House of Representatives———

That no Governor, Lieutenant Governor, nor Senate be appointed.

That, a Council or Committee be annually Chosen by the House of Representatives, of the Number of [sixten?] one to be elected out of each County, and one Chosen at Large who shall be president of Said Council and Chief Majistrate of this Common wealth, who shall sign all Commissions Given to Civil officers, and warrants for Drawing money out of the Publick Treasurer———

Said Council to Sit in a Seperate Body for the purpose of giving advice and Council to the House, and to be invested with the Powers which in Said Constitution are given to a Governor in Chapter 1. Section 1. article 2 and 4. to the Senate in Section 2. article 6 and 8, to a Governor and Council in Chapter 2. Section 1. article 11. Excepting that the Major votes of the House of Representatives shall finally Decide all Questions——

Said Council to keep their Seats untill a New Council be Duly chosen and sworn in their steads, and that not Less then the major part of the members of Said Council make a Quoram,——In Case of the Death or removal of the Chief majistrate Said Council or the major part of them shall have full power to transact Buisness without one untill such times as a new Majistrate shall be Chosen by the House.

That a Captain General, or Commander in Chief be appointed by the General assembly who Shall hold his office During Good Behavour who Shall be invested with all the powers Given to a Governor in Chapter 2 Section 1. article 7, 10 and 12. and shall Sign all Military Commissions Said Captain General to make returns to the General assembly a true account of the State of all Military affairs that come under his care once in three months, and Shall be accountable to the House for his Conduct,——

That all other powers mentioned in said Constitution to reside either in a Governor or Senate shall be in the House of Representatives——

That Every Corporate Town in this Common Wealth have the privilidge of sending one Member to the General Court and that all Towns be allowed to send a greater number, according to what was practiced, in the year 1770——

That not Less then the Major part of the members of the General assembly make a Quoram,——

That no person be Deprived of Being elected for a Representative for want of an Estate,——

That every male person of the age of 21 years, and free shall have the priviledge of voting for a Representative——

That the members of the General assembly be paid out of the publick Treasurer of the Commonwealth——

That every Corporate Town in this Commonwealth be obloiged to elect, and return one member of the General assembly, under penalty of a Large fine——

That every member thus elected and returned be obloiged to give constant attendance at all times of the Setting of the General Court under penalty of a Large fine, unless he can give Sufficient Reason therefor to the House———

That no person be freed from any process or arrest in any civil action on account of his Belonging to, or attending the General assembly.———

That no Standing Salleries or pentions be ever made by the General assembly—But that all Civil and Judicial Officers have their salleries annually Granted, and hold their office During the pleasure of the Electors.———

That Every Town be the Judge of the Qualifications of those they Chuse to Represent them———

That every Corporate Town in Commonwealth have the privilidge of Chusing a Justice of the peace, who shall hold his office During the pleasure of the Electors

That a Convention of Delegates of this Common Wealth be called within Seven years for Revising the Constitution

for the above amendments, yeas 118. Nay, 0

a true Coppy of the Votes of Said Meeting

attest, Hiram Newhall, Abner Graves — Selectmen of Athol

Barre (277/84)

To the Honarable the Convention of Deligates for fraiming a Constitution of civil government for the State of Massachusetts Bay

The town of Barre Having Deliberated upon the form of civil government presented to us by your Committee and at a town meeting legally Esembled for that purpose on the 31th day of May 1780 the town on the whole Declaration of Rights thair was But 11 Desenting votes and on the Legistative Execetive and Judiciary powers they Have Nothing of any objections But the following Remarks

First that no person shall be elegible to offices either as governour, Lieutenant governor, Counsilor Senator or Representitive unless he shall Declare Himself to be of the protestant Relegion———

2ly that No person shall be Elegible to any office in the Legislative who Dos not contribute to the support of civil government in the Way of taxation the Reason we give is we think he who pays part of the publick charges will be more likly to Expend our money frugally then He who bares No part of the Burthan

3ly We think that the important servants of this comon welth viz. the governour Lieutenant governor Council or Sanetor Representitive ought Not to be admited to sustain or sarve in offices more than four years out of seven at most the reason we give is that this Restriction will be a check upon Enterprising and Designing men and of consequence Have a tendency to sarve the Libertyes of the people and Render the Comon Welth more safe.

4ly that No person shall Have a seat in Congress and either Branch in the Legislature at the same time We think such a practice would open A way for some persons to have an undue influence in government and Derogetory to the liberties of the people.

5ly We choose that a cartain Day should appointed for the Choice of Representetives throughout this Comonwelth as it will save the trouble and Expence of a anuel precept

6ly think that Each town in this comon welth ought to have the previledg of nominating one Justice of the peace it being our opinion that the Representitive towns are under a grater advantage to Determine with Rispect to the Qualifications and abilities of their townsmen then the first majestrate of this Common Welth Can possibly be etc

the Number of Voters present in said meetting 104 the yeas 104 Nays 4

gentlemen of the Convention we are far from thinking that our Sentiments upon the Constitution are perfect all that We Hope from them is that they may convey Light in this important Business our Real Desier is that upon Examination if you find any Room to make the Constitution more perfect you will do it.

Which is humbly submitted.

Done in town meeting May 31th A:D. 1780

William Henry Selectmen of Barre
Benj. Nye
Timothy Hasten

Bolton (277/85)

At a meating of the male Inhabitants of the Town of Bolton Twenty one years of age and upwards held by adjournment on Monday the 15th Day of May 1780

The Question was put to see whether the Town Did approve of the Constitution or form of Government and it passed in the affirmative viz. Thirty nine for it and Eleven against it.

N.B. Since said meeting Three of those that voted against said Constitution have Declared their approbation of it and also six that was not present at said meeting have Declared their approbation thereof.

James Goddard
David [Nicol?] Selectmen
William Sawyer the 3d.
Jacob Moor

A true copy Attest Nathaniel Langley town clerk
Bolton May 31st 1780

Brookfield (277/86)

At a Meeting of the Freeholders and other Inhabitants of the Town of Brookfield legally warned and assembled on Monday the 8th Day of May A.D. 1780 and continued by Adjournment to Wednesday the 24th Day of said Month——.

IT HAVING pleased Almighty GOD in his Providence to afford to the Inhabitants of the State of Massachusetts-Bay an opportunity, which seldom happens in the Course of human Affairs, voluntarily and peaceably to deliberate, agree upon and establish without Fraud, Violence or Surprize, such a Frame or Constitution of Civil Government as the united Wisdom of all the People, assembled in their respective Town-Meetings, and, by their Representatives freely elected, assembled in General Convention, shall dictate as most conducive to their Welfare and Happiness in political Society:——And it being an object of the highest Importance that a Form of Government organized and balanced in such Manner as to promote, establish and secure the Happiness of all the different Classes of the People should now be adopted and fixed, on a Basis as lasting and permanent as possible:——

THE FREEHOLDERS and other Inhabitants of the said Town of Brookfield, therefore, impressed with a high Sense of the Necessity of Government being established and of the goodness of divine Providence in giving them the present opportunity of agreeing upon a Constitution of Government calculated to promote the general Happiness of the People, have proceeded to take into their most serious and deliberate Consideration "the Constitution or Frame of Government agreed upon by the Delegates of the People of the State of Massachusetts-Bay, in Convention begun and holden at Cambridge on the first of September A.D. 1779 and continued by Adjournment to the second of March A.D. 1780"—signed by "JAMES BOWDOIN," President—" and attested by *"Samuel Barrett,* Secretary," of said Convention and transmitted to this Town for their Sentiments thereon———

THE SAID Constitution and Frame of Government, with the address of the Convention prefixed thereto, having been read in open Town-Meeting and considered with all that seriousness and Attention which the high Importance of the Subject deserves, the Inhabitants of said Town, acting upon the Principles of general Benevolence and yielding some opinions of smaller Moment to the essential Considerations of general utility, in order that some Form of Government might be consolidated and established, proceeded to give their Sentiments relative thereto—and the Question being proposed—*"Whether the said Inhabitants would agree to adopt and establish the said Constitution in its present Form without any Amendments or Alterations"?*—and the Votes being taken by Yeas and Nays, there appeared ONE HUNDRED AND SEVENTY EIGHT Yeas, or Votes for establishing said Constitution in its present Form—and ELEVEN Nays, or Votes for not establishing it without some Amendments or Alterations———.

WHEREUPON it is voted and resolved as the Sentiments and opinions of the Inhabitants of this Town, by a Majority of One hundred and seventy eight to eleven, that the said Constitution or Frame of Government be adopted and established as the Constitution or Frame of Government of the State of Massachusetts-Bay and become a Part of the Laws of the Land———

Certified by order and on behalf of said meeting
By Dwight Foster Moderator
Attest Caleb Hitchcock Town Clerk

At a Meeting of the Freeholders and other Inhabitants of the town of Brookfield, legally warned and assembled on Wednesday the 24th Day of May A.D. 1780———

WHEREAS the Delegates of the People of this State, in the Convention begun and holden at Cambridge on the first Day of September 1779 and continued by Adjournment to the second of March 1780, for the Purpose of agreeing upon a Constitution or Frame of Government for the said State, to be submitted to a Revision of their Constituents, have "Recommended to the Inhabitants of this State to empower their Delegates, at the next Session of said Convention, to agree upon a Time when the said Frame of Government shall take place without returning the same again to the People:——PROVIDED that two thirds of the Male Inhabitants of twenty one years of age and upwards, voting in the several Town and Plantation Meetings, shall agree to the same, or the Convention shall conform it to the Sentiments of two thirds of the People aforesaid"——

AND as it is of the utmost Importance for the Welfare and Happiness of the People of this State that the said Constitution or Frame of Government should be agreed upon and established as soon as possible—And as there is now no Delegate appointed to represent this Town in said Convention——

IT IS THEREFORE VOTED AND RESOLVED

That DWIGHT FOSTER Esquire be and he is hereby elected and appointed to represent this Town in the Convention to be holden at Boston on the first Wednesday in June next to compleat the Constitution or Frame of Government lately agreed on by said Convention and submitted to a Revision of their Constituents——

And that the said DWIGHT FOSTER be, and he is hereby empowered, in Behalf of this Town, in Conjunction with the Delegates from the other Towns in this State, to agree upon a Time when the said Frame of Government shall take Place without returning the same again to the People, pursuant to the said Recommendation——.

The foregoing is a true copy extracted from the records of the town of Brookfield this 25th of May A.D. 1750.

Witness. Caleb Hitchcock, Town Clerk

Charlton (277/87, 88)

Votes and proseedings of the town of Charlton respecting the Constitution or form of government proposed——

At a meeting of the inhabitance of Charlton Legally assembled at our meeting hous on monday the fifteenth day of May 1780 to act on the Constitution or form of government proposed

Voted and Chose Jacob Davis Esquire moderator

Voted to attend to the reading of the Constitution

Voted to begin with the bill or rights, and read article by article and act upon them

Article 1st—49 for—19 against

article 2—96 for———

article 3—15 for 69 against

Voted to Chuse a Committe to state the objections against the third article in the bill of rights—

Voted and Chose Mr. Caleb Ammidown
Voted and Chose Mr. David Lamb
Voted and Chose Mr. Caleb Curtis
} Committe

---

article 4th—39 for———
article 5th—35 for———
article 6th—41 for———
article 7th—44 for———
article 8th—48 for———
article 9th—42 for———
article 10th—42 for———
article 11th—43 for———
article 12th—42 for———
article 13th—36 for———
article 14th—36 for———
article 15th—17 for———
article 16th—32 for———
article 17th—23 for———
article 18th—32 for———
article 19th—27 for———
article 20th—30 for———
article 21st—29 for———
article 22d—32 for———
article 23d—32 for———
article 24th—33 for———
article 25th—33 for———
article 26th—33 for———
article 27th—34 for———
article 28th—31 for———
article 29th—22 for—21 against
article 30th—37 for———

Fraim of Government Chapter first

Section first
article first—37 for none against
article 2d——35 for———
article 3d——21 for———
article 4th——32 for———
Section 2d all acted on at once 14 for 8 against
Section 3d
article 1st——10 for 14 against
article 2d——27 for 1 against
article 3d——22 for———
article 4th——9 for———

article 5th—28 for——
article 6th—20 for——
article 7th—22 for——
article 8th—25 for——
article 9th proposed an amendment that a quorum of the hous be an hundred members
Voted—26 for——
article 10th 27 for——
article 11th 23 for——

Chapter Second Section first

article 1—17 for——
article 2d—with this amendment the word protestant in the room of Christian
Voted—24 for 2 against
article 3d—24 for——
article 4th—25 for 2 against
article 5th—23 for 1 against
article 6th—36 for——
article 7th—26 for 2 against
article 8th—29 for——
article 9th—16 for 9 against
article 10th— 7 for 34 against
Voted to Chuse a Committee of 3 men to propose amendments on the 10th article
Voted and Chose Mr. Caleb Ammidown }
Voted and Chose Mr. Samel. Robinson } Committee
Voted and Chose Mr. Peter Sleman }
article 11th—18 for——
article 12th—23 for——
article 13th—19 for——

Chapter Second Section Second

article 1st—27 for 2 against
article 2d—22 for——
article 3d—34 for——

Chapter 2d Section 3d

article 1st—17 for 2 against
article 2d—8 for——
article 3d—15 for——
article 4th–19 for——

article 5th—15 for——
article 6th—16 for——
article 7th—18 for——

Chapter Second Section 4th

article 1st—14 for——
article 2d—14 for——

Chapter 3d Judiciary power

article 1st—8 for 3 against
article 2d—18 for——
article 3d—17 for 2 against
article 4th—11 for 6 against
article 5th—11 for——

Chapter 4th—16 for——

Chapter 5th—Section first

article 1st—15 for——
article 2d—16 for——
article 3d—13 for——

Chapter 5th Section 2d

Voted——10 for——

Chapter 6th with this amendment of the Christian relidgeon as Exersised by protestants

article 1st—6 for——
article 2d—12 for——
article 3d—13 for——
article 4th—16 for——
article 5th—17 for——
article 6th—15 for——
article 7th—10 for——
article 8th—16 for——
article 9th—16 for——
article 10th with this amendment that the Constitution be revised once in five years
voters ——12 for——
article 11th—15 for——

Voted that if the Constitution be accepted by two thirds of the people or if it be Conformed to the minds of two thirds of the people—that it take place in September next——

Voted that our Former Delegates to Convention be Continued.

A true copy taken off the minits of the town meeting in Charlton respecting the Constitution etc.
test Nehemiah Stone town Clerk
Charlton June 2d - 1780.

Samuel Lamb
John Cobourn Select men
Jonathan Mower of Charlton

The following was substituted instead of the 3d article in the Declaration of Rights
In order that no coercive Measures Shall ever take place within this Common Wealth in any eclesiastical Matters, the Several Towns, Parishes, Precincts and other bodies politic or religious Societies Shall at all times have the exclusive right of electing their own public Teachers, and supporting and maintaining the Same in a manner most agreeable to the dictates of their own Conscience; but no Person Shall be compelled thereto by Law. And every Denomination of Christians demeaning themselves peaceably and as good Subjects of this commonwealth Shall be equally under the protection of the Law; and no Subordination of any one Sect or Denomination to another Shall ever be Established by Law.
The within written is the report of the Committee whose names are of followeth

David Lamb
Caleb Ammidown Committee
Ebenezer Davis
Isaiah Blood

Voted and accepted the within writen report twenty for none against
test Nehemiah Stone Town clerk

Chapter 2 Executive Power,
Article 10th The Captains and Subalterns of the Militia shall be elected by the written Votes of the train band and alarm List of their Respective Companies who are called upon to do Duty at Home or to Serve in the Continental Army. And all Officers chosen in the Manner aforesaid Shall not hold their Commissions for any longer Term than three years from the Time of their Election. Except Elected again in the manner Aforesaid Which is Humbly Submitted

Voted on the within amendment 38 for none against

Caleb Ammidown
Peter Sleeman Committee
Samuel Robinson

The Committee appointed by the Town of Charlton To make Some Addition to the dicleration of the Rights Beg leave to Report it is their opinion that to the 16th Article those words be added that the privelidge of printing the Bible under proper Direction of the Sivil Authority is Necessary and that the Inhabitants of this Common Wealth shall forever be indulged with the free use thereof

Voted and accepted the within writen report 21 for none against

Which is submitted Caleb Curtiss per order

Douglas (277/89)

In the Declaration of Rights

Article 1 For 18 Against

2——24
3—— 6
4——27
5——27
6——27
7——25
8——29
9—— 9——24
10——22
11——28
12——31
13——28
14——29
15——25 (26 [25] objected to the Article. 15. Object only to the 4th Paragraph. viz. And all monies paid by the subject etc. Objected to Because we apprehend the paragraph leaves room for one Denomination to convert the Monies of other Denominations, to uses contrary to their consent; and tends to oppression: at

least leaves room for unhappy Disputes, dishonorary to Religion.

We wish the paragraph stood agreeable to the following. No laws of this State Shall ever enable one Denomination of professing Christians, for the Support of public teachers, to levy taxes upon other Denominations of professing Christians)

16——26
17——27
18——36
19——39
20——32
21——32
22——33
23——32
24——32
25——34
26——36
27——30
28——32
29——9 ——37 Praying the Judges may be chose annually
30——15

Frame of Government

Chapter 1

Legislative power Section 1

article 1—— 6 for against

2—— 9
3——13
4——12

Section 2 Senate

1—— 9——13—wishing the number of Senators may be less

2——11——19—Because we conceive a Smaller number will perform business more expeditiously——

3——11
4—— 9
5—— 4——15—The ninth Article of rights and Several Articles founded upon it. Objected to Because the objectors Suppose they have a right to Such men, to represent them, whether rich or poor, as will feel

the distresses of the poor—It is their opinion also that all rational men above twenty one years of age should have the privilege of voting governors, Senators and Representatives: otherwise, all men cannot be said to be born free and equal.

6— 8
7—10
8—10
9—10

House of Representatives

Article 1—15 for 0 against
2—16— 0
3— 7— 8 To Article 3 Chapter 1. Section 3 Provided estate is to be the qualification for a Representative: The objectors and others wish to have added—if he lose his estate by his own imprudence.
4— 8— 9
5—12
6—13
7—16
8—13— 2
9—18
10—17
11—18

Chapter 2 Executive Power. Section 1. Governor

Article 1—18 For
2—21—wishing, Protestant may stand instead of Christian
3—15
4—15
5—15
6—15
7—14
8—11
9— 8—Against 1—
10—13—with this amendment Sixteen instead of twenty one as youth will be more teachable under officers of their own choice
11—14

12—19

13— 7

Section 2 Lieutenant Governor

Article 1— 8 for

2—14

3—14

Section 3.

Article 1— 8

2— 7

3—10

4—11

5—12

6—12

7— 9

Section 4.

Article 1—15

2—14

CHAPTER 3 Judiciary Power

Article 1— 6 for 3 against

2—16

3— 7 9 desiring the Justices may be annually chosen by their Town

4—15

5—17

Chapter 4 13 For

Chapter 5 Section 1 University

Article 1—14 For

2—14

3—14

Section 2 Literature, encouragement

14 For

Chapter 6 Oaths etc.

Article 1—16

2—16

3— 9

4—15

5—13

6—15

7——11
8——12
9——15
10——18—— With the amendment Seven years instead of fifteen
11——16

It was voted that the same delegate Mr. Stearns attend the convention for this town with full liberty to vote as he sees fit as to the time of the Constitution's taking Place

Caleb Whiting
Aaron White Selectmen of Douglass
Daniel Tiffany

Douglass June 2, 1780

Dudley (277/90)

At a Town-Meeting held in Dudley in the County of Worcester in the State of the Massachusetts Bay
On the 29 day of May 1780
Firstly voted that the Following amendment be made viz. On the third article of the Bills of rights that the Word (not otherwise be added after the decleration relative to attendance, on the Teachers of Piety religion and Morality
For it 48 against it 16
2ndly voted that all male Persons that are twenty one years of age and Upwards that have Paid taxes, and are Inhabitants in any Town have a right to vote for a Governor Senet and Representtitive for it 52.———
3ly voted the Quorom of the House of Reprsenttitives be 100 For it 42———
4ly Voted that the word Protestant shall be added where it Saith the Governor declares himself to be of the Christian Religion before the word Religion for it 52———
5ly voted to have the General Court by joint ballet to Chuse A Governor out of the two that hath the most votes from the People Provided no one Hath a Majority of votes from the People for it 42.———
6ly voted that the representation of Each County shall nominate the justices of the Peace for their County and thier Nomination to be made yearly, and the Governor shall Commission them accordingly for it 42———

7ly voted that the Revition of the Constitution be made Certain and that it be in the year of our lord 1790 for it 42——

8ly voted that our deligates be impowered to set the time where said Constitution shall take Place, without having it sent out to the People again Provided it be agreeable to two thirds of the People, or can be made agreeable to the minds of two thirds of the People for it 42——

Jedidiah Marcy
Benj. Morris Select men of Dudley
Jonathan Willard

Fitchburg (277/91)

At a legal meeting of the Inhabitants of the Town of Fitchburg May 23d 1780

The Question was put, whether this Town will adopt the Constitution or Form of Goverment, as set forth by the Convention lately formed for said Purpose; It passed in the affirmative Nem.con.—The Number voting Sixty five——

By order of the Selectmen of the town of Fitchburg

Test. Thomas Cowdin T. clerk

To Samuel Barrett Esq. Secretary for the Convention

Grafton (277/91)

Agreable to a Request of the Convention for framing a New System of Government We the Subscribers Caused the Town of Grafton to be Legally assembled and Laid the Constitution or form of Government before them and Said Town have acted as follows viz——

Article first in the Bill of Rights
approved by voters 39—
Article 2 approved by 30
Disapproved by 31
(Because we Conceive that our duty shall not be included with a declaration of Rights wherefore let the Clause (as well as the duty) be erased)—
article 3 approved by—19
Disapproved by—43 Because we conceive the free Exercise of Religeon is Restricted and that Some Clauses may be Construed to injure

pratercally our Rights of Conscience and upon the whole is very ambiguously Expressed.

From 3rd article to 12th approved by 39

Article 12th Disapproved by—43 Because it is not mentioned in said article that the Jury Shall be Chosen as usual and that it is not mentioned that the number Shall be as usual in this State.

From 12th to 18 approved by 41

article 18th approved by 24

Disapproved by .... 39 because we apprehend their may be an allusion to the third article and Confirming the same

From article 19 to the——29th approved by 38

Disapproved by 3.

article 29th approved by——16

Disapproved by 27 Because they are for having the Judicial officers Chosen annually and their Salaries granted anually.

article 30th approved by——37

Part 2d. the frame of Government approved by 37——

Chapter 1 the Legislative power Section 1st the General Court

[Art.] 1 approved by 29

Disapproved by 18 Because they are for having but one house

article 2d. approved by 16

Disapproved by 32 they apprehend the Governor hath part in Legislation Contrary to the 30th article in the Bill of Rights

article 3d approved by 14

article 4th approved by 6

Disapproved by 12 Two of them object Because they apprehend it Connects with the 3rd article in the Bill of Rights, also Two disapprove because it says the Court are to make laws not Repugnant to this Constitution whereas they Dont allow it to be a Constitution as it now Stands

Chapter 1st Section 2 the Senate

article 1 approved by 7

Disapproved by—10 apprehending there is ten too many for the Council and Senate

article 2 approved by 9

disapproved by—6 being against having more than one house

article 3 approved by—11

disapproved by—8
article 4th and 9th inclusive
approved by———11
disapproved by———9 against having more than one house

Chapter 1st Section 3rd Representatives article 1: 2d approved by 1 disapproved by 19 Being of opinion that Largest Town in the State ought to send no more than thru Representatives and none less than one
article from 2d to 9th. approved by 19 disapproved by 5
article 9th. approved by 8 Disapproved by 12 Being of opinion that 60 members is not Enough to Constitute a Quorum
article 10th approved by 18
disapproved by—2 one objects against the whole Book and the other Because it doth not mention that no man ought to be assaulted as well as the members of the House
article 11th approved by 10
disapproved by—5 because it mentions more than two Branches in the Court

---

Chapter 2 Executive Power Section 1st. Governor viz.
article 9th Disapproved by 24 Because we are for having all Estates intestate to be Settled in the Towns where such Estates ly.

Chapter 6th article 2 objected by 22 Because they are of opinion that all Justices out to be Excluded having any hand in Legislation

Jona Stow
Moses Holbrook — Select men of Grafton
Elijah Drury
Joseph Bruce

Grafton June 6th 1780

Hardwick (277/92)

To the Honorable Convention of the State of the Massachusetts Bay convened at Boston for the purpose of taking into consideration the Constitution or form of Government, with the proposed amendments from the several towns within this State.

Gentlemen. The weight and importance of the business now under your consideration makes it indispensably Necessary, that you should be rightly informed with regard to the true spirit and meaning of your Constituents.

We therefore, the Inhabitants of the town of Hardwick think ourselves in duty bound to inform the Honorable Convention, that in the amendments proposed in our last meeting, and sent down by a Member then chosen; you have by No means got the minds of the Major part of the inhabitants. We shall give you an extract from the Town Records, of the proceedings of those several Meetings, by which it will appear that there has been an omisstion with regard to the Number of Votes for, and against several articles in the Constitution. Monday May 8th 1780 Voted that 80 Members be a Quorum of the House of Representatives by a majority of 45 to 14———Voted, not to have a Governor 27 to 15———Monday May 22———Voted, the 3 article of the Bill of rights, 68 to 10———The first article in the Constitution passed in the Negative 50 to 24———Chapter 1st article 2 passed in the Negative 46 to 3——— Chapter 1 article 4 Negatived 36 to 6———Chapter 1st Section 4th passed in the affirmative 30 to 15———Chapter 1st Section 3 Negatived by 35 to 12———Adjourned to Thursday May 25———The proceedings of the Committee were laid before the Town and accepted. by 40 to 2——— These are true extracts from the Town Records, which may be compared with the Report sent from this Town and you will be able to determine wheather or not it is a true representation.

any further light relative to the matter may be had of the member sent from the Town, who was one of the Committee———Monday June 5th met by a Warrant issued by the Select Men in the consequence of a Petition from a number of the Inhabitants of the Town:—

1st—Made choice of Brigadier Jona. Warner Moderator of said meeting: 2—voted to choose a Committee of 5 to take into consideration the Records of the Town with regard to the Constitution; and to amend what was omitted by a late Committee; in order to have the same transmitted to the Convention.———

3 The Report of the Committee accepted, by 128 Nem.Con. So far as respected the records of the former meeting;

4 Voted to accept the following amendments of the Committee; viz; page 33 Section 12

That after the Commissary General and Commanding Officers etc. etc. have made their Returns to the Governor that he shall Previous to the

expiration of his appointment, make out those Returns and Lodge them in the Secretary's Office.———
Reason, That the house may inform themselves of the State of the Publick Stores etc. without the formality of a Requisition to his Excellency: ———Voted, by 128 Nem.Con.———Page 39. Chapter 3 Section 4—We propose, that in stead of leaving it to future Legislation to appoint one or more Probate Courts in each County that it should be exprest in the Constitution, that each County should be divided into proper Districts, with a Probate Court in each, with proper times and places appointed in each, for transacting the business.———Reason, Because some counties are so large, that by reason of time and cost in traveling and attendance for the setteling Estates, Widows and orphans are put to great expence, which might be lessened by the proposed amendment.———65 voted for the above amendment and 53 for the amendment as sent down by the Member chosen at the former meeting.
Page 50 Section 10 That in stead of issuing Precepts for the purpose of forming a Convention to revise the Constitution, in the year of our Lord 1795.
We would propose to have this Revision made in 1787———Reason, Because 7 years experience is time sufficient in our opinion to find the good or ill Effects of the present Constitution———
passed in the affirmative by 128—Nem.Con.———Voted, that one of the former Delegates, (viz Brigadier Jona. Warner) do attend at the Convention and Represent the Town with regard to the proceedings of this Meeting, and as a member of the Convention.———
Voted, to accept the Constitution with the above amendments 47 yeas—2 nays.———
Voted, to instruct their Delegates to determine with the Convention when the Constitution shall take place agreable to their Resolves.

A true coppy from the Town records

Attest.

Sylva. Washburn Town Clerk
Hardwick Stephen Rice
June 5, 1780 John Hastings
Elijah Warner
Abraham Knowlton
Select Men

[Lucius R. Paige, *History of Hardwick, Massachusetts* (Boston, 1883), 116–118, contains the following account, drawn from town records.]

The town held four meetings, May 1, 8, 22, and 25, 1780, to act on the proposed Constitution. At the second meeting, it was "voted that there be no Governor appointed, by a majority of 27 against 15." At the third meeting, it was "voted, that if there be a Governor, that he be of the Christian Protestant Religion," instead of "the Christian Religion." At the fourth meeting, a committee, consisting of Joseph Allen, William Paige, Aaron Barlow, Thomas Robinson, and John Sellon, submitted a report, embracing several amendments to objectionable articles, with the reasons therefor; which report, with the proposed amendments, was accepted by a vote of 40 against 2. Some of the objections and amendments were as follows:—

"In the Bill of Rights, Article I, page 7, objected to and amended: it reads thus,—'All men are born free and equal, etc., amended,—'All men, whites and blacks, are born free and equal,' etc.; Reason: lest it should be misconstrued hereafter, in such a manner as to exclude blacks."[1] Article III. "Voted, That a person that does not attend the public worship of God at any place ought not to be taxed in the place where he lives. Every other article in the Declaration of Rights approved."

Article 1, page 15, objected to, because the two branches have a negative on each other; whereas it ought to be but for a given time, and at the expiration of said time, if non-agreed, that both houses meet, and by a majority decide the controversy."

"Article 2, objected to, because the majority of the court can't make a law, without being exposed to a negative by the Governor."

The qualifications of voters was objected to, "because every male, being twenty-one years of age, must have an annual income of three pounds, or an estate worth sixty pounds, to be qualified to vote for a senator. Reasons : That every male, being twenty-one years of age, ought to vote in all cases."

The mode of filling vacancies in the senate objected to: "Reason : The persons having the highest number of votes in the District ought to be the men."

The office of Governor was disapproved: "Provided, nevertheless, that if the inhabitants of this State shall see meet to choose a Governor, Lieutenant-Governor, and Council, they should by no means have power over the militia; but the militia shall be under the order and direction of the General Court; and that they or either of them shall not prorogue, adjourn, nor dissolve the General Court without their request; and that

[1] This question was decided by 68 yeas against 10 nays.

they by no means appoint any officers, either civil, judicial, or military."

It was further recommended by the committee, and the town voted its approval, to wit:—

"That the power of pardon always be in the hands of the Legislature:

"That the Justices of the Superior Court be appointed by the General Court:

"That the Justices of the Inferior Court be chosen by the people of their county, as the Registers now are:

"That all Justices of the Peace shall be chosen annually by the people in each town in which they dwell, by ballot:

"That the Register of Deeds for each town in this State be annually chosen by ballot:

"That the Judges of Probate for each town in this State be annually chosen by the people of each town, by ballot, to serve in that town only:[2]

"That the captains and subalterns of the militia shall be elected by written votes of the alarm list and training band of their respective companies, of twenty-one years of age and upwards:

"That the colonels and majors be chosen by their respective regiments, the brigadiers and brigade majors by their respective brigades, the adjutants and quarter-masters by their respective regiments, by ballot."

Acting upon the suggestion of the Convention before mentioned, the town now "voted to dismiss the former delegates to the Convention, and dismissed them accordingly; and voted to choose one man to attend said Convention on the first Wednesday in June next, to be held in Boston, and made choice of Deac. William Paige for said delegate."[3]

Harvard (277/93)

The Town on due notice being assembled Proceeded to hear and consider the Constitution or frame of Government. first voted to accept the 3d. article in the bill of rites, 78 voting for and 28 voting against the said

[2] June 5, 1780. The town proposed a different amendment, "that each county should be divided into proper districts . . . because some counties are so large that by reason of time and cost in travelling and attendance in the settling of estates, widows and orphans are put to great expense which might be lessened by the proposed amendment."

[3] June 14, 1780. The town modified its action in regard to delegates, as quaintly expressed by the town clerk: "Voted, that the town does approve of Brig'r Jonathan Warner as their delegate at the Convention; also voted, that the Honorable William Paige be considered as a member in full communion of said convention."

article. Then voted that the following amendments be made in said Constitution.

1st. That there be a new Convention within the term of 15 years to Consider what amendments may be made in the Constitution.

2ly. That the Suspension of the habeas Corpus act shall be confined to the time of war invasion or rebellion and not to exceed the term of six months

3ly. To give the Governer power in the recess of the General Court to march or transport the inhabitants of this State for the relief of a neighbouring State invaded or threatened with immediate invasion.

4ly. That the Governer shall be of the protestant relegion.

Then voted to accept the whole of said Constitution with the above amendments (except the 3d. article in the bill of rites which has been already voted) 81 voted for accepting and not one against.

Then voted to accept the Constitution as it now Stands provided the above amendments cannot be obtained, 35 voting for and 16 voting against the same.

likewise voted to send two Delegates to the Convention one of each Denomination.

Voted and chose Colonel Josiah Whitney Mr. Joseph Stone Delegates.

Caleb Sawyer — Selectmen
Joseph Willard — of
Richard Harris — Harvard
William Burt

Holden (277/94)

To the honorable convention for forming anew Constitution for the State of Massachusetts.——

Gentlemen,

Agreeable to your request we have taken under consideration the form or constitution of goverment sent out to the several towns, and embrace, and improve our liberty to make objections to some parts of the constitution, and desire some alterations. [As to the third article in the declaration of rights, desire it may be specified, that, where a person attends on a teacher of a different sect, or denomination from the stated teacher in the place where he resides, his producing evidence that he has satisfied his own teacher shall exempt him from any tax to any other teacher]

We object against the 1st Article of 2d Section Chapter 1st—which makes provision for the election of 40 Councellors, and Senators, and request that it may be altered to a number not exceeding 30. Our reason is, that a number exceeding 30 would occasion an increase of publick expence, without any advantage arising therefrom, sufficient to justify it.

We object also against the expression christian religion mentioned 2 Chapter Section 1 Article 2d and Chapter 6th article 1st, as being too vague, and indeterminate as to its meaning, or import, and not sufficiently expressive of what we suppose the Convention designed by it, and desire it may be clearly and fully expressed that the protestant religion is intended. We object likewise to that part of article 10th Chapter 2d Section 1st that impowers the Governor with advice of council to appoint all continental officers and officers of forts, and garisons, and desire the power of appointing them may be lodged in the representative body. and Lastly, We object against article 10th Chapter 6th as to the meeting of a new convention to make such alterations in this form of Goverment as shall be found necessary; We apprehend it highly expedient that the meeting of a new convention in 1785 shoud be made certain. and that the people also should have full power, whenever the major part judge it necessary, for the publick weal, to instruct, or require their representatives to order precepts to be issued from the Secretary's office to the several towns to elect delegates to meet in Convention for the pusposes aforesaid. and if the representative body fail of doing this, that the Selectmen of the several towns shall have power to call together their respective towns for the purpose of choosing delegates to form a convention for the purposes above expressed. If the above alterations are adopted according to their true meaning, and import, we consent to the ratification of the present form, altered as above, (if not in words, in Spirit, and meaning by the present convention—At publick Town-Meeting For the Comstitution with these amendments. Yeas 82 Nays 2

Holden June the 5th. 1780

Moses Smith
Amos Heywood Select men of Holden
Samuel Thomson

Lancaster (277/94)

To Mr. Samuel Barrett Secretary of the Convention for forming a Constitution or frame of government for the State of the Massachusetts Bay.

Sir.

Agreable to the Request of the Convention contained in their Resolve of March 2 1780—the Inhabitants of the Town of Lancaster, at a Meeting legally Called, have had Said Constitution or Frame of Government laid before them———at which meeting they Passed the following Votes. Viz———

Voted to receive the Constitution as it now stands, 103 for it and 7 against it. Voted to empower the Delagates at their next Session to agree upon a time when this Constitution Shall take Place without returning the Same again to the People; provided that two Thirds of the Male Inhabitants of the Age of twenty one years and upwards, voting in the several Town and Plantation Meetings shall agree to the Same, or the Convention Shall Conform it to the Sentiments of two Thirds of the People as aforesaid.———

Voted that the Members of the Convention be Directed, if any exceptions be lodged with them, with regard to the Constitution, to State those objections, and endeavour to enforce the Reason therefore in Convention, any previous vote notwithstanding———

A true coppy of the records attest Josiah Leavitt Town Clerk

Benja. Richardson
Josiah Kendall Jr.
Samuel Sawyer
Solomon Jewett
David Jewett

Selectmen of Lancaster

Leicester (277/95)

At a Town-Meeting legally Warned and continued by Adjournment from April 27th to June 1st 1780 to consider the Frame of Government sent out by the Convention—The Inhabitants of the Town of Leicester came to the following Votes.

Voted Colonel William Hinshaw Moderator

Voted that the Constitution or frame of Government be read through
Voted that it be taken up by Articles then Adjourned to 15th May
Voted unanimously that they approve of the 1st and 2d Articles in the Declaration of rights. 67 present———
Voted to refer the 3d Article to a Committee for Amendment, the other Articles in the declaration of Rights were Voted unanimously.
The frame of Government

The 1st 2d and 3 Articles passed Unanimously the 4th, 40 for and 1 against it.

Senate

Article 1st. 37 in favor of and 5 against it: the 8 next Articles voted Unanimously———

House of Representatives

The 8 first Articles Voted Unanimously, the 9th: 55 in favour of and 6 against it 10th and 11 Voted Unanimously———

Governor

Article 1st Voted Nem. Con. Article 2d. Voted to dele the word Christian and insert the word Protestant

the next 12 Articles Voted Nem. Con.

Lieutenant Governor—

The three Articles 2 Chapter voted Nem. Con.

Council

The seven Articles in the 2. Chapter 3d Section Voted Nem Con. The Committee on the 3d Article of the declaration of Rights reported an Amendment 29 in favor of the Amendment and 36 against it. Adjourned Met etc. Voted 43 in favour of deleing the word Protestant in the 3d Article of the declaration of Rights and 18 against it—and for erasing the whole Sentence in the said Article begining at the word And all Monies etc. 49 in favour of said erasement and 3 against it. Adjourned —Met etc. and reconsidered the foregoing 3d. Article Voted 54 in favor of the word Protestant standing in the 3d Article and 13 against it——— Voted 48 in favour of that Sentence in the 3d Article beginning at the word And all monies etc. being retained and 14 for erasing it.———
Secretary etc. The 1st and 2d Articles voted Nem Con.
Judiciary Power Chapter 3d the 5 Articles in it voted Nem. Con
Delegate to Congress Chapter 4 Voted Nem Con.
University Chapter 5th. Voted Nem. Con.
Literature Chapter 5th. Section 2 Voted Nem Con.
Oaths Chapter 6th Article 1st. Voted Nem. Con. 2d Article Voted Nem

Con that the Clergy be excluded a seat in the House of Representatives the 7n next Articles Voted Nem Con the 10th Article 4 in favour of it and 51 for calling a new Convention in 7 years to revise the Constition, The 11th Article voted Nem Con.——It was then moved whether they would accept of the Frame of Government if the Convention should not alter any part of it, being put—61 Voted to Accept it and 13 desired not to be counted either way——Voted that Major Seth Washburn and Colonel William Hinshaw are empowered to agree with the other Delegates in Convention on the Time the New Constitution or frame of Government shall take place, agreeable to the Resolve of the Convention.

P.S. Captain John Brown by infirmity of Body being unable to attend the meeting requests that he may be counted as voting in favour of every Article in the Constitution as sent out to the People and be added to the above Number who Voted in like manner;—which is submitted to the Convention by the Town.

William Henshaw Moderator

Attest John Lyon Town Clark

The Committee assigned to make the amendment in the 3d article of the Bill of rights, Present the following reasons for Dealing the word Protestant in the 1st Paragraph. and the whole of the 4th Paragraph in said article——

1st In the 1st Paragraph the Legisture is authorized and required to authorize and require the Severall Towns Parishes Precincts and other Bodies Politic or Religious Societys to make Suitable Provision at there own Expence for the Support of Protistant Teachers of Piety Religion and Morality in all Cases where such Provision is not made Voluntarily —and whereas there is, and may be diffirent Sects and religious Societys that in Conscience Cannot maintain and attend on Protestant Teachers for the aforesaid Purposes. therefore Persecuting or Compeling them (in our oppinion) would Tend to gain them more Proselites and Disturb the peace of the Commonwealth, and is inconsistant with the Last Paragraph, but that Every Denomination of religious Societys Demeaning themselves Peaceably and as Good Subjects Should be Equally under the Protection of Law.——

2ly we apprehend that the 4th paragraph implies a ministereal Taxation upon the whole of the Subjects, and that Each Subject paying his money it Shall go to the Publick Teacher or Teachers of his own Religious Sect or Denomination. If he Require it. otherwise it may be paid for the Support of the Teacher or Teachers of the Parish or Precinct in which the moneys are raised——and whereas it is against the Principles of a great part of the Community to pay any ministeril Tax at all. other then by a free Contribution by there own hands, we are of oppinion that it is oppressive to the Subjects against whose principle it is paid by a Tax, and is in Consistant with the 2d Article of the Bill of rights——

John Lyon Town Clark

Leominster (277/96)

At a Legal Meeting of the Inhabitants of the Town of Leominster on the 15th of this instant May and Continued by several adjournments to the 29 of this instant Did then pass the following votes viz——
voted to approve of the Constitution Excepting the articles that contain the suspention of the Habeas Corpus act and the qualifications for officers as to Relegian 25 yeas and 7 nays——
Also voted that the word Protistant should be insarted in the Begining of the oath to be subscribed to by the several officers specefied in the Constitution and that the Habeas Corpus act should not be suspended for more then six months by the Legesliture 25 yeas and 6 nays——
Likewise voted to impower there Deligate at there Next session to agree upon a time when the form of government shall take place in case two Thirds of the male inhabitants shall vote in favour of it.

Dated at Leominster May the 29: 1780
Thomas Gowing
David Wilder Select men for Leominster
Timo Boutell

Lunenburg *

At a meeting of the inhabitants of the town of Lunenburg assembled May 1st 1780. Voted and chose Mr. Benjamin Redington Moderator, then the Constitution or frame of Government was read and the meeting adjourned to Monday the Eight instant at twelve o'clock at this place; the town being met agreeable to adjournment May the Eighth 1780.

* Town records, Massachusetts Historical Society.

Voted to allow Capt. Kimball 375 pounds for his service in attending in the convention for framing a Constitution.

Voted that the Selectmen be directed to draw orders on the town treasurer for the payment of Capt. Kimball's amount.

Voted that the Selectmen take back the list of jurymen to revise and make return at the next town meeting,

Voted further to adjourn this meeting to the day that shall next be appointed by the Selectmen for choosing a Representative at one o'clock in the afternoon at this place.

The Town being met agreeable to adjournment May 22, 1780.

Voted to accept the return of Jurymen made by the Selectmen.

Voted to chose a Committee to estimate the Rev. Mr. Adams Salary for said Committee. Voted and Chose Capt. George Kimball, Mr. Asahel Hartwell, Jedidiah Bailey, Mr. Benjamin Redington and Capt. Joseph Bellows.

Voted that the Committee be instructed to call upon the tresurer for the money that was assessed for Mr. Adams Salary and when the money is ready to Estimate the same agreeable to a former vote of the town by the Necesaries of Life.

Voted to raise £224 for the use of the school.

Voted to accept the Constitution or Frame of Government as there was present 75 for and 18 against the same.

Voted that Capt. Kimball be Directed to attend in Convention and use his influence to agree upon a time when this form of Government shall take Place without Returning the same to the town.

A true record Per Jedidiah Bailey Town Clerk.

Mendon (277/97)

We the Subscribers Committee of the Town of Mendon have taken into our mature Consideration a number of articles acted upon in the Constitution or Form of Goverment and find in Som articles matters Contained, which would be gratly Destructive to this Common welth——

article 1th. voted 70 for 1 aganst in the Bill of Rights——

article 2 65 for and none aganst——

article 3. 4 for 56 aganst it——Rejected for this reason we judge that no Lejesletive body hath or ought to have power to make a Law to Controle any matter of an Eclesastical Nature Espesialy in matters of Conscience, for in the second article we find no Subject Shall be hurt or molised or Restrained in his parson Liberty or Estate for worshiping god in the maner and Season most agreable to the Dictats of his own Consience. Therefore we think that no parson or parsons ought to be holden to pay any thing toward the Suport of the Publick Worship of God or to pay any taxes tiths Dutys or any other way whatsoever to Suport Publick Teatchers in matters of Religon without his own parsonal free Consent

4 article voted 52 for 2 aganst—

5 article voted 42 for

6 article voted

7 article voted

8 article voted

9 article voted with amendment that no parson shall Elect or be Elected into Publick office Except those that pay publick taxes to this Common welth———

10 article voted———

11 article voted

12 article voted

13 article voted 14 voted 15 voted 16 voted 17 voted 18 voted 19 voted———

20th article voted 11 for 8 aganst 21 voted 22d. voted 23d voted 24 voted 25 voted 26 voted 27 voted 28 voted———

29th voted with good Behaver to stand five years 30 voted———

The Frame of Goverment the Lejesletive Power

Chapter 1 Section 1 article 1 voted article 2d 15 for 21 aganst it 3 article voted 4 article voted 20 for 17 aganst

Article the 5th Chapter 1 Section 2d article 1 voted with the mendment for the Senet to Concist of 19 in the afermative 36 in the negative 2 and for the Governor's Councill to Consist of 9 for it 25 against it 11. voted that there be not more than one Counciler in any one County 37 for 1 aganst it———

article 2d voted with the amendment that no man Shall Elect or be Elected into any Publick office but shuch as pay Taxes to this Common welth

Article 3d. 20 for 8 aganst it 4th voted 12 for 1 aganst it

article 5th vot for 16 aganst it 2

Article 6 voted article 7 voted article 8 voted 9 voted with a eleven for a Corom insteid of Sxteen

House of Representatives

Chapter 1 Section 3d article 1 voted article 2d voted not to Except. and Substitute in Lew of it that the Representative Body of this State do not Exed 150 in Number that the whole State be Devided into Equal Districts Eatch to Send one Representative making in the whole 150 the Mode of Representation in the proposed Constitution is not Eligable because it will admit of so larg a number of members as will form un weildy Body for Doing Business, 2dly it will be atended with grat and unnessesary Expence to the publick 3d. because Every small Corporation being alowed to send a Representative is no Real advantidge to them as it can amount to no more than a nominal Representation they being unable to Suport one where as the whole State were Divided into Equal Districkts of a proper Bigness [werby?] part would injoye an Equal Representation and the Burden an[d] Expence would be inconsidarable articles 3 4 5 6 7 all voted. 8th voted. 9 voted with this amendment that not less than 40 members of the house of representives should Constitute a Corom for Doing Business in the rom of [*blotted*]

article 10 voted article 11th vot 11 for it 2 aganst it———

Executive Power

Chapter 2d Section 1 article 1 13 for 3 aganst it 2d article voted with this amendment———Protestant in the sted of Cristion Religon———

Article 3d voted 4 and 5 article voted 6 7 8 voted 9th. voted with the amendment—that the Judges and Regesters of probate and Regestors of Deeds be apointed by the several towns and that all probate bisiness and Registry of Deeds be Done in Eatch town voted that the Select men of Eatch town Boath apoint and licence Retalers and Tavern keepers.———

10. 11. 12 articles voted article 13 not voted as it now stands but in Lew thereof there shall be reasonable grants and adiquate to there service Respectively be annuelly made and to the Governer and Justices of the judishal and Supream Court acording to the Directtion of the Genarel Coart for the time being———

Chapter 2d. Section 2d. Leiutenant Governer———

Article 1th voted article 2 and 3 voted———

Chapter 2d. Section 3d. Cuncill—Articl 1st voted 2 and 3d articles voted article 4th not Exeped and voted in the Lew thereof that not more than one Cunceler shall be Chosen out of any one County.

article 5 6 7 all voted Chapter 2d. Section 4th. Secretry article 1th 2d. voted Chapter 3d. Judisary Power. article 1th. not Exeped voted in Lew thereof that judisary officers shall not hold thre office not more than 5 years without a new apointment article 2d voted and 3d voted with the amendment of 5 years insted of seven

Chapter 3d. Continued. article 4 not Exepted for this reason we think it will be attended with grate Cost and troble when the Same Biseness may be Done in Eatch town in the State with more Ease less Charge and Troble———

article 5 voted

Chapter 4 Delegats to Congress———

article 1th voted 9 for 5 aganst it

Chapter 5 Section 1 The University

Article 1th voted not to Exept for this Reason we judge that if our rights and Privledges are Secured to us by this Constitution the same securs them and their priviliges 2 for 4 aganst it.

article 2 voted—not to Exept for the same reason as ofered in the first article in the 5 Chapter and first Section 2. for it 4 aganst it

Article 3d voted aganst it 4 aganst [12?] for.

Chapter 5 Section 2d. 5 for 3 aganst———

Chapter 6th. article 1 voted 2 3 4 all voted article 5 voted article no 6 voted 8 for 6 aganst———article 7th. 8.9. all voted

article 10 voted 6 for 8 aganst—for this reason we judge it nesesary that there shall be a Convention once in Seven years to Revise this Constitution.

Article 11th voted to impower our Deligate in conjuntion with other Members of the Convention at there Next Session to agree upon the time when this Constitution shall take place———

Mendon June 5th 1780

Stephen Torney
John Benson
William Thayer

Select Men of Mendon

Milford (277/98)

To Mr. Samuel Barrett Secretary of the Convention begun and held at Cambridge on the first of September 1779 for the purpose of framing a new Constitution of Government for the State of Massachusetts Bay to be submitted to the revision of their Constituants in conformity to said convention.

We the Select men of the Town of Milford in the County of Worcester have appointed a meeting for the Revision of the constitution or form of Government Put out by the Honourable Convention above mentioned, and we have attended said meeting in said Town of Milford and the votes on the Constitution or form of Government appears to be as followeth. viz: Votes on the Declaration of Rights

Article first accepted

2	Ditto
3	36 against it. 1 for it
4	Accepted
5	Ditto
6	Ditto
7	Ditto
8	Ditto
9	Ditto
10	Ditto
11	Ditto
12	Ditto
13	Ditto
14	Ditto
15	Ditto
16	Ditto
17	Ditto
18	Ditto
19	Ditto
20	Ditto
21	Ditto
22	Ditto
23	Ditto
24	Ditto
25	Ditto
27	Ditto
28	Ditto
29	12 for it 8 against it.
30th	accepted

Part the Second form of Government

Article first accepted

2— Ditto

3— Ditto with this amendment that the Select men of the Several Towns within this State be impowred to Prove wills and Grant

Administration on Intestate Estates and to Settle all Estates of Testate and Intestate persons Deceast agreeable to Law: that Each Town in This State be Impowrd to Chuse a Regester of Deeds within their Respective Towns

Chapter 1 Section II Senate

Article 1 Rejected Voted to have but 28 Councilors and Senators
2 accepted
3 Ditto
4 Ditto
5 Ditto
7 Ditto
7 Ditto
8 Ditto
9 Rejected Voted that 12 Senators Should make a Quorum

Chapter 1 Section 3 House of Representatives

Article 4—Voted that all persons Should have a Right to Vote for Repersentatives that pays Taxes

Chapter 2 Executive Power Sextion 1 Governor—

Voters 8 against it

Ditto 18 for having the Governor to have the advice of his Council in all Cases

Article 10 Rejected 13 against it. but Voted that all Soldiers should have a Right to Vote for their officers.

Milford June the 3: 1780

Jesse Whiting Select men of Milford
Caleb Cheeney
Ebenr Read

New Braintree (277/99)

New Braintree May the 31 1780

At a Leagul meeting of the Mail Inhabitants of the town of New Braintree being Twenty one years of age and upords to Consider and act on the Constituon or form of Government———

1 Voted and Chose Major James Wood moderator for said meeting———

2 the Question Being put Wheather they would accept the Constituon as it now Stands 15 for and 42 against it

3 Voted to make the following a mendments 42 in favior and 15 against viz.———

Part first article 3d	[any Person of what Sect or Denomination Soever residing in any Place Diffiring from his in Sentiment Shall have full Liberty to Covenant and Engage to Support the gospell with Those of his one Sect or Denomination and Shall Be Exempt from any Tax to Support the gospell where he resides unless by his own Consent———] etc.———
Legislative Chapter 1st Section 1st Article 3d	The Recording of Deeds and the probate office ought to be Established in Every Town or in other words Every Town vested with power to appoint Persons for or to Do that Bisness———
Senate Chapter 1st Section 3d Article 3d	Not less then one hundred members ought to Constitute a Quoram to Do Business———
Executive Chapter 2d Section [?] Article 2d	The word Christion ought to have bin Protastant———
Judiciary Chapter 3d Article 3d	That no Justice of the pice Be Commisioned unless Recommended By the Major part of the people where he resides———
Executive Power Chapter 2d Section 1st Article 12th	That the governer be obliged to render an accompt. once in the year to the Legislature or oftner if required.

Joseph Bowman
Jacob Pepper — Select men of
John Barr — New Braintree
Joseph Barr

Northborough (277/100)

At a Legal meeting of the inhabitants of the Town of Northborough from twenty one years of age and upwards being duly notifyed and Convened at the meeting-house in said Northborough on monday the first day of may 1780.—And Continued by ajournments to the eighteenth instant, for the purpose of taking under their Serious Consideration, a new Constitution or frame of Government, provided by the Convention of the State of Massachusetts bay, appointed for that purpose. The Town then proceeded in the following manner, (viz)———

1st. Voted to accept of the 30, articles in the bill of rights yeas 34 Nays 1———

2ly Voted unanimously to accept of the whole Constitution or Frame of Government, with only the following proposed alterations———

In Chapter 1st Section 3d. article 4th the Town would propose every Male person of twenty one years of age who pays to the Support of Government Should have a right to vote in the Choice of a Representative———

In Chapter 2d Section 1st article 2d. The Town would propose the Governer Should declare himself to be of the protestant Religion

Chapter 6th. The Town would propose that in order to keep the legeslative and judicial departments distinct, that the Several Counties may not Suffer through a delay of justice, the justices of the inferior Court of Common Pleas Should be excluded from a Seat in the house of representatives and Senate; at least in the Senate.

Chapter 6th. article 10th. The Town would propose that the term for Calling a new Convention, for revising the Constitution in order for amendments, Should be Shortned to five or at most to Seven years from the time of its first taking place. these alterations and amendments the Town proposed if they Can easily be obtained; but if a Major part of the people in the State, acting in the Meetings accept of these Articles as they now are, then this Town Consents to have it established as it is.———

Number present at said meeting and acting in favour of the foregoing amendments 34———

3ly. Voted to impower their deligate at the ajournment of the Convention to agree upon a time when the form of Government Shall take place provided that two thirds of the male Inhabitants of the age of twenty one years and upwards voting in the Several Town and plantaation meetings Shall agree to the same, or the Convention shall Conform it to the Sentiments of two thirds of the people as aforesaid.

Northborough
May 29th 1780 Seth Rice Jr.
John Ball
Solomon [Gadded?]
Abraham Monroe
Selectmen for Northborough

Northbridge (277/101)

Northbridge June the 5th 1780

In Town Meeting agreeable to adjunment for a Consideration of the proposed Constitution and Fraim of Government for the Common Welth of Massachusetts (viz The Vote was tried in favour of the Constitution as Exhibited By the Late Convention for that porpose
for the Said Constitution none against it 38
on the first article in Diclarition of Rites Yeas 12—Noes—6
on article Second .... Yeas 23—No: 0
article third without amendment———yeas 6—No: 17
with amendment Begining the third article in the following maner——— Viz.———

As the Great Creator of All Things and Goviner of all Events Hath Given the Strongest Intimation that He will Honour those that Honour Him and Hath anexed a Blessing to and observence of the Sabath and as it is obvious and observable that Religeon Florisheth or decayeth acording to our observance of Said Day it must be Considered as the Indispencable Duty of the Legesliture of this Common Welth to Injoin a Strich observance of the Lords Day———

Voted that the Word (and) in the Begining of the Last Sentence in the third article of the Diclaration of Rites be Left out and the following Claus be Substituted for the Satisfaction of Difrent Religious Sects (Viz)———

(Provided further that no Interpitation of this article may admit those of one Religeous Sect or Denomination for the porpose of Supporting a teacher or Teachers of there own to Inpose any Tax or assesment on those Evidently of a *Difrent Denomination*). But that Every etc. (with the fore going amendment Yeas 27 No : 23.

The Question was then put Respecting the Rest part of the Book and with the following amendments. the Yeas was 20 Nos. 0.

Viz article 30th in the Dicleration of Rites

As we aught to ward against Roman Catholicks Pagons or Mahomitents from Having any Seat in Government, from whom the People of God Have So much Suffred in past ages the following amendment is proposed which may be added to the 30th. article of the Decliration of Rites (Viz—and no one Shall be Eligible to any office in Either of the fore going Departments Unless He be of the Christian Protestant Religion.—

---

to Chapter 1th. Section 2d article 1th etc.

Considering the Number of Councelers and Senetor to be More Numorous then wold be adventagous to this Common Welth the following amendment is proposed to Chapter first Section Second article first etc. Viz.———

In Stid of forty Councelers and Senetors. Read. 27.

article 9th. let Eleven of the Senate Consitute a Quorum—for etc.

Chapter 2nd Section 1th article 13

As all Men and Bodies of Men are falable our Lagislature may be Pregidic or by Reason of other frailties. or by Reason of the Extrodinary Times (for Silver and Gold do not always Hold the Same Vallue) Set Salaries to Excessive High yet according to the proposed Constitution there is no liberty for loring the Same there fore the following amendment is proposed to Chapter 2d. Section 1th. article 13th.

at the Close of the Sentance—Viz.

and if to High they may be Lowred.

Chapter 2nd Section 3 article 1th and 2d.

The Councel being Considered as larger than Nessasary the following amendment is proposed to Chapter 2nd. Section 3d article 1th and 2d Viz.——

Seven Councelers to be Chosen of which four may be a Quorum

As it is Considred of Publick Utility that Probate Business and Likewise that of Recording Deeds be performed in Every Town and that Justises of the Peace be not Commishoned but by Recommendation of their Respective Towns it is Requested that there be an article added to this Constitution to that Effect and that this Constitution be conformable there to.——

The foregoing is agreeable to the Votes of this town
Attest William Park Town Clerk

Northbridge June the 5th 1780

Oakham (277/102)

At a legal Meeting of the Male Inhabitants of the Town of Oakham in the County of Worcester, being free and Twenty one years of age on the 18 of May 1780 and continued by adjournment to the 25th. day of the same month

for the purpose of considering a Constitution or frame of goverment agreed upon by the Deligates of the People of the State of Massachusetts Bay in Convention begun and held at Cambridge on the first of September 1779 and Continued by adjournments to the Second of March 1780——

Voted as folows—This Town impressed with a Sense of the many disadvantages this State are labouring under for want of a good Constitution or Goverment and the necessity that such a Constitution should be established as soon as may be—having duly perused and Considered said frame of goverment are of oppinion that the most of the articles therein contained well calculated for the good goverment peace and Safety of this State and we do approve of the greater part thereof accordingly, but are constrained to say we disapprove of the following particular parts thereof (viz)

Part the 2d. Frame of Goverment

Chapter I, Article I Objection, that the Senate Should have a compleat negative on the House as it Stands Expressed——

Reasons, the House of Representatives are in the most compleat maner the Representatives of the People at large, and much Superiour in numbers

Amendment—In Case the Senate non concur any Bill or Resolve the House of Representatives shall reconsider the same and two thirds of the House present to give it a Sanction or force of Law.———

Article II whole rejected———

Reasons 1st. We view this article in its consequences very little short of the Governors having a full negative.

2d We cant think it reasonable to confide more in the wisdom of any one man than in the wisdom of the General Court———

3d. We cannot be assured the Governor will allway act with integrity.

4th. It is, we conceive, in consistant within any good article in said frame of goverment, wherever it is mentioned that the General Court shall have full Power to make Laws etc.

5th. we apprehend, lifting one man so much higher than the rest has a direct tendency to introduce compleat Monarchy, That Monarchy is destructive both to the Temporal and spiritual intrest of Mankind.———

Chapter I. Section II

Article I. Ob. we object against the number of forty Persons to be Elected Councellors and Senators———

Reason, we see no necessity of any Council at all Seperate from the General Court That the Senate may with propriety Council the first Majistrate or Executive Officer, and with as much safety and far less expence, in every particular mentioned in the frame of Goverment.

Amendment—Thirty one persons to be Senators———

Chapter I. Section III

Article I Ob. we object against the mode of Representation———

Reasons 1st. If every Town should send their full numbers allowed, and they should generally attend the House would be unweildy———

2d. If the members should take turns to attend, new members constantly coming in the business would be protracted to the great detriment of the Public.

3d. How ever this mode of Representation may on first view appear on paper in point of equallity, yet considering the local circumstances of the several Towns in this State, it is not practicable in its nature, and consequently the large Towns near the seat of goverment would have an undue advantage above the rest.

4th In after Times many Towns not having 150 R. Polls would be deprived of being represented, which we think unjust.——

Amendment—Every Incorperated Town shall have the Priviledge of sending one Representative and no Town in the State more than one Except large Sea-Ports (viz) Boston 5 or 6 and other large Sea Ports in proportion——or otherways this mode (viz) Every Incorporated Town send one any Town having 500 Ratable Polls may send two, 1000 three and so on still allowing the additional number of 500 to give another member——either mode we should be content with, and we apprehend it would have a great tendency to remove jealousy between and Country

Executive Power

Chapter III. Section I. ——

Article II Ob. Respecting the Qualifications of a Governor "and unless he declare himself to be of the C. Religion"

Reasons. we esteem is very dangerous to open a Door for a papist to be Governor, or to have a Seat or Voice in the Legislative or Judiciary Department

Amendment—and unless he be of the Protestant Christian Religion. and the same amendment to be observed in every other place where the Christian Religion is mentioned as a qualification.——

The Governour and Lieutenant Governour shall have a Seat and Single voice in Senate——.

Article IX Ob. Judicial officers etc. Safer for the General Court to appoint

Amendment—all Judicial officers etc. shall be appointed by both Houses, each having a negative on the other.——

Article XIII and last article of Executive Power

Ob. "it is necessary that he Should have an honourable Stated Salary of a fixed and permanent value and so on to the End of the Article—to us conveys a most abhorent Idea——.

Reasons 1st. no Servant of the Public how ever dignified ought wholly to be independant of the Public, but every one ought to have a Reasonable Reward and no more, according to Service and as circumstances may Require

2d. This article, whither designed or not, is so constructed that if any General Court, however thin both Houses may be, should grant the Governour and Judges half the Income of this State No General Court in futre could lessen their Salories untill the State Should be thrown into Such Convultions as to annihilate the Constitution.

Amendment. Honorable Salories shall be granted annually,——

Chapter VI Article X

Ob. fifteen years to long a time for tryal of the Constitution.
Amendment—in the year of our Lord 1787——Voted to accept said Frame of Goverment with the proposed amendments and such others as shall be found necessary to make it conformable to said amendments. 63 Voters were present at said meeting 61 Voted as above 2 against the whole
number of 63 against Reciving said Frame as it Stands—— ((If two thirds can be agreed the Delegate is Instructed to Establish it))

true Copy Attest
William Crawford Town Clerk

Oxford *

At a legal meeting in Oxford on Monday the 25th Day of August, 1779.

2dly. To see if the Town will choose some person to set with the State Convention at Cambridge to assist in Forming a Constitution of Government, Agreable to a resolve of the General Court of the State.
2dly. (At said Meeting) Chose by Ballot Ebenezer Learned Esquire and Mr. Ezra Bowman, Delegates to set with the State Convention at Cambridge to act in forming a Constitution of Government for this State: And voted to instruct them to Return to the Town a copy of their proceedings, for the Town to concur, or non concur as they see fit.

Legal meeting of Monday 22d. of May 1780.

5thly. To see if the Town grant Ebenezer Learned Esquire, and Mr. Ezra Bowman pay for their services and expenses for attending a Convention for forming a Constitution, at Cambridge.

Voted Ebenezer Learned Esquire and Mr. Ezra Bowman 30 dollars per Day for their services at the Convention for forming a Constitution of Government.

The meeting then adjourned to Monday the 29th. Day of May at one o'clock in the afternoon; Then met and,
6thly. Further to hear and consider the proposed Constitution and act thereon as the Town shall think proper. Voted further to hear and consider the proposed constitution at a future meeting.

* Town records, Massachusetts Historical Society.

At a legal meeting on above warrant on June 27, 1780.
2ndly. Further to hear and consider the proposed Constitution of Government and to act thereon as the Town shall think proper. 2ndly, Read and considered the Constitution and voted to accept the several articles therein contained, except the 1st., 2nd. and 3rd. and 29th., in the Bill of Rights. For the first article 13, against it 2: for the 2nd. article 18, against it 22; for the 29th. 3: against 5: [*illegible*] the first article for it 2; against it 2

Paxton (277/103)

At a town Meeting of the inhabitants of Paxton 21 years of age Legally assembled for to Consider of the Late proposed Constitution or form of Government for the State of Massachusetts Bay begun May 1d. 1780—(and Continued by Several Adjournments to the 29 of May Current) and the Town agreed to the said form of Government with the Several amendments as follows (Viz).

On the Declaration of the Rights of the Inhabitants of Massachusetts Bay

	Yeas	Nays
Article 1	32	00
2	21	00
3	00	12

for we Donot heir find that the Legislative body are empowered to Make Laws to prevent the breach of the Sabbath——but by insarting in the Second paragraft after the Word (athority) To Enact Laws to prevent the Breach of the Christian Sabbath and also.——in so doing the yeas 12 nays 00

	yeas	Nays
article 4	17	00
5	19	00
6	21	0
7	21	0
8	21	0
9	21	0
10	20	0
11	20	0
12	20	0
13	20	0
14	20	0
15	20	0
16	20	0
17	19	0
18	19	0
19	19	0
20	19	0
21	12	0
22	12	0
23	12	0
24	12	0
25	12	0
26	12	0
27	12	0

	yeas	Nays
28	12	0
29	12	0
30	12	0

On the form of Government

		yeas	Nays
Article	1	9	0
	2	9	0
	3	9	0
	4	8	0

Section——2

		yeas	Nays
Article	1	13	0
	2	19	0
	3	20	0
	4	20	0
	5	19	0
	6	19	0
	7	19	0
	8	20	0
	9	20	0

Section——3

		yeas	Nays
Article	1	14	0
	2	13	0
	3	16	0
	4	15	0
	5	13	0
	6	14	0
	7	14	0
	8	13	0
	9	13	0
	10	13	0
	11	15	0

Chapter 2 Section 1

Article 1 ...... 14 00

2 ...... 00 ...... 17 for our fore fathers Did not onely go under that Extencive word Christians but Protestants and we Mean Not to have any other but protestants to Rule us but as occasion May Requier in the army——but by Dealing the word Christian and insurting the word protestant——the
——

...... 18 00

		yeas	Nays
Article	3	16	0
	4	16	0
	5	15	0
	6	15	0
	7	14	0
	8	14	0
	9	10	0
	10	13	0
	11	11	0
	12	12	0
	13	15	0

Section——2

Article 1 00 14 — for the same Reasons as Mentioned in the preseeding Chapter article 2—but by bringing this article to agree with what we have Expressed under the foresaid article—the

14 00

		yeas	Nays
Article	2	13	0
	3	14	0

Section——3

		yeas	Nays
Article	1	12	0
	2	10	0
	3	10	0
	4	10	0

	yeas	Nays
5	12	0
6	10	0
7	9	0
Section——4		
Article 1	10	0
2	9	0
Chapter 3 Judiciary Power		
Article 1	10	0
2	10	0
3	10	0
4	11	0
5	11	0
Chapter 4		
Article 1	11	00
Chapter——5		
Article 1	9	0
2	9	0
3	9	0
Section——2		
Article 1.	12	0
Chapter——VI		
Article 1.	00	12 but by Dealing the word Christian and insarting the word Protestant for the Reasons before Mentioned—— then the
	12	00
Article 2	11	0
3	8	0

	yeas	Nays
4	10	0
5	10	0
6	10	0
7	9	0
8	11	0
9	9	0
10	00	11 —

for we think fifteen years is two Long a time to improve upon a New Constitution (without any Right to alter it) for fear the Rights of Men Should be Violated some way or other when it Never was intended——but by dealing the words Ninety five and insarting the words Eighty Seven the yeas 11. Nays 00

article 11 ..... 11 0

then it was put to vote to see if it was their Minds that this Constitution (when agreed upon) should take place as soon as May be with Conveniency and it Past in the affermetive

Yeas 11 .... nays. 00

a tru copy from the minutes test

Adam Maynard : Moderator
.... Phine. Moore : Town Clerk

Paxton. June 5th. 1780

Abraham Smith
Daniel Steward
Selectmen of Paxton

Petersham (277/104)

To the Honorable Convention of Diligates for forming a Constitution of Civil Government for the State of Massachusetts

The town of Petersham Taking into their Serious Consideration the frame of Government presented to them By your Honors would ask your Candor when we offer to your Consideration the Following Remarks in the same and Firstly we think the time given us For its Revisal much too short Considering its Importance. Therefore we hope if it should appear that We have Committed any Errors we may have Charritable Allowance on that Account.

The Consequences in the third Article of the Declaration of Rights we think Does not answer to its Introduction Nor Coincide or flow from the Second Article. For if No person shall be Hurt Mollested or Restrained in his person Liberty or Estate for Worshiping God in the Manner and Season most agreable to the Dictates of his own Conscience and as you justly say in your Address that Religion is a Matter Between God and Individuals in such Case Can Individuals with Safety Delegate a Power to others to Be Judges for them of the proper Institutions of Divine Worship and Be their absolute Dictators as to the times and Seasons of such Worship We grant that the Happiness of a People and the good order and Preservation of Civil Goverment Greatly Depends upon Piety Religion and Morality. But we Can by no Means Suppose that to Invest the Legislature or any Body of men on Earth with a power absolutely to Determine For others What are the proper Institutions of Divine Worship and To appoint Days and seasons for such Worship With a power to impose and Indow Religious Teachers and by penalties and punnishments to be able to Enforce an Attendance on such Publick Worship or to Extort Property fom any one for the Support of what they may Judge to be publick Worship Can have a Tendency to promote true piety Religion or Morality But the Reverse and that such a Power when and where Ever Exercised has more or Less Been an Engine in the Hands of Tyrants For the Destruction of the Lives Liberties and Properties of the People and that Experience has abundantly Taught Mankind that these are Natural Rights which ought Never to be Delegated and Can with the greatest propriety be Exercised by Individuals and by every Religious Society of men. Therefore we think the third

Article ought to be amended in the Following Manner or in some Manner similar. [Viz. as the Happiness of a people and good order and preservation of Civil Goverment Greatly Depend upon piety religion and Morality therefore it shall be the Duty of the several Branches of Delegated Power Effectually to protect the people in the Exercise of the Natural Rights of Conscience and of Worshiping God According to its Dictates and by Example to Encourage those Natural and Christian graces and to Discountenance and Punnish Vice and to see that Immorallity is not Encouraged or Countenanced in the Name of Religion or Divine Worship and Every Denomination of Christians Demeaning themselves peaceably and as good Members of the Commonwealth shall be Equally under the protection of the Laws and No subordination of any one Sect or Denomination to another shall ever be Established By law.]

The Fourth Article we think ought to Be amended By an Addition of the Following Nature Viz. and no power shall Be Delegated to Congress Incompatible with the Freedom of this Commonwealth.

The Fifth Article we think might Be amended By an addition of the following Nature Viz. of consequence the people ought to Establish in their Constitution a Regular and peaceable mode of Rendering them Ameniable to Justice Agreable to the Nature of Civil Goverment and Notwithstanding their Annual Election of Legislatures they ought to Reserve in their own Hands a power to Recall their Representatives at any time and To Elect others in their Stead.

The Sixteenth Article we think might Be Amended in the following Manner Namely. as the Liberty of Speech Writing and Printing More Especially on the principles of government and Religion are Necesary for the Support of Freedom therefore Such Liberties shall Never be Restrained in this Commonwielth.

The Seventeenth Article we think might Be amended in the Following manner Viz. the People have a Right to keep and Bear arms For the Common defence and as in time of Peace Armies are Dangerous to Liberty therefore in time of peace Armies shall not be kept up without there may be Danger of Invasion, and not without the Consent of the Legislature. And the Executive power shall Never make use of Mercenary Troops For the Administration of Civil Government but shall have Recourse to the People only For Assistance and the Military Power shall always Be Held in Exact Subordination to the Civil Authority and Be governed by it.

The Nineteenth Article we think ought to be amended with an addition of the Following Nature Viz. and if in this way they may not be able to obtain Redress they may and ought to have Recourse to a Coart of Convention Established in their Constitution to Sit and to be Impowered to act For that Purpose.

The Twentyeth Article we think ought to be Expunged For if the Legislature Have the power of Making Laws and of Repealing Laws we think that a Power of Suspending all Law may be Dangerous and we think in its own Nature Militates against the last Clause of the thirtieth Article which seems to prefer a goverment by Laws and not of Men if the Legislature should Suspend the Exercise of all law which By this Article they would Be Impowered to do, it must most Surely Introduce Anarky or a Government of Men and why should we open a door in our Constitution for Either.

The Thirtieth Article we think might be amended by an Addition in the Following Manner Namely, and Such Seperate Departments of Government shall ever be Exercised in Seperate and Distinct hands and if it should at any time So Happen that any one person who may Sustain any office or offices in any one of such Departments should Be Elected or Appointed to office in any of such Different Departments or that any person shall be Elected or appointed to office in such Different Departments in such Case such person or persons shall hold and Sustain office in But one of the aforesaid Departments and may chuse in which he Will Hold this Measure We think we are Justified by your Reasonings in your address Viz. (that the History of the Rise and Fall of the empires of the World affords us ample proof that when the same man or Body of men Enact interpret and Execute the Laws property Becomes too precarious to be Valuable and a people are finally Borne Down with the force of Corruption Resulting from the union of those Powers) Besides we think that Such a Seperation of those Departments Would Be a Natural Spring to the Rising Generation to Quallify themselves For Office and a Necesary opening and introduction to that useful Learning ever Requisite for the protection of the government of a free and Happy Commonwielth. the people we think would Soon Be able to Distinguish a Suitable Number of Men sufficient to Fill every Department with propriety and Safety to the Body Politick.

We Chuse that the Forepart of the First article in the Frame of Goverment should stand something in the Following manner Viz: the Department of Legislation shall Be Formed By two Branches, a Senate and

House of Assembly which shall be Composed of the Representatives of the People who at their First meeting Annually shall form themselves into a Convention and Proceed to Elect out of their own Body one third Part or one Half of their Members who may be Stiled the Senate and the Remainder may Be Formed into a Seperate Body and Stiled the assembly Such Seperate Bodies may be impowered Compleatly to organize themselves with Proper Officrs and Seperately to Establish Proper Rules For their own Governmint. Such Convention if they please may Proceed to Elect Five Senators at Large the Senate and Assembly thus Composed Shall Have a Power of Negative upon Each other For the Term of Seven Days at the Expiration of which Either Branch Demanding of the other a Convention of the Legislature it shall be Immidiately complyed with and in Such Convention or Conventions From time to time shall all matters thus Negatived Be Determined By the Major Vote that Cannot otherwise be Concured By the two Branches Aforesaid Some way agreable To the Befor Recited Method of Composing the Legislative Body we think Preferable. The people in this way will Be Saved the Expence of a Seperate Election and Be more Likely to obtain the Best wiscest and most Virtuous Legislative Body Every Corporation may Be as Amply Represented in one Department as in the other and no Department at so great a Remove from the people But that any act Resolve etc. may originate in Either Department the people in this way Insured the Choice of their Legislators all Excepting five we think to establish a power of perpetual Negative in Either Department that in such Case in Some Instances the people might Suffer for the want of a Determination and is in its own Nature Inconsistant with good Government In this way of Constituting a Legislature it will Lessen the Number of the General Coart and Render it more Wieldy and fit for Business and less Expensive and Burthensome to the people.

The Second article we chuse Should Be Totally Expunged. That part of the Fourth article Empowering the General Coart to Impose and Lay Duties and Excises on the Intirnal Consumption produce and Manufacturies of the Commonwealth we think to be Injurous to the Happiness of the People Money thus raised is in a great measure Swallowed up in Collecting and may be Easily kept out of the knowledge of the people as to its Expenditure and officers of Trust less Accountable and we think the Experience of many of the aged People of this State Forbids Such a Measure if it should be thought Prudent to Empower the General Coart to levy Duties and Excise on Imported Manufactured Articles we have no objection But the Common Method of Raising money to Supply the Exigencies of the State on Poles and Estates etc. we much prefer. And we Chuse in Every Part where the Governor or Lieutenant Governor is Mentioned it may be Expunged and that if the General Coart should Be Impowered to Costitute any new officers or Departments of office heretofore Not in use such officers shall Be appointed By the Election of the Quallified Voters in the District or Districts For which they may act. The President of the Senate with the advice and Consent of a Committee Chosen Annually by the General Coart may Exercise all the Powers of Goverment Necsary to be Exercised By a Governor and Be amply paid For their Services with less Expence than to Support a Governor and the People Eased of the Expence of Electing a Governor Lieutenant Governor and saved from being Droved into parties By the influence of Rich and Powerful Men who will act in Competition with each other for the obtaining the office of Governor and their Morals Saved From the Corruption that Naturally Flows From Bribery and undue Influence. The Constituting the General Court a Judiciary For the Tryal of all officers we think Inconsistant with the thirtyeth Article which Expressly makes provition that Such Departments shall not Interfere in the Duties of the others we rather Chuse that all officers Shall Be Inditable and Tryable at the Superior Coart and that all officers thus tryed shall have the priviledge of Being tryed By a Jury. This will in Some Measure keep up and Support the Supremacy of the People.

We Chuse that the present Method of Drawing the Jurors out of the Box which has Been Experienced to be Safe and Free from Corruption Should Be Established in our Constitution.

We think that a Majority of Either Branch of Legislation is Best to Establish as a Quorum For Doing Business.

We Greatly approve of the Travel of the Coart being paid By the State and Should be Exceedingly Glad if the whole Expence of the Coart might be paid in the same manner. This we think would Create a Full Representation and prevent partial and ruinous Measures from being Carried into Execution which would much more than Counter balance the Extra Expence which might arise From a General Attendence Men that Expect to Enjoy the Blessings of a Free and good Goverment ought to be willing to pay in a Direct Manner for its Support Near as much as others pay in an Indirect Manner For the Support of Arbitrary Power.

We think that a Certain Day in the year ought to Be Fixed for the

Choice of Representatives which will prevent the Expence and Necessity of Precepts By which the people may Annually be impowered to chuse a new Legislature without Being prevented By waiting for precepts as was the Case with the people of Britain in King Charles the First's time.

The Quallification of Electors and the Elected we think ought to be Determined so Far as it Respects property by Taxable property and the Last Tax list we think the Best Rule to Stear By this we think would be to prevent the Multiplicity of Needless oaths and may be a Safe Rule By which to Determine the Number of Representatives Each Corporation May Send A much Better Rule than to Determine By the Number of Rateable Pools we think that such person as does not participate with the people in the Support of goverment ought not to be Either an Elector liable to Be Elected that Such ought not to be Impowered to bind Heavy Burdens Who do not Touch Even with one of their Fingers.

We think that quallified Electors ought to have the power to Elect any Quallified Elector to Be a Legislature. Riches and Dignity Neither Makes the Head Wiser nor the Heart Better the overgrown Rich we think the most Dangerous to the Liberties of a Free State and we object against a Discretionary power in the General Coart to alter Such Quallifications in Future.

We Can have No Conception of the propriety of your Distinction Between the Representation of the persons and property of the people. Neither if we must have a Govenor do we Se the Consistency of the Legislatures having a power to Increase and not Decrease his Salary.

We think that the officers of which the People have the Election ought to Return to private life at Certain periods and the peopl have a right of a New Election and that the Electors of Each County ought to have the Election of their County Officers Such as County Treasurer Register of Deeds Judge of Probate and Sheriff and once in five years at Most and that each Town ought to have the Election of one Justice of the peace and one at most in five years in such Case the Coart of Quarter Sessions Would be the Representative of the People and Might with propriety Grant and assertain County Taxes. And we think that Town and Corporate officers ought to be Confirmed to the Election of the people and not be left in the Precarious tenor of the old Laws on which they Depend which the General Coart may at Any time Repeal.

We also are of the Mind that Effectual Provition ought to be made against the Slave Trade a Wicked and Ruinous practice Established By Custom Equal to a Law.

Provition we think ought also to be Made against Entailing Estates for any longer time than for one life only.

Some Rules we think ought to be Established for the Goverment of the General Coart Such as that they shall ever be obliged to Hold open Coart Save Only in Such Matters as Absolutely Require Secrecy and that any One Member shall have a Right to have his Dissent against any vote etc. Entered on the Journals of the House and any five Members Demanding any Vote to be tryed by Yeas and Nays Such Demand Shall be Complyed With and that all such Dissents and Yeas and Nays shall be printed in the Journals of the House and Timely Transmitted to the people that they may be able to Investigate the Doings of the Important Servants of the publick.

In the 3d. Chapter Article 5th. Determining all Appeals from Judges of Probate all Causes of Marriage Divorce and allimony to be Heard and Determined by the Governor and Council we chuse should be Transfered to the Superior Coart.

We think it too much to give the Corporation of the university at Cambridge a Section in Our Constitution we are of the Mind that it might with Safety be left to the Care of the Legislature and that it may be possible that the Legislature in time may find it Necesary to Curtail that Rich and Growing Corporation Least it should Endanger the Liberties of the Commonwealth.

We think that the Provition For Amending the Constitution is not Sufficiently Full and ample According to the principles held up in the Decleration of Rights for if the people have at all times a Right Why Should they not at all times have a Constitutional Power we think that when a Majority of the Corporations May Coincide that there is Need of Such a Coart of Convention they ought to be impowered to Make Regular Movements to Bring Forward the Choice of Such a Coart and that when Such Coart are Convened they ought to be impowered Not only to propose Amendments to the people and to Ratify them if Approved of But they Ought to Be Enabled to Repeal and Remove Every Encroachment Made By the Legislature or otherwise on the Constitution or the Reasonabl Liberties of the people and also be impowered to Set as a Coart of Tryal for Legislators and all other Great Officers of State who may have Been Guilty of Male Administration or Treason against the State and Impowered Forever to Disquallify From Holding any office post of Honor or trust in the State For why should the people Be Impowered to Mend thir Constitution without at the same time Reserving a power in their own Hands By the Means of such a Coart to oblige their most Dignified Servants to attent to it in their Administrations of Goverment and we think that such Coart ought Periodically to Sit at Most once in thirty years and that a Section ought to Be inserted in the Constitution making of it the Highest Treason To oppose the Free Exercise of the Constitution Either By Force of Arms or By Acts Resolves or Doings of the Legislature.

The Habeas Corpus Act we Cannot Consent Shall Ever be Suspended By any power on Earth the Danger of such a power in the Hands of any Human Beings is Much gre[ater and] Counter Balances any advantages that Can in the Nature of things [appear to] us to arise from the Exercise of it.

Some Few of our proposed Amendments we have Neglected to Enforce by Reasons Least we should Render our Address to the Honorable Convention too lengthy and Tedious. We apprehend you will Be able to see the force of such proposed amendments without Such Reasons a Word to the wise is Sufficient.

We Feel our Selves Much Perplexed when we take into View the Extensiveness of our Proposed Amendments Least we Should be Taxed with Arogance By the Great the Wise and the Powerful But we ask the Candor of the Honorable Convention when we assure them that our anxiety for obtaining the Best Constitution of Civil Government in which the Happiness of Mankind is so Greatly Interested has been our Greatest Inducement and we hope will appollogise in our Favour We hope that you will not attend to any of our Errors but that if any of our Remarks may have a Tendency to perfect this great Work our Wishes Will be Accomplished Our Desire is that you Would Revise the Constitution with Diliginc and Wisdom and if you find any Room to amend it you will do it let the present sentiments of the people Be what they will For we are Fully of the Mind that the People will Finally Submit to the Best we should Chuse it should be Adopted by at Least two thirds of the people But if that Cannot finally Be Obtained We are Willing to submit to a Majority so Far as respects Civil Goverment But the Rights of Conscience we Beg leave to reserve We think that the More this Matter is Agitated the more likely to be perfect and that the people Would not think much of the Expence of Divers times submitting of it to their Revisal if by that means they may obtain a Free Happy Social Compact Founded upon Natural and Christian principles in such a Manner that By Divine and Human assistance it may Increase in perfection.

We Cannot at present Fix upon a time when we should be Willing to have it Confirmed without a Further Revisal unless it shall appear that two thirds of the people have Agreed to it in gross and if that should be the Case We petition For a Reserve of the Liberties of Conscience.

All which is Humbly Submitted———

at a Town meeting held at Petersham on Monday the 29 of May by adjornment to Take into Consideration the frame of Government Reported to the Town by the Honorable Convention the Question was put whether the Town would accept of such Constitution and it passed in the Negative unanimously 24 votes against it———and at an adjournment [of] the same meeting held on the sixst Day of this Instant June the beforegoing adress to the Honorable Convention as the sence of the Town Respecting the frame Reported by the Convention was voted In Town meeting and ordered to be sent to the Convention.

attest.
David Sanderson
Town Clerk

Princeton (277/105)

Princeton, June 1st. 1780

At a Meeting of the Inhabitants of Princeton upon the 4th day of May 1780 the Constatution or Form of Goverment, which is sent out for the Concurrence of the people was then Read the Town voted to adjourn the meeting till the 29th of said May. The Inhabitants being assembled upon the adjournment, it was Read a second time and a vote Called upon it and there appeared to be 32 in favour of said Constatution without any alteration and five opposers———four of which have enclosed their reasons—also voted that said Constatution take place assoon as said Convention may judge it most proper.———

Benja. Holden
John Mirick Selectmen of Princeton
Paul Mather Jr.

a True Coppy attd—William Dodd Town Clerk

We the subscribers do object against the third article in the Declaration of the Rights of the inhabitants of the Commonwealth of Massachusetts:

for we think that if the legislature are to be invested with that power to make aney law or laws that will inable any sosiety or Denomination of Christions in this Commonwealth to tax aney person or persons without his or their free and volinterey Consent (as such measures aire plainely implyed to us thoe they are not so plainly Expresed as they might have been) to the seting up or supporting of aney of those public protestant teachers of piety, which we suppose to mean Christs ministers—such measures (meaning a Taxing power to support those Teachers above mentioned) will naturally bring on disputes that will tend more to Confution and disorder then to peace and union———

For the legislature to be invested with a powr as above said [appears] to us to be a infringment on the natural rights of the inhabitants as mentioned in the first and second articles in the above said Declaration.

Thaire is in the frame of government things that aire not so agreable to us as we Could wish for. If the above Dificulty Can be Removed it will make the burthen hear liter. We mean to be frinds to good government

Princton June the 1t 1780

Sadey Mason
Nathan Smith
John Gleason
Stephen Rolph

Royalston (277/106)

At a legal Town meeting in Royalston on Wednesday the 25 day of May 1780 and Continued by ajornments to the 31 of May and first of June following then meet to Consider the Frame of Goverment agreed upon by the Deligates of the People of the State of the Massachusetts in there late Conventition—after reading said Form Several times over: they Reed articule by articule and Voted to every articule Singaly—and Voted unanimously by all at Said meeting to approve of the Frame of Goverment and to have the Same approved and agreed on for a Form of Goverment for the State of Massachusetts———Except Some Small amendments in the fillowing articules viz———

[in the third articule of the bill of Rights we find Some people uneasy in there minds to be any ways obliged to pay or Support Teachers whoes principals are Contrary to the Dictates of there Consciances. The addition proposed as an amendment we think remadys this Difficulty and will prevent any consconcious persons being any ways unreasonably burdoned with the following addition the Town unanmiously voted to approve of the articule

viz———Provided neverthe less: that if the lot of any person is cast at so great a Distance from the place where those of his own Denomination assemble for Instruction or worship that he cannot conveniently attend yet if he has Joyned a Christian Society and is a regular member thereof He Shall be Exempt from paying toward the Support of the Teacher of the parish where his lot is Cast]

In the Frame of Goverment Chapter first Section 3 articule 9 the Town is of a mind that the House of Representetives will Consist of Three Hundred members or more Sixty will be to Small a porpotion for a Quorum as by that means the Representetion of a few Towns may transact buisness of the most important nature with out the knowledg or consent of the far greater part of the House therefore we think one Hundred members ought to be a Quorum it will be but one Third of the House not less than that number ought to Transact business the unhapy consequences of allowing to Small a number to be a Quorum are but to well known

Chapter 2nd Section 1 articule 2 and Chapter 2nd Section 2nd articule 1st and Chapter 6 articule 1: the objections to these articules as it must be Disagreeable to the people in General in this State So we view it inconsistant with the [known] Sentimants in Religion to intrust the principal officer in civel goverment to men whose religiouss Sentiments are [directly against] to those of the people of this State

therefore we think the words: viz———Christian religion: ought to be the of the Reformed protestant Christian Religion———

Chapter 3 articule 3 and 4 we think it ought to be left to the Determination of each Town to have a Justice of the peace in the Town and that they are the best Judges who are Qualified to Exercise in that office amingst them that the people appoint there one Justies of peace and the Govenour to Commisionate them and further we think it necesary for the ease and Comfort of the Widow and Fatherless that the Setlements of Estates of which in the best manner it is in our oppinion Judges Should be appointed in the Respectives Towns for Such matters we therefor for which Reasons we object against the Govenor and Councel nominating and appointing Judges of Probate and Reigesters of probate

Chapter 6 articule 7: we think the writ Habeas Coupus ought not to be Suspended above Six months many and Sufficiant Reasons might be given therefor

The 16 articule in the Bill of rights the word ought we think Should be Shall not be Restraned——

Then the Town unanimously that if Two Thirds of the Inhabitants Voted to approve of Said Form of Goverment as is Contained in the Said frame or by amendments there Deligate to agree with the other Deligates in Convention to appoint the time when Said Frame of Goverment Shall Take place——Numbers present 63

John Fry
Silvanus Hemenway
Benjamin Waite
Selectmen
for Royalston

Rutland (277/107)

The Town of Rutland being Legally warned and Assemblyed on the Twenty ninth day of May one thousand Seven hundred and Eighty Voted to except of the new Constitution or frame of Government agreed on by the Convention at Boston, with this alteration (Vizt) in Chapter Second, Article Second and all other places where Relegion is mentioned that all officers Shall Declare them Selves of the protestant Christian Religion

Number in Town Meeting 31
Yeas 27, Nays 4

Phinehas Walker
John Stone
Silas Bent
Jonas Howe
Selectmen of Rutland

Shrewsbury (277/108)

At a Meeting of the Inhabitants of the Town of Shrewsbury Regularly Assembled on Monday the first day of May A.D. 1780 for the purpose of hearing and Considering of a Constatution or Frame of Goverment after Reading———

Doctor Edward Flint was Chosen Moderator for said meeting the meeting being Opened The form of Goverment was read and Conversed upon. Then the Town Voted to Adjorn the meeting to a future time, Accordingly the Town meet on the 25 day of May agreable to the Adjornment. The Town then Proceded on the Constatution Article by Article and on the Bill of Rights, their Appeared Ninety two in favor of all the Articles except the third and twenty Ninth, in favor of the 3. was 61: and against it 35: and the 29 Article there was in favor 58: and against it 35 Part the Second Frame of Goverment Chapters The Legistative Power. Sextion first The General Court—Article 1. 42 in favor and 37 against it Article 2: 34 in favor 38. aganst Article 3: 41 in favor 26 aganst. Article 4: 38 in favor 36 aganst Chapter 1 Section 2. Senate Article 1: 36: in favor 40 against Article 2: 39 in favor 35 against. Article 3: 39 in favor 35 againt the Six following Articles 40: in favor and 35 against

Sextion 3 Article 1: 47 in favor. 21 against Article 2: 37 in favor 23 against Article 3: 39 in favor 20: against, Article 4: 39 in favor 20 against Article 5: 38: in favor 21: against Article 8 and 9 40 in favor 17 against Article 10: 34 in favor 28. against Article 11: 34 in favor 22 against Chapter 2 Sextion 1 Govenor Article 1: 40 in favor 39: against Article 2: 34 in favor 22 against Then the Town Voted to Adjorn this meeting to Monday Next at one of the Clock Afternoon at this place and it was accordingly Adjorned. According to the foregoing Adjornment The Town meet at time and place being the 29 day of May and Doctor Edward Flint was Continued Moderator The Town then Voted to Choose a Committe to make an Amendment on the Third Article of the bill of rights and the Committe Reported as follows. Page 8 and line 1 and 2 leave out the woord and require the two places and line 8 leave out the three last woords and the whole of line Ninth and the Seven next following lines After that Clause which Provides that all Societies etc. Shall have the Exlusive right of Electing and Supporting their own teachers, then add but None Shall be held to Contribute to their Support that are of another Sect or perswasion in matters of religion provided he or they Congregate else where, Forth: 5. and 6 lines from the bottom to be left out, page 9 line 1 instead of Subordination put in Superioraty, Then the Town Voted to Reconsider the third Article on the bill of rights and accept of the Above Amendment and in favor of the Amendment 44 aganst the

Amendment, 15 Then the Town Voted to read the remainder of the form of Goverment which was not acted upon Already and if any Article Should not be agreable they have Liberty to Object.. The Article 7. 32 in favor as it now Stands and 27 against it. Article 9th Amendment, All Juditial Officers as it is Set forth in said Article be Appointed by the Legislative body 35 in favor of said Amendment and 20 as it now Stands Article 10 54 in favor of an Alteration That the Senate and house of Representatives to Nomenate all Continental Officers to be Commissioned. Article 13: 54 in favor of an Alteration that the Governor and Justices of the Supreme Court have their Salaries Granted Yearly, The Town then Voted to Adjorn this meeting Next Thirsday at one of Clock afternoon Edward Flint moderator Accordingly the Town meet on said day being the first day of June Doctor Crosby was Chosen Moderator and Then proceded on said meeting and the following Objection wer brought Against the 29 Article in the bill of rights which are as follows That the Superiour Judges ought to be Chosen once in five Years as their Office is of Great importance to the publick it ought therefore to revert into the hands of the people at Certain periods for in makeing them Independant of the people we Make them Dependant on the Govenor and open a Door for Setting up their Commissions to the highest bider or we may expect that Relations and favorites must be first Served Then it was put to Se if the town would reconsider their Vote on the 29 Article in the bill of Rights and accept of the above amendment, and in favor of the Amendment 39. and against 11

Chapter 6 Article 2 page 48 for an alteration line 3 Setled Minester Line 8 all see men to be excluded a Seate in the house for the Alteration 41 and 8 against it and a further Alteration that No Man Shall hold more then one Commission Civil or Military at the Same time 31 in favor of this alteration and 20 against it, Chapter third Article 3 page 39 22 in favor as it now Stands and 21 against it Chapter 6 page 50 Article 10: in favor of Reviseing the Constatution within five Years 26 and 22 against revising So Soon, 26 in favor of a Leiutenant Govenor and 14 against it 25 in favor of Council for Adviseing with the Govenor and 15 against it 26 in favor of the manner of Setling Elections and 13 against it 39 in favor of Secretary and Commasary etc. Chapter 3 Article 1 Page 39 line 9 instead of may, read Shall 27 in favor of the Alteration and 7 against it 26 in favor of the Manner of Sending Deligates to Congress and 7 against 33 in favor Universaty Litarature Oaths and what is Contained in Chapter 6 excepting what has been Objected to before the remaining part of the Cnostatution not before acted upon was accepted Unanimosly present in the House 39.

Att Samuel Crosby Moderator

Shrewsbury June
6th. 1780

Job Cushing Town Clerk
by Order of the Selectmen

Southborough (277/109)

At a Legal Town Meeting began and held att South borough May the first and Continued by Adjournment to May the 26th. 1780 att Which Meetings the Constitution or form of Goverment being Several times Destinkly Read and acted upon the Same as followeth viz
The Vote being put to See how many would accept of the Constitution as it now Stands there were Twenty two for it and Forty against it
Then the Vote was put to See how many would accept of it with the following Amendments Forty Eight for it and fourteen against it
Then a Vote was put to See how many would accept of the Constitution if after the most Strenuous Exertions of the Delagate to obtain the Amendments if Agreable to Two thirds of the Inhabitants of the State, and Rather than have the Constitution fail would accept it without the amendments Forty one for it and fourteen against it———
The Objections or Amendments are as followeth viz———

Amendment 1t [*illegible*] on Chapter 1t. Section 1t. article 1t. that the Legislative body Consist of two braches only—that the Governor and Council Constitute one Branch—and the house of Representatives the other Branch The Council to Consist of Twenty Eight members to be chosen in the Same manner and Proportion in the Several destricts as the Senetors were to be chosen, the Govenor and Council to have all the Powers that were to be Lodged in the Senate

Amendment 2d on Chapter 1t. Section 3d, article 2d. accepted with this amendment that Each and Every Town that Shall be here after Incorperated not having one Hundred and fifty Ratable poles be Inteteled to Elect a Representative

amendment 3d on Chapter 1t. Section 3d. and article 3d. accepted leaving out the last Clause in said Article—

amendment 4th. on Chapter 1t. Section 3d and article 4th—Every Ratable Pole being Free and Twenty one Years of Age and Subject to Taxes have a Right to Vote for Coucil and Representatives

amendment 5th on Chapter 2d. Section 1t and 9th article accepted with this amendment that the house of Representative have an Equal Right in the Nomination of these Officers as any others in this Constitution

amendment 6th on Chapter 6th. and article 7th accepted with this amendment that Six months be Incerted Instead of Twelve months

amendment 7th on Chapter 6th and article 9th [10] accepted with this Amendment that one Thousand Seven Hundred and Ninty be Incerted Instead of one Thousand Seven Hundred and Ninty five

amendment 8th. the Last amendment on the Last article of the 6th Chapter accepted with this addition that the Laws Mentioned in this article and in the 6th article of this Chapter Shall be all the Laws that Shall be In force and Practiced upon in Courts within this State and all Laws that Shall be hereafter made Shall be Emediately Sent to Each and Every Town in this State, to the End that Every Individual may know all the Laws he is to be Governed by

And Where Ever the Senate and house of Representatives are Mentioned, the Govenor and Council, and house of Representatives be Incerted

Further Wee desire that Each and Every part of this Constitution that Millitate with these amendments may be made Conformable to these amendments

To the Honorable the Convention For forming a form of Goverment for the State of Massachusetts Bay agreable to the Dircetion in your form of Goverment we have Considered the same, and have made the foregoing alterations and hereunto Subjoin our Reasons therfor. viz———

on the first alteration or amendment that the having a Govenor Council Senate and house of Representatives is Multiplying too Large a body of men to the Retarding of Publick Business and Creating Unnescesary Charge to the State

on the 2d. alteration That Taxation and Representation are and of Right ought to be Insepperably Connected together

on the 3 alteration that a Person Quallified in good abillities to Serve his Constituants in the General Court Yet if meeting with any adverse Providence to the Lessning his Estate to a Sum Less than £ *200*—Should leave his Seat in the house which we Judge to be a Disparagement to a Gentleman

on the 4th. alteration Referred to the 2d. being of the Same Nature on the 5th. alteration as all Money bills Originate in the house of Representatives So ought all the Officers of the State

on the 6th. alteration That the Write of Habeas Corpus is held so dear to the Subject Six month is time Sufficient to have said Write Suspended

on the 7th. alteration That Ten Years will Reduce to Practice the Constitution Whereby the Good or Ill Effects will be Sufficiently known for Revision

on the 8th. alteration That our Former Province Laws were so Little Practiced on in Courts the Subject in General Scarce Ever kenw when he was to be defended by the Laws of the State, wherby Numberless Law Suits were Commenced that would not have been if the whole Laws that were Practiced upon in Courts were Contained in one Volume and depossated with the Clerk of Every Town

Southborough June the 5th 1780

A True Extract from the Minutes
Attest Joshua Smith Town Clerk

Spencer (277/110)

At a Meeting of the Inhabitants of the Town of Spencer Legaly Assembled on May the 22. 1780—And Continuand By Ajournments till May the 24th To take into Consideration the Form of a constitution or Frame of Government and Acted on the Same as Follows Viz——

Part the First

Article	1d.	Voted to accept in Favor	62	
	2	Voted to accept in Favor	62	
	3	Voted to accept in Favor	55.	against article 3d.—20
	4	Voted to accept in Favor	71	
	5	Voted to accept in Favor	69	
	6	Voted to accept in Favor	52	
	7	Voted to accept in Favor	55	
	8	Voted to accept in Favor	61	
	9	Voted to accept in Favor	61	
	10	Voted to accept in Favor	60	
	11	Voted to accept in Favor	60	
	12	Voted to accept in Favor	60	
	13	Voted to accept in Favor	60	

14 Voted to accept in Favor 60
15 Voted to accept in Favor 60
16 Voted to accept in Favor 60
17 Voted to accept in Favor 60
18 Voted to accept in Favor 60
19 Voted to accept in Favor 60
20 Voted to accept in Favor—60
21 Voted to accept in Favor—60
22 Voted to accept in Favor—60
23 Voted to accept in Favor 61
24 Voted to accept in Favor 60
25 Voted to accept in Favor 60
26 Voted to accept in Favor 59
27 Voted to accept in Favor 59
28 Voted to accept in Favor 59
29 Voted to accept in Favor 60
30 Voted to accept in Favor 60

Part the Second Chapter the 1d. and Section the 1d.

Article the 1d. Voted to accept in Favor 63
2 Voted to accept in Favor—71
3 Voted to accept in Favor—75
4 Voted to accept in Favor—77

Chapter the 1d. Section the 2d.

Article the 1d. Voted to accept in Favor 75
2 Voted to accept in Favor—67 against article 2d. 3
3 Voted to accept in Favor 76
4 Voted to accept in Favor 74
5 Voted to accept in Favor—54 against article 5th—10
6 Voted to accept in Favor 78
7 Voted to accept in Favor 76
8 Voted to accept in Favor 76
9 Voted to accept. in Favor 77

Chapter the 1d. Section the 3d

Article 1d. Voted to accept in Favor 77
2 Voted in Favor 9 Against article 2d. 51—Amendment of the Town of Spencer. in Legal Town Meeting Assembled on the 24 May 1780——Chapter the 1d. Section the 3d. article 2d. in the Constitution or Frame of Government—— it appears to the Inhabitants of Spencer that the Representa-

tion is Not Equal on the Account of Towns to be Hereafter Incorporated and plantations Having No previlege of Representation Excepting they have one Hundred and Fifty Rateable pools. we think it no more then Reasonable that the Above Mentioned Towns and plantations should have the privlige of joining two or More of them to Geather in Choosing a Representative or Joining Sum other Ajacent Town for that purpose———

Voted to accept of article the 2d. with the Amendment in Favor 35—
Article 3d. Voted to accept in Favor 71
4 Voted to accept in Favor 51 against article 4th.—15
5 Voted to accept in Favor 63
6 Voted to accept in Favor 61
7 Voted to accept in Favor 61
8 Voted to accept in Favor 61
9 Voted in Favor of the article 31. against article 9th. 29—
10 Voted to accept in Favor 63
11 Voted to accept in Favor 60

Chapter the 2d. Section the 1d.

Article the 1d. Voted to accept in Favor 53 against article 1d. 7
2. Voted to accept in Favor 59 against article 2d—[4]
3 Voted to accept in Favor 57 against article 3— 3
4 Voted to accept in Favor 67 against article 4: 3
5 Voted to accept in Favor 69 against article 5.— 1
6 Voted to accept in Favor 67 against article 6: 3
7 Voted to accept in Favor 70—against article 7. 5
8 Voted to accept in Favor 68 against article 8— 6
9 Voted to accept in Favor—68 against article 9: 6
10 Voted to accept in Favor 39 against article 10th. 31
11 Voted to accept in Favor 69 against article 11: 1
12 Voted to accept in Favor 40 against article 12— 25
13 Voted to accept in Favor 51 against article 13- 6

Chapter the 2d. Section the 2d—

Article the 1d. Voted to accept in Favor 50: against article 1d. 5
2 Voted to accept in Favor—53 against article 2: 3
3 Voted to accept in Favor 55 against article 3— 1

Chapter the 2d. Section 3d———

Article the 1d. Voted to accept in Favor 51 against article 1d.—4
2 Voted to accept in Favor 51 against article 2 4

	3	Voted to accept in Favor 55 against article 3— 2
Article the	4	Voted to accept in Favor—57
	5	Voted to accept in Favor 56
	6	Voted to accept in Favor—53
	7	Voted to accept in Favor—51 against article. 7th—2
		Chapter the 2d Section the 4th.
Article	1	Voted to accept in Favor—54
	2	Voted to accept in Favor—54
		Chapter the 3d
Article	1d	Voted to accept in Favor—53
	2	Voted to accept in Favor—53
	3	Voted to accept in Favor—52
	4	Voted to accept in Favor—52
	5	Voted to accept in Favor—51
		Chapter the 4th
		Voted to accept of the 4th. Chapter in Favor—51
		Chapter the 5th. Section 1d
Article—	1d	Voted to accept in Favor—50
	2	Voted to accept in Favor—48
	3	Voted to accept in Favor—48
		Chapter the 5 Section 2d.
		Voted to accept of Chapter 5. Section the 2d. in Favor—51
		Chapter the 6th.—
Article	1d	Voted to accept in Favor—60: against article 1—4
	2	Voted to accept in Favor—60
	3	Voted to accept in Favor—57 against article 3—1
	4	Voted to accept in Favor—58
	5	Voted to accept. in Favor—57
	6	Voted to accept in Favor—57
	7	Voted to accept in Favor—57
	8	Voted to accept in Favor—57
	9	Voted to accept in Favor—57
	10	Voted to accept in Favor 58
	11	Voted to accept in Favor—58———

At a Meeting of the Inhabitants of Spencer Legaly assembled on May the 22. 1780—and Continuand by ajournment till May the 24th. To take Into Consideration the Form of A constitution or Frame of Government and a Monge other Votes—Voted that the Dilegate be Impoward and Authorized to Agree when this Constitution Shall Take place if he finds that Two thiards of the people are in Favor of the Same without Returning it again to the people at Large———

attest.

Ebenezer Mason. Town Clerk

Spencer June the 5th. 1780———

Sturbridge (277/111)

Agreeable to the request of the Convention Chosen to form a new Constitution or frame of Government we have laid the Same before the male Inhabitants of the age of Twenty One Years and upwards of the Town of Sturbridge, at a Town Meetting Called for that purpose, who unanimously agreed to the Same except the following articles, viz.———

The 3d. article in the Declaration of Rights 120 voters present, 73 voted for and 47 against said article, for the Objections and Reasons we refer you to the Paper herein enclosed.———

The 2d. Article in the 3d. Section of the 1st. Chapter. Frame of Government. Objection. The Number of Representatives according to that calculation will be so large that it will Retard Public business rather than forward it, and enhance the Public charge, for that reason we Judge that Representatives ought to be chosen according to the number of Quallifyed voters, rather than the number of Rateable Polls———

The above said article 32 voted for, and 15 against———

The 8th. Article in the first Section of the 2d. Chapter the Power of Pardoning offences is confered on the Governor by and with the consent of the Council, which we think belongs to no meer Man [or] Men.

in the 9th. Article of the 2d. Chapter all Judicial officers etc. are to be appointed by the Governor with the advice and consent of the Council, whereas the Justices of the Peace for each County ought to be Nominated and recommended by the Representatives of the County where the said Justices belong. The two last mentioned articles 14 voted for and 34 against———Objection against the 2d Article in the 3d. Section of the 2d Chapter is, the Chusing any one of the Council out of the People at large, for this reason, the number Forty being so large we think the choice ought to be confined to that number. 6 Voted for 36 against said article.

Sturbridge 30th, of May 1780

Henry Fisk | Aaron Allen | Ralph Wheelock — Selectmen for Sturbridge

At a town meeting Sturbridge May. 8th. 1780 according to the warrant for that purpose 3d. article in the Decaration of rights was read which occationed a long dispute at length decided by yeas and nays. We who are of the number of the Nays ware the minor. Who could not receiv or comply with said 3 article; Have the following reason to render for our conduct. 1. the vallew or invaluable price we hold our rights of concience. 2 as they are inallinable we cant devest our selves of them. 3. The mischeifs that must Ensue if confirmed we will jest hint at some of the many that might be named,—article a right to invest there legislator with power to authorize and require the several town etc. to make sutable provision for the worship of God etc, the people of this common welth have this power this privilidge in there own hand, for ther use and improvement, but when the people have invested the Legislator with this power there is none left for themselvs to injoy. Which the Legislator are to improve from time to time in matters Excleastical what times are sutable and what money is sufficent what peneltys to enex in case of failure seizur of good imprisoment etc. in ther power Finally if this 3 article obtains which we hav no reason to Expect but it may—a Just Soveraign God for the crying sins of the land Especially for the sin of sitting light by and misimproving our privilidges and libertys, while we had them—Who left our Delligats to form said articles may have two thirds of the people of this State to confirm it. as it now stands, from that moment we may wright Jehabod on all our Glory we fear———

Sturbridge May 31—1780

Henry Fisk. In Behalf

Sutton (277/112)

Att a Legal Town Meeting of the Inhabitants of the Town of Sutton May 1th 1780 Warned for the purpose of considering and acting on the Constitution or Frame of Government sent out by the convention Which Meeting was continued by several adjournments to the 30th day of Said May In which Town Meeting Said Constitution passed with the following amendments;

the several Articles according to the following List

Declaration of Rights

	Article	Yea	Nay	Referance to the Town votes.
Chapter 1. article	1	91	0	
	2	91	0	amendment, article 1
	3	92	55	amendment, article 2
	4	48	0	
	5	55	0	
	6	60	0	
	7	89	0	
	8	87	0	
	9	93	0	
	10	85	0	
	11	92	0	
	12	90	0	
	13	98	0	
	14	95	0	
	15	100	0	amendment article 3
	16	101	0	
	17	98	0	
	18	100	0	
	19	105	0	
	20	100	0	
	21	101	0	
	22	100	0	
	23	102	0	
	24	101	0	
	25	98	0	
	26	102	0	
	27	106	0	
	28	100	0	
	29 unanimously voted out, article 4			
	30	84	0	

Frame of Government

Preface accepted unanimosly

	Article	Yea	Nay	
Chapter 1s. Section 1. article	1	103	0	
	2	103	1	
	3	106	0	
	4	117	0	amendment, article 1

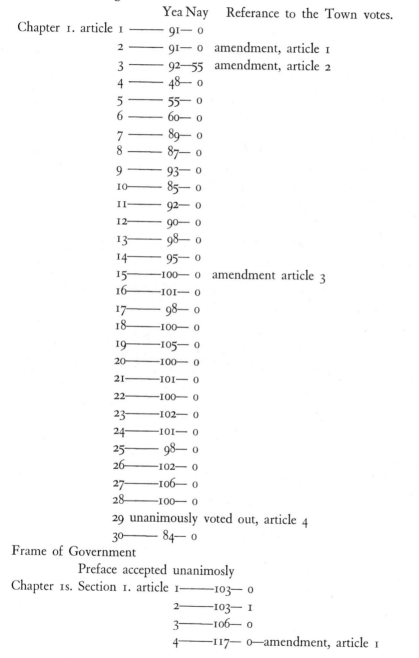

Chapter 1. Section 2d. article 1——44— 0
2——63— 0
3——54— 0
4——80— 0
5——73— 0
6——75— 0
7——72— 0
8——76 0—amendment, article 5
9——66— 0

Chapter 1 Section 3. article 1——74— 0
2——46— 0—amendment, article 6
3——48— 0
4——55— 0
5——56— 0
6——56— 0

Chapter	Section	article	yea	nay	Referance to the Town votes
1	3	7	44	0	
		8	50	0	
		9	57	0	—amendment, article 6
		10	57	0	
		11	42	2	
2	1	1	73	9	
		2	63	1	—amendment article 7
		3	67	1	
		4	55	2	
		5	59	0	
		6	57	0	
		7	55	3	
		8	48	16	
		9	57	0	—amendment by substitute, article 8
		10	19	7	—first paragraft, amendment article 9 Last paragraft save one, amendment article 10
		11	35	0	
		12	27	0	
		13	34	0	—amendment, article 11
2	2	1	38	0	
		2	34	2	

Chapter	Section	article	yea	nay	Referance to the Town votes
		3	33	0	
2	3	1	38	2	
		2	24	0	
		3	33	0	
		4	33	1	—amendment, article 12
		5	36	0	
		6	37	0	
		7	36	0	
2	4	1	40	0	
		2	42	0	
3		1	44	0	—amendment, article 13
		2	31	0	
		3	38	0	—amendment, article 13
		4	34	0	
		5	31	0	
4			36	0	
5	1	1	28	0	
		2	34	0	
		3	35	0	
5	2		38	0	—amendment by dele, article 14.
6		1	41	0	—amendment, article 15
		2	44	0	
		3	45	0	
		4	45	0	
		5	47	0	
		6	47	0	
		7	40	0	
		8	50	0	
		9	54	3	
		10	53	0	—amendment, article 16
		11	52	0	

The following Objections Reasons and proposals for amendments were Voted in Said Town Meeting viz.

1 The Town object against the Constitution because there is no provision made for the observation of the Sabbath. which we look upon to be coeval with the creation. Therefore propose that one day in Seven as a Sabbath of Rest from all Servile Labour be asserted as a Right in

the 2d article of Rights. And that in the Frame of Government Chapter 1st Section 4 page 11 the Legislature be authorized and required to make Laws enjoining the due observation of the Sabbath or Lords Day

2 Article 3d of Rights page 8. Paragraft 4 at the end of the 6 line incert. *and no where else.*

3 Object, because there is no provision for the securing the present mode of returning and making up juries which appears to be as necessary, as the tryal by jury. For if they might be packed by the Sheriff or any other partial or sinister Method, it would frustrate the whole Privilege.

Therefore propose that the present method of returning jurors be confirmed and secured by an amendment or addition to the 15 article of Rights.

4 Object against the 29. Article of Rights because we dont see that it is any Right or advantage for Officers to be so independant as there expressed but a disadvantage. There propose that the whole article be droped out.

5 Object against the having power to disqualify Parsons from holding offices as in Article 8. Page 23 Because it puts it into the Power of the Senate arbitrarily to destroy mens Characters and usefulness and there is no way for redress or Restoration. Therefore propose that the Part of the Article impowring the Senate to disqualify persons for holding Offices be cast out.———

6 Object against the mode of Representation Page 24, 25, 26 because it makes too large a Body for the dispatch of Business, and unnecessary Burden if the Towns general send, and their Representatives attend; an unequal Representation; fluctuating House if they don't attend, and that any part of the pay of Representatives should be laid upon their own Towns we object because their Business is for the whole State. Therefore propose that the whole State be divided into Districts not exceeding 150 each District to send one Representative and a proper Rotation of choosing the Representatives in each District so as that every Town may still retain its proportional Right as near as may be and that the whole of the Representatives Pay be out of the publick Chest. We also object against so small a Quorum of the House as 60, because it admits of so small a part of the State giving Law to the whole. and is unpresedented generally in other Bodies which requires a majority to do Business. Therefore propose that a Quorum always be a majority of the whole House whatever the number may be

7 Object against the Qualifications of in Page 27. Article 2. because he may be a Papist notwithstanding any thing therein, and makes it necessary for men to put themselves up candidates for Governor by declaring themselves etc.——Therefore that the last calause of said article Shall read thus "and unless he Shall be of the Protestant Christian Religion."

8 Object against the appointment of civil Officers as in the 9. article Page 31 because the Governer cant properly know in so extensive a State who are proper for Officers sufficient to nominate every one, and gives the utmost opportunity for men to buy Places and Offices of the Governor and for the Governor to sell offices to the highest bidder. Therefore propose that all Offices be new appointed by the General Court annually, the Representatives of each county to first nominate their county Officers, then to pass the House after that the Senate, and then commissioned by the Governor. The Judges of the Superior Court to be first Chose by the House pass the Senate and Commissioned by the Governer.

9 In article 10 Page 32, Line 4 instead of 21 Years of age, incert, *18 years of age*

10 Object against the Governer appointing all the Officers of the Continental Army and of Forts and Garrisons as in the first Paragraft 33. Page: Because he may according to that appoint them in some few Towns when the Men are [quotared?] to be raised in the several Towns in the State, and men will not be willing to go under officers they are stranger to and while they think they have not justice done by being allowed a proper proportion of Officers. Therefore propose that the Governor in appointing such officers shall always be limeted to appoint such Field Officers within the Brigades the Captains and Subalterns within the Rigiments where the men are to be raised, and in proportion to the Men to be raised within the several and respective Brigades and Rigiments

11 Object against the 13. Article 34 Page appointing a Stated Salary for the Governor and Judges of the Superior Court and no provision for altering of it unless to enlarge it; because that no court can determine through the vicissitudes of Time what shall never be too much, any more than what shall never be too little. Therefore propose that as they are annually to be appointed their Salaries Shall be annually granted by the general Court some of the first Acts of their may Sessions.

12 Object against 4th Article 37. Page that two counsellers are allowed

to a District by which means the greater part of the State is liable to have no voice in the Counsel which is the supreme executive Department of the whole state. Therefore propose that not more than one counseler be chosen out of a Senator Distirict and no one in the District where the Governor or Lieutenant Governor belong

13 In Page 39. Article 1st instead of *"during [good be]avior"* incert *one year* and in the 3d. Article instead of "seven years"—incert "one Year".

14 In Page 43: 3d. Line from the Bottom propose that the word Grammer be deled. Because we are and have long been of the opinion that the obloiging every Town to keep a Grammer School is rather a stagnation to the learning of Youth than any promotion of it.

15 Object against the Declaration of the Officers in the 44 Page because the Word *Protestant* is not incerted, We think that all possible bars should be laid against Papists holding important seats in Government among us. Therefore propose that the word *Protestant* shall be incerted in said Declaration

16 Object against the 10 Article 50th Page seting the Time so long before the constitution is to be revised, and than precarious whither there shall be a convention. By being so long, if there should be any things very disagreable, it would be unreasonable to suffer it so long. If things should go on easy people would loose sight of the Principles of the Constitution as expressed in the begining of the Article and so not likely to vote for having a Convention whereby designing mischevious Men by degrees by taking the People inattentive might work in great mischief. Therefore propose; that it be absolute in the Year one thousand Seven hundred and ninety.

A True extract from the minutes of the Transaction of the Town Meeting

Attest Follansbe Chase Town Cler

In Town Meeing Sutten May 30th 1780

On the Resolve of the Convention of March 2d 1780

Voted that the within be laid before the town for the Instruction of their Delagates.

In Town Meeing Sutton May 30th 1780. On the resolve of the Convention of March 2d 1780. Voted to instruct the Delegates in Convention that if upon Returns it appears that two thirds of the Inhabitants of the state meeting and voting in the several towns shall appear in Favor of the Constitution that the Delegates from this Town be hereby impowered to join in convention to agree and Determine when the constitution shall take place ratify the same as the constitution of this State and to do all things necessary to put it in Execution as soon as conveniently may be But if there should not appear to be 2/3 in favor of it as aforesaid that then should there be two 3ds of the Towns present by their Delegates who have returned Delegates and the major part of them have similar Instructions in such case the Delegates from this Town are hereby impowered to join in convention to make amendments according to the general sense of the State as near as they can and proceed to ratify etc. as afforesaid without sending out to the people again.

Attest

Nathan Putnam Moderrator
Follansbe Chase Town Cler

Templeton (277/113)

We the Subscribers Selectmen of Templeton in the County of Worcester having received the Constitution or Frame of Government agreed upon by the Delegates of the People of the Massachusetts Bay and laid the Same before the Town at a Legal Town Meeting, and after Considering the same throughly—Voted as follows Viz. that the Declaration of Rights be approved of Excepting the 3d article

Forty three in affirmative—three in the Negative

The 3d article Excepting the Last Paragraph approved by 43—and 8 aginst it———

the Last paragraph passed 38 for it as it Now Stands, and ten for having the word Protestants in the Room of Christians———

in the frame of government Chapter 2d Section first (Governor) article second—at the end of the Second Line be added the following words "a Native of this Common-wealth, and"

further in Bottom Line of said article Protestant be inserted in the Room of Christian; and all other Places where the word Christian is mentioned in the frame of Government the word Protestant be inserted in its Room. The several votes Respecting the frame of government passed Fifty Seven for, and one against and the other part of the Frame of government approved of by 57—one against it

Templeton June the 5th 1780

Ebenr. Wright
Ezekiel Knowlton
Silas Cutler
Charles Baker

To the Convention of Delegates to meet at Boston on the first Wednesday of this instant June

Upton (277/114)

At a meeting of the male Inhabitants of the Town of Upton. of the age of Twenty one years and upwards upon Due warning Assembled at the meetinghouse in Said Town on the 15 Day of May 1780 and Continued by adjornment to June 2d. Said meeting was to hear and take into Consideration a Constitution and form of Government for the State of Massachusetts Bay agreed by the Convention of Said State March. 2. 1780.

Said Town's Votes are as follows

Part the first a Declaration of the Rights etc.

Two first articles Voted by 45 yeas nays. 1

Third article voted by——8 yeas nays 26

Third article Voted by 33 yeas nays 17. with this amendment by adding these words at the end of the fourth paragraph But no person owning himself to be of the Sect of Baptist or Quaker Denomination Shall Ever be Required by Law to pay any Tax or Rate for the Support of the ministers of Religion or for Building or Repairing houses for Divine worship in any way or form Either for their own or any other Denomination or Sect of Religion whatsoever unless as individuals they Request this power as a priviledge for them Selves

The 4th article to the 29th

Voted by 31 yeas nays none

29th article Voted by 22 yeas nays 17

30th article Voted by 32 yeas nays none

Part the Second

The frame of Government

Voted to accept the Introdction

by—39 yeas nays none

Chapter 1 the Legislative Power

Section 1 The General Court

1 article Voted by 36 yeas nays none

2 article Voted by 31 yeas nays none

3 article Voted by 31 yeas nays none

4 article Voted by 23 yeas nays 11

Chapter. 1. Section 2. Senate
1 article Voted by 25. yeas. nays. 17
2 article Voted by 35 yeas nays 4
3 article Voted by 27 yeas nays 4
4 article Voted by 34 yeas nays none
5 article Voted by 39 yeas nays 1
6th and 7th articles Voted by 33 yeas nays none
8 article Voted by 27 yeas nays none
9 article Voted by 29 yeas nays none

Chapter 1 Section 3rd House of Representatives
1 article Voted by 16 yeas nays none
2 article Voted by 16 yeas nays 9
3 article Voted by 23 yeas nays none
4 article Voted by 21 yeas nays none
5th and 6 articles Voted by 21 yeas nays none
7 article Voted by 12 yeas nays none
8th and 9 articles Voted by 17 yeas nays none
10 article Voted by 28 yeas nays 1
11 article Voted by 21 yeas nays none

Chapter 2 Executive power
Section 1 Governor
1 article Voted by 18 yeas nays 2
2 article Voted 24 yeas nays 7 with this amendment
by adding the word protestant in the Last Line
3 article Voted by 21 yeas nays none
4 article Voted by 18 yeas nays none
5 article Voted by 13 yeas nays none
6 article Voted by 14 yeas nays none
7 article Voted 15 yeas nays 1
8 article Voted by 11 yeas nays none
9 article Voted by 25 yeas nays. 2 with this amendment
all Judicial officers Excepting the Judges of probate Shall be nominated and appointed by the Governor by and with the advice and Consent of Council the attorny-General and Solicitor-General Shall be Chosen annually by Joint ballot of the Senators and Representatives—all Judges of the probate Registers of probate all Sheriffs and Coroners to be Chosen by their Respective Counties in Such manner as the legislature shall provide.

10 article Voted by 20. yeas nays none
11 article Voted by 16 yeas nays none
12 article Voted by 16 yeas nays none
13 article Voted by 13 yeas nays none

Chapter 2 Section 2 Leiutenant Governor
1st, 2nd and 3rd articles Voted by 14 yeas nays none

Chapter 2 Section 3 Council and the manner of Settling Elections by the Legislature
1st, 2nd, 3rd, 4th, 5th, 6 and 7 articles Voted by 14 yeas nays none

---

Chapter 2nd. Section 4th Secretary Treasurer Commissary etc.
1 article Voted by 19 yeas nays none
2 article Voted by 24 yeas nays none

Chapter 3 Judiciary Power
1 article Voted by 18 yeas nays none
2 article Voted by 32 yeas nays none
3 article Voted by 24 yeas nays none
4 article Voted by 23 yeas nays none
5 article Voted by 23 yeas nays none

Chapter 4th Delegates to Congress
Voted by 25 yeas nays none

Chapter 5 the University at Cambridge and Encouragement of Literature etc. Section 1 the Unversty
1,2, and 3 articles Voted by 11 yeas nays 1

Chapter 5 Section 2. the Encouragement of Literature etc
Voted by 7 yeas nays 6

Chapter 6. Voted by 18 yeas nays none

Voted to Leave it to the Delegates to
Set a time when the Constitution
Shall Take place in Case it Shall
be Accepted

A True Copy attest Ephraim Whitney Town Clerk
Upton June 6 1780

P.S. The Reason given for the amendment in the third article in the bill of Rights—is to ease the minds of the Baptist and Quakers and that the Said article may be better undersood.
The Second chapter Section 1 in the frame of Government
the Second article the word protestant Because more safe
Second Chapter Section 1 article 9th
that there may be a Due Ballance btween the Powers of the State
attest Ephraim Whitney

Uxbridge (277/115

Return of the Proceedings of the Inhabitants of the Town of Uxbridge upon the Constitution or Frame of Government Agreed "upon by the Deligates of the People of the State of the Massachusetts Bay in Convention Begun and held at Cambridge on the first of September. 1779. and Continued by Adjournments to the Second of March 1780." Voted to Accept of the whole of the Articles as they now Stand in Said form of government Except such Articles as are hereafter Mentioned [Objected to the 3rd Article in the Bill of Rights. 117 against it and 11 in favour. the objection Stated that no Subject be held to pay taxes to any Teacher or Teachers of Piety, Religion, and Morality, unless to such Teachers as are of their own Religious Sect or Denomination]—Chapter 1st Section II Senate, Article first—Objected to the Number of the Senate and Councill as being larger then Necessary. 48 Against it 9 in favour. Objections stated that the Senate Consist of but 25 and the Council of 7———Chapter 1st Section III Article 2nd Against it 28 in favour None. Objections Stated that 150 as therein Mentioned Send one. that 450 send Two, and that 600 Hundred [sic] be the Next mean increasing Number and so on———9th Article. Objectors 29—in favour none. Objections Stated, that no less than 80 Members of the House of Representatives Shall Constitute a quorum for doing Business.

Uxbridge June 15th 1780

Abner Rawson
[Nicks?] Baylies
Benja. Green
Jesse Taft
Gershom Taft
Selectmen of Uxbridge

Ward (277/116)

The proposed form of Government for Massachusetts agreed upon by the late Honorable Convention being laid before the Town of Ward and having been read and Carefully considered at a regular meeting of Said Town may the 26th 1780 Voted 1 that we Cordally approve of said Constitution as to the Substance therof as what appears to us to be Salutary and well adopted———

2. We beg leave however with Du defference to the Convntion to Suggest that we look upon the great Disproportion proposed in the matter of representation betwen the greater and less Towns meerly on the account of Numbers to be pregnant with dngerous consequences with regard to som very Important matters———therefrom. We could heartily wish that representation might be weighed by Towns rather then by the Numbers of polls, which would be Similar to the proceedings of the Honorable Congress and Some Neighbouring, well regulated States that have been attended with very wholsome Effects———

3 that we are greatly Dissatisfyd with the long time of fifteen years proposed for the run of Constitution previous to any Revisions amendments or alteration for that we conceive the most wise and wholesom system of government Supposable must be likely to need Some alterations and amendments at least as to certain appendages in less then half the Number of fifteen years and we pray this matter may be Duly cnsidred———

4 We hope to be pardoned in this freely opening out thots in these affairs as we never had a member in Convntion———

Respectfully Submiting thejse matters therfore to the wisdom and candor of that venerable Body: we shall Rejoyce to See a happifying Establishment of Government Compleeted as Soon as my be

Humbly submitted
Ward May 30th 1780

Samuel Eddy
Jacob Stevens
Jesse Stone
Select men of Ward

N.B. the numbers Voting for the above ware 23—
Dessenters 9

Westborough (277/117)

A Return of the Proceedings of the Town of Westboro on the Constitution sent from the Honorable Convention,———at a Town meting May

1. 1780. and at several adjournments voted to accept of the Constitution in the manner following viz. with the Amendments Specified.

	Yeas	Nays
1st the Declaration of Rights——	61——	—
Part 2d Frame of Government——	71——	—
Chapter 1st Legislative Power. Section 1st		
Article 1st——	64——	3
2d——	70——	2
3d——	76——	—
4th——	76——	—
Section 2d Same chapter Senate		
Article 1st——		80
voted to have 31 Councellors and Senators instead of 40 (as an amendment)——	80——	—
Article 2——	83.	
3——	1——	82
voted 3 Counsellors instead of 5, (as an amendment.)——	71——	5
Article 4——	70——	1
5——	71——	—
6——	73——	—
7——	72——	1
8——	74——	—
9——	2——	73
Voted that 13 Senators be a Quorum instead of 16 (as an amendment.)——	55——	—
Chapter 1 Section 3 House of Representatives,		
Article 1st——	70——	—
Article 2d——	1——	80
Voted the following Amendments. (viz) for the 3d Representative 675. for the 4th. Representative 1200 Ratable poles making 525 the mean increasing number for every additional Representative. Slaves not to be numbered in matters of Representation	83——	0
Article 3d——	83——	1

	Yeas	Nays
Article 4th——	90——	—
Article 5th——	90——	—
Article 6th——	89——	—
Article 7th——	88——	—
Article 8——	89——	—
Article 9——	96——	1
Article 10——	96——	1
Article 11——	78——	—

Chapter 2d Executive Power

	Yeas	Nays
Section 1. Governor: Article 1st——	74——	—
Article 2——	2——	86
voted to have at the *Christan, PROTESTANT* Relgion (as an amendment)——	83——	—
Article 3th——	80——	—
Article 4th——	1——	85
Voted to have it 3 Counsellors in Stead of 5 (as amendment)	85	
Article 5th——	88.	
Article 6——	76	
Article 7——	58——	3
Article 8——	57——	
Article 9——	47——	4
Article 10——	59——	
Article 11——	56	
Article 12——	59	
Article 13——	59	

Chapter 2 Section 2d Lieutenant Governor

	Yeas	Nays
Article 1st——	58	
Article 2d——	59	
Article 3d——	38	

Chapter 2 Section 3d Council and Manner of Sitling. Elections etc.

	Yeas	Nays
Article 1——		30
voted to have 5 Councillors instead of 9 and that 3 be a Quorum (as an amendment)—32		

	Yeas	Nays
Article 2d——— ———	———	34
Voted to have 5 instead of 9 (as an amendment)	35———	
Article 3———	35———	
Article 4———		35
Voted to have one Counsellor instead of two in a district (as an amendment)	35	
Article 5———	35	
Article 6———	35	
Article 7———	38	
Chapter 2. Section 4th Secretary of Treasury Commissary etc.		
Article 1st———	38———	
Article 2d———	39	
Chapter, 3 Judiciary Power.		
Article 1st———	38	
2d———	38	
3d———	35	
4th———	41	
5th———	41	
Chapter 4th Delegates to Congress———	39	1.
Chapter 5 The University at Cambridge and Encouragement of Literature etc.		
Section 1st Article 1st———	43———	5
Article 2———	46———	
Article 3———	48———	
Chapter 5 Section 2 The encouragement of Literature etc.	48———	
Chapter 6 The Oaths and Subscriptions etc.		
Article 1———	1———	46
—in the oath Christian, protestant Religion (as an amendment)—Voted——— and in the Next Paragraph to have 3 Counselors instead of 5———	49———	

	Yeas	Nays
Article 2d——	25——	14
Voted that the Minsters of the Gospel and the Judges of the Inferior Court be added to those who shall not have a seat in the General Court	48——	
Article 3d.——	41	
4th——	41	
5th——	39	
6th——	36	
7th——	37	
8th——	38	
9th——	39	
10th——	0——	41
Voted. that the Revision of this Constitution or amendment of it be within Ten years——	38	
Article 11——	40	

Voted unanimously (except one dissenter) to Accept of the Constitution with the Several amendments aforesaid.——the one dissenting vote was for it as it was sent to the People.

Ebenr. Maynard
Barnabas Newton
Eli Whitney
Abijah Gale

Select Men of Westborough

Westminster (277/118)

At a Legall Meeting of the Inhabitants of the Town of Westminster in the County of Worcester for the Purpose of Considering the Proposed Form of Government for the State of Massachusetts Bay, on Tuesday the Sixth day of June Instant when after duely weighing said Form of Government It was Voted by a Majority of Thirty that said Form of Government be Accepted making the Alterations hereafter Mentiond—and five against said alterations who are in favor of said Form of Government without alteration——

said alterations Agreed to are as follows Vizt.——

Alteration 1st: In the 12th. Article of the Bill of Rights

Immediately after the words by himself be added or any other Person or Persons he shall apoint, whether he or they so appointed be sworn Attorneys or not———

The Reason is that by the word Councill in the Article may be Explained in such manner as to oblidge the Subject to Imploy none in his Cause but such as are sworn Attorneys which may be a Restraint on the Liberty of the Subject———

ditto—2d In the 29th Article of the Bill of Rights Provision is made for the Judges of the Superior Court to have Honorable Salarys assertained and Established by Standing Laws—in the Room of which we think it ought to be Granted by the Legislators anually—our Reason is that the Uncertainty of humane affairs make it Necessary that the Salarys of the Supream Judges should be annually Granted———

ditto—3. In the 3d Article of the frame of Goverment after the words other Courts be added such as have been used or Practiced in this State—the Reason of which is to prevent all Unconstitutionall Courts Beeing Erected———

ditto—4—In the first Article Section Second we are of opinion that therein ought to be no Councill and that the Number of Senators be Reduced to Thirty one—Our Reason is Because we Apprehend a Number of Senators may be as proper for advisers to the Govenor as a Councill might be———

Alteration 5th: In the Third Section upon a Representation in the Second Article we Judge an alteration is Necessary and in particular with Regard to the Increasing Number of Voters to Send a Second Representative in a Town, we Conceive that 500 Rateable poles ought att Least to be the mean Increasing Number to send the Second Representative in any Town, we Judge allso that Every Town that from the time that this Constitution shall Take place which may be Incorporated and taxed to the Charge of Goverment ought to be allowed to send a Representative Lett their Number be moor or Less Observing the above Rule for an additionall Representative———

The Reason of our Increasing the Number of Voters to send a Second Representative is Because that so small a Number of Voters as 225 will Increase the Number of Members so Greatly as that Buisness will be much obstructed, and the charge of Goverment Greately Increased———

ditto 6—The 11th Article Accepted only that part that Respects a Privey Councill———

ditto—7—In the 8th Article we are of opinion that the Power of pardoning should Lie with the Governor and Sennate

ditto—8—In the 9th Article we are of the Opinion that the House of Representative ought in the Room of the Govenor in the same manner to make the Nominations of all Civill and Judiciall Officers and to be Complied with or Rejected by the Governor and Senate and Commissionated by them—Our Reason is that we Judge that it is much Safer to the Subject to have the Nomination of Officers to be in the hands of the people by their Representatives then in the hands of an Individuall

ditto—9—In the 13th. Article we are of Opinion that the Governor and Supream Judges Salaries should be Annually Granted by the Legislators as the particuliar Exigencies of the times may Require the Reason is as Given heretofore in the 29th. Article of the Bill of Rights with Respect to the Salaries of the Superior Judges———

ditto. 10—Section 3d. Chapter 2d. Voted to Expunge the whole of this Section———

and Voted that the Constitution be Revised in Seven Years after it shall take place———

Then a Vote was Called for to know what time was Judged Best to have the Constitution take place whereupon it was Unanimously Voted that the time for said Constitution to take place Could Best be Determined by the Convention and we therefore Refer that to [their] Consideration Accordingly.

A True Coppy

Westminster June 7. 1780 [J.] M Gill Town Clerk

Winchendon (277/119)

At a Legal Meeting of the Male Inhabitants of Winchendon be free and twenty one years of age on the 15th Day of May 1780 After Reading the Constitution Voted and adjurned to the 24th Day of May Instant and then Met and after Deliberately Reading the Declaration of Rights and Debateing thereon the Question was put Voted for it 30 against it one then adjurned to the 29 Day May aforsaid and then Voted After Reading the frame of government [several] Amendments were Proposed Viz.

II article in the II Section I Chapter Frame of Government

That amng those who are Qualifyed as to Estate to Vote in Elections there be an Exception Made against Common Drunkards Comon thieves and other Capitol offenders and that Every Person before he Proceeds to Vote in Electing Oficers etc. be Required to take an oath obliging him self for ever After to use the Best of His Skill and Judgment in Electing persons to office

---

I Chapter Section III Article II

that two or More unincorporated Towns or Plantations haveing in them 115 Rateable Polls May Join togeather and Elect one Representative

---

Chapter II Section I article I and Chapter 6th Article I

That the Word Christian be Epunged and the Word Protestant Substituted

---

The Question being Put upon the frame of government with the Foregoing Amendments Voted for it 21 against it. none

It was then Moved to have the frame of Government Put as it Stands— Voted for it 9 against it two

A true Coppy Taken from the Minutes Attest
Abel Wilder Town Clerk

Western (277/119)

A Return

The Proceedings of the town of Western with Respect to the Constitution at a Legul Town meeting of the Inhabitants of Said Town on monday the Eighth Day of May 1780 Voted to Except of the whole of the Constitution Except three artickeles Eighty five In Noumber Voted for the above 1 Voted that the first artickel In the 19 Page that the Number of Counsellers and Senators Should Be Reduceed to 32 In Sted of 40 and the Reson we give is that the Representatve Body Be Large and that a Smaller Number in the Counsell and Senet will Be as Likely to Do the Business of the State as Quick and as well as a Larger and Besides it will be Less Cost and will Take of good men that we Trust will be Imployd in Publick Business In the State Ealeswhere 85 voters for the above amendment if it Can Be obtainde if Not to Take it as it is In the Constitution 27 Voted that the 2 artickele In 24 page Should Stand as it is In the Constitution

22 Voted that the mean Increasing Number Should Bee 300, In Sted of 225 for Every additional Representative and the Resin We give is that the Representative Body will Be Two Large and that the Large Towns under Every Surcomstans will have as good a Chans as the Small ons to have the meane Increesing Noumber 300: 57 Voted that the 10 artickele In the 50 page Should Be altered So that at the Experation of 15 years or Soonner if may Be Should Be Conveoned Togather and Not Be Left uppon unsartainties.

Voted to Except of the Whole Constitution if it Cant Be altered. But we Live it with our Dellagate to Do what he thinks is Best and we mean to Comply with it and have Impowered him to Let the Time for the Constitution to Take place etc.——

The above is the Proceedings of Said Town attested to By us——

Danforth Keyes
Solomon Rich
John [Barnes?]
Select
men
of
Western

Worcester (277/120)

We the Select Men of the Town of Worcester in pursuance of Advice from the said Convention have lately laid before this Town the proposed Constitution or Plan of Government and make return of the doings of said Town as follows viz——

Part first—

Article 1st and 2d The first and second Articles passed unanimously—70 present on the first and 73 present on the 2d—

Article 3d—The 3d. Article was rejected. 53 present—4 for the Article. 49 Against it——in Lieu of which the Town adopted the Amendment proposed by the Town of Boston for the reasons that Town have assigned and upon Counting the numbers there appeared to be 56 for the Amendment and 3 against it

Article 4th—passed unanimously —67 present
5th—Unanimosly —75 present—
6th—Unanimously —71 present—

7th—Unanimously —37 [73?] present—
8th—Unanimously —73 present
9th—Unanimously —74 present
10th—Unanimously —75 present
11th—Unanimously —73 present
12th and 13th. Unanimously—74 present
14th. Unanimously —70 present
15th. Unanimously —68 present
16. Unanimously —69 present
17. Unanimously —73 present
18th. Unanimously —70 present
19th. Unanimously —74 present
20th—4 for 61 against the Article as it stands. An Amendment was made that all the words after the word Legislature in the third line should be erased. 61 for 4 against the Amendment——
21st—Passed unanimously —67 present
22d.— Unanimously —75 present
23d— Unanimously —72 present
24— Unanimously —66 present
25— Unanimously —72 present
26— Unanimously —72 present
27— Unanimously —78 present
28th— Unanimously —73 present
29th— Unanimously —61 present
30th— Unanimously —80 present

Part the second. The frame of Government——

Paragraph 1st—63 for. 1 Against it——

Chapter 1st. Section 1st.—The General Court

Articles 1st and 2d.—passed Unanimously.—63 present

Article 3d.—63 for 1 Against it——

4th.—8 for 55 against it—An Amendment was proposed that from and after the word *Commonwealth* in the 4th. line of the 11 page the paragraph should be erased 54 for the Amendment. 9 against it——

Chapter 1st Section 2d. Senate

Article 1. 54 for 4 against it——

2d. 53 for 7 against it——
3d. 57 for 3 against it——
4. 60 for. 1 against it
5th. 6th. 7th. 8th. 9th. 57 for. 2 against those Articles

Chapter 1st Section 3d. House of Representatives

Article 1st.—50 for the Article 6 Silent upon the Question——

2d. Rejected Unanimously 57 present—for the following Reason It is calculated for forming a most unwieldy legislative body. In process of time should the probable degree of population take place the house of Representatives will be so numerous that the dispatch of business will be greatly retarded, and such languor in legislation produced as will, in a great measure, defeat the design of the political existence of the Assembly—For it is well Known *that great bodies move slowly.* If the proposed mode is established there will be a continued Jealousy in the minds of the people as a very few of the most populous Towns will have it in their power to constitute a Quorum of the house of Representatives, and being near the State house (should the place of Assembly be and continue in the present Capital of the State) their members can easily and constantly attend; while those at a distance from their local situation and many other Causes, be unavoidably absent at the opening or close of a Session *whereby in* a thin house Laws might be passed which would not be calculated for the General Good——

The following Amendment afterwards passed 24 for 21 against it——

That the mode of Representation should be set and established in the Constitution in the same way as Elections in the now State were practiced and had according to Law in the Year 1774. and that the two last paragraphs in this Article be and remain as proposed by the Honorable Convention with this Alteration viz. That the members of the house of Representatives receive their pay and expenses out of the publick Treasury as well for their attendance as their Travels—and this because we apprehend that Each member of said house is the Representative of the whole State and not meerly of the Corporation by which he is elected.

Article 3d.—51 for. 3 against it—
4—20 for. 28 against it

5. 6. 7. 8. Passed Unanimously 44 present

9th. Article 20 for it stands 24 against it—

An Amendment was made which passed 31 for the Amendment and 24 Against and is as follows—

That no less than one third of the Members returned to serve as Representatives shall constitute a Quorum.

The Reasons are as follows———

Should the proposed mode of Representation be agreed on the proportion of be to the whole number that may compose the house will be too inconsiderable to transact matters of great importance, as it may afford opportunities for designing men to seize the advantage of a thin house and wrest it to their own particular purposes———

10th. and 11th. Passed Unanimously 44 present———

Chapter 2d. Executive Power

Article 1st.—30 for. 16 against it—

2d.—29 for. 17 against it

3d.—30 for 19 against it

4. —26 for 23 against it

5. 35 for 9. against it

6. —34 for 10 against it

7. —38 for this article with the following Amendment.

6. Against it.

The Amendment is. Provided that the said Governor shall not at any time hereafter by virtue of any power by this Constitution granted or hereafter to be granted to him by the Legislature, transport any of the Inhabitants of this Commonwealth or oblige them to march out of the limits of the same without the Consent of the General Court. if it should be then sitting or if otherwise, that the General Court should be convened as soon after as may be, and that the Inhabitants aforesaid shall not be compelled to remain without the limits of this Commonwealth without the Consent of the General Court after they shall be convened.———

Reasons for the Amendment. Because in Case of an Invasion of a neighbouring State when the General Court of this State shall not be sitting, the Enemy before a vigourous opposition can be made, may have Opportunity to strengthen themselves in such a manner as may render it extremely difficult to remove them by a large force, whereas a comparatively small number might be able to repel them and defeat their intentions by an early opposition———

Article 8.—34 for 11. against it
9. 29 for. 14 against it
10. 25 for. 19 against it
11. 30 for. 11 against it
12. 33 for. 7. against it—
13. 31 for. 8 against it

Chapter 2d. Section 2d.
Lieutenant Governor

1st. 2d. and 3d. Articles. 38 for 1 against them

Chapter 2d. Section 3d
Council etc.

The Whole Section) 38 present. Unanimous———

Chapter 2d. Section 4th
Secretary etc.

The whole Section) 38 present—unanimous

Chapter 3d. Judiciary Power

The whole Chapter.) 38 for. 1 against it—

Chapter 4. Delegates to Congress
38 for. 1 against it

Chapter 5. The University etc
Section 1

The whole Section)—33 for 7 against it—

Chapter 5. Section 2d
30 for. 12 against it—

Chapter 6

Article 1st.—4 for. 1 against it
Article 2d.—41 for this Article and 4 Against it provided on each side that members of Congress and Settled Ministers of the

Gospel are excluded a Seat in either house of the Legislatur

Article 3d. 11 for. 27 against this Article as it stands after which the following Amendment was made, that the Article remain as it stands adding the word *"not"* after the word *be* in the 4th line and erasing these words which end the paragraph *As the Circumstances* of the Commonwealth shall require.

Articles 4. 5. 6 Passed Unanimously 38 present

Article 7th. The following Amendment was made and passed Unanimously 40 present———

After the Word *Legislature* in the 5th. line to read thus Except in times of War, Invasion or Rebellion and for a limited time not exceeding six months———

Reason of the Amendment is Because these Words upon the most urgent and pressing Occasions are vague and Indefinite and the time of six Months being sufficiently long.

Article 8th and 10 on to the End Passed Unanimously 38 present———

The Town also unanimously voted—Present 35—That their Delegates at the next Session of the Convention be impowered to agree upon a time when the form of Government shall take place without returning the same again to the people with the proviso mentioned in the Resolve of the Convention.

Worcester, June 6th. 1780.

John Green	Select Men
Joseph Barber	of
Edward Crafts	Worcester

Amesbury *

Warrant dated April the 28th 1780

Art 2. to take into consideration the Constitution or form of Goverment agreed upon by the delegate of the State of the Massachusetts Bay and accept the same or reject it, or make such alterations upon it as they shall think best when meet——
And as the business is of the utmost importance it is earnestly desired that all that can conveniently, would attend and also to choose other Delegates instead of the present members to meet in Convention in the first Wednesday of June next if they see fit and to do any other business they shall think proper when met

May the 4. 1780
At the same meeting voted to choose a Committee to peruse the form of Government for amendment and make report at the adjournment of this meeting
At the same meeting voted to choose 5 persons to be the Committee which are as follows Col Jonathan Bagley. Mr. Simeon Bartlett, Christoper Sargent, Capt. Timothy Barnard Mr. Willis Patten were chosen

May the 22. 1780
At the same meeting voted to suspend whole plan and form of Goverment for further consideration till nex Monday at 2 oclock afternoon at this place

May the 29, 1780
At the same meeting voted the 3 articles of the Bill of rights 13 yeas 14 noes For the remainder of the Bill rights 8 yeas 2 noes. For the form of Government 21 yeas and 19 nays At the same meeting voted not to send a delegate to the Convention

Andover †

Andover May 1st. 1780

at a Meeting of the Male Inhabitants that are free and twenty one years of Age and upwards being legally warned and convened on said Day—

* Town records, Massachusetts Historical Society.

† Andover Town Records, Andover, Mass. For different reports on the vote, see Abiel Abbot, *History of Andover* (Andover, Mass., 1829), 62; and S. L. Bailey, *Historical Sketches of Andover* (Boston, 1880).

The Honorable Samuel Phillips Esquire was chosen Moderator [*illegible*] Chose the Reverend Mr. William Symmes, the Reverend Mr. Jonathan Ire [*illegible*] the Honorable Samuel Phillips Esquire Deacon Joshua Holt, Capt. John Farnu [*illegible*] Mr. Nehemiah Abbot, Mr. Moody Bridges, Mr. Asa Abbot, [Cap.?] Osgood, Mr. Philemon Chandler, [Lieutenant?] Oliver Peabody, a Com [*illegible*] join with the Members of Convention for said Town; to make such remarks and amendments [wp?] the Form of Constitution (now [before?] them) as they shall think proper, and lay the same before the Town at the Adjournment of this Meeting for their Considerat[ion?]

Voted to Adjourn to the 15th. instant at One O Clock afternoon—[at?] which Time one Hundred Sixty Six Met; and said Form of Government was take up and deliberatly read, and the following observations made upon Part 1st. Art. 3d. in the Declaration of Rights by the aforesaid Committee—Part 2d. Chap. 1st. Sect. 1 Ar[*illegible*] by Mr. Moody Bridges—And Chap. 1st. Sect. 1st. Art. 4th. by [*illegible*] Amos Stevens, And Chap. 1st. Sec. 3d Art. 2d. by said Committee [*illegible*] and Chap 2d. Sec 1st. Art. 2d. by said Committee—

Then the Question was put, whither the parts of the Form of Constitution not remarked upon as [proposed] by the Members of Convention be approved by the [Town] as a Bill of Rights and Form of Government for this State

Past in the Affirmative. Nem Con.

Voted to Adjourn to the 22d. instant at 12 O Clock at Noon [*illegible*] One Hundred and Eighty One Voters Met. and proceeded to [*illegible*] aforesaid Objections and following amendments (vez) [*illegible*] The paragraph in the 3d. Art. in the Declarition of Rights [*illegible*] paid by the Subject for the Support of Publick Worship and [*illegible*] ought to be rendred more explicit and less liable to Mis[con?]struction.

We conceive the true intent of a Declaration of Right, is to defend and Express those Rights of a Society or Individuals in it which are Unalinable; and which no Laws can superceed, Alter, or set aside consequently such Rights ought to be expressed in Plain and intelligible Terms, levelled as much as may be to the Capacities of the Subjects in common. We are of opinion therefore that, that paragraph ought to be rendred, "All Monies levied by Assessments upon the Subject for the Support of publick worship and publick Teachers as aforesaid shall, if he require it be uniformly applied for the Support of the publick Teacher or Teachers of a Different religious Denomination from those among whom he resides provided there be any on whose Instructions he attends.

otherwise it shall be paid towards the support of the Teacher or Teachers of the Parish or Precinct in which the said Monies are raised.

past in the Affirmative Unanimously—

The 2d. Art. in Chapt. 1st. Sec. 1st was put as it stands in said Form of Constitution as proposed by Convention

past in the Affirmative 180
Negative—1

Voted. An Amendment upon the 4th. Art. in Chap 1st. Sec 1st. be as follows (viz) To impose and levey reasonable Duties and Excises upon all Spirituous Liquors distilled in the State; upon all Articles that shall be deemed by the Legislature Superfluous and upon Goods, Wares, Merchandize and Commodities whatsoever brought into the same—In the Affirmative 167

Negative— 2

Voted, That it as the Opinion of the Town; that the Governor Leut. Governor, Counsellors, and Senators, and Representatives ought to be of the protestant Religion, and that no others should be eligable to either of those Offices; and would therefore propose that this restriction should be maded in the qualifications for a Governor, in Chap. 2d. Art. 2d. page 27th. And also in the Declaration Chap 6th. Art. 1st. page 44th. for the following reasons (viz)

1st. We consider it as one of the natural and civil rights of a free People, forming a Constitution for themselves to determine and assert the qualifications of all their Officers of Government, that they cannot be truly free and Independent without this Right—

2. We Suppose the Declaration in Chap 6th. pages 45th and 46th Art. 1st. was intended to answer the purpose of such a restriction; that is, that it was intended to prevent any except Protestants from holding Seats in Government—And if so then

3d. We think it consistent with Honestity and sound Policy, publickly and Explicitly to declare this intention—And cannot conceive it would be a matter of Offence to any Nation in the World to do it

4. There is not any Thing which has a greater tendency to give Dignity to a people and command respect from others, than to act with firmness from principles and consistantly with themselves. To adhere therefore steadily to these principles and Express this intention in the Constitution. instead of offending any Nation in the world would give us Dignity in the Eyes of all Europe, as every nation there knows the design for which our fore Fathers came into this Land and Settled this Country, and the principles upon which they and we; under God, have

hitherto defended it, and have no right, to expect we should depart from them—

In the Affirmative 180
Negative— 1

Voted That it is the Opinion of this Town that an alteration in Chapt. 1st. Art. 2d. That instead of making two Hundred twenty five rateable poles the Mean increasing number for every additional Representative, the Mean Increasing Number itself should be enlarged Thirty in every such Addition for the following Reasons (viz)

1st. Because the Art. as it now stands would make a larger House of Representatives than would be convenient for the publick—
2.—Because it would give the large and more populous Towns more than their just proportion of Influence in the General Court which Evils we conceive would be remidied by the proposed Alteration

past in the Affirmative—Nem Con—

Voted Unan: That it is the Opinion of said Town that provision be made for a revisal of the Constitution by a Convention chosen by the people at large and distinct from the General Court for that purpose in Ten or fifteen years from this one's taking place—

[*illegible*] A Question was proposed—whither the Town would umpower [*illegible*] Delegates at the next Session of Convention to agree and fix upon a Time when this Form of Government shall take place without returning the same to the People again—Provided that two thirds of the Inhabitants of this State shall agree to the same, or that a Convention shall conform it to the Sentiments of two thirds of the People—past in the Affirmative

A Question was put, whither it be agreeable to the Town that the Members of Convention from the Town be directed to use their influence that the present Form of Constitution as it now stands be established as a Constitution or Form of Government for this State provided the Alterations Amendments and Additions proposed cannot be obtained

past in the Afft.

Meeting Dissolved—

Beverly *

[At a Meeting of the Selectmen May 11th 1780 They ordered that a Town Meeting Should be warned and Held on Tuesday the Twenty 3d

* Town records, Massachusetts Historical Society.

day of May Instant at one o'Clock in the afternoon at the Stated place for Holding Town meeting in said and the following is a Copy of the warrant that was Issued out agreeable to there order Viz]

Essex ss. To Mr. Benjamin Obear one of the Constables of the Town of Beverly Greeting.

In the Name of the Government and peple of the State of the Massachusetts Bay You are hereby required forthwith to Notify and warn the Freholdors and other Inhabitents of the said Town that are qualified as the Law Directs to Vote in the Choice of Representatives to the Great and General Court and in Town affairs as also all the Male Inhabitents of said Town that are Free and Twenty one years of age being qualified by law to Vote relative to the Makeing receiving or rejecting of the Constitution and form of Government for the State of the Massachusetts to assemble and meet together on Tuesday the 23d day of May instant at one of the Clock in the afternoon at the Stated Place for holding of Town Meetings in said Town

* *

2ly To Take under Consideration the Constitution and form of government for the State of the Massachusetts as proposed by the State Convention appointed for that purpose and approved or reject the Same or any part thereof or propose Such amendments thereon as they in their wisdom Shall think best" and also To Impower their Deligats at the next Session of the Convention when the Said Form of Government Shall Take place in such way and manner as is Prescribed by a resolve of the said Convention and to Choose other Deligates in the Room of the Present members if they think Proper.

* *

hereof fail not at your perrel in the Law and make Due returns of this warrent to the Selectmen with your doing thereon before the above said Time.

By order of the Selectmen of Beverly May 11th 1780

Joseph Wood T. Cler

At a A Meeting of the Male Inhabitants of the Town of Beverly that ware free and Twenty one Years of age Duly warned and assembled on the 23d day of May 1780 Josiah Batcheldor Esq was Chosen Moderator

The Constitution and Fram of Government for the State of the Massachusetts Bay as proposed by a Convention appointed for that Purpose was Taken under Consideration which after being read and Considerably Debated upon Josiah Batcheldor Esq Capt George Cabot and the Revd Mr. Joseph Willard ware Chosen a Committee to revise and Examen and make such remarks on the above said Constitution and form of Government as they Shall think best and report the same to the Town on their adjornment of this meeting

Voted that the Town Meeting be adjorned to Monday the 29 day May Instant at 9 o'clock in the four noon and the Town meeting was adjorned accordingly

At a meeting of the Male Inhabitants of the Town of Beverly that Ware free and Twenty one Years of age Duly warned and Assembled on the 29 day of May 1780 being on adjornment.

The Constitution and Form of Government was further Considered and the Committee appointed to examine and revise the Same reported and Duly Considered and the Question was put To See if the Town will approve of the Constitution and Fram of Government proposed by the State Convention appointed for that purpose to gather with several amendments and Instructions in Several papers on file and it passed unanimously in the affermitive

No present 53

Boxford, May 30, 1780 *

Boxford, May 30, 1780.

The committee appointed to inspect the Constitution beg leave to inform the town that as far as we are able, according to the time we have had, we have endeavored to investigate the Constitution, and point out the errors, and shall lay before the town our objections and remarks thereon.

First objection: As the third article in the 'Declaration of Rights' is rather obscure and ambiguous, we therefore want some further explanation on said article before we can accept it.

Second objection: We object against the freemen of any town or plantation being excluded from giving their votes for the choice of a representative while they are subjected to pay their proportion of State taxes.

Third objection: The House of Representatives being intended as the

* Sidney Perley, *History of Boxford* (Boxford, Mass., 1880), 249–250.

representative of the people, we object against any free inhabitant twenty-one years of age being excluded from giving his vote in the choice of a representative.

Fourth objection: We object that the quorum of the House of Representatives is too small where the House consists of three or four hundred members, and where they are invested with power to levy duties and exises on all wares, merchandise, and commodities whatsoever.

Fifth objection: We object the Governor's simply acknowledging himself of the Christian religion is not sufficient,—that he ought to declare himself a Protestant.

Sixth objection: We object against the Legislature's being invested with power to alter the qualifications of any officer in the State whatever until this Constitution shall be revised.

Seventh objection: Fifteen years we think too long for this Constitution to stand: we think eight years is long enough.

First remark, or addition: That settled ministers of the Gospel shall not have a right to a seat in the Council, Senate, or House of Representatives.

Seventh objection: Fifteen years we think too long for this Constitu-
a month lay before their constituents the several votes that may be determined by yeas and nays in said House, that the people may be able to judge who are friends to their country and who are not.

Third remark: That the towns may have authority to recall their representatives at any time when they shall act any thing inimical to the liberties of this Commonwealth, and to choose others to succeed them.

Fourth remark: That the House of Representatives be subjected to a trial by jury for any failure of their promises to the people of this Commonwealth.

Capt. Jonathan Foster
Capt. Isaac Adams
Capt. John Robinson
Dr. William Hale
Thomas Perley, jun.

Bradford *

At a Meeting of the Male Inhabitants of the town of Bradford, twenty one years of age and upward, held on May 25th 1780; and Continued By

* Town records, Massachusetts Historical Society.

Adjournment untill June 5th. Daniel Thurston Moderator of Said Meetings.

The Constitution was Read and after due deliberation on the important affair, the following votes were Passed Viz.

The Question was put ? Whether the Town would accept of the Constitution as it now Stands, Except the third Article, and it passed in the Affirmative.

Then a Vote was tryed upon the third Article and their Appeared to be 51 for it as it Stands, and 11 against it. Voted, that on the Article concerning the Qualification of the Governor: that the Word, Protestant be inserted after the word Christian.

Gloucester *

The Convention completed their work in March, 1780; and submitted the Constitution they had agreed upon to the people of the State. A town-meeting to consider it was held here on the 8th of May; when a committee was chosen to report concerning it, at an adjourned meeting to be held on the 22d of the month. On that day, the Constitution was accepted by a vote of forty-eight in its favor. No negative votes are recorded; nor is any thing more known of the debate on the subject than that Captain Sargent and Colonel Foster said that they objected to it.

Haverhill †

At a Town Meeting held in Haverhill on Tuesday, May 2nd 1780, warned by the Constable by Virtue of a Warrant received from the Select Men for his so doing

The Articles in the Warrant, are as follows

"Viz. 1 To see if the Town will approve of the Form of Government "for the State of Massachusetts Bay, as agreed upon by their Delegates "in a Convention lately held at Cambridge, for the sole purpose of form- "ing a Constitution for said State or disapprove of the Whole; or any

* John J. Babson, *History of the Town of Gloucester, Cape Ann* (Gloucester, Mass., 1860), 442.

† Town records, Massachusetts Historical Society.

"Part thereof; and make such Alteration in any Article as they, upon "mature Consideration, may think proper; giving their reasons for the "same.

" 2d. To see if the Town will impower their Delegates at the next "Session of said Convention, for forming a Constitution, to agree upon "a time when their proposed Form of Government shall take place; "provided that Two thirds of the Inhabitants of twenty one years of age "and upwards, shall agree to the same.

" 3d. As the Convention has submitted it to the several Towns, to "choose other Delegates, instead of the present members, to meet in "Convention on the 1st Wednesday in June next, this is to see if the "Town will proceed to such a Choice, or act on that Affair as they may "think proper."

General Jas. Brickett was chosen Moderator: who publickly read the form of Government as published by the Convention. The Moderator numbered the Voters in the Meeting and declared them to be one hundred and nineteen.

The 1st Article in the Bill of Rights being read, and proposed to the People, for their Approbation and Acceptance; it was, by a unanimous Vote, agreed to.

The 2d Article was also unamously voted and agreed to. The 3d Article was a Subject of considerable Debate, and no vote tried upon it. The Meeting was adjourned to Monday next at 1 Clock, P.M.

The Town met pursuant to the Adjournment; and the Moderator opened the Meeting.

After a little Time spent in talking upon the 3d Article in the Bill of Rights; on motion made, it was voted to postpone the Consideration of this Article for one Hour; and the Town proceeded to act upon the Subsequent Articles. The Moderator numbered the Voters present, and declared them to be 175. The 4th, 5,6,7,8 and 9th Articles in the Bill of Rights being read by the Moderator, and severally proposed to the Town, were approved of by a unanimous Vote.

The 10th Article was approved of by a Majority of 104; there being 26 against it, and 130 in favour of it.

The 11, 12, 13, 14, 15, 16, 17, 18, 19, and 20 Articles, being put up sepperately, were unanimously approved of.

The Towne then resumed the consideration of the 3d Article, which was a subject of much Altercation, and considerable Time was spent in arguing upon it. The following Vote was passed, viz. 91 voted to have it stand as it was published by the Convention; and 85 voted for an Amendment. This last Vote was reconsidered by a Majorety of 64 and on a second Tryal there were but 40 for the Article and 104 against it. A Division then took place in this last Number, concerning the Alteration and amendment. Two Plans were proposed; one by the Honbl. Nat. P. Sargent Esqr. and, the other by the Reverend. Mr. Hezekiah Smith. A Vote was tried on each of their Amendments; and there were 79 in favour of the former and 66 for the latter.

The Meeting was then adjourned till the next Day, at 1 Clock P.M.

The Town met according to Adjournment.

The Moderator opened the Meeting. The Number of Voters present was 33. The 21, 22d, 23d. 24, 25, 26, and 27th Articles were agreed to, without one Dissentient. The Number of Voters present, were from 33 to 43. The 28th Article was agreed to by 47 and but 1 against it. The 29th ditto had 19 in favour of it, and 19 against it. The 30th do. was unanimously agreed to by 56 Voters.

Then the Moderator proceeded to lay before the Town, the Frame of Government. The 1st Article of which was approved of by a unanimous Vote.

The 1st Chapter was then proposed, Article 1st which was agreed to unanimously. The 2d Article in this Chapter had 17 votes for it, and 17 against it (62 Voters present)

The 3d and 4th Articles in this Chapter, were voted unanimously. The Moderator proceeded to the 2d Section in Chapter 1st. The whole 9 Articles in this Section, were approved of. Voters 66 The 3d Section in this Chapter was approved of, except the 2d Article, and but 2 voted against that.

The 2d Chapter was then proposed. Section 1st. The 1st Article was agreed to unanimously, The 2d Article had 23 for it, and 12 against it. The 3d, 4, 5, 6, 7, 8, and 9th Articles were approved of unanimously 50 Voters present. The 10th Article had 12 for it, and 20 against it. The 11 and 12 Articles were approved of unanimously. For the 13th Article, were 22, and 4 against it.

The Meeting was adjourned to Monday 22d Inst.

1780

May 22d The Town met, pursuant to the Adjournment; and The Moderator opened the Meeting, and proceeded to lay before the Town, the Frame of Government begining at Chapt. 2d Section 2d. The 1st Article of which was voted unanimously Present 42

Voters The 2d Article was voted, with 1 dissenting Voice. The 3d Article voted unanimously 48 Voters.

Section 3d was then considered.

Article 1st was voted, by 62 2 Dissentients. The 2d,3d and 4 Articles were approved of and voted The 5th Article was objected to by 1, The 6th and 7th Articles were accepted.

Section 4th was then proposed. The 2 Articles of which were approved of.

Chapter 3d was then considered. The whole 5 Articles of it were approved of.

Chapter 4 considered, was voted unanimously.

Chapter 5 Section 1st acted upone. The 3 Articles contained in this Section were voted and accepted.

The 2d Section was voted and agreed to.

Chapter 6 was voted with the Amendment, at the Word "Christian" and Protestant. 75 Voters present.

All the Articles in this Chapter were voted and agreed to, except 1 Dissentient against Article 3d.

On the 2d Article in the Warrant, the following Vote was passed, to leave it with the Convention, for fixing a time when the Form of Government shall take place.

General James Bricket was chosen a Delegate to for this Town, to meet in Convention the 1st Wednesday in June next.

On motion made, it was voted to lay befor the Town, the 3d Articles in the Bill of Rights; and next Thursday is fixed upon for further considering it

This Meeting is adjourned to Thursday 25th Instant at 4 o Clock in the afternoon.

The Town, pursuant to the Adjournment, met together.

Voted, to consider all that has been acted on, respecting the Third Article in the Bill of Rights. Seventy one Voted for the above. On a Motion made it was put to vote, to see how many were for the 3d Article. There were Eighty five for and Sixty nine against it The Reverend Mr. Smith then offered an Amendment, which, being read, was voted, and accepted by 69.

The following Vote was passed, viz. Though the Town have thought fit to propose to the Convention some Alterations and Amendments in some of the Articles in the Form of Government they have made for the Common Wealth of Massachusetts, are, notwithstanding of Opinion, and do consent that the Whole of said Form, as published by the Convention, be established, rather than the same should be returned to the People for farther Revision; which will prevent its taking place, and being established so soon as we wish to have it. The Meeting was dissolved by the Moderator.

Ipswich *

[6/15/1780] "Voted not to accept the Constitution, unless the proposed amendments are allowed."

Marblehead †

The new State Constitution proposed by the legislature having been rejected by the people, a convention of delegates from each town was called to meet at Cambridge on the 28th of October, for the purpose of forming another. On the 30th of September, Azor Orne, Joshua Orne, Thomas Gerry, and Jonathan Glover, were elected delegates from Marblehead. The instrument framed by this convention was ratified by the people, and on the 22d of May, 1780, the vote of Marblehead was cast in favor of its adoption.

Middleton ‡

1ly At a legal town meeting of the Inhabitants of the town of Middleton assembled May the 30th Day 1780 Capt Benjamin Peabody was chosen moderator of said meeting.—

2ly The Town Voted to choose a Committee to take under consideration the frame of Government agreed upon By the Delegates of the People of the State of the Massachusetts Bay in Convention Begun and Held at Cambridge on the first Day of September 1779 and continued by adjournment to the second of March 1780

3ly. Mr. Elias Smith Mr Isaac Kenney [*illegible*] Amos Curtis. Mr. Israel Kenney [*illegible*] Johnathan Seamon was chosen committee to take under Consideration the frame of Government and make report

* Joseph B. Felt, *History of Ipswich, Essex, and Hamilton* (Cambridge, Mass., 1834), 134.
† Samuel Roads, Jr., *The History and Traditions of Marblehead* (Boston, 1880), 130.
‡ Town records, Massachusetts Historical Society.

to said Town then the Moderator adjourned Said Meeting to the 5th day of June at one of the clock in the afterNoon—then the town meet and proceded as followeth.
the first article 35 for it and 12 against it
Article the Second 42 for it 5 against it.
Article the third with amendments 36 for it 9 against it
Article the forth 32 for it 6 against it
Article the fifth 35 for it 5 against it
Then they voted to Except of all the articles from the 5th to the 30th 32 for it and Seven against it.
the town Excepted of the article of Common Wealth 33 for it and 7 against it
25 Do Except of the 4 article of the Legestative Power with the amendments and thirteen against it
30 for the three first articles and 7 against it
Chapter the first Sextion the 2 Senate 31 for it 7 against it
Chapter the first Sextion the 3—26 for it 2 against it
Chapter the Second Executive power Sextion the first Governor 24 for it 1 against it
Chapter the 2 Sextion Let Governor 24 for it with amendments.
Chapter 2 Sextion the 3 Council and manner of Setling Election By the Legeslative 24 for it.
Chapter 2 Sextion 4 Secretary Commersary 24 for it.
Chapter the 3 Judicatory Power 22
Chapter 4 Delegates to Congress 30 for it
Chapter 5 the university at Cambridge Encouredgement of the Legislation[Literature?]. Sextion the unversity 30 for
Chapter 5 Sextion 2 Encouredgement of the Legislation, and 28 for it.

Newbury *

On the twenty-ninth day of May, [1780] Enoch Sawyer, Esq., Mr. Richard Adams, and Mr. Ebenezer March were re-elected to represent Newbury in the examination of the returns; and at the same meeting it was also voted, "that the Delegates from this Town be authorized to Joyn with their Brethren in Convention and Determine when the Constitution shall take Place, Provided that two Thirds of the male inhabitants of this state vote for the same."

* John J. Currier, *History of Newbury, Mass. 1635–1902* (Boston, 1902), 290.

Newburyport *

At a legal meeting of the freholders and other inhabatants of the town of Newburyport qualified to vote in town affairs, held the ninth day of May Anno Domini 1780

Voted—Nathaniel Carter Esq Moderater.

voted that Patrick Tracy, Theophilas Bradbury and Micajah Sawyer Esq. be a committee to Take into consideration the constitution or form of government, proposed to the inhabitants of the State, by the late convention, held at Cambridge, and make report on the adjournment

Voted, that the town do impower their delegates at the next convention to be held on the first Wednesday in June next, to agree on a time when the form of government shall take place without returning the same again to the people

Voted. that the Selectmen be a committee to wait on the several ministers of this town and desire them to impress on the minds of their hearers, the necessity of a general attendance at the town meeting on the adjournment, when the constitution or frame of government is to be voted upon.

Voted—that Mr. Moses Hoyt be a committee to wait on the proprietors, of the first meeting house in Newburyport, to obtain liberty to meet in said house on adjournment

Voted to adjourn this meeting to Monday next 9 oclock A.M. at the Rev. Mr. Carey's meeting house.

May 15 Voted unanimously that the town do approve of the frame of the Government with the amendments and alteratives which have been made and reported by the committee, chosen by the town for that purpose. Except the 7th Article of Chap. 2nd Section 1 which was approved by 102 voters and disapproved by 132

May 18 Met according to adjournment

Voted unanimously to accept the report of the Committee appointed to take into consideration the constitution or frame of government agreed upon by the delegates of the people of Massachusetts Bay in convention held at Cambridge the first Tuesday of September A. D. 1779 and continued by adjournment to the second Tuesday in March 1780, viz

* Town records, Massachusetts Historical Society.

They concieve it to be of great importance that the governor as supreme executive magistrate should have with the advice of the council a negative upon all the acts of the legislature that so the executive branch of the constitution may ever be kept distinct from and independent of the legislature, and the due balance between the two powers preserved, they are of aprehensive that without this check the legislative will encroach by degrees on the judicial as well as the executive till at length, both of the latter will be stripped of all their rights and powers. and united with the former, and if ever this event happens, if ever the legislative body shall become the judicial and executive also, if in other words, the same body of men may make interpret and execute the laws, there will be an end of civil liberty, for such a body will enact such laws, and such only as it chooses to execute, it will cause the laws in being to speak what language it pleases, and affix such a sense to them as it finds convenient, and there and then justify such interpretation, and their doings in consequence of it, However tyranical by a retrospective law, declare such sense to be the true one. By such retrospective laws, it may also make such past actions as it wishes to punish criminals though they were not so when committed, and then annex the most grievous even capital punishment to them and thus the most arbitrary and opressive measures may be justified by law. In short this union which each of these powers has ever attempted to effect, and against which the proposed negative of the supreme executive is the only effectual security, has in all ages been productive of innumerable mischief and the greatest calamnities —the provision made by the proposed plan, that the supreme executive magistrate, shall revise all the bills and resolves passed by the legislature and if he has any objection may require a concurrence of two thirds of the house and senate to give them authority of law, will have a good tendency to preserve the executive, legislative and judicial departments distinct and independent of each other. But no provision is made to check the legislative power in its encroachment upon the executive, whenever two thirds of the house and senate shall unite to make them and whenever such encroachments as [are] so made, they will be more alarming, because there will be less probability that the executive power will be able to regain its rights where stripped of them by the concurrence of two thirds of the legislature than by bare majority. to give the governor a negative with the advice of his council in convenience [is convenient?] and as he is annually elected by and is the representative of all the people, this town conceives no danger can accrue from it, but many solid advantages too many here to enumerate. [1]

2 The town are of opinion, the number of representatives which may be chosen by the plan proposed is made far too large and unwieldy and in the course of a few years will become intollerable and they never will be able to debate with deliberation and coolness, that the public can never be conducted with despatch but will be protracted to unmeasurable lengths and that the expense criated, [thereby] will be enormous unless no more than a quarter part, perhaps of the members attend at once, this indeed would in some degree remove the evil last mentioned, but at the same time create a greater mischief for the frequent change of members during the same session would produce crude indigested and inconsistant acts and resolutions and by this means this important branch of the legislature would soon lose its dignity, importance and usefulness. The town therefore think that the number of legislators ought to be greatly reduced and fixed, and that the number should be proportioned in the principle of equality, upon the electors by dividing the state into new and larger districts, or otherwise as shall be found most expedient. The proposed constitution fixes the number necessary to form a quorum of sixty, and this the town think is a proper and sufficient number to do business, if so it suggests a further strong argument for reducing the whole number of the house, for upon the present plan, thirty one members only, that is to say, not more than one tenth part of the representative body and in a few years, perhaps not more than a twentyth are or will be necessary to make the most important laws, affecting the property the liberty and even the life of every subject, and the whole society will be bound by such laws to which they can with no propriety be said to have given their consent in person or by their representatives against the most fundamental principle of a free government.

3 When the town considers the great importance of a regular and well disciplened militia they cannot but wish that the mode of electing and appointing of officers might be altered. The choosing such officers by the people at large has been found by experience productive of disorder and confusion and ever will be so, very undue miasures and improper influence may be used and most probably will on such elections, and there is great danger that unworthy and unfit persons will be invested with the command of important body. The electers will be apt to consider and look down upon the elected as their creatures and servants and of course

it will become impossible to establish and preserve that due subordination and proper discipline, without which the militia will be of no service to the state. Past experience since the commencement of the present war, The town conceive has fully proved the truth and justice of the foregoing observations. The town therefore think the power of nominating and appointing all militia officers should be vested with the governor as commander in chief, who will have every inducement to appoint the best officers and such as we can confide in, whenever he shall have occasion to call out that body into actual service especially as he may possibly sometimes be called to command them in person and considering him as the representative of the whole people and depending upon them annually for his existance and that all such officers are removable only by court martial upon a fair trial there is no danger of his exerting his power to the injury of the people or for his own emolument.

4 The town considers the right of every subject to the writ of habeas-corpus as an inestimable privilege and cannot think but that the power granted to the legislature (by the plan proposed) to suspend it for a term not to exceed twelve months to be very dangerous to liberty. The proviso that they shall not do it but upon the most pressing and urgent occasions does not in the opinion of the town does not afford a sufficient security, for the legislature are and must be sole judges of such necessity and are amenable to no superior authority in the state should they do wrong. The town therefore think that even the legislature ought never to be invested with such suspending power except in time of actual or expected war invasion or rebellion and then they should have power to suspend that right for no longer a space then three months. With regard to the 7th article in the second Chap. The town are of the opinion that the General Court should be vested with the power from time to time to detach and march out of the state, such part of the militia as they may judge necessary to oppose the enemies thereof and that the Governor should have the like power in the recess of the General Court, but that neither the governor or general court should have power to detain in service any of the militia taken by draught or impress for a term exceeding three months. Besides these principle alterations and amendments the town would suggest a few more of less importance as

Suggest

1 If a negative of the supreme executive cannot be obtained the 2nd art. of the 1st Chap. of the second part should be amended by inserting

the word *and* instead of the word *or* between the words Senate and House, least it should seem to be implied that a bill or resolve of either house might have the force of a law, of not objected too by the governor as proposed by that article and least the governors right to object to a bill or resolve of both houses might be hereafter disputed

Sug 2 The town are of opinion that the senates power to determine disputed elections of their own members, should not be limited to the last Wednesday in May, but left at large as that of the house of representatives is, for persons who may appear on that day to have a majority of votes, may afterward appear unduly elected

Sug 3 The mode of electing a governor or lieutenant governor in case there is no majority of votes for any person, should be the same, in case the person having such majority of votes should refuse to accept. The town are also of opinion that proper qualifications for the delegates of Congress ought to be required, as well as for the officers of the state.

Sug. 4 The latter part of the 2nd Article of the 6th Chap. does not appear to be clearly expressed and the town think may be amended by saying that none of the officers there mentioned shall at the same time have a seat in the council senate or house of representatives, but if a councillor, senator or representative shall be chosen or appointed to any of these offices and accept thereof such acceptance shall vacate his seat in the council, senate or house of representatives and if any person holding any of these offices shall be chosen and accept a seat in the council senate or house of representatives, such acceptence shall vacate such office. And the town are further of opinion that some of the principle militia officers should be excluded from a seat in the council senate or house of representatives for in the choice of members for any of those places the influence of such officers, considering their peculiar station and connections may sometimes be as great as the force of bribery and corruption

Sug 5 There appears to the town an impropriety that a judge of the superior court, should be at the same time a justice of the peace. they conceive there is danger however upright the Judge may be that by acting in the latter capacity on matters that may afterward come in judgement in the former, he may be unduly although insensibly predjudiced and biased in cases of the greatest importance even of life and death

The town then voted that the Hon Benjamin Greenleaf, Hon Jonathan Greenleaf Jonathan Jackson Theoplilus Parsons and Nathaniel Tracy Esq their former delegates be desired to attend the convention at their adjournment on the first Wednesday of June next, and use their endeavors to obtain the several alterations and amendments aforesaid, especially the four first mentioned as far as they may find it prudent but if this cannot be effected yet, considering that from the variety of opinion, generally formed on matters of an interesting nature by reason of prejudices arising from education and influence of interests and various other causes it is not to be expected that a form of government can ever be devised that will be perfectly agreable to all the members of the community and that consequently mutual concessions must be made considering further the necessity of a speedy establishment of a form of government for the state, and that provision is made that the one now proposed for the revision of the same at some future period, and esteeming it in general a wise and good one. The town do vote and declare their approbation of the same in its present form, and that their said delegates be empowered and they are hereby empowered on behalf of this town to agree in the said convention upon a time when said form of government shall take place without returning it again to the people provided that two thirds of the male inhabitants of the age of 21 years and upward, voting in the several towns and plantations shall have agreed to the same, or the convention shall conform it to the sentiments of two thirds of the people as aforsaid

This meeting is dissolved

A true record Attest M. Hodge Town Clerk

Salem *

At a Meeting of the Freeholders and other Inhabitants of Salem, lawfully qualified to Vote in Town Affairs at the Townhouse, on Thursday the 18th day of May, at 10 OClock in the Morning. Voted Captain Benjamin Goodhue Junior Moderator. Then came before the Town, the form of a Constitution or Frame of Government, to be Revised considered and acted upon. a Motion was made that the said book should be read, that contains the Bill of rights etc.——

Accordingly it was read by the Moderator, then each Article was taken up seperately and Considered and Voted as in the Minutes appears,—as far as the 30th Article. then the Meeting was Adjourned untill half past 2 OClock in the Afternoon; The 3rd Article in the first part was referred. to a Committee.——

* Salem Town Records, City Hall, Salem, Mass.

The Town met according to adjournment at half past 2 oClock in the Afternoon, the Moderator Present. The Town then took the second part of the Bill of Rights under Consideration, and Voted as may bee seen in the Minutes Viz. Chapter 1. Section 3d. Article 2d referred:——

Chapter IV Refered, Chapter VI. Article 7th a Motion was made that a Committee should be Chosen to take this 7th Article into Consideration, and make report at the Adjournment.

Voted Severally

The Honorable John Pickering Esquire William Pinchon Esquire and William Witmore Esquire

be Said Committee

then t'was Voted that this Meeting be adjourned untill Monday next, being the 22d Instant at 9 OClock in the Morning AD 1780: and that the Reverend the Ministers of the Gospel in this Town be presented with a Copy of said Vote, and be desired to read the same after Service to their Several Congregations.—

The Town Met according to Adjournment on Monday Morning at 9 OClock the 22nd Day of May 1780.——

The Moderator being present Then was taken into Consideration, (Seperately)—sundry Articles which were Reffered to this Adjournment, and proceeded as far as the 5th or last clause of the 3rd Article of the Bill of rights.——

Then the Meeting was adjourned untill half past two OClock in the Afternoon.——

in this 3rd Article the Clauses were taken up Seperately and Considered.——

The Town met according to Adjournment. the Moderator being present. Then the Second part of the Bill of Rights was taken up and considered Seperately and debated upon very largely by divers learned Gentlemen, and concluded on as in the Minutes may more largely appear.——

Voted. That the Delegates at the next Sessions of this Convention, be instructed to use their Influence to get the Amendment, as far forth as they can and to agree upon a time when this form of Government shall take place.——

Then the Meeting was dissolved.

At a Meeting of the Freeholders and other Inhabitants of Salem, legally qualified to Vote in Town Affairs, held at the Town House in

Said Salem, May 24th 1780 for the purpose of taking into Consideration the form of a Constitution and Frame of Government agreed upon by the Delegates of the People of Massachusetts Bay, begun and held at Cambridge on the first day of September 1779 and Continued by adjournment to the 2d March 1780.

Captain Benjamin Goodhue junior Moderator The town proceeded to take into Consideration, the said proposed form of a Constitution etc. Article by Article as reccommended by the Convention.

The Bill of Rights

		Nays
Article the 1st	130	None
Article 2d.	132	None

Article 3d. the following amendment proposed in the first paragraph, viz. in all Cases where such Teachers receive pay and provision shall not be made Voluntarily.——

The fourth Paragraph, the Words if he require it to to be deled.——

The Question was then put upon the Article with the Amendment.——

	Yeas	Nays
Amendment	77	10
Article 4	122	None
Article 5	129	None
Article 6	134	None
Article 7	129	None
8	133	None
9	133	None
10	115	2
11	131	
12	130	
13	122	
14	129	
15	122	
16	118	
17	124	
18	121	
19	126	
20	122	
21	119	
22	121	
23	122	

	Yeas	Nays
24	119	
25	117	
26	121	
27	121	
28	120	
29	119	
30	122	

Frame of Government.

Preamble	Yeas	No's
	64	

General Court.

	Yeas	No's
Chapter 1, Section 1, Article 1	61	
Article 2	65	
3	64	1
4	73	

Senate

Section 2d	Yeas	No's
Article 1	69	
2	65	
3	68	
4	70	1
5	70	
6	76	
7	75	
8	74	
9	73	

Section 3 House Representatives

	Yeas	No's
Article 1	75	
2. 1st and 2d Clauses	1	95

And then the following was proposed to be substituted in the room of Said 1st and 2d Clauses in the Said 2d Article—Representation ought to be upon principles etc.———

85

In the third Clause of Said 2d Article to Dele the word Town and Substitute the Word District.

79

Fourth Clause Chapter 1 Section 3d Article 2d Pay of Representatives to enquire about it.

			Yeas	Nays
Article	3d		68	
	4		82	
	5		83	
	6		83	
	7		81	
	8		82	
	9		81	
	10		83	
	11		83	
Chapter	2d			
Section	1	Governor		
Article	1		83	
	2		83	
	3		84	
	4		79	
	5		79	
	6		71	
	7		70	
	8		85	
	9		83	
	10		84	
	11		86	
	12		87	
	13		84	
Section	2—Lieutenant Governor			
Article	1		88	
	2		85	
	3		84	
Section	3	Council etc.		
Article	1		86	
	2		85	
	3		85	
	4		86	
	5		82	
	6		89	
	7		86	
Section	4—Secretary etc.			
Article	1		84	

		Yeas	Nays
	2	86	
Chapter	3	Power	
Article	1	80	
	2	81	
	3	86	
	4	83	
	5	81	
Chapter	4	Delegates to Congress	
		3	68

It was then Moved That that part of the Chapter, from the being to word Room be deled and the following Words Substituted in their stead Viz.

The Delegates of his Common Wealth etc.

The Question upon the Chapters as it stand with the Amendment was then put

		Yeas	Nays
		49	
Chapter	5		
Section	1		
Article	1	73	
	2	77	

3 Amendment proposed to dele the Word Congregational and to Substitute the word Protestant. Also to dele the Words mentioned in the Said Act.——

The Question upon the Said 3d Articles as amended.

		Yeas	Nays
		33	2
Section	2d Literature	Yeas	
		76	
Chapter	6	Oaths etc.	
Article	1	68	1
Article	2	67	1
Article	3	53	
	4	60	
	5	55	
	6	59	

7 Amendment. That the Words Except upon the most urgent and pressing Occasions, be expunged, and the Words Except in Case of Rebellion, or Hostile Invasion,

Substituted etc. The Question was put upon the Article as Amended....

	Yeas	Nays
	49	
Article 8	45	
9	52	
10	62	
11	53	

The Town then Voted Unanimously that their Delegates be impowered to agree upon a time, when the said Constitution shall take place.

Salisbury *

At a meeting in Said Town the 18th of May 1779 the question was put whether the Town would Send two Representatives. Voted in the Negative—put to vote Whether they would send one. Voted in affirmative—the Votes were called for and Major Joseph Page was Chosen to Represent the Town in the Great and General Court of this State at the same meeting put to vote whether the town Chuse at this time to have a New Constitution or form of Government made. Number Voted in the affirmative twenty two and one in the Negative—at the same meeting—Voted that Major Joseph Page our Representative be and is hereby instructed to Vote for the Calling a State Convention for the purpose of forming a New Constitution.

At a meeting of the Inhabitants of the Town of Salisbury Legally assembled at the West meeting House the 5th of August 1779. Major Joseph Page was Chosen Moderator for said meeting—the proceedings of the Convention at Concord the 17th of July Last being Read and after some Deliberate Considerations thereon first Voted Unanimously that we will Endeavor to the utmost of our power to Support and Carry into Execution the measures agreed upon and Recommended by the Convention at Concord for puting our Currency upon a more Respectable footing and for promoting the Public Happiness.——

Capt Johathan Evans was Chosen a Delegate to Represent this town at a Convention to be held at Concord on the first Wednesday in october next.

At a meeting May 24th 1780

Voted to axcept of the Constution in every article, by fifty none against—2ly Voted that except those which follow in the third Article in the bill

* Town records, Massachusetts Historical Society.

of Rights after these words. and all moneys paid by the Subject to the Support of publick Worship and the public Teachers aforesaid shall if he requir it be uniformly applied to the Support of the publick Teachers of his own religoues Sect or Denomination provided there be any on whose Instructions he attends. It is the mind of this Town that these words shoud be added——provided also that he signify his mind publickly and enter his Dissent at the Settlement of a Minister as being of a Different Denomination

This we Judge ought to signified at the time of contracting with and Settleing a minister for the sake of his fellow Contractors as well as for him who Settles For otherwise neither will be safe. The people being left at an utter uncertainty who is to support their minister even after an unanimous Vote: and the Minister at an uncertainty whether he can have any Support at all. More over it appears to us unreasonable that a man should be allowed to break his civil Contract with a minister or any other man, unless because he changed his religous Sentiments. And further it appears to us Downright Injustice for one part of the Contracter to Shift their burthen on the rest when they please after having explicitly or even implicitly bound themselves to bear their propotion of it. nor do we think it comes within the power of any Government to dissolve such a Contract while there is no forfeiture of it——forty five for the above mentioned and Twelve for no amendment.

Voted that it would be agreable to this Town if at the Close of the Seventh Section in the Second Chapter the following words added—— or in case of actual invasion by the Enemy—Because in that case immeadiate Help may be necessary which Power in a single Person can best afford—forty for the word added none against.

Voted that in the 6th Chapter Section 7th respecting the Habeas Corpus Act—the words except upon the most urgent and pressing occasions appears to us as to indefinite and we could with them alter thus—Except in times of War, Invasion or Rebellion, and we could with the limited times not to exceed six months instead of the twelve mentioned in the Article.—forty for the amendment and none against.

Voted that it the mind of this Town that it would to have the Constitution revised at the end of ten years.

Voted that if two thirds of the Male Inhabitants of this State twenty one years of age, Voting in their several Meetings shall agree to this Constitution if it shall be altered by the Convention so as to be Conformable to two thirds of the Voters aforesaid not Essentially different from it as

it now stands—Then it is the mind of this Town that their Delegate in the next Convention be impowered and he is hereby impowered to agree upon the time when this Form of Government shall take place.
fifty for and non against.

Topsfield *

[Question of adopting the Constitution first came up at a town meeting held May 8, 1780. The action of the town was as follows:]

Samuel Smith Esq was Chosen moderator for said meeting——upon reading the proposed Constitution and form of Goverment Sent to the Several Towns in the State of Massachusetts, by a Convention of Said State Elected to frame a Constitution and form of Goverment for their Consideration thereon, The Town made Choice of Samuel Smith Esquire Mr. Abraham Hobbs, Mr. Thomas Porter, the reverend Daniel Breck, Messrs. Solomon Dodge, Moses Perkins, David Balch Junr., David Towne, and David Perkins, To Revise Said Constitution and form of Goverment, and make proposals for amendments or alterations of Such articles in Said Constitution as they Shall think wants amendment, and make report to the Town at the adjournment of this meeting.

The meeting adjourned to May 23rd and again adjourned to June 5th and again to June 12th and then to June 15th.

[The organization of the June 15th meeting is recorded in the records and is followed by two and one-half pages left blank, presumably with the intention of recording the proceedings, which never was done. No further record occurs.]

* Town records, Massachusetts Historical Society.

CUMBERLAND COUNTY

Brunswick *

At a meeting held May 15th, the town postponed voting in regard to a change of the State Constitution until the next meeting. Probably the next meeting of the town occurred too late for the vote of Brunswick to have any effect, since no vote of the kind was recorded at any subsequent meeting this year.

Cape Elizabeth †

At a legal meeting of the male Inhabitants of the Town of Cape Elizabeth on Wednesday the 3d day of May A. D. 1780

Voted Mr. Nathaniel Staple Moderator

Voted to choose a Committee to examine the New Constitution of Government and make their report to this Town on adjournment of this meeting

Voted Colonel Jordan—Captain Skillin—Captain Leach—Clement Jordan—and David Strout Esquire—Deacon Dyer—Major Thrasher—Captain Wentworth—and Mess James Maxwell—Zebulon Trickey—Joseph Mariner—Jeremiah Jordan Junior—Jno Armstrong—Barzillia Delano—Jno Ficket—Joseph Cobb—James Dyer be the said Committee

Voted this meeting be adjourned to the 31 day of May Instant.

Attest

David Strout Town Clerk

The Town met according to Adjournment Viz:—May 31st 1780 and Voted to accept the said Committees Report which is as follows,

This Committee being chosen to Examine and report to the Town what Articles ought to be revised and altered in the present form of Government offered to the Commonwealth, have carefully Examined the same and report as follows, That in Chapter First Article 4th ought to

* G. A. Wheeler and H. W. Wheeler, *History of Brunswick, Topsham, and Harpswell, Maine* (Boston, 1878), 128.

† Town records, Massachusetts Historical Society.

stand thus, Once in Six Years at the least and as much oftener as the General Court shall order—

Chapter Second Article Second should stand unless he shall declare himself to be of the Protestant Christian Religion—

If these Amendments be not received the whole to be accepted as it now stands.

For the said report 27 Yeas, Nays 1

Recorded by David Strout
Town Clerk

Falmouth *

On the 22d of May, 1780, the consideration of [the constitution's] adoption came before this town, and a committee of seven was appointed to examine the instrument and report whether any amendments were necessary; they were specially instructed to report on the objections to the third article of the bill of rights.

The Constitution was approved, "the vote in this town on the third, the most objectionable article, being forty-nine for and thirty-four against it."

New Gloucester †

[Our records show a call for a Meeting on April 1 1780. To see what method the Town will come into to raise the men as required by order of the General Court, dated March 15, 1780, and to act there on and pass such votes as may be thought proper in said meeting.—In May a meeting was held (May 22) "Article 3" To see if they will accept the new form of Goverment and to act upon the whole or any particular part of article of the said form of Government as shall be thought proper when mett: Twenty nine voters on this article. Nineteen voted to accept of the whole of the new form of Government.]

* William Willis, *The History of Portland, From 1632 to 1864* (Portland, Maine, 1865), 542–543. The name of Falmouth was changed to Portland.

† Town records, Massachusetts Historical Society.

APPENDIX

The Massachusetts Towns of 1780

The Massachusetts Towns of 1780

The editors have been unable to establish a meaningful correlation between the social conditions in specific towns and the attitudes expressed in the responses. The closest relationship is between grievances about Article III and the places in which Baptists were numerous; but even in this matter the correlation is not exact. The introduction therefore made no effort to describe the almost three hundred towns of the Commonwealth, each of which, of course, had its own character. The following tabulation presents some indices useful in identifying the communities from which the responses emanated.

All town and county names are given as used in 1780, with notations of significant changes thereafter.

The date of first settlement, when known, is an approximate indication of distance from frontier conditions. The date of incorporation (or recognition as a corporate district or precinct) is generally a reflection of the strength and stability of local institutions. In both cases, however, there are important exceptions, for new towns were sometimes created by the division of old ones, and incorporated towns, especially in Maine, sometimes remained empty for years and sometimes, though settled for a while, were depopulated and revived decades later. This information has been drawn from *Acts and Resolves,* I, II, XIX, XXI; F. W. Cook, *Historical Data Relating to Counties, Cities and Towns in Massachusetts* (Boston, 1948); Florence S. M. Crofut, *Guide to the History and the Historic Sites of Connecticut* (New Haven, 1937), I, 194, 329; II, 811, 871; town and county histories; John Warner Barber, *Historical Collections* (Worcester, Mass., 1839); and from Elias Nason, *Gazetteer of the State of Massachusetts* (Boston, 1878).

The most useful available indicator of the wealth of each community is the assessment of the state tax of 1780. The figures arrived at by the General Court are approximations of the ability of each town to pay a share of the tax based on estimates of the value of its property. The data are given in *Acts and Resolves,* V, 1139–1162.

BARNSTABLE

Town	Date Settled	Date Incorporated	State Tax (£)
Barnstable	1639	1639	18,095
Chatham	1665	1712	4,503
Eastham		1646	8,458
Falmouth		1686	9,100
Harwich		1694	9,741
Sandwich	1637	1639	12,973
Truro		1709	4,293

Town	Date Settled	Date Incorporated	State Tax (£)
Wellfleet		1763	4,223
Yarmouth		1639	11,771
	BERKSHIRE [1]		
Adams		1778	7,361
Alford		1773	2,216
Ashawelot [2]	1755	1784	2,100
Becket		1765	3,488
Egremont		1760	4,036
Great Barrington		1761	10,150
Hancock	1760	1776	6,685
Lanesborough		1765	11,970
Lee	1760	1777	4,141
Lenox	1750	1767	6,790
Loudon [3]		1773	1,843
Mount Washington	1753	1779	
New Ashford [4]		1781	1,983
New Marlborough	1739	1759	6,708
New Providence [5]	1767		3,033
New Salem		1753	
Partridgefield [6]		1771	3,406
Pittsfield	1752	1761	10,955
Plantation No. 7 [7]	1778	1792	1,843
Richmond	1760	1765	8,015
Sandisfield	1750	1762	6,941
Sheffield		1733	13,813
Stockbridge		1739	7,175
Tyringham	1739	1762	5,378
Washington	1760	1777	3,756
West Stockbridge		1774	4,048
Williamstown		1765	7,991
Windsor [8]	1768	1771	5,133
	BRISTOL		
Attleborough		1694	16,333
Berkley		1735	4,911

[1] Some territory transferred later to Franklin County.
[2] Became the town of Dalton.
[3] Became a part of Otis in 1810.
[4] Made a town in 1835.
[5] Became a part of Adams in 1780; incorporated as Cheshire in 1793.
[6] Name changed to Peru in 1806.
[7] Became the town of Hawley. Became part of Franklin County.
[8] Incorporated as Gageborough; name changed to Windsor in 1778.

Town	Date Settled	Date Incorporated	State Tax (£)
Dartmouth		1664	41,136
Dighton		1712	9,088
Easton		1725	7,630
Freetown		1683	10,196
Mansfield		1770	6,568
Norton		1711	9,963
Raynham	1650	1731	7,000
Rehoboth		1645	25,585
Swansey and Shawamet		1667	13,685
Taunton		1639	22,248
	CUMBERLAND [9]		
Bakerstown			280
Bridgeton		1794	210
Brunswick		1737	6,580
Cape Elizabeth			8,260
Falmouth		1658	14,420
Gorham	1736	1764	7,011
Gray		1778	1,505
Harpswell		1758	4,900
New Gloucester		1774	4,340
North Yarmouth		1732	13,265
Pearsontown [10]			2,333
Raymondtown [11]	1771	1804	560
Royalsburgh			1,341
Scarborough		1658	10,885
Sylvestertown [12]			280
Windham		1762	3,045
	DUKES		
Chilmark		1714	7,443
Edgartown	1645	1671	6,906
Tisbury		1671	5,915
	ESSEX		
Amesbury [13]		1666	12,098
Andover		1646	31,896

[9] Separated as part of the state of Maine in 1820.
[10] Became part of Standish in 1785.
[11] Raymond incorporated in 1804.
[12] Probably Sylvester Canada, settled in 1777 and incorporated in 1786.
[13] Name changed from Salisbury new town in 1668. Also known as Almsbury.

Town	Date Settled	Date Incorporated	State Tax (£)
Beverly	1630	1668	23,193
Boxford	1645	1685	10,721
Bradford	1658	1675	12,541
Danvers		1757	21,443
Gloucester	1631	1642	24,710
Haverhill	1640	1643	19,600
Ipswich	1633	1634	37,100
Lynn	1629	1637	16,800
Manchester		1645	5,238
Marblehead	1629	1649	35,735
Middleton		1728	7,595
Methuen		1725	10,243
Newbury		1635	34,230
Newburyport		1764	37,800
Rowley	1638	1639	17,313
Salem	1628		56,618
Salisbury		1639	13,253
Topsfield		1650	9,846
Wenham		1643	5,320

HAMPSHIRE[14]

Town	Date Settled	Date Incorporated	State Tax (£)
Amherst		1759	8,306
Ashfield	1745	1765	4,981
Belchertown		1761	7,420
Bernardston	1735	1762	3,920
Blandford		1741	6,965
Brimfield		1731	8,785
Charlemont		1763	3,616
Chesterfield		1762	6,486
Chesterfield Gore[15]			1,081
Colrain		1761	4,526
Conway		1767	7,676
Cummington[16]	1770	1779	3,021
Deerfield		1682	9,135
Enfield[17]		1816	
Granby		1768	4,340
Granville		1754	10,721
Greenfield		1753	5,658
Greenwich[18]	1732	1754	5,775

[14] Later divided into Franklin, Hampshire, and Hampden counties.
[15] Became part of Cummington, Plainfield, and Goshen.
[16] Known as Plantation No. 5 until incorporation.
[17] Part formed to Greenwich in 1787; remainder in Connecticut.
[18] Taken by the Metropolitan Water Commission in 1938.

Town	Date Settled	Date Incorporated	State Tax (£)
Hadley		1661	8,120
Hatfield		1670	7,851
Leverett		1774	2,473
Ludlow	1750	1774	2,566
Merryfield [19]		1785	1,703
Monson	1715	1760	6,043
Montague		1754	4,200
Murrayfield [20]		1765	4,480
New Salem		1753	7,128
Northampton		1654	13,253
Northfield		1713	6,591
Norwich [21]		1773	1,831
Palmer	1727	1752	5,670
Pelham		1743	6,241
Shelburne		1768	6,265
Shutesbury		1761	3,698
South Brimfield [22]	1730	1762	5,191
Somers [23]			
South Hadley	1721	1753	4,036
Southampton	1732	1753	5,891
Southwick	1734	1770	3,605
Springfield	1635	1636	16,835
Suffield [24]			
Sunderland		1714	3,780
Ware		1761	3,628
Warwick	1744	1763	4,946
West Springfield		1774	16,858
Westfield		1669	12,576
Westhampton		1778	2,193
Whately	1735	1771	3,418
Wilbraham	1730	1763	9,695
Williamsburg		1771	4,153
Worthington		1768	4,678

LINCOLN [25]

Belfast		1773	571
Boothbay		1764	5,448
Bowdoinham		1762	1,621

[19] Also known as Myrifield; incorporated as Rowe in 1785.
[20] Originally No. 9. Name changed to Chester in 1783.
[21] Name changed to Huntington in 1855.
[22] Name changed to Wales in 1828.
[23] In Connecticut.
[24] In Connecticut.
[25] Separated as part of the state of Maine in 1820.

Town	Date Settled	Date Incorporated	State Tax (£)
Bristol		1765	5,716
Edgecomb	1744	1774	2,601
Georgetown		1716	10,208
Hallowell		1771	3,803
Medumcook [26]	1750	1808	1,411
Newcastle		1753	4,060
Pittston		1779	4,106
Pownalborough		1760	8,260
St. George's Lower Town [27]		1777	1,820
Thomaston		1777	2,076
Topsham		1764	4,736
Vassalborough		1771	4,433
Waldoborough		1773	3,920
Warren		1776	2,076
Winslow		1771	2,823
Winthrop		1771	4,200
Woolwich		1759	3,208

MIDDLESEX

Town	Date Settled	Date Incorporated	State Tax (£)
Acton	1656	1735	7,070
Ashby		1767	3,220
Bedford		1729	6,358
Billerica		1655	11,200
Cambridge	1631	1633	21,420
Charlestown	1628	1629	7,000
Chelmsford		1655	10,710
Concord	1635	1635	13,440
Dracut		1702	8,236
Dunstable	1673	1673	6,568
East Sudbury [28]		1780	
Framingham	1675	1700	13,020
Groton		1655	13,020
Holliston		1724	7,560
Hopkinton		1715	8,493
Lexington	1642	1713	9,065
Lincoln		1754	6,580
Littleton		1715	8,446
Malden		1649	8,353
Marlborough	1660	1666	16,800
Medford	1630		10,920

[26] Became part of Friendship in 1808.
[27] Became part of Thomaston.
[28] Became Wayland.

Town	Date Settled	Date Incorporated	State Tax (£)
Natick [29]		1745	4,690
Newton		1691	12,810
Pepperell		1753	7,956
Reading		1644	14,525
Sherborn		1674	6,790
Shirley		1753	5,086
Stoneham	1645	1725	3,115
Stow	1650	1683	7,770
Sudbury		1639	18,106
Tewksbury		1734	6,416
Townsend		1732	6,066
Waltham		1738	8,400
Watertown		1630	9,730
Westford		1729	9,730
Weston		1713	9,251
Wilmington		1730	5,320
Woburn		1642	14,630
	NANTUCKET		
Sherburn [30]		1687	30,881
	PLYMOUTH		
Abington		1712	9,275
Bridgewater		1656	36,960
Duxbury		1637	7,221
Halifax		1734	4,631
Hanover	1649	1727	6,860
Hingham	1633	1635	
Hull		1644	
Kingston		1726	6,603
Marshfield		1640	9,111
Middleborough		1669	30,216
Pembroke		1712	12,390
Plymouth		1620	15,225
Plympton	1680	1707	11,118
Rochester		1686	13,568

[29] The "praying Indians" and the proprietors of the lands had had some sort of corporate existence earlier; but in 1745 Natick was formally constituted a precinct or parish. In 1762 it was established as a "district" and the general act of 1775 may have made it a town. Doubts on that score were resolved in an act of incorporation of 1781. See also D. H. Hurd, *History of Middlesex County, Massachusetts* (Philadelphia, 1890), I, 521.

[30] Name changed to Nantucket in 1795.

Town	Date Settled	Date Incorporated	State Tax (£)
Scituate		1636	21,980
Wareham		1739	4,048

SUFFOLK [31]

Town	Date Settled	Date Incorporated	State Tax (£)
Bellingham		1719	4,900
Boston	1630	1630	154,000
Braintree	1625	1640	27,300
Brookline		1705	9,380
Chelsea	1630	1739	6,650
Cohasset		1770	6,020
Dedham		1636	28,000
Dorchester		1630	17,360
Foxborough		1778	8,120
Franklin		1778	10,686
Hingham [32]	1633	1635	15,493
Hull [32]		1644	1,726
Medfield	1650	1651	9,800
Medway		1713	10,640
Milton		1662	12,133
Needham		1711	11,503
Roxbury		1630	23,216
Stoughton		1726	18,200
Stoughtonham [33]		1765	8,411
Walpole		1724	9,053
Weymouth		1635	13,300
Wrentham		1673	13,440

WORCESTER

Town	Date Settled	Date Incorporated	State Tax (£)
Ashburnham		1765	3,640
Athol		1762	6,020
Barre [34]		1774	11,620
Bolton		1738	9,870
Brookfield		1718	21,700
Charlton	1750	1755	10,290
Douglas	1722	1746	4,270
Dudley		1732	6,720
Fitchburg		1764	5,600
Grafton	1728	1735	7,735

31 Later divided into Norfolk and Suffolk counties.
32 Later in Plymouth County.
33 Name changed to Sharon.
34 Incorporated as Rutland District in 1753 and as the town of Hutchinson in 1774; name changed to Barre in 1776.

Town	Date Settled	Date Incorporated	State Tax (£)
Hardwick		1739	11,200
Harvard		1732	10,430
Holden		1741	5,600
Hubbardston		1767	3,990
Lancaster		1653	22,166
Leicester		1714	5,320
Leominster		1740	8,400
Lunenburg		1728	9,800
Mendon		1667	16,380
Milford		1780	
New Braintree		1751	7,700
Northborough		1766	5,180
Northbridge		1772	2,800
Oakham		1762	3,990
Oxford		1713	6,720
Paxton		1765	5,600
Petersham		1754	8,680
Princeton		1771	5,740
Royalston		1765	5,051
Rutland		1714	9,660
Shrewsbury	1717	1727	14,700
Southborough		1727	7,560
Spencer		1753	8,400
Sturbridge		1738	9,660
Sutton		1715	20,440
Templeton		1762	7,490
Upton		1735	4,340
Uxbridge		1727	9,310
Ward [35]		1778	3,278
Westborough		1717	7,921
Western [36]		1742	7,140
Westminster	1737	1770	7,490
Winchendon		1764	4,060
Woodstock [37]			
Worcester	1713	1722	20,580
YORK [38]			
Arundel [39]		1653	6,650
Berwick		1711	23,613

[35] Name changed to Auburn in 1837.
[36] Name changed to Warren in 1834.
[37] In Connecticut.
[38] Separated as part of the state of Maine in 1820.
[39] Incorporated as Cape Porpoise in 1653; town privileges lapsed; re-established in 1718 as Arundel.

Town	Date Settled	Date Incorporated	State Tax (£)
Biddeford [40]		1653	7,210
Brownfield		1802	560
Buxton		1762	5,320
Coxhall		1778	1,750
Fryeburg		1777	4,200
Kittery		1647	18,935
Lebanon		1767	4,025
Limerick		1787	560
Little Falls [41]		1798	980
Massabesec [42]		1784	2,030
Pepperellborough		1772	6,720
Sanford		1768	3,745
Wells		1653	15,400
York		1647	17,453

[40] Town privileges lapsed, re-established in 1718.
[41] Plantation until 1798 when incorporated as part of Phillipsburgh. Name later changed to Hollis.
[42] Plantation until 1784 when incorporated as Waterborough.

Index

This index includes subject and personal and place names in full for the introduction, but only proper names for the documents. Samuel Barrett and John Avery who were secretaries of the conventions, are listed where they appear as signers of a document, but not in the salutation, for almost every return was directed to them.